STUDIES IN THE EARLY HISTORY OF BRITAIN

General Editor: Nicholas Brooks

The Northern Danelaw

The Northern Danelaw

Its Social Structure, *c.* 800–1100

D. M. Hadley

Leicester University Press
London and New York

Leicester University Press
A Continuum imprint
Wellington House, 125 Strand, London WC2R 0BB
370 Lexington Avenue, New York, NY 10017-6503

First published 2000

© D. M. Hadley 2000

British Library Cataloguing-in-Publication Data
A catalogue record for this book is available from the British Library.

ISBN 0-7185-0014-8

Library of Congress Cataloging-in-Publication Data

Hadley, D. M. (Dawn M.), 1967–
　　The Northern Danelaw: its social structure, *c.* 800–1100/D.M. Hadley.
　　　　p.　cm.–(Studies in the early history of Britain)
　　Includes bibliographical references and index.
　　ISBN 0-7185-0014-8 (hb)
　　　　1. Great Britain–History–Anglo-Saxon period, 449–1066. 2. Land tenure–England,
Northern–History–To 1500. 3. Peasantry–England, Northern–History–To 1500.
4. England, Northern–Social conditions. 5. Great Britain–History–Invasions.
6. Vikings–England, Northern.　 I. Title. II. Series.

DA158.H34 2000
333.3′22′0942809021–dc21　　　　　　　　　　　　　　　　　　　　99-087413

Typeset by BookEns Ltd, Royston, Herts.
Printed and bound in Great Britain by The Cromwell Press, Trowbridge, Wilts.

Contents

Foreword

The aim of the *Studies in the Early History of Britain* is to promote works of the highest scholarship which open up new fields of study or which straddle the barriers of traditional academic disciplines. As scholarship becomes ever more specialized, interdisciplinary studies are needed not only by students and lay people but also by professional scholars. This series has therefore included research monographs, works of synthesis and also collaborative studies of important themes by several scholars whose training and expertise has lain in different fields. Our knowledge of the early Middle Ages will always be limited and fragmentary, but progress can be made if the work of the historian has secure foundations in philology, archaeology, geography, literature, numismatics, art history and liturgy – to name only the most obvious fields. The need to cross and to remove academic frontiers also explains the extension of the geographical range of this series to include the whole island of Britain, where its predecessor had been limited to 'early English history'. The change would have been welcomed by the previous editor, the late Professor H.P.R. Finberg, whose pioneering work helped to inspire, or to provoke, the interest of a new generation of early medievalists in the relations of Britons and Saxons. The approach of this series is therefore deliberately wide-ranging. Early medieval Britain can only be understood in the context of contemporary developments in Ireland and on the Continent.

In this volume Dr Dawn Hadley offers a much-needed synthetic re-evaluation of the society of the northern Danelaw. Ethnic interpretations of social history, as characterized by the fundamental work of Sir Frank Stenton on the peasantry of this region, are no longer in fashion. Preferring to follow Maitland's advice 'to be careful how we use our Dane', she provides a new assessment of the Scandinavian impact and of the nature of the indigenous inheritance against a wide European background. She pulls together modern historical and archaeological approaches to ethnography, to the linguistic and toponymic evidence, to the analysis of the landscape and of early ecclesiastical structures, to artistic and sculptural styles, as well as to the traditional issues of peasant freedom in the face of manorial lordship. The resulting picture of the northern Danelaw is much richer and more complex than we have seen hitherto. Scandinavian influence can no longer be a *deus ex machina* to explain every distinctive feature of Danelaw society; but we can now hope to gauge that impact more clearly. I am delighted to welcome a volume to the series which brings students and lay people up to date on some of the most controversial issues of English social history.

N.P. Brooks
University of Birmingham
July 1999

Acknowledgements

This book owes a great debt to the many friends and colleagues who have offered encouragement and advice during its genesis and composition. In particular I would like to acknowledge the major influence on my research played by the various members of the Department of Medieval History at the University of Birmingham, and its 'Friday Night Seminar', who have helped me to formulate my ideas and have forced me on many occasions to rethink assumptions and to look beyond the narrow focus of the northern Danelaw. I am, in particular, indebted to Steve Bassett for his patience and support during my years as a postgraduate student, and my Ph.D. examiners, John Blair and Nicholas Brooks, for their advice and encouragement as the thesis was developed into a book. Both Chris Dyer – who initially inspired me, through his work, to study the medieval period – and Chris Wickham have provided much advice and encouragement over many years. Chris Dyer, Chris Wickham, John Blair and Nicholas Brooks also kindly read part, or all, of the text and saved me from numerous errors.

The book has also benefited from discussion with other friends and colleagues, some of whom have assisted by making available to me unpublished work: I am particularly grateful to Lesley Abrams, Ross Balzaretti, Julia Barrow, Andrew Chamberlain, Katy Cubitt, Ros Faith, Margaret Gelling, Guy Halsall, Carenza Lewis, Keith Lilley, Patrick Mitchell-Fox, Julian Richards, David Roffe, David Stocker, Alan Thacker and Gabor Thomas. I would like to thank John Palmer for making the Hull University Domesday database available to me and for his advice about the construction of my own database, the Cambridge Population Studies Group for funding my database, and Gill Bullock for helping me with data in-putting. My thanks are also due to Colin Merrony, Jo Mincher and Alex Norman for the other illustrations. I am also grateful to the British Academy for funding the period of post-doctoral research out of which this book developed, and to Bruce, Ron and Molly Coley for their support and hospitality during the earliest stages of research for this book.

Finally, I would like to acknowledge the help and encouragement of a number of friends whose support helped me to finish this book. Kate Peters helped me to want to finish this project, which, in the end, made me do so. The final stages of the completion of this book were far more enjoyable than they would otherwise have been thanks to the love and support of Patrick Major. The book is dedicated to the people without whom it would not have been started or completed, my parents and CJW.

Abbreviations

Æthelweard	*The Chronicle of Æthelweard*, ed. A. Campbell (1962)
AASRP	*Associated Architectural Societies' Reports and Papers*
Ag. Hist., I.II	H.P.R. Finberg (ed.) *The Agrarian History of England and Wales* I.II *AD 43–1042* (1972)
Ag. Hist., II	H.E. Hallam (ed.) *The Agrarian History of England and Wales* II *1042–1350* (1988)
AgHR	*Agricultural History Review*
ANS	*Anglo-Norman Studies*
Antiq. J.	*Antiquaries Journal*
Arch. J.	*Archaeological Journal*
ASC	*Anglo-Saxon Chronicle (EHD,* I, no.1)
ASE	*Anglo-Saxon England*
ASSAH	*Anglo-Saxon Studies in Archaeology and History*
Asser	Asser's *Life of King Alfred,* in *Asser's Life of Alfred the Great and Other Contemporary Sources*, trans. S. Keynes and M. Lapidge (1983)
B	W. de G. Birch, *Cartularium Saxonicum* (3 vols, 1885–93)
BAR	British Archaeological Reports
Burton Abbey Charters	*Anglo-Saxon Charters, II: Charters of Burton Abbey*, ed. P.H. Sawyer (1979)
CBA	Council for British Archaeology
Cox	J.C. Cox, *Notes on the Churches of Derbyshire* (4 vols, 1875)
DAJ	*Derbyshire Archaeological Journal* (formerly *Derbyshire Archaeological and Historical Journal*)
DB	*Domesday Book* (ed. J. Morris, Nottinghamshire, 1977; Derbyshire, 1978; Lincolnshire, 1986; Yorkshire, 1986)
EcHR	*Economic History Review*
EHD, I	*English Historical Documents I,* c. *500–1042,* ed. D.W. Whitelock (1955; 2nd edn 1979)

EHD, II	*English Historical Documents II, 1042–1189*, ed. D.C. Douglas and G.W. Greenaway (1953; 2nd edn 1981)
EHR	*English Historical Review*
EME	*Early Medieval Europe*
EPNS	English Place-Name Society
EYC	*Early Yorkshire Charters*, ed. W. Farrer and C.T. Clays (12 vols, 1914–65)
Flores Historiarum	Roger of Wendover's *Flores Historiarum: Rogeri de Wendover, Chronica sive flores historiarum*, ed. H. Coxe, Rolls Series, 84 (4 vols, 1841–2)
HE	*Bede's Ecclesiastical History of the English People*, ed. B. Colgrave and R.A.B. Mynors (1969)
HSC	*Historia de Sancto Cuthberto (Symeonis monachi Opera omnia*, ed. T. Arnold, Rolls Ser., 1882–5), I, 196–214 (selected chs trans. in *EHD* I, no.6)
IBGT	*Institute of British Geographers, Transactions*
JBAA	*Journal of the British Archaeological Association*
JEPNS	*Journal of the English Place-Name Society*
JHG	*Journal of Historical Geography*
K	J.M. Kemble, *Codex Diplomaticus Aevi Saxonici* (6 vols, 1839–48)
LHA	*Journal of the Society for Lincolnshire History and Archaeology*
Life of Saint Guthlac	*Felix's Life of Saint Guthlac*, ed. B. Colgrave (1956)
PN Berks	M. Gelling, *The Place-Names of Berkshire*, 3 pts, EPNS, 51–3 (1973–6)
PN Derbs	K. Cameron, *The Place-Names of Derbyshire*, 3 pts, EPNS, 27–9 (1959)
PN ERY	A.H. Smith, *The Place-Names of the East Riding of Yorkshire*, EPNS, 14 (1937)
PN Notts	J.E.B. Glover, A. Mawer and F.M. Stenton, *The Place-Names of Nottinghamshire*, EPNS, 17 (1940)
PN NRY	A.H. Smith, *The Place-Names of the North Riding of Yorkshire*, EPNS, 5 (1928)
PN WRY	A.H. Smith, *The Place-Names of the West Riding of Yorkshire*, 8 pts, EPNS, 33 (1961–3)
RA	*The Registrum Antiquissimum of the Cathedral Church of Lincoln*, ed. C.W. Foster, 3 pts, Lincoln Record Society, vols 27–9 (1931–5)

S	P.H. Sawyer, *Anglo-Saxon Charters: An Annotated List and Bibliography* (1968)
s.a.	*sub anno*
Settimane	*Settimane di studio del Centro italiano di studi sull'alto medioevo*
Sym. Op.	*Symeonis monachi Opera omnia*, ed. T. Arnold, Rolls Ser. (2 vols, 1882–5)
Thoroton	M.W. Barley and K.S.S. Train (eds) *The Antiquities of Nottinghamshire. Robert Thoroton. Edited and Enlarged by John Throsby* (first pubd. 1790–6; this edn, 3 vols, 1972)
Tithe Files, vol. 219	*Tithe Files, 1836–c.1870. Bedfords. to Leics.*, List and Index Society, 219 (1986)
Tithe Files, vol. 225	*Tithe Files, 1836–c.1870. Lincs. to Southampton*, List and Index Society, 225 (1987)
Tithe Maps, vol. 68	*Tithe Maps and Apportionments. Part I, Bedfords to Lincolns.*, List and Index Society, 68 (1971)
Tithe Maps, vol. 83	*Tithe Maps and Apportionments. Part I, Notts. to Yorks.*, List and Index Society, 83 (1972)
TRHS	*Transactions of the Royal Historical Society*
TTS	*Transactions of the Thoroton Society*
Valor	*Valor Ecclesiasticus temp. Henr. VIII* (5 vols, 1817)
VCH Derbs	W.M. Page (ed.) *The Victoria History of the County of Derbyshire*, vol. II (1907)
VCH Lincs	W.M. Page (ed.) *The Victoria History of the County of Lincoln*, vol. I (1914)
VCH Notts	W.M. Page (ed.) *The Victoria History of the County of Nottingham*, vol. II (1910)
VCH E. Riding	K.J. Allison (ed.) *The Victoria History of the County of Yorkshire. The East Riding*, vol. 6 (1989)
VCH N. Riding, I	W.M. Page (ed.) *The Victoria History of the County of York, North Riding*, vol. I (1914)
VCH N. Riding, II	W.M. Page (ed.) *The Victoria History of the County of York, North Riding*, vol. II (1923)
VSW	*The Life of Bishop Wilfrid by Eddius Stephanus*, ed. B. Colgrave (1927)
YAJ	*Yorkshire Archaeological Journal*
YAS	Yorkshire Archaeological Society

1 Introduction: past and current controversies

... we must be careful how we use our Dane

– F.W. Maitland[1]

This study examines the rural society and institutions of the northern Danelaw (Derbyshire, Nottinghamshire, Lincolnshire and Yorkshire) in the period *c.* 800–1100. It focuses on forms of lordship and the structure of peasant society, the development of the estate structure, the rural settlement pattern, and ecclesiastical organization and the emergence of the parish system. Each of these aspects of rural society is examined individually, although their mutual influence is of central importance. The peculiarities of the region have long been recognized, but explanations for them are still open to great debate. The impact of the vikings remains a controversial subject, although it is one that has experienced few innovations since the 1970s, and discussion continues to revolve around long-standing debates. This study offers new perspectives on the Scandinavian impact on parts of northern England, by combining a detailed local study with a consideration of wider issues concerning the society of Anglo-Saxon England. Clearly, the Scandinavian settlement differentiates the experiences of the various parts of the Danelaw from those of the rest of Anglo-Saxon England in the ninth and tenth centuries, but this can offer only a partial explanation for the peculiarities of northern and eastern England. Although decreasingly fashionable in other branches of scholarship, 'ethnic' explanations have not been wholly abandoned where the history of the Danelaw is concerned, despite the fact that every institution and every peculiarity of the social structure can, in fact, be paralleled elsewhere. Particularly prominent in the scholarship of the region is an emphasis on the impact of invasion and conquest as the major paradigm for explaining its characteristic features. There is also a tendency to treat the Danelaw as a single entity, without sufficient regard to the diversity of social, tenurial and ecclesiastical organization within the region. These are all issues which require revision.

---

1. F.W. Maitland, *Domesday Book and Beyond* (1897), 139.

Accordingly, this study has five main aims. First, it sets the societies of the northern Danelaw in a wider context. The region is compared with other parts of Anglo-Saxon England and also with contemporary Continental societies. From a purely Anglo-centric perspective explanations of the perceived contrasts between the societies of the Danelaw and of the rest of England have tended to emphasize the Scandinavian influence as the major differentiating factor. However, set within a broader context the region appears less unusual, and comparison with contemporary Continental societies offers both a necessary corrective to the emphasis on the Scandinavian factor, and a perspective that reveals a society not nearly as different as is sometimes supposed. Second, the study identifies regional variations within the northern Danelaw. Third, this study of the rural societies and estate structures of the northern Danelaw confronts a number of methodological problems. Various models have been generated in recent decades for uncovering the nature and organization of Anglo-Saxon society, which draw on a diverse body of evidence. This study offers a critique of several of these models using the evidence of the northern Danelaw; it also draws on contemporary analogies, from both elsewhere in Britain and the Continent, which suggest alternative ways of examining early medieval society. Fourth, it shifts the focus away from the impact of political conquest and invasion on the societies and institutions of the northern Danelaw, and examines longer-term developments and short-term changes unrelated to successive conquests. Finally, the study questions some of the old assumptions about the Scandinavian impact, and seeks to provide a new impetus to the debate by posing and addressing new questions.

This book, then, combines detailed local study of the society and institutions of the northern Danelaw with a broad survey of early medieval society in both Anglo-Saxon England and on the Continent, and in doing so seeks both to generate a new understanding of the history of the northern Danelaw and to offer new thoughts on aspects of Anglo-Saxon society that have received little attention of late. This introductory chapter highlights the evidence available for studying the northern Danelaw between *c.* 800 and *c.* 1100, considers the characteristics of the societies of the region and outlines the controversies surrounding them.

The northern Danelaw: its history and historiography

The term 'Danelaw' is first used in a law-code of 1008, and is more commonly used in the twelfth century to define those areas of northern and eastern England where Danish law, as opposed to Mercian or West Saxon law, was thought to prevail. The composition of the 'Danelaw' in the eleventh and twelfth centuries generally included the area of England to the east of, and including, Yorkshire, Derbyshire,

Leicestershire, Northamptonshire and Buckinghamshire (Fig. 1).[2] In addition to the legal definition of the Danelaw, historians tend to use the term to denote the areas of Scandinavian conquest and settlement in the ninth and tenth centuries. However, despite the fact that the Danelaw as a whole has many characteristics which distinguish it from the rest of England, there are also distinct regional differences within the Danelaw. Sir Frank Stenton recognized this in 1910 in his seminal study *Types of Manorial Structure in the Northern Danelaw.* The

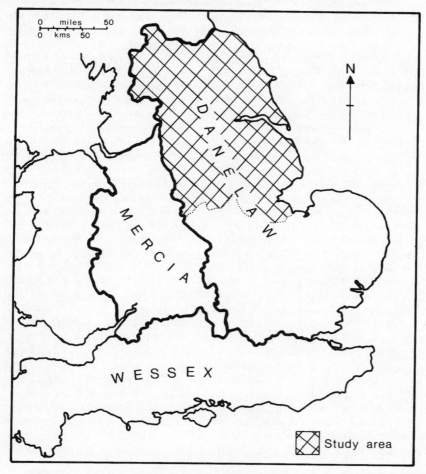

Figure 1 The Danelaw. Note that the Danelaw was not a consistently defined territory in the eleventh and twelfth centuries; this map shows those areas said at various times to be in the Danelaw

2.   H.M. Chadwick, *Anglo-Saxon Institutions* (1905), 198–201.

northern Danelaw in this study comprised Yorkshire, Lincolnshire, Nottinghamshire, Derbyshire, Rutland and Leicestershire, and he described it as a region characterized by the following features:

> by local names of Scandinavian origin, by the occurrence, within its limits, of a form of local division, the wapentake, otherwise unknown, by its ancient assessment on lines distinct from those which prevailed elsewhere in England, by the persistence of its political individuality until a late period, a reasonable uniformity of tenurial custom ... expressed with remarkable clearness in the terminology of the Domesday survey.

In the present volume the northern Danelaw is taken to mean an area smaller than that discussed by Stenton: Leicestershire and Rutland are omitted, mainly on account of the fact that the available evidence for those two counties is rather different from that available further north.[3] This study also goes further than that by Stenton and examines the distinctive nature of ecclesiastical provision in the region, the nature of lordship and peasant status, and the prevalence of a distinctive material culture heavily influenced by Scandinavian styles and motifs.

Following the pioneering work of Stenton, numerous studies have described the characteristic phenomena of the northern Danelaw in greater detail and many have sought to determine how far they were shaped by the Scandinavian settlers. Every perceived peculiarity of the region has at some time been ascribed to Scandinavian influence; but whether these were real or semantic has been a point for great debate. Two extreme views have been taken. Stenton believed that the region was characterized by the Danish element, which – although it varied across the region – was everywhere the dominant strain.[4] For him it was no accident that 'a social organization to which there is no parallel elsewhere in England occurs in the one part of the country in which the regular development of native institutions had been interrupted by a foreign settlement'.[5] The Scandinavian settlement not only overturned the existing political system but fundamentally altered the basis of social and economic organization. At the other extreme, Peter Sawyer later commented that 'apart from their settlements and their influence on the language and consequently on names and on some of the terminology of law and administration, the Scandinavians do not seem to have made a distinctive mark on England'.[6] Although Sawyer's additional comments on the small size of viking armies have been rejected,[7] more attention has been paid in the wake of his work to the

---

3. In particular, Domesday Book does not provide the same detail about estate organization or the church in Leicestershire and Rutland as it does further north.
4. F.M. Stenton, *Anglo-Saxon England* (3rd edn, 1971), 502–25.
5. *Ibid.*, 519.
6. P.H. Sawyer, *The Age of the Vikings* (2nd edn, 1971), 172–3.
7. See pp. 19–20 below.

similarities between the regions of the Danelaw and other parts of Anglo-Saxon England; rather than being regarded as Scandinavian innovations, many of the peculiarities of the Danelaw have now been assigned pre-viking origins.

Much recent work on the social organization, estate structure and the church in the northern Danelaw makes virtually no reference to the Scandinavian impact.[8] But this is to go too far, and is misleading. Although the characteristic features of the region can no longer be ascribed largely or solely to Scandinavian influence, there is still a need to assess the Scandinavian impact on the society and culture of the region. However, it is no longer adequate to map the distribution of, for example, Scandinavian place-names, or of metalwork and stone sculpture with Scandinavian-style ornamentation, and present it as an index of Scandinavian settlement and impact. A more sophisticated approach is required. Although none of the features of the northern Danelaw is a straightforward index of Scandinavian activity, all, in context, have much to reveal about it.

It is not difficult to see why such diverse interpretations of the Scandinavian impact could be generated from the same body of evidence. The major Anglo-Saxon narrative sources maintain a comparative silence on the northern Danelaw following the Scandinavian settlement and we are left to plot the unrecorded history of the region through an analysis of the combined evidence of non-narrative sources and much later narrative accounts. These sources appear to give contrasting impressions of the history of the region. It is worth briefly considering each type of evidence in turn, to establish its limitations and to identify the debates to which it has given rise.

Documentary sources

Our knowledge of the northern Danelaw before the tenth century is extremely scanty. No contemporary manuscript of any Anglo-Saxon northern chronicle has survived. However, the so-called D manuscript of the Anglo-Saxon Chronicle was compiled towards the end of the eleventh century and draws on earlier annals from York, as do parts of the E manuscript, the archetype of which seems to have been maintained at Canterbury in the mid-eleventh century and the surviving copy of which was produced at Peterborough in the early twelfth century.[9] The other

---

8. See, for example, the work of Glanville Jones on multiple estates (nn. 85 and 91) and R.K. Morris, *Churches in the Landscape* (1989), 133–9, 140–67, where the Scandinavians are not mentioned in his discussion of the church in the Danelaw during the tenth century.

9. P.H. Sawyer, 'Some sources for the history of Viking Northumbria', in *Viking Age York and the North*, ed. R.A. Hall (CBA Research Report 27, 1978), 3–7. On the various manuscripts which comprise the Anglo-Saxon Chronicle, see *EHD*, I, 109–19; P.A. Stafford, *Unification and Conquest: a political and social history of England in the tenth and eleventh centuries* (1989), 6–9; G.P. Cubbin (ed.) *The Anglo-Saxon Chronicle: a collaborative edition, Volume 6, MS D* (1996), xxvi.

Figure 2 Places referred to in this chapter

most notable sources for the history of Northumbria were apparently
produced by the community of St Cuthbert at Durham: the anonymous
Historia de Sancto Cuthberto (which was probably compiled in the mid-
tenth century, although the earliest surviving manuscript is in a late
eleventh-century hand), and the early twelfth-century writings
attributed to Simeon of Durham, which also drew on earlier annals.[10]

---

10.   Sawyer, 'Sources for the history of Viking Northumbria', 4.

Together these sources provide us with patchy evidence about the activities of kings, nobles and leading ecclesiastics. A more detailed understanding of the society of the region is hampered by the absence of any extant law-codes and the extremely small corpus of reliable pre-viking charters. This is a particular problem for attempts to analyse the impact of the Scandinavians; so little is known about the societies of the northern Danelaw on the eve of their settlement that it is not safe to assume that the idiosyncrasies of the region can be explained only by reference to Scandinavian influence.

The events surrounding the Scandinavian raids, political conquests and settlement are chiefly known to us from sources compiled outside the areas of Scandinavian settlement and political control. These include various manuscripts of the Anglo-Saxon Chronicle, the histories produced by the community of St Cuthbert, and a number of Irish and Scandinavian sources.[11] The West Saxon conquest of the northern Danelaw can be traced through the same sources, which are supplemented by the so-called Mercian Register entered in the B and C manuscripts of the Chronicle and the charters issued by the kings of Wessex. A brief account follows of the documented history of the region from the advent of the vikings to the expulsion of the last viking king of York.

The coming of the vikings in 793 was noted in dramatic style by the D and E manuscripts of the Anglo-Saxon Chronicle:

> In this year, dire portents appeared over Northumbria and sorely frightened the people. They consisted of immense whirlwinds and flashes of lightning, and fiery dragons were seen flying in the air. A great famine immediately followed those signs, and a little after that, on 8 June, the ravages of heathen men miserably destroyed God's church on Lindisfarne, with plunder and slaughter.[12]

There were other raids around the same time: for example, the Northumbrian monastery at *Donemuthan* (erroneously identified by Simeon of Durham as Jarrow) was plundered in 794.[13] Little more is heard of viking armies until 835, when they began to attack parts of southern England. Although the raids and battles recorded by the Anglo-Saxon Chronicle were mostly in the south, raids in other parts of England are recorded, such as that on Lindsey, East Anglia and Kent in 841. In addition, there was a raid on Northumbria in 844 in which King Rædwulf and one of his ealdormen were killed.[14] A new development

---

11. On the latter, see A.P. Smyth, *Scandinavian York and Dublin: the history and archaeology of two related kingdoms* (2 vols, 1975-9).

12. *ASC*, D, E, *s.a.* 793.

13. *ASC*, D, E, *s.a.* 794; on the identification of *Donemuthan*, see Dorothy Whitelock's comments in *EHD*, I, 182, n. 2; 830, n. 3.

14. The existence of King Rædwulf is recorded only in Roger of Wendover's *Flores Historiarum*, I, 282–3. His account is corroborated by the survival of a number of coins bearing Rædwulf's name: J.J. North, *English Hammered Coinage, I: Early Anglo-Saxon to Henry III, c. 650-1272* (1994), 72.

followed in 851, when for the first time a viking army stayed through the winter, on Thanet (Kent). The nature of the viking threat appears to have changed again in 865 with the arrival of the great army (*micel here*) under the leadership of Ivarr the Boneless and Halfdan.[15] It was seemingly a composite army which was much larger than any of the previous raiding bands; furthermore, it remained in England, camping in winter and raiding in summer.

In 866 the army occupied York. The Northumbrian attempt to regain York failed, during which Kings Ælle and Osberht and eight ealdormen died, and the vikings established an Englishman, Egbert, as king.[16] In the following years the army moved around Northumbria, Mercia (where it was besieged at Nottingham by Mercian and West Saxon forces in 868), East Anglia (killing King Edmund along the way) and Wessex, raiding and fighting, during which time it received only one major set-back – at Ashdown (Berks) in 871.[17] In the autumn of 872 the army returned to Northumbria, where a revolt against Egbert had caused him to flee along with the archbishop of York, Wulfhere. It is not clear what ensued, but a Northumbrian candidate, Ricsige, emerged as king, although probably only ruling north of the Tyne, and the archbishop returned. This may have been a compromise solution, and in any case Egbert had died.[18] The viking army spent the winter at Torksey (Lincs) and then moved to Repton (Derbs), after which the Mercian king, Burgred, left for Rome. The kingdom of Mercia was then given to Ceolwulf II; 'a foolish king's thegn', according to the common stock of the Anglo-Saxon Chronicle. Burgred and Ceolwulf were members of rival royal lines, and the viking involvement in Mercia may have been precipitated by Mercian factionalism.[19]

Wintering and raiding appears to have then turned to settlement: in 876 Halfdan went north with half of the army, where he 'shared out the land of the Northumbrians, and they proceeded to plough and to support themselves'. In 877 the other half of the army (under Guthrum, Oscytel and Anund) divided half the kingdom of Mercia among its members, and granted the rest to Ceolwulf.[20] Having made peace with Alfred of Wessex and accepted baptism in 878, Guthrum subsequently went into East Anglia in 880 and 'settled there and shared out the land'.[21] However, hostilities between the viking army in East Anglia and the West Saxons continued, and Alfred made another

---

15. *Æthelweard*, 35; *ASC*, s.a. 866; on the confusion over the names of the leaders of this army, see *EHD*, I, 192, n. 6; Stenton, *Anglo-Saxon England*, 246 and n. 2.
16. The events in Northumbria are described in Simeon of Durham's *Libellus de exordio atque procursu istius hoc est Dunelmensis ecclesie* in *Sym. Op.*, I, 3–169 at 55; in the *Historia Regum* attributed to Simeon, *ibid.*, II, 3–283 at 106, 110; and in *Flores Historiarum*, I, 298–9.
17. For a summary, see Stenton, *Anglo-Saxon England*, 248–51.
18. *Sym. Op.*, I, 56, 225; II, 110; *Flores Historiarum*, I, 325; *ASC*, s.a. 867.
19. *ASC*, s.a. 874; see p. 233 below on Mercian politics in the ninth century.
20. *ASC*, s.a. 876, 877.
21. *Ibid.*, s.a. 878; Asser, 85.

peace with Guthrum, in 886 or thereabouts, which involved the definition of a boundary between their areas of jurisdiction. The boundary ran along the rivers Lea and Ouse north from London to Bedford and from there ran along Watling Street for an unspecified distance. Although this is often regarded as a significant moment in defining the limits of viking control in England, it is, in fact, apparent that the boundary was not long respected, and by the early tenth century places to the west of the boundary, such as Hertford, Buckingham and Bedford, were under Danish control.[22] Most of the attention of the Anglo-Saxon Chronicle during the 880s and 890s was focused on subsequent raids and battles in Wessex and East Anglia, which intensified following the arrival, in 885 and 892, of new armies which had previously been raiding in France. Although they had made peace with Alfred, the existing viking armies in East Anglia and Northumbria did not desist from joining raids on Wessex. In 896 the new army divided and one force went to East Anglia and the other to Northumbria, and raids on Wessex continued.[23]

The shifting political allegiances of Northumbria in the later ninth and tenth centuries may be pieced together, although the history of the east Midlands (roughly Derbyshire, Nottinghamshire and Lincoln-shire) is less certain. The community of St Cuthbert, which had left Lindisfarne in 875, settled at Chester-le-Street (Co. Durham) c. 883, and shortly afterwards was instrumental in helping the local viking army to choose one of its number, Guthfrith, as king. He died in 895 and was buried in York Minster.[24] Little is known of his immediate successors as king, although Sigfrith and Knutr both issued silver coins in their names at York.[25] Accommodation with viking armies continued to be an option for indigenous lords, including Æthelwold, the nephew of Alfred, who 'went to the Danish army in Northumbria, and they accepted him as king and gave allegiance to him', following the death of Alfred in 899. He was subsequently accepted by the viking army in Essex, but was soon after killed by the army of Alfred's

---

22. *ASC*, *s.a.* 885, 886; *EHD*, I, no. 34; R.H.C. Davis, 'Alfred and Guthrum's frontier', *EHR*, 97 (1982), 803–10. The treaty has traditionally been dated to 886, after Alfred's capture of London, but a case for dating it earlier, perhaps to 878, is made in D. Dumville, 'The treaty of Alfred and Guthrum', in his *Wessex and England from Alfred to Edgar* (1992), 1–27. Whatever the date of this document, the political circumstances of the late ninth century were too complex for us to maintain that the 'Danelaw' was first defined at this time.
23. Stenton, *Anglo-Saxon England*, 263–9.
24. This assumes, as seems likely, that the Guthfrith referred to by Æthelweard is the same person as the *Guthred* mentioned in the *Historia de Sancto Cuthberto*, the *Libellus* and the *Historia Regum*: Æthelweard, 51; *Sym. Op.*, I, 203; *ibid.*, II, 82, 92, 110, 119; see also *EHD*, I, no. 6.
25. Sawyer, 'Sources for the history of Viking Northumbria'; M. Dolley, 'The Anglo-Danish and Anglo-Norse coinages of York', in *Viking Age York and the North*, ed. Hall, 26–31; I. Stewart, 'CVENNETTI reconsidered', in *Coinage in Ninth-Century Northumbria*, ed. D. Metcalf (1987), 345–59; North, *English Hammered Coinage*, 110–11.

successor, Edward the Elder. One of those who died alongside
Æthelwold was Brihtsige, son of the aetheling (throneworthy prince),
Beornoth; the names of Brihtsige and Beornoth and the use of the
term *aetheling* suggest that these were men of one of the Mercian royal
lines, and indicates another English faction who preferred to side with
the Danes rather than the West Saxon kings.[26]

Western Mercia came under West Saxon overlordship at some point
following the disappearance of Ceolwulf II from the historical record
after 877. It was ruled in the 880s by the Mercian ealdorman
Æthelred, who recognized Alfred as his lord and was married to
Alfred's daughter, Æthelflaed.[27] The fate of the rest of Mercia is less
clear. Although the east Midlands is often referred to as the territory
of the Five Boroughs (that is, Nottingham, Derby, Leicester, Lincoln
and Stamford), it is not known when this grouping came into existence,
nor when the region came to be conceived of as a single political unit.
The Five Boroughs are first linked together in an alliterative poem
incorporated in the Anglo-Saxon Chronicle entry for 942 (to
commemorate the capture of the region by King Edmund of Wessex).
That this grouping was more than a mere device of the poet who
composed the entry is shown by its appearance in Æthelred II's law-
code issued at Wantage (978 × 1008), which reveals that the Five
Boroughs had their own court, administration and legal identity, and in
the Chronicle entry for 1013.[28] The confederacy of the Five Boroughs
need not be a Danish institution, as has often been supposed, and
might as plausibly have resulted from administrative reorganization
instituted by the house of Wessex. However, it is not certain where
control over the various parts of the east Midlands lay in the later
ninth and early tenth centuries. An otherwise unknown king, Halfdan,
ruled somewhere in the north-east Midlands *c*. 900, where coins were
struck in his name. Elsewhere in that region military rulers exercised
control from towns, such as Jarl Thurcytel at Bedford, Jarl Thurferth at
Northampton and Jarl Toli at Huntingdon, and our evidence suggests
that political control was fragmented and fluid, although it is possible
that some form of political authority over the region lay between the
armies of East Anglia and Northumbria.[29] It is alleged by the late tenth-
century chronicler Æthelweard that King Alfred of Wessex sent an
ambassador to York in 894 to negotiate over land to the west of
Stamford (Lincs), which suggests that there had been a revival of

---

26.   *ASC*, *s.a.* 900, 902, 903; note that the A manuscript of the Chronicle does not
        mention Æthelwold's acceptance as king in Northumbria or the submission to
        him in Essex. On the coin associated with Æthelwold, see North, *English
        Hammered Coinage*, 111.

27.   For a discussion of the relevant charter evidence, see Stenton, *Anglo-Saxon
        England*, 259–60; Dumville, 'The treaty of Alfred and Guthrum', 7.

28.   *ASC*, *s.a.* 942, 1013; *EHD*, I, no. 43; P.A. Stafford, *The East Midlands in the
        Early Middle Ages* (1985), 112–16.

29.   M. Dolley, *Viking Coins of the Danelaw and of Dublin* (1965), 18; *ASC*, A, *s.a.*
        914, 917; *Liber Eliensis*, ed. E.O. Blake, Camden 3rd ser., 92 (1962), 98.

ancient claims of Northumbria to rule south of the Humber.[30] Such claims may also have lain behind the later attempt by the viking king of York, Olaf Guthfrithson, to extend his rule to the south in 939.[31]

Little can be established about political and military events in the northern Danelaw during the early tenth century, but it is known that the West Saxon king Edward the Elder encouraged some of his nobles to purchase land from the Scandinavians in advance of the wars of conquest by the house of Wessex.[32] The conquest of the territories controlled by the Scandinavians began in earnest in 909, when Edward dispatched an army against the Northumbrian Danes. In 910 his army defeated them at Tettenhall (Staffs), and killed their kings *Eowils* and Halfdan.[33] From then on Edward and his sister Æthelflaed attended to the defence of Mercia, and subsequently proceeded to capture and fortify the major strongholds of the Danelaw. In 912 Edward went to Hertford (Herts) and Witham, where *burhs* were built, while Æthelflaed built a *burh* at Bridgnorth (Shrops), and in the following three years she built *burhs* at Tamworth (Staffs), Eddisbury, Chirbury and Runcorn (Cheshire). In 914 Edward went to Buckingham, where he built two *burhs*, one on either side of the river, and received the submission of numerous Danish earls (*holds*) 'who belonged to' Bedford and Northampton. The following year he captured Bedford, and in due course Derby, Towcester, Tempsford, Colchester (917), Leicester, Stamford and Nottingham (918) fell to Edward or Æthelflaed. Æthelflaed also gained a promise from the people of York that they would be under her control, although she died before this could be effected. Who the 'people of York' included is not explained, but it is reasonable to assume that this was only one faction: perhaps indigenous lords intent on driving out Scandinavian rulers, although it is possible that they included Danes, who faced competition for control of York from the Norse who had been based in Dublin. Following the death of his sister, Edward took control of Mercia by removing Æthelflaed's daughter to a southern monastery. He then received the submission of the inhabitants of Mercia, at first Tamworth

---

30. *Æthelweard*, 51. Alfred's interest may have been connected with claims to the traditional dowry-land of the Mercian queens, given that his daughter was married to the Mercian ruler, Æthelred; Stafford, *East Midlands*, 112–14.

31. He took Tamworth (Staffs), but met resistance at Northampton and was eventually besieged by King Edmund of Wessex at Leicester; nonetheless, he succeeded sufficiently well in extending his authority for coins to be struck in his name at Derby: *ASC*, D, *s.a.* 943 (although these events clearly belong several years earlier); Dolley, *Viking Coins of the Danelaw and of Dublin*, 18.

32. S 396 (B 659), and see also *EHD*, I, no. 103; S 397 (B 658); F.M. Stenton, *Types of Manorial Structure in the Northern Danelaw*, Oxford Studies in Social and Legal History, ed. P. Vinogradoff, 2 (1910), 3–96, at 74–5.

33. *ASC*, *s.a.* 910; *Æthelweard*, 53, where a third king, Ivar, is mentioned; *The Chronicle of John of Worcester, I: the annals from 450 to 1066*, ed. R.R. Darlington, P. McGurk and J. Bray (1995), 365, where another king, Inguar (possibly the same person as Æthelweard's Ivar), is noted; for discussion, see Stenton, *Anglo-Saxon England*, 319–63.

and then Nottingham.[34] We do not know when Lincoln was captured, and although it may have been towards the end of the second decade of the tenth century, when the rest of the east Midlands fell to Edward or Æthelflaed, it is possible that it remained under the control of York, as it seems to have been at the end of the ninth century: coins minted at Lincoln in the 920s were similar to those being minted in York.[35] It may not be appropriate to describe the events of the early tenth century as evidence of a fusion of West Saxon and Mercian interests: the spheres of activity of Edward and Æthelflaed were clearly demarcated, with the latter defending Mercian territory, and are described separately in the main body of the Chronicle and the Mercian Register, respectively, and the two royal courts remained separate. Yet it is clear that a common threat in the north saw Mercia and Wessex drawn together.[36]

Meanwhile, Northumbria experienced fresh conquest by Norse raiders from Ireland, the history and consequences of which may be pieced together from the various northern sources, from Irish sources and from numismatic evidence. Ragnald, the grandson of Ivarr, occupied the land of Ealdred, reeve of Bamburgh, c. 914, and divided the lands of Alfred, a tenant of the community of St Cuthbert, between his followers, Scula and Onlafbal. He subsequently defeated the Bernicians and Scots in battle at Corbridge (Northumberland) in 914. In the following years he was active in the Isle of Man and Ireland, but returned c. 918 and fought a second battle at Corbridge, after he which he divided out the land he had acquired in battle among his followers, including the Englishmen Esbrid and Ælstan.[37] It is not certain when Ragnald took York: the *Historia Regum* dates this event to 919, the Anglo-Saxon Chronicle gives the date 923, but the *Historia Dunelmensis Ecclesiae* indicates that Ragnald took York before the first battle of Corbridge. Support for the earliest date comes from numismatic evidence, as Ragnald may be associated with an issue of coins from York which bear the name 'RAIENALT', and which have been dated on numismatic grounds to c. 910–15, owing to their similarity with the St Peter coins minted at York c. 905–10 (Fig. 3).[38]

Further south, in 920 Edward the Elder built a new *burh* at Nottingham and then went into the Peak District to Bakewell (Derbs), where he received the submission of Ragnald, the sons of Eadwulf and 'all who lived in Northumbria', the king and people of Strathclyde, and

---

34. ASC (including the Mercian Register), *s.a.* 912–18.
35. Stafford, *East Midlands*, 114.
36. Stafford, *Unification and Conquest*, 32.
37. *HSC*, 210; translated in *EHD*, I, no. 6; these events are discussed in C.D. Morris, 'Viking and native in northern England: a case study', in *Proceedings of the Eighth Viking Congress*, ed. H. Bekker-Nielsen (Odense, 1981), 223–44.
38. *Sym. Op.*, I, 72–3; II, 93; *ASC*, *s.a.* 923. On the coinage, see Smyth, *Scandinavian York and Dublin*, I, 103–6.

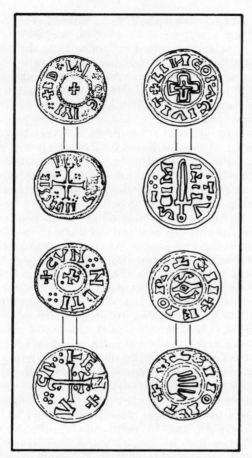

Figure 3 Coinage from the northern Danelaw

of the Scots.[39] This, however, gave Edward no direct authority over the north, although it doubtless did much for the prestige of the West Saxon monarchy, and may have been a necessary expedient for Ragnald. Moreover, it did not lead to a period of peace or stability and was followed, rather, by a protracted struggle between the dynasty of Ivarr and the kings of Wessex.[40] Ragnald was succeeded as king in York in 920 by his kinsman Sihtric from Dublin, and in 924 Edward the Elder died and was succeeded to the West Saxon kingdom by his son Athelstan. Athelstan gave his sister in marriage to Sihtric, who also

39. *ASC*, s.a. 920.
40. Evidence for the family links of the rulers at York is contained in the *Annals of Ulster*; Smyth, *Scandinavian York and Dublin*, I, 111.

accepted Christianity, although Roger of Wendover claims that the marriage and conversion were short-lived.[41] Following the death of Sihtric in 927, Athelstan asserted influence over the north, when the kings of Scotland, Strathclyde and Gwent and the lord of Bamburgh, Aldred, became his men and 'came under his rule', and he took control of York.[42] In 927 a king called Guthfrith was expelled from York by Athelstan, who then destroyed the viking fortress at York and minted coins in his name there.[43]

Until his death in 939 Athelstan appears to have ruled York, yet the West Saxon control of the north was far from secure. It was challenged in 937 when Olaf, the son of Guthfrith, sailed for northern Britain from Dublin, but Athelstan maintained his position in the north when Olaf was decisively defeated at the Battle of Brunnanburh. However, upon Athelstan's death in 939 Olaf invaded again and took York. The following year he raided the Midlands as far south as Northampton, accompanied by Archbishop Wulfstan. Returning northwards he was met by the army of the new king of Wessex, Edmund, at Leicester, but battle was averted by the archbishops of York and Canterbury, who arranged a peace which gave to Olaf the territory between Watling Street and Northumbria.[44] This success for the kingdom of York was to prove short-lived. The following year Olaf died and was replaced by his cousin Olaf Sihtricson, who in 942 lost to Edmund the lands which had been won in 940. Following this, Olaf Sihtricson made peace with Edmund and accepted baptism, as did another little-known viking leader, Ragnald Guthfrithson. Little more is known of the situation in York at this time, but in 944 Edmund drove both these kings out.[45]

The chronology of the final phase of the so-called First Viking Age in England is confused. It appears that Archbishop Wulfstan and 'all the councillors of the Northumbrians' gave their pledges to King Eadred in 947, but that shortly afterwards Northumbrian allegiances switched to Eric 'Bloodaxe', who had arrived from Norway. Eadred then invaded Northumbria and burned the church at Ripon (Yorks). Although Eadred's army was defeated at Castleford (Yorks), his threat to return to Northumbria and 'destroy it utterly' prompted the councillors of the Northumbrians to desert Eric. Olaf Sihtricson returned to Northumbria in 949, but was driven out upon the return of Eric in 952. At

41. The death of Ragnald is noted in the *Annals of Ulster* for 921; Smyth, *Scandinavian York and Dublin*, I, 112–13. On Sihtric and Athelstan, see *ASC*, D, *s.a.* 926; *Flores Historiarum*, I, 385. The coinage from Sihtric's reign is discussed in North, *English Hammered Coinage*, 113.
42. *ASC*, D, *s.a.* 927.
43. *Willelmi Malmesbiriensis Monachi. De Gestis Rerum Anglorum*, ed. W. Stubbs, Rolls Series, 90 (2 vols, 1887–9), I, 147; *ASC*, *s.a.* 927; *Sym. Op.*, II, 93; *The Annals of Ulster (to AD 1131)*, ed. S. MacAirt and G. MacNiocaill (1983), 378–9; North, *English Hammered Coinage*, 135, 137.
44. *The Annals of Ulster*, ed. MacAirt and MacNiocaill, 382–7; *ASC*, *s.a.* 937, 940, 943; *Sym. Op.*, II, 93–4.
45. *Sym. Op.*, II, 94; *ASC*, *s.a.* 943, 944.

some point in the early 950s Archbishop Wulfstan was imprisoned by King Eadred, although it is not clear whether this was before or after Eric's return. Eric ruled Northumbria until he was expelled two years later and Eadred took Northumbria.[46] Although it may not have been immediately apparent, the expulsion of Eric brought the age of viking rule in northern England effectively to an end.

The narrative sources provide a partial record of the succession of rulers in northern England, and of the battles and treaties that brought about changes in political control. To move beyond this fragmentary record in order to establish motives and intentions is no easy task. Nonetheless, it is certain that the political fortunes of the northern Danelaw cannot be understood simply in terms of a changing balance of power between 'English' and 'Scandinavian' interests. There were many divisions between the various English and Scandinavian factions, and political and military allegiances were not formed solely along 'ethnic' lines. The previous histories and identities of the various regions of the northern Danelaw remained important, and to some extent determined the actions of successive rulers in the later ninth and earlier tenth centuries, although new allegiances and areas of political control continued to be formed. Divisions among the Scandinavians may also have been significant in the rapidly changing political situation in the north, and may have lain behind the readiness with which 'the people of York' agreed to come under Æthelflaed's control, and the submission of Ragnald and then Sihtric to successive West Saxon kings as they attempted to gain legitimacy in the north. The church also played an important role in underpinning the authority of successive rulers. It is not certain that there was a deliberate West Saxon attempt to create an 'English' kingdom; even if such an ambition existed, the political reality of separate kingdoms with long traditions had to be addressed. The taking of the kingdom of York was much less straightforward than had been the capture of Mercia, where alliances and family politics had prepared the ground for West Saxon success more effectively. In the north, the ground had been less well prepared, and the emergence of successive claimants from Dublin with potential allies to hand in Northumbria complicated matters still further.[47]

There are sufficient pointers to allow us to believe that the accounts provided by the narrative sources are far from the whole story, even where political and military issues are concerned. The various manuscripts of the Anglo-Saxon Chronicle and related accounts provide a partial version of events. Some were written under the aegis of the West Saxon court and were concerned to promote the image of successive West Saxon kings and to justify West Saxon expansionism; others were written

---

46. *ASC*, s.a. 946–9, 952, 954; *Sym. Op.*, II, 94; *Flores Historiarum*, I, 402–3 (for an account of Eric's death); Smyth, *Scandinavian York and Dublin*, I, 155–6. P.H. Sawyer, 'The last Scandinavian kings of York', *Northern History*, 31 (1995), 39–44, suggests that Olaf may have ruled from 947 to 950 and Eric from 950 to 952.
47. Stafford, *Unification and Conquest*, 31–4.

long after the events, although relying on earlier accounts, and all have a particular perspective and agenda which they promote, such as, for example, the role of the community of St Cuthbert and the fate of its landed endowments.[48] In general there is little comment on the damage inflicted on the church in the Danelaw by successive Scandinavian raids, but there is contemporary evidence from other regions, particularly in charters, that individual churches did often suffer great depredations and that contemporaries feared for the future of the church, and this must also have been true of the church in the Danelaw.[49] Nonetheless, the well-documented relations of the community of St Cuthbert and successive archbishops of York with various viking rulers indicates that relations between vikings and ecclesiastics were not invariably based on hostility, and these documented cases may have been the tip of the iceberg. It is also clear that viking rulers and armies regularly reached accommodations with English rulers and aristocrats, lay and ecclesiastical, in the north.[50] On the other hand, even if, as Sawyer put it, the vikings were but a complication, 'and for some a welcome one', they certainly did great damage.[51] The disappearance of bishoprics, the loss of independence of three kingdoms and the deaths of a number of their kings, and the apparent loss of most of the books, charters and libraries of the Danelaw should not be overlooked. We should not abandon the idea that the vikings could be 'dangerous to know'.[52]

There are, then, grounds for maintaining that the perspectives reflected in the various narrative sources leave much undisclosed, or only summarily recorded. The picture of Scandinavian involvement in England presented by narrative sources appears to be particularly one-dimensional when compared with the evidence of place-names, of archaeology, of later law-codes and of the social structure and ecclesiastical organization of the region revealed in later sources. These sources have been the subject of much debate, not least because they seem to suggest that the settlement of the Scandinavians may

---

48.   J. Bately, 'The compilation of the Anglo-Saxon Chronicle 60 BC to AD 890: vocabulary as evidence', *Proceedings of the British Academy*, 64 (1980 for 1978), 93–129.

49.   R.I. Page, *A Most Vile People: early English historians on the vikings* (1987). The only reference in the Anglo-Saxon Chronicle to the destruction of religious houses in the late ninth century is a twelfth-century interpolation in the E manuscript produced at Peterborough: *EHD*, I, 192, n. 6; discussed in Sawyer, *The Age of the Vikings*, 19–20.

50.   Notable examples of collaboration include the community of St Cuthbert and the viking leader Guthfrith; the English lords Esbrid and Ælstan with the viking leader Ragnald (above, n. 37); and Archbishop Wulfstan and successive viking rulers. Wulfstan's actions are discussed in D.W. Whitelock, 'The dealings of the kings of England with Northumbria in the tenth and eleventh centuries', in *The Anglo-Saxons: studies presented to Bruce Dickins*, ed. P. Clemoes (1959), 70–88.

51.   Sawyer, *The Age of the Vikings*, 147.

52.   To use the words of P. Wormald, 'Viking studies: whence and whither?', in *The Vikings*, ed. R.T. Farrell (1982), 128–53, at 148.

have been on a substantial scale, that the Scandinavian settlement and periods of control were not completely inimical to the fortunes of the church, that trade was boosted by the wide contacts of the Scandinavian newcomers, and that the society of the Danelaw was fundamentally transformed through its contact with Scandinavian settlers. It is, then, necessary to consider the non-narrative evidence for the impact of the Scandinavians, which permits us an insight into aspects of this impact that extend beyond the documented military and political activity, and enables us to consider the social, economic and cultural consequences of Scandinavian settlement.

Linguistic evidence

The significance of the density of wholly or partially Scandinavian or scandinavianized place-names, field-names, terms to describe the features of the landscape and personal names in the Danelaw has been hotly disputed (Fig. 4).[53] Philologists have long argued that this linguistic impact can only be explained by reference to a mass settlement of Scandinavians.[54] This argument is apparently strengthened by the massive impact of the Scandinavian languages on Old English, including the adoption of Scandinavian nouns and verbs in Anglo-Saxon speech and the formation of words according to the grammatical rules of Old Norse (such as the use of the Scandinavian genitival forms *-ar* and *-s* rather than the Old English *-es* in place-name formation).[55] In the following summary of the main arguments about linguistic evidence, it will become apparent that there has traditionally been a polarization of opinion between linguists and place-name scholars on the one hand, and historians on the other. More recently, however, matters have partially improved: the work of the philologist Gillian Fellows Jensen, in particular, has kept pace with changing historical interpretations, and John Hines has elsewhere demonstrated

---

53. On place-names, see n. 54. On field-names, see N. Lund, 'The settlers: where do we get them from – and do we need them?', in *Proceedings of the Eighth Viking Congress*, ed. Bekker-Nielsen, 147–71, at 162–5; K. Cameron, 'Early field-names in an English-named Lincolnshire village', in *Otium et Negotium*, ed. F. Sandgren (Stockholm, 1973), 38–43; K. Cameron, 'The minor names and field names of the Holland division of Lincolnshire', in *The Vikings*, ed. T. Andersson and K.I. Sandred (Uppsala 1978), 81–8. On other landscape features, see M. Gelling, *Signposts to the Past* (1978), 215–16.
54. K. Cameron: *Scandinavian Settlement in the Territory of the Five Boroughs: the place-name evidence* (1965); K. Cameron, 'Scandinavian settlement in the territory of the Five Boroughs: the place-name evidence, pt II: place-names in thorp', *Mediaeval Scandinavia*, 3 (1970), 35–49; K. Cameron, 'Scandinavian settlement in the territory of the Five Boroughs: the place-name evidence, pt III, the Grimston-hybrids', in *England before the Conquest*, ed. P. Clemoes and K. Hughes (1971), 147–63; G. Fellows Jensen, 'The vikings in England: a review', *ASE*, 4 (1975), 181–206.
55. G. Fellows Jensen, *Scandinavian Settlement Names in the East Midlands* (Copenhagen, 1978), 272–3.

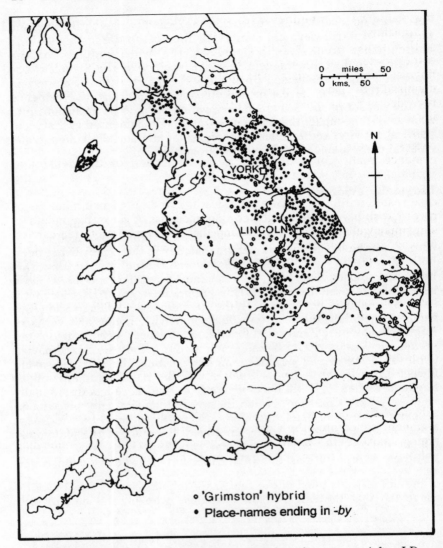

Figure 4 Distribution map of Scandinavian place-names (after J.D.
Richards, *Viking Age England* (1991), fig. 17). Names formed with the
element *-thorp* have been omitted, as there is uncertainty about whether
they should all be regarded as being formed with a Scandinavian, as
opposed to an English, place-name element.

the value of combining historical, archaeological and linguistic approaches.[56]

Historians have generally been less convinced that the linguistic evidence testifies to a massive influx of Scandinavians than have linguists and philologists. The historian R.H.C. Davis, for instance, dismissed the idea that the plethora of Danish personal names recorded in East Anglia in the tenth to twelfth centuries betokened the invasion of large numbers of Danes; in the same way that the Normans were to do later, the Danes had merely started a new fashion in names.[57] Peter Sawyer questioned the extent to which the place-name evidence really could be used as an indication of the density of Scandinavian settlement, since he believed that the armies of the vikings were to be numbered in hundreds rather than thousands.[58] His case rested on the fact that early raids involved only small numbers of recorded ships, and he suggested that accounts of greater numbers of ships may well be exaggerations and that the numbers of men carried on any given ship may not have been much in excess of thirty.[59] Further, the Anglo-Saxon Chronicle uses the term *here* to describe the viking raiding parties, and it has been observed that since the seventh-century laws of King Ine of Wessex earlier used the term to mean a band of marauders in excess of thirty-five men, it need not signify great numbers.[60] However, philologists have not been convinced by Sawyer's argument. The Norman conquest of England has been used as a control case; it was an aristocratic conquest achieved by a few thousand aristocrats and their followers, and their effect on place-names was minimal.[61] By contrast the Scandinavian invasions would seem to have been much more massive.

The continuing belief that the linguistic evidence proved a substantial Scandinavian presence necessitated nullifying Sawyer's argument. Accordingly, it was argued by Kenneth Cameron that although the size of the armies may not have been substantial, there must have been a settlement of significant magnitude, a secondary migration, that followed in the wake of the military conquest of the region.[62] Nicholas Brooks subsequently suggested that the Anglo-Saxon Chronicle probably did not, in fact,

---

56. G. Fellows Jensen, 'Scandinavian settlement in Yorkshire: through the rear-view mirror', in *Scandinavian Settlement in Northern Britain*, ed. B.E. Crawford (1995), 170–86; see a reference to the work of John Hines in n. 75.

57. R.H.C. Davis, 'East Anglia and the Danelaw', *TRHS*, 5th ser., 5 (1955), 23–39, at 29–30.

58. Sawyer, *The Age of the Vikings*, 169–70.

59. P.H. Sawyer, 'The density of the Danish settlement in England', *University of Birmingham Journal* 6 (1) (1957), 1–17; Sawyer, *The Age of the Vikings*, 124–5.

60. G. Jones, *A History of the Vikings* (2nd edn, 1984) 218, n. 1.

61. Gelling, *Signposts to the Past*, 236–40; Stafford, *The East Midlands*, 77.

62. The point was made in H.R. Loyn, *Anglo-Saxon England and the Norman Conquest* (1962), 54, and expanded on by Cameron in his three papers on the place-names of the territory of the Five Boroughs (n. 54, above). See also N. Lund, 'The secondary migration', *Mediaeval Scandinavia*, 1 (1969), 196–201; Lund, 'The settlers'.

greatly exaggerate the numbers of ships involved in the viking raids, as its figures show remarkable consistency with those of Continental sources.[63] Sawyer's estimation of the numbers carried by individual ships has also been questioned.[64] Whatever the size of the armies, it has become common to distinguish between a period of conquest and a period of colonization, and Sawyer himself conceded that the Scandinavian impact on England could not be measured by the original conquest and colonization alone.[65]

The situation concerning the numerical impact of the Scandinavians is far from resolved.[66] Whatever the size of the armies, it is not clear how many of them actually settled, and although the concept of a mass peasant migration holds some attractions – not the least the fact that it apparently makes sense of the linguistic evidence – the narrative sources are concerned with the aristocratic and royal levels of society, not with rural society, and therefore offer little to support, or to disprove, the argument for a mass migration. For example, in the tenth century the Scandinavians were still referred to in terms of armies, and when faced with the threat of conquest by the armies of Edward the Elder and Æthelflaed the Scandinavians apparently regrouped within the defences of the *burhs* of eastern England and the north Midlands; this does not suggest a mass invasion.[67] On the other hand, however, it is impossible to know what the size of the catchment area of any given *burh* would have been, or whether the viking leaders would have been concerned to protect all Scandinavian immigrants. This, and what we know of the perspective of the narrative sources, renders the recourse to the *burhs* of little use in determining the number of Scandinavians in the Danelaw. Neither the reference in the Anglo-Saxon Chronicle to the fact that King Edgar 'attracted hither foreigners and enticed harmful people to this country' and his separate legislation for 'the Danes' in his fourth law-code,[68] nor the massacre of Danes in 1002 on the instructions of Æthelred II, can be safely used to support an argument for a mass migration.[69]

Hence, the linguistic evidence remains the strongest indication of a large-scale Scandinavian settlement. This is not, however, to accept the linguistic argument as traditionally presented. There are in fact a number of important issues to be addressed concerning the absorption

63. N.P. Brooks, 'England in the ninth century: the crucible of defeat', *TRHS*, 5th ser., 29 (1979), 1–20, at 3–8.
64. A.L. Binns, 'The navigation of Viking ships around the British Isles in Old English and old Norse sources' in *The Fifth Viking Congress*, ed. W.F.H. Nicolaisen (1968), 107–8.
65. P.H. Sawyer, 'Conquest and colonization: Scandinavians in the Danelaw and in Normandy' in *Proceedings of the Eighth Viking Congress*, ed. Bekker-Nielsen, 123–131, at 130.
66. Lund, 'The settlers'.
67. F.M. Stenton, 'The Danes in England', *Proceedings of the British Academy*, 13 (1927), 5.
68. *ASC, s.a.* 959; see Whitelock's comments, *EHD*, I, 225, n. 4; *EHD*, I, no. 41.
69. *ASC, s.a.* 1002; *EHD*, I, no. 127; Stafford, *Unification and Conquest*, 66.

of a new language into an existing one which have yet to be considered in most work on the linguistic evidence. The introduction of a new language into law and administration could easily have been achieved by a small group of legislators and administrators, but it can hardly be envisaged that the rulers of the Danelaw could have, on their own, facilitated the adoption of Scandinavian words into Anglo-Saxon speech and nomenclature.[70] It should also be remembered that not all Scandinavian place-names were necessarily coined during the period of Scandinavian control of the Danelaw, or the initial phases of settlement. Certainly some place-names contain Scandinavian personal names that appear to have dropped out of use by the eleventh century, and this suggests that they were coined much earlier.[71] However, there is evidence that some place-names containing Scandinavian words and names emerged later. For example, Bleasby (Notts) incorporates the Danish element *by*, but until at least 956 was known as *Blisetune*, which incorporates the Old English *tun*.[72] A number of studies have concluded that many Scandinavian place-names may have been coined as late as the eleventh or twelfth century, although whether this betokens an ongoing influx of Scandinavian settlers is not apparent.[73] This brings us no nearer to determining the density of Scandinavian settlement, but it does at least warn against using the distribution of Scandinavian place-names as an index of the earliest phases of Scandinavian settlement.

The debate about the linguistic impact of the Scandinavian settlers has been fierce. It has been dominated by a concern to relate the linguistic impact to the scale of the settlement, and by discussion of the ways in which the distribution of Scandinavian place-names reveals the location of Scandinavian settlement. However, as I have observed elsewhere, there are many reasons why these older approaches require critical re-evaluation.[74] For example, in other branches of early medieval scholarship few would now attempt to use place-name evidence to establish a chronology of settlement, and place-name distribution maps have been shown to be too unsophisticated, when used in isolation, to identify the locations or movements of peoples. The Scandinavian impact on place-names needs to be considered alongside the Scandinavian impact on aspects of material culture, and within the context of territorial organization and estate structure, which

---

70. K. Cameron, 'Linguistic and place-name evidence', his reply to Sawyer's 'The two viking ages', *Mediaeval Scandinavia*, 2 (1969), 176–7.
71. G. Fellows Jensen, 'Of Danes – and thanes – and Domesday Book', in *People and Places in Northern Europe, 500–1600*, ed. I.N. Wood and N. Lund (1991), 107–21.
72. Fellows Jensen, *Scandinavian Settlement Names in the East Midlands*, 293.
73. Fellows Jensen, 'Scandinavian settlement in Yorkshire'; Fellows Jensen, 'Of Danes – and thanes'; *PN Berks*, pt 2, 330; J. Insley, 'Toponymy and settlement in the North-West', *Nomina*, 10 (1986), 69–76; B.K. Roberts, 'Late -*by* names in the Eden Valley, Cumberland', *Nomina*, 13 (1989–90), 25–40.
74. D.M. Hadley, ' "And they proceeded to plough and to support themselves": the Scandinavian settlement of England', *ANS*, 19 (1997), 69–96, at 71–5.

we know to have been important in determining the coining of place-names. Recent work on language change in other contexts also needs to be incorporated into the debate, not least because it questions the extent to which it can be directly correlated with the numerical impact of speakers of a particular language; the importance of examining the broad social contexts within which language change might occur has recently been emphasized, and provides a method for bringing linguistic data into an interdisciplinary approach to social and cultural change.[75]

Social structure and estate organization according to Domesday Book

Domesday Book appears to reveal great contrasts between the northern Danelaw and other parts of eleventh-century England – contrasts traditionally associated with Scandinavian settlement. The free peasants of the Danelaw (*sochemanni* and *liberi homines*) have long been figures of fascination; to Maitland, for example, they testified that the Danelaw was 'the home of liberty'.[76] The debate about the significance of these peasants has been almost as fierce as that concerning Scandinavian place-names. The key factor is the distribution of these peasants, who according to Domesday Book are largely limited to eastern and northern England (Fig. 5). To Stenton this distinctive group within rural society could be ascribed to the Scandinavian settlement of the region; they were the descendants of the rank and file of the viking armies.[77] In the case of Lincolnshire, where half the population recorded in Domesday Book were sokemen, this would seem to indicate that there was a massive settlement of Scandinavians. However, Stenton's argument has long since been undermined. First, R.H.C. Davis observed a similarity between socage tenure, Kentish tenure by gavelkind and the tenure of the '*ceorl* who sits on *gafolland*' who was named in the treaty of Alfred and Guthrum.[78] All three forms of tenure appeared to have their origins in freehold land held under payment of tribute to the king. The significance of this association was that the '*ceorl* who sits on *gafolland*' existed before c. 890, which means that, by analogy, socage tenure was not an innovation. Hence, the necessity of explaining it, and by extension sokemen, to the Scandinavians was removed. Second, there is no precise correlation between the distribution of Domesday

75. See, for example, J. Hines, 'Scandinavian English: a creole in context' in *Language Contact in the British Isles*, ed. P.S. Ureland and G. Broderick (Tübingen, 1991), 403–27.
76. Maitland, *Domesday Book and Beyond*, 23.
77. F.M. Stenton, 'The free peasantry of the northern Danelaw', *Bulletin de la Société Royale des lettres de Lund* (1925–6), 73–185; Stenton, 'The Danes in England', 145.
78. Davis, 'East Anglia and the Danelaw', 33; *EHD*, I, no. 34. See also *The Kalendar of Abbot Samson of Bury St. Edmunds*, ed. R.H.C. Davis, Camden 3rd ser., 84 (1954), xlv–xlvi.

	Freemen	Sokemen	Villeins	Bordars	Cottars	Slaves	Others	Total
Yorkshire								
W. Riding	16	281	1,727	1,043	16	–	107	3,190
N. Riding	15	44	1,592	322	–	–	41	2,014
E. Riding	26	123	1,714	441	–	–	58	2,362
Derbyshire	42	124	1,776	734	–	20	50	2,746
Nottinghamshire	3	1,704	2,611	1,176	–	24	55	5,573
Lincolnshire	–	10,882	7,029	3,379	–	–	172	21,462

Figure 5 The rural population of the Danelaw according to Domesday Book (figures taken from H.C. Darby and I.S. Maxwell, *The Domesday Geography of Northern England* (1962))

free peasants and Scandinavian place-names. For example, Yorkshire has relatively few sokemen but many Scandinavian place-names; conversely East Anglia has many sokemen and *liberi homines* but Scandinavian place-names are comparatively less common.[79] In other words, the two major bodies of evidence usually invoked to demonstrate the density and extent of Scandinavian settlement present different impressions.

Third, to make any sense the connection between sokemen and Scandinavians requires large areas to have been depopulated or else for there to have been large areas awaiting colonization, but such an argument cannot easily be substantiated. It now seems unlikely that there were many areas devoid of settlement in the Danelaw. Neither the distribution of sokemen/*liberi homines* nor that of Scandinavian place-names can confidently be used, therefore, to indicate areas of colonization in the period following the Scandinavian conquest of the Danelaw.[80] All that can really be said about the sokemen/*liberi homines* of the Danelaw is that they are generally found, as are Scandinavian place-names, in areas which in the late ninth and early tenth centuries came under Scandinavian control. This does not prove that they were of Scandinavian descent; still less does it offer proof of a mass migration of Scandinavians. Indeed, it is as plausible to believe that they were in essence of Anglo-Saxon descent but that the Scandinavian settlement in some way either altered or preserved their status, and we might do as well to ask what happened to the free peasants of the rest of Anglo-Saxon England.[81] To develop this point it will be necessary to examine the nature of the Anglo-Saxon peasantry and how

79. Sawyer, *The Age of the Vikings*, 154–71.
80. P.H. Sawyer, *From Roman Britain to Norman England* (1978), 132–67, esp. 161–3; C.D. Morris, 'Aspects of Scandinavian settlement in northern England: a review', *Northern History*, 20 (1984), 1–22, at 13–15.
81. *The Kalendar of Abbot Samson*, ed. Davis, xliii–xlvii; Sawyer, 'The density of the Danish settlement in England', 2; Sawyer, *The Age of the Vikings*, 171; E. John, 'The age of Edgar', in *The Anglo-Saxons*, ed. J. Campbell (1982), 160–89, at 164.

the structure of society changed through the Anglo-Saxon centuries. The peasantry has received less attention of late than it has within Continental scholarship, and debates on the Continent will be summarized in order to highlight possible analogies in the evidence and approaches taken. An attempt to set the society of the Danelaw in a wider context was attempted more than twenty years ago by Anne Kristensen, but it has received little attention; there are certainly problems with her interpretation, but her approach warrants more detailed consideration.[82] The recent study by Rosamond Faith of the peasantry and lordship in early medieval English society renders a new look at the social structure of the northern Danelaw especially timely.[83]

The second striking feature of the society of the Danelaw is its complex estate structure, which appears to have been rather different from that of other parts of late Anglo-Saxon England. It is characterized by large, multi-vill manors which had numerous attached properties, and which were known as sokes. For Stenton the sokes were the result of the settlement of the rank and file of the army around one of the leaders of the invasion, and he suggested that the greater sokes of the Danelaw may well have been the product of the sharing out of the lands of the kingdoms of Northumbria, East Anglia and Mercia that is recorded in the Anglo-Saxon Chronicle.[84] However, more recent accounts have assigned the sokes of the Danelaw origins in the pre-viking period. The basis for such an argument is that the sokes resemble other 'multiple estates' known to have characterized rural organization in the pre-viking period.[85] As in the case of the sokemen, the sokes of the Danelaw, according to a number of studies, must represent the remnants of an earlier form of organization which for some reason survived the Scandinavian conquest of the region.[86]

The possibility of exploring this proposition has been created by the great advances made in recent decades in our understanding of territorial organization in the seventh to the ninth centuries, using both contemporary and later documentary sources combined with the evidence of place-names, archaeology and parish boundaries.[87] The northern Danelaw has been less intensively investigated than other

---

82. A.K.G. Kristensen, 'Danelaw institutions and Danish society in the viking age: *sochemanni, liberi homines* and *königsfreie*', *Mediaeval Scandinavia*, 8 (1975), 27–85.
83. R. Faith, *The English Peasantry and the Growth of Lordship* (1997).
84. Stenton, *Anglo-Saxon England*, 510–12; Stenton, 'The Danes in England', 4–5, 16–18.
85. See, for example, G.R.J. Jones, 'Multiple estates and early settlement' in *English Medieval Settlement*, ed. P.H. Sawyer (1979), 9–40; Stafford, *The East Midlands*, 30–2; *The Kalendar of Abbot Samson*, ed. Davis, xliv–xlvii.
86. *The Kalendar of Abbot Samson*, ed. Davis, xlvi.
87. J. Campbell, 'Bede's *reges* and *principes*', in his *Essays in Anglo-Saxon History* (1986), 85–98, at 95–6; S.R. Bassett, 'In search of the origins of Anglo-Saxon kingdoms', in *The Origins of Anglo-Saxon Kingdoms*, ed. S.R. Bassett (1989), 3–27; J. Blair, *Early Medieval Surrey* (1991), 12–34.

regions, partly because of the absence of early documentary evidence. Moreover, whereas studies of other regions have confidently used late evidence to infer much earlier patterns of organization, students of the Danelaw have perhaps been more cautious, owing to the reputation of the vikings and the expectation that they caused great changes to the socio-economic organization of the region. Nonetheless, once the impact of the Scandinavians had been questioned, the large sokes of the Danelaw came to be seen as comparable to the large multi-vill estates uncovered elsewhere.[88] G.W.S. Barrow, who found traces of such a system in Scotland, remarked that there was a system of 'extensive' royal lordship from Kent to Northumbria based on a unit known variously as a lathe, soke, shire or *manerium cum appendiciis* which survived long enough for its features to be still discernible in the eleventh and twelfth centuries.[89]

The identification of earlier parallels, and of analogies outside the Danelaw, for the sokemen and sokes of the Danelaw serves to reduce the level of change that can be attributed to the Scandinavians. However, little attempt has been made to pursue the implications of this for furthering our understanding of how the Scandinavians, and later the West Saxons, secured their control of the Danelaw, beyond the suggestion that they may have adopted and exploited the existing territorial organization.[90] Glanville Jones did, however, long ago devise a model concerning the sokes of the northern Danelaw which also accounted for the proliferation of Scandinavian place-names. He has suggested that the viking leaders took over the focal points of the large sokes, but rarely changed their names, whereas their followers were endowed with intermediate rights over the appendages of the sokes, and their closer association with individual hamlets or villages saw the more frequent adoption of Scandinavian names for the dependencies of the sokes.[91] In contrast, other studies have observed that although the territorial soke may represent an ancient form of organization, it is not unlikely that some of the sokes recorded by Domesday Book may, in fact, be more recent creations.[92] However, this observation has yet to be explored systematically.

---

88. W.E. Kapelle, *The Norman Conquest of the North: the region and its transformation, 1000–1135* (1979), 62–6.
89. G.W.S. Barrow, *The Kingdom of the Scots* (1973), 27.
90. Morris, 'Viking and native in northern England', 227.
91. G.R.J. Jones, 'Early territorial organization in northern England and its bearing on the Scandinavian settlement', in *The Fourth Viking Congress*, ed. A. Small (1965), 67–84, at 77, 83.
92. Sawyer, *The Age of the Vikings*, 237–8, n. 40; P.H. Sawyer, 'The two viking ages: a discussion', *Mediaeval Scandinavia*, 2 (1969), 163–207, at 170; *The Kalendar of Abbot Samson*, ed. Davis, xlvi; D.C. Douglas, *The Social Structure of Medieval East Anglia*, Oxford Studies in Social and Legal History, ed. P. Vinogradoff, 9 (1927), 180–90, 205–19; Stenton, *Anglo-Saxon England*, 518–19; D.R. Roffe, 'Great Bowden and its soke', in *Anglo-Saxon Landscapes in the East Midlands*, ed. J. Bourne (1996), 107–20; D.M. Hadley, 'Multiple estates and the origins of the manorial structure of the northern Danelaw', *JHG*, 22 (1) (1996), 3–15.

Recent emphasis on continuity raises new questions. Given the paucity of contemporary documentary evidence for the northern Danelaw, any argument for continuity in the nature and organization of society involves great leaps of faith based on back-projection from much later evidence and a reliance on models generated for other parts of Anglo-Saxon England, models which are themselves open to much critical re-evaluation. Certainly, the methods devised for uncovering early territorial organization have the great merit of utilizing a variety of sources, which makes them especially attractive methodological approaches to the early history of a region such as the northern Danelaw for which early documentary sources are but few. However, a number of studies have questioned the validity of using later sources to uncover earlier organization, whereas others have disputed the regularity of organization which has been reconstructed.[93] Again, this is an aspect of Anglo-Saxon society that would merit reconsideration. Until we have resolved these problems it is difficult to assess the antiquity of the estate structure of the northern Danelaw as revealed in largely tenth- and eleventh-century sources, and virtually impossible to begin to discuss the impact of the vikings on it. Therefore, before we permit the pendulum to swing fully towards a continuity model, we need to explore the preconceptions of this model. There has been much recent work, in England and elsewhere in Europe, on early medieval social organization and estate structures, and it is timely to contribute to this debate and to examine the evidence from the northern Danelaw in this light. Regional studies are at their most valuable when they are firmly located within wider debates, and when they examine the locally specific evidence within the context of the evidence from other contemporary societies. One cannot hope to understand what is unique about a region unless the broader context is first established.

Archaeological evidence

The archaeological evidence for the viking period adds another dimension to the debate. It is often observed that there is surprisingly little archaeological evidence for Scandinavian activity throughout the Danelaw. Although many late-ninth- and tenth-century sites have been excavated in the Danelaw, it is difficult to assign them to a specifically 'Scandinavian' context, inasmuch as there is a paucity of artefacts

---

93. On the problems of the 'multiple estate' model, see N. Gregson, 'The multiple estate model: some critical questions', *JHG*, 11 (1985), 339–51; Bassett, 'The origins of Anglo-Saxon kingdoms', 20, and n. 52; Hadley, 'Multiple estates'; W. Davies, *Wales in the Early Middle Ages* (1982), 43–7. On using the evidence of parish boundaries and the pattern of ecclesiastical organization, see E. Cambridge and D.W. Rollason, 'The pastoral organization of the Anglo-Saxon church: review of the "minster hypothesis"', *EME*, 4 (1) (1995), 87–104; and this book, Chapter 2, pp. 88–90.

either displaying Scandinavian influence or of Scandinavian origin. Yet even if we find artefacts of Scandinavian origin or influence, can we be certain that they were used or deposited by people of Scandinavian descent? Does the absence of such artefacts necessarily betoken the absence of Scandinavian settlers? Without a more detailed discussion of the role of material culture in early medieval society, and of the extent to which 'ethnic' identity may be identified archaeologically, the significance of the corpus of Scandinavian-style artefacts will remain doubtful. These are, as we shall see, discussions that have taken place in other branches of archaeology but not hitherto in the study of the vikings.

Also striking is the apparent scarcity of evidence for 'pagan' practices. This is, perhaps, unexpected since the chroniclers of the period lay so much emphasis on the heathenism of the invaders. Yet what do we expect 'paganism' to look like archaeologically? Scandinavian pagan burials have been identified on the grounds that they contain grave goods at a time when the Anglo-Saxons are thought to have long abandoned the practice. As few as twenty-five such burial sites have thus far been discovered in the Danelaw, and most of these sites are of single burials (Fig. 6).[94] Their significance is rendered ambiguous by their not infrequent location in a Christian context, such as the burials in the churchyards at Repton (Derbs), Kildale and Wensley (Yorks).[95] In addition to these churchyard burials, a substantial cremation cemetery at Ingleby (Derbs) has been excavated and dated, on the basis of the funerary rite and the associated artefacts, to the later ninth or earlier tenth century.[96] In contrast to the churchyard burials, it is not plausible that a cremation cemetery was used by a community that had embraced Christianity. Yet it is an isolated example. This burial evidence has given rise to various interpretations. The comparative paucity of evidence for 'pagan' burial is thought by some to signify the rapid conversion of the Scandinavians. Meanwhile, pagan burials that occur in churchyards are thought perhaps to indicate that the Scandinavians had become Christian but were slower to abandon their traditional burial practices. On the other hand, this could signify no more than that the Scandinavians were merely using existing burial grounds, irrespective of belief; continuity of burial need not

---

94. D.M. Wilson, 'Scandinavian settlement in the north and west of the British Isles: an archaeological point-of-view', *TRHS*, 5th ser., 26 (1976), 95–113; D.M. Wilson, 'The Scandinavians in England', in *The Archaeology of Anglo-Saxon England*, ed. D.M. Wilson (1976), 393–403. It should be noted that accompanied, pagan, burials have been identified solely on the basis of the discovery of weapons and jewellery in churchyards in a number of cases.
95. J.D. Richards, *Viking Age England* (1991), 111–16.
96. For a summary of earlier investigations and more recent examination of the burials at Ingleby, see J.D. Richards, M. Jecock, L. Richmond and C. Tuck, 'The viking barrow cemetery at Heath Wood, Ingleby, Derbyshire', *Medieval Archaeology*, 39 (1995), 51–70, and this book, Chapter 6, pp. 322–3.

Figure 6 Viking Age burials (after D.M. Wilson, 'The Scandinavians in England', in *The Archaeology of Anglo-Saxon England* (1976), 393–403). Note that these burials, which form the standard corpus of Viking burials in England, are identified on the basis of the presence of grave goods or of cremation. There are many other burials of the ninth and tenth centuries in the region

signify continuity of cult.[97] Equally, the 'pagan' burials may have preceded the church concerned. We cannot resolve this issue until we address the fundamental question of how far grave goods should really be associated with Scandinavian and 'pagan' burial practice. There is, in fact, no necessary connection.[98] We know very little about the attitude of the Anglo-Saxon church to burial practice at this date, and it is not easy to predict how it would have begun to convert the newcomers to Christianity and how it would have reacted to the traditional burial practices of the Scandinavians, which, in any case, were varied.[99] Consequently, it is dangerous to assume religous belief or ethnic affiliation on the basis of grave goods. We need to place burial rite in its broader social context to further our understanding of the funerary archaeology from the northern Danelaw.

Further questions about the attitude of the Scandinavian settlers and their rulers to Christianity are raised by the discovery of numerous coins minted in the Danelaw carrying Christian motifs or a combination of Christian and traditional Scandinavian motifs, as well as by the corpus of Anglo-Scandinavian stone sculpture carrying a similar combination of motifs. In the late ninth century coins were minted in East Anglia which bore the legend 'St Edmund', commemorating the East Anglian king Edmund who had been murdered by vikings in 870. In the last decade of the ninth century coins were minted by the viking rulers Knutr and Sihtric in York which followed Carolingian designs, and the crosses and latinized forms of names suggest an ecclesiastical influence. From *c.* 905 a new coinage appeared in York with 'an overtly ecclesiastical flavour', which bore the legend 'St Peter', and from *c.* 920 coins were minted in Lincoln which bore the name of St Martin (Fig. 3).[100]

The stone sculpture of the Danelaw is perhaps the most visible legacy of the Scandinavian influence on England. Although picture-stones and rune-stone memorials are known in the Scandinavian homelands, there was virtually no stone sculpture produced in

---

97.　These arguments are summarized in J. Graham-Campbell, 'Pagans and Christians', *History Today*, 36 (October, 1986), 24–8.

98.　J. Blair, *Anglo-Saxon Oxfordshire* (1994), 70–4; A. Morton, 'Burial in middle Saxon Southampton', in *Death in Towns*, ed. S.R. Bassett (1992), 68–77 at 71; more recently, see H. Geake, *The Use of Grave-Goods in Conversion-Period England, c. 600–c. 850* (BAR British Series, 261, 1997).

99.　If the Anglo-Saxon church really had attempted to suppress the burial of artefacts in graves, it is perhaps surprising that there is no mention of this in contemporary or later narrative accounts of the early church in England: D. Bullough, 'Burial, community and belief in the early medieval West', in *Ideal and Reality in Anglo-Saxon and Frankish Society*, ed. P. Wormald, D. Bullough and R. Collins (1983), 177–201, at 185–6. For other aspects of post-conversion burial practices, see D.M. Hadley, 'The historical context of the inhumation cemetery at Bromfield, Shropshire', *Transactions of the Shropshire Archaeological and Historical Society*, 70 (1995), 145–55. On Scandinavian burial practices, see Chapter 6, pp. 319–23.

100.　Dolley, 'The Anglo-Danish and Anglo-Norse coinages of York', at 26 for the quotation; I. Stewart, 'The St Martin coins of Lincoln', *British Numismatic Journal*, 36 (1967), 49–54.

Scandinavia before the end of the tenth century. In England, in contrast, there was a flourishing tradition of stone sculpture, and the Scandinavian conquest had a significant impact on its production. Pre-existing Anglo-Saxon motifs were not entirely lost, but they were combined with Scandinavian motifs and ornamentation and, most strikingly, warriors and weapons.[101] It is generally assumed that the Anglo-Scandinavian crosses were grave-markers, but since none has been found in association with a specific burial they could equally well be memorial stones for individuals buried elsewhere, although the fact that most crosses are found in churchyards would suggest a funerary context.[102] Grave slabs and the so-called hogback tombs form the rest of the corpus of stone sculpture in the northern Danelaw. The distribution of this sculpture is also telling: many sites which have pre-viking sculpture also have Anglo-Scandinavian sculpture, although Anglo-Scandinavian sculpture is also found at many sites with no pre-existing sculpture. As Richard Bailey has observed, irrespective of who the patrons of such sculpture were, 'stone carving did not just continue into the viking period but was *enthusiastically* taken up' both at sites where it had been found previously and at places where it had not.[103] This body of numismatic and sculptural evidence presents a rather different impression of the vikings from that derived from much of the written evidence, and it provides an insight into the implications of the acceptance of Christianity or of allegiance with Christian leaders by viking rulers that is but fleetingly documented. The material culture of the region was heavily influenced by the Scandinavian incomers, but native traditions were not overwhelmed; again, this seems to have much to reveal about the nature of the relations between groups of peoples in the region. Moreover, the commissioning of stone sculpture, whoever the patrons, betokens enduring power and status, and suggests that the Scandinavian settlement both had a long-lasting cultural impact and also led to the establishment of some of the settlers as important lords in the northern Danelaw, a development that lies beyond the scope of the narrative sources.

The archaeology of the northern Danelaw has also served to modify some of the arguments based on place-name evidence, and the dialectic between the two bodies of evidence has been an important factor in the development of new interpretations of the Scandinavian settlement. There is a limited amount of archaeological evidence that can be offered to demonstrate pre-viking settlement at sites with Scandinavian place-names. The Yorkshire Wolds have been identified

101.   W.G. Collingwood, *Northumbrian Crosses of the Pre-Norman Age* (1927); J.T. Lang (ed.) *Anglo-Saxon and Viking Age Sculpture and Its Context* (BAR British Series, 49, 1978); J.T. Lang, 'Anglo-Scandinavian sculpture in Yorkshire', in *Viking Age York and the North*, ed. Hall, 11–20; R.N. Bailey, *Viking Age Sculpture in Northern England* (1980).
102.   Richards, *Viking Age England*, 119.
103.   Bailey, *Viking Age Sculpture*, 81.

as one of the major areas of Scandinavian colonization on the basis of a preponderance of Scandinavian place-names; yet the fact that this area had been heavily settled in the Roman period, has yielded numerous early Anglo-Saxon cemeteries and had high Domesday assessments suggests that the region was well exploited in the period preceding the Scandinavian conquest.[104] Furthermore, occupational debris has been excavated and dated to the pre-viking period at a number of places with Scandinavian place-names.[105] However, the number of sites which have rendered evidence of pre-viking settlement is limited and one ought to be wary of sweeping generalizations; individual sites may have had very different experiences. Although it is doubtless true to say that on the eve of the viking settlement much land was divided up among estates, it would be inaccurate to assert that no new land was taken into cultivation subsequently.[106]

Excavation has also established that there was rapid economic development under Scandinavian rule. Urban expansion has been identified in the northern Danelaw at York, Lincoln and Stamford, and elsewhere in the Danelaw (for example, at Thetford and Norwich), in the late ninth and early tenth centuries (Fig. 7).[107] Although little is known of pre-viking manufacture and trading centres, it is difficult to avoid the conclusion that urban expansion was directly associated with Scandinavian influence, although it is not easy to identify precisely when the various examples of urban expansion began, and attempts to link archaeological phases to recorded events are hazardous.[108] The major kiln sites of England in the tenth century were located in the northern and eastern Midlands: Nottingham, Thetford, Ipswich, Norwich, Torksey, Lincoln and Northampton (Fig. 7). These places also seemingly developed as markets and urban centres during the tenth century.[109] This evidence reveals that whatever the disruptions attendant upon the rapidly changing military and political situation in northern and eastern England in the ninth and tenth centuries, trade and manufacture seemingly were boosted in the long term. This is not

---

104. Sawyer, *From Roman Britain to Norman England*, 162.
105. *Ibid.*; P. Everson, C.C. Taylor and C.J. Dunn, *Change and Continuity: rural settlement in north-west Lincolnshire* (1991), 8–9.
106. Morris, 'Aspects of Scandinavian settlement', 13–15.
107. J. Moulden and D. Tweddle, *Anglo-Scandinavian Settlement South-West of the Ouse* (CBA Archaeology of York, 8/1, 1986); A.J. Mainman, *Anglo-Scandinavian Pottery from Coppergate* (CBA Archaeology of York, 16/5, 1990); R.A. Hall, *Viking Age York* (1994); D. Perring, *Early Medieval Occupation at Flaxengate, Lincoln* (CBA, Archaeology of Lincoln, 9, 1981); M. Atkin, B. Ayers and S. Jennings, 'Thetford-type ware production in Norwich' in *Norfolk: waterfront excavations and Thetford ware production*, ed. P. Wade-Martins (East Anglian Archaeology Report, 17, 1983), 61–104; R.A. Hall, 'The Five Boroughs of the Danelaw: a review of present knowledge', *ASE*, 18 (1989), 149–206; D. Hinton, *Archaeology, Economy and Society: England from the fifth to the fifteenth century* (1990), 82–94.
108. R.A. Hall, 'Vikings gone west? A summary review', in *Developments around the Baltic and North Sea in the Viking Age*, ed. B. Ambrosiani and H. Clarke (Stockholm, 1994), 32–49 at 36–7.
109. Hinton, *Archaeology, Economy and Society*, 82–7.

Figure 7 Excavated urban and rural sites of the ninth and tenth centuries in the Danelaw (after J. Graham-Campbell (ed.) *Cultural Atlas of the Viking World* (1994), 134)

to say, however, that the Scandinavian influence was the only impetus, and the production of pottery, especially the wheel-thrown wares, which arguably surpassed those of the West Saxon potters, owed much to Continental techniques. Similarly, the quality of coinage produced in the Danelaw was improved from the debased issues of the last English Northumbrian, Mercian and East Anglian kings, as silver was used to strengthen the currency. This saw the moneyers of the Danelaw imitating Continental coinage, and it has been suggested that Continental moneyers came to England in the wake of the Scandinavian settlement.[110] Moreover, the artefactual evidence includes relatively little of Scandinavian provenance, suggesting that it was broader international trade and also national trade that was stimulated by the Scandinavian settlement. This evidence serves as a reminder that the Scandinavian impact is not solely identifiable in terms of artefacts from Scandinavia, or artefacts bearing Scandinavian-style motifs. It is ironic, but telling, that one of the major influences of the Scandinavian settlers on Anglo-Saxon England survives in the artefactual record in the form of items which are *not* of Scandinavian provenance!

The archaeology of rural settlement has thus far proved disappointing to students of the vikings; in a rural context the Scandinavians are difficult to identify. The evidence excavated at sites in and near the northern Danelaw such as Goltho (Lincs), Wharram Percy, Cottam, Ribblehead (Yorks), Simy Folds (Co. Durham) and Raunds (Northants)[111] cannot easily be associated with the vikings, and little progress has been made in our understanding of whether such processes as the emergence of nucleated villages and the development of manorial sites preceded the Scandinavian settlements or were subsequent to them (Fig. 7). If it was the latter, it is not apparent whether the vikings were 'catalysts for or coincidental to change'.[112] It appears that the extent of the settled area was expanded in the tenth and eleventh centuries in areas such as the Cambridgeshire fens, the Peak District and the Yorkshire Dales, but again it is difficult to associate this directly with

---

110. R. Hodges, *The Anglo-Saxon Achievement* (1989), 161–2.
111. G. Beresford, *Goltho: the development of an early medieval manor, c. 850–1150* (1987), but note that the interpretation of each stage in the development of this site by the excavator has been open to significant revision elsewhere: P. Everson, 'What's in a name? "Goltho", Goltho and Bullington', *LHA*, 23 (1988), 93–9; M. Beresford and J.G. Hurst, *Wharram Percy Deserted Medieval Village* (1990); D. Haldenby, 'An Anglian site on the Yorkshire Wolds', *YAJ*, 62 (1990), 51–62; D. Haldenby, 'An Anglian site on the Yorkshire Wolds', *YAJ*, 64 (1992), 25–40; A. King, 'Gauber High Pasture, Ribblehead: – an interim report', in *Viking Age York and the North*, ed. Hall, 31–6; D. Coggins, K.J. Fairless and C.E. Batey, 'Simy Folds: an early medieval settlement in Upper Teesdale', *Medieval Archaeology*, 27 (1982), 1–26; G. Cadman and G. Foard, 'Raunds: manorial and village origins', in *Studies in Anglo-Saxon Settlement*, ed. M.L. Faull (1984), 81–100.
112. Hall, 'Vikings gone west?', 36; see also T.H. Unwin, 'Towards a model of Anglo-Scandinavian rural settlement in England', in *Anglo-Saxon Settlements*, ed. D. Hooke (1988), 77–98.

the period of Scandinavian control.[113] The rural archaeology of the Danelaw indicates that sweeping generalizations about the nature of pre-viking settlement and the subsequent impact of the Scandinavians are inappropriate. Nonetheless, this archaeological evidence of settlement growth and development, though it is difficult to tie it clearly to the Scandinavians themselves, has been instrumental in counteracting the traditional view that the Danelaw experienced only catastrophe and decline as a result of the Scandinavian conquest.

The landscape of the northern Danelaw was characterized in the medieval period by nucleated villages, although some regions, especially upland zones, displayed a more dispersed settlement pattern. It is now widely accepted that the medieval village came into existence sometime in the period between the ninth and thirteenth centuries.[114] The Anglo-Saxon centuries appear to have been characterized by a great deal of rural settlement mobility, in which the nucleated village was a late and anomalous feature.[115] Research into village origins and development in the region has focused on a handful of major excavations – such as those undertaken at Wharram Percy (Yorks), Barton Blount (Derbs) and Goltho (Lincs)[116] – and on the analysis of the morphology of villages.[117] A recent survey of rural settlement in Lincolnshire brought together the evidence of archaeological excavation, field-walking and morphological analysis in order to explore the origins and development of rural settlement in that region.[118]

This study examines the rural settlement pattern of the northern Danelaw within the context of the social organization of the region. The relationship of the complex tenurial structure of the region and of the complexity of village communities to the form of rural settlement will be examined. In particular, it proves instructive to examine the relationship between the social and tenurial structure of a village and the form of its plan; an important issue to resolve is the extent to which complex village plans, termed by Christopher Taylor 'polyfocal',

113. Hodges, *Anglo-Saxon Achievement*, 154–62, 166–77; Hinton, *Archaeology, Economy and Society*, 72–4, 82–97; Hall, 'Vikings gone west?', 33–8.
114. C.C. Taylor, *Village and Farmstead* (1984).
115. C.C. Taylor, 'Aspects of village mobility in medieval and later times', in *The Effect of Man on the Landscape: the lowland zone*, ed. S. Limbrey and J.G. Evans (CBA Res. Rep., 21, 1979), 126–34; H. Hamerow, 'Settlement mobility and the "Middle Saxon Shift": rural settlements and settlement patterns in Anglo-Saxon England', *ASE*, 20 (1991), 1–17.
116. Beresford and Hurst, *Wharram Percy*; G. Beresford, *The Medieval Clay-Land Village: Excavations at Goltho and Barton Blount*, Society for Medieval Archaeology Monograph Series, 6 (1975).
117. P. Allerston, 'English village development: findings from the Pickering district of north Yorkshire', *IBGT* 51 (1970), 95–109; J. Sheppard, 'Medieval village planning in northern England: some evidence from Yorkshire', *JHG*, 2 (1) (1976), 3–20; B.K. Roberts, *The Making of the English Village* (1987).
118. Everson, Taylor and Dunn, *Change and Continuity*.

reflected the complexity of social and tenurial organization.[119] Complex, or polyfocal, village plans deserve more attention than they have hitherto been given in the region, not least because their very form precludes monocausal explanations, as they seem likely to have developed gradually rather than in a single act of village planning. It is the more regularly arranged villages that have received greatest attention in the northern Danelaw, especially those of Yorkshire. Monocausal explanations have tended to be sought; replanning after either the viking invasions or the apparently devastating effects of the 'harrying of the North' carried out by William the Conqueror in the 1070s have been recurrent themes.[120] However, more recent work suggests that the level of destruction experienced in the 1070s may not have been as great as was once thought, and, in any case, such an explanation seems too simplistic to be useful.[121] It is also important to analyse the extent to which regular villages can be said to have been 'planned', and if so, by whom: by lords or by peasant communities?[122] Did regular village plans coincide with less complex tenurial arrangements? Finally, it has often been suggested that the fragmentation of the 'multiple estates' characteristic of Anglo-Saxon England may, in part, account for the creation of nucleated villages; but in a region in which 'multi-vill' sokes long remained a characteristic feature of rural society this hypothesis may require modification.[123]

The ecclesiastical organization of the northern Danelaw

It is perhaps for violence against the church that the vikings have been most seriously vilified. Long after the vikings had ceased raiding the English coast, chroniclers still wrote with horror about the atrocities that they had allegedly committed against ecclesiastical targets. Although admitting that there may have been some later embellishments, modern scholars have, until recently, accepted the picture painted by medieval chroniclers of an English church brought to

---

119. C.C. Taylor, 'Polyfocal settlement and the English village', *Medieval Archaeology*, 21 (1977), 189–93.
120. Beresford and Hurst, *Wharram Percy*, 84.
121. D.M. Palliser, 'Domesday Book and the"harrying of the North"', *Northern History*, 29 (1993), 1–23.
122. This issue is considered in C.C. Dyer, 'Power and conflict in the medieval English village', in *Medieval Villages: a review of current work*, ed. D. Hooke (1985), 27–32; P.D.A. Harvey, 'Initiative and authority in settlement change', in *The Rural Settlements of Medieval England*, ed. M. Aston, D. Austin and C.C. Dyer (1989), 31–43.
123. H.S.A. Fox, 'The people of the wolds in English settlement history', in *The Rural Settlements of Medieval England*, ed. Aston, Austin and Dyer, 85–96; H.S.A. Fox, 'The agrarian context', in *The Origins of the Midland Village*, Papers prepared for a discussion at the Economic History Society's annual conference, Leicester (1992), 36–72, at 60–2; R. Faith, 'Estates, demesnes and the village', *ibid.*, 11–35.

near-ruin by a vicious band of heathens.[124] In fact, however, the contemporary evidence is contradictory. Certainly the remarks of chroniclers seem to be supported by the long gaps in the episcopal lists for northern and eastern England, and by the scarcity of wealthy and heavily endowed churches in the Danelaw during the tenth and eleventh centuries.[125] On the other hand, however, the great wealth of Anglo-Scandinavian sculpture which is almost always found in an ecclesiastical context, the readiness with which at least some Scandinavians adopted Christianity alongside the general absence of evidence for pagan Scandinavian practices, and the clear indications that viking leaders and native lords, including ecclesiastics, could forge harmonious working relationships with each other bring into question the traditional image of the vikings.

Admittedly, narrative sources present a dire picture of the viking invaders, in which they inflicted terrible, sometimes irreparable, damage on the Anglo-Saxon church. Although later chroniclers provide more colourful accounts, it is clear that contemporaries did fear for the safety of the church.[126] However, although it is undeniable that the vikings posed a real threat, they were not alone in behaving in a manner that was inimical to the fortunes of the Anglo-Saxon church.[127] The struggle among kings, bishops and lay lords for control over monasteries and their possessions was a characteristic feature of the ninth century, and by this time not only had gifts to the church declined, but in some cases its endowments had actually been diminished by royal seizure of ecclesiastical land and revenues.[128] In other words, the vikings were but one factor, if a particularly brutal one, in what may have been a general change in the fortunes of the church. Indeed, Asser commented on the apathy of potential recruits to the church, and Alfred bemoaned the lack of learning and literacy.[129] It is notable that contemporaries were inclined to balance viking attacks on the church with their own failings as explanations for the

---

124. Stenton, *Anglo-Saxon England*, 433.
125. R.K. Morris, 'Churches in York and its hinterland: building patterns and stone sources in the 11th and 12th centuries', in *Minsters and Parish Churches: the local church in transition, 950–1200*, ed. J. Blair (1988), 191–200, at 197; see also John Blair's comments in the introduction to this volume, 2.
126. The use of the clause 'as long as the Christian faith shall last' in ninth-century charters reveals the extent to which contemporaries feared for the safety of the church and Christianity in Anglo-Saxon England: N.P. Brooks, *The Early History of the Church of Canterbury: Christ Church from 597 to 1066* (1984), 150–2, 201–3.
127. See, for example, the accusation made in the *Historia de Sancto Cuthberto* that the Northumbrian kings, Ælle and Osbert, had robbed the community of St Cuthbert of land: *HSC*, 201–2; P. Wormald, 'The ninth century', in *The Anglo-Saxons*, ed. Campbell, 132–59, at 135, 139.
128. Brooks, *Canterbury*, 184–6; see also Chapter 5, pp. 283–5.
129. Asser, ch. 93, 103; Alfred's translation of Gregory the Great's *Pastoral Care* in *Asser's Life of Alfred the Great and Other Contemporary Sources*, trans. S. Keynes and M. Lapidge (1983), 124–30, at 124–5.

state of the Anglo-Saxon church. However, although vikings may have been seen as a form of divine retribution for a deterioration in Christian standards, this does not argue that the Scandinavian onslaught was not serious.[130]

Although it is possible to balance the Scandinavian impact on the church by examining it in the wider context of ongoing assaults on ecclesiastical fortunes, the traditional view that the viking invasions did great harm to the church in the Danelaw does appear to be corroborated by Domesday Book.[131] Houses of secular and monastic clergy were much less common in the Danelaw than they were in many parts of southern and Midland England, and the amount of land held by the church was much less in the Danelaw (around one-tenth) than in the south of England (around one-fifth to one-third in some counties).[132] In interpreting this evidence we must remember that we have little surviving evidence for the fortunes of the church in the Danelaw on the eve of the viking attacks, and that we are not especially well informed about the way in which the West Saxons treated the region as they conquered it in the tenth century.[133] A recent suggestion that the house of Wessex made use of ecclesiastical lands to reward their followers warrants consideration.[134] The idiosyncrasies of ecclesiastical organization in the northern Danelaw must owe much to the vikings, but may also have been determined by both earlier regional differences and the role of the West Saxon kings as they conquered the region in the tenth century.

Nonetheless, even if we were to allow that the impact of the vikings might have been less cataclysmic than has generally been believed, the fact remains that ecclesiastical organization in the Danelaw was different from that in other regions. The recent development of the so-called 'minster model' as a framework for the evolution of the Anglo-Saxon church has increased the sense of contrast. The 'minster model' was developed in a series of papers published in the 1980s and 1990s, although a few earlier studies by William Page, Brian Kemp and Patrick

---

130. Alcuin, for example, believed that the raid on Lindisfarne was not entirely unexpected: *EHD*, I, no. 193.
131. For example, Stenton, *Anglo-Saxon England*, 433–8; A. Rogers, 'The origins of Newark: the evidence of local boundaries', *TTS*, 77 (1974), 13–26, at 15; Morris, 'Churches in York', 191–9.
132. J. Blair, 'Secular minster churches in Domesday Book' in *Domesday Book: a reassessment*, ed. P.H. Sawyer (1985), 104–42; R. Fleming, 'Monastic lands and England's defence in the viking age', *EHR*, 100 (1985), 247–65, at 249. The main exception to this is in the fenlands, where tenth-century monastic reformers had heavily endowed their foundations.
133. Wormald, 'The ninth century', 135.
134. Fleming, 'Monastic lands and England's defence'. This paper has, however, received considerable criticism, not least for its reliance on late sources; see D. Dumville, 'Ecclesiastical lands and the defence of Wessex in the First Viking Age', in his *Wessex and England*, 29–54.

Hase prefigured and influenced these discussions.[135] A coherent model emerged which not only proposed the nature of early medieval ecclesiastical organization, but also offered a methodology for uncovering this organization through the use of documentary and topographic evidence. It came to be generally accepted that there was everywhere a basic sequence of development in the provision of pastoral care which can be summarized as follows.[136] In the seventh and eighth centuries each Anglo-Saxon kingdom acquired a network of churches which provided pastoral care through a coherent system of *parochiae*. Although these churches were of diverse origins and were described by various terms, and the composition and size of their communities varied, all performed, or else supported, pastoral work in the vicinity, and have come to be known by the contemporary term 'minster' (Old English *mynster*). Between the tenth and the eleventh centuries this so-called 'minster parish system' gradually fragmented as local manorial churches proliferated; these new foundations apparently included both daughter churches of the minster, founded to provide pastoral care at a distance from the minster, and manorial chapels at the estate centres of secular lords. In time these churches commonly acquired partial or full parochial rights, and their priests were able to perform all or most pastoral functions. By the twelfth century, developments in canon law served to inhibit the proliferation of local churches, and the parish system of the later Middle Ages came to be more or less fixed at this time. It has been argued that the essentials of the earlier minster system may be uncovered through the use of contemporary and later documentary evidence and the pattern of parish boundaries, which allow the identification of minster churches on the basis of their 'superior' characteristics and which reveal the extent of former minster parishes through indications of the subordination of one church to another (such as the payment of

---

135.   The most important papers in the development of this model are contained in the volume edited by John Blair, *Minsters and Parish Churches*, and that edited by Blair and Richard Sharpe, *Pastoral Care before the Parish* (1992). Other notable contributions include M.J. Franklin, 'The identification of minsters in the Midlands', *ANS*, 7 (1985), 69–88; Blair, 'Secular minster churches in Domesday Book'; J. Blair, 'Local churches in Domesday Book and before', in *Domesday Studies*, ed. J.C. Holt (1987), 265–78. Earlier studies out of which the minster model grew are W. Page, 'Some remarks on the churches of the Domesday Survey', *Archaeologia*, 2nd ser., 16 (1915), 61–102; B.R. Kemp, 'The mother church of Thatcham', *Berkshire Archaeological Journal*, 63 (1967–8), 15–22; B.R. Kemp, 'The churches of Berkeley Hernesse', *Transactions of the Bristol and Gloucester Archaeological Society*, 87 (1968), 96–110; P.H. Hase, 'The development of the parish in Hampshire' (Ph.D. thesis, University of Cambridge, 1975), ideas from which are discussed in his 'The church in the Wessex heartlands', in *The Medieval Landscape of Wessex*, ed. M. Aston and C. Lewis (1994), 47–81; C.N.L. Brooke, 'Rural ecclesiastical institutions in England: the search for their origins', *Settimane*, 28 (2) (1982), 685–711.

136.   J. Blair, 'Introduction: from minster to parish church', in *Minsters and Parish Churches*, ed. Blair, 1–19; J. Blair and R. Sharpe, 'Introduction', in *Pastoral Care before the Parish*, ed. Blair and Sharpe, 1–10.

tithes or pensions, or the status of chapelry to another church, and so on).

Hitherto, studies of the northern Danelaw have conveyed little sense of a minster framework.[137] This book will show that some parts of the northern Danelaw do appear to conform to the minster model, but others do not. It will be necessary, hence, to consider why this is so, and to determine the extent to which the minster model is an appropriate model for analysing the development of ecclesiastical organization in the northern Danelaw. The coherence of the model and the uniformity expected in its application give cause for concern, as does the fact that some authors have presented a rather different view of early ecclesiastical organization from that proposed by the minster model.[138] Four main points need to be raised and addressed. First, we need to consider whether it is plausible that ecclesiastical provision could have been established in such an orderly manner; was there really a moment in time when there was a coherent minster network, which it is reasonable for us to attempt to reconstruct? Second, given the argument that will be developed in subsequent chapters about the fluidity of territorial and social organization, it seems questionable that the ecclesiastical organization of Anglo-Saxon England was substantially more stable, given the clear relationship between patterns of secular and ecclesiastical organization. Third, and a related point, is that the use of late medieval evidence to uncover earlier patterns of organization poses a series of methodological issues that need to be addressed. Finally, the extent to which there was pastoral care at an early date requires consideration.

Conclusions

It is clear that the society of the northern Danelaw, as described by Domesday Book, was rather different from that of Midland and southern England. This contrast has traditionally been explained by reference to the Scandinavian invasions and settlement of the late ninth and early tenth centuries. However, this explanation has received recent modification, as a number of scholars have sought to limit the extent of the changes that can be ascribed to the Scandinavians. Now it is generally considered to be more likely that the free peasants of the Danelaw have origins in an earlier period and that they should not be thought of as the descendants of the viking armies. The sokes of the Danelaw are no longer

---

137.   Blair, 'Introduction', 2.
138.   E. Cambridge, 'The early church in county Durham: a reassessment', *JBAA*, 137 (1984), 65–85; Cambridge and Rollason, 'The pastoral organization of the Anglo-Saxon Church'; C.R.E. Cubitt, 'Pastoral care and conciliar canons: the provisions of the 747 council of *Clofesho*', in *Pastoral Care before the Parish*, ed. Blair and Sharpe, 193–211; C.R.E. Cubitt, *Anglo-Saxon Church Councils c. 650–c. 850* (1995), 113–18; P. Sims-Williams, *Religion and Literature in Western Britain, 600–800* (1990).

considered to be the creations of Scandinavian army leaders but the remnants of a once universal system of territorial organization characteristic of the early Middle Ages. If such interpretations are to be accepted, we need to offer explanations for the survival of the social structure of the Danelaw during a period of undoubted upheaval. Is it possible to accept the implications of much recent research that far from undergoing a revolution in its social structure, as was once believed, the northern Danelaw was in fact to some extent moribund in the later Anglo-Saxon period? In the light of evidence for the expansion of trading networks and urban centres, this seems unlikely. We also need to consider whether the institutions of the northern Danelaw, in particular the distinctive nature of the peasantry and the estate structure, really are representative of pre-viking society.

An important aim for this book is to reconcile the apparently contradictory nature of the various types of evidence concerning the impact of the vikings on the society of the Danelaw. There seem to be two major areas which would repay further exploration. The first concerns the nature of the contact between the existing inhabitants of the region and the Scandinavian newcomers; one might add that the reaction of both groups to the arrival of West Saxon overlords is also worth considering. Many studies have sought to distinguish Scandinavian sites and artefacts from those of the native population, but this hinges on a belief that these groups long remained distinctive. If, however, such a distinction was not maintained, then the questions we ask of the archaeological evidence may need to be reformulated to take account of this. The second area for particular attention concerns the recent emphasis on the pre-viking origins of some of the most characteristic features of the region. It is not at all certain that the recent emphasis on continuity can be supported; the sokemen and the sokes of the Danelaw may indeed have pre-viking antecedents, but that is not to say that they were unaffected by the Scandinavian conquest and settlement, or, indeed, that of the West Saxons. Moreover, we must also look at the long-term changes to social and estate organization, in addition to examining the short-term change attendant on conquest. Such undertakings are not, however, entirely straightforward since the very methods used to uncover early medieval society, and the models that have been generated, have been open to great criticism. Hence, in order to pursue the idea that the sokemen and sokes of the Danelaw have their origins in the pre-viking period, it is necessary to grapple with the methodological and historiographical problems that confront any study of early medieval society.

In recent times, the nature of the Anglo-Saxon peasantry has attracted little interest; however, the recent book in the present series by Rosamond Faith has reopened a debate that has been dormant for too long.[139] Furthermore, many studies of early estate organization

---

139.   Faith, *The English Peasantry*.

have employed models that do not withstand rigorous scrutiny. These historiographical and methodological problems hamper attempts to assess the Scandinavian contribution to the societies of the northern Danelaw by means of a comparison with other parts of Anglo-Saxon England. We cannot hope to elucidate aspects of the history of the northern Danelaw if we import uncritically models developed for elsewhere. Nonetheless, it is essential to move beyond a purely local, or even Anglo-centric, perspective. If we examine the northern Danelaw in a wider context – that of contemporary Continental society – new analogies and methods of interpretation can be brought to bear, which, as we shall see, render the region and its society rather less unusual than does an exclusively Anglo-Saxon perspective.

Accordingly, Chapter 2 offers an updated and wide-ranging analysis of early medieval society, with particular reference to forms of lordship, the nature of land tenure, the status of the peasantry and types of estate structure and organization. Chapters 3 and 4 provide a detailed examination of the social organization and estate structures of the Danelaw, placed firmly within the context of the models offered in Chapter 2. The most influential studies of the society and institutions of the northern Danelaw were written within an older historical framework; Chapters 3 and 4 offer a new perspective. Chapter 5 details the development of ecclesiastical organization in the northern Danelaw, with particular emphasis on the debates concerning the extent of viking destructiveness and the emergence of the parochial system. Finally, Chapter 6 provides a new examination of the experiences of the northern Danelaw during the period of Scandinavian conquest and settlement. This is unashamedly a regional study, but one which places regional issues and evidence within a broader conceptual framework. This perspective enables new questions to be asked of the evidence from the northern Danelaw, from which new understandings will emerge. This introductory chapter ends, then, where it began, with the words of F.W. Maitland: 'If only we can ask the right questions we shall have done something for a good end.'[140]

---

140. Maitland, *Domesday Book and Beyond*, 2–3.

2 Early medieval societies

> the documents themselves show societies not nearly as different
> as they appear in ... national historiographies
> – C.J. Wickham[1]

Previous studies of the rural society of the Danelaw have been dominated by discussion of the considerable numbers of 'free' peasants and of the apparently distinctive nature of its estate structures. Few would now seek to argue that the sokemen and the *liberi homines* of the Danelaw are the descendants of the Danish armies. It is currently more fashionable to believe that they were primarily the descendants of the English peasantry of an earlier era.[2] Furthermore, the extensive Domesday estates (sokes) of the Danelaw are now believed to be comparable with the 'multi-vill estates' thought to have characterized pre-viking England. This chapter explores the validity of these oft-cited, but poorly evidenced, assertions. Comparison with other parts of England will be shown to be, in fact, only partially useful. It is not clear which regions provide the most suitable points of comparison, and the tendency to aggregate the scarce, chronologically and geographically dispersed evidence renders comparison still more difficult. This chapter also suggests that viewed in isolation, the structure of Anglo-Saxon society is much less understandable than when examined in its broader early medieval context. Such a comparison reveals the extent of regional variation in early medieval society, which enables us to view the apparent dichotomy between the Danelaw and the rest of England in a new light.

A brief outline of earlier traditions concerning early medieval society is followed by a discussion of recent studies of a variety of early medieval Continental societies as a prelude to examining the Anglo-Saxon evidence. Subsequent chapters then examine the evidence from the northern Danelaw in this light. This juxtaposition of a broad comparative approach with a regional study demonstrates the value of approaching the problems of early medieval history on a variety of scales.

---

1. C.J. Wickham, 'Problems of comparing rural societies in early medieval western Europe', *TRHS*, 6th ser., 2 (1992), 221–46, at 224.
2. E. John, 'The age of Edgar', in *The Anglo-Saxons*, ed. J. Campbell (1982), 160–89, at 164.

Previous studies of early medieval societies

The society of the Danelaw has been explicitly analysed in a European context once before. Over twenty years ago Anne Kristensen commented that whatever various English historians had made of the ethnicity of the sokemen and freemen of the Danelaw, most of them had the basic idea that they were a class of free land-owning peasants of the type that were a characteristic constituent element of early Germanic societies.[3] She alleged that the English historical tradition concerning the notion of a free peasantry was stuck with a concept rooted in nineteenth-century German doctrine, and that it had failed to take account of recent developments in the study of early medieval society. Where once the free peasantry were regarded as part of a democratic association of freemen, the free peasantry of the early medieval period had now, according to German historians of the 1930s to 1960s, become *freedmen* who owed their freedom to royal favour. The sokemen and free men of the Danelaw were, she alleged, comparable to these freedmen. Although the so-called new tradition can itself be called into question, this study was immensely important in that it set the Danelaw into a wider context, and provided new frameworks for examining the idiosyncrasies of Danelaw society.[4]

Although the German tradition has not been unknown to English historiography, its findings have rarely been applied systematically, or have been applied only very tardily, and in recent years the status of the peasantry has been of little interest to most studies of Anglo-Saxon society.[5] It is necessary to describe briefly the development of German scholarship and to examine the extent to which Anglo-Saxon historiography has mirrored its findings. As we shall see, there have been some comparable developments in the two branches of scholarship, but recent developments in Continental research have yet to be extensively received in Anglo-Saxon studies.

Gemeinfreie and the democratic association of freemen

A tradition developed in eighteenth- and nineteenth-century German scholarship that the basis of Germanic society was a democratic association of freemen, and that land-ownership was essentially the privilege of an equal and free land-owning peasantry.[6] These were

---

3. A.K.G. Kristensen, 'Danelaw institutions and Danish society in the viking age: *sochemanni, liberi homines* and *königsfreie*', *Mediaeval Scandinavia*, 8 (1975), 27–85, at 33.
4. This study has scarcely been acknowledged, but see P.A. Stafford, *The East Midlands in the Early Middle Ages* (1985), 79.
5. A notable exception is R. Faith, *The English Peasantry and the Growth of Lordship* (1997).
6. For summaries, see E.W. Böckenförde, *Die deutsche verfassungsgeschichtliche Forschung im 19. Jahrhundert*, Schriften zur Verfassungsgeschichte, 1 (Berlin,

dubbed the 'common freemen' or 'Gemeinfreie'.[7] Such a society was envisaged as having few slaves and only a small noble class, from which kings were drawn, although in a variant of the basic model it was argued that kings were chosen by the people and that their powers were limited by the popular assemblies. In this democratic polity the free landholder–warrior–farmer stood side by side with the noble in the army and at the assembly. This is how the Salic Law, the sixth-century codification of Frankish law, was interpreted; it mentioned *ingenui* (freemen), *liti* (half-free) and *servi* (serfs), and it was believed that the nobility must have been included among the *ingenui*. In the late eighteenth century Justus Möser had contended that this polity was organized on the basis of individual farms which were virtually independent 'states' as a result of the power of the householder, but this was later rejected in favour of a model which depicted a polity based from the start on larger communal groupings, a genuine state organization.[8] The natural expression of this social system was thought to have been the nucleated village surrounded by its open-field system, with the inhabitants having equal shares in the common pasture and woodland.[9] The inequality that emerged among the Gemeinfreie was the result of a number of developments: some lost ownership of their property and with it their status, others rose in importance owing to service in the king's retinue, which gave them office and new lands, and with them control over other free landholders. It was manorialism and the development of lordship that were inimical to the initial liberty of the Gemeinfreie.[10] It was suggested by Möser that the class of equal shareholders finally split into nobles, commoners and serfs during the reign of Louis the Pious because this ineffectual king was no longer able to control the power of the emergent nobility.[11]

To some extent these ideas were adopted by Anglo-Saxon historians such as William Stubbs and J.M. Kemble, and since then political

---

contd.

   1961), 15–22; J. Schmitt, *Untersuchungen zu den Liberi Homines der Karolingerzeit*, Europäische Hochschulschriften, Reihe III, Geschichte und ihre Hilfswissenschaften, Band 83 (Frankfurt, 1977), 1–41. For summaries of these ideas in English, see R. Aris, *History of Political Thought in Germany from 1789 to 1815* (1936); L. Krieger, *The German Idea of Freedom: history of a political tradition* (1957); F. Staab, 'A reconsideration of the ancestry of modern political liberty: the problem of the so-called "king's freemen" (königsfreie)', *Viator*, 11 (1980), 51–69, at 52–6.

7.   Staab, 'Modern political liberty', 54–5.
8.   Before the mid-eighteenth century it was considered that the nobility were the most important group among the *ingenui*, but the work of Johann Sorber and Justus Möser placed greater emphasis on the role of the villagers, the independent land-owning farmers; Staab, 'Modern political liberty', 52–4.
9.   Böckenförde, *Die deutsche verfassungsgeschichtliche Forschung*, 134–6; Schmitt, *Untersuchungen zu den Liberi Homines*, 16–17; Staab, 'Modern political liberty', 55–6.
10.   Schmitt, *Untersuchungen zu den Liberi Homines*, 16–17.
11.   Aris, *History of Political Thought*, 222–34; Krieger, the *German Idea of Freedom*, 72, 179–80.

liberty has tended to be attributed to Germanic origins.[12] In the twentieth century Sir Frank Stenton was the champion of these ideas. He believed that whatever aristocracy there had been was wiped out during the migrations and that the free-peasant land-holder was at the basis of English society, 'without claim to nobility, but subject to no lord below the king'.[13] For him the development of bookland and of private estates was a solvent of the original primitive equality which characterized early Anglo-Saxon society.[14] The wholesale transplantation of this type of society from the Germanic homelands was entirely in keeping with the belief current at the time that the countryside had been largely cleared of its indigenous population and had large areas awaiting colonization and exploitation.[15] Again the natural expression of this social order was believed to have been the nucleated village with its open-field system, planted *de novo* by the Anglo-Saxons in a largely empty landscape.[16]

Königsfreie and the king's freemen

From the beginning of the twentieth century there was a significant reaction against these ideas within German scholarship.[17] Alfons Dopsch, for example, thought that manorialism was a basic element in Frankish society from the Merovingian period, and that royal, aristocratic and ecclesiastical landlordship existed at that time. He demonstrated that there were great inequalities in the land-holdings of the Gemeinfreie. He also highlighted acts of emancipation as a corrective to earlier models which sought only acts of subjection and suppression to explain the disintegration of the Gemeinfreie polity.[18] Further objections were raised elsewhere: other Germanic tribal laws do allow for a noble class; and detailed local studies revealed that the nobility had huge possessions, family monasteries and high posts in the army, church and judiciary. This undermined the argument that the

---

12. J.M. Kemble, *The Saxons in England*, 2 vols (1849); W. Stubbs, *The Constitutional History of England in Its Origin and Development* (3 vols, 1880); see also P. Vinogradoff, *Villainage in England* (1892); F.M. Stenton, *Anglo-Saxon England* (3rd edn, 1971), 277–9, 470–1; J. Campbell, 'Epilogue', in *The Anglo-Saxons*, ed. Campbell (1982), 240–6, at 242–4.
13. Stenton, *Anglo-Saxon England*, 277, 304.
14. *Ibid.*, 471–2.
15. See, for example, W.G. Hoskins, *The Making of the English Landscape* (1955; 3rd edn 1988, with a commentary by C.C. Taylor), 39, 52–3, 71–2, 77–82.
16. C.S. Orwin and C.S. Orwin, *The Open Fields* (1938); Stenton, *Anglo-Saxon England*, 280–1, 285–7; H.R. Loyn, *Anglo-Saxon England and the Norman Conquest* (1962; 2nd edn 1991), 42, 51, 162–9.
17. Böckenförde, *Die deutsche verfassungsgeschichtliche Forschung*, 15–22; Staab, 'Modern political liberty', 56–9.
18. A. Dopsch, *Die Wirtschaftsentwicklung der Karolingerzeit vornehmlich in Deutschland* (Darmstadt 1912–13); A. Dopsch, *Wirtschaftliche und soziale Grundlagen der europäischen Kulturentwicklung aus der Zeit von Cäsar bis auf Karl den Grossen* (Aalen, 1918–20).

nobility was a relatively unimportant class. Further, it was argued that the late medieval village custumals, once regarded as representing a record of the original peasant freedoms passed down through the ages, reflected rather the sum of the privileges acquired as a result of the benevolence of the nobility and the king, often following in the wake of land clearance. The fundamental freedom of this peasantry was diminished, to be replaced by a freedom which was given to the peasants by the king on admittance to the army, in return for various dues and services. The name given to the free peasantry was 'king's freemen' or 'Königsfreie', and their characteristics were most fully enumerated in the work of Theodor Mayer and Heinrich Dannenbauer. The Köngisfreie were identified as the *liti* of early sources, and their numbers were thought to have expanded greatly under the Frankish kings.[19] To be free now meant to be protected, and the land-holdings of the free were not fully free – they were not, that is, allodial; they could not be disposed of outside the family without the permission of the king.[20] Furthermore, the state was no longer thought to have been based on a political alliance between peasant freeholders and the king, but rather, royal power was balanced by the equal rights of the nobility, whose status was self-generating, and which had not come into being by means of acquiring the possession of royal privileges.[21] This model presented a new picture of northern Europe in the post-Roman era. It was now thought that the early Frankish kings took over from existing institutions by settling these soldier-colonists throughout their realm in territories called 'centenae'. There was an attempt to demonstrate that the late medieval administrative units, the hundreds, could, because of their military functions, be regarded as having originated as the basic units of this soldier-colonist organization.[22]

Anne Kristensen's thesis compared the sokemen and *liberi homines* of the Danelaw with the königsfreie soldier-colonists of mid-twentieth-century German historiography. Ultimately she was unable to say whether the bulk of them were of Anglo-Saxon or Scandinavian descent, but whatever their ethnicity, she claimed, they were not freemen but freedmen whom the Danish leaders, and later the West

---

19.   The königsfreie literature is vast. A representative selection is: the work of H. Dannenbauer, collected in his *Grundlagen der mittelalterlichen Welt* (Stuttgart, 1958); the work of Theodor Mayer, collected in his *Mittelalterliche Studien: gesammelte Aufsätze* (Lindau, 1959); O. Brunner, *Land und Herrschaft: Grundfragen der territorialen Verfassungsgeschichte Österreichs im Mittelalter* (Vienna, 1939); W. Schlesinger, *Die Entstehung der Landesherrschaft: Untersuchungen vorwiegend nach mitteldeutschen Quellen* (Darmstadt, 1941).
20.   A. Waas, *Herrschaft und Staat im deutschen Frühmittelalter*, Historische Studien, 335 (Munich, 1938); W. Schlesinger, 'Herrschaft und Gefolgschaft in der germanisch–deutschen Verfassungsgeschichte', *Historische Zeitschrift*, 176 (1953), 225–75.
21.   A.K.G. Kristensen, 'Free peasants in the early Middle Ages: freeholders, freedmen or what?', *Mediaeval Scandinavia*, 12 (1988), 76–106, at 78–80.
22.   Dannenbauer, 'Hundertschaft, Centena und Huntari'.

Saxons, had used to settle and control their newly won territories.[23] The main evidence for this, beyond mere analogy, was that according to Domesday Book every *liber homo* and sokeman, and every piece of sokeland (the land of a sokeman), was annexed to a royal manor or else to a manor over which some lord exercised delegated regalian rights. According to this model, the sokes and wapentakes (subdivisions of the shire) recorded in Domesday Book were the remnants of the equivalent to a system of centenae.[24]

Although there are clear merits to examining Anglo-Saxon society within a broader Continental context, Kristensen's work also highlights the potential pitfalls. First, scholars of Anglo-Saxon England did not on the whole find the Königsfreie model as appealing as the preceding Gemeinfreie model. As a result, there was not a receptive historical tradition for Kristensen's model. Although some scholars had questioned older assumptions about the freedom of the Anglo-Saxon peasantry, none had gone as far as to suggest that they were part of some overarching military colonization, neither had they framed their objections to the old German tradition explicitly in the context of the Gemeinfreie–Königsfreie debate.[25] Significantly, however, a distinct part of Anglo-Saxon historiography did develop ideas that mirror to some extent the Königsfreie model; although they appear to be chronologically unconnected, and largely uninfluenced by Continental scholarship. In the late nineteenth century Seebohm had claimed that 'English history begins not with free communities but with serfdom',[26] and later Carl Stephenson dismissed the free village community as 'a figment of the romantic imagination'.[27] Trevor Aston argued in the 1950s that the free peasants of Domesday Book were difficult to relate to the peasants of earlier sources, and therefore could most plausibly be explained by postulating a growth of freedom during the pre-Conquest period; that is to say, the free peasants of Domesday owed their freedom to what they had acquired over the immediately preceding centuries.[28] H.P.R. Finberg later spoke of a 'highly class-conscious society ruled by powerful monarchs' and aided by a strong aristocracy to whom the peasantry, as tenants, owed labour

---

23. Kristensen, 'Danelaw institutions and Danish society', 69.
24. *Ibid.*, 52–60; she argued that the sokes were Scandinavian creations and the wapentakes, which often fail to coincide with sokes, were established by the West Saxons.
25. See the dismissal of Dannenbauer's ideas in N.P. Brooks, 'The development of military obligations in eighth- and ninth-century England', in *England before the Conquest*, ed. P. Clemoes and K. Hughes (1971), 69–84, at 70, n. 5.
26. F. Seebohm, *The English Village Community* (1883), 423.
27. C. Stephenson, *Medieval Institutions* (1954), 244.
28. T.H. Aston, 'The origins of the manor in England', *TRHS*, 5th ser., 8 (1958), 59–83. See also E. John, *Land Tenure in Early England*, Studies in Early English History, 1, ed. H.P.R. Finberg (1960); E. John, 'English feudalism and the structure of Anglo-Saxon society', in his *Orbis Britanniae and Other Studies*, Studies in Early English History, 4, ed. H.P.R. Finberg (1966), 128–53.

services.[29] More recently, in his study of Anglo-Saxon military organization Richard Abels has likened those who served in the *fyrd* to königsfreie peasants.[30] Although to some extent, then, the classical Germanist tradition has been questioned by Anglo-Saxonists, the Königsfreie model was effectively ignored and has not played any significant part in the study of Anglo-Saxon England.

The second major problem with the comparison drawn by Kristensen is the fact that the Königsfreie model has been more or less abandoned on the Continent after receiving substantial critical reappraisal.[31] It has been argued that the term *liberi*, far from being used of königsfreie peasants, was employed very broadly in the tribal laws and capitularies to refer to a wide spectrum of people: nobles, vassals – including those of the king, nobility and church – free men who held allodial land and free men who were linked to an ecclesiastical or secular lordship. Unlike the Königsfreie, the *liberi* owned their allodium (where they had any) and were able to dispose of it as they wished.[32] The Königsfreie model had held that the inhabitants of the king's land paid a tax for the privilege called Königszins.[33] However, later research suggested that it was also paid both by the holders of precarious tenure of royal land, and by land-holders within the more narrowly defined royal estates (the royal Grundherrschaft). Dannenbauer had considered the hundreds to be an integral part of the Carolingian royal fisc, but Wolfgang Metz demonstrated that this was not the case.[34] Studies of Frankish legislation, sources ignored by Dannenbauer and Mayer, came to elaborate very different results from those of the major proponents of the Königsfreie model. The model has now been almost universally rejected. It is also important to note that Italian, French, Catalan and Castilian historians had never really adopted the Königsfreie model,

29. H.P.R. Finberg, 'Anglo-Saxon England to 1042', in *Ag. Hist.*, I.II, 385–525, at 446–8.
30. R. Abels, *Lordship and Military Obligation in Anglo-Saxon England* (1988), 11–42.
31. See, for example, E. Müller-Mertens, *Karl der Grosse, Ludwig der Fromme und die Freien: wer waren die 'Liberi Homines' der karolingischen Kapitularien 742/743–832? Ein Beitrag zur Sozialgeschichte und Sozialpolitik des Frankenreiches*, Forschungen zur mittelalterlichen Geschichte, 10 (Berlin, 1963); H.K. Schulze, *Die Graftschaftverfassung der Karolingerzeit in den Gebieten östlich des Rheins*, Schriften zur Verfassungsgeschichte 19 (Berlin, 1973); H.K. Schulze, 'Rodungsfreiheit und Königsfreiheit: zur Genesis und Kritik neuerer verfassungsgeschitlicher Theorien', *Historische Zeitschrift*, 219 (1974), 529–50; Schmitt, *Untersuchungen zu den Liberi Homines*; H. Hunke, *Germanische Freiheit im Verstandnis der deutschen Rechts- und Verfassungsgeschichtsschreibung* (Göttingen, 1972); for a summary in English, see Staab, 'Modern political liberty', 59–69; Kristensen, 'Free peasants in the early Middle Ages', 82–105.
32. Müller-Mertens, *Karl der Grosse*, 88; Schmitt, *Untersuchungen zu den Liberi Homines*, 41–103.
33. Dannenbauer, 'Königsfreie und Ministerialen', 319.
34. W. Metz, *Das karolingische Reichsgut: eine verfassungsgeschichtliche Untersuchung* (Berlin, 1960), 193–4.

and that they had always had little difficulty in envisaging the presence of both aristocrats and peasant landholders in early medieval societies.[35]

Recent studies of early medieval societies

More recent Continental research has exposed the variety of social organization found throughout early medieval Europe. In contrast, and in the absence of detailed local sources, ideas about the Anglo-Saxon peasantry have developed in few significant ways in recent decades, and the old dichotomies still prevail. A recent exception is the study by Rosamond Faith, which reopens the debate about the peasantry, and her study is important to the discussion that follows.[36] Despite the fate of Kristensen's attempt, it proves instructive to examine recent Continental models to bring a different perspective to the study of early medieval social structures in the northern Danelaw.

Despite the diversity of the terminology employed in contemporary sources and the varying nature of the surviving evidence, it is possible to detect a number of characteristics shared by most rural communities before *c.* 900. Most communities in the seventh, eighth and ninth centuries were characterized by a spectrum of lords, free landowners, tenants and slaves. Lords ranged in significance from the great lay aristocrats and major churches to prosperous peasants who rented out a little of their land to neighbouring peasant tenants. Recent studies have consistently argued that across Europe landed property was normally thought of as being held by free persons who had acquired it by inheritance; as the Franks put it, it had come to them *de alode parentum*.[37] Everywhere allodial land appears to have been freely alienable, through sale, bequest, dowries, and so on. However, although there may have been no need to seek the permission of a superior, restrictions may in practice have been placed on alienation by the claims of kin.[38]

Land-ownership is a complex concept. In attempts to identify and define early medieval land-ownership much confusion has arisen from the fact that few people had totally unrestricted rights over land. Yet this should not be surprising; one can envisage few social contexts in which individuals had no obligations attendant on their control over land, whether to superiors, the family, the wider community, potential heirs, and so on, but this does not mean that individuals and families

---

35. Wickham, 'Rural societies', 224.
36. Faith, *The English Peasantry*. One of the most recent syntheses of Anglo-Saxon England essentially returned to a Stubbsian view of the peasantry: Campbell, 'Epilogue', 242–4.
37. S. Reynolds, *Fiefs and Vassals: the medieval evidence reinterpreted* (1994), 75–84 (on France); 182–8, 207–9 (on Italy); 398–403 (on Germany).
38. A.C. Murray, *Germanic Kinship Structure* (1983), 183; Müller-Mertens, *Karl der Grosse*, 66–89; Reynolds, *Fiefs and Vassals*, 76–7, 183–4.

were not perceived as landowners. In any discussion of land-ownership we need to discuss the ways in which given societies defined and controlled rights over land, and how the restrictions placed on control over land were maintained and understood. This is no easy task. It is apparent that the ways in which historians have often categorized land, and distinguished between, for example, land that was 'owned' (for which the landowner owes nothing more than public taxation) and land that was simply 'rented' (in which a payment is made for the right to enjoy someone else's property), do not always stand up to scrutiny. In an early medieval context, it can often be difficult to distinguish taxation from rent, rulers from landlords and rights of property from rights of government, 'not because people confuse them but because the distinction does not exist', as Susan Reynolds has observed.[39] Land-ownership is, in fact, determined in socially and culturally specific contexts. It is the bundle of rights over land that are recognized and protected by a society, and, as such, it requires social or governmental recognition.[40] Peasants can accordingly be considered as landowners in a social system which recognizes their rights of property in the way that it does those of the aristocracy.

The term 'peasant' is also contentious. Teodor Shanin has provided a general definition of peasants as 'small agricultural producers, who, with the help of simple equipment and the labour of their families produce mostly for their own consumption, direct or indirect, and for the fulfilment of obligations to the holders of political and economic power'. He also suggests that for the peasantry the family farm is the basic multidimensional unit of social organization, that land husbandry is the main means of livelihood, and that the peasantry occupy the 'underdog' position and are dominated by outsiders.[41] In the early medieval period our ability to go beyond Shanin's fairly uncontentious generalizations are limited; we do not have, for example, the manorial court records or, with few exceptions, the estate surveys available to the late medievalist. In many ways this discrepancy in evidence lies at the root of the reluctance of early medievalists to consider the peasantry. We must, then, conceptualize the problem differently. Ultimately the term 'peasant' is an abstraction, although medievalists rarely address this fact. Abstractions cannot be used as 'simple descriptions of a really-existing society somewhere' but serve more appropriately as 'points of reference for the comparison of such societies'.[42] Chris Wickham offers a working definition of early medieval 'free peasant owners' which provides us with a starting-point: they are 'direct cultivators who possess their own land with

---

39. Reynolds, *Fiefs and Vassals*, 53.
40. *Ibid.*, 54.
41. T. Shanin, 'Introduction: peasantry as a concept' in *Peasants and Peasant Societies*, ed. T. Shanin (2nd edn, 1988), 1–14, at 3 for the quotation.
42. Wickham, 'Rural societies', 228.

more or less full property rights'.[43] It is the nature of rights over land, and the social pressures which determine attitudes to land, that are crucial to definitions of peasantry in an early medieval context.

Recent studies have revealed that the obligations that rested on the holders of allodial land were everywhere similar, whatever the social standing of the individual: taxes had to be paid (where they could be exacted); other miscellaneous tributes might be demanded by kings of free landholders; there were obligations to provide military service; and to attend the public courts.[44] As a result, even the humblest of free landholders had a direct link to public authority. There seems to have been a general belief that both nobles and lesser free men could have rights in land that were broadly similar, and equally protected by law, although, certainly, there may have been differences in the precise details of inheritance customs, or in the rules governing alienation. However, although freedom was important in theory, in practice it was no protection against economic hardship, and many free peasants were economically no more advantaged than their unfree neighbours. This was apparently an important factor in enabling the greater lay and ecclesiastical lords to usurp the rights of their less advantaged neighbours, and bring them increasingly under their jurisdiction.

Although there is evidence for communal co-operation in agricultural activities and for communal rights in resources such as woodland and meadow, there is little to indicate that land was normally held communally; in general land appears to have been thought of as being held by individuals or by families.[45] Agricultural practice and land-owning were related, but different, aspects of local organization.

Early medieval tenants might be either legally free or unfree. Some, although not all, were closely involved in the economy of the lord whose land they cultivated, and they were heavily burdened with labour services. The proportion of peasant proprietors to peasants holding land on restricted tenancies varied enormously from region to region, or even from village to village.[46] Indeed, it is often difficult to distinguish easily between these two groups, since freeholders might also hold land on a tenancy. It has been suggested that the presence of these small freeholders may have served to undermine the ability of lords to coerce their tenants; groups of free peasants might provide a

---

43. *Ibid.*, 223.
44. P. Bonnassie, *From Slavery to Feudalism in South-Western Europe* (1991), 299–301; Reynolds, *Fiefs and Vassals*, 80–2, 185–6.
45. Murray, *Germanic Kinship Structure*, 183–215; E. James, *The Origins of France* (1982), 84–7; C.J. Wickham, 'Land disputes and their social framework in Lombard-Carolingian Italy', in *The Settlement of Disputes in Early Medieval Europe*, ed. W. Davies and P. Fouracre (1986), 105–24; Reynolds, *Fiefs and Vassals*, 76, 183. In Catalonia, however, there is evidence that some land was held communally, but this was far from common, and was the result of ecological factors: Bonnassie, *From Slavery to Feudalism*, 116.
46. C.J. Wickham, 'Rural society in Carolingian Europe', in *The New Cambridge Medieval History, II, c. 700–c. 900*, ed. R. McKitterick (1995), 510–37.

refuge to which fleeing *coloni* and slaves could escape.[47] Slavery was known to all parts of Europe, though the numbers of slaves and the capacity for manumission varied enormously from region to region.[48]

As we shall see, the social structure of rural communities was not static throughout our period. It is now time to look at a number of these issues in a little more detail. What follows is by no means a comprehensive survey; a few widely drawn examples must suffice. The intention is merely to present a cross-section of recent research on early medieval societies in continental Europe, and to use this survey to generate ideas and to broaden our perspective on early medieval English society in general, and, in turn, on the societies of the northern Danelaw in particular.

Regional Continental studies

Studies of the 'great estate' (*villa*) in Carolingian Frankia have tended to propose the estates of a handful of great monasteries as the archetypal form of rural organization.[49] On the supposedly typical estate, such as that described by the early ninth-century polyptych of the abbey of Saint-Germain-des-Prés in Paris, slaves and others of servile status (*servi fiscalini*) can be found among the tenants (*coloni*) of the *mansi* who worked on the abbey's reserve, or demesne (*mansus dominicatus*), in return for their holdings.[50] This model for rural organization has influenced many studies of the period. However, it is now clear that estates of this type did not dominate the countryside, that they were typical really only of the area around Paris which was under the shadow of the Frankish kings, and are particularly to be found in association with the great monasteries.[51] Indeed, the bipartite estate of the polyptychs has come to be seen in a new light recently; it is now recognized that the documents are not mere descriptions but are normative sources by which the lord of the estate tried to establish a coherent 'estate custom'.[52] However, if that was so, it was not always

47. J.P. Poly and E. Bournazel, *The Feudal Transformation 900–1200* (1991), 126–7.
48. R. Karras, *Slavery and Society in Medieval Scandinavia* (New Haven, Connecticut, 1988), 5–39.
49. M. Bloch, *Feudal Society* (2 vols, trans. 1961), I, 241–54; R. Latouche, *The Birth of Western Economy; economic aspects of the Dark Ages* (trans. 1961), 176–89; G. Duby, *The Early Growth of the European Economy: warriors and peasants from the seventh to the twelfth century* (trans. 1974), 83–97.
50. Latouche, *The Birth of Western Economy*, 176–89, 191–4; C. Perrin, 'Observations sur le manse dans la région parisienne au début du ixe siècle', *Annales d'histoire économique et sociale*, 2 (1945), 39–52.
51. G. Duby, *Rural Economy and Country Life in the Medieval West* (trans. 1968), 47–8; *The Early Growth of the European Economy*, 83–8; Latouche, *The Birth of Western Economy*, 196–202; Poly and Bournazel, *The Feudal Transformation*, 246–71; A. Verhulst (ed.) *Le Grand Domaine aux époques mérovingienne et carolingienne* (Ghent, 1985).
52. Duby, *The Early Growth of the European Economy*, 84–5, 90; J.P. Devroey, 'Les premiers polyptyques remois, viie–viiie siècles', in *Etudes sur le grand domaine carolingien*, ed. J.P. Devroey (1993), 78–97.

a very successful attempt. Even among the lands of the abbey of Saint-Germain-des-Prés there are a number of holdings that do not fit the 'great estate' model; these are scattered holdings often called demesnes but supported by the labour of slaves rather than by tenants on adjacent *mansi*, a striking contrast to the classic *villa* system.[53]

The importance placed on slave labour appears to have varied enormously, both geographically and chronologically. It was apparently of greater importance in the east Frankish economy, and this was doubtless linked to the eastward expansion of the Empire, which replenished the stocks of slaves. However, the number of slaves was reduced everywhere by manumission, ecclesiastical sanctions and intermarriage with the free.[54] Slave labour seems to have been less important in the heartland of the Frankish Empire by the ninth century, as greater emphasis was placed on exploiting the labour services of tenants who had been granted land in return for these services. Indeed, the imposition of labour services seems to have been a feature of the seventh to ninth centuries, and may have been the result of a shortage of slaves.[55] Labour services entailed a greater level of servility for the peasantry than did renders and rents, which carried a clearer association with free status. However, it is clear that labour services were not universally important on great estates: in the Midi, for example, much less use was typically made of labour services.[56]

There is also evidence that some 'great estates' did not have a demesne, and that the lords of such estates relied instead on food rents and other renders from their tenants. On the estates of the abbey of Saint-Martin of Tours (France) the occupants of the tenements in the late seventh century owed enormous renders of wheat and wood, but apparently did not provide labour services on a demesne to any great extent. On the estates of the abbey of Marseilles (France) in the early ninth century little emphasis was placed on the demesne and more attention was paid in surviving documents to tenants than to tenements; the only dues specified, and still irregular, are pasturage,

---

53. Latouche, *The Birth of the Western Economy*, 194–7.
54. Duby, *The Early Growth of the European Economy*, 31–3; Bonnassie, *From Slavery to Feudalism*, 1–59; P. Bonnassie, 'La Croissance agricole du haut moyen âge dans la Gaule du Midi et le nord-est de la péninsule ibérique', in *Croissance agricole du haut moyen âge: chronologie, modalités, géographie*, Flaran, 10 (Auch, 1990), 13–35; P. Toubert, 'La Part du grand domaine dans le décollage économique de l'Occident (viiie–ixe siècles)', *ibid.*, 53–86; A. Verhulst, 'Étude comparative du régime domanial classique', *ibid.*, 87–101; P. Dockès, *Medieval Slavery and Liberation* (trans. Chicago, 1982), 92–8, 101–5; Poly and Bournazel, *The Feudal Transformation*, 120–2.
55. Verhulst, 'Étude comparative'; A. Verhulst, 'Die Grundherrschaftsentwicklung im ost-frankischen Raum vom 8. bis 10. Jahrhundert', in *Strukturen der Grundherrschaft im frühen Mittelalter*, ed. W. Rösener (1989), 29–46. Chris Wickham has suggested (pers. comm.) that the emphasis placed on slave labour in studies of the eastern part of the Frankish Empire may be misplaced, and that they are likely to have been servile tenants.
56. Poly and Bournazel, *The Feudal Transformation*, 252, 261.

pannage, *tributum* of one penny, hens and eggs. They must also have had to provide a portion of their produce, given the apparent absence of a demesne of any significance.[57] It is widely believed that demesne exploitation was less common east of the Rhine. There, renders rather than labour services appear to have been more common, especially on lands situated any distance from the estate centre.[58] The classic system did, however, exist in some places beyond the Rhine. A diploma issued by Louis the German in 840 described 'a lord's *mansus* with houses and other buildings and twenty other *mansi* making renders and doing service there' which was presented to the abbey of Corvey (Germany).[59]

In Lombard Italy Pierre Toubert has distinguished three types of estate structure.[60] On the first type little or no importance was placed on a demesne, with manorial profit gained from grazing or wine-growing, or with peasant tenants providing a proportion of their harvest to the lord. On the second, exploitation was concentrated into areas of specialized profit, in which tenant labour services were limited to a few weeks' work per year. The third type of estate more closely resembles the classic 'great estate', with great emphasis on cereal production, in which tenant labour services were extremely important. In other words, not only did the means by which lords exploited the countryside vary, often depending on the nature of the terrain, but the pressures placed on the peasant tenants varied accordingly. This must be a universal truth. Adriaan Verhulst, for example, has identified a variety of types of estate organization in modern Belgium which are similar to those described by Toubert.[61]

Another important variable in the structure and exploitation of large estates was the extent to which the estate either formed a coherent block or else was widely scattered. On dispersed estates the emphasis on labour services tended to be less, partly because of the great distance at which many tenants lived, and partly because the scattered nature of the estates rendered economic planning difficult, and the tight control required for the enforcement of labour services was hard to maintain.[62]

It has become increasingly apparent that interspersed with the 'great estates' were both 'small estates' and the lands of small

---

57. *Ibid.*, 249.

58. For a summary of the eastern Frankish economy, see T. Reuter, *Germany in the Early Middle Ages, 800–1056* (1991), 94–102.

59. Reuter, *Germany in the Early Middle Ages*, 99; the term *mansus* is equivalent in meaning to 'hide'; that is to say, it had a meaning that was susceptible to change, but essentially was used to describe a unit of land sufficient to support a family, for which services were demanded of its tenants.

60. P. Toubert, 'L'Italie rurale aux viie–ixe siècles: essai de typologie domaniale', *Settimane*, 20 (1973), 95–132; P. Toubert, *Les Structures du Latium médiéval: le Latium méridional et la Sabine du IXe à la fin du XIIe siècle* (Paris, 1973).

61. A. Verhulst, 'La Genèse du régime domanial classique en France au haut moyen age', *Settimane*, 13 (1966), 135–60.

62. See, for example, C.J. Wickham, *Early Medieval Italy: central power and local society, 400–1000* (1981), 105–7.

freeholders. Small estates have been identified and discussed in many regions, and a recent study of such estates in the vicinity of Cluny (France) has shown them to have been unstable, constantly being formed and re-formed through the workings of inheritance, gifts and exchanges, and to have been based on small-scale exploitation involving slave labour, but with little evidence for a strict division of land into demesne and tenanted land.[63] Although it is often difficult to identify the status of landholders named in the available sources, the possibility that the fabric of rural organization in so many documented cases was formed by communities of free peasant property-holders is suggested by the small size of the lands referred to, by the number of the transactions, by the lack of restrictions placed on such transactions by great lords and by the absence of references to tenants.[64] Beyond the world of the 'great estate', peasant freeholders and small estates have been identified in recent studies of, for example, Picardy (once generally considered to be a region dominated by the 'great estate'), the Mâconnais, Provence and Auvergne (France).[65] Recent work on Catalonia has emphasized the continuing importance there of independent peasant communities into the eleventh century. There were certainly aristocrats in Catalonia but the extent of their landed possessions was rarely substantial.[66] The number of smallholders there, whose holdings and prosperity were diverse, may be accounted for by several factors: the role of the free village communities (the *concejos*) in the fight against Islam, and as the weapon of the monarchy against seigneurial ambition; and the clearance of land by individuals who were subsequently accorded free disposal of it.[67]

A number of recent studies of the social fabric of early medieval societies emphasize that although there were broad similarities across Europe, there was also great diversity between regions, and even between neighbouring villages. For example, a distinctive social structure

---

63. G. Bois, *The Transformation of the Year One Thousand* (trans. 1992), 122–9.
64. Latouche, *The Birth of the Western Economy*, 177–8; Wickham, 'Rural societies', 228–32; Wickham, 'Rural society in Carolingian Europe', 512–26.
65. R. Fossier, *La Terre et les hommes en Picardie jusqu'à la fin du XIIe siècle* (Paris, 1968), 210–11; Bois, *The Transformation of the Year One Thousand*; see the various contributions to R. Delort (ed.) *La France de l'an mil* (Paris, 1990); see also A. Verhulst, 'La genèse du régime domanial classique'; Poly and Bournazel, *The Feudal Transformation*, 126; L. Genicot, 'Sur le domaine de Saint-Bertin à l'époque carolingienne', *Revue d'Histoire Ecclésiastique*, 71 (1976), 69–78; Duby, *The Early Growth of the European Economy*, 89–90; E. Magnou-Nortier, *La Société laïque et l'Eglise dans la province ecclésiastique de Narbonne de la fin du VIIIe siècle à la fin du XIIe siècle* (Toulouse, 1974), 156, 207, 284; J.P. Poly, *La Provence et le société féodale, 879–1166* (Paris, 1976), 87, 104; Bonnassie, *From Slavery to Feudalism*, 296–304; C. Lauranson-Rosaz, *L'Auvergne et ses marges du VIIIe au XIe siècle: la fin du monde antique?* (Le-Puy-en-Velay, 1987), 397–9.
66. Bonnassie, *From Slavery to Feudalism*, 296–313.
67. *Ibid.*, 116, 243–54; P. Bonnassie, *La Catalogne du milieu du Xe siècle à la fin du XIe siècle; croissance et mutations d'une société* (Toulouse, 1975), 305; P. Friedman, *The Origins of Peasant Servitude in Medieval Catalonia* (1991), 4–25; M. del C. Carle, *Del concejo medieval castellano-leonés* (Buenos Aires, 1968).

in early medieval Brittany has recently been discussed, which, although it may have been atypical, serves as a reminder that peasant communities could organize themselves to resist the encroachment of lordship.[68] There the activities of villages (*plebes*) were presided over by machtierns, who, although they were aristocrats in the sense that they were commonly substantial landowners and fulfilled public duties, had little direct control over the villagers. The latter (the *plebenses*) were land-owning peasant cultivators, who dominated the affairs of the villages. Any machtiern who wished to dominate them had to negotiate and win their support; they were not landlords in the sense understood elsewhere. The active resistance of rural communities to the acquisition of too much power by any of its members has also been argued for the continental Saxons in the period before the Frankish conquest and for the Slav confederation of the Liutizi in the tenth century.[69]

The detail provided by the surviving records of land transactions permits us to trace the history of individual estates and even villages in various parts of Europe. A recent study of early medieval Italy has demonstrated that individual village communities might have very different experiences during the eighth and ninth centuries. A comparison of Varsi (in the Appennines) with Gnignano (in the Lombard plain) reveals that while the former had a relatively stable pattern of social organization and land-holding (the number of land transactions was small, the local church acquired land only piecemeal and no family appears to have given away more than a fraction of its land), the latter experienced great upheavals (during the period *c.* 798–856 the church of S. Ambrogio in Milan acquired a great deal of land there) and there was more outside interest in lands in the village (from both S. Ambrogio and urban artisans from Parma).[70]

The variation and complexity of lordship and the varied nature of relations between lords and peasants is evident from numerous modern studies of early medieval society across Europe. Lordship was not invariably expressed as land-ownership, in the Roman sense, and lords clearly sometimes enjoyed rights over people who themselves enjoyed property rights over their own lands. It is extremely difficult to clarify the nature of property rights in the early medieval period, not least because the dichotomy between the terminology employed in contemporary documents and socio-economic and legal reality may have been substantial in many parts of Europe. It has been suggested, for example, that forms of property rights that did not conform to the Roman legal tradition were respected even in the heartlands of the

---

68. W. Davies, *Small Worlds* (1988).
69. Wickham, 'Rural societies', 240, and references therein; Reuter, *Germany in the Early Middle Ages*, 66–7.
70. Wickham, *Early Medieval Italy*, 101–5; for further studies of individual regions and villages, see Wickham, 'Rural societies', 228–30, 234–6; Wickham, 'Rural society in Carolingian Europe', 512–26.

former Roman Empire; in less romanized areas this may have been even more in evidence.[71] An additional development complicated patterns of land-ownership, and that was the emergence of forms of land-holding which were on limited terms (usually for a life or with limitations on inheritance) and were known as *beneficia* or *precaria*. It did not, however, take long before land held in benefice and allodial property became indistinguishable, especially in periods of ineffective kingship when there was little regulation of benefices; 'the working of political favour, power politics, the growth of a land-market, and the drift of custom' all served to blur the divisions between types of property-holding.[72]

Peasant freeholders were constantly under threat from coercion by their more powerful neighbours. They were especially vulnerable during times of harvest failure or warfare, when they were often forced to resort to giving up their land, only to receive it back on a limited tenancy.[73] The expansion of the estates of great lords often led to the absorption of the lands of allodialists. Lords can also be witnessed attempting to enforce new exactions from peasants, and placing limitations on their freedoms.[74] Across Europe throughout the early medieval period, and particularly from the eighth century in northern Frankia and perhaps a little later further south, the status of the free peasant landholders was becoming increasingly undermined by changes in the nature of lordship, of estate organization and of the state. Although, of course, not all seigneurial power was the result of delegation, the increasing number of grants of royal land and of royal rights over land to other lords did serve to compromise the position of the free peasants, who became increasingly subject to a more local seigneurial authority. Delegated regalian rights were increasingly transformed by coercion, violence and the development of new rights, or 'bad customs' (*malus usus*) as they came to be known. Lordship in the tenth and eleventh centuries was increasingly based on castles, and on military and judicial powers. The fate of the free proprietors depended on the nature of the lordship to which they became subject; ecclesiastical lordship was a great leveller of social status, and churches were not averse to regarding all peasants as tenants regardless of their status, whereas lords with widely dispersed estates often found it difficult to enforce exactions, particularly labour services, and in such circumstances the free fared better.[75]

---

71. C.J. Wickham, 'European forests in the early Middle Ages: landscape and land clearance', *Settimane*, 37 (1990), 479–545, at 495–9.
72. Reynolds, *Fiefs and Vassals*, 48–52, 57 (for the quotation), 78–9, 84–113 (on Frankia), 425–47 (on Germany).
73. Poly and Bournazel, *The Feudal Transformation*, 126, 259; Bonnassie, *From Slavery to Feudalism*, 297.
74. Friedman, *The Origins of Peasant Servitude*, 63–4; Wickham, 'European forests in the early Middle Ages', 494–7.
75. Duby, *The Early Growth of the European Economy*, 172–6; Duby, *Rural Economy*, 224–31; Bonnassie, *From Slavery to Feudalism*, 164–5, 217–21, 232–7.

There is, however, evidence to suggest that the deterioration in the status of the free peasantry was not unopposed. In a notable example from 900, eleven men of Cusago, near Milan, claimed that they were free on the grounds that they held small amounts of property even though they did do labour services for other parts of their property; unfortunately for the count of Milan, the men called upon to prove his case swore that the men of Cusago were right.[76] However, it is not generally demonstrable whether peasants were successful in their attempts to find legal redress for their changed circumstances, but it seems unlikely that they often were.[77] Nonetheless, the very fact that peasants were able to make representation to a court in defiance of a lord indicates an initial expectation that lords were not entitled to demand more than the king had previously claimed; and a number of these court cases involved areas where monasteries had recently acquired land from other lords and were trying to exert greater central control over it.[78] Kings sometimes legislated on behalf of the free, which may suggest that their status was under threat. Charlemagne, for example, sought to preserve a system for recruitment in which poor freemen could serve in his armies.[79] It has also been suggested that in the Peace of God movements of the eleventh century the peasantry found élite support in the shape of some churchmen, and that, in turn, the movements gained considerable peasant support.[80] More dramatically, peasants sometimes resisted new demands with violence. The best known example was the peasant uprising in Normandy in 997.[81] This sort of uprising was probably rare, but there is evidence to suggest that lords had to guard against resistance from both the independent landholders and their own dependent peasants. Legislation by Carolingian kings against sworn associations of peasants and the emphasis placed by theologians on the duty of slaves to obey their masters suggest a concern with maintaining order among the rural population.[82]

Nonetheless, despite the evidence for the vitality of free peasant communities, they did increasingly succumb to seigneurial pressures. The main developments were the merging of the free and unfree classes of rural society into a single semi-servile group; the fragmentation of public power; the usurpation of public rights; and the development of new ones by a wider section of lords. The pace of these developments doubtless varied. But recently a number of studies

---

76. Wickham, *Early Medieval Italy*, 109–10.
77. For examples, see Wickham, 'European forests in the early Middle Ages', 494–5; Wickham, *Early Medieval Italy*, 109–11.
78. Wickham, *Early Medieval Italy*, 110.
79. Dockès, *Medieval Slavery and Liberation*, 100.
80. Bonnassie, *From Slavery to Feudalism*, 307–11; Bois, *The Transformation of the Year One Thousand*, 136–7, 164; cf. R.I. Moore, 'The first European peace movement, or virtue rewarded', *Medieval History*, 2 (1) (1992), 16–25.
81. Bonnassie, *From Slavery to Feudalism*, 310.
82. Reuter, *Germany in the Early Middle Ages*, 102.

have spoken of a swift transformation, a veritable revolution, in social structure which occurred in the tenth and eleventh centuries.[83] In addition, the blurring of distinctions between allodial land and land acquired on more limited terms had a concomitant effect on the peasantry.[84] The development of what may be termed 'full' property rights by lords over the lands they acquired varied across Europe, but in many areas it was a process occurring from the eighth and ninth centuries and was associated with the increasing acquisition of land by the church.[85] In such circumstances, the peasantry were prone to be merged into a single status-group.

In a study that is concerned with the Scandinavian impact on England, it would be desirable to consider the nature of social organization in contemporary Scandinavia. This, however, is not as straightforward as simply making a comparison with other parts of continental Europe, because Scandinavia does not provide us with contemporary written records. Later written sources, contemporary written perspectives from outside Scandinavia and archaeological evidence allow some tentative conclusions to be drawn about what Scandinavian society may have been like in the Viking Age.[86] There has been much discussion of the relative proportions of free peasants and slaves in early medieval Scandinavia. It now seems to be the consensus that the uniformity of the free class was not as great as was once thought, a conclusion that has been drawn, as we have seen, in studies of many parts of early medieval Europe. Archaeological evidence for substantial earthwork defences in the eighth century and the existence of rune-stones in the tenth and eleventh centuries recording the names of lords emphasize the importance of powerful lordship and kingship during the Viking Age in Scandinavia. Moreover, slavery was clearly important, as was an intermediate class of freed slaves. This was no peasant democracy. Nonetheless, it is clear from contemporary written evidence that the powers of kings were limited by the collective voice of at least some of their subjects. For example, the late ninth-century *Vita Anskarii*, by Rimbert, bishop of Hamburg–Bremen (Germany), describes the missionary activity in Birka (Sweden) of Anskar, his predecessor as bishop, where the king had to consult with two assemblies before he could allow Anskar to continue his work.[87]

83. Poly and Bournazel, *The Feudal Transformation, passim*; Bonnassie, *From Slavery to Feudalism*, 104–31, 288–313; Bois, *The Transformation of the Year One Thousand, passim*. A useful summary in English of recent studies of this subject is B.G.H. Ditchum, 'The feudal millennium? Social change in rural France *circa* 1000 in recent French historiography', *Medieval History*, 3 (1993), 86–99.
84. Reynolds, *Fiefs and Vassals*, 77–84.
85. Reynolds, *Fiefs and Vassals*, 53–4, 59–65 and *passim*.
86. See, for example, Karras, *Slavery and Society*; B. Sawyer and P. Sawyer, *Medieval Scandinavia: from conversion to Reformation, c. 800–1500* (Minneapolis 1993), 1–26, 129–43; N. Lund, 'Scandinavia, c. 700–1066', in *The Cambridge New Medieval History*, ed. R. McKitterick (1995), 202–27; J. Graham-Campbell (ed.) *Cultural Atlas of the Viking World* (1994), 38–75.
87. P.H. Sawyer, *King and Vikings: Scandinavia and Europe AD 700–1100* (1982), 39–64 at 54 for the *Vita Anskarii*.

Moreover, both the documentary and the archaeological evidence suggests that power was distributed among a multiplicity of lords. There is rarely any indication that the lords with whom western kings had dealings had much power in the Scandinavian homelands, many of the kings named in genealogies are not commemorated on rune-stones and those rulers who are commemorated do not appear in genealogies, suggesting limitations on the powers of the kings named in the genealogies. Furthermore, the elaborate nature of some of the burials from the Viking Age may suggest a fragile social and political authority that needed to be underpinned by an elaborate burial rite.[88] The lure of wealth in western Europe may have been one cause of the viking raids, but another seemingly important factor was the departure of rulers and their followers, who in the face of the growing authority of some 'royal' dynasties went off overseas in search of somewhere to rule.[89] The available evidence suggests differences with other parts of Europe, not least the later arrival of the Christian influence on social and political organization, but also many similarities.

In sum, this necessarily brief survey of recent work on early medieval society in Europe reveals the complexity and variety of forms of organization and of social structures found across the Continent, and indicates that the pace of change varied from region to region. If the histories of these better-documented regions provide any lessons for the following survey of early medieval society in England, it is that we should be wary of simple models, and we should not expect to find a uniform society across all regions of England. Nor should we expect developments in social organization, the estate structure and patterns of land-holding to have occurred at the same rate across the whole of the country. Such comparisons also alert us to the dangers of aggregating evidence from different regions of Anglo-Saxon England and from different centuries, and place question marks against much received wisdom about the nature of early medieval society in England. With this established it is now time to turn to the evidence for early medieval England.

Early medieval England

It is arguable that the old paradigms within which early medieval societies have been studied have yet to be completely abandoned where early medieval English society is concerned. Yet the comparatively meagre early medieval English evidence for rural organization will sustain re-evaluation. A number of recent studies

---

88. G. Halsall, *Settlement and Social Organization: the Merovingian region of Metz* (1995), 251–4, 264–7, interprets early medieval funerary rituals in this manner. For the Scandinavian material, see Graham-Campbell (ed.) *Cultural Atlas of the Viking World*, 31–5, 40–3.
89. P. Wormald, 'Viking studies: whence and whither?', in *The Vikings*, ed. R.T. Farrell (1982), 128–53, at 144–8.

have discussed Anglo-Saxon land-ownership and lordship in a Continental context. This chapter builds on those studies and also offers new insights into other aspects of Anglo-Saxon society, in particular the structure of rural society, peasant status and estate organization.[90] What sort of society did the Scandinavian settlers of the ninth and tenth centuries encounter?

Lordship and land-holding in Anglo-Saxon England

It is pertinent to begin by examining the nature of lordship in the period to *c.* 900. Very little can be discerned of lordship, including kingship, before the seventh century, by which time the influence of the Christian church had probably effected important changes.[91] Nonetheless, two possible scenarios have been proposed concerning the nature of lordship in the early Anglo-Saxon centuries, and for the emergence of kings and kingdoms at that time. On the one hand, it has been argued that Germanic settlers moved into the remnants of the Romano-British estate structure, merged with the existing population and forged a mixed British–Germanic community out of which emerged dominant 'tribes' or extended families. Increasingly hierarchical leadership within the dominant family gave rise to leading members who established themselves at the head of their family or tribe through both force and, eventually, inheritance. Some of these were eventually successful in extending their territories and in establishing themselves at the head of other families or tribes, and this coalescence of territories was the catalyst for the process of state formation to begin in earnest. On the other hand, it has been proposed that kingship emerged following the conquest of an existing British territory by an outside group. One effect of such a takeover was the emergence of centres of sub-Roman kingdoms as important Anglo-Saxon royal centres.[92] Either way, many recent accounts have emphasized the emergence of the more important and successful Anglo-Saxon kingdoms out of smaller political units and settlement areas – the *regiones* and *provinciae* referred to in early written sources.[93] There have, however, been some dissenting voices, influenced by a Continental perspective. Wendy Davies and Hayo

90. Reynolds, *Fiefs and Vassals*, 323–95; P. Wormald, *Bede and the Conversion of England* (1984); Faith, *The English Peasantry*.
91. J. Campbell, 'The first Christian kings', in *The Anglo-Saxons*, ed. Campbell, 45–69 at 53–8; S.R. Bassett, 'In search of the origins of Anglo-Saxon kingdoms', in *The Origins of Anglo-Saxon Kingdoms*, ed. S.R. Bassett (1989), 3–27, at 4.
92. Bassett, 'The origins of Anglo-Saxon kingdoms', 23.
93. *Ibid.*; T. M. Charles-Edwards, 'Early medieval kingships in the British Isles', in *The Origins of Anglo-Saxon Kingdoms*, ed. Bassett, 28–37; J. Blair, *Early Medieval Surrey: landholding, church and settlement before 1300* (1991), 12–34; C.J. Arnold, 'Territories and leadership: frameworks for the study of emergent polities in early Anglo-Saxon southern England', in *Power and Politics in Early Medieval Britain and Ireland*, ed. S.T. Driscoll and M.R. Nieke (1988), 111–27.

Vierck have proposed that some of the peoples and population groups named in the Tribal Hidage (a seventh- or eighth-century list of tribute assessments) may not have constituted kingdoms, and that other forms of socio-political organization may have prevailed. Moreover, social grouping and kingdom may not have been straightforward alternatives, and groups of peoples may have existed alongside but outside the kingdom structure.[94] Guy Halsall has also questioned the notion that the territories named in early documents were necessarily separate kingdoms or proto-kingdoms, rather than subdivisions of larger kingdoms.[95]

There may, then, have been several processes which gave rise to the kingship and aristocratic lordship of the seventh and eighth centuries when our sources first allow us to see them in action. By that time kings were itinerant, and hospitality was enjoyed at the halls of magnates or in monasteries, or else in the kings' own halls or vills (*villa regia*), which might be spread throughout their territories.[96] Kings were supported by a tribute-collecting economy, although we have only a vague notion of the sorts of dues owed to them. Kings declared land to be free from *feorm* and *tributum* in the charters they issued, and these dues had presumably formerly been enjoyed by kings, but it is not clear what they included, how they were levied, how regularly they were enforced, or how heavy they were.[97] There may have been a big difference between the way in which kings exploited land in the vicinity of royal vills, and land at more distant locations. As kingdoms grew, the royal itinerary could no longer adequately incorporate the whole territory, and there was, in any case, presumably a limit to how many food renders the king and his entourage could consume. The renders owed from more distant parts of the kingdom are less likely to have taken this form, and it has been suggested that livestock, for example, would have been a more appropriate render from such territories.[98] By the late seventh century the kings of Wessex had regularized their food renders to the extent that they could legislate for a fixed rate at which they were to be levied. According to the law-code of Ine, an estate of ten hides was expected to render ten vats of honey, three hundred loaves, twelve ambers of Welsh ale, thirty of clear ale, two cows or ten wethers, ten geese, twenty hens, ten cheeses, an amber full of butter, five salmon, twenty pounds of fodder and one hundred eels.[99] The variety and specificity of

---

94. W. Davies and H. Vierck, 'The contexts of Tribal Hidage: social aggregates and settlement patterns', *Frühmittelalterliche Studien*, 8 (1974), 223–93, at 229, 240.
95. G. Halsall, 'The origins of Anglo-Saxon kingdoms: a Merovingianist speaks out' (forthcoming).
96. J. Campbell, 'Bede's *reges* and *principes*', in his *Essays in Anglo-Saxon History* (1986), 85–98, at 95–7; J. Campbell, 'Bede's words for places', *ibid.*, 99–119, at 108–16; Charles-Edwards, 'Early medieval kingships'.
97. F.W. Maitland, *Domesday Book and Beyond* (1897), 236–40.
98. Charles-Edwards, 'Early medieval kingships', 29–30.
99. See the law-code of Ine, c. 70.1 [hereafter Ine], in *EHD*, I, no. 32.

this render implies a formidable level of organization, both of the king's support system and of the estates themselves, presumably by their lords.[100] The establishment of regular tribute circuits based on royal vills can be seen in action: when King Offa of Mercia granted land at Westbury and Henbury (Glos) to the bishop of Worcester, he stipulated that he was to receive a food render delivered to the royal vill (*ad regalem vicum*).[101] Many such dues survived into later centuries, although those recorded in Domesday Book were probably the result of relatively recent innovations on royal estate management, which had seen royal dues subject to increasing regularization.[102] The royal household of any kingdom may not simply have included the king and his entourage, as it is also possible that the queen, sub-kings, royal *duces* and *praefecti* had their own households, which may plausibly have also been supported by the system of food renders.[103]

Kings of the seventh and eighth centuries surrounded themselves with entourages, the members of which they rewarded with administrative offices and grants of land. Gift-giving was also an important means of retaining the support of their followers.[104] The more successful kings incorporated new lands into their kingdoms and in doing so had to establish new administrative structures and appoint rulers to the new territories; sometimes these were appointed from cadet branches of the kings' own family, although on occasions the existing rulers of the newly subjugated lands were retained for this purpose. The political organization of early Anglo-Saxon England was rooted in delegated power. The powers of sub-kings and ealdormen over once independent kingdoms were similar to those exercised by kings, and they had the authority to command both tribute and loyalty.[105] Not all power in Anglo-Saxon England was, however, delegated from above, and the leaders who emerged out of the extended families of the post-migration period doubtless had, and long maintained, power bases in their localities.[106] Bede's lack of precision in the application of titles to rulers and members of the aristocracy (*rex, princeps, dux, praefectus,*

100. Stenton, *Anglo-Saxon England*, 288; Faith, *The English Peasantry*, 38–9.
101. S 146 (B 272); *EHD*, I, no. 78.
102. P.A. Stafford, 'The "farm of one night" and the organization of King Edward's estates in Domesday', *EcHR*, 2nd sec. 33 (1980), 491–502; P.H. Sawyer, 'The royal *tun* in pre-Conquest England', in *Ideal and Reality in Frankish and Anglo-Saxon Society*, ed. P. Wormald, D. Bullough and R. Collins (1983), 273–99. Not all royal estates in the late eleventh century had long, or continuously, been in royal hands.
103. Charles-Edwards, 'Early medieval kingships', 31–2.
104. Abels, *Lordship and Military Obligation*, 11–42; Campbell, 'The first Christian kings', 54–8.
105. Campbell, 'Bede's *reges* and *principes*'; T.M. Charles-Edwards, 'The distinction between land and moveable wealth in Anglo-Saxon England', in *English Medieval Settlement*, ed. P.H. Sawyer (1979), 97–104.
106. Faith, *The English Peasantry*, 5–11; Bassett, 'The origins of Anglo-Saxon kingdoms', 23.

sub-regulus) – the 'messiness and ambiguity' of his terminology – undoubtedly reflected something of the world in which he lived.[107]

The main form of royal rewards came to be grants of territory. The earliest surviving land-books were intended to provide the church with a substantial, secure and permanent endowment, and they were awarded to individual churches, or to a secular lord for the foundation and endowment of a church.[108] Indeed, it was the permanence of the endowment and the alienability of the land by the recipient that probably distinguished grants by land-book from whatever provisions were made for the church before the advent of bookland. The benefits of a land-book (which included access to the rights the king had previously enjoyed) were attractive enough for laymen to go to the length of acquiring them by fraudulent means, according to Bede. He also informs us that this could be a dangerous practice for kings to allow as it diminished the stock of land at their disposal with which to reward faithful followers and warriors.[109] However, the granting of land was an important means of securing the support of the church and secular aristocracy for the king.[110] Moreover, churches were often useful repositories for royal children, and endowing a royal monastery was a means for a royal dynasty to retain land. Kings did not lose all interest in land once it had been booked; failure to meet the *trinoda necessitas* – bridge-work, *burh*-work and service in the *fyrd* – could result in forfeiture.[111]

That there were great differences in status in the early medieval period is first suggested by the evidence of grave goods and burial rite in the fifth to eighth centuries. Yet while the different treatment accorded individuals in death suggests social differentiation, it would be folly to try to 'read off' status directly from this evidence, or to try to equate it to the distinctions in status drawn in documentary sources. Archaeological evidence cannot provide a simple index of social status, and status as marked in the funerary ritual may not necessarily relate directly or predictably to status in life; it was doubtless also mediated by factors such as ethnicity, gender, stage in the life-cycle, and so on, which may have been as important as 'class' in determining the appropriate burial display.[112] Burial displays may nonetheless have

---

107.   Campbell, 'Bede's *reges* and *principes*', 87; see also A.T. Thacker, 'Some terms for noblemen in Anglo-Saxon England, *c.* 650–900' in *ASSAH*, II, ed. D. Brown (BAR British Series, 92, 1981), 201–36.

108.   P. Wormald, 'The age of Bede and Æthelbald', in *The Anglo-Saxons*, ed. Campbell, 70–100, at 95–100; P. Sims-Williams, *Religion and Literature in Western England, 600–800* (1990), 147–54.

109.   The complaint is expressed in Bede's letter to Ecgberht, the archbishop of York, written in 734: *EHD*, I, no. 170.

110.   N.P. Brooks, 'The development of military obligations in eighth- and ninth-century England', in *England before the Conquest*, ed. Clemoes and Hughes, 69–84.

111.   B. Yorke, *Wessex in the Early Middle Ages* (1995), 246.

112.   For a review of these themes, see R. Gilchrist, 'Ambivalent bodies: gender and medieval archaeology', in *Invisible People and Processes: writing gender and childhood into European archaeology*, ed. J.M. Moore and E. Scott (1997), 42–58, at 44–50.

much to reveal about social identity and status: elsewhere in early medieval Europe it has been demonstrated that lavish burial may mark an unstable social structure, subject to competition, and that conversely an absence of lavish burial display may signify not an absence of powerful or wealthy people, but a society in which wealth and power were less open to challenge.[113] There is clear evidence of regional variation in burial practices, which renders universal interpretations of burial rite inappropriate, but which may have much to reveal about difference in the social fabric of early kingdoms and territories.[114] Excavation of settlement sites also suggests distinctions in status between their inhabitants, in the form of varying sizes of houses, and in the number of ancillary buildings associated with each house. However, where it has been possible to compare a settlement with a contemporary cemetery (for example, at Mucking (Essex), Bishopstone (Sussex) and West Stow (Suffolk)), it has been shown that the burials in the cemetery often show greater diversity than do the buildings in the settlement.[115] This is an important reminder that status may be signified in different ways according to context. In sum, although the archaeological evidence is difficult to interpret, it does suggest that great differences of wealth and status existed in the earlier Anglo-Saxon centuries, and implies that the Anglo-Saxon kingdoms had an aristocratic stratum beneath that of their kings.

According to documentary sources, Anglo-Saxon lordship was based on status at birth; on office-holding and economic factors, such as the amount of land held; on rights over the inhabitants of this land; and on the types of dues of which the lord was the recipient. The variety of terms which were used to describe noblemen and high officials reflect something of the variety of the obligations and prerogatives associated with lordship. The Latin and Old English terms employed in various sources frequently do not correspond, and the terminology used to describe those of high rank was not consistent either within or between kingdoms, or over time. Proximity to the king might result in a lord acquiring administrative or military office (as *praefectus, subregulus, dux*), from which would follow rights over new territories, as well as new status and, perhaps, greater wealth; some of these terms were, however, sometimes applied to the rulers of once independent territories which had become subordinated to greater kingdoms.[116] The way in which an aristocratic family might see itself need not have coincided with the way in which others viewed it: for example, the

---

113. This theme is developed at length in Halsall, *Settlement and Social Organization*, esp. 251–4, 264–7. The implications of this study have yet to be examined in an Anglo-Saxon context, but see H. Hamerow, 'Settlement mobility and the "Middle Saxon shift": rural settlements and settlement patterns in Anglo-Saxon England', *ASE*, 20 (1991), 1–17, at 9.
114. See, for example, C.J. Arnold, *An Archaeology of the Early Anglo-Saxon Kingdoms* (1988), 142–93.
115. Hamerow, 'Settlement mobility', 9.
116. Thacker, 'Some terms for noblemen', *passim*.

rulers of the Hwicce may have continued to regard themselves as kings but to their Mercian overlords they were *sub-reguli, comites* or *ministri*; the context in which an individual operated and was referred to determined the title most appropriately bestowed upon him.[117] Distinctions within the aristocracy must have been created when some of its members acquired interests over wider areas, through fulfilling administrative roles, in contrast to those whose interests were limited to their own lands and locality.[118] According to the law-codes, administrators could be removed for neglect of duty, but they may have proved difficult to dislodge if they were socially and economically entrenched in a region.[119]

Lordship had many facets in the early medieval period, and rights over people, land, services, the produce of the countryside, justice, and so on could be separable, and became increasingly so. The seventh-century law-code of Ine establishes that people of noble status did not necessarily hold land.[120] Exile and eviction were not uncommon fates for nobles, and such men had to seek their fortunes elsewhere, such as the court of a rival king; indeed, many kings (such as Oswald, Oswy and Aldfrith of Northumbria and Cenwalh and Caedwalla of Wessex) experienced a period of exile. Royal households were a potential source of refuge and patronage, and many young nobles took themselves off there hoping to seek advancement, including Bishop Wilfrid, who went at the age of 14 to be presented to Queen Eanfled in the mid-seventh century.[121] Although there has been much debate about this, it now seems clear that lordship was central to the social fabric of early medieval society in England. However, it would be reasonable to suppose that the nature of lordship varied from region to region, and over time. The rights and privileges enjoyed by lords, especially as alleged in the idealized world of the law-codes, must have varied according to a number of factors: family connections; proximity to the king and his court; the amount of land inherited or subsequently acquired, whether by grant, forfeiture or outright usurpation; the nature of the terrain over which they exercised their rights (upland and woodland environments may have been less easily intensively exploited); the extent to which their lands were concentrated or dispersed (the latter probably being more difficult to exploit); and the pre-existing social structure on the lands over which they had authority. These are some of the most obvious factors that would

---

117. Campbell, 'Bede's *reges* and *principes*', 87; Thacker, 'Some terms for noblemen', 213, 222.
118. For comparable east Frankish examples, see Reuter, *Germany in the Early Middle Ages*, 35.
119. Ine, c. 36.1.
120. *Ibid.*, c. 51.
121. *Ibid.*, c. 30, 68; *VSW*, c. 24, 40, 67. On the opportunities open to young nobles, see Charles-Edwards, 'Early medieval kingships', 29, 31–2; Campbell, 'The first Christian kings', 56.

have mediated the exercise of lordship, and all find parallels elsewhere in contemporary early medieval society, as we have seen.

One further factor was important in determining the nature of Anglo-Saxon lordship: patronage. It is not easy to elucidate the working of patronage networks, but their importance is apparent in our earliest written sources, which demonstrate the extent to which kings built up entourages and took exiles into their courts: even a 15-year-old Mercian noble, Guthlac, was able to gather together 'comrades of diverse peoples' as he went out pillaging *c.* 690, doubtless as a result of the promise of adventure and booty.[122] The late ninth-century case of the thief Helmstan is instructive on the importance of patronage.[123] Helmstan was accused of stealing the belt of one Æthelred, and if found guilty Helmstan would no longer have been capable of representing himself in the face of the law. His rivals began to claim his lands, even those for which he had written title, and Helmstan was forced to turn to an old patron, Ealdorman Ordlaf, who offered him life tenure of his lands if he stayed out of trouble. Ordlaf also interceded with King Alfred on behalf of Helmstan and arranged the court procedure. Helmstan won the case, and his ability to gain powerful patronage was clearly an important element in his success. The case of Helmstan gives us a rare insight into the processes and concerns that lay behind the law-codes and charters, and although it is difficult to provide many examples, we ought not to underestimate the extent to which 'local political and social relationships, between a person and his or her kin, friends, neighbours, patrons and enemies, created the practically relevant world in which each person lived'.[124] For insights into this social network, legal documents are only partially useful.

Although there has been a great deal of debate about the nature of land-holding in the pre-viking centuries and the evidence concerning these centuries is less than comprehensive, it is unlikely that Anglo-Saxon England was radically different from the rest of north-western Europe. Thus, there should be little difficulty in envisaging a nobility that had freely held hereditary lands as well as a free land-holding peasantry. Indeed, this assertion has found widespread acceptance; with the proviso that we know little about the unfree, and the relative proportions of free and unfree.[125] The noble and the peasant may, of course, have had very different obligations to meet, and their capacity to maintain their free status and to retain their lands must have varied,

---

122. *Life of Saint Guthlac*, 81.
123. The events took place around 897, but are recorded in a letter from Ealdorman Ordlaf to Edward the Elder: *EHD*, I, no. 102; P. Wormald, 'A handlist of Anglo-Saxon law-suits', *ASE*, 17 (1988), 247–81; S. Keynes, 'The Fonthill letter', in *Words, Texts and Manuscripts: studies in Anglo-Saxon culture presented to Helmut Gneuss*, ed. M. Korhammer (1992), 53–97.
124. Wickham, 'Rural society in Carolingian Europe', 511.
125. P. Wormald, *Bede and the Conversion of England* (1984), 21–2; see also Campbell, 'The first Christian kings', 59; Stafford, *The East Midlands*, 29–34; Reynolds, *Fiefs and Vassals*, 325–7, 331, 334–5.

but in principle their rights over land were similar. Although there is little enough evidence concerning land tenure before the introduction of grants of bookland, and this in itself cause material changes to the nature of land-holding, there are few reasons to doubt that hereditary land was known before the introduction of the land-book. Certainly, in his letter to Bishop Ecgbert of York, Bede complains that nobles and thegns caused, among other things, lands 'to be ascribed to them in hereditary right by royal edicts (*in ius sibi haereditarium regalibus edictis*)', and he is clearly talking about charters. But it 'strains one's credulity' to suppose that the charter introduced the Anglo-Saxons to the very concept of inherited property.[126] Indeed, in another context Bede describes the fact that Benedict Biscop regarded hereditary succession as 'the *worldly* norm' in the late seventh century.[127] No reliable early charter discusses hereditary right; it is freedom of disposition that is commonly of central concern. It is more plausible to maintain that land may have passed by inheritance within kins, but that the creation of bookland changed the rights of the recipient to dispose of the property, and effectively created new inheritances. In granting the holders of bookland perpetual right, the charters served to enhance acquired property with the characteristics of inherited property, and it may be, as Wormald suggests, for this reason that Bede '*in disgust*, could call it *"ius haereditarium"* '.[128]

In order to accept recent assertions concerning the existence of a significant stratum of free landowners, peasant as well as noble, we need to address a number of issues relating to land tenure. In particular, we need to recognize that the corpus of Anglo-Saxon charters presents a number of problems for this model. If we are to argue that there was in Anglo-Saxon England everywhere a nobility that had hereditary lands, not to mention a free land-owning peasantry, then we have to reconcile this with the evidence of the charters, which shows huge tracts of land being granted by kings to the church and, eventually, to select members of the lay aristocracy. The world of the charter is a very simple and ordered one, but it sits uncomfortably alongside the evidence we have for the complexity of social organization, and any argument for the existence of numerous free landholders. A number of questions must be addressed. What was the intention of a charter: to convey land or to grant rights over land and its inhabitants? How did the issue of such a charter affect the inhabitants of the land concerned; could they object, did they know about it? How did the granting of charters affect the organization of the countryside in the long run?

The charters certainly use the language of land-ownership; they speak of *terra iuris mei*, and they employ a terminology (*manentes*,

---

126.   *EHD*, I, no. 170; Wormald, *Bede and the Conversion of England*, 19–23.
127.   *Venerabilis Baedae Opera Historica*, ed. C. Plummer (2 vols, 1896), I, 374–6.
128.   Wormald, *Bede and the Conversion of England*, 23; the foregoing section is influenced by *ibid.*, 19–23.

cassati) that is common currency for dependent tenancies.[129] This might lead us to believe that they were conveyances of land, made in a countryside inhabited by dependent tenants.[130] But it cannot have been like that. Kings could surely grant only what they themselves were able to command from the land concerned, and a major obstacle to seeing the land-books as conveyances of land-ownership is the very size of the grants made; these seventh- and eighth-century kings would have had to have been landowners on an immense and unparalleled scale.[131] However, the oft-cited alternative, that land-books granted, rather, 'rights over land', is equally problematic. This traditional dichotomy, over which much ink has been spilled, is in fact a rather blunt instrument with which to dissect Anglo-Saxon society – not least because, as Susan Reynolds has observed, 'rights in land are seldom simple'.[132] Accordingly, we need an explanatory framework that eschews simple and dichotomous definitions of land-owning.

Reynolds has observed that the hereditary property of peasants and nobles looks much like Frankish allods, while land held on fixed-term leases, from kings and churches (*laenland*), looks much like Frankish benefices.[133] Bookland, however, appears to be a rather more anomalous category of rights over property. In attempting to understand bookland, we might do well to bear in mind that it is unlikely to have embodied a stable concept of rights and obligations. For example, although technically it was freely alienable, it is probable that social and familial pressures combined to limit the possibilities for alienation of bookland: the terms by which Dudda was granted land by King Offa of Mercia in 779 stipulated that he was free to choose among his heirs, but it was not supposed that he should ignore them all.[134] After bookland had been inherited once, it is likely that families would have expected it to continue to be inherited within the family. Furthermore, the ability of the recipient of bookland to exploit it must have been mediated by the rights of those who occupied the land. Within a large area of land granted by charter there must have been inhabitants of varying status, some of whom surely had more or less full property rights, and the right to alienate their land and to seek other patrons; the interests of the recipient of the charter in these peoples and their lands must similarly have varied. It is not at all clear that the lands of such people were considered to be part of the lord's bookland. Late Anglo-Saxon charters, the late Anglo-Saxon estate survey known as the *Rectitudines*

---

129. Maitland, *Domesday Book and Beyond*, 335.
130. John, *Land Tenure*, 64–79.
131. Wickham, 'Rural societies', 235.
132. Reynolds, *Fiefs and Vassals*, 327.
133. The development of the concept of loan-land enabled the church, and other lords, to make grants for one or more lives. The church was forbidden from permanently alienating its land: N.P. Brooks, *Early History of the Church of Canterbury: Christ Church from 597 to 1066* (1984), 159; R.V. Lennard, *Rural England 1086–1135: a study of social and agrarian conditions* (1959), 159–70.
134. Reynolds, *Fiefs and Vassals*, 328.

Singularum Personarum and Domesday Book can all be shown to take a greater interest in recording and regulating the activities of the most burdened peasants, those whose dues and labour contributed the most to the lord's income; by contrast, the freer peasants, although not beyond the remit of such sources or beyond the grasp of the lord, were much less clearly part of the lord's estate, and the information required to be recorded about them and their lands was much more limited.[135] Thus, the interests that lords had in the lands of the peasantry who came in some way under their control varied, and if this is true of the tenth and eleventh centuries it is even more likely to have been so at a much earlier date. As we have seen from Continental examples, it was not necessarily easy for lords to extend demands placed on the inhabitants of recently acquired land, and the ways in which lords exploited their land must have varied according to local custom and the ability of the inhabitants of the land to resist.

From the seventh century it is clear from the charters that control over land was indeed conceived of as land-ownership, but at the same time it is not difficult to suppose that the earliest grants of land to lords did not entail a uniform body of rights, and that the ways in which lords then exploited the land they acquired proceeded at different rates.[136] It is difficult to know what to call the rights that lords enjoyed over bookland, or, indeed, how to describe the lords who held bookland. We should not expect to distinguish, if contemporaries could not, rights of land-ownership from rights of jurisdiction or administration, or rights to tax or tribute (which were public in origin) from rights to rent (which derived from dependent tenure).[137] Rosamond Faith has recently described such lordship in the following terms: the 'dominance of considerably developed local political authorities over a society based on a still relatively undeveloped agrarian economy [that] took the form of a complex of rights to services and renders from the people of a given territory'. This form of exploitation, which she calls 'extensive lordship', saw tribute flowing from farmers to rulers not because lords owned the land, but because they ruled the people.[138] Consequently, 'governors' rather than 'landlords' may be a more appropriate term to use of the earliest holders of bookland.[139]

By the time of Domesday Book, lordship and the rights of lords over land were rather different from those of, say, 700. By that time the free disposition of land that had been conferred by royal land-books was now seemingly enjoyed by a wide spectrum of people. In the tenth century the purchases made by Bishop Æthelwold in East Anglia for

---

135. See pp. 80–1 below.
136. Reynolds, *Fiefs and Vassals*, 337–8.
137. *Ibid.*, 53–7, 327.
138. Faith, *The English Peasantry*, 2–4; The term 'extensive lordship' was previously used by Geoffrey Barrow in his *The Kingdom of the Scots: government, church and society from the eleventh to the thirteenth century* (1973), 25.
139. Reynolds, *Fiefs and Vassals*, 326.

his monastic foundations reveal that fairly humble-looking people were able to dispose freely of their land, and they 'surely did not all have royal land-books'. Domesday Book commonly comments on whether people could alienate their land, and although it is concerned primarily with freedom from seigneurial control, it would not have been worth noting if families were normally able to constrain disposition.[140] One reason for the extent of freedom of disposition in the tenth and eleventh centuries might be the authority and power that English kings had, certainly in comparison with their Frankish counterparts, such that they may have had less need than contemporary Continental rulers to control the alienation of land. By the later tenth century it seems to be the case that bookland and other hereditary property had ceased to be distinguishable; the will of King Eadred is the last to state whether land bequeathed was bookland, and Edgar was the last king known to have turned land into bookland. Where the term bookland was used at all, it may then have meant nothing more specific than one's own property.[141] By the later Anglo-Saxon centuries, society was very unequal, but matters of status, on the one hand, and land-holding and tenurial organization, on the other, were not necessarily directly related. Power and authority over people did not always equate to a hierarchy of tenure, and the hierarchy of government was also distinct from the hierarchy of property. Great lords might, for example, have jurisdictional rights of sorts, or soke rights, over other landowners but that did not necessarily constitute a tenurial hierarchy, as those under their jurisdiction, or soke, had property rights, most notably the right of alienation, themselves. Neither was commendation or patronage necessarily directly related to matters of tenure. There seem to have been many ways in which lords might have rights over others, but it is not helpful to describe them all in the same terms; being commended to a lord, coming under his soke, leasing land from him, holding land on restricted terms or serving him in some way were all different types of relationship that an individual might have with a lord, and although they sometimes went together it does not, in general, help to conflate these relationships or to describe the individuals concerned as tenants.[142]

There are some important contrasts with parts of the Continent by this date, not least because public authority was seemingly much stronger and less open to challenge in England than in many other places.[143] It is this, and the perceived impact that the Norman Conquest had, that has prevented English historians from using 'feudal' terminology in the context of late Anglo-Saxon England. But if we recognize much more clearly that 'feudalism' is an abstraction, and,

---

140. *Ibid.*, 334–5.
141. S 715 (B 1118), S 727 (B 1127), S 1515 (B 912); Reynolds, *Fiefs and Vassals*, 333–4.
142. *Ibid.*, 332–42, discussed further below, pp. 80–1.
143. P. Wormald, 'Lordship and justice in the early English kingdom', in *Property and Power in the Early Middle Ages*, ed. W. Davies and P. Fouracre (1995), 114–36.

from a socio-economic point of view, open to a wider range of interpretation than was once the case, it is possible to propose that this terminology is not out of place in Anglo-Saxon society. That is to say, we can speak of a gradual 'feudalization' of society if we take that to include 'the exclusive nature of rights to land [and] the unmediated control by landholders over the tenant cultivators of that land'.[144] This is not to say that we would describe all lordship or all social relations in these terms, because it is clear that across Europe social systems could and did vary, even in areas of close proximity. The rate at which these processes of 'feudalization' occurred clearly varied, and it is only in a local context that we can begin to understand the emergence of new systems of dependence in the Anglo-Saxon period. I shall say more on this matter in subsequent chapters in relation to the northern Danelaw. It is now time to consider the Anglo-Saxon peasantry.

The peasantry of Anglo-Saxon England

The non-noble free elements in early Anglo-Saxon society are grouped under the contemporary but ambiguous term *ceorl*.[145] The *ceorl* has been the subject of much debate and the available sources are admittedly few, but there are sufficient grounds for believing in the essential freedom of the *ceorl*, although the term could cover a wide variety of people. This chapter will pursue the idea that *ceorls* included people who were analogous to the free peasant landholders identified in contemporary societies; that is to say, legally free, holding their own land, and subject to dues and services (tribute, military service, and so on) which were owed initially to the king, but which were increasingly acquired by other lords.[146] In time the freedoms of the *ceorls* were submerged, as were the freedoms of free peasants everywhere, although not uniformly.

It is not possible to offer a single description of the status of the *ceorl* because Anglo-Saxon society was not static and status must have varied according to a variety of factors, including the nature of agrarian exploitation and the proximity and form of seigneurial control in any given region. *Ceorls* had a direct relationship with the king, who legislated on their behalf and to whom they owed dues and services, including an obligation, at least theoretical, to serve in the *fyrd*.[147] The status of a *ceorl* was expressed in terms of his *wergild*, his blood-price in the event of

---

144. Wickham, 'Rural societies', 237.
145. Maitland, *Domesday Book and Beyond*, 58–9; Stenton, *Anglo-Saxon England*, 277–9, 290–1.
146. See J. Campbell, 'Early Anglo-Saxon society according to written sources', in his *Essays in Anglo-Saxon History*, 131–8 at 135.
147. See Ine, c. 45, 51, where the penalties for failing to perform *fyrd*-service are described. The role of the *ceorls* in the *fyrd* is, however, unclear and they are perhaps more likely to have served as auxiliaries than to have formed the fabric of the army: Abels, *Lordship and Military Obligation*, 13–14, 65–6, 175–9.

death at the hands of another.[148] However, this tells us nothing about the economic prosperity of the *ceorl*. It is evident by the eleventh century that *ceorls* were able to improve their position by acquiring additional land.[149] Such marks of freedom may, however, have been of little significance at an earlier date if the opportunities to buy and sell land were limited, by the interests of the kin-group, for example.

The role of the kin-group was clearly an important factor in the organization of *ceorlisc* society.[150] The law-codes of early medieval England give numerous details about the role of the kin-group when one of its members was the perpetrator or the victim of a crime: it was responsible for avenging the death of a member; it could vouch for the innocence of one of its members; the kindred could stand surety for an accused member; and it could ransom one of its members from penal slavery. The kin-group acted as a restricting force on marriage: the laws of Æthelred II forbade marriage within six degrees of kinship. The kindred also undertook to look after children in the event of the death of the father.[151] The role of the kindred – if not the effective shape of it – was precisely definable in legal terms, and it was clearly necessary for a man to belong to a kin-group. As well as its legal role, the kindred also had an important social function. A coherent identity may have been forged by kin-groups, perhaps through belief in a common ancestor. Place-name evidence may reflect this. Place-names which are formed with a personal name and the element '*ingas*', meaning 'the sons/followers/dependants of X', may signify the presence of a kin-group in a particular area, although it should be stressed that not everyone in that locality was necessarily a member of, or thought of themselves as being in any way connected with, that kin-group.[152]

There is no evidence that land was ever held communally by kin-groups. Certainly the kindred may have sought to ensure that every member had a suitable land-holding, for reasons both of economic security and the preservation of legal status.[153] Consequently, alienation of land

---

148. See the early seventh-century law-code of Æthelbert of Kent [hereafter Æthelbert], c. 6, 16, 21, 25; the late seventh-century law-code of Hlothhere and Eadric of Kent [hereafter Hlothhere and Eadric], c. 3; and the late seventh-century law-code of Wihtred of Kent [hereafter Wihtred], c. 26: *EHD*, I, nos. 29, 30, 31; see also Ine, c. 30.

149. The early eleventh-century text describing status states that if a *ceorl* prospered so that he possessed five hides of land, then he was entitled to the rights and *wergild* of a thegn: *EHD*, I, no. 52.

150. L. Lancaster, 'Kinship in Anglo-Saxon society, I', *British Journal of Sociology*, 9 (1958), 230–50; L. Lancaster, 'Kinship in Anglo-Saxon society, II', *British Journal of Sociology*, 9 (1958), 359–77; T.M. Charles-Edwards, 'Kinship, status and origins of the hide', *Past and Present*, 56 (1972), 3–33.

151. Hlothhere and Eadric, c. 5, 6, 8, 9, 10, 11, 16, 16.1, 16.2; Wihtred, c. 21, 26; Æthelbert, c. 81; Ine, c. 38.

152. Charles-Edwards, 'Kinship, status and the origins of the hide', 30; Bassett, 'The origins of Anglo-Saxon kingdoms', 18–23. There is the alternative possibility that place-names of that sort could indicate a dominant household and its followers rather than a kin-group: Lancaster, 'Kinship in Anglo-Saxon society', 373–4.

153. Charles-Edwards, 'Kinship, status and the origins of the hide', 8–14.

may have been proscribed to preserve the equilibrium, and to protect the interests of the family and of the extended kin-group. Moreover, it is undeniable that communal co-operation was a necessary part of agrarian life, and neighbours who were involved in such activity may well have been members of the same kin-group. Indeed, village communities and whole neighbourhoods may have sometimes been composed of members of a single kin-group. This would have been a natural outcome of a system of partible inheritance among sons; a patrilocal group of kinsmen occupying neighbouring farmsteads.[154] This has nothing to do with the old concepts of communal ownership of land. It is more helpful, and more appropriate, to think of families holding land individually, and in theory free to dispose of their land as they wished, but in practice restricted by local agricultural conditions and the needs and influence of their kinsmen. This is entirely in keeping with patterns of land-ownership found elsewhere in the Germanic world, and there is little reason to suppose that Anglo-Saxon society was radically different in this respect.[155]

The law-codes give us no idea how much land *ceorls* held or what their agricultural duties are normally likely to have been. The standard holding of the normal *ceorlisc* family was, however, expected to be, at least in theory, one hide; this is the land of one family, the *terra unius familiae* referred to by Bede.[156] The area of the hide was not standard, it was rather an assessment that might vary depending on the quality of the land in question; although it has been suggested that a hide might be anything up to 120 acres.[157] What mattered was that the hide should provide sufficient to support a family comprising a husband and wife, their children and any dependants they might have.[158] The relationship between the hide and the *ceorlisc* family is, however, unlikely to have remained constant. The possibility of acquiring more land is clearly allowed for at a later date since an eleventh-century text (known as *Geþyncþo*, or 'the promotion law', and often attributed to Archbishop Wulfstan II) remarked that a *ceorl* who prospered could attain the status and *wergild* of a thegn by acquiring five hides of land.[159] The likelihood of such advancement is unknown, but one supposes that it was relatively uncommon. Population growth and increasing subdivision of holdings through partible inheritance may have resulted more commonly in those of *ceorl* status coming to hold less than the norm of

154. *Ibid.*, 29–30.
155. Murray, *Germanic Kinship Structure*, 183–215; James, *The Origins of France*, 84–7; Reynolds, *Fiefs and Vassals*, 75–6.
156. Charles-Edwards, 'Kinship, status and the origins of the hide', 5–15.
157. Maitland, *Domesday Book and Beyond*, 357–520.
158. Charles-Edwards, 'Kinship, status and the origins of the hide', 4–14.
159. To be worthy of thegnly status he would also need to have 'a church and kitchen, a bell and a *burh-geat*, a seat and special office in the king's hall'; *EHD*, I no. 52. The land was, however, the key; a clause in the *Norðleoda laga* states that 'even if he prospers so that he possesses a helmet and a coat of mail and a gold-plated sword, if he has not the land, he is a *ceorl* all the same'.

a single hide.[160] Indeed, the very fact that some *ceorls* might prosper presupposes that they sometimes did so at the expense of other, less fortunate *ceorls*. *Ceorls* must also have been at the mercy of the ravages of warfare and natural disaster. The ability of *ceorls* to restock their lands after such events must have been limited, and in such cases more restrictive, yet at least secure, terms of land tenure offered by greater lords must have proved attractive.[161] Such a process is undocumented in the Anglo-Saxon kingdoms, but analogy with elsewhere renders it a plausible scenario.[162] Throughout European society it can be seen that freedom and land-holding are no guarantee of prosperity. As R.V. Lennard has aptly commented, ' "freedom" may mean freedom for the enterprising or the fortunate to prosper and obtain more land and stock; but it also means freedom to become indebted, freedom to sell one's land, freedom to sink into poverty'.[163]

As a concomitant of owning land, *ceorls* might have slaves and dependants; this was not an egalitarian society. *Ceorls*, as much as great nobles, might have their *hlafæta* (loaf-eater), and could utilize the labour of dependants to maintain their hide of land.[164] Indeed, if the standard hide ever extended to 120 acres, as has been postulated, then the *ceorlisc* family would of necessity have had to draw on additional labour. The law-code of Ine of Wessex depicts *ceorls* who were involved in agricultural activities: they had cattle, perhaps enjoyed shares in communal resources and fenced their homesteads. For example:

> If *ceorls* have a common meadow or other land divided in shares to fence, and some have fenced their portion and some have not, and [if cattle] eat up their common crops or grass, those who are responsible for the gap are to go and pay to the others, who have fenced their part, compensation for the damage that has been done there.[165]

This implies that there must have been some communal forum for discussing and supervising such arrangements, although no record of this survives.[166]

That particular clause from Ine's law-code reveals very little about the social or economic position of the average *ceorl*, and does little to

---

160. By way of comparison, a seventh-century Irish law-code states that a man could be deprived of the status of *boaire* (the equivalent of the *ceorl*) if he had numerous heirs, and, hence, the property requirement could not be met: Charles-Edwards, 'Kinship, status and the origins of the hide', 9.
161. W.G. Runciman, 'Accelerating social mobility: the case of Anglo-Saxon England', *Past and Present*, 104 (1984), 3–30.
162. See, for example, Wickham, *Early Medieval Italy*, 108–11.
163. Lennard, *Rural England*, 355.
164. Æthelbert, c. 16, 25.
165. Ine, c. 40, 41, 42, 42.1.
166. Loyn, *Anglo-Saxon England*, 174; comparison is drawn here with the communal forum (*thing*) found in later Scandinavian society, where the seigneurial hierarchy was not all-embracing.

define his relationship with lords. An influential article by T.H. Aston argued that in another clause of the laws of Ine traces of the manorial system can be found, with its necessary dichotomy between a lord's demesne and the holdings of peasant tenants who worked the demesne.[167] It is stated there that if a nobleman (*gesiðcund mon*) wishes to leave an estate, he must prove that a certain proportion of the land is *gesett land*: twelve hides if he has twenty hides of land; if ten, then six must be *gesett*; and one and a half if he has three hides. Aston interpreted the *gesett land* of Ine's laws – often taken to mean 'sown land' or 'cultivated land' – as land occupied by tenants.[168] On the basis of this interpretation Aston concluded that the manorial economy was in existence in seventh-century Wessex, suggesting that the *gesett land* formed some 50 to 60 per cent of the arable land of the whole estate and that this was the peasant tenant land, with the rest of the estate forming the demesne.

However, before we deduce from this that the *ceorl* was akin to a manorial tenant, heavily dependent on his lord, a number of observations should be made. First, even if we allow that there were elements of a manorial economy in seventh-century Wessex, it is not clear on what scale. Should we imagine it to have been universal? Should we expect that there were small single-vill units divided into demesne land and tenant land, or should we think in terms of large multi-vill territories divided in this way, with whole vills reckoned as demesne or tenant land?[169] Second, there is no necessary connection between the activities of *ceorls* and the *gesiðcund mon* who was instructed to leave a portion of his land *gesett*, because there is no reason to suppose that those who occupied the *gesett land* were normally *ceorls*. Third, even if we did suppose that some of the occupants of *gesett land* were *ceorls*, the fact that some *ceorls* could be subject to a lord in a relatively dependent context does not mean that all were.

Fourth, the early law-codes of Kent and Wessex do not suppose that there was always or normally a lord between the *ceorl* and the king.[170] The very fact that Ine should have bothered to legislate for the minutiae of agricultural activity, including that of *ceorls*, presupposes that there was not everywhere close aristocratic supervision, or else there would have been little point in legislating. Indeed, at a later date such matters were left to manorial courts, and the king had no interest in supervising them.[171] This is not to say that lordship was not a part of

167.   Aston, 'The origins of the manor'.
168.   Ine, c. 63, 64, 65, 66; Aston, 'The origins of the manor', 65–6; see also J.F. McGovern, 'The meaning of "gesette land" in Anglo-Saxon land tenure', *Speculum*, 45 (1971), 589–96; Faith, *The English Peasantry*, 103–4.
169.   For further criticisms, see Bassett, 'The origins of Anglo-Saxon kingdoms', 20, and n. 52.
170.   Æthelbert, c. 6; Loyn, *Anglo-Saxon England*, 172–3.
171.   Stenton, *Anglo-Saxon England*, 280; see also the observations in Wickham, 'Rural societies', 235.

early and middle Anglo-Saxon society, nor is it to deny that Anglo-Saxon society was hierarchical: the earliest law-codes demonstrate a concern with distinctions of social and economic status, and references to the *tuns* or *villae* or *hams* of noblemen abound in early sources. The incidence of personal names in place-names in conjunction with habitative elements – which increased towards the end of the pre-Conquest period – points in the same direction.[172] However, this does not prove that all or most *ceorls* were subordinated to 'manorial' structures. Fifth, and in contrast, whichever way one chooses to interpret the *gesett land* of Ine's law-code, it is clear that kings and nobles did take an interest in how the agrarian economy operated, although this is not sufficient to deny the freedom of the *ceorlisc* class nor to undermine the importance of their direct links to the king and to public authority.[173] What our evidence does suggest is that no matter how important was this link with public authority, on a more mundane level it was often locally based lords who dictated affairs. Indeed, this is emphasized by another clause from Ine's code, which reveals that lords were normally involved in maintaining law and order on their lands:

> If a nobleman comes to terms with the king, or with the king's ealdorman or with his lord, on behalf of his dependants, free or unfree, he, the nobleman, shall not have any portion of the fines, because he has not previously taken care at home to restrain them from evil doing.[174]

It would be wrong to over-emphasize the freedoms of the Anglo-Saxon *ceorls*. From our earliest sources they were under threat, and in some sources, especially of the tenth century, the *ceorl* appears to have been heavily dependent on estate structures, and at the mercy of seigneurial exploitation. The term *ceorl* is imprecise, and it is not unreasonable to expect that even at an early date it could be applied to people of a wide variety of economic and social standings. Nonetheless, there are equally good reasons why we cannot altogether dismiss the notion that the *ceorlisc* class included at least some free landholders. The evidence presented in this chapter – notably the discussion of the law-code of Ine, the nature of bookland and other forms of land tenure, the very size of the territories granted by charters – leads us to the conclusion that *ceorls* cannot all have been dependent tenants of the type familiar to

---

172.   Loyn, *Anglo-Saxon England*, 174; M. Gelling, *Signposts to the Past* (1978), 112–16, 162–90; B. Cox, 'The significance of the distribution of the English place-names in *ham* in the Midlands and East Anglia', *JEPNS*, 5 (1973), 15–73; J. Campbell, 'Bede's words and places', in *Names, Words and Graves: early medieval settlement*, ed. P. H. Sawyer (1979), 34–53; Seebohm, *The English Village Community*, 126, 148–59; Finberg, 'Anglo-Saxon England to 1042', 511–14.
173.   Stenton's view that the law-code revealed 'no trace ... of any private lord' (*Anglo-Saxon England*, 280) cannot stand: Loyn, *Anglo-Saxon England*, 171.
174.   Ine, c. 50.

later medieval manorial organization, although some certainly may have been. As a class they are more likely to have been equivalent to the relatively autonomous peasants found in many regions of Continental Europe in the early Middle Ages.

This is not, however, to deny that the *ceorls* were prone to having their freedoms denuded. The general depression of the peasantry and its subjection to the exploitative powers of lords cannot be precisely traced, but a number of general processes may be identified. Although not explicitly referring to *ceorls*, another clause from Ine's law-code indicates the pressures that were placed on peasants and helps to explain why the free slipped into dependent relationships. Clause 67 states that

> if anyone accepts a yardland or more at a fixed rent and ploughs it, then, if the lord requests rent and work from him, he need not comply unless the lord gives him his dwelling; he does, however, lose the crops.

This suggests that the peasants were involved in decisions about their fate, and that lords did not necessarily act in a completely arbitrary fashion.[175] It also reveals that some peasants were tied to labour-service if they took on a house. This suggests that the process towards the fully fledged manorial economy had begun, in however small a way, in the seventh century.[176] It also raises questions about the implications of the creation of nucleated villages: if the lord was responsible for these developments, then the offering of a house in the village to the peasants may have obliged those who accepted to take on more dependent terms in return.[177] Clause 67 of Ine's law-codes does not refer to *ceorls* – and may not have been intended to apply directly to them[178] – but it demonstrates that once peasants became involved in contractual obligations with lords their rights over land might come under threat, notably if they failed to comply with the demands of the lord over any land they had acquired.

Anglo-Saxon society was not static, and the nature of lordship and the status of the peasant classes continued to change. These changes can be explained by reference to a number of general processes. The increasing weight of the burdens placed on the free peasantry (Danegeld, ecclesiastical tithes, demands of local lords and the pressures of incipient 'manorialism', the king's food rent, and the fact that formerly public dues were being exacted by private lords who had been granted the right to do so) served to weaken their economic

---

175. See further, Charles-Edwards, 'The distinction between land and moveable wealth', 184–7.
176. *Ibid.*, 174.
177. Yorke, *Wessex in the Early Middle Ages*, 271–4.
178. Faith, *The English Peasantry*, 76, where it is argued that the clause more appropriately refers to those of a less free status – such as the *geburs* who appear in the *Rectitudines Singularum Personarum*.

position, which in turn must have made them prone to give up some of their legal freedoms (in particular the right to their lands) in return for seigneurial patronage and protection. That some, at least, of the *ceorls* were subject to extensive seigneurial exploitation and regarded as having limited freedoms can be demonstrated in the ninth and tenth centuries. For example, the ninth-century translation of Orosius's *Histories against the Pagans* equates the *ceorl* with *libertinus* – that is, freedman – and the heavily burdened *ceorls* of Stoke (Hants) *c.* 900 owed week-work and ploughing rent, and payments in cash and in kind which were owed 'from each *hiwisc*' (hide) to the estate centre at Hurstbourne.[179] This need not, however, indicate that all *ceorls* had been relegated to such a lowly status, and were so heavily burdened and involved in a lord's estate. The more successful and ambitious *ceorls* may have been able to improve their position through the purchase of land, performance of local administrative and estate offices (the *Rectitudines* lists several estate officers which were filled by the peasantry), military service (although its increasing specialization must have excluded all but the most prosperous *ceorls*) and service in the lower offices of the church.[180] It is difficult to comment on patronage, but legal success, social advancement and economic prosperity might all depend on *ceorls*, as much as anyone else of free status, having the right network of patrons.[181]

By the tenth century royal law-codes demanded that every man should have a lord to stand surety for him in front of the legal machinery.[182] Hence, recourse to the kin was declining in scope and dependence on lords was growing. It is nonetheless notable that in the eleventh-century *Northumbrian Priests' Laws*, which refers to a region in which the royal administrative structure was less comprehensively established, the *ceorl* is still permitted to have compurgators from his kin: in response to the accusation of carrying on any heathen practices, 'if a man of the *ceorl* class denies it, then ... selected compurgators of his equals are to be nominated for him ... if that fails, he is then to pay *lahslit* [a fine varying with the rank of the offender]'. Even in Northumbria, however, lords were still clearly important in the organization of local society, as they are said to have been involved in, for example, the collection of church tithes and in the suppression of heathen practices.[183] It is highly unlikely, thus, that many *ceorls* could

---

179. The *Old English Orosius*, ed. J. Bately, Early English Text Society, Suppl. ser., 6 (1980), 87, 274; H.P.R. Finberg, 'The churls of Hurstbourne', in his *Lucerna: studies of some problems in the early history of England* (1964), 131–43; *EHD* II no. 173.
180. Lennard, *Rural England*, 328; Runciman, 'Accelerating social mobility', 17.
181. *EHD*, I, no. 102; Wickham, 'Rural societies', 510–11; Wickham, 'Rural society in Carolingian Europe', 531–3.
182. See, for example, the law-codes of Athelstan [hereafter Athelstan] and Edgar [hereafter Edgar] in *EHD*, I, nos. 35–7, 40–1: II Athelstan, c. 2, 2.1, 4; III Edgar, c. 6; Loyn, *Anglo-Saxon England*, 310–11.
183. See the 'Law of the Northumbrian priests' in *EHD*, I, no. 53, c. 53 (for the quotation); c. 54.1, 57.2 (on the lord's obligations).

have escaped the attentions of some lord, but that is not to say that they became, or were thought of as, tenants of that lord. By the time of Domesday Book, although peasants and others held land under (*sub*) or from (*de*) a lord, this did not necessarily mean a reduction in their property rights, nor did it mean that all were tenants of that lord.[184]

A major influence on the status of the peasantry was the granting of bookland. Whatever the nature of the rights initially granted, in the long run the granting of bookland interposed lords between the peasantry and the king, and doubtless facilitated the exaction of more regular and onerous dues from the peasantry. The granting of bookland also caused a blurring of the distinctions between the free land-holding peasantry and the less free and unfree peasants. Although in origin the dues owed by the various groups within rural society were very different, they were now often owed to the same lord and formed part of the income from his estates, and they came to differ really only in degree; they all became, essentially, a form of rent. The evident decline in slavery through the Anglo-Saxon centuries must also have had concomitant effects on the demands lords made of peasants: a diminution in the labour provided by slaves must have prompted lords to rely on the labour services of an increasingly dependent peasantry. The distinctions in the seventh century between what lords claimed from the various members of rural society were seemingly much greater than they were to be on many estates by the time of Domesday Book.[185]

Nonetheless, by the later Anglo-Saxon period there was still much variety in the status of the various strata of the peasantry. The late Anglo-Saxon estate survey known as the *Rectitudines Singularum Personarum* describes the services performed and dues owed by the inhabitants of an unidentified estate, which was probably located in Wessex.[186] According to the *Rectitudines*, the *geneat* owed a money rent for his lands, paid the freeman's due of church-scot and provided a number of light services on the estate, involving riding and carrying messages but not ploughing; the bee-keeper and the swineherd rendered honey and pigs, respectively, and owed odd ploughing and carrying services; by contrast the *kotsetla* did not owe rent and consequently owed substantial labour services, and the *gebur*, who unlike the *kotsetla* might have his own plough-team, both paid rent and owed labour services, and when he died the lord took what he left. The peasantry appear to be greatly burdened in the world of the *Rectitudines*. The *geneat* can possibly be numbered among the

---

184. Maitland, *Domesday Book and Beyond*, 72–3, 154–5; Reynolds, *Fiefs and Vassals*, 338–9, where such phrases are compared with their use in France.
185. Yorke, *Wessex in the Early Middle Ages*, 261–4; C.C. Dyer, 'St Oswald and 10,000 west Midland peasants', in *St Oswald of Worcester: life and influence*, ed. C.R.E. Cubitt and N.P. Brooks (1996), 174–93, at 185–6.
186. For the text of the *Rectitudines*, see *EHD*, II, no. 172; for discussion, see P.D.A. Harvey, '*Rectitudines Singularum Personarum* and *Gerefa*', *EHR*, 108 (1993), 1–22. A compelling case for the production of the *Rectitudines* at Worcester is made in Dyer, 'St Oswald', 183–4.

peasantry, but he looks much like the *radmen* of Domesday Book, who owed light services and carried messages, and who resembled the lesser ranks of the leaseholders on the Worcester estates – who can, as Christopher Dyer has observed, scarcely be counted as peasants.[187] The bee-keeper and swineherd seem to be free peasants, owing light services, although we are not told much about their land-holdings. The *gebur* and the *kotsetla*, then, seem to be representative of the peasantry at large, and, as Dyer has commented, 'these heavily burdened tenants were far removed from the independence characteristic of some Continental peasants at this time'.[188] Yet rather than demonstrating that the free peasant was no longer an important part of the rural economy, it may suggest that sources like the *Rectitudines* and, later, Domesday Book are more concerned to record the major contributors to the labour supply of the estate. This may help to explain the seemingly small populations on some Domesday manors – a conclusion supported by the fact that later manorial surveys regularly reveal the presence of freer peasants who were presumably the descendants of peasants whom Domesday Book does not record. The *Rectitudines* and Domesday Book present the information of concern to lords, and reinforce the notion that the obligations owed to the lord were the most important part of a peasant's life. Yet reference in the *Rectitudines* to local custom in the context of peasant duties 'hints at other activities and relationships' regulating the lives of peasants, beyond those relating to the obligations of the peasants to the lords.[189] The *Rectitudines* may have served – like the Continental polyptychs are believed to have done – to establish, as much as to record, estate custom.[190] It is reasonable to assume that lords throughout the Anglo-Saxon period exploited their lands in different ways, and that there would have been differences according to the status of the lord, the size of his estates, and the sorts of obligations that he was expected to meet as a result of the very possession of his estate.

It has been observed that the nucleation of villages in the tenth and eleventh centuries was a product of seigneurial intervention, and that this process of 'putting men in cells', as Robert Fossier put it, was an important element in the extension of the rights of lords over the peasantry. Indeed, we have already seen the possible implications of accepting a house from a lord according to Ine's law-code. Yet we have to be careful not to attribute a disproportionate level of entrepreneurial endeavour to early medieval lords. At a later date lords did not exert great control over the daily lives of their subordinates, and peasant communities are as likely to have been involved in the

---

187. *Ibid.*, 186–7.
188. *Ibid.*, 187.
189. *Ibid.*, 189–90.
190. Harvey, '*Rectitudines Singularum Personarum* and *Gerefa*'; Faith, *The English Peasantry*, 59, for the quotation.

ordering of settlements as their lords.[191] If this argument may be made of the later medieval period, when the administrative machinery of the manor had been imposed everywhere, it is likely to have been even more true of the earlier period. In some regions there was certainly an increasing regularization of space in rural settlements through the Anglo-Saxon centuries, as settlement became nucleated, but this need not necessarily imply that it was the product of seigneurial initiative, as has sometimes been assumed.[192] The earliest nucleated sites were commonly abandoned in the later Anglo-Saxon, or post-Conquest, period, which suggests that the organization of settlements was open to much renegotiation.[193] Furthermore, variations in building construction and alignment may be observed within plots, which indicates independent agency in the construction of aspects of the settlement on the part of those who lived there.[194] This suggests that if lords attempted to impose their will on the peasantry, they were not necessarily successful. Whatever the implications of village nucleation for the exercise of lordship, we should not ignore the amount of settlement dispersal which may be observed even in those regions commonly regarded as nucleated village zones.[195] Furthermore, we should also be aware that the domination of a village by a single lord was not a universal phenomenon. In many regions multiple lordship was common, and yet the nucleated village was still the dominant form of settlement organization.[196] There is a striking correlation between villages with multiple lordship and those with polyfocal plans, and those with multiple manor houses and churches, suggesting that each manor left its mark on the layout of the community. However, at the same time it is generally the case that such villages developed single open-field systems, suggesting that the village community itself was instrumental in influencing the organization of the community.[197] Independence on the part of the peasant communities within their villages may have been expressed through such facets of their lives as building construction, or choices over the crops to be grown on their plots in the fields, or the use made of the crofts attached to their homesteads. Furthermore, village communities were not isolated, or self-sufficient; interaction with neighbouring communities in the market-place or through the sharing of common resources such as woodland, marsh or fenland was instrumental in determining the daily

191.   C.C. Dyer, 'Power and conflict in the medieval village' in *Medieval Villages: a review of current work*, ed. D. Hooke (1985), 27–32.
192.   T. Saunders, 'The feudal construction of space: power and domination in the nucleated village', in *The Social Archaeology of Houses*, ed. R. Samson (1990), 181–96; R. Dodgshon, *The European Past: social evolution and spatial order* (1987), 166–92.
193.   H. Hamerow, 'Settlement mobility'.
194.   *Ibid.*, 2–6.
195.   P. Everson, C. C. Taylor and J. Dunn, *Change and Continuity: rural settlement in north-west Lincolnshire* (1991), 12–13.
196.   *Ibid.*, *passim*.
197.   T. Williamson, *The Origins of Norfolk* (1993), 158.

experiences of villagers.[198] These are all issues which we are able to discuss more readily in relation to the later Middle Ages, but which were clearly important at a much earlier date.

It should not be overlooked, finally, that Anglo-Saxon society was also characterized by much unfreedom and even slavery. The laws of Æthelbert refer to three classes of *laets*, who were semi-free, and three classes of slaves, as well as the 'loaf-eaters' of the *ceorls*, who were presumably some sort of dependant.[199] There are references to slaves in the laws of Ine, and those of Alfred indicate that even *ceorls* might have their own slaves.[200] They could be bought and sold, and disposed of in wills. Warfare and trade were important sources of slaves, and enslavement was the punishment for certain crimes.[201] Slavery was not, however, an inescapable state, and acts of manumission are commonly recorded in wills.[202] It is difficult to assess the widespread significance of slavery and unfreedom, although it probably varied enormously from region to region. In the immediate sub-Roman period slavery may have been more prevalent in the more heavily romanized regions, especially in those instances where some level of continuity in organization has been posited.

Although a case can be made for the existence of a significant stratum of land-owning peasants, we should not overlook other forms of social relationship and forms of exploitation which may have been characterized by a much lower incidence of freedom. The church in particular required regular and reliable supplies of foodstuffs, and this need led to the much more intensive exploitation of some parts of their estates. Faith has described this directly exploited core area as representing a transitional point between an economy based purely on tribute and the manorial system; this core area commonly came to be known as 'inland'. The inhabitants of this area, which need not have been geographically coherent or even mostly or exclusively adjacent to the lord's residence, were much more heavily encumbered than were the *ceorls*.[203] She suggests that lords organized the 'inland' of their estates in a distinctive way, often with core areas located close to the lord's residence, but that this level of organization was not necessarily extended to the rest of their land-holdings.[204] The level of seigneurial exploitation of both the inland and other land (which Faith labels

---

198. C.C. Dyer, 'Were peasants self-sufficient? English villagers and the market, 900–1350', in *Campagnes mediévales: l'homme et son espace*, ed. E. Mornet (Paris, 1995), 653–66.
199. Æthelbert, c. 16, 25, 26.
200. Ine, c. 3.2, 7.1, 11, 23.3, 24, 47, 53, 62; and Alfred's law-code [hereafter Alfred], in *EHD*, I, no. 33, c. 25. For discussion, see D. Pelteret, *Slavery in Medieval England: from the reign of Alfred to the twelfth century* (1995).
201. Such as theft, and it was also the punishment for a freeman who worked of his own free will on a Sunday: Ine, c. 3.2, 7.1.
202. D.W. Whitelock, *Anglo-Saxon Wills* (1930), no. 3 for the will of Wynflaed.
203. Faith, *The English Peasantry*, 56–88.
204. *Ibid.*, 15–55.

'warland'), and the extent to which labour services were imposed on sections of the peasantry, are open to debate. Faith suggests that labour services were less common than has sometimes been supposed, and looks to an extension of this imposition in the decades after the Norman Conquest. However, there is much in the limited Anglo-Saxon evidence, especially the *Rectitudines*, that displays similarities with later medieval organization in which labour services played an important part.[205]

A major obstacle to understanding Anglo-Saxon society is presented by attempts to classify that society either as one dominated by free peasant communities with relatively little seigneurial control or, at the opposite extreme, as one characterized by a peasantry highly subordinated to strong seigneurial authority. We have consistently been presented with this dichotomy by historians. This central debate in Anglo-Saxon studies is brought sharply into focus by a comparison with contemporary Continental societies. We should not expect to find a pattern of *either* free peasant communities knowing no lord, *or* dependent *ceorls* closely tied to manorial structures under close seigneurial supervision. Rather, we should expect to find elements of both. This is the only interpretation that makes sense of the diverse evidence from Anglo-Saxon law-codes, charters and surveys. Of course, we should also expect to find marked regional variations. In the heavily romanized and arable areas a greater emphasis on slavery, large estates and demesne exploitation may have prevailed. The terrain must also have played an important role in determining social organization. We should also expect to find that different regions developed through into the later Anglo-Saxon period in very different ways; the demands of lords were not everywhere uniform. In fact, incipient manorialism (with strong lordship and dependent peasants) and free peasant communities are not mutually exclusive, and if Continental parallels reveal anything it is that alternative forms of exploitation can be found in close juxtaposition in many regions. To accept that there was such variation at an early date makes the variety of social organization and estate structures recorded in Domesday Book at the end of our period more readily explicable. It was not the case that a uniform society became increasingly complex throughout the Anglo-Saxon centuries; rather, a very diverse society remained diverse and complex thoughout the period.

The geography of lordship

This discussion has implications for the way in which we perceive territorial organization in Anglo-Saxon society. Of the various models that have been devised for uncovering and explaining early medieval

---

205. Dyer, 'St Oswald', 183–8.

territorial organization, the most influential of these in Britain is the so-called 'multiple estate' model. A number of important papers by Glanville Jones have argued that the basic unit of organization in the early medieval period was the 'multiple estate', a large territory comprising numerous vills and their inhabitants. The latter typically owed a variety of dues and services at the estate centre, which might be a royal, aristocratic or ecclesiastical vill. Royal grants or the pressures of inheritance caused these 'multiple estates' to be broken up, and in many areas by the eleventh century they had fragmented to form the single-vill manors common in Domesday Book. Jones evolved this model from the evidence of north Wales, where a group of law-texts of the thirteenth century appear to describe a system of estates comprising numerous homesteads and vills. Developing the work of J.E.A. Jolliffe, Jones has proposed that such a system is similar to that of, for example, the *scirs* of Northumbria, the lathes of Kent and the rapes of Sussex, and that such similarities can be accounted for only if it is accepted that the system was a pre-Anglo-Saxon survival.[206] It has been proposed that enough evidence of the former 'multiple estates' survives to the eleventh and twelfth centuries that such a system can be uncovered in most parts of Britain. Numerous studies have identified a network of such estates across Britain through the use of documentary, cartographic and place-name evidence, and it has been observed that the only significant difference is in the choice of local terminology: the *scir* of Northumbria, the soke of the Danelaw, the lathe of Kent are, in fact, analogous.[207]

A number of historians have, however, rejected the 'multiple estate' model, not least because it rests on very late evidence.[208] That in itself is no reason to dismiss the model, but it is certainly doubtful whether the social structure and forms of exploitation found in later medieval sources were widespread in the early medieval period. Estate structures involving a subject peasantry and a division between the lord's 'demesne' land and the peasant tenant land were not universal, nor necessarily especially common, at least not in the seventh and eighth centuries. Nonetheless, Anglo-Saxon charters and narrative sources do suggest that the countryside was divided into numerous multi-vill 'territories' in the seventh and eighth centuries, through which local administration, settlement and agrarian exploitation were organized.[209] Charters of the seventh and eighth centuries often

---

206. See, for example, G.R.J. Jones, 'The multiple estate as a model framework for tracing early stages in the evolution of rural settlement', in *L'Habitat et les paysages ruraux d'Europe*, ed. F. Bussat (Liège, 1971), 251–67; G.R.J. Jones, 'Early territorial organization in Gwynedd and Elmet', *Northern History*, 10 (1975), 3–25; G.R.J. Jones, 'Multiple estates and early settlement', in *English Medieval Settlement*, ed. P.H. Sawyer (1979), 9–40.
207. Barrow, *Kingdom of the Scots*, 23.
208. Bassett, 'The origins of Anglo-Saxon kingdoms', 20, and n. 52; N. Gregson, 'The multiple estate model: some critical questions', *JHG*, 11 (1985), 339–51.
209. Campbell, 'Bede's *reges* and *principes*', 95–6.

describe the dependencies of the estates concerned as named and hidated units, incorporating a wide variety of resources, indicating that the countryside was already well exploited and assessed.[210] Place-names which incorporate elements relating to particular resources or dues imply quite sophisticated estate organization, with vills possibly either specializing in the production of particular crops or meeting specialized tribute obligations.[211] As well as being the basic units of socio-economic organization, these early multi-vill territories formed the basis of political organization. They have recently been identified as the units out of which the greater kingdoms of the eighth century and later were created through a process of amalgamation.[212]

Much effort has been expended on identifying networks of multi-vill territories using a range of evidence. This endeavour faces four distinct difficulties. Is it really possible to use late and, often, indirect evidence to uncover early patterns of territorial organization? Was early medieval society really so uniform? Did the Anglo-Saxon period really witness a general transition from large territories of exploitation to smaller ones? What other features of early medieval territorial organization do we need to identify in order to assess the practically relevant world in which early medieval peasants and lords operated?

It is now a commonplace that early medieval territorial organization was characterized by networks of interconnected vills which left their mark on the countryside and can be recoverd through the use of, *inter alia*, Anglo-Saxon charters and narrative sources, Domesday Book and contemporary surveys, the parochial geography and place-names. However, it must be emphasized that these sources require sensitive handling, not least because they refer to different functions of society, and the patterns they reveal (particularly in the cases of place-names and parish boundaries) lack clear chronological parameters. To conflate evidence drawn from different facets of early medieval society leads to the projection of units of territorial organization that may never have existed, and raises more problems than many studies have allowed for. Moreover, we must remember that the exploitation of land by lords developed in significant ways during the Anglo-Saxon period, and that this may have had implications for the ways in which the countryside was divided up; the tribute territories of an early date need not necessarily be exactly the same as the estates of later lords, and the 'privatization' of territorial organization may have occurred at varied pace and with divergent results.[213]

210. P.H. Sawyer, *From Roman Britain to Norman England* (1978), 138–50.
211. Blair, *Early Medieval Surrey*, 30; N. Higham, *The Origins of Cheshire* (1993), fig. 5.2; Faith, *The English Peasantry*, 12.
212. Bassett, 'The origins of Anglo-Saxon kingdoms', 17–18, 23–7.
213. Faith, *The English Peasantry*, 11–12.

Anglo-Saxon sources

Although early narrative sources and charters often record the names of estate centres, they rarely indicate the extent or precise locations of the territories which were attached to them. Even when the land granted by a charter is defined, can we assume that charters habitually granted old-established territories which already had some sort of economic or administrative cohesion? This is certainly implied when boundaries are said to be well known, and the land included in the terms of the charter may already have owed dues of some sort to the main vill named by there.[214] On the other hand, this may not invariably have been the case. John Blair has argued that the endowment of the early religious community at Chertsey in Surrey was carved out of an existing *regio* focused on Woking; that is to say, the charter included only part of an existing territory and in doing so established a new focal point.[215] Furthermore, as kings granted ever-smaller territories they were instrumental in breaking up earlier and larger patterns of territorial organization.

Anglo-Saxon charters have little to say about the internal workings of the estates they grant. A handful of Anglo-Saxon estate surveys provide some insights, but they are late and not necessarily widely representative. Moreover, they concentrate on what was owed to the lord from the more dependent and burdened inhabitants of the estate.[216] Hence, Anglo-Saxon sources provide only a partial view of the extent of early estates and forms of exploitation, and the relationship of such estates to much earlier forms of territorial organization is generally unclear.

Domesday Book

Domesday Book apparently has much to reveal about earlier patterns of territorial organization, and the manors with numerous dependencies recorded there have been identified as the remnants of such a system of earlier 'multiple estates'.[217] This is not an unlikely scenario, but we must also consider the possibility that Domesday estates were sometimes of more recent origin. Della Hooke has, for example, suggested that portions of woodland in the Warwickshire Arden which were attached to lowland manors were probably acquired in the later Anglo-Saxon period, and that, as a result, such associations should not

---

214. See S 8 (B 45), in which Hlothere granted land in Thanet which was defined 'by the well-known bounds indicated by me and my reeves'; *EHD* I no. 56.
215. Blair, *Early Medieval Surrey*, 20–1, 27.
216. Dyer, 'St Oswald', 183–93; *EHD* II nos 172–5.
217. J.E.A. Jolliffe, *Pre-Feudal England: the Jutes* (1933), 44–6; H.M. Cam, '*Manerium cum hundredo*: the hundred and the hundredal manor', *EHR*, 57 (1932), 353–76; Stafford, *The East Midlands*, 29–39; Barrow, *The Kingdom of the Scots*, 7–68; *Kalendar of Abbot Samson*, ed. R.H.C. Davis, Camden 3rd ser., 84 (1954), xlvi.

be used as evidence for earlier 'multiple estates'.[218] It is not difficult to envisage that settlement expansion and changes in land use (from transhumance to permanent settlement, for example) could cause new territories to be built up, and that the division of marginal, lightly settled land into fixed territorial groupings may have occurred at a relatively late date.

In a number of regions the presence of small self-contained units has been identified at an early date, equating to single farmsteads or hamlets, which preceded and were sometimes later integrated into multi-vill estates, but which often survived as separate small estates.[219] The existence of smallholdings is suggested by the evidence of personal names associated with the features named in charter boundaries, and by the minor place-name elements 'worthy' (meaning 'a small enclosed farm', or 'a piece of land farmed severally') and 'huish' (derived, like the word 'hide', from a root-word meaning 'family').[220] These may have been the holdings of small lords or *ceorls*, and may have lain outside the organization of the larger estates. We have little evidence concerning the existence at an early date of the 'small estates' known to have characterized early medieval societies elsewhere, although from the ninth century charters increasingly refer to small estates assessed at just a few hides, which may conceivably have long been in existence. The number of small estates was increased by the leasing of such estates in the later Anglo-Saxon period: for example, in the later tenth century much of the estate of the bishopric of Worcester was leased to laymen who held estates varying in size from one to six hides.[221] The small manors of Domesday Book may, then, have been of diverse origins.

If we are to use the evidence of Domesday Book to identify much earlier estate organization, we must recognize that the estate structure it describes came into existence over a protracted period of time, and in response to diverse factors.

Parish boundaries

It has often been argued that the parochial geography can be used to uncover early forms of territorial organization, on the grounds that the *parochiae* of the so-called minster churches founded in the seventh and

---

218. D. Hooke, *Anglo-Saxon Landscapes of the West Midlands: the charter evidence* (BAR British Series 95, 1981), 68–73; see also C.C. Dyer, *Lords and Peasants in a Changing Society* (1980), 25.
219. Blair, *Early Medieval Surrey*, 21–2, 27; Hooke, *Anglo-Saxon Landscapes of the West Midlands*, 68–73, 87–100; *PN Berks*, pt 3, 808–9; C.C. Taylor, *Dorset* (1970), 49–75.
220. M. Costen, 'Huish and worth: Old English survivals in a later landscape' in *ASSAH*, 5, ed. W. Filmer-Sankey (1992), 65–83; Yorke, *Wessex in the Early Middle Ages*, 268, 271; *PN Berks*, pt 3, 629–30.
221. Dyer, *Lords and Peasants*, 17.

eighth centuries were coterminous with pre-existing secular territories.[222] The starting-point for this approach is the frequent correlation between the boundaries of territories recorded in Anglo-Saxon charters and those of ancient ecclesiastical parishes recorded in late medieval and post-medieval documents and maps.[223] This correlation suggests that parish boundaries may be an important guide to early medieval territorial organization, and an important source to compensate for an absence of early charters.[224] The territories on which the minster *parochiae* were apparently based fragmented in the Anglo-Saxon period through the booking of land and inheritance customs. This commonly resulted in the foundation of new churches to serve the newly created smaller estates; initially they would have remained subordinate to the minster church, but many in time acquired full parochial rights. It was a process of fragmentation that proceeded at different rates across the country. In some instances the newly founded churches remained highly subordinate to the minster church, and it is such signs of subordination (commonly represented as payments of pensions from the daughter church to the minster, or by the limited functions performed by the former) that can be used to reconstruct the minster *parochiae* and, in turn, to identify early secular territories.[225]

However, although this provides a useful additional body of evidence with which to work, we should be aware of the dangers of this model, which has been the subject of a number of sharp critiques recently. We should also make no mistake: parishes were not the same thing as estates, *provinciae*, *regiones*, or any other type of secular territorial unit. Their boundaries may, of course, have coincided, but there are

---

222. C.N.L. Brooke, 'Rural ecclesiastical institutions in England: the search for their origins', *Settimane*, 28 (2) (1982), 685–711.

223. For sources of such maps, see J.B. Harley, *The Historian's Guide to Ordnance Survey Maps* (1964); J.B. Harley, *Maps and the Local Historian* (1972).

224. *PN Berks*, pt 3, 617–22; Hooke, *Anglo-Saxon Landscapes of the West Midlands*, 34–8; C.D. Drew, 'The manors of the Iwerne Valley, Dorset: a study of early country planning', *Proceedings of the Dorset Natural History and Archaeological Society* 69 (1948), 45–50; Taylor, *Dorset*, 49–72; M. Reed, 'Buckinghamshire Anglo-Saxon charter boundaries', in *The Early Charters of the Thames Valley*, ed. M. Gelling (1979), 168–87; D. Hooke, *The Landscape of Anglo-Saxon Staffordshire: the charter evidence* (1983), 32–7, 63–109; Blair, *Early Medieval Surrey*, 31–4; C. Phythian-Adams, *Continuity, Fields and Fission: the making of a Midland parish*, Department of English Local History, no. 8 (1975), 5; Gelling, *Signposts to the Past*, 191–5; Bassett, 'The origins of Anglo-Saxon kingdoms', 19–21; J.N. Croom, 'The minster *parochiae* of south-east Shropshire' in *Minsters and Parish Churches: the local church in transition, 900–1250*, ed. J. Blair (1988), 67–82.

225. See, for example, Bassett, 'The origins of Anglo-Saxon kingdoms', 19–23; Croom, 'The minster *parochiae* of south-east Shropshire', 67–8; B.R. Kemp, 'The mother church of Thatcham', *Berkshire Archaeological Journal*, 63 (1967–8), 15–22; B.R. Kemp, 'The churches of Berkeley Hernesse', *Transactions of the Bristol and Gloucester Archaeological Society*, 87 (1968), 96–110; P.H. Hase, 'The mother churches of Hampshire', in *Minsters and Parish Churches*, ed. Blair, 45–66.

important functional and chronological issues to address before we can confidently substitute parish boundaries for evidence of secular organization.

Place-names

Place-names can also be used to help reconstruct Anglo-Saxon territorial organization. It was once thought that a chronology of place-name formation could be used as an indication of the chronology of Anglo-Saxon settlement. This hypothesis has now been largely abandoned, although it is considered that topographical place-names are more likely on the whole to be earlier than habitative place-names. More useful for reconstructing early territorial organization are place-names containing the element -*ingas*, directional place-name elements and adjacent place-names containing the same element. The element -*ingas* appears to have meant 'the people/followers of' in place-name formations, and is found combined with personal names (as in Hastings (Sussex), meaning 'the people of Hæsta'), with river names (such as Avening (Glos) or Blything (Suffolk)) or with topographical terms (such as Nazeing (Essex), meaning 'the people of the spur of land'). Such place-names seemingly indicate the location of a group of people associated with a particular person or topographical feature, that location being in a particular region to which this relationship gave its name.[226] Such place-name forms cannot be dated precisely, but they seem likely to have been early formations, although perhaps not belonging to the migration period, as was once thought.[227]

The extent of the territories to which these place-names related cannot normally be identified. However, a notable exception is found in Essex, where eight ecclesiastical parishes, which incorporated some sixteen Domesday estates, have the place-name Roding (meaning 'the people of Hrotha'). It has been suggested that this distribution of place-names can be used to reconstruct an early settlement district which existed in the Middle Saxon period if not earlier.[228] Place-names that contain directional elements, such as 'north' or 'east', can also be used to identify Anglo-Saxon territorial organization, since their names suggest that they belonged to some larger unit, and they indicate their location in respect of the focal point of that territory.[229] Other place-

---

226.   Gelling, *Signposts to the Past*, 106–12.
227.   *Ibid.*; J.McN. Dodgson, 'The significance of the distribution of English place-names in -*ingas* and -*inga*- in south-east England', *Medieval Archaeology*, 10 (1966), 27–54.
228.   P.H. Reaney, *The Place-Names of Essex*, EPNS, 12 (1935), 490–1; Bassett, 'The origins of Anglo-Saxon kingdoms', 21–2.
229.   When combined with the ubiquitous element *tun* this would produce the names Norton and Aston. Other directional place-names are Weston ('west *tun*'), Sutton ('south *tun*'), Middleton ('middle *tun*'), Upton ('upper *tun*').

names suggest dependence on somewhere else: names such as Thorpe (*þorp*, 'secondary settlement') or Barton (*bere, tun,* 'barley farm'), for example.[230] Place-names in close proximity which contain the same elements may suggest that those places had once formed part of the same territorial unit.[231] Finally, place-names incorporating words for particular resources might conceivably indicate that the inhabitants of the place concerned had, at some point, been responsible for a specialized render within a larger territorial grouping.

Place-name evidence is useful, but we must remember that place-names could, and did, change, and that it is rarely possible to determine precisely when a place-name was coined. Furthermore, places commonly retained names related to their position or role within some larger territory long after that context had ceased to be relevant to the inhabitants of that place.

Synthesis

This combination of evidence can provide a persuasive picture of territorial organization at an early date, especially when different types of evidence reveal the same pattern. However, the patterns to emerge are not always so neat. Moreover, we must question just what it is that we are reconstructing. Is it the earliest settlement units of peoples, extended families or kinship groups? Or is it the bookland estates acquired by churches and lay lords? Or is it administrative units created, perhaps, in the tenth century? Any, all or none of these units of territorial organization might conceivably be revealed by the methods and evidence outlined above.[232]

There are sufficient grounds to caution against the urge to fit every piece of land into some former extensive 'multiple estate'. The likelihood that estates were built up over the course of the Anglo-Saxon period, and that unitary 'estates' had, as Trevor Aston warned, long been part of the landscape is too great to be ignored. Small unitary 'estates' and both large and small 'multiple' estates were not mutually exclusive at an early date. We have to think in terms of both forms of organization existing simultaneously. Although our evidence is likely to have more to reveal about large estates, we should not discount smallholders and the lands of the peasantry from our mental picture of early medieval society even if it is not possible to map out their lands in the way that we can for the king, the aristocracy or the

---

230. Gelling, *Signposts to the Past,* 227; Faith, *The English Peasantry,* 36–7.
231. Bassett, 'The origins of Anglo-Saxon kingdoms', 21.
232. Blair, *Early Medieval Surrey,* 12–39. See also N.P. Brooks, 'Rochester Bridge, AD 43–1381', in *Traffic and Politics,* ed. N.P. Yates and J.M. Gibson (1994), 1–40, in which it is shown that the early administrative territories from which the resources were drawn for building and repairing Rochester bridge changed over time to mirror changing patterns of lordship and estate organization.

church. By combining different types of evidence we may be identifying not the earliest units from which all other estates were eventually carved, but rather the end-products of generations of both fragmentation and amalgamation of estates.

One of the fundamental flaws of much research into early medieval social and territorial organization is the underlying assumption that there was a universal form of organization in the early medieval period. Comparison with contemporary Continental societies, with their richer body of evidence, reveals complex and varied patterns, and reasons why we should be wary of such models. A few examples drawn from different regions of the Continent suggest very varied societies, while some historians of early medieval England seem to expect that a single model will fit the whole country. The simplicity of such models and the uniformity of organization that they depict sits uneasily alongside the evidence from more extensively documented Continental societies. This brief survey is far from comprehensive but it does highlight possible further lines of enquiry for research into Anglo-Saxon England and suggests alternatives and modifications to existing models.

Implications for the study of the northern Danelaw

As we turn to the evidence of the northern Danelaw we have established a framework for analysing it which differs from those used by previous studies of the region. It is now apparent that the sokemen of the northern Danelaw have definite analogues in pre-viking English society, and elsewhere in contemporary Europe, and that therefore we do not necessarily have to posit a relationship between the sokemen and the Scandinavian settlers, even though the arrival of the latter may have had some impact on the free peasants of parts of England. We have also demonstrated that Continental parallels reveal some of the possible complexity and variation that may underlie the society portrayed in the more limited Anglo-Saxon documentary sources; they also reveal, and present challenges for, some of the assumptions inherent in many discussions of Anglo-Saxon society.

This analysis of lordship and the land-holding patterns of lords highlights the possibility that the land-holding pattern revealed in the northern Danelaw in tenth- and eleventh-century sources derived from various forms of earlier land tenure and territorial organization. We should, then, strive to establish a chronology for the development of territorial organization presented by Domesday Book. We must also examine the internal organization of the multi-vill sokes: did lords have the same rights over all parts of the soke and over all the inhabitants? Or does the superficially similar pattern of Domesday sokes disguise a more complex reality? We have also highlighted the fact that the issue of continuity or change cannot solely be a matter for students of the impact of the Scandinavian settlement. Elements of continuity and change were, of course, found in all the Anglo-Saxon centuries.

The traditional isolation of discussions of Anglo-Saxon social organization from Continental parallels has arguably been detrimental to the development of new ideas and approaches. It would, of course, be inappropriate simply to borrow from Continental scholarship – not least because it is hardly a coherent body – and we must continue to identify difference as much as similarity. But a major point to emerge is that what Chris Wickham calls 'the interpretative inconveniences of the early Middle Ages' are not simply a product of the documentary sources, but are also a product of our analytical frameworks.

Having established the broad context of Anglo-Saxon society, we can now turn to consider the northern Danelaw in detail. The following chapters do not normally refer back to the wider context; in part to avoid repetition, and in part because analogy can offer only a partial explanation for the peculiarities of the northern Danelaw.

3 Territorial organization

> It appears that the basic unit of government and exploitation was quite often an area ... centred on a royal vill. All free inhabitants owed some services and dues to that vill, the services being of a non-servile kind, and the dues partaking of the nature of a uniform rent. ... Within it there were sometimes or generally particular villages which were more strictly bound to the lord and owed heavier services
>
> – J. Campbell[1]

By the eleventh century the various routines of daily life in the countryside were conducted within numerous territorial institutions (vills, manors, parishes, shires and their subdivisions, wapentakes and so on). Some of these were of great antiquity; others, however, were of more recent creation. This chapter examines the territorial structures of the rural society of the northern Danelaw and their relationships to each other, assesses the balance between continuity and change in rural institutions during the Anglo-Saxon period and offers a relative chronology for their formation. As we shall see, the distribution and juxtaposition of manors, vills, parishes and wapentakes have much to reveal about social, economic and political developments in early medieval society, which is especially invaluable in a region lacking narrative sources.

Territorial organization in the Anglo-Saxon period can be uncovered through the use of Anglo-Saxon charters and narrative sources, Domesday Book and contemporary surveys, place-names, and secular and ecclesiastical boundaries. Although each type of evidence has its shortcomings, each offers its own insights into early medieval society, which have generated different models for uncovering and understanding early medieval territorial organization. This chapter offers a critical appraisal of how we may use such evidence in a regional study, and in particular reveals the problems of conflating different types of evidence.

---

1. J. Campbell, 'Early Anglo-Saxon society according to written sources', in his *Essays in Anglo-Saxon History* (1986), 131–8, at 135–6.

Domesday Book and rural organization

The Domesday survey provides our first glimpse of most parts of the northern Danelaw, and it has been the traditional starting-point for discussions of the territorial organization of the region during the Anglo-Saxon period. There are obviously dangers in arguing backwards from later evidence, and we must avoid teleological explanations. It is also important to recognize that Domesday Book offers an insight into just a moment in time of the history of the region. Furthermore, the picture it presents is the result of numerous processes, and there is much diversity underlying the superficially consistent ways in which the survey records its information. How, and in what ways, then, did the territorial organization recorded by Domesday Book come into being?

Vills

The basic unit of exploitation in the Anglo-Saxon period was the individual farmstead. Commonly farmsteads were dispersed, but increasingly they came to be grouped together into nucleated clusters, the predecessors of the later medieval village.[2] Whatever the precise spatial arrangement of the farmsteads, all were grouped together into larger units – vills – to meet the requirements of agricultural activities, the sharing of common resources and the demands of the exploitative and administrative machinery of great lords.[3] Although the names of most are first recorded in Domesday Book, the vills find their origins long before the survey was compiled. Some studies have placed the origins of the vills long before the Anglo-Saxon settlements; others, however, have located them at a much later date. Some studies have looked to the essentially communal nature of the vill whereas others have emphasized the seigneurial role in its formation, and looked to moments of political upheaval following successive conquests for its origins.[4] As we shall see, it is probable that vills of the region were established over a protracted period of time in response to a variety of requirements and influences.

Much can be discerned about the origins and development of vills from their boundaries. However, since it is rare to find Anglo-Saxon charters or medieval surveys which delineate the boundaries of vills,

---

2. See Chapter 4, pp. 197–201.
3. H. Cam, 'The community of the vill', in *Medieval Studies presented to Rose Graham*, ed. V. Ruffer and A.J. Taylor (1950), 1–14; A. Winchester, 'The medieval vill in the western Lake District: some problems of definition', *Transactions of the Cumberland and Westmorland Archaeological and Antiquarian Society* 78 (1978), 55–69.
4. For a summary, see T.H. Unwin, 'Towards a model of Anglo-Scandinavian rural settlement in England', in *Anglo-Saxon Settlements*, ed. D. Hooke (1988), 77–98, at 83–5, 92–6.

we must turn to post-medieval evidence to recover those boundaries. The fact that the parochial system attached itself to existing secular organization means that many vills came to be mirrored by ecclesiastical parishes, and the essentially conservative nature of parish boundaries through to the nineteenth century, when they can first be mapped, provides the best means of recovering the boundaries of medieval vills. The validity of this method is confirmed by those Anglo-Saxon charters which incorporate boundary clauses: when mapped they can regularly be shown to conform to later parish boundaries. This confirms that parish boundaries commonly mirror much earlier secular territorial divisions and, in turn, that the boundaries of some vills had been defined by the end of the first millennium. The basic coincidence of charter boundaries recorded in Anglo-Saxon charters and parish boundaries has been demonstrated in Nottinghamshire at Sutton, Lound, Scrooby, Ranskill, Torworth and Bilby, at Southwell and its dependencies Normanton, Upton and Fiskerton, in Derbyshire at Weston-upon-Trent and Ballidon, and in Yorkshire at Newbald, Patrington and Drax.[5] The high level of correspondence between places named in Anglo-Saxon charters, places named in Domesday Book, and parishes (or the chapelries into which the parishes were divided) suggests a basic level of continuity in the organization of vills from at least the late Anglo-Saxon period.

Prior to the late Anglo-Saxon period, the main evidence for the origins of vills lies in the relationships between the boundaries of those vills (as reflected in parish boundaries) and features in the landscape. It is possible that the boundaries of some vills follow prehistoric boundaries. It has been suggested, for example, that some of the boundaries of some of the vills on the North York Moors may have such early origins, given the frequent location of Bronze Age barrows on those boundaries. The location of prehistoric barrows on boundaries may be an indication that the boundaries were first defined when those barrows were still in use. In this region the association between lowland and highland zones was crucial, and whatever the political or military situation in the region, survival demanded an efficient and continuous farming husbandry of which the continuity of land divisions may have been a part (Fig. 8).[6] Conversely, aerial surveys have suggested that in other parts of the northern Danelaw,

---

5.   G.T. Davies, 'The Anglo-Saxon boundaries of Sutton and Scrooby, Nottinghamshire', *TTS*, 87 (1983), 13–22; P. Lyth, 'The Southwell charter of 956 AD: an exploration of its boundaries', *TTS*, 86 (1982), 49–61; C.R. Hart, *The Early Charters of Northern England and the North Midlands* (1975), 219; N.P. Brooks, M. Gelling and D. Johnson, 'A new charter of King Edgar', *ASEP*, 13 (1984), 137–55; M.H. Long, 'Newbald', in *Yorkshire Boundaries*, ed. H.E.J. Le Patourel, M.H. Long and M.F. Pickles (1993), 134–41; M.H. Long and M.F. Pickles, 'Patrington' *ibid.*, 143–50; *EYC*, 1, 14; M.H. Long, 'Howden and Old Drax' *ibid.*, 125–34 at 132–4.

6.   D.A. Spratt, 'Prehistoric and medieval boundaries on the North York Moors', in *Yorkshire Boundaries*, ed. Le Patourel, Long and Pickles, 85–94, at 93.

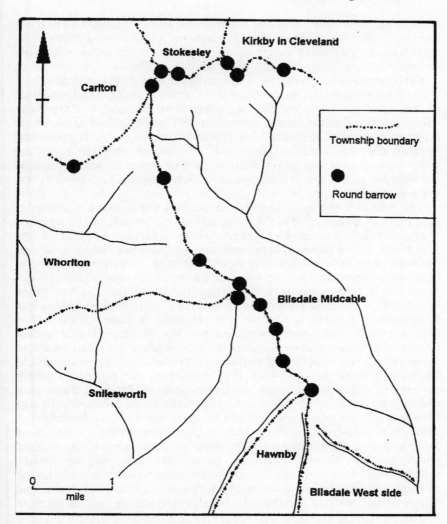

Figure 8 Townships on the North York Moors (after D.A. Spratt, Prehistoric and medieval boundaries on the North York Moors', in *Yorkshire Boundaries*, ed. H.E.J. Le Patourel, M.H. Long and M.F. Pickles (1993), 85–94)

such as north Nottinghamshire, the boundaries of vills must be of post-Roman origin, since they do not conform to Romano-British field systems.[7] A pre-Roman origin is also precluded for those vills with boundaries that follow the course of Roman roads.

Early Anglo-Saxon cemeteries are often located on the boundaries of vills.[8] For example, the barrow burial at Caenby (Lincs) is located close to the junction between the boundaries of Hemswell, Harpswell, Glentham and Caenby, and a charter of 963 granting land at Newbald (Yorks) includes 'Saxferth's *hlaw* (mound/tumulus)', which may have been another such early burial mound.[9] Presumably such burials either were located on existing boundaries, or were used to mark out new boundaries; either way it suggests that such boundaries existed in the early Anglo-Saxon period.

The territory of most vills was continuous, but outlying portions of vills are not unknown. This was apparently the result of the need to provide the inhabitants of a particular vill with access to resources not found adjacent to their settlement. When and by whom these detached portions were allocated is not clear, although they may sometimes have been formalizations of earlier patterns of inter-commoning.[10] Many more vills may once have had detached portions, or have incorporated neighbouring vills from which they had subsequently become detached. In particular, vills located on poor-quality arable land may once have been attached to vills in more fertile areas. Sometimes such former relationships are suggested by the fact that other vills in the vicinity still contained a cross-section of types of land when they were first mapped. For instance, the so-called 'ladder pattern' of vills to the north of Lincoln utilizes Ermine Street as a common boundary, and many of the vills incorporate a cross-section of high and low-lying land; and in Ryedale there are a series of elongated vills running north–south so that each incorporates a stretch of moorland (Fig. 9). Interruptions to these patterns may, then, be later developments. Elsewhere, parish boundaries may hint at former relationships between vills: upland vills often contain chapelries of churches in river valley settlements, as has been demonstrated in the Wolds of the Nottinghamshire–Leicestershire border and in parts of Kesteven (Lincs).[11]

---

7.   D.N. Riley, *Early Landscapes from the Air: studies of crop marks in south Yorkshire and north Nottinghamshire* (1980); T.H. Unwin, 'Townships and early fields in north Nottinghamshire', *JHG*, 9 (4) (1983), 341–6.
8.   P.H. Sawyer, *From Roman Britain to Norman England* (1978), 147–8.
9.   P. Everson, 'Pre-viking settlement in Lindsey', in *Pre-Viking Lindsey*, ed. A. Vince (1993), 91–100, at 94–7; Long, 'Newbald', 135–7.
10. P. O'Hare, 'Yorkshire boundaries and their development', in *Yorkshire Boundaries*, ed. Le Patourel, Long and Pickles, 9–23; M. Ecclestone, 'Townships with detached parts', *ibid.*, 75–84. Most detached portions were rationalized and awarded to neighbouring vills or turned into separate vills in the nineteenth century.
11. See pp. 150–1 below.

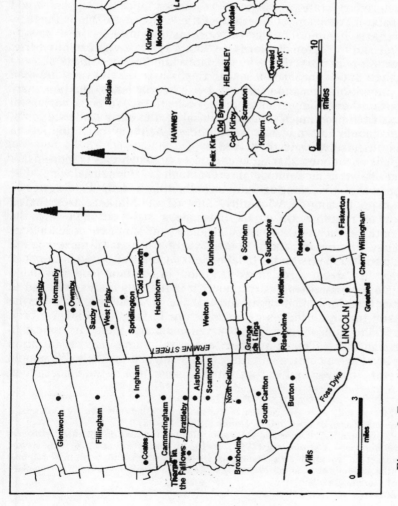

Figure 9 Townships north of Lincoln, and in north Yorkshire

The boundaries of many vills may also hint at the motives for their creation. The regularity of vills in some regions, and the fact that their boundaries often incorporated a mixture of types of soil and resources, has encouraged speculation that lords must have imposed the pattern of vills. But it is difficult to see what their interest in agricultural activity at this level would normally have been. The sharing of types of soil between neighbouring vills certainly suggests an economic and agrarian motive for the delineation of vills, but one which would have been more pressing for individual communities than for great lords. The latter could expect to have a cross-section of resources on their lands by virtue of the fact that they had control over, and could demand tribute and services from, large amounts of land spread over wide areas, thus the organization of the territories of individual communities to incorporate a range of resources and soil types would presumably have been of relatively little concern to them. Furthermore, the laying out of vills by lords seems unlikely in a society characterized by 'extensive lordship' and a relatively unexploited free land-owning peasantry. Even in the later Middle Ages, lords showed themselves to be concerned less with the daily routine of rural life than in the receipt of dues and services; it was largely left to the peasantry to organize themselves to meet those obligations. We must be careful not to attribute too much entrepreneurial zeal to early medieval lords, and we should not underestimate the capacity of communities to organize themselves and their land.[12]

The not uncommon sharing of resources between vills is more likely to have been a community interest than a seigneurial one. For example, the Lincolnshire vills of Buslingthorpe, Faldingworth, Friesthorpe, Lissington, Wickenby, Linwood and Market Rasen shared an area of meadow known as Lissingleys right through into the nineteenth century. Although this arrangement is not recorded before the thirteenth century, there is little doubt that it is of more ancient origin, and it appears to be independent of tenurial arrangements in the area.[13] In areas of reclaimed land, and of common land in which a number of communities had interests, it is the vills themselves rather than manorial lords that organized the use of such land. This can be witnessed in the fen edges of Lincolnshire in the thirteenth century, and as Nellie Neilson long ago observed, such arrangements appear to be pre-manorial.[14] This is another reason to believe that organization at this level had a communal rather than a seigneurial basis. We should be careful, however, not to regard the organization of the landscape at

---

12.   C.C. Dyer, 'Power and conflict in the medieval village' in *Medieval Villages: a review of current work*, ed. D. Hooke (1985), 27–32.
13.   P. Everson, C.C. Taylor and C.J. Dunn, *Change and Continuity: rural settlement in north-west Lincolnshire* (1991), 9–10, for other examples of vills having shares in common areas (such as Blyton, Scotton and Scotter Commons, Madgin Moor and Caistor Moor); D.R. Roffe, 'Lissingleys and the meeting-place of Lindsey' (forthcoming).
14.   *A Terrier of Fleet, Lincolnshire*, ed. N. Neilson (1920), xli.

this level as a product of communal rights in land. The previous chapter discussed reasons why this is an inappropriate concept; rather we should think of the division of the landscape into vills as one of the products of a notion of 'equal entitlement' to resources. Furthermore, it should be noted that it may have been the most substantial peasants who were responsible for organizing local agricultural routines rather than the whole community.[15]

There are, as we have seen, regions where an otherwise regular pattern of vills is interrupted by what appears to be the subdivision of a vill, and it is reasonable to conclude that the topography of vills was not immutable prior to the eleventh century. For example, the relationship between Harpswell, Glentworth and Hemswell (Lincs) indicates that Harpswell was an interpolation into what is an otherwise fairly regular pattern. Similarly Aisthorpe, Brattleby and Thorpe in the Fallows (Lincs) appear to have been carved out of a single pre-existing vill (Fig. 9). In Domesday Book the entries for these three places link them together, and together they were assessed at twelve carucates, which may indicate that they formed a 'hundred', a pre-manorial administrative and agrarian arrangement into which all land in Lincolnshire was enrolled.[16] All three vills have Scandinavian place-names and it is not implausible that the alterations to the pattern of vills occurred sometime after the Scandinavian settlement, which also caused new place-names to be coined. All three places also have tenth-century sculpture, which is further evidence that they were separate vills, with their own churches, by that time.[17]

Thus, it appears that in the northern Danelaw, as elsewhere, the patterns of medieval vills were of diverse origins; as we shall see, they were also cross-cut in various ways by other forms of land division.

Hundreds

Domesday Book intermittently records a rural institution peculiar to the northern Danelaw, the twelve-carucate hundred (not to be confused with the so-called English hundred, which finds its Danelaw equivalent in the wapentake). Hundreds are most frequently recorded in Lincolnshire, although they are also found in Derbyshire and Nottinghamshire. Virtually all land in Lincolnshire was enrolled in a hundred: the entry for Coulsuain's manor in Pickworth notes that 'these 2 carucates are not enumerated in any hundred nor have they their like in Lincolnshire'.[18] Domesday Book and later sources reveal a

---

15. Cam, 'The community of the vill'; R. Faith, *The English Peasantry and the Growth of Lordship* (1997), 146–7.
16. *DB*, fos. 340c, 354c, 356d, 371a; Everson, Taylor and Dunn, *Change and Continuity*, 9. Hundreds are discussed below, pp. 101–4.
17. See Chapter 5, p. 287.
18. *DB*, fo. 377c.

variety of functions for the hundred: it was associated with the collection of geld; it was seemingly associated with the provision of military service; it had a responsibility for maintaining law and order; it may have had a court, and certainly it is found witnessing charters and pronouncing on matters of tenure; the community of the hundred acted as a legal body and provided information on tenure to the Domesday commissioners; and it was sometimes responsible for agrarian organization.[19] It is rarely possible to reconstruct the hundreds of Domesday Book, since the survey does not record the hundredal names consistently, but there is sufficient information to reveal that a hundred might comprise a single vill (as in the case of Leverton), or conversely that a single vill might incorporate more than one hundred (such as Blankney and Long Bennington, which incorporated two hundreds[20]). Equally, a hundred might comprise land in several vills (the hundred of Swaby, for example, included land in Belleau, South Thoresby, Claythorpe and Tothill, as well as in Swaby itself). Where it is possible to reconstruct them, it has been shown that hundreds normally formed a coherent territorial unit, and that they were often unrelated to either the manorial or the parochial structure (Fig. 10).[21]

In Lincolnshire the importance of the hundred renders the Domesday record especially complex. The initial enquiries in Lincolnshire appear to have been conducted through the hundred, and any land belonging to a given lord within a particular hundred would be recorded together. Only where appurtenant land was located in berewicks or sokeland which lay outside the hundred does the survey normally differentiate the location of the manorial resources, other than in exceptional cases where the manorial appurtenance was held by someone other than the lord of that manor.[22] In other words, land might be recorded under the name of the hundred but actually lie in a different vill. For example, later evidence reveals that four of the six Domesday manors described as being in Bourne were actually located in Austerby. Bourne was the hundred to which they belonged.[23] Occasional interlineations above the hundredal name record where the land concerned actually lay. For example, above the entry for Drew de Beurere's manor of Keelby '*vel Cotes*' has been interlined, which indicates a distinction between the hundred name and the precise location of the property.[24] That there was a distinction to be drawn is

---

19.   D.R. Roffe, 'The Lincolnshire hundred', *Landscape History*, 3 (1981), 27–36; F.M. Stenton, *Documents Illustrative of the Social and Economic History of the Danelaw from Various Collections* (1920), 60–2, nos. 93, 94.

20.   *DB*, fos. 361b, 348a–b.

21.   Roffe, 'The Lincolnshire hundred'; for a reconstruction of Nottinghamshire hundreds based on groups of vills assessed at twelve carucates, rather than on hundredal rubrication, see C.R. Hart, *The Danelaw* (1992), 411–27.

22.   Roffe, 'The Lincolnshire hundred', 31.

23.   For this and other examples, see D.R. Roffe, 'Place-naming in Domesday Book: settlements, estates and communities', *Nomina*, 14 (1990–1), 47–60, at 50, and n. 12.

24.   *DB*, fo. 360b.

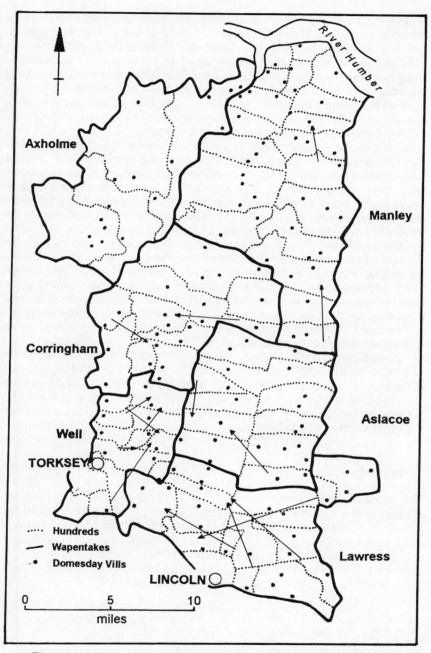

Figure 10 Lincolnshire hundreds (after C.R. Hart, *The Danelaw* (1992), fig. 11.1)

occasionally noted in the text: Count Alan's various lands in Drayton are said to lie 'in Drayton hundred', 'in the same Drayton' and 'in Drayton itself'.[25] In general, however, Domesday Book is not as helpful, and the structure of Domesday estates was often more complex than the text suggests. The Domesday Book entries were artificial creations of the hundred, and we have to conclude that there were many more composite estates, incorporating land in more than one vill, than the survey reveals, since it was the hundred, and not the estate, that formed the basic unit of enquiry.[26]

It is difficult to assign origins to the hundredal system. The twelve-carucate assessment need not mean that the hundred was a post-Scandinavian institution, as has sometimes been suggested, since it could have been a reassessment of a pre-existing unit. The general lack of coincidence between hundreds and manors suggests that they were created independently of each other. This, and the communal role of the hundred, suggests that the hundreds originated in essence in the social conditions of a pre-manorial society. It is, perhaps, no coincidence that the role of the hundred survived longest in the fen edges in Lincolnshire where manorial organization was slower to develop. However, in general, by the thirteenth century the hundred had ceased to exist, and there is some evidence to show that even at the time of Domesday Book its role was being usurped by that of the manor: for example, the three hundreds of Frieston, Normanton and West Willoughby pertained to the manor of Caythorpe, according to the survey.[27]

Although lords and their estates dominated many aspects of the lives of peasants, the role of the hundred, and indeed that of the vill, is a reminder of the importance of the links between and within communities in the organization of society, a point that is prone to be overlooked by the traditional emphasis on the hierarchical links between manorial centres and dependencies, and between lords and peasants.

Wapentakes

The shires of the northern Danelaw were divided in the eleventh century into a number of wapentakes, which were the equivalent of the hundreds of southern and Midland England (confusingly, however, there were also hundreds in the East Riding of Yorkshire). The wapentakes served as communal meeting-places and had courts which sat in judgement on trespasses and disputes over land, and were responsible for monitoring the policing of the area and the muster of its levies.[28] The

25.   *Ibid.*, fos. 348a–b.
26.   Roffe, 'The Lincolnshire hundred', 33.
27.   *DB*, fo. 363b.
28.   D.R. Roffe, *The Lincolnshire Domesday*, Alecto Historical Editions (1992), 32. The wapentakes in Yorkshire were also grouped into three ridings. Lincolnshire was divided into the 'parts' of Lindsey, Kesteven and Holland, and Lindsey was further subdivided into three ridings.

rubrication of wapentakes in the Domesday text is often sporadic and it is not easy to reconstruct the extent of wapentakes from the survey alone. Where it is possible to reconstruct the wapentakes, using the survey and later evidence, it emerges that they varied in size and in the number of vills that they contained. Generally they were coherent, but sometimes they included isolated areas of land. The wapentake is first recorded as an institution in Edgar's law-code of 963, and David Roffe has suggested that the influence of the West Saxon kings lies behind this administrative organization as they took control of the region.[29] However, the distinctive use of local terminology more probably suggests earlier origins, as does the similarity of names and of topographical settings of public assemblies in both the northern Danelaw and elsewhere in England. Moreover, the variations in the size and assessments of wapentakes may suggest that in some instances they were framed around pre-existing administrative units or estates.

The wapentakes and the sokes of the northern Danelaw were fundamentally unrelated institutions, both geographically and functionally. Manors and their dependencies were often located in different wapentakes, and unlike some of the hundreds in other parts of the country, the wapentakes of the northern Danelaw were generally not appurtenances of a major manor.[30] In the few occasions where wapentake and soke centre coincided, such as at Newark-on-Trent (Notts), Horncastle and Bolingbroke (Lincs), the jurisdiction and organization of each were clearly distinguished.[31] The meeting-places of wapentakes in the eleventh century were commonly located at a distance from the major soke centres. For example, in Derbyshire the eleventh-century wapentakes were named after, and met at, relatively unimportant places in the manorial hierarchy: these included Hamston wapentake (which seems to have met at Hamston Hill in Thorpe vill, which was part of the manor of Ashbourne); Morleystone (apparently named after some prominent stone in Morley vill, a minor holding in 1066); Scarsdale (which met somewhere in the Scarsdale valley); Appletree (which later met in Sutton-on-the-Hill, and which may have been the site of the eponymous tree); Blackwell (a berewick of Ashford); Litchurch (a manor on the edge of Derby); and *Walecros* (a lost name, somewhere in the vicinity of Repton) (Fig. 11).[32] Similarly, in Lincolnshire wapentake meeting-places were often located away from major soke centres: for example, Ashwardhurn wapentake met at Kirkby Mount (in Kirkby la Thorpe), rather than at Kirkby la Thorpe

29. Roffe, *The Lincolnshire Domesday*, 40–1.
30. H. Cam, *Liberties and Communities in Medieval England: collected studies in local administration and topography* (1944; reprinted 1963), 64–90.
31. M.W. Barley, *Documents Relating to the Manor and Soke of Newark-on-Trent*, Thoroton Record Society Series, 16 (1956), xxxliii; F.M. Stenton, *Types of Manorial Structure in the Northern Danelaw*, Oxford Studies in Social and Legal History, ed. P. Vinogradoff, 2 (1910), 3–96, at 44; Roffe, *The Lincolnshire Domesday*, 37.
32. D.R. Roffe, *The Derbyshire Domesday*, Alecto Historical Editions (1990), 36–7.

Figure 11 Wapentakes and ridings in the northern Danelaw (after C. Hart, *The Danelaw* (1992), fig. 8.1)

itself, or one of the other major manors in the wapentake (such as Quarrington or Old Sleaford). In Nottinghamshire and Yorkshire wapentakes are usually not named after, nor did they meet at, major manorial centres.[33]

---

33. Roffe, *The Lincolnshire Domesday*, 32; K.M. Hall, 'Pre-Conquest estates in Yorkshire', in *Yorkshire Boundaries*, ed. Le Patourel, Long and Pickles, 25–38, at 27–33; D.R. Roffe, *The Nottinghamshire Domesday*, Alecto Historical Editions (1995), 20–30.

Although seigneurial interests were, in theory, separate from those of the wapentakes, in practice they did have an impact on each other. The division of some vills between two wapentakes (such as Staunton (Notts), which was divided between the wapentakes of Newark and Bingham, and Bearwardcote and Dalbury (Derbs), which were divided between Litchurch and Appletree wapentakes[34]) seems to indicate the importance of seigneurial control in determining where the wapentake boundary was drawn. Isolated portions of wapentakes may also have arisen as a result of the influence of lords and the structure of their estates. The fact that many sokes were regularly confined within the boundaries of one or other wapentake may indicate either that the wapentakes were drawn around their estates, or conversely that the sokes were created in part through grants of land within a given wapentake.[35]

Scirs

Domesday Book occasionally provides evidence for another unit of territorial organization, the *scir*, but one which had largely ceased to have any practical role. Geoffrey Barrow has argued that the *scir*, a small region with administrative functions, owing tribute to a lord and, perhaps, enjoying a sense of cultural identity, was a common form of early medieval organization that pre-dated the estate structure recorded by Domesday Book. The remnants of such a system in Yorkshire may be indicated in Domesday Book by the wapentake names of Burghshire and Cravenshire, and later sources reveal other *scirs*, including Howdenshire, Hallamshire, Richmondshire, Sowerbyshire, Allertonshire, Coxwoldshire, Gillingshire, Riponshire and Mashamshire.[36] These were not necessarily all early creations, although some of the *scirs* were attached to important early medieval estate and ecclesiastical centres. The term was used in the later Middle Ages to describe whole estates, parts of estates (Sowerbyshire was part of the manor of Wakefield) and new creations, such as the Honour of Kirkby Malzeard, which was known as Kirkbyshire.[37] The name Morthen (*Mōr-thing*) may indicate another such regional territory, and Holderness ('the headland (ON *nes*) of the earl (ON *holdr*)') may have been another, possibly of Scandinavian origin.[38]

---

34. *DB*, fos. 273b, 275d, 276a, 281d, 288c; Stenton, *Types of Manorial Structure*, 46.
35. See p. 152 below.
36. *DB*, fos. 379d, 380b; Hall, 'Pre-Conquest estates in Yorkshire', 35–6; G.W.S. Barrow, *The Kingdom of the Scots: government, church and society from the eleventh to the thirteenth century* (1973), 10–11.
37. Hall, 'Pre-Conquest estates in Yorkshire', 35.
38. The traditional etymology of Morthen ('the moorland district with a common assembly (OScand *thing*)') has recently been questioned, and it may derive rather from a name in *-ingas*; M.S. Parker, 'Morthen reconsidered', *YAJ*, 58 (1986), 23–9. On Holderness, see B. English, *The Lords of Holderness, 1086–1260: a study in feudal society* (1979), 1.

None of these territories, as far as we are able to define them, appears to relate directly to the manorial structure of Domesday Book.

The manorial structure

The complex manorial structure of the northern Danelaw as it is presented in Domesday Book stands in marked contrast to that of southern and Midland England.[39] The region is characterized in Domesday Book by large estates or 'sokes', which consisted of a central manor with outlying dependencies (known as berewicks and sokelands) which not uncommonly were many miles away from the manorial centre. The term 'manor' (*manerium*) has been the subject of great debate, but it was seemingly employed by Domesday Book when a lord's hall (*aula*) was present; the hall was the collection point for geld, and was doubtless also a focal point for organizing agricultural activities and settling grievances.[40] In many parts of the country the typical manor comprised a lord's hall and home farm (or demesne) and land on which the tenants who worked the lord's home farm lived. Furthermore, as Henry Loyn put it, in the 'classic' manor 'the tenurial unit which was the manor ... equated exactly with the agrarian unit that was the village'.[41] But such consolidated manors were more common in Midland and southern England than they were in the northern Danelaw. Even those manors which appear to include property in only one named place can often be shown to have included property in other vills. In practice, the many manors in the region comprised land scattered around a variety of places, varying rather in scale than in kind.[42]

The berewicks and sokelands that were attached to so many of the manors of the northern Danelaw have long been regarded as contrasted types of subsidiary local organization. Sir Frank Stenton emphasized the fact that the lord of the manor owned the soil of the berewick; it was a detached piece of the lord's demesne land, and in the northern Danelaw the term was used interchangeably with the term 'inland'. In contrast, sokeland was owned by the men who lived on it, although it also carried a liability to render services and dues at the manorial centre to which it was attached.[43] On the 'classic' manor we expect to find the lord's hall, demesne, land of his peasant tenants and perhaps also freer holdings of the more privileged stratum of the peasantry, all located within the confines of a single vill. In the northern Danelaw, by contrast, manor and vill rarely coincided, and whole vills were regularly reckoned as

---

39.   H.R. Loyn, *Anglo-Saxon England and the Norman Conquest* (2nd edn, 1991), 194–6, 352–3.
40.   F.W. Maitland, *Domesday Book and Beyond* (1897), 107–28; Loyn, *Anglo-Saxon England*, 169–76, 194–205, 351–6; Stenton, *Types of Manorial Structure*, 57–8.
41.   Loyn, *Anglo-Saxon England*, 353.
42.   See Chapter 4, pp. 166–76.
43.   Stenton, *Types of Manorial Structure*, 4–5.

sokeland or berewicks. The survival of so many large sokes meant that the distinctions between types of tenure were often drawn at the level of the soke as a whole rather than at the level of the individual vill. Such a system may be of considerable antiquity, and is in contrast to the manorial organization of other regions, where the ties between vills had ceased to be relevant to estate organization.

It is important to note here that, confusingly, the term 'inland', which is used as a synonym for berewick, carries a much wider meaning in the northern Danelaw than it does in its usage elsewhere, including both the lord's land and that of the peasants, as opposed to a relatively limited intensively exploited core area of an estate.[44] The synonymity of the terms inland and berewick is demonstrated by a number of entries in Domesday Book, in which land is identified as a berewick in the margin, but as inland in the text:[45]

B & S.   In (Little) Ouseburn [there are] 5 carucates for geld. Land for 3 ploughs. [They are] inland and soke in Knaresborough

B & S.   In the same Coleby there are 12 carucates of land [assessed] to the geld. There is land for as many ploughs. Of these 1 carucate is inland in Washingborough, but 11 are soke[land]

In these cases the marginal 'B' indicates a berewick, and the 'S' indicates sokeland.

Berewicks and sokelands are always described by Domesday Book as pertaining to some manor, and the survey generally enters them immediately after the account of the manor itself. In the Yorkshire folios, which were probably the first to be compiled in the production of the Exchequer Domesday, there is, however, commonly little attempt to group the berewicks and sokelands of a manor with the manorial *caput*.[46] Since the Domesday survey sometimes gives overall totals for the resources and assessment of manors and their dependencies, it is not always possible to determine how they were distributed between, and derived from, the component parts of the manor. For example, the manor of Hope (Derbs) and its berewicks were assessed at ten carucates, there was land for ten ploughs, thirty *villani* and four *bordarii* with six ploughs, and its resources included meadowland and woodland pasture 'in places'; but there is no

---

44. See Chapter 2, p. 83–4.
45. *DB*, fos. 301c, 337d.
46. D.R. Roffe, 'Domesday Book and northern society: a reassessment', *EHR*, 105 (April, 1990), 310–36, at 315. The normal formula is 'In *x* there are *y* carucates of land; the soke is in *x*' or 'In *x* there is soke of *x*; *y* carucates to the geld'. However, in the case of the larger sokes the formula is often 'To this manor pertains the soke of this land ...', followed by a list of vills and their assessments.

indication how these assessments and resources were distributed.[47] By contrast the resources, population and assessments of the major sokes of Lincolnshire are recorded in much greater detail and the information for each of the dependencies is commonly recorded separately. For example, the entries for the royal manor of Horncastle give information on the population and resources of each of fifteen sokelands and inlands (the equivalent of berewicks) in addition to an overall total.[48]

Although manors outside the northern Danelaw often had dependencies in neighbouring vills, it is the number and the extent of the dependencies of such manors which distinguish the northern Danelaw from many other regions. These composite manors ranged in size from, for example, Stainton-by-Langworth (Lincs), which had a single berewick in Reasby, to Tuxford (Notts), which had sokeland in Kirton, Walesby, Egmanton and West Markham, to Beverley (Yorks), which had numerous dependencies spread throughout much of the East Riding of Yorkshire, and Mansfield (Notts), which had dependencies widely distributed over most of northern Nottinghamshire.[49] Such variety in manorial structure can be found right across the region. Some of the larger sokes incorporated a significant amount of underdeveloped land: the sokelands of Wakefield and Bolton-in-Craven (Yorks) both included much land on the Pennine uplands (Fig. 12). However, this was not invariably the case, and many large sokes are found on the most favoured agricultural land. As example is the manor of Southwell (Notts) in the Trent valley, which included twelve berewicks spread through a number of neighbouring vills.

Despite the high incidence of manors which included land in several vills, there were, nonetheless, manors in the northern Danelaw which were seemingly confined to single vills, or even to fractions of vills. In the Trent valley in Derbyshire and Nottinghamshire such manors are very common, and our ability to see them in the Domesday text is aided by the fact that the hundreds were too big to be used to identify land, and most entries seem to relate more precisely to vills than in Lincolnshire.[50] Such a pattern of territorial organization appears to go back to at least the mid-tenth century, when the grant to Wulfsige *Maur* of a number of properties in the Trent valley in 942 lists them individually by name, in such a manner as to suggest that they were already at that date separately managed properties.[51]

---

47.   *DB*, fos. 272d, 273a.
48.   *Ibid.*, fos. 339a–b.
49.   *Ibid.*, fos. 281b–c, 284d, 285a, 304a–b, 349c.
50.   Roffe, 'Place-naming in Domesday Book', 52–3.
51.   S 479 (B 771); S 484 (B 772); S 1606 (B 773); translated in *Burton Abbey Charters*, 10–12. The properties were Alrewas, Bromley, Burton, *Tatenhyll*, Branston, Stretton, Rolleston, Clifton, *Hagnatun*, Newbold (Staffs), Walton-on-Trent, Coton-in-the-Elms, Cauldwell, Drakelow, Linton, Croxall, Stapenhill, Cotton (Derbyshire). It should be noted that Stapenhill included property in Brislingcote and Stanton in the twelfth century and may have done so earlier (see p. 160, below).

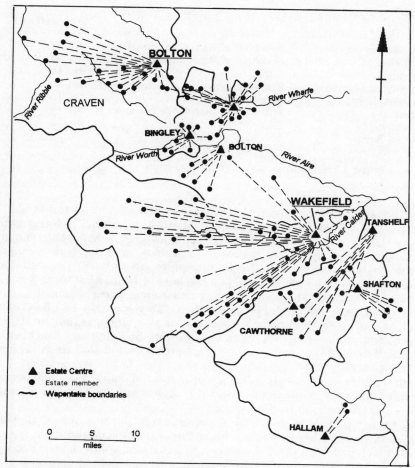

Figure 12 The sokes of Wakefield and Bolton-in-Craven (after K.M. Hall, 'Pre-Conquest estates in Yorkshire' in *Yorkshire Boundaries*, ed. H.E.J. Le Patourel, M.H. Long and M.F. Pickles (1993), 25–38)

A further characteristic feature of the northern Danelaw in the eleventh century was the extreme fragmentation of territorial organization; many vills contained a multitude of manors, berewicks and sokeland. In 1066 Winterton (Lincs), for example, included four small manors, separate berewicks of the manors of Whitton, Coleby and Roxby, and sokeland of the manors of Kirton in Lindsey, West Halton and Scawby and Sturton (Fig. 13).[52] At Eaton (Notts) six and a

---

52.   *DB*, fos. 338b–c, 349b, 353c, 361c, 362c–d, 365a, 371b. For additional examples of the complexity of tenurial organization, see Hart, *The Danelaw*, 337–85.

Holder	Type of holding	Assessment
Earl Edwin	sokeland of Kirton in Lindsey	4c, 0b
Earl Harold	sokeland of West Halton	4c, 0b
Fulcher	2 manors	1c, 4b
Fulcher & Grimbald	2 manors	1c, 3b
Wege & Baret	berewick of Coleby	0c, 1b
Edwin	sokeland of Scawby & Sturton	0c, 4b
Merlswein	berewick of Roxby	0c, 2b
Siward Barn	berewick of Whitton	0c, 2b

Figure 13 Domesday holdings in Winterton

half bovates were divided in 1066 between the manors of ten thegns, each of whom had his own hall; at Carlton in Lindrick (Notts) two carucates were divided between six thegns, who each had a hall; and at Killingholme (Lincs) ten carucates and two bovates were divided between ten manors.[53] In Nottinghamshire, in only 40 per cent of named vills did a single lord hold all the land in 1066, whether it was as a manor, berewick or sokeland.[54] The situation in parts of Lincolnshire was even more complex. For example, in the wapentake of Elloe only Lutton and Gedney were held by one lord as a single manor in 1066; Tydd, Holbeach, Whaplode, Weston Moulton, Spalding and Pinchbeck were all divided into multiple manors, berewicks and sokelands, which were generally held by different lords (Fig. 14).[55] By contrast, in Staffordshire only twenty vills out of a total of more than 350 were divided between more than one lord in 1086, and in Wiltshire it was equally rare for vills to be divided.[56]

The complexity of manorial organization in the northern Danelaw appears to have been reduced after the Norman Conquest, as many vills which had been divided into two or more manors were acquired by a single lord. It is possible that the people named as holding manors in a particular vill in 1066 sometimes held their land of the same 'overlord', perhaps for a period of a life or lives.[57] Hence, it is difficult to judge whether the Norman takeover of the region saw a concerted effort to simplify land-holding and to reduce the number of manorial lords, or whether it saw the pattern of 'subtenancies' disrupted. Nonetheless, even if multiple-manor entries represent land held from a single greater lord, there was still an ensuing simplification of organization since the new Norman lords rarely seem to have

53. *DB*, fos. 284d, 285b, 347a, 350c, 361d.
54. T.H. Unwin, 'The Norman aggregation of estates and settlement in eleventh-century Nottinghamshire', *Landscape History*, 9 (1987), 53–64, at 55.
55. *DB*, fos. 338a–b.
56. Loyn, *Anglo-Saxon England*, 354–5.
57. D.R. Roffe, 'The early history of Wharram Percy' (forthcoming). The subject of 'overlords' and 'subtenants' is discussed in Chapter 4, pp. 171–3.

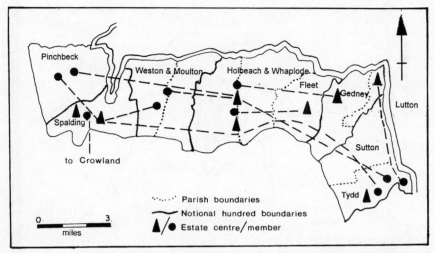

Figure 14 Domesday manorial structure in Elloe wapentake (after D.R. Roffe, 'The Lincolnshire hundred', *Landscape History*, 3 (1981), 27–36)

maintained the number of subdivisions. For example, some of the Bishop of Bayeux's manors in Lincolnshire had been held by more than one person in 1066, but in 1086 they were held of the bishop by only one named person: Sturton had been held in 1066 by Ulfketill, Asfrothr, Restelf and Wulfmaer, but in 1086 was held of the bishop by Ilbert alone; Glentham had been held by Æthelstan and Wulfmaer, but later by only Wadard; and Firsby by Alwige and Asketill, but later by Ilbert.[58]

There was significant diversity in the size, spatial distribution, population and level of exploitation of the manors and sokes of the northern Danelaw.[59] Manors varied enormously in size from those that coincided with fractions of vills assessed at just a few bovates or less, to manors such as that of Sherburn in Elmet (Yorks), which extended into numerous places and which along with its berewicks was assessed at 96 carucates.[60] Manors were not always coherent, and were often interspersed with other manors. For example, Earl Edwin's pre-Conquest soke of Kirton in Lindsey (Lincs) was interspersed with the holdings of other lords: in Glentworth the manor of Kirton held sokeland assessed at six carucates and two and a half bovates, but in Glentworth there was also sokeland of the manor of Glentham, which was held by Steinn, and manors held by Godric, Gamall and Sotr; and in Grayingham, in addition to the sokeland of Kirton, assessed at four

---

58. *DB*, fo. 342a.
59. See Chapter 4, pp. 166–76.
60. *DB*, fo. 302c.

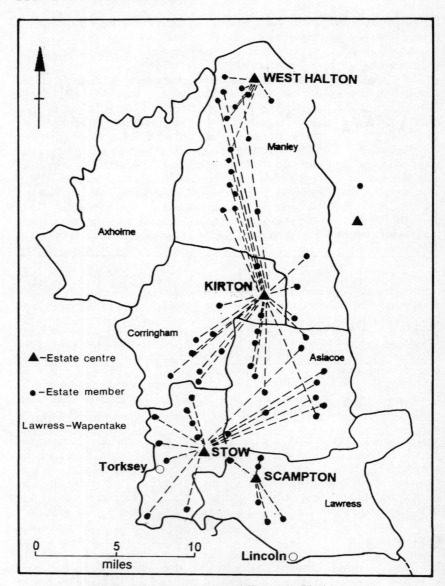

Figure 15 The Domesday soke of Kirton in Lindsey

carucates, there were two manors held by Halfdan and Eadgifu (Fig. 15).[61] It is difficult to ascertain patterns of land-holding below the level

---

61.   *DB*, fos. 338c, 342a, 344b, 359a, 362c, 365b, 366a.

of royal and ecclesiastical estates because of the difficulty of identifying and distinguishing lesser landholders, but an analysis of the holdings of such people in Nottinghamshire revealed that their holdings tend to have been scattered in 1066.[62]

The populations of manors also varied, especially in respect of the proportion of sokemen to *villani* and *bordarii*, – that is to say, in the proportion of peasants with greater or lesser freedoms and privileges. Accordingly, the rights that manorial lords enjoyed over their manors varied depending on the status of their inhabitants, the proximity of the dependencies of the manor to the manorial centre, and the extent to which they owed dues to some greater lord. The implications of the complex manorial structure for the inhabitants of those manors is not made explicit in Domesday Book, but later evidence can supplement our picture. The pattern of sokes recorded in Domesday Book persisted in parts of the region for centuries, and it was not uncommon for the inhabitants of appurtenant places to continue to owe services at manorial centres many miles away. In the thirteenth century the inhabitants of the berewicks of the archbishop of York's manor of Ripon still owed labour services (including ploughing work), construction duties on Rogation days, transport obligations and military service at Ripon. The inhabitants of Denton owed ploughing services and reaping at Otley until at least 1315, and the men of some eighteen vills attached to the manor of Knaresborough were burdened with boonworks and the obligation to feed the lord's dogs. In the thirteenth century the inhabitants of Ledston still owed ploughing services at Kippax, and those of Levisham were obliged to do harrowing at Pickering.[63]

How did the estate structure of the northern Danelaw described by Domesday Book come into being? It is important to state at the outset that we cannot use the evidence of Domesday Book to uncover in any detail what territorial organization was really like at an earlier date, even if we supplement it with other sources. The text presents much to debate about the nature of land-holding and territorial organization in 1086, and still more so at an earlier date. What we can profitably do, however, is to identify trends in territorial organization, and to suggest the ways in which it emerged and developed through the Anglo-Saxon centuries. It will be shown that the manorial organization of Domesday Book had evolved piecemeal in response to the diverse demands of politics, agriculture, lordship, community and settlement.[64]

---

62.   Unwin, 'The Norman aggregation of estates and settlement'.
63.   W.E. Kapelle, *The Norman Conquest of the North: a region and its transformation 1000–1135* (1979), 68–70.
64.   Faith, *The English Peasantry*, 12.

The Domesday text

If we propose to argue backwards 'from the known to the unknown', then we must be clear about what Domesday Book actually tells us about rural organization. Although the northern Danelaw undoubtedly had a complex manorial structure, some of the complexity of the Domesday survey of the region arose from the process of data collection and presentation. It used to be thought that the relatively confused nature of the Yorkshire folios was a product of an extremely complicated tenurial structure, and of the disruptions caused by the so-called 'harrying of the North' by William I in 1069–70; that is to say, the complexities in the Domesday *text* reflected the nature of society and estate structure in Yorkshire.[65] However, more recent textual analysis has suggested that the irregularities in the Yorkshire folios result from experimentation on the part of the scribes. Some of the irregularities even arise from postscriptal additions of conventions adopted later in the process of compilation. David Roffe has argued that the Yorkshire folios of Domesday Book were the first to be compiled, given that the formulas employed vary so much. Twelve formulas were experimented with before the scribe settled on the formula which was then used for the rest of the northern circuit ('In x a had y carucates; land for z ploughs. Now b has it.')[66] The complexities and ambiguities of the Yorkshire folios may also arise to some extent from the late organization of the region by the Normans, and from the ignorance of the new Norman lords about their possessions.[67]

Experimentation on the part of the scribes even extended to decisions about whether or not to enrol land as a manor. In the Yorkshire folios of Domesday Book there were proportionately more manors than in Lincolnshire, and changes in scribal convention may help to explain this contrast. The record of service due from one manor to another and references to people holding manors from a greater lord have prompted David Roffe to suggest that these were what he calls 'intermediate tenures' held on limited terms. It is not in fact clear that these entries reflect tenurial arrangements, as we shall see,[68] but they certainly indicate that some other lord had interests in the land of the immediate lord. By the time that the Lincolnshire folios were compiled, the scribe had developed his concept of the manor and ceased describing such holdings as manors, but rather entered them as sokeland. Support for this suggestion comes from those entries in which lords of sokeland are recorded. For example, Ernuin the priest and four sokemen held five bovates of sokeland in Gonalston, which was attached to the king's manor of Arnold (Notts). Furthermore, it has been suggested that the sokemen who enjoyed the services of

---

65. D.M. Palliser, 'Domesday Book and the "harrying of the North"', *Northern History*, 29 (1993), 1–23.
66. Roffe, 'Domesday Book and northern society', 313–23.
67. Palliser, 'Domesday Book and the "harrying of the North"', 22.

villani and *bordarii* at Northorpe, Brant Broughton, Barton upon Humber and Baumber (Lincs) would probably have been assigned manors in the Yorkshire portion of the text.[69] Duplication of material was also a product of the complexity of tenurial and jurisdictional organization. This was especially likely if a lord had rights over land which pertained to the manor of another lord. A further complexity of the Domesday text lies in the grouping of manors in the 'soke', or jurisdiction, of other manors. Sometimes this is made explicit, as in the case of Robert of Stafford's manor of Denton, which was in the soke of the king's manor of Grantham (Lincs), but there were no doubt instances where such relationships between manors were not noted.[70] In other words, the Domesday text cannot be taken as a reliable guide to the subtleties of tenurial or jurisdictional organization, and we should not expect that it invariably describes similar forms of organization in the same terms, or that the terms it employed were used consistently.

The term 'manor' was seemingly used flexibly by the Domesday survey to incorporate a variety of forms of social, tenurial and territorial organization. The manor was an emerging concept, and the term was rarely used in the century following the compilation of Domesday Book.[71] Put simply, the Domesday 'manor' can be said to have been a focal point for the collection of tribute, other dues and services – 'a nexus of tribute', as David Roffe has put it.[72] This fact underlies the way in which the Domesday text was compiled. It was important to record the centres through which dues and services were collected, and as a result many settlements and vills in existence in 1086 went unrecorded.[73] Some lords exercised extensive rights, often called 'sake and soke', over their manors, but many other parcels of land which were described by Domesday Book as manors were holdings which were in some way intermediate between the manors of great lords, who held them with obligations only to the state and the king, and the holdings of the peasantry.[74] The lords of such manors did not necessarily have unequivocal rights to them, but held them in some way from another lord, and for this reason we sometimes find manors grouped together under the jurisdiction of some greater manor. Elsewhere, some of the small manors into which many vills were divided were often said to be in the soke of another of the manors in that vill: for example, Carle's manor in Carlby (Lincs) was under the soke of Dane's manor in the same vill.[75]

Numerous holdings in Yorkshire are described by the survey as

---

68.   See Chapter 4, 171–3.
69.   *DB*, fo. 293b; Roffe, 'Domesday Book and northern society', 328–33.
70.   *DB*, fo. 368c.
71.   Stenton, *Social and Economic History of the Danelaw*, lx.
72.   Roffe, 'Domesday Book and northern society', 329.
73.   Roffe, *The Derbyshire Domesday*, 6–7.
74.   These rights are akin to the rights of bookland: Chapter 4, pp. 168–72.
75.   Roffe, 'Domesday Book and northern society', 329–33; *DB*, fo. 368c.

'waste'. This has long been regarded as an indication of the destruction
inflicted by William I's army in 1069–70, during the so-called 'harrying
of the North'. So serious was this onslaught believed to have been that
seventeen years later the region had still apparently not recovered.
More recently, however, such interpretations have been called into
question. Some holdings described as waste have a value, population
or resources assigned to them, which suggests that the term *wasta est*
does not indicate land lying deserted in 1086. It is much more likely
that the term, as it can be shown to do at a later date, should be taken
to indicate land which was not paying taxes, or for some other reason
was of no value to its lord.[76]

As we have already seen, Domesday Book sometimes disguises the
complexity of manorial organization because of its administrative
devices: in Lincolnshire, holdings in the same hundred as the manorial
centre are not always enumerated even if they lie in other vills.[77]
Furthermore, near-contemporary surveys reveal that Domesday Book
is concerned to record the resources and inhabitants of a manor which
contributed to the lord's income, and may omit the less burdened
peasants and their holdings.[78]

The manorial structure depicted by Domesday Book was far less
coherent and stable than has sometimes been supposed. It seems clear
that there was still much fluidity in territorial and tenurial organization. What Domesday Book reveals is a complex web of rights over
land, and the competing and sometimes contradictory nature of those
rights. Its rigid formulas sit very uneasily on the social reality of the
region. Few previous studies of Anglo-Saxon territorial organization in
the northern Danelaw have recognized this problem with their
traditional starting-point, Domesday Book.

The early origins of the manorial structure of the northern Danelaw

It is clear that the grouping of vills and settlements into multi-vill
territories was a central feature of Anglo-Saxon territorial organization. Recent studies have proposed that such territories often survive
into the eleventh century, when they were recorded by Domesday
Book. Do the multi-vill manors of the northern Danelaw represent,
then, the remnants of a much earlier and once widespread pattern of
territorial organization? This is indeed true of *some* of the multi-vill
sokes of the region, although it is not invariably true, and we need to
take account of *re*-grouping and reorganization. Moreover, whatever
survivals there are from an earlier era had been transformed as a
result of changes in the nature of lordship and seigneurial exploitation,

---

76.   Palliser, 'Domesday Book and the "harrying of the North"', 12–13.
77.   See p. 103 above.
78.   See Chapter 4, pp. 181–2.

administrative factors and the very process of the compilation of the Domesday survey itself.

It is important to be clear about what it is possible to achieve. In starting our discussion of Anglo-Saxon society with the evidence of Domesday Book and supplementing this with Anglo-Saxon charters, we are primarily concerning ourselves with evidence for lordship and aspects of tenurial organization, both of which had developed in significant ways through the Anglo-Saxon centuries. If we are to explore the notion that the sokes represent the remnants of earlier forms of organization, we must recognize that the relationship of sokes to other forms of territorial organization (tribal, royal, administrative, agrarian or ecclesiastical) is not necessarily straightforward or predictable. Accordingly, when we attempt to supplement our picture of early territorial organization with other types of evidence we must be aware that they may reveal aspects of territorial organization that were quite unconnected with lordship and tenurial organization.

Domesday Book and beyond

There is evidence to suggest that some of the larger sokes of the northern Danelaw were of great antiquity by the time that they were recorded in Domesday Book. A series of essentially reliable charters reveals that some of the sokes had origins in at least the mid-tenth century. For example, in 959 King Edgar granted Howden (Yorks) and its dependencies to 'the matron Quen'.[79] The dependencies of Howden which are named in the charter were all berewicks of the Domesday manor of Howden.[80] Clearly, then, the Domesday soke of Howden had existed in essence for over a century, and it had remained intact despite the fact that Howden had changed hands several times between 959 and 1086.[81] Howden is perhaps the clearest example from the region, but origins in or before the mid-tenth century can be suggested in a number of other instances. Although the berewicks of the manors of Sherburn in Elmet (Yorks) and Southwell (Notts) are unnamed in Domesday Book, later sources reveal that they must have included those places which are already recorded as their dependencies in charters dated to the mid-tenth century.[82] The Domesday manor of Parwich (Derbs) had berewicks at Alsop, Cold Eaton and Hanson,

---

79. S 681 (B 1052); *EYC*, 1, 12–15.
80. *DB*, fo. 304c. See Figure 31, below, p. 153.
81. Hugh Candidus records that Howden was granted to Peterborough Abbey by Edgar, then lost in the early eleventh century: *The Chronicle of Hugh Candidus*, ed. W.T. Mellows (1949), 64. In 1066 Howden was held by the king; it was later given to the Bishop of Durham: *DB*, fo. 304c. Howden had other Domesday berewicks, which are discussed below, pp. 152–3.
82. Stenton, *Types of Manorial Structure*, 79–80; S 659 (B 1029) and S 712 (B 1112); W. Farrer, 'Introduction to the Yorkshire Domesday', in *The Victoria History of the County of York*, vol. II, ed. W.M. Page (1912), 210.

and it is likely that this arrangement had its origins in the tenth century since another charter dated to 966 and issued by Edgar granted a relatively sizeable estate assessed at ten *mansae* at Parwich to the thegn Ælfhelm.[83] The manors of Ashford and Hope (Derbs) also each had large dependent sokes in the eleventh century. These also appear to have had origins in at least the early tenth century, for sometime before 911 Uhtred had purchased 60 *manentes* of land from vikings at Ashford and Hope.[84] Although the charter does not name any dependencies, it is likely that they already included the Domesday berewicks of the two manors.[85] It is apparent that these important soke centres were the focal points of substantial territories over a century and a half before the compilation of Domesday Book, and it is quite plausible that their Domesday berewicks belonged to the territories referred to by charters of the tenth century.

The division of individual vills into multiple manors, berewicks and sokelands may also be of some antiquity (although the component parts were not necessarily known by these terms at an earlier date). A few tenth- and eleventh-century charters indicate that lords at that date might possess rights over only portions of vills. For example, of the dependencies of Southwell recorded in 956, only portions of four of them pertained to Southwell: 'In Farnsfield the land of two men's lots pertain to Southwell; in Halam every sixth acre and three men's lots; in Normanton every third acre; in Fiskerton the two parts and four men's lots of all the land.'[86] In 1086 two bovates in Farnsfield were held by Walter d'Aincourt, although soke over one of those bovates belonged to Southwell; similarly, Walter held six bovates in Fiskerton of which the archbishop held the soke (presumably through his manor of Southwell). In Normanton three and a half bovates were held in 1086 by Gilbert of Ghent, and again the soke lay with Southwell.[87] Although the berewicks of Southwell are not named by the Domesday text it is almost certain that they included these three places; hence the tenurial divisions recorded by Domesday Book appear to have their origins in or before the middle of the tenth century. Similarly, in the cases of Sherburn in Elmet, Otley and Ripon the archbishop possessed rights over only parts of many of their dependencies in the tenth and eleventh centuries. Memoranda of the late-tenth century record that the archbishop's estates of Sherburn, Otley and Ripon had lost land, including half of Burley, Denton and *Byllinctun* from Otley; one hide in Stanley and two hides in Poppleton from Ripon; and half of

83. S 739 (B 1175); *Burton Abbey Charters*, 23–5; *DB*, fo. 272c.
84. S 397 (B 658); *DB*, fos. 272d, 273a.
85. Stenton, *Types of Manorial Structure*, 74–86.
86. *EYC*, 1, 5–10. The term 'manslot' is of Scandinavian origin, and means 'man's share'. It is a term that is used rarely, although it survived in usage as a familiar unit of land division in Norfolk into the thirteenth century: F.M. Stenton, *Anglo-Saxon England* (3rd edn, 1971), 514–15.
87. *DB*, fos. 288d, 290d.

Ceoredesholm and half of Cawood from Sherburn.[88] Pertaining to Sherburn *c.* 1030 were the following:

> two parts of Cawood ... two oxgangs in Flaxley, and half Barlow, and all Brayton except half a ploughland ... and all Burton except half a ploughland ... and five oxgangs in Haddlesey ... and all Fairburn except two and a half ploughlands, and two ploughlands in Ledsham and one in Newthorpe ... and all Fenton except half a ploughland, and two ploughlands and five oxgangs in Barkston.[89]

This suggests either that other lords may have had an interest in other parts of those vills, or that they were free of close seigneurial involvement.

It is not clear whether, or how far, such divisions antedate the tenth century. However, it seems likely that patterns of landholding were always sufficiently complex for them to have been present at an early date. Within any given vill it is plausible to expect that peasants of varying status lived alongside each other in the same rural communities, and we might expect there to have been free peasant landowners and their dependants, alongside the tenants of greater lords. Consequently the interests of great lords in the inhabitants of given vills may from an early date have been restricted to only those who were, strictly speaking, their tenants; lords did not necessarily have a close involvement with all the inhabitants of the lands over which they acquired rights, nor did they necessarily impinge on the property rights of those inhabitants. It seems clear that the land over which lords had the closest control, which they exploited most intensively (their inland, as it is often known), need not have been geographically coherent or located in the immediate vicinity of their dwelling-places. Again, this is an arrangement that goes back to at least the mid-tenth century, as can be seen from the example of Sherburn in Elmet, where in 963 the inland was spread among a number of places located up to ten miles away:

> These are the land-boundaries of the 20 hides at Sherburn of the inland. First on the south side: west along the brook to the 'herepath', northward along the way to 'Scearpan' bridge, eastward thence along the slade until it come to the way. And half a hide at *Hibaldestoft*, one hide at Fryston, two oxgangs at Hillam, two oxgangs at Lumby, two and a half hides at Milford and at Steeton and at Mickleford two hides and all at Lotherton except one hide and another half hide at Fenton and another half hide at Cawood.[90]

As we have seen, a similar situation seems to have obtained at Southwell at about the same time, where the Bishop Oscytel had rights

---

88.   *EHD*, I, no. 114.
89.   *EYC*, 1, 21–3; *EHD*, I, no. 114.
90.   *EYC*, 1, 19–21. See Figure 17 below, p. 127.

over scattered vills, and in some cases his rights were limited to the holdings of individual peasants.

In the entries for the larger sokes, Domesday Book sometimes appears to apply a formula which includes listing the dependent vills in groups of three, six, nine or twelve. This may reflect administrative arrangements, since it can often be shown that the sokes concerned had land in other vills. Although it is not certain where the origins of such a system lay, it is possible that they lie in at least the tenth century. In northern Derbyshire, for example, it is possible to identify a group of interlocking manors and sokes comprising five groups of twelve vills (including the manors of Darley, Bakewell, Ashford, Hope and Hathersage and their sokes, the twelve manors of Longendale and a number of other separate Domesday manors), and it has been suggested that these 60 vills are identical with the 60 *manentes* at Ashford and Hope acquired by Uhtred in the first decade of the tenth century. This arrangement was independent of the precise details of the Domesday manorial structure, since some of the vills were divided between manors.[91] The duodecimal arrangement of manors and their dependencies is a widespread phenomenon in the northern Danelaw, and it is possible that this is everywhere of much earlier origin than Domesday Book.[92] It would not be wise to press these numerological matters too far. Nonetheless, whatever the precise significance of these duodecimal groups of vills, Domesday Book reveals a layer of organization connected with estate management that is separate from that of the basic units of exploitation and which finds its origins before the later eleventh century.

Before the tenth century

There is circumstantial evidence to suggest that the origins of many Domesday sokes may lie before the tenth century. Several of the most important Domesday manors with large appurtenant sokes are known to have been important royal or ecclesiastical vills with substantial appurtenant territories before the viking settlements. In the late seventh century the abbot of Breedon on the Hill (Leics) acquired 31 *manentes* at Repton (Derbs), the site of a major Mercian royal monastery.[93] It is at least possible, then, that the origins of the Domesday soke of Repton lay many centuries earlier. In the seventh century Bishop Wilfrid acquired a monastery and 30 hides of land at

---

91.   D.R. Roffe, 'The origins of Derbyshire', *DAJ* 106 (1986), 102–22, at 120–1; *DB*, fos. 272b, 272d, 273a, 275c, 276a, 277b.
92.   Kapelle, *The Norman Conquest of the North*, 79–81.
93.   S 72 (B 48); for the identification of the *Hrepingas* named in the charter with Repton, see A. Rumble, '*Hrepingas* reconsidered', in *Mercian Studies*, ed. A. Dornier (1977), 169–71.

Ripon (Yorks).[94] The soke of Ripon recorded in documents of the later tenth and early eleventh centuries and in Domesday Book could therefore in principle have derived in essence from the grant to Bishop Wilfrid. Many other centres of the larger sokes were important ecclesiastical or royal vills in the pre-viking period, and we may assume by analogy that they would all have sat at the centre of a relatively substantial territory: these include Beverley, Whitby, West Gilling, Catterick, Conisbrough (Yorks), Southwell (Notts), Wirksworth and Bakewell (Derbs). Although we know little about the sokes of the region before the tenth century, and in most cases not before the compilation of Domesday Book, and it is, of course, likely that the composition of sokes may have changed over time, it is plausible that the Domesday sokes attached to these vills may have been derived in essence from much earlier estates. Moreover, whatever changes had taken place to the composition of estates between the pre-viking period and the compilation of Domesday Book, it is clear that the distribution of major estate centres across the region was broadly similar in the later eleventh century to the situation in the pre-viking period.

The possibility of continuity in the locations of major territorial focal points is suggested by documentary evidence, and is supported by both the locations and the place-names of some of the major soke centres, which suggest that they had long been places of importance. Many of the major manors with large appurtenant sokes are located near to Roman roads or ancient trackways, and thus were presumably in regionally accessible locations. A number of important territorial centres are located at, or very near to, important Roman sites. Derby, for example, is located close to the site of the second- to fourth-century fort at Little Chester, while Chesterfield, York and Lincoln were all the sites of Roman forts.[95] Southwell was preceded by a Roman villa, and Horncastle, Caistor (Lincs) and Catterick were the sites of Roman walled towns.[96] Continuity of occupation has not been demonstrated except at Lincoln, which, it has been postulated remained an important ecclesiastical and administrative centre through the fifth century and beyond, and one whose defences continued to be used.[97] The significance of the correspondence may be that the Roman sites were recognizable as former centres of authority, they provided accessible

---

94.   *HE*, iii, 25; *VSW*, c. 8; for a discussion of these lands, see G.R.J. Jones, 'Some donations to Bishop Wilfrid in northern England', *Northern History*, 31 (1995), 22–38.

95.   H. Wheeler (ed.) 'Roman Derby', *DAJ*, 105 (1986), *passim*; P. Ellis, 'Roman Chesterfield', *DAJ*, 109 (1987), 51–130; M.J. Jones, 'Roman Lincoln', in *Roman Lincolnshire*, ed. J.B. Whitwell (revd edn, 1992), xvii–xxiv.

96.   Lyth, 'The Southwell charter', 59; Whitwell, *Roman Lincolnshire*, 69–74; A. Tyler, *Survey of Roman Sites in North Yorkshire* (1980), 28–9.

97.   K. Steane and A. Vince, 'Post-Roman Lincoln: archaeological evidence for activity in Lincoln from the fifth to the ninth centuries', in *Pre-Viking Lindsey*, ed. A. Vince (1993), 71–9.

but defensible sites, and they provided a legitimacy to lordship which harked back to an earlier era. Indeed, it is not necessary to demonstrate, or to expect, continuous occupation to believe that lords recognized the importance of earlier centres of power in affirming their authority.[98] Many of the major estate centres are in topographically striking locations. Repton sits on a bluff overlooking the Trent, and Derby was situated in the peninsula created by the Derwent and the Markeaton Brook.[99] Sherburn is located on an outlier of the limestone ridge on which it sits, and in the East Riding of Yorkshire many of the more important soke centres were located along the coast (these include Bridlington, Mappleton, Aldborough, Withernsea, Easington and Kilnsea (Fig. 16)). Many of the major manors with large appurtenant sokes are located on good agricultural land, but are often on the edge of upland, and less extensively exploited and settled land, which is where many of their dependencies are located. The Domesday sokes of Pickering and Kirkby Moorside (Yorks) both contained land in the Vale of Pickering but also extended up to the high moors to the north, and, as has been mentioned, the sokes of Wakefield and Bolton-in-Craven both included numerous holdings located on the Pennine uplands.[100] It is also clear that where a major manor did not lie adjacent to a river, it often had access to one through its dependencies which were located near to one: this can be demonstrated in the cases of Gilling, Northallerton, Sherburn in Elmet and Kippax (Yorks).[101] It is notable that a number of the greater sokes straddle major rivers: for example, the soke of Otley lay on either side of the river Wharfe, and that of Ripon on either side of the river Ure. Such arrangements may well have early origins; if nothing else, the disposition of the great sokes reveals a concern to include a variety of resources, and they look much more like the tribute territories of an earlier era than the heavily exploited and more compact estates that emerged later.

The place-names of these important estate centres are commonly of the type deemed to be of early origin. Many refer to topographical features: for example, Southwell ('south spring', *wielle*); Ashbourne ('ash-tree stream', *burna*); Hope ('valley', *hop*); Mansfield ('open space near a river called Maun', *feld*); and Howden ('head valley', *heaford*, *denu*).[102] Others, such as Repton and Ripon, refer to groups of people. Waltham (Lincs) has a place-name derived from Old English *wealdham*, which has elsewhere been associated with important places connected

---

98. R. Bradley, 'Time regained: the creation of continuity', *JBAA*, 140 (1987), 1–17. It should, however, be noted that not all major Roman sites became Anglo-Saxon estate centres.
99. M. Biddle, 'Archaeology, architecture and the cult of saints in Anglo Saxon England' in *The Anglo-Saxon Church*, ed. L.A.S. Butler and R.K. Morris (CBA Res. Rep., 60, 1986), 1–31, at 22.
100. Hall, 'Pre-Conquest estates in Yorkshire', 26.
101. *Ibid.*, 25–6, 29.
102. *PN Derbs*, pt 2, 341; *PN Notts*, 123–4, 17500; *PN ERY*, 250–1.

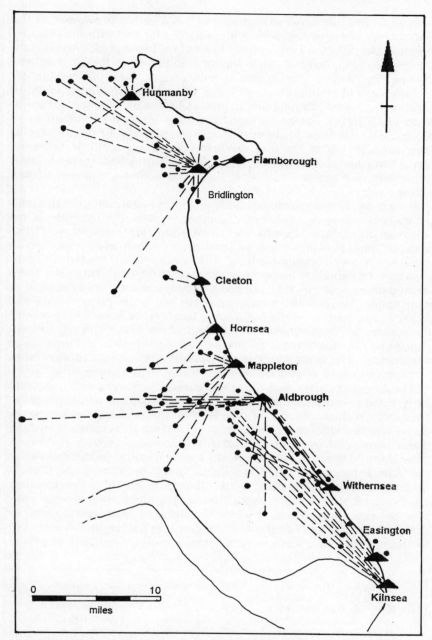

Figure 16 Major soke centres in the East Riding of Yorkshire

with royal hunting in woodland areas.[103] A significant number of the focal points of major sokes have place-names formed with the element *ingatun*: Bridlington, Doddington, Easington, Lissington, Nunnington, Patrington, Pocklington, Quarrington, Ridlington, Ruskington and Waddington.[104] The place-name element *-ingas*, meaning 'people of' or 'followers of', is regarded as being of early origin, and is found in conjunction with both personal names and the names of topographical features.[105] In the absence of early recorded forms it is difficult to be categorical, but it is likely that these place-names in -ington derive from the addition of *tun* to a name formed in *-ingas*. Little is known about the pre-viking status of these places, but by analogy with other important soke centres it is not unlikely that they were important pre-viking centres.

Such a pattern of characteristic features and continuity in the major estate centres has been observed in other regions. For example, in his work on Kent, Alan Everitt identified some forty places which he termed 'seminal places'; that is, focal places which were important in each successive development of the shire. They tended to have primitive Old English place-names (usually topographical); they were located on or near major rivers and trackways; most were located at or near major Roman settlements; and they were the *villae regales* and major estate centres of the region, the locations of 'minster' churches, the centres of hundreds and the locations of markets.[106] This pattern of continuity in the 'seminal places' of a region has now been demonstrated in many parts of the country, and seems to have been a common feature of Anglo-Saxon territorial organization.[107]

The frequent correlation of major Domesday manors with important early royal or ecclesiastical vills may, then, indicate a basic level of continuity in the territorial organization of the region from before the Scandinavian settlements. Is it, then, justifiable to suppose that if the major manors of Domesday Book were pre-viking territorial centres, their Domesday sokes may also be of such antiquity? In the absence of pre-tenth century charters it is difficult to say, but it might be thought to be plausible by analogy with other regions. This proposition, however, requires further exposition, and a number of caveats must also be expressed. First, it must be stressed that any element of continuity is first and foremost geographical in nature, and relates only to the constituent members of the sokes concerned. That is to say,

---

103. R. Huggins, 'The significance of the place-name *wealdham*', *Medieval Archaeology* 19 (1975), 198–201.
104. Hart, *The Danelaw*, 265.
105. J.McN. Dodgson, 'The significance of the distribution of English place-names in *-ingas*, *-inga-* in south-east England', *Medieval Archaeology*, 10 (1966), 1–29; M. Gelling, *Signposts to the Past* (1978), 104–21.
106. A. Everitt, *Continuity and Colonization: the evolution of Kentish settlement* (1986), 259–301.
107. J. Blair, *Early Medieval Surrey* (1991), 19–34; and the various contributions to S.R. Bassett (ed.) *The Origins of Anglo-Saxon Kingdoms* (1989).

although certain places may long have been associated with a given major vill, the nature of lordship, of forms of exploitation, of the obligations owed by the inhabitants of those places to the lord of the central vill, in addition to the settlement pattern, could and doubtless did change over time. We know that such changes had taken place in the decades prior to the compilation of the Domesday survey. For example, although the archbishop of York's estates at Otley, Ripon and Sherburn remained more or less intact between *c.* 1030, when they were recorded in memoranda, and 1086, the status of some of the members of those estates had changed during that time. In the memoranda there was a distinction between dependencies which were *agenland* (which seems to have included *inlande*, and is likely to have been synonymous with the term 'berewick') and sokeland; yet by 1086 the estates of Otley and Sherburn consisted solely of berewicks, and five of Ripon's earlier sokelands were described by Domesday Book as berewicks.[108] Assuming this to be more than merely a scribal convention, this suggests that the organization of these estates had changed between *c.* 1030 and 1086, and serves as a reminder that continuity of estate geography may mask changes in agrarian organization. If such a change could occur in the half-century before Domesday Book was compiled, then the likelihood that similar changes had taken place over the preceding centuries has to be allowed.

Second, it is certain that some sokes recorded in Domesday Book represent only the remnants of once larger estates. Late tenth-century memoranda record that the archbishop of York had lost land from his estates at Sherburn, Otley and Ripon (Figs. 17, 18, 19). It is not clear when the losses occurred, and while it is possible that they had occurred relatively recently, since the archbishop had only acquired Sherburn at some point since 963, when it had been granted to one Æslac, the memoranda may refer to much earlier losses – as a result of Scandinavian incursions, or even earlier attacks on their endowments (Fig. 17).[109] It also seems clear that the Domesday soke of Repton was significantly smaller than the estate of 31 *manentes* granted there to the abbot of Breedon in the seventh century. In 1086 the soke included just three berewicks and four sokelands. Together the manor of Repton and the berewick of Milton were assessed at six carucates, and the rest of the soke totalled just over nine carucates.[110] The land at Parwich granted to Ælfhelm in 966 was assessed at ten *mansae*, whereas in the eleventh century it, together with its berewicks, was assessed at four carucates. Assuming that this is more than a reassessment, it suggests that the territory attached to Parwich may have been diminished at some point between 966 and 1066. The dependencies of many sokes commonly incorporate only a portion of a

---

108. *EYC*, 1, 21–3; *DB*, fos. 302c, 303c, 303d.
109. *EHD*, I, no. 114; N.K. Blood and C.C. Taylor, 'Cawood: an archiepiscopal landscape', *YAJ*, 64 (1992), 83–102, at 83–5.
110. *DB*, fo. 272d.

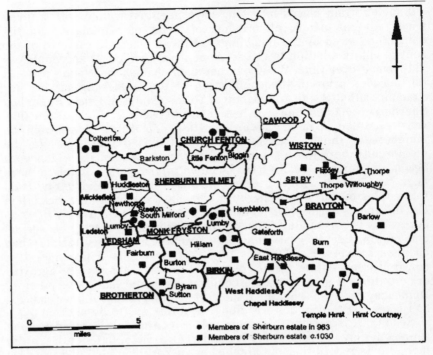

Figure 17 The soke of Sherburn in Elmet

vill, and although it is not impossible that this was an original feature of the estate, it may reflect in some instances the loss of parts of the soke, as would appear to be the implication of the late tenth-century memoranda concerning the estates of the archbishop of York's estates, which comment on the losses of portions of vills.[111] It is also often suggested that separate manors which are interspersed with the members of the larger sokes had once belonged to that soke. For example, were the separate Domesday manors which are interspersed with members of the sokes of Wakefield, Conisbrough, Mansfield, Newark, Kirton in Lindsey once part of the soke? This, however, is a dangerously circular argument, since it starts from the assumption of an earlier coherent pattern of territorial organization. We must, in sum, remain open to the possibility that many Domesday sokes represent the remnant of a once much larger predecessor, but we must caution against believing that all anomalies in the patterns of sokes can be explained only by reference to the diminution of a once larger soke, otherwise we could end up reconstructing sokes covering most of the region, and this would surely be approaching the absurd.

111.   *EHD*, I, no. 114.

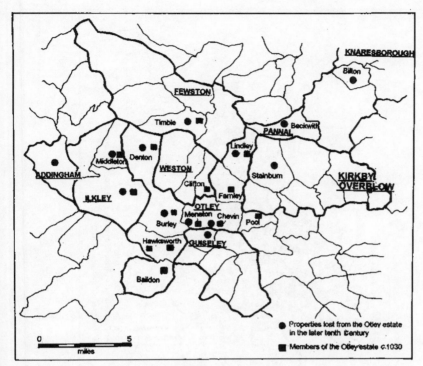

Figure 18 The soke of Otley

The suggestion that the large sokes of the northern Danelaw may have origins in the pre-viking period cannot be directly proved, but is plausible. We know from the evidence of the *Historia de Sancto Cuthberto* that further north, the leaders of the Scandinavian conquerors simply took over existing estates as going concerns and distributed them among their followers.[112] Meanwhile, the grants of large estates made by the West Saxon kings in the northern Danelaw generally give the impression of transferring or confirming existing arrangements, not of creating new estate structures.[113]

Setting aside these caveats, is it possible to develop the argument that some of the sokes of Domesday Book were of early origin? This suggestion that many of the sokes of the region were in essence of great antiquity by the eleventh century finds some support from the indirect evidence of parish boundaries and place-names. There are obviously difficulties inherent in using indirect evidence to reveal

---

112. C.D. Morris, 'Northumbria and the viking settlement: the evidence for land-holding', *Archaeologia Aeliana*, 5th ser., 4 (1977), 81–103.
113. Exceptions to this are discussed below, pp. 155–6.

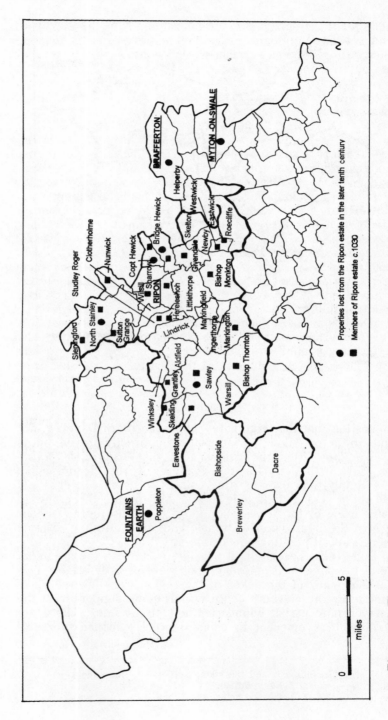

Figure 19 The soke of Ripon

patterns of territorial and estate organization. Nonetheless, some interesting and consistent patterns do emerge and it would be folly in a poorly documented region to dismiss this complementary body of evidence.

Parish boundaries

In southern and Midland England recent studies have suggested that the parochial geography of a region can reveal the extent of secular territories that existed as far back as the seventh and eighth centuries, as we have seen.[114] Despite the debates that have ensued about the antiquity of parish boundaries, few could plausibly deny that the pattern of parishes was established by the tenth century and that the main changes to this, subsequently, resulted from the subdivision of existing parishes. It is also apparent that parishes often remained intact even when the local estate structure changed.

That the parochial geography is useful to our discussion of Anglo-Saxon territorial organization is, then, suggested by studies undertaken in other regions, and, more to the point, by the evidence from the northern Danelaw itself. It is, for example, striking that many of the larger Domesday sokes of the region, including those known to be of tenth-century origin, are mirrored by the parochial geography; that is to say, outlying members of the soke are commonly located within the parish of the church which sat at the centre of the soke. Some parishes appear to have remained intact even when parts of the parish had been granted away as separate estates. For example, in Derbyshire, Newton (in Repton parish), Ballidon (in Bradbourne parish), Parwich (in Ashbourne parish) and Stanton (which was either Stanton-in-the-Peak in Youlgreave parish, or Stanton-by-Newhall in Stapenhill parish) were all the subject of mid-tenth-century charters but are known from later sources to belong to the parish of churches sited elsewhere.[115] Ranskill, Torworth and Bilby (Notts) were included in the estate of Sutton-by-Retford granted to the archbishop of York in 958, yet were members of Blyth parish.[116] The fact that Ashford was recorded as the focal point of a large territory by *c.* 911 and yet was a member of the parish of Bakewell may indicate that the parish had been defined by the first decade of the tenth century (Fig. 20).[117] Most

---

114. See Chapter 1, 38–9; Chapter 2, 88–90.
115. *Burton Abbey Charters*, 23–6, 37–9; Brooks, Gelling and Johnson, 'A new charter of King Edgar', 137–55; Hart, *Early Charters of Northern England*, 185–6. It is possible that the grant of two *manentes* at *Stantune* to Alchelm *c.* 900 indicates that one of the Derbyshire Stantons was a separate estate by 900.
116. D.M. Hadley, 'Danelaw society and institutions: east midlands' phenomena?' (Ph.D. thesis, University of Birmingham, 2 vols, 1992), 355–7.
117. It has, however, been argued that the land attached to Ashford in the early tenth century included Bakewell. Certainly the size of the assessment of the estate of Ashford and Hope (60 *manentes*) suggests that it included an area greater than the two Domesday sokes of Ashford (assessed at 22 carucates) and Hope (10

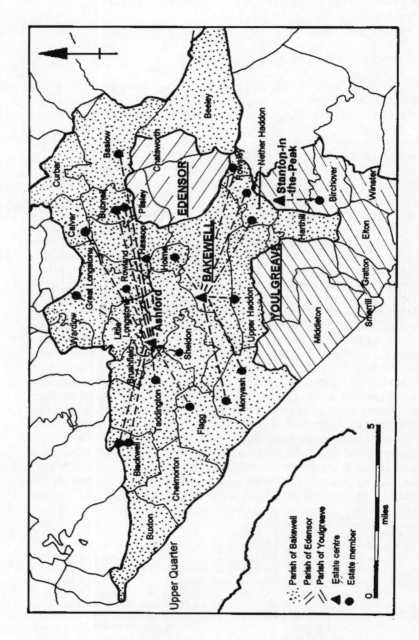

Figure 20 The sokes of Ashford and Bakewell

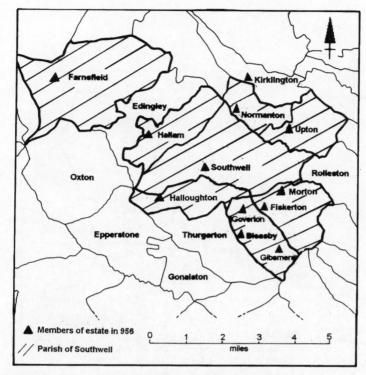

Figure 21 The parish and soke of Southwell

of the major Domesday sokes are not recorded before the later eleventh century, but many are mirrored by the parochial geography, and given that the estate centre is known to have been the location of an important pre-viking church (examples include Wirksworth, Southwell, Otley, Gilling and Masham[118]), it suggests that the pattern revealed by both the parochial geography and Domesday Book is, in essence, of great antiquity (Figs 21 and 22).

Given the apparently turbulent history of the region and the paucity of pre-Conquest documentary evidence, it is significant that one can demonstrate *any* correlations between secular territorial organization and the parochial geography, yet a remarkably consistent pattern does

---

cont.

carucates). It must, then, be allowed that Bakewell may have been a member of the Ashford estate; even so, it would provide a further example of a parish which mirrored an estate that existed as early as the early tenth century: see Roffe, 'The origins of Derbyshire', 120–1.

118. Hadley, 'Danelaw society and institutions', ch. 5, *passim*; R.K. Morris, *Churches in the Landscape* (1989), 134–8.

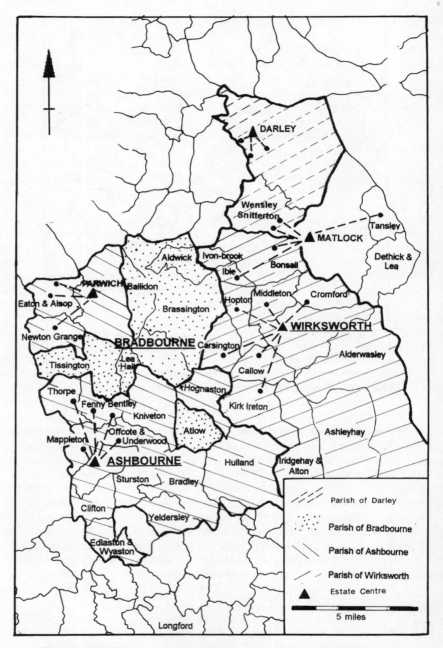

Figure 22 The parishes and sokes of Ashbourne and Wirksworth

emerge. In fact, the northern Danelaw, with its corpus of late Anglo-Saxon charters which record the dependencies of given vills, and the detailed Domesday record, which gives similar information, provides some of the best examples with which to test the hypothesis long since propounded that the parochial geography commonly mirrored secular territorial organization. Certainly there are difficulties with the approach: we cannot be certain of the types of territories mirrored by the parochial geography, and the date at which the parishes were created is unknown. Nevertheless, even allowing for these uncertainties, the pattern of parishes should not be dismissed, as it offers an additional, if indirect, perspective on territorial organization. A few examples demonstrate the potential of mapping the parochial geography of the region. The Domesday soke of Ashbourne was mirrored by its parish, although the parish also included the smaller soke of Parwich and a number of separate Domesday manors (Fig. 22). It is tempting to suggest that the soke of Ashbourne once included Parwich and these other manors.[119] The parish of Bradbourne is surrounded by members of the parish of Ashbourne and, again, we have to consider whether this is indicative of a once much larger soke and parish of Ashbourne. Similar conclusions might be drawn about the neighbouring soke of Wirksworth.

A number of unremarkable Domesday manors, and manorial dependencies, sit at the centre of large parishes, and it remains an interesting possibility that these parishes indicate the former extent of correspondingly large secular territories which had fragmented by the eleventh century. Examples include Blyth, West Markham (Notts), Stapenhill (Derbs), Wharram Percy, Darfield, Silkstone and Wath upon Dearne (Yorks).[120] Western Derbyshire was characterized in 1066 by single-vill manors, and by manors that comprised only a portion of a vill, yet a number of the parishes of the region are much larger, and include two or more vills (Fig. 23). The parochial geography of the region is complex, and the juxtaposition of neighbouring parishes suggests the probable outline of once larger parishes, which may, in turn, reveal the former existence of once larger estates. Despite the multiplicity of manors in given vills, most vills in the region were held as a single manor in 1086 by Henry de Ferrers, and this may be an indication that the whole area had once been held by a single lord. The

---

119. *DB*, fos. 272c, 273c, 274d, 275a–b, 276d, 277c.
120. *DB*, fo. 285b; *The Cartulary of Blyth Priory*, ed. R.T. Timson (2 vols, 1968), 1, xxxiii, lv–lix (Blyth); *DB*, fos. 284d, 285a; *Thoroton*, 3, 227 (West Markham); *DB*, fos. 273b, 278a; Hadley, 'Danelaw society and institutions', 236, n. 62 (Stapenhill); *DB*, fos. 301b, 331a; M. Beresford and J.G. Hurst, *Wharram Percy Deserted Medieval Village* (1990), 26 (Wharram Percy); *DB*, fo. 330c; P. Ryder, *Saxon Churches in South Yorkshire*, South Yorkshire County Archaeology Monograph, 2 (1981), 12 (Darfield); *DB*, fo. 316c; Ryder, *Saxon Churches*, 12 (Silkstone); see also Figure 47, below, p. 255; *DB*, fos. 319c, 330c; *Fasti Parochialis*, ed. A.H. Thompson and C.T. Clay, YAS Record Society, 107 (1943), 72 (Wath upon Dearne).

Figure 23 Parishes and Domesday manorial structure in western Derbyshire

location of Norbury ('north *burh*') and Sudbury ('south *burh*') to the north and south of this region respectively may offer some support to the speculation that the whole area once formed a single territory.[121] This may stretch the available evidence too far, but the fact remains that the parochial geography of western Derbyshire hints at larger groupings of vills than can be found in Domesday Book, where small manors predominate.

The parochial geography and the evidence of Domesday Book combine to provide many insights into Anglo-Saxon patterns of territorial organization. However, caution must be exercised. Derby provides an example of the difficulties of using this combination of

---

121. Hadley, 'Danelaw society and institutions', 285–97.

Figure 24 Derby and its vicinity

evidence in a sensible manner (Fig. 24). By the eleventh century the rural land attached to Derby comprised only Quarndon, Little Eaton and Little Chester. That Derby had once been the centre of a much larger territory is, however, suggested by the geography of the parishes attached to its numerous churches. The parish of St Peter's included Normanton, Osmaston and Boulton; St Michael's parish included Alvaston; and there are grounds for believing that the parish of the lost church of St Mary included Mickleover and possibly Willington.[122] If this can be taken as an indication of a large rural territory attached to Derby, its usefulness as evidence is limited by the lack of chronological parameters: neither its origins nor its

---

122. *Ibid.*, 336–43.

fragmentation into separate manors can be dated. Furthermore, it creates additional problems that have to be confronted: its amorphous shape, which lacks any clear boundaries between it and neighbouring parishes/sokes, and the fact that a number of the places referred to either had further dependencies or else were themselves dependencies of places other than Derby poses the problem of whether the territory attached to Derby was once even larger.[123] This matter cannot be easily pursued in the absence of any supporting evidence, but as the site of a pre-viking church associated with a saint's cult, and one of the early tenth-century *burhs*, it is not at all unlikely that Derby was the focal point for a substantial territory; but whether it was a unit of 'extensive lordship', an estate, a proto-shire, a proto-kingdom or some form of administrative unit is difficult to say. The available evidence suggests that it may have served as the focal point for any, or all, of those units, although they were not necessarily coterminous and the pattern of Domesday estate organization and parishes does not necessarily correspond consistently with any of them. What this evidence may indicate is the complexity of territorial organization at an early date – a complexity that cannot easily be unravelled by projecting ever larger sokes as we draw on ever more diverse bodies of evidence.

In sum, the parish boundaries of the region, because they were framed around secular territorial units that existed at some point in the Anglo-Saxon period, serve both to confirm the essential antiquity of some Domesday sokes, and to supplement the evidence of Domesday Book and Anglo-Saxon charters by suggesting the outline of secular territorial organization at an earlier date. However, new problems arise from the lack of correlation of estates and parish boundaries, which are, as we shall see, not necessarily resolved by the conflation of different types of evidence.

Place-names

The evidence of place-names lends further support to the argument that some Domesday sokes were of great antiquity. It has long been recognized that place-names of the type where a personal name is combined with *tun* (for example, Wollaston, 'Wulfric's *tun*', 'the estate/village of Wulfric') reflect changes in patterns of land-holding in the later Anglo-Saxon period.[124] As the large multi-vill territories believed to have characterized early medieval agrarian organization were dismembered, the closer association of individual lords with ever smaller estates commonly led to the commemoration of such lords in place-names. For example, it has been established that the place-

---

123.   *DB*, fos. 272d, 273b, 276d.
124.   N. Lund, 'Personal names and place-names: the persons and the places', *Onoma*, 19 (1976), 468–86; P.H. Sawyer, 'English medieval settlement: new interpretations', in *English Medieval Settlement*, ed. P.H. Sawyer (1979), 1–8.

names East Garston, Uffington, Woolstone (Berks), Bibury (Glos) and
Tredington (Worcs) all incorporate the personal name of a man or
woman who acquired that place at some point between the eighth and
eleventh centuries (Esgar, Uffa, Wulfric, Beage and Tyrdda, respectively).[125] Presumably these place-names replaced earlier names. Such
a process cannot be documented in the northern Danelaw, but it
presumably did occur, to judge from the numbers of place-names that
incorporate personal-name elements. The place-names of separate
manors commonly combine a personal name with *tun* or some other
habitative term (notably Old Norse *by*); *tun* carries an implication of
habitation ('farmstead' or 'village') or else of estate division ('enclosed
piece of land'; that is, 'a territory defined by a boundary').[126] Such
place-names are prevalent in the Trent valley in Nottinghamshire and
Derbyshire, where single-vill manors are comparatively more common.[127]

It may be significant, then, that by contrast such place-names are
comparatively rare among the constituent members of many of the
large sokes. These more commonly possess topographical place-names
and do not generally have place-names that incorporate personal
names, and this would appear to reflect the continuing integrity of
these sokes through the later Anglo-Saxon period. Where personal
names do occur among the place-names of these sokes, the second
element tends to be a topographical feature rather than a habitative
term. Whatever process saw individuals commemorated in such place-
names, it was seemingly not the same as that which resulted in the
creation of 'personal name + *tun*' place-names; that is to say,
apparently the dismemberment of large sokes to create small estates,
or 'manorial' holdings, and the more intensive exploitation of the land
and its inhabitants.[128] The presence of some personal names among
the place-names of these sokes may be accounted for both by the
fluidity of territorial organization – land might become attached or
reattached to a larger estate, having at some point been a separate
estate – and by the overlapping nature of rights over land, providing
contexts within which individuals could become associated with given
vills while at the same time the vill remained associated with some
larger grouping. However, the processes by which personal names
were combined with *tun*, or some other habitative element, seems to
mark a departure, and signals the point at which land was removed,
often permanently, from some larger territorial grouping to form a
separately controlled manorial-style property.

It is also striking that the members of the sokes likely to have been

---

125. Gelling, *Signposts to the Past*, 123–4, 180–3. Tredington is now in Warwickshire.
126. A.H. Smith, *English Place-Name Elements*, pt 2, EPNS, 26 (1956), 183–93.
127. K. Cameron, 'Scandinavian settlement in the territory of the Five Boroughs: the
      place-name evidence, pt III: The Grimston-hybrids', in *England before the
      Conquest*, ed. P. Clemoes and K. Hughes (1971), 147–63.
128. Gelling, *Signposts to the Past*, 185–6.

of greatest antiquity rarely have place-names of Scandinavian origin. For example, of the members of the tenth- and eleventh-century estate of Sherburn, almost all had Old English place-names; a few reveal scandinavianization in spelling or pronunciation, two combine a Scandinavian personal name with Old English *tun*, there are three names in *thorp* (which need not necessarily be of Scandinavian origin), but only one name (Lumby) is unambiguously Scandinavian.[129] Of the dependencies of Ripon named in tenth- and eleventh-century documents, there are very few examples of Scandinavian place-name elements (only Littlethorpe, which is not certainly Scandinavian, and possibly Wilsill, although that may contain an Old English rather than a Scandinavian personal name). Again personal names are rare, and occur only in conjunction with topographical elements. Of the dependencies of Howden named in the charter of 959, all but two had Old English place-names. Among the dependencies of Otley recorded in tenth- and eleventh-century sources, personal names are uncommon and Scandinavian elements less common still. The coining of Scandinavian place-names not uncommonly seems to have been associated with changes to estate organization, and it is significant, then, that many of the larger sokes have few Scandinavian place-names. The larger sokes, especially those that remained in ecclesiastical hands, seem not to have undergone major organizational changes, and therefore did not need new Scandinavian names, or names incorporating personal names, for parts of the estate.

In conclusion, the place-name evidence supports the conclusions that may be drawn from other forms of evidence, notably Anglo-Saxon charters, Domesday Book and parish boundaries, and permits us to suggest that a number of the large sokes described by Domesday Book were, in essence, of great antiquity. Our evidence is far from conclusive, but it is sufficiently consistent, and hence persuasive, to suggest that some of the characteristic features of the region in the eleventh century owe their origins to a much earlier time, although it is also apparent that there was change and development, as we should expect, and it is this that we now need to discuss in greater detail.

The diverse origins of the manorial structure of the northern Danelaw

It has often been assumed that the major dynamic in territorial organization during the Anglo-Saxon period was the fragmentation of large units into smaller, single-vill manors. There is some evidence to demonstrate that this process did indeed occur; but there is also

---

129.   P.H. Sawyer, *Kings and Vikings: Scandinavia and Europe, AD 700–1100* (1982), 103–4.

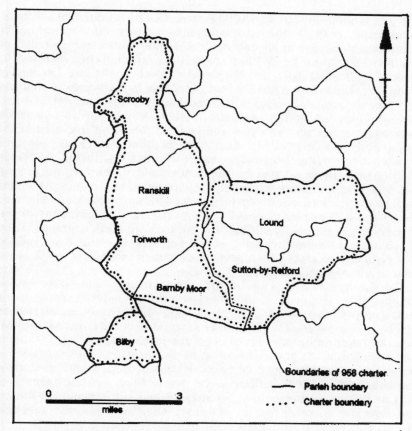

Figure 25 The tenth-century estate of Sutton-by-Retford

evidence to suggest that multi-vill sokes continued to be built up and to change their composition during the later Anglo-Saxon centuries.[130]

Although a number of the sokes of the northern Danelaw were undoubtedly of great antiquity, others were of recent origin or had been recently augmented. In 958 the archbishop of York acquired ten *cassati* of land at Sutton-by-Retford (Notts). The boundary clauses of the charter suggest that the grant included land in Lound, Scrooby, Torworth, Barnby, Ranskill and Bilby (Fig. 25). By 1066 only Lound and Scrooby were berewicks of Sutton, but a new group of sokelands had been attached to the estate.[131] There is little indication from the

130. E. Miller, 'La Société rurale en Angleterre (xe–xiiie siècles)', *Settimane*, 13 (1966), 111–34.
131. S 679 (B 1044); Davies, 'The Anglo-Saxon boundaries of Sutton and Scrooby', 13–22; *DB*, fo. 283b.

will of Wulfric Spott (*c*. 1004) that Conisbrough had a large appurtenant soke in the early eleventh century, but according to Domesday Book it had an enormous soke stretching across much of southern Yorkshire.[132] A charter of 1011 granted five *mansae* to Morcar of land at *Ufre*, or Mickleover (Derbs), yet the Domesday account of this manor suggests that the estate had undergone changes by 1066. In Domesday Book Mickleover and its three berewicks were assessed together at ten carucates, and its widely spread sokelands were assessed at six carucates and two bovates. The five *mansae* do not readily correspond to any part of the Domesday soke of Mickleover.[133] The Domesday soke of Howden included places additional to those named in the tenth-century charter, suggesting that new land had been acquired.[134] A charter of 963 names a number of dependencies of Sherburn in Elmet, and additional dependencies are named in a survey of *c*. 1030 (Fig. 17). The fact that many of the dependencies named *c*. 1030 are located at some remove from Sherburn and its dependencies of 963 suggests that these are indeed new acquisitions rather than properties named separately for the first time in the eleventh century.[135]

The Domesday sokes of Barrow upon Humber and Barton upon Humber (Lincs) appear to be different from the estate recorded in a tenth-century charter. A charter of 971, which granted Barrow to Bishop Æthelwold for the re-endowment of the monastery at Peterborough, indicates that only neighbouring Barton upon Humber was included in the grant. However, by the later eleventh century the situation was rather more complex: Earl Morcar's manor in Barrow had sokeland in Goxhill; there were two further separate manors in Barrow held by Earnwine and Siward in 1066; Ulfr's manor of Barton had sokeland in South Ferriby and Horkstow; and there was sokeland of Earl Harold's manor of Barnetby le Wold in Barton.[136]

These examples emphasize that although the core of Domesday sokes may be of great antiquity, land might have been lost and gained from the soke over time. Admittedly, it is possible that the charters and memoranda concerned did not consistently record dependencies of estates, and may, for example, have concerned themselves only with the dependencies whose inhabitants owed particular kinds of dues (the inland, perhaps). However, there is other evidence to suggest that the augmentation of estates was not uncommon.

On a general level it is of significance in this context that there is evidence to demonstrate that lords were clearly able to purchase land in the Danelaw, and that this may have been done with little

---

132. The will stipulated that the recipient of Conisbrough, Ælfhelm, had to give Burton Abbey 'a third of the fish', which might suggest that the estate then included the large fisheries at Tudworth: *Burton Abbey Charters*, xxv.
133. S 924; *Burton Abbey Charters*, 66–7; *DB*, fo. 273b.
134. *DB*, fo. 304c.
135. *EYC*, 1, 18–23.
136. *DB*, fos. 349b, 354c–d, 360b.

reference to the king. This is exemplified by the purchases made by Bishop Æthelwold for his abbey at Ely,[137] and a recension of the foundation charter of Thorney Abbey, written between 973 and 975, which records that Bishop Æthelwold had purchased a number of estates in Holland (Lincs) from Ealdorman Æthelwine, and soke over these lands was purchased later from the king.[138] A charter issued by Eadred to the thegn Ulfketel in 949 records that Ulfketel was to receive four *ruris cassatae* in 'Sutton' (probably Sutton on the Hill), with licence to buy a fifth hide.[139] By way of comparison, there is evidence that the community of St Cuthbert purchased land, or acquired land that someone else had purchased, in Northumbria in the tenth and eleventh centuries in what is now County Durham.[140] Late tenth-century memoranda concerning the archbishop of York's estates in Yorkshire also make references to both losses and recent acquisitions:

> These are the lands which Archbishop Oscytel obtained in Northumbria with his money and which were given to him in compensation for illegal marriage: one in Appleton which he bought for 24 pounds from Deorwulf. He bought Everingham for 44 pounds from Osulf's father ... and he bought the estate at Newbald for 120 mancuses of red gold from King Edgar; and Helperby was given to him in compensation for illicit cohabitation – there were two brothers who had one wife. ... And he bought Skidby for 20 pounds, and three hides at Bracken he bought from King Edgar.

At the end of the enumeration of the archbishop's lands it is stated that he held all of these lands until Æthelred II ascended, 'then St. Peter's [of York] was afterwards robbed [of them]'.[141] Even though none of these examples provides evidence of the creation of a soke, they suggest that the building up of estates by purchase, seizure or forfeiture was not uncommon.

The loss and acquisition by lords of parts of their multi-vill estates was clearly not uncommon, but it is rarely possible to be certain about the mechanisms by which land was lost or gained. The case of Helperby provides a rare, though partial, insight: as we have seen, Helperby and its soke were lost from the archbishop's soke of Ripon, but were later forfeited to the archbishop because the two brothers who held it were living in illicit union with one wife. Irrespective of the precise reasons for the changing composition of sokes, however, it is apparent that whatever the upheavals caused by the events of the late

---

137. *Liber Eliensis*, ed. E.O. Blake, Camden 3rd ser., 92 (1962), 75–117; S. Reynolds, *Fiefs and Vassals: the medieval evidence reinterpreted* (1994), 333–5.
138. C.R. Hart, *The Early Charters of Eastern England* (1966), 168, 170–1.
139. S 549 (B 876).
140. HSC, 208–9, 213–14.
141. EHD, I, no. 114.

ninth and early tenth centuries, they do not on their own account for disruptions to estate organization across the whole two centuries prior to the compilation of Domesday Book.

Once a lord had acquired land by purchase or forfeiture or any other means, there was little to prevent him from grouping and regrouping his lands as he saw fit. There would be little to prevent him from transferring the dependencies of one estate centre to another, or from attaching newly acquired, and separate, properties to one of his existing estate centres.[142] This may have been true especially in those cases where the lord enjoyed rights over the land concerned that were administrative and jurisdictional in nature, rather than being based on more intensive exploitation involving the imposition of labour services. The concerns of late Anglo-Saxon estate management may also have been instrumental in causing significant alterations to be made to existing patterns of estate organization. For lords with dispersed holdings it may have proved more attractive to group them under the control of a single administrative centre, rather than try to maintain some form of administrative machinery on every parcel of land they held.

There is reason to think that the recorded examples of sokes losing or gaining dependencies between the mid-tenth century and the later eleventh century may have been just the tip of an iceberg. We should consider, in turn, the evidence of the complex spatial distribution of the Domesday sokes, of their place-names, and of the lack of correspondence between sokes and either wapentakes or parishes. This evidence suggests that the sokes of the northern Danelaw had many different and piecemeal origins and that the fashion for interpreting them all as relics of ancient organization should be resisted.

The spatial distribution of sokes

Many sokes present such a complex and overlapping pattern on the ground as to raise questions about their antiquity. One possible explanation for such complex arrangements lies in the fragmentation of larger sokes into a number of smaller sokes. Where neighbouring manors each have dependencies in the same vills, such an explanation appears appropriate. For example, the Domesday manors of Sleaford, Kirkby la Thorpe and Ewerby Thorpe (Lincs) each had dependencies in Howell, Heckington, Quarrington, Laythorpe and Evedon (Fig. 26), and it has been proposed that that was the result of the subdivision of a single soke, based probably on Sleaford.[143] It is not implausible that the requirements of inheritance, for example, might have resulted in the division of a single soke into such a complex and interwoven pattern of smaller sokes.

---

142. For examples in another region, see Faith, *The English Peasantry*, 171–2.
143. Roffe, *The Lincolnshire Domesday*, 11.

Bishop of Lincoln	The king	Kolsveinn
M Sleaford	M Kirkby la Thorpe	M Ewerby Thorpe
S Ewerby	S Ewerby Thorpe	M Heckington
S Howell	S Howell	S Howell [of Kirkby la Thorpe]
S Heckington	S Heckington	M Laythorpe
S Quarrington	S Quarrington	B Evedon [of Kirkby la Thorpe]
S Laythorpe	B Evedon	
S Evedon		

Figure 26 Manorial organization in the vicinity of Sleaford

Similarly, the double sokes of Claxby, Rigsby, Kirkby-on-Bain and Great Sturton (Lincs) may well have resulted from the division of four single sokes, since the two soke centres located in each vill had dependencies in the same neighbouring vills.[144] It is possible that estates were dismembered in this way, rather than divided into separate blocks, because it allowed the recipients of the divided estate to maintain the existing administrative arrangements in the vills. Very rarely is there explicit evidence that a soke had once formed part of some larger soke, although in the case of Helperby it seems probable that its small soke (which included Myton, *Wisbustan*, Tholthorpe, Youlton and Thorpe) was carved out of the soke of Ripon, as we have seen, but the composition of neighbouring sokes suggests the fragmentation of a once larger estate.

Some of the sokes recorded by Domesday Book were, then, simple divisions of pre-existing estates. However, other overlapping sokes may indeed reflect ancient arrangements. It has been suggested that the reason the Domesday manor of Bardney (Lincs) had sokeland located at some distance in Candleshoe wapentake was that the ecclesiastical community at Partney had been a daughter cell of Bardney in the pre-viking period, and the Candleshoe sokelands represent the initial endowment of Partney.[145] This hypothesis reminds us that Anglo-Saxon lords had long had interests spread over wide areas, and it is not implausible that their lands should have, from an early date, been dispersed, and that early medieval territories may not have been regular and coherent. We certainly need not suppose that all the land between a soke centre and its furthest-flung dependency had once belonged to that soke, despite a recent attempt to do just that in Nottinghamshire.[146] Any such interpretation necessitates entirely arbitrary judgements about which overlapping sokes should be given chronological priority. Why, for example, should

---

144. *DB*, fos. 340c–d, 355b, 355c, 359d, 365c; see also Hart, *The Danelaw*, 239, 244.
145. Hart, *The Danelaw*, 243.
146. For an extreme example of this approach, see M.W. Bishop, 'Multiple estates in late Anglo-Saxon Nottinghamshire', *TTS*, 85 (1981), 37–47, at 42–5.

M Conisbrough	Members of the soke:	
	Ravenfield*	Bramley
	Clifton*	Aughton
	Braithwell*	Whiston
	Barnbrough	Warmsworth*
	Hoyland	Dinnington*
	Bilham	Anston
	Dalton*	Stainforth
	Wilsic*	Kirk Bramwith
	Harthill*	Fishlake*
	Kiveton	Thorne*
	Aston*	Tudworth*
	Kirk Sandall*	Hatfield*
	Greasbrough*	Streetthorpe*
	Cusworth*	Long Sandall*

* Within the parish of Conisbrough

Figure 27 The soke of Conisbrough

we believe the recent suggestion that Mansfield once included the manor and soke of Southwell, on the grounds that the Domesday soke of the former overlaps Southwell and its soke, rather than vice versa?[147] A similar problem is presented by the extensive soke of Conisbrough (Fig. 27). Certainly Conisbrough was the site of a probable eighth-century church, and the church or its founder may have been provided with a sizeable landed endowment, but it is quite another matter to reconstruct that endowment from the Domesday soke and the smaller sokes which it overlapped, not least because the early eleventh-century will of Wulfric Spott gives no indication that Conisbrough had an appurtenant soke at that date.[148] Similarly questionable is the suggestion that the sokes of Ripon, Aldborough and Knaresborough once formed a single estate, on the grounds that a few vills contained dependencies of two of these manors in the eleventh century. Even if this were the case, it would be difficult to determine the original estate centre.[149] Many studies of the northern

147. The same applies to the other major manors whose sokes are interspersed with that of Mansfield, such as Dunham, Laneham, Sutton and Bothamsall; *ibid.*, 45.
148. *DB*, fos. 307d, 308b, 319a, 319d, 321b–d. On the possibility that Doncaster was an Anglo-Saxon *burh*, see M.S. Parker, 'Some notes on the pre-Norman history of Doncaster', *YAJ*, 59 (1987), 29–43.
149. G.R.J. Jones, 'Multiple estates and early settlement', in *English Medieval Settlement*, ed. Sawyer, 9–34, at 29–32. It is argued that the three sokes were subdivisions of the wapentake of Burghshire, which, it is postulated, had its origins in the territory attached to the Roman cantonal capital of the Brigantes, *Isurium Brigantum* (Aldborough). Although this is not impossible, the map produced by Professor Jones omits to record that the estate of Ripon is not confined to the wapentake, and that manors outside the wapentake, including Otley and Cundall, included land within Burghshire.

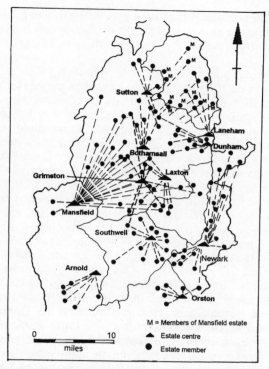

Figure 28 Manorial organization in northern Nottinghamshire

Danelaw have adduced fragmentation of once larger sokes to explain
the complex pattern revealed by Domesday Book, and in the context of
a study of a handful of sokes this is an appealing explanation. Yet when
we look at the region as a whole, the pattern is too complex for such an
explanation to carry much validity. It is surely an over-simplification.
The Domesday soke of Mansfield, for example, stretched right across
northern Nottinghamshire, as did the soke of Sutton-by-Retford (Fig.
28). Along with the sokes of Laneham and Bothamsall this created an
extremely complex pattern of territorial organization. Several vills
were divided between two or more of these sokes in the eleventh
century: Ranby was a sokeland of Mansfield and was also described as
being 'of Bothamsall';[150] similarly, both manors had attached sokeland
in Hodsock.[151] That this represents the remnants of a former single
soke may not be the only plausible explanation in this instance, or in
the case of many other examples of complex soke distribution. Rights
over land were complex and varied throughout early medieval society,

---

150.   *DB*, fo. 281b.
151.   *Ibid.*, fo. 285b.

and there is reason to doubt that land was invariably organized in neat and coherent units, or that the situation in the eleventh century could only have come into being through the dismemberment of a once orderly pattern.

It is also striking that many sokes are divided in Domesday Book into two groups, one comprising dependencies clustered around the manorial centre, the other dependencies in far-flung vills. This may simply reflect administrative convenience, but it may be an indication that the two groups had different origins. For example, the soke of Mansfield was divided into two groups by Domesday Book, and the second group, in Oswaldbeck wapentake, may have been a more recent acquisition. Rights of soke in Oswaldbeck wapentake had clearly been divided, and soke over much land there was attached to the archbishop of York's manor of Laneham; the rights of the king were granted to the archbishop in a writ of 1065, but the thirteenth-century Hundred Rolls confirms that the archbishop's lands in Oswaldbeck had formerly been part of a larger estate in Oswaldbeck.[152] Similarly, the soke of Newark-on-Trent comprised two groups, one near to the manor, the other further away (Fig. 28). That the latter group had undergone some changes is suggested by its anomalous protusion into Lincolnshire and by the fact that the sokeland at South Scarle is in Nottinghamshire whereas adjacent North Scarle is in Lincolnshire.[153] Domesday Book lists the sokeland of Greetham (Lincs) in a number of groups, each with a shared assessment, list of resources and liability for the geld; the first three are in Calcewath wapentake, the next two in Candleshoe, the next two are on the coastal marshland and the last one comprises members of Hill wapentake (Fig. 29).[154] This soke has all the hallmarks of a piecemeal creation. The members of some sokes were clearly recent additions since they lay on newly reclaimed lands. These tend to be vills on the fen edges and along the coastal plain. The soke of Gayton (Lincs), for example, is a most unusual soke in that most of its members were located many miles away on the coastal marsh; it is likely to have been of late foundation.[155] Such a soke need not, however, have been the result of reclamation conducted by the lord of Gayton manor; it may well have been carried out by the sokemen situated there, whose lands were later attached to the manor of Gayton.

---

152. *Ibid.*, fos. 281a–c, 283a; *Anglo-Saxon Writs*, ed. F.E. Harmer (1952), no. 119; Roffe, *The Lincolnshire Domesday*, 11, n. 56.
153. *DB*, fo. 283d.
154. *Ibid.*, fo. 349a; Hart, *The Danelaw*, 240–1.
155. Hart, *The Danelaw*, 239, 241, 244.

Entry	Dependencies of Greetham	Wapentake
1	Legbourne	Calcewath (detached part)
2	Swaby, Belleau, Thoresby, Claythorpe, Tothill	Calcewath
3	Withern, Aby, Haugh, Calceby	Calcewath
4	Sutterby, Dalby, Dexthorpe	Candleshoe
5	Fordington, Ashby, Bratoft, *Langene*	Candleshoe
6	Wainfleet, Haugh, Calceby, Theddlethorpe, Mablethorpe	Calcewath (ex. Wainfleet)
7	Huttoft, Thurlby, Sutton, Trusthorpe, Bilsby, Markby	Calcewath
8	Langton, Hagworthingham, Salmonby, Tetford, Brinkhill, Winceby, Claxby	Hill

Figure 29 The soke of Greetham

Parochial geography and sokes

It is certain that there was no uniform or linear progression in territorial organization in the region; the very distribution of sokes and the organization of manors in the eleventh century argues against this. It is, furthermore, not uncommon that the evidence of Domesday Book, of tenth-century charters, of place-names and of parochial geography quite fails to reveal neat patterns of ancient arrangements. We have already seen the difficulties exposed by parochial geography and manorial structure around Derby, and across the region there is the recurrent danger that in combining the evidence of the spatial distribution of sokes in Domesday Book with that of tenth-century charters, parochial geography and of place-names, it would be possible to link any number of places to each other and to project a whole host of putative earlier sokes that may in fact never have existed.

The example of Chesterfield (Derbs) raises a number of questions concerning the combination of types of evidence. The parish of Chesterfield included the chapelries of Wingerworth, Walton and Brampton and also included Tapton, Whittington, Brimington, Calow, Hasland, Newbold, Eckington and Boythorpe.[156] In Domesday Book Chesterfield was a berewick of Newbold along with Whittington, Brimington, Tapton, Boythorpe and Eckington. Presumably Newbold ('new building/*bodl*') had recently, and seemingly temporarily, replaced Chesterfield as the estate centre, since shortly afterwards Chesterfield was referred to as a manor in its own right.[157] According to Domesday

---

156. See Hadley, 'Danelaw society and institutions', 268–75. The Eckington in the Domesday entry is probably to be associated with the place of this name in Newbold, rather than the parish of Eckington to the east of Chesterfield: P. Riden, *History of Chesterfield* (1984), 2–3.
157. It has, however, been suggested that estate centres and early churches were commonly located adjacent to, but not at the exact same location as, each other: J. Blair, 'Minster churches in the landscape', in *Anglo-Saxon Settlements*, ed. D. Hooke (1988), 35–58, at 40–8.

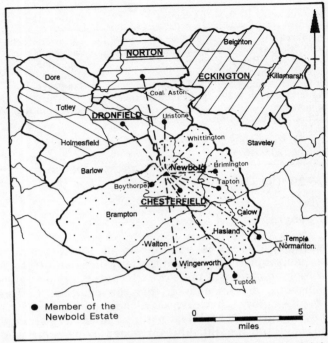

Figure 30 Manorial organization and parishes in the vicinity of Chesterfield

Book, Newbold also had sokeland in ten other places, many of which were outside the parish of Chesterfield (Fig. 30).[158] That both the soke and the parish were of early origins is plausible given the status of Chesterfield as the only Roman military site in north-eastern Derbyshire, and possessing what was clearly a church of superior status.[159] However, the fact that the Domesday manorial pattern and parochial geography in the area show such a lack of correspondence gives cause for concern about the merits of combining types of evidence. This evidence suggests, at the very least, that the manorial organization described by Domesday Book had arisen piecemeal, at a different rate from the creation of the local parish structure, and not through a straightforward process of dismemberment of a once larger estate.

On a related issue, it is possible to cite examples in which the evidence of Domesday Book and that of the parochial geography appear to point in contrary directions. For example, the inhabitants of the sokeland of

158.　*DB*, fo. 272b.
159.　Hadley, 'Danelaw society and institutions', 268–75; *DB*, fo. 272b. On the church at Chesterfield, see Chapter 5, pp. 273–4.

Melbourne located in Osmaston and Normanton were members of the parish of St Peter's in Derby;[160] in seeking to reconstruct earlier territorial organization would we be better advised to place our faith in the evidence of Domesday Book or of parish boundaries? Or should we combine our evidence, in which case we would have to bring the estates and parishes of Repton and Derby into the equation?

The fact that some parts of sokes are mirrored by the parochial geography whereas others are not may, in fact, indicate that the composition of sokes had altered. For example, the parish of Sutton-by-Retford included Lound and Scrooby, which had been part of the estate of Sutton since at least 958, but none of the places either lost or gained between 958 and 1066. Some of the places lost from the estate were in the neighbouring parish of Blyth, suggesting that parish boundaries remained at least partly resistant to changes in the estate structure.[161] The relationship between the soke and parish of Mickleover suggests that the soke was created piecemeal. The Domesday soke was comparatively widely spread and contained most of the recorded sokeland in the wapentake of Appletree, although Mickleover itself was in Litchurch wapentake. Mickleover's three berewicks are located close to the manor and were within the parish of Mickleover, whereas its sokelands were widely spread and were not members of the parish. The evidence of place-names, supports the conclusion that the sokelands were recent additions: the three berewicks of Mickleover have topographical place-names whereas two of its sokelands (Snelston and Dalbury) have a place-name containing a personal name.[162] The place-name evidence, the spatial distribution of the sokelands, the relationship between the soke and the wapentake, and the parochial geography suggest possible stages in the construction of the soke of Mickleover. In addition, the early eleventh-century charter relating to Mickleover also indicates change, given the discrepancy in assessment between then and 1086, as we have seen.[163]

The relation of the various rural institutions to each other was rarely simple and in many parts of Lincolnshire and Yorkshire, in particular, their relationship was especially complex. In Kesteven a recurrent pattern has been identified of parish churches situated on the better soils and dependent chapels in the less accessible, less favourable locations. This has been used to support an argument for settlement expansion: the distribution of churches apparently represents the primary settlement zones, and the chapelries reflect the later colonized land.[164] Yet when compared with the evidence of

---

160.   *DB*, fos. 272c–d; *The Cartulary of Darley Abbey*, ed. R.R. Darlington (2 vols, 1945), nos. F45, F108, F112, O12, Axiii, Axvi.
161.   Davies, 'The Anglo-Saxon boundaries of Sutton and Scrooby'; Hadley, 'Danelaw society and institutions', 355–7.
162.   *PN Derbs*, pt 2, 464–5, 478–9, 483–4.
163.   See p. 140 above.
164.   D.M. Owen, 'Chapelries and rural settlement: an examination of some of the Kesteven evidence', in *English Medieval Settlement*, ed. Sawyer, 35–40.

Domesday Book it can be seen that the parochial geography is sometimes at odds with the pattern of manorial organization. For example, Marston, which was a chapelry of Hougham, contained a number of Domesday manors, a sokeland belonging to Hough-on-the-Hill, a berewick of Haceby, and sokeland in Dry Doddington and Hougham. The crucial point is that the only connection between the two places in the manorial sphere shows Hougham to have been a dependency of Marston, yet in the ecclesiastical sphere Marston was a dependency of Hougham.[165] Similarly, a cogent argument presented by Harold Fox concerning the development of settlement on the Wolds sits uneasily with the evidence of both Domesday Book and the parochial geography. He has argued that Wolds settlement commonly originated as dependent holdings of low-lying, valley estates, and were probably used as summer pastures. Later they became separate estates and permanent settlements, and they were often characterized as small villages, with relatively small vills and two open fields. This is a persuasive and plausible conjecture.[166] Yet it is sometimes contradicted by the evidence of Domesday Book, since some of the Wolds settlements in Lincolnshire were major manors with dependencies in valley settlements (such as Barnetby-le-Wold and Caistor on the Wolds), and by the evidence of the parochial structure, since some Wolds settlements had churches with chapels, rather than themselves being chapels of valley churches, which is what the Fox thesis would lead us to expect.[167] In general, the organization of Domesday manors and parishes reveals a more complex series of developments than either Owen or Fox allows for. This does not discredit their arguments, but rather reveals that developments in agrarian exploitation, estate structure and ecclesiastical organization did not always coincide, and cautions against reliance on any one type of evidence as a means of understanding the origins and development of territorial organization.

Wapentakes and sokes

Another reason for believing that sokes might be put together piecemeal derives from the juxtaposition of wapentake and soke boundaries. There are a number of manors which have attached to them most of the sokeland and sokemen in a given wapentake. For example, Mansfield, Newbold, Mickleover and Melbourne (Derbs) have Domesday sokes which include most of the recorded sokeland and sokemen in the wapentakes of, respectively, Oswaldbeck, Scarcliff,

---

165. *DB*, fos. 347d, 357b, 358c, 366c, 367d; Owen, 'Chapelries and rural settlement', 36.
166. H.S.A. Fox, 'The people of the wolds in English settlement history', in *The Rural Settlements of Medieval England*, ed. M. Aston, D. Austin and C.C. Dyer (1989), 77–101.
167. This is not an oversight on the author's part as Harold Fox does not discuss the Lincolnshire evidence in his article. On estates on the Wolds, see Hart, *The Danelaw*, 233–6.

Litchurch and Appletree. Stenton observed that such sokes give the impression of having resulted from 'a royal grant to thegn or earl of the king's rights over all the unattached free men dwelling within a given wapentake'.[168] A similar conclusion may be drawn from the disposition of sokes. The soke of Greetham, for example, overlaps the smaller sokes of Rigsby, Candlesby, Claxby and Willoughby.[169] It is open to debate whether these smaller sokes were carved out of the soke of Greetham, or whether the last was created by attaching to Greetham all the sokemen and sokeland of the wapentakes of Calcewith and Candleshoe that were not already at that point attached to other sokes. Such complex soke arrangements would be what we might expect to find if there had been a process of 'mopping up' the unattached sokemen and sokelands of a region.

Place-names and sokes

It is also significant that many of the sokes of the region include members with place-names that incorporate personal names. As has been noted, this is not a feature common to those sokes known to be of greatest antiquity. One possible explanation of this phenomenon is that part of a vill had been granted away to a person after whom the whole vill subsequently became known. However, many of the places which incorporate personal names in their nomenclature belonged totally to a larger soke, according to Domesday Book. This lends support to the argument that such places had not always formed part of that soke, but had formed a separate estate, presumably held at some point by the person whom the place-name commemorates. As we have noted, all but two of the dependencies of Howden named in a charter of 959 possess Old English place-names; yet the dependencies recorded in Domesday Book, which include more named properties than in 959, include a much higher percentage of Scandinavian place-names. These places may have been acquired since 959, or else they represent newly founded settlements, or settlements separately assessed for the first time (Fig. 31).[170] It is also notable that several of these new Scandinavian place-names incorporate personal names.[171] This suggests that changes to the organization of territories might result in the coining of new place-names, and in the cases of sokes not recorded before 1086 we might be able to conclude that many of the places with

---

168. Stenton, *Types of Manorial Structure*, 45.
169. *DB*, fos. 339d, 343a–b, 349a, 355b–c, 356c, 360a, 370d.
170. *DB*, fos. 304c, 381c. The boundaries of the Howden charter of 959 pose some problems. It is not obvious whether the western boundary should be taken to include Asselby and Barmby (which are not named in the charter) or whether it followed the later vill boundary between Knedlington and Asselby (thus excluding Asselby and Barmby). Recent work has suggested that the latter solution is the more appropriate: Long, 'Howden and Old Drax', 129.
171. *PN ERY*, 247–66.

Members of the Howden estate in 959	Members of the Howden estate in Domesday Book
Knedlington	Knedlington
Barnhill	Barnhill
Cavil	Cavil
Thorpe**	Thorpe
Hive	Hive
Eastrington	Eastrington
Belby**	Belby
Kilpin	Kilpin
	Owsthorpe**
	Portington
	Yokefleet
	Cotness
	Saltmarshe ~
	Laxton
	Skelton ~
	Asselby**
	Barmby**
	Babthorpe**
	Barlby*

**   Scandinavian place-name
*   Partly Scandinavian place-name
~   Scandinavianized name

Figure 31 The soke of Howden

Scandinavian place-names or personal name elements in their names had undergone various transformations in their status.

There are, however, alternative interpretations of the distribution of place-names incorporating personal names. We have already discussed the fact that some of the groupings of property in Domesday Book were artefacts of the Domesday text. Some vills were held by one lord as a separately managed estate, but one over which some other lord had residual rights, which might result in the vill being entered as a sokeland rather than as a separate manor. Thus a property might be for all intents and purposes a separate estate, which might in time come to adopt the name of its lord, yet still owe some dues to the lord of another estate. The incidence of place-names comprising a personal name and a habitative element among the larger sokes is so great, even among the berewicks, that we have to suppose one of two explanations: either they reflect newly acquired (or reacquired) property, or they are the product of complex arrangements in which more than one lord had interests in the same land, both the lord of the soke and an immediate lord whose name was borne by the property.

Synthesis

A common pattern emerges from a study of the sokes of the northern Danelaw concerning the distribution of berewicks/inland and soke-lands. Berewicks were normally located closer to the manorial centre. This is not surprising since the inhabitants of berewicks were more likely to have been burdened with regular labour services than were the sokemen inhabitants of sokelands. Although the renders from sokelands were certainly important to the income of the manor, it would have been much easier for lords to transfer them to another manor, or to sell or grant them to other lords because they owed little in the way of labour services on the lord's demesne. Berewicks tend to be located within the parish of the manor to which they were attached, and to have Old English, rather than Scandinavian, place-names, which less commonly incorporate personal names. Hence a combination of evidence indicates that the berewicks of the region had, on the whole, long been associated with the soke centre to which, according to Domesday Book, they were attached. By contrast, there are grounds for believing that the sokelands of manors may often have been more recent acquisitions, and were much more fluid in their attachment.

Thus there is evidence to suggest that although continuity was certainly one characteristic feature of territorial organization in the northern Danelaw during the later Anglo-Saxon period, some of the larger sokes of the northern Danelaw were put together piecemeal, were more fluid in their organization and were not of great antiquity when they were first recorded in Domesday Book. This serves as a warning against the unquestioning acceptance of later sources as a guide to earlier territorial organization, as well as revealing the continuing complexity and vitality of society and its organization in the later Anglo-Saxon centuries.

Lordship and royal authority in the tenth and eleventh centuries

Despite the scarcity of evidence relating to lordship and royal authority, there are sufficient pointers to suggest that patterns of land-holding may not have been especially stable in the northern Danelaw during the tenth and eleventh centuries. The viking raids and settlement are likely to have disrupted existing patterns of land-ownership, especially that of the church. However, it is also important to note that we have evidence that some land held by the church in the mid-tenth century, or the early eleventh century, had passed out of ecclesiastical control by 1066.[172] Moreover, the conquest of the Danelaw by the West Saxons changed patterns of land-holding. The West Saxon rulers seem to have prepared for the conquest of the

---

172. See Chapter 5, pp. 285–6.

region by encouraging their nobles to purchase land from the Scandinavians. The charter issued by Athelstan to Uhtred concerning land at Ashford and Hope stated that Uhtred had purchased this land from the heathens for 20 pounds of gold and silver at the command of King Edward and Ealdorman Æthelred.[173] At the same time, Athelstan confirmed to one Ealdred land at Chalgrave and Tebworth (Beds) that he had purchased from the heathens for ten pounds.[174] There are other indications of the interest of the West Saxon kings in land-holding in the Danelaw. It has been noted that there is a peculiar lull in the issuing of grants of land in the reigns of Alfred and Edward the Elder, with a complete cessation in the period 910–24. Assuming this to be more than chance, David Dumville has argued that this was deliberate policy on the part of the West Saxon kings, and that this may have been a time when they rewarded loyal followers with land in the Danelaw.[175] The *Liber Eliensis* alleges that Edward the Elder redistributed land on a massive scale in Huntingdonshire after he captured Huntingdon in 917.[176] Whatever, if any, documentation followed on from this we do not know; it certainly does not survive. However, even with limited documentary evidence, it is clear that there was a substantial transfer of land in the Danelaw in the early tenth century, involving the kings of Wessex both directly and indirectly.

This was followed in subsequent decades by royal grants to leading secular and ecclesiastical figures of often substantial amounts of land.[177] For example, the grant to Wulfsige *Maur* of a large block of land around Burton upon Trent in 942 comprised a group of separately named places. These places correspond to Domesday vills and there is little reason to suppose that they had formed part of some larger estate when they were granted to Wulfsige. However, the very fact that he received this cluster of vills on either side of the river Trent suggests that the intention was to create a new, large multi-vill territory by granting a number of separate small parcels of land.[178] It is claimed that Athelstan granted to the church of Beverley the right to collect grain from each working plough in the East Riding of Yorkshire.[179] If genuine, this looks very much like a pre-existing royal render. Crucially, the granting of royal rights over large districts was not detrimental to Athelstan and his descendants since they had never

---

173. Stenton, *Types of Manorial Structure*, 74.
174. S 396 (B 659); *EHD*, I, no. 103.
175. D. Dumville, 'Between Alfred the Great and Edgar the Peacemaker: Athelstan, first king of England', in his *Wessex and England from Alfred to Edgar* (1992), 141–71, at 151–3.
176. *Liber Eliensis*, ed. Blake, 98–9; Hart, *The Danelaw*, 226–7.
177. Stenton, *Types of Manorial Structure*, 74.
178. S 479 (B 771), S 484 (B 772), S 1606 (B 773); *Burton Abbey Charters*, 9–13; P.H. Sawyer, 'The charters of Burton Abbey and the unification of England', *Northern History*, 10 (1975), 28–39, at 34–9.
179. S 451 (B 644); Hart, *Early Charters of Northern England*, 118–19.

before received such renders, whose collection would have been difficult for kings not resident in the northern Danelaw.

Both Dorothy Whitelock and Peter Sawyer have suggested that an important part of the extension of West Saxon royal control to northern England was the role played by leading noblemen. Whitelock interpreted the early eleventh-century will of Wulfric Spott to reveal 'how there were by the end of the tenth century thegns in English areas who possessed also large estates in the districts settled by the Danes', and she supposed that they got their possessions together by both grant and purchase.[180] The people on whom the house of Wessex relied included leading southern lords, such as Wulfsige and Wulfric, but also possibly northern lords, of whom Uhtred may have been one. It has been suggested that Uhtred was a member of the Bernician rulers of Bamburgh, perhaps a son of Eadwulf of Bamburgh who died in 912, on the grounds that most bearers of the name Uhtred recorded in documents from the eighth century were members of this family.[181] The family of Uhtred possibly maintained an interest in the region after Uhtred died, sometime around 950; this is suggested by a charter of 955 which granted land at Chesterfield to one Uhtred *cild*, who was probably a kinsman of the earlier Uhtred.[182] Both Uhtred and Wulfsige acquired land in the region at a time when the West Saxon kings had little authority there, and 'there is therefore a strong suspicion that it was left to the beneficiaries themselves to take and hold what they had been given'.[183] The grants of two large estates in Nottinghamshire in 956 and 958 to Bishop Oscytel of Dorchester, who was later to become archbishop of York, by Eadwig and Edgar respectively, may have been another means by which the southern kings attempted to secure their control in the north, by granting land to magnates in the south who they then hoped would take control on their behalf further north.[184]

There are grounds for believing, then, that the West Saxon kings conquered and secured the northern Danelaw in part by creating new, large estates for the leading lay and ecclesiastical lords, on whom they relied to control a region which the kings themselves rarely visited. The annexation of disparate pieces of land to a single centre would have substantially increased the value of that estate centre and would have made a very handsome reward for loyal service. It was also a means of concentrating power. This practice is mirrored in the ecclesiastical sphere by the manipulation of ecclesiastical tithes, which often followed the foundation of new churches in the Danelaw by the

---

180.   D.W. Whitelock, 'The dealings of the kings of England with Northumbria in the tenth and eleventh centuries', in *The Anglo-Saxons*, ed. P. Clemoes (1959), 70–88, at 81 for the quotation; Sawyer, 'The charters of Burton Abbey', 29–31.
181.   Sawyer, 'The charters of Burton Abbey', 33–4.
182.   S 569 (B 911); *Burton Abbey Charters*, 21–2.
183.   Sawyer, 'The charters of Burton Abbey', 31.
184.   S 659 (B 1029); S 679 (B 1044); see also J. Barrow, 'Oscytel' in *The New Dictionary of National Biography* (forthcoming).

West Saxon royal family.[185] Not only did men such as Uhtred, Wulfsige, Uhtred *cild* and Wulfric help to secure royal control in the northern Danelaw, they also eventually benefited royal land-holding in the region by maintaining widespread possessions which eventually came under direct royal control. Many of the properties referred to here were royal estates by the time that Domesday Book was compiled, but it is not clear how or when this transfer happened – although the presence of records of the acquisition of many of these properties in the Burton Abbey archive suggests that they were not yet in royal hands by the early eleventh century when the abbey was endowed by Wulfric.[186]

However, we should try to look beyond the circumstances of successive conquests in order to explain the form taken by territorial organization in the northern Danelaw. It is clear that the manorial organization of Domesday Book should not be attributed solely to royal initiative. The purchase of land and a burgeoning landmarket seem certain to have been a contributory factor to the form of the manorial structure recorded in 1086. Uhtred's purchase of land in the northern Danelaw may well be only a documented example of a much more widespread practice of purchasing land from the Scandinavians. Nobles were instrumental in shaping the estate pattern as they purchased land in the region, and this may have been carried out with little reference to the king. At a later date the *Libellus Æthelwoldi* makes no reference to land-books or to the king when discussing the acquisitions of Bishop Æthelwold for his monastic foundations in East Anglia.[187] The market in land was apparently well advanced in tenth-century East Anglia, and numerous writs, charters and chronicles refer to the buying and selling of land, often by fairly humble people. The sale and purchase of land, and the survival of a stratum of the peasantry that had been able to alienate land, were arguably everywhere major factors in the dismantling, as also the creation, of large multi-vill territories. The great numbers of place-names which contain personal names indicate the emergence of a group of lords closely involved with small estates, some of which may have been created by purchase in response to a burgeoning land market.[188] The usurpation of land by tenants or other individuals may also have been a factor during undoubtedly troubled times. Perhaps this is what lies behind the archbishop of York's complaints that land, often single vills or portions of vills, had been taken from his estates of Ripon, Otley and Sherburn.

Pauline Stafford has discussed the reorganization of royal lands in the later Anglo-Saxon period; in her study of the royal demesne in

---

185. J. Blair, 'Secular minster churches in Domesday Book', in *Domesday Book: a reassessment*, ed. P.H. Sawyer (1985), 104–42, at 118–19.
186. Sawyer, 'The charters of Burton Abbey', 34.
187. Reynolds, *Fiefs and Vassals*, 333–5.
188. P.A. Stafford, *Unification and Conquest: a political and social history of England in the tenth and eleventh centuries* (1989), 132–3, 209–10, 214.

Domesday Book, she distinguishes between ancient royal renders on the one hand, and the more recent regularization of the nature and distribution of those dues, on the other. Fluctuation in the royal demesne, largely as a result of the alienation of land, must have necessitated continual changes to the organization of the demesne. The grouping of royal land in Domesday Book into large units in order to provide 'the farm of one night' betokens recent restructuring of the royal demesne.[189] It is not implausible that the estates of the greater landholders similarly underwent periods of reorganization in the later Anglo-Saxon centuries, as a result of the process of conquest and redistribution of lands and the need to provide suitable systems of support for lords, many of whom were absentee.

The Norman Conquest of the northern Danelaw also had an impact on its estate structure. As we will see in the next chapter, there is evidence to suggest that the acquisition of land by Norman lords caused some alterations to be made to patterns of land-holding, and the very enquiries that followed from the Norman takeover of land, including the Domesday survey, caused material changes to attitudes to land-holding. There is also some evidence to suggest that some Norman lords exploited their lands in different ways from their predecessors, although we should probably not over-emphasize the level of change, since there is no reason to presume that pre-Conquest lords did not periodically make changes to the ways in which they exploited their lands. Rosamond Faith has recently argued that many Norman lords adopted a more systematic exploitation of the lands they acquired than had previously been the case, and created demesnes where previously there had been none.[190]

In sum, although it is rarely possible to be specific, it is clear that the manorial structure of the northern Danelaw which was recorded in Domesday Book was of diverse origins, and that it cannot be wholly explained and understood either by reference to the Scandinavian settlement or by invoking continuity from an earlier period as the sole explanation. From what we know of the tenth century it would indeed be highly unlikely that that period should not have contributed a great deal to the territorial organization of the region. During the tenth century demands by lords and kings on their estates increased enormously, owing to the requirements of warfare, the development of the market-place, the refoundation and endowment of monastic communities, church-building, and the establishment of regular local courts.[191] We have already commented on the way in which tenth-century estate management may have tended towards the imposition of regular dues and heavier obligations on the peasantry. The circumstances of the West Saxon conquest of the region and the

---

189. P.A. Stafford, 'The "farm of one night" and the organization of King Edward's estates in Domesday', *EcHR*, 2nd sec. 33 (1980), 491–502.
190. Faith, *The English Peasantry*, 178–200.
191. Stafford, *Unification and Conquest*, 204–16.

extension of royal authority northwards also played an important role in the development of territorial organization in the northern Danelaw. As we have seen, the West Saxon kings encouraged their nobles to buy land in the Danelaw before the main campaigns of conquest; and doubtless the documented examples were accompanied by other, unrecorded, examples of this. They also made grants of land in the region, although our knowledge of how this proceeded, who the recipients were (and they were surely not all southern noblemen) and how it was recorded is patchy. Nonetheless, there is sufficient evidence to reveal that patterns of land-holding were subject to much upheaval in the tenth century.

Beyond the sokes

There is a tendency to emphasize the sokes of the northern Danelaw in any discussion of territorial organization because they are one of its most characteristic features, and also because they are deemed to be typical of much earlier patterns of organization. Yet it is clear that units of administration, lordship and exploitation of much smaller size were also found in the Anglo-Saxon centuries. Although it is not possible to uncover much about such units, we must take care not to underestimate their importance by assigning them to some larger 'multiple estate' or other, which tends to be the consequence of some of the geographers' approaches to Anglo-Saxon society.

Although the large multi-vill soke has received the most attention from students of the northern Danelaw, equally characteristic are small estates, which often have the same structure as the large sokes, although on a reduced scale.[192] Some such small estates appear in tenth-century charters, as we have seen in the examples of Drax, Parwich, and the various properties acquired by Wulfsige *Maur* in the Trent valley in 942. Domesday Book has many small estates comprising a manor and a few berewicks or sokelands. There were, indeed, more such estates than Domesday Book makes explicit; often it does not record the individual settlements that were part of a manor, and the entry for those places is subsumed in the entry for the manorial centre. The entry for Stapenhill (Derbs), for example, can be shown from near-contemporary evidence to have included the resources for neighbouring Stanton and Brislingcote.[193] The evidence of parish boundaries may reveal the former existence of others in those instances where a parish includes a number of separate Domesday manors.

The creation of these small estates was an important development in the pattern of seigneurial land-holding in the later Anglo-Saxon period. Some were seemingly carved out of the earlier extensive

---

192. Faith, *The English Peasantry*, 153–77, discusses this feature of early organization at length.
193. D.R. Roffe, *Domesday Derbyshire* (1986), 8–9.

tribute territories that had hitherto been characteristic of territorial organization. However, we should also be open to the possibility that this type of estate was created 'from below', and was not always the result of the actions of some great lord. The ability of the lords of such estates to build up their holdings based on hereditary land by coercing, or otherwise receiving land from, their neighbours must account for some of the pattern of manorial organization presented by Domesday Book. It may be such processes that, in part, account for the dispersed manors of Domesday Book which sprawl awkwardly over the vills of the region, and the frequent division of vills among numerous lords.[194] Such estates may not have been especially stable, and the very process of recording them in Domesday Book may have contributed to freezing such estates as they appeared in the later eleventh century. The presence of place-names incorporating personal names among the members of the larger sokes may be a reflection of the fact that many more places had formerly been separate estates than was the case at the time of the survey.

The lords of these small estates were not able to draw on the extensive tributes and food-renders available to greater lords and had to find new ways to exploit their land – forms of exploitation that increasingly subjected the peasant inhabitants of the estate to the will of the lord, and drew them into the cultivation of his land.[195] It is not surprising, then, that these small estates have a very low incidence of sokemen and free peasants by the eleventh century.

Rosamond Faith has recently suggested that the emerging small estates were associated with a range of features including a seigneurial dwelling-place, a complex of buildings including a court, a defensible area and a church. These core areas, she argues, formed the embryos of later medieval villages.[196] Such a phenomenon is attested in the northern Danelaw at Goltho (Lincs): by the tenth century there was an enclosed area, a dwelling-place, and a range of other buildings including a church.[197] The proliferation of local churches in the tenth century in some parts of the region may well have been associated with the emergence of these types of small estate, since many were located on small manors and sokes according to Domesday Book.[198] Across England this type of estate is often associated with place-names combining personal names (the names of lords who in some way

---

194. Maitland, *Domesday Book and Beyond*, 325–6.
195. *Ibid.*, 175.
196. Faith, *The English Peasantry*, 163–7.
197. G. Beresford, *Goltho: the development of an early medieval manor* c. *850–1150* (1987). There are, however, doubts about the date ranges suggested for the various phases and about the association of the site with the documentary evidence for Goltho: P. Everson, 'What's in a name? "Goltho", Goltho and Bullington', *LHA*, 23 (1988), 93–9. It should also be noted that in this instance the village developed much later than the seigneurial centre, which must, here, have acted as a delayed magnet for settlement.
198. See Chapter 4, pp. 287–8.

'owned' or possessed the estate) with *tun* or another habitative element. It is not implausible that the element *tun* emerged, in part, to describe an enclosure of a small area with a building or buildings inside it, and that it was used to describe the manorial curias and inlands of their eponymous owners.[199]

The economy of these small estates is not generally visible in our sources. One document does, however, survive that gives an insight into the workings of just such a small estate. During the reign of Æthelred II, one Ærnketel and his wife Wulfrun gave to Ramsey Abbey their land of Hickling and Kinoulton (Notts), from which an annual rent was forthcoming: the rent included malt, groats, flour, hams, cheeses, cows and salmon.[200] Whether labour services of any kind were owed is not stated. Such an estate was on the way to becoming the fully manorialized estate with which we are more familiar at a later date. In such situations it is not difficult to see how a food render might be translated into services once lords found it too inconvenient to travel to enjoy the food render; and once they had established an overseer on the estate, to ensure regular supplies, it would only be a short step before they increased their demesne and demanded services instead.[201] Lordship was turning decisively away from distant tribute-taking to closer involvement in estates, necessitating a real presence within individual settlements and neighbourhoods and the receipt of regular payments of rents, dues and taxes.[202] Such forms of exploitation may, however, still have been relatively isolated, 'seigneurialized islands' amid the holdings of the relatively independent peasant farmers.[203]

Conclusions

The territorial organization of the northern Danelaw, as it is presented by Domesday Book, contrasts sharply with that of other regions. This is, in part, the product of the ways in which the survey was compiled and ordered, but it is also the result of the competing and conflicting rights over land in the region. Furthermore, the diverse evidence from the region presents a pattern of territorial organization that cannot easily be fitted into the frameworks of the 'multiple estate' model, and indeed of related models. It is far too complex to be readily reassembled into neat and contiguous units, and it forces us to reconsider our approaches to early medieval territorial organization. It

199. Gelling, *Signposts to the Past*, 178–81.
200. S 1493; *Chronicon Abbatiae Ramesiensis*, ed. W.D. Macray, Rolls Series, 83 (1886), 66–7.
201. Maitland, *Domesday Book and Beyond*, 319–20; Stenton, *Types of Manorial Structure*, 37–8.
202. B.K. Roberts, *The Making of the English Village* (1987), 72.
203. Faith, *The English Peasantry*, 176–7.

is likely that most regions were divided up at an early date into more or less coherent territories, the settlement districts of tribal groups or kin-groups, and administrative units, through which kings and their followers exploited the land. It is, however, quite another matter to suppose that much later evidence (in the form of Anglo-Saxon charter boundaries, Domesday Book, place-names and parish boundaries) necessarily provides a direct means of access to those earlier patterns of organization. The settlement districts of tribal groups were not the same kinds of units as later bookland estates (any more than were parishes or administrative units, such as wapentakes). As such, they need not necessarily have coincided, although it was doubtless in the interests of some that they did. The recognition that these units were in essence different from each other provides the means to understand the complexity of the Danelaw evidence. The rate at which early patterns of Anglo-Saxon organization were 'privatized' into estates proper clearly varied, and seemingly occurred on different scales across the region. Large multi-vill estates are everywhere found alongside small estates.

It may be pertinent to envisage the following processes which gave rise to the complex manorial organization revealed by Domesday Book. We begin with a landscape peopled with landowners, who varied in social status from the *ceorl* to the great noble, who owed tribute to greater lords by virtue of the latter's military authority rather than in their capacity as landlords. The landscape was seemingly divided into large territories which not uncommonly conformed to the natural topography, and through which tribute was directed. Within these large territories were smaller subdivisions, later known as vills, which were possibly created by communities to ensure access to natural resources. Some of these were of prehistoric origins, although others were defined during the Anglo-Saxon centuries. From the seventh and eighth centuries great blocs of land were transferred to churches, possibly, although not invariably, in the form of coherent territories. The interests of ecclesiastical lords in the land of the inhabitants of these bookland territories were probably minimal initially, but the possession of bookright and its perpetual nature meant that over time the burdens placed on the inhabitants were easily increased. The creation of bookland estates was a source of, and a starting-point for, the diminution of freedom. The evidence from the northern Danelaw reveals that these bookland estates did not survive intact until the time of Domesday Book; members might be lost and gained, transforming what was a relatively coherent estate into a more uneven and fragmented estate. In addition to the breaking up of large early territories 'from above', the creation of small estates also went on 'from below'. Together these processes gave rise to the complex and varied pattern of estate structures recorded by Domesday Book, which the survey often found it difficult to categorize.

The overlapping pattern of sokes was, to some extent, the product of the creation of bookland estates, and the product of the efforts of diverse lords to acquire a variety of rights over land and its inhabitants. Some sokes were surely the result of the fragmentation of earlier territorial groupings; others were clearly the product of amalgamation. Consequently, we cannot safely use the spatial distribution of sokes to reconstruct earlier patterns; as 'estates' they may from the start have been complex and dispersed. And since their relationship to earlier patterns of territorial organization (the settlement districts of tribal groups, or extended families) is uncertain, it seems a futile attempt to try to use the pattern of Domesday sokes to uncover such arrangements. It may, broadly speaking, be true that the manorial structure of the northern Danelaw in the eleventh century had more in common with much earlier patterns of territorial organization and socio-economic exploitation than is the case in other parts of the country, but that is not to say that the precise arrangements recorded by Domesday Book were of very great antiquity. Our evidence refutes this in many instances.

It is important not to confuse the various territorial divisions of early medieval society, as there are important functional and chronological distinctions to be drawn between the tribal, administrative and tenurial units of Anglo-Saxon England, even if in many parts of the country they were related physically. It is equally important not to conflate the evidence for multi-vill territories which existed in the Anglo-Saxon period; certainly the evidence from different sources sometimes tells the same story, but where it does not, we should resist the urge to make it conform. Inconsistencies in the patterns revealed by different types of evidence often tell us real things about regional, and temporal, variation.

It is rarely possible to be specific about the origins and development of the territorial organization depicted by Domesday Book, and this chapter has stretched the available evidence as far as, and sometimes further than, is permissible. Nonetheless, it is evident that there was great variation across the region. The evidence of Anglo-Saxon charters, Domesday Book, place-names, parish boundaries and so on also reveals that the manorial and administrative structure which can be first examined in detail in the later eleventh century is a palimpsest of centuries of development. Furthermore, as we move backwards in time from Domesday Book, the reconstruction of a simple and orderly past is a difficult, and perhaps inappropriate, undertaking. We must now move on to consider the nature of lordship and of the social structure of the region; from this, even greater diversity of manorial organization will be revealed in the eleventh century, as it will be shown that even within superficially similar manors, the social structure and forms of exploitation might vary enormously.

4 Lords and peasants

The free peasant of the Danelaw was something more than an
interesting exception

– F.M. Stenton[1]

Who were the inhabitants of the vills, manors, parishes and multifocal
estates of the northern Danelaw? This chapter seeks to set out, and
account for, the peculiarities of lordship and of the peasant classes in
the northern Danelaw. Once again, it is best to begin with the sources
available at the end of our period. We have seen that the social
structure of the northern Danelaw was characterized in the eleventh
century by great numbers of relatively free peasants (*liberi homines*
and *sochemanni*) among the rural population, by the comparatively
fragmented nature of tenurial organization, and by dispersed patterns
of land-holding and of lordship. It is only really from the later evidence
of estate surveys of the eleventh and twelfth centuries that we can
uncover the rights and obligations of *liberi homines* and *sochemanni*,
and we must consider the antiquity and uniqueness of their status as it
is described by such sources. The evidence of Domesday Book can be
supplemented by a number of near-contemporary documents from the
abbeys of Burton, Ely, Peterborough and Bury St Edmunds. From that
foundation an explanation can be offered of how the social structure of
the later eleventh century had emerged through the Anglo-Saxon
period in response to the demands and pressures of the king and the
state, the judicial machinery, the agricultural regime and estate policy.
It is clear, however, that the Domesday text greatly simplifies the
social structure of the region and we must also guard against thinking
that there was everywhere a linear or predictable progression towards
the social structure depicted by Domesday Book. This chapter
attempts to identify those aspects of lordship and peasant status that
were of great antiquity by the eleventh century, and also those that
were of more recent origin. There is evidence that the nature of
lordship and the structure of peasant society developed in divergent
ways and at different speeds across the region, and at the time of
Domesday Book both were still in a state of flux.

---

1. F.M. Stenton, 'The Danes in England', *Proceedings of the British Academy*, 13
   (1927), 31.

Lordship at the time of Domesday Book

The pattern of seigneurial land-holding in the northern Danelaw distinguishes the region from other parts of the country in the eleventh century. According to Domesday Book, royal and ecclesiastical land was generally less extensive and less compact than in other parts of the country.[2] Common to all major lords was the fragmented nature of the estates they held, which often included only portions of vills and which were commonly interspersed with those of others. As we have seen, many of the major Domesday estates of the region had been created piecemeal over preceding centuries. Moreover, much royal and ecclesiastical land had been acquired only during the course of the later tenth and eleventh centuries.[3] For example, the major sokes of Derbyshire had not been in royal hands in the early tenth century, and therefore the Domesday organization of the estates of Darley, Wirksworth, Ashbourne, Matlock, Parwich, Bakewell, Ashford and Hope to provide a royal render of cash, honey and wagon-loads of lead must have been a relatively recent arrangement.[4]

Domesday Book names a pre-Conquest holder of virtually every manor in the northern Danelaw. Below the level of the king, and major ecclesiastical lay lords, it is difficult to identify with any certainty the holdings of any given individual in 1066 since it is unclear whether or not each reference to Godric, Sveinn, Gamel and so on relates to the same person. Even where the versions of the name were spelt differently it is not certain that they refer to different people. Furthermore, the text cannot be relied upon to have employed epithets consistently: for example, the opening entry of the section, or breve, recording the lands of Gilbert of Ghent in Lincolnshire names his predecessor as Ulfr Fenman, but although it seems likely that the following references in that breve to an 'Ulfr' are to the same person, one cannot be equally sure that this is the Ulfr mentioned in other breves.[5] The problem of the identification of lesser lords is acute, but some conclusions may nevertheless be drawn. In Nottinghamshire, for example, most pre-Conquest lords held, at best, only a few manors: 57 named individuals (46 per cent of the total) each held a single manor,

---

2.   J.D. Hamshere, 'Domesday Book: estate structures in the west Midlands', in *Domesday Studies*, ed. J.C. Holt (1987), 155–82; R. Fleming, 'Monastic lands and England's defence in the viking age', *EHR*, 100 (1985), 247–65 at 249.

3.   See Chapter 3, pp. 154–7.

4.   *DB*, fos. 272b–c, 272d, 273a. On royal estate organization, see S.J. Harvey, 'Royal revenue and Domesday terminology', *EcHR*, 2nd ser., 20 (1967), 221–8; S.J. Harvey, 'Domesday Book and its predecessors', *EHR*, 86 (1971), 753–73; P. Stafford, 'The "farm of one night" and the organization of King Edward's estates in Domesday', *EcHR*, 2nd ser., 33 (1980), 491–502.

5.   *DB*, fo. 354c. The *Clamores* refer to Ulfr Fenman as the predecessor of Gilbert (fo. 377b), and they reveal that the Ulfr named as holding a manor in Belton, which later passed to Geoffrey of La Guerche, was also the same person, although this is not indicated in the main body of the text (fos. 369b, 377b).

and 22 (18 per cent) held only two manors. Many of these lords held extremely small manors, and holdings of the larger landholders were usually widely scattered.[6] Although the text rarely states explicitly the status of the people named as holding manors in 1066, it is evident that they did not form a homogeneous group. As we shall see, the rights that these lords enjoyed over their lands varied, and some of those named in the text in fact probably held their land on limited terms from someone else, or their rights in their land were limited by obligations to another lord.

Lords and their estates

A characteristic feature of late Anglo-Saxon lordship in the northern Danelaw was the possession of large multi-vill estates (or 'sokes') comprising a manorial centre and numerous dependent properties (berewicks and sokelands), which were often distributed over wide areas. However, the structure of the Domesday record sometimes obscures the extent of particular estates. Contemporary surveys reveal that on occasions a lord's estate extended into more vills than the one named in the Domesday entry. For example, an early twelfth-century survey of the lands of Burton Abbey records the same assessment for the combined holding of Brislingcote and Stapenhill (Derbs) as did Domesday Book for the manor of Stapenhill alone, which suggests that Brislingcote was not recorded separately in Domesday Book because it was included under the entry for Stapenhill.[7] As we have seen, the survey does not always specify the precise location of land if it is located in the same hundred as the manorial centre, and this may diguise the fact that parts of the manor are actually located in another vill. Hence, the estates which lords held were sometimes more complex, and spread over more vills, than Domesday Book reveals.

The Domesday text repeatedly refers to the rights that lords exercised over their estates as 'soke' or 'sake and soke'; they have sometimes been treated as if they are identical, but there are, in fact, important differences between them. Soke is a word that was used in different ways. The Old English word *socn* means essentially 'the act of seeking', and carries the implication of seeking justice or jurisdiction. In Domesday Book and later sources the term and its derivatives are employed in four main contexts: i) to describe the obligations resting on land and its inhabitants; (ii) as a term for a territorial unit or estate (the dependencies of a manor are commonly described as its soke);

---

6.   Although some of these manors included property in more vills by virtue of the berewicks and sokeland attached to their manors: T.H. Unwin, 'The Norman aggregation of estates and settlement in eleventh-century Nottinghamshire', *Landscape History*, 9 (1987), 53–64, at 55.

7.   *DB*, fo. 273b; C.G.O. Bridgeman, 'Burton Abbey twelfth-century surveys', *Collections for a History of Staffordshire*, new ser., 23 (1918 for 1916), 209–300, at 238–40.

(iii) to describe land (sokeland or *terra in soca*); and (iv) as a descriptive word for a stratum of the peasantry (*sochemanni*).[8] Soke is therefore an imprecise term, employed by Domesday Book with diverse meanings. Soke could be enjoyed over a mill, woodland, a fishery, a garden or a church, as well as over land and people.[9] Sir Frank Stenton believed that rights of soke implied nothing more than rights of jurisdiction, and in some contexts this is a not unreasonable definition: in many instances the land was held by one lord but the soke was held by another, and in such cases jurisdiction is an apt modern rendering of 'soke'.[10] Thus, for instance, two bovates of land at Great Coates (Lincs) were held in 1086 by Alfred, but Durand Malet had the soke of them.[11] This type of entry in which the rights of the lord who held the land are distinguished from the rights of the lord who held the soke is not uncommon, especially in Lincolnshire. What this 'jurisdiction' amounted to probably varied: some lords received fines incurred in courts by their subjects as a result of having rights of soke over them, and rights of patronage may also have been involved. The lord's jurisdiction may have been over what would later be called his 'manorial' court, and does not imply that royal jurisdiction had been usurped by seigneurial or franchisal courts.[12]

In many other cases the same lord held both the land and its soke; in these instances the lord's rights were termed 'sake and soke' (*saca et soca*); '*sac*' means cause, or dispute, in the legal sense. It is clear that the term 'sake and soke' had a rather more specific meaning than mere soke (i.e. jurisdiction), with which it was conflated by Stenton. Both David Roffe and Susan Reynolds have argued that 'sake and soke' is a term 'indicative of and synonymous with tenure by book'.[13] That is to say, the estates of lords who enjoyed the benefits of sake and soke were akin to bookland estates (although it is not necessarily the case that all had acquired land-books), and the terms by which the land was held implied extensive rights over the land concerned and its inhabitants.[14] It was these rights that formed the basis of the

---

8. F.W. Maitland, *Domesday Book and Beyond* (1897), 84ff.; *The Kalendar of Abbot Samson of Bury St. Edmunds*, ed. R.H.C. Davis, Camden 3rd ser., 84 (1954), xlff; A.K.G. Kristensen, 'Danelaw institutions and Danish society in the viking age: *sochemanni, liberi homines* and königsfreie', *Mediaeval Scandinavia*, 8 (1975), 27–85, at 74–85.

9. C.A. Joy, 'Sokeright' (Ph.D. thesis, University of Leeds, 1972), 77–89.

10. F.M. Stenton, *Types of Manorial Structure in the Northern Danelaw*, Oxford Studies in Social and Legal History, ed. P. Vinogradoff, 2 (1910), 3–96, at 4; D.R. Roffe, 'From thegnage to barony: sake and soke, title and tenants-in-chief', *ANS*, 12 (1990), 157–76, at 164–5.

11. *DB*, fo. 375d.

12. S. Reynolds, *Fiefs and Vassals: the medieval evidence reinterpreted* (1994), 338; P. Wormald, 'Lordship and justice in the early English kingdom', in *Property and Power in the Early Middle Ages*, ed. W. Davies and P. Fouracre (1995), 114–36, at 129–30.

13. Roffe, 'From thegnage to barony', 165–6; S. Reynolds, 'Bookland, folkland and fiefs', *ANS* 14 (1992), 211–27, at 219 for the quotation.

14. Reynolds, *Fiefs and Vassals*, 333–5.

acquisition of land by the Norman newcomers; mere soke did not confer title to land. This is demonstrated by a dispute recorded in Domesday Book about the land of Karli in Billingborough (Lincs). Robert of Stafford claimed it in 1086, presumably on the grounds that Karli was his antecessor elsewhere, but his claim was rejected on the grounds that Karli held this particular land from Ralph the Staller, who had rights of sake and soke over Billingborough; the land was therefore conferred on Count Alan, who was the recipient of the rest of Ralph's possessions.[15] Many of the disputes that are recorded in Domesday Book emerged because Norman lords were attempting to claim more than their predecessors had enjoyed; the former may have taken a conveniently broad view of the rights that their antecessors enjoyed, and this came to light when the rights of other lords were compromised.[16]

Bookright, or rights of sake and soke, signified that the lord was to receive from land the dues and services that had once been owed to the king. The dues and services owed to lords are often described by Domesday Book as *consuetudines*, a vague term which incorporated right to taxes and rents as well as to miscellaneous services and dues.[17] Included in the privileges of sake and soke were the profits of justice and the rights of 'toll and team', that is, the regalian privileges of market and toll.[18] The distinction between lords who enjoyed rights of sake and soke and those who did not was felt to be important, and the Domesday accounts of each of the counties of the northern Danelaw include a list of the lords who were privileged to enjoy these rights in 1066. Some 35 individuals are listed at the beginning of the Lincolnshire folios, although this list cannot have been exhaustive, as others with such rights are named in the main body of the text (Fig. 32).[19]

The benefits accruing from these rights of sake and soke varied in practice, however, according to the status of the land the lord held and the status and rights of the inhabitants of that land. In particular, the rights of a lord over his sokeland were limited by the interests of the sokemen, who had property rights of sorts of their own, whereas over his own manors and berewicks the lord had much less restricted rights.[20] As Susan Reynolds has observed, sokemen were not strictly speaking tenants of the lord, and the relationship between sokemen and lords did not, in theory, compromise the rights the sokemen had

---

15. *DB*, fos. 337a, 377c; D.R. Roffe, *The Lincolnshire Domesday*, Alecto Historical Editions (1992), 12–15.
16. Reynolds, *Fiefs and Vassals*, 339.
17. Maitland, *Domesday Book and Beyond*, 77; A. Williams, *The English and the Norman Conquest* (1995), 74.
18. Roffe, *The Lincolnshire Domesday*, 13; *Anglo-Saxon Writs*, ed. F.E. Harmer (1952), 73–8.
19. *DB*, fo. 337a; Roffe, *The Lincolnshire Domesday*, 13.
20. D.R. Roffe, 'The *Descriptio Terrarum* of Peterborough Abbey', *Historical Research*, 65 (1992), 1–16, at 13.

Bishop of Lincoln	Rothulfr son of Skjaldvor
Queen Edith	Godric son of Thorfrothr
The Abbot of Peterborough	Aki son of Siward and Vigleikr his brother
The Abbot of Ramsey	over their father's land
The Abbot of Crowland	Leofwine son of Alwine
Earl Harold	Atsurr son of Svala
Earl Morcar	Ælfric son of Mergeat
Earl Waltheof	Auti son of Atsurr
Earl Ralph	Æthelstan son of Godram
Ulfr Fenman	Thorir son of Roaldr
Merlesveinn	Toli son of Alsige
Thorgautr	Atsurr son of Burg
Toki son of Auti	Wulfeard White
Stori	Ulfr
Ralph the Constable	Hemingr
Siward Barn	Barthi
Harold the Constable	Sveinn son of Svafi
Fiacc	

Figure 32 Domesday lords in Lincolnshire who enjoyed sake and soke and toll and team

over their own land.[21] Indeed, sokemen were, or had been, able to alienate their lands and to seek lords outside the soke to whom they could commend themselves. Certainly, by the eleventh century alienation of land was fairly limited, but earlier evidence suggests that this had not always been the case. That rights of alienation were spread widely in Danelaw society is suggested by Bishop Æthelwold's purchases of land in East Anglia in the tenth century, which were rarely opposed by disgruntled heirs of the vendor. Freedom of disposition seems to have been possible 'by people who surely did not all have royal landbooks'.[22] Moreover, commendation did not carry any necessary implication of tenurial involvement between lord and peasant, although commendation did provide a means for a sokeman to form another social bond beyond that of the one he had with his soke lord. The more detailed Domesday accounts of East Anglia show that, for example, lords might only enjoy the commendation of *liberi homines* or sokemen but have no interest in, or rights over, their land. Indeed, it is likely that such people would have sought to commend themselves to lords other than their soke lord as a means of gaining additional patronage. The rights of lords over sokemen and *liberi homines* did not interfere with the participation of the latter in public courts, which was, in fact, one of their defining characteristics.[23] Hence although great lords exercised control over vast tracts of land, even where they enjoyed rights of sake and soke they did not precisely

---

21. Reynolds, 'Bookland, folkland and fiefs', 222; this is discussed further below, pp. 180–96.
22. Reynolds, 'Bookland, folkland and fiefs', 220.
23. F.M. Stenton (ed.), *Documents Illustrative of the Social and Economic History of the Danelaw* (1920), cix–cx; Stenton, *Types of Manorial Structure*, 21.

'own' most of it; rather, they were entitled to a series of dues and services from its inhabitants, whose own rights in land were both socially and legally recognized.

Domesday Book does not distinguish between land that had been acquired by a grant of bookright and hereditary land. By the eleventh century such a distinction was no longer drawn, and this had probably long been true.[24] Susan Reynolds has suggested that by *c.* 1000 the term 'bookland', if and when it was used, might mean nothing more specific than 'one's own land', which might be of diverse origins and include both inherited and acquired lands.[25]

Although a number of important lords had rights of sake and soke over their lands, many other lords did not have such comprehensive rights over their manors. A group of lords has been identified who collected tribute, labour services and other dues from the peasantry on their manors but who nonetheless held those manors precariously, probably for a 'farm', or some sort of payment; rights to the land itself and to the soke over land, however, remained with another lord. For example, although Siward held the manor of Scrivelsby (Lincs) with its appurtenant berewicks and sokelands in 1066, his lord, Achi, retained the soke of Scrivelsby in his manor of Thornton. Achi also apparently had residual rights to the land in Scrivelsby since it was as the successor of Achi and not of Siward that Robert the Steward later claimed the manor.[26] Other intermediate holdings existed, in which a lord received certain dues from the land but owed renders to another lord. This is true of lands held in thanage; those who held thegnland were not at liberty to alienate it.[27] Pre-Conquest tenures of this type are not recorded systematically in the Domesday text, but there are sufficient miscellaneous references for us to believe that they are not uncommon, and that some of the recorded holders of manors in Domesday Book were, in fact, probably holding their land from a greater lord.[28] One indication of 'overlordship' is provided by the presence in the lists of lords who had rights of sake and soke over their lands (which appear at the beginning of the folios for the counties of the northern Danelaw) of individuals who are not then named in the main part of the text as holding land. One must conclude that they enjoyed these rights over land recorded by Domesday Book as being held by someone else. In Lincolnshire, for example, Fiacc and Atsurr son of Svala are said to have had rights of sake and soke in 1066 but neither of them is mentioned in the text as holding land in the county. However, the *clamores* record that Robert Malet was entitled to claim soke over four bovates in Ingoldsby through his predecessor, Atsurr;

---

24. Reynolds, *Fiefs and Vassals*, 333; Chapter 2, p. 71.
25. Reynolds, *Fiefs and Vassals*, 334.
26. D.R. Roffe, 'Domesday Book and northern society: a reassessment', *EHR*, 105 (April, 1990), 310–36, at 329.
27. Williams, *The English and the Norman Conquest*, 75.
28. P.H. Sawyer, '1066–1086: a tenurial revolution?', in *Domesday Book: a reassessment*, ed. P.H. Sawyer (1985), 71–85, at 72.

the main entry for Ingoldsby says that it was held by Godwin, who must have this land in some way from Atsurr.[29] There is a further indication of overlordship in the Domesday text. In many instances vills were divided into two or more manors in 1066; the number of manors is indicated by a number written above the normal marginal M. Such vills often passed to a sole Norman lord. This may well have been because the multiple manors of 1066 had, in fact, been held of a single Anglo-Saxon 'overlord'; furthermore, it is notable that these multiple-manor vills are described as a single manor in cases where dependencies are attached and are accorded a single assessment.[30]

We have to be careful, however, about the assumptions that we draw from this evidence. The common use of terms such as 'overlord' and 'tenant' is prone to give misleading impressions. It is now apparent that the rigid hierarchy of property held from the king by a range of tenants-in-chief and subtenants that is described in much literature on Domesday Book is in part a fiction of both the Domesday text and later historiography. Although there were certainly people who held land on restricted terms from other lords, we should not assume that all those who had relations with other lords concerning their land were necessarily restricted in their rights over that land. Although all those who held land had restrictions placed on their control over it – by law, social pressure and the requirements of loyalty – all also had their rights protected in law and by social expectation. Susan Reynolds has presented a cogent argument for not describing the many facets of the social, estate, seigneurial and administrative structure described by Domesday Book as a 'tenurial hierarchy'. Although we know something about the terms by which people held land from the church, and by which thegns held royal land, we have to be careful, she points out, about extrapolating out from this. The nature of the rights that the men described as 'overlords' in much secondary literature actually had over their so-called 'subtenants' is very unclear; the rights of kings mattered and were recorded, as were those of the immediate lord of land, but the rights of other lords and other layers of property are comparatively rarely recorded in the post-Conquest period.[31] Lords who 'held from' others may have had their rights to their land restricted, but the term could also be used to describe relationships based on patronage or some other form of authority, with few implications for their property rights.[32] These considerations have considerable implications for those studies that have used Domesday Book to trace the development of 'multiple estates', because many of the relationships that may be identified between people and places should not be interpreted as part of some tenurial hierarchy, and it is

29.   *DB*, fos. 368b, 377b.
30.   On the alternative explanation, that such entries reflect estate amalgamation after the Conquest, see Unwin, 'The Norman aggregation of estates', 58–9.
31.   Reynolds, *Fiefs and Vassals*, 359–60.
32.   *Ibid.*, 346–8.

misleading to conflate the various links that are recorded and to project integrated estates.

On the eve of the Norman Conquest there was an extremely complex mosaic of lordship, and of overlapping and competing rights, in the northern Danelaw, of which Domesday Book allows us only a glimpse. The very nature of the survey and the information which it presented created the appearance of a more rigid hierarchy of property and lordship than was often really the case. The bonds between lords, and between lords and peasants, might be personal, tenurial or jurisdictional, and lords did not invariably enjoy the same relationship with all the lords and peasants with whom they had dealings. This was something that the limited and relatively rigid terminology of Domesday Book does not easily capture.

There has been much recent debate about the impact of the Norman Conquest on patterns of land-holding. Two methods have been identified by which land was distributed after the Norman Conquest. The first was antecessorial acquisition, in which Norman lords acquired all the lands of given pre-Conquest landholders. For example, in Nottinghamshire Walter d'Aincourt took over all the lands of Thori, Gilbert of Ghent took over all the lands of Ulfr, and Roger de Buisli took over all of the lands of Odincar.[33] The second method of land distribution saw certain Norman lords acquire land in contiguous blocks which paid little attention to earlier patterns of land-holding. Robin Fleming has remarked that the great honours of William de Peveril and Roger de Buisli in Nottinghamshire, for example, formed fairly coherent groupings of land, which contrasts with the apparently more confused arrangements of 1066; she argues that this was the result of the grouping together of the lands of numerous pre-Conquest landholders.[34] However, Fleming's analysis has been subject to criticism from Peter Sawyer and David Roffe, who have both emphasized the overriding importance of antecessorial acquisition, on the grounds that there are sufficient indicators in the Domesday text to suggest that many of those named as the holders of manors in 1066 were in fact holding their land from some greater lord.[35] It is possible that both methods of land acquisition characterized the Norman takeover (subject to the caveats expressed above about the use of terms such as 'overlord' and 'subtenant'); but only rarely can we be certain which process prevailed in any given instance. It should be stated, however, that we must not assume that because there is some evidence for 'overlordship', all holders of small manors in 1066 held them from some greater lord. For example, Gilbert of Ghent

---

33. *DB*, fos. 284–286c, 288c–289a, 290c–d.
34. R. Fleming, 'Domesday Book and the tenurial revolution', *ANS*, 9 (1987), 86–102.
35. Sawyer, '1066–1086: a tenurial revolution?'; Roffe, 'From thegnage to barony'. For the differing results produced by the opposing views, compare the treatment of the Peveril fee in Roffe, 'From thegnage to barony', 173–4, with that of R. Fleming, *Kings and Lords in Conquest England* (1991), 148–9.

apparently tried to claim that Brown and Odincar had held Shipley (Derbs) from his predecessor, Ulfr Fenman, but the 'sworn men' called upon to adjudicate stated that the two men had held the land in such a way that 'they could grant or sell to whom they would'; this suggests that Brown and Odincar held their land with full rights, and that that is why Gilbert had no claim through his regular predecessor, Ulfr Fenman.[36] As we have seen, lords might be under some sort of authority or jurisdiction of another lord, but that did not necessarily mean that they held their land precariously from that lord. Whatever the means by which land was transferred to new Norman lords, there is no doubt that many vills held by a single lord in 1086 had had several manorial lords in the pre-Conquest period. Although it is possible that some pre-Conquest lords held their land under the jurisdiction of another lord, it is, nonetheless apparent that in many instances the number of lords with an interest in a particular vill was reduced after the Conquest.

Lords received from those who came under the authority of their manors combinations of rent or money payments, which may have been a commuted food render of earlier times, the profits of justice, perhaps military services, and the labour services of some of the peasantry. Only for the royal manors are we given much detail of dues in kind. For example, in Derbyshire the royal manors owed sesters of honey and wagon-loads of lead, and at Dunham and Arnold (Notts) the inhabitants owed sesters of honey to the king.[37] Near-contemporary evidence demonstrates that the lords of Domesday manors often received far more than is revealed in the text. A charter from the reign of Æthelred II (978–1016) relating to Hickling and Kinoulton (Notts) by which Ærnketel and his wife Wulfrun granted land there to Ramsey Abbey states that the inhabitants of those vills owed renders in kind, yet there is no indication of this in Domesday Book.[38] Similarly, there is no indication in Domesday Book of the dues owed by the inhabitants of Blyth (Notts), which was a sokeland of Hodsock; yet the charter issued in 1088 by Roger de Buisli for a Cluniac priory at Blyth records that the inhabitants of Blyth were obliged to plough, do carrying services, reap, mow, make hay, pay merchet and maintain the dam of the mill-pond.[39]

Some lords may have had a home farm (demesne) on their manors, that is to say land directly exploited by the lord for his subsistence, but Domesday Book gives little information on this. The survey does, however, consistently record the numbers of plough-teams on the

36. *DB*, fo. 277d; D.R. Roffe, *The Derbyshire Domesday*, Alecto Historical Editions (1990), 10.
37. Stafford, 'The "farm of one night"'.
38. S 1493 (K 971); *Chronicon Abbatiae Ramesiensis*, ed. W.D. Macray, Rolls Ser., 83 (1886), 66–7; *DB*, fos. 283a, 289a, 291b, 293a. It is difficult to know which of the Domesday holdings in Hickling and Kinoulton relate to lands granted to Ramsey Abbey at an earlier date: Stenton, *Types of Manorial Structure*, 37–8.
39. Stenton, *Types of Manorial Structure*, 22–3; *The Cartulary of Blyth Priory*, ed. R.T. Timson (2 vols, 1968), 1, xx–xxix, 207–9.

lord's land and the numbers owned by the peasants; this enables us to evaluate the relative importance of the home farm within given vills. Few lords had substantial home farms, and this is not surprising given the paucity of major ecclesiastical landholders, since in other regions it is they who are most commonly associated with large home farms and high relative percentages of plough-teams.[40] The resources listed by Domesday Book (such as woodland, pasture, mills, fisheries and so on) are those that contributed to the income of the lord's manor, and they should not be taken as a guide to the resources generally available to the rural population. There were doubtless many more mills or acres of pasture than Domesday Book records. The survey is primarily a record of the assets of a manor and as such is of little use as a guide to the organization of the land for economic exploitation. For example, the failure of Domesday Book to record pasture in the fen edges of Lincolnshire may have been because the fenland provided pasture; the resources of the fens may already have been being inter-commoned under the guidance of the vill and the hundred – as they were known to have been at a later date – and of no interest to the survey since they did not contribute to manorial income.[41] Furthermore, resources were often recorded at the place from which they were exploited, even though they were physically remote from the manorial centre. For example, two salt-pans are recorded at North Witham (Lincs) even though it is located twenty miles from the coast; twelfth-century evidence reveals that they were located at Bicker Haven.[42]

Lords' rights over their various estates had a basis both in law and in social expectation. Their ability to exploit their estate and its inhabitants was restricted on the one hand by the obligations that they had to the state, the king and to other lords (for example, if they were holding the land on limited terms from another lord, or if another lord had soke over their land), and on the other by the rights that the peasant inhabitants of the lands enjoyed. Divergent estate policy produced different results. The survival of large numbers of free peasants and the relative amount of land which was exploited as inland depended to a large extent on the successes of successive lords of the estate in bringing the peasantry into dependence, and in the capacity of the peasantry to resist this.[43] The creation of dispersed estates comprising only portions of given vills, whether through subdivision or amalgamation, was also a major factor in determining the nature of lordship and the forms of exploitation in the northern Danelaw. This had a concomitant effect on the peasantry: variations in their numbers

40. S.J. Harvey, 'The extent and profitability of demesne agriculture in England in the late eleventh century', in *Social Relations and Ideas*, ed. T.H. Aston, P. Coss, C.C. Dyer and J. Thirsk (1983), 45–72; Roffe, *The Lincolnshire Domesday*, 18.
41. *A Terrier of Fleet, Lincolnshire*, ed. N. Neilson (1920), v–xxxv, xlix–lviii; H.E. Hallam, *Settlement and Society: a study of the early agrarian history of south Lincolnshire* (1965), 161–6.
42. Roffe, *The Lincolnshire Domesday*, 22.
43. R. Faith, *The English Peasantry and the Growth of Lordship* (1997), 87–8, 121–2.

had much to do with landlord policy.[44] As the early eleventh-century *Rectitudines Singularum Personarum* puts it, 'The estate-law is fixed on each estate: at some places it is heavier, at some places, also, lighter because not all customs about estates are alike.'[45]

An important feature of lordship in the northern Danelaw was the complexity of rights over land. Particularly striking is the fact that more than one lord might have interests in the same piece of land. This has implications for our understanding of how sokes functioned. Although some sokes were integrated economic and agrarian units, in which the peasant population of the various dependencies owed dues and services at the soke centre, in other instances this was not the case since dues and services were intercepted by people other than the lord of the soke. It is also important to recognize that the rights of lords over their sokes were limited by the property rights of the sokemen.[46] This calls into question the traditional view of early medieval multi-vill estates, of which it has been stated that there is 'a strong impression of a functional integration between the components of the larger ... multiple estates'.[47] Certainly there was some integration of the component parts of the sokes of the northern Danelaw, and by the eleventh century they were not merely fluid associations of free peasants, as Stenton had believed. But neither were they fixed and immutable institutions: the composition of sokes continued to change, as did the rights that lords enjoyed over the component parts of the soke. Recent attempts to reconstruct patterns of early medieval territorial organization have arguably underestimated the complexity of rights over land, which are not easily translated into dots and lines on maps. We would do well to keep this in mind when considering the plethora of recent attempts at 'reconstruction'.

The peasantry of Domesday Book

As in other parts of the country in the eleventh century, the counties of the northern Danelaw had a rural population comprising of peasants of varying status. The most commonly used categories are *villani*, *bordarii*, slaves (although they are rare in the Danelaw), sokemen and *liberi homines*. The distribution of the various peasant classes described by Domesday Book is uneven across the region. Any discussion of this distribution is subject to the caveat that Domesday

---

44. A point made by John Moore about the distribution of slavery, but which obviously has wider significance: 'Domesday slavery', *ANS*, 11 (1988), 191–220, at 205.
45. *EHD*, II, no. 172; the text is discусssed in P.D.A. Harvey, '*Rectitudines Singularum Personarum* and *Gerefa*', *EHR*, 108 (1993), 1–22.
46. Roffe, 'The *Descriptio Terrarum*', 13; Reynolds, 'Bookland, folkland and fiefs', 222.
47. G.R.J. Jones, 'Multiple estates and early settlement', in *English Medieval Settlement*, ed. P.H. Sawyer (1979), 9–34, at 32.

Book can be unreliable as a guide to population distribution; in particular, entries which describe a manor with numerous appurtenant sokelands and berewicks do not always describe the population of each of those dependencies, often giving only an overall total. For example, the Domesday manor of Southwell with its twelve unnamed berewicks was populated by 10 sokemen, 137 *villani* and 62 *bordarii*, but we cannot go beyond this and say precisely where they were located; presumably both in Southwell and scattered among the berewicks.[48] Composite entries are a particular feature of the Yorkshire folios, and it tends to be the material added postscriptally that contains more detailed information about individual berewicks.[49] The Lincolnshire folios, by contrast, provide more detailed information concerning the distribution of people within the great sokes: for example, the entry for the soke of Caistor records for each dependency an assessment in carucates or bovates, the number of sokemen, *villani* and *bordarii*, and whether it was sokeland or inland.[50]

Villani

Villanus is a vague term, apparently equivalent to the Old English *tunesman*, and most appropriately understood to mean nothing more specific than a member of the vill, or a 'villager'.[51] The *villani* of Domesday Book did not form a homogeneous group. The term *villanus* was employed to describe people of varying status and prosperity; the early twelfth-century Laws of Henry I describes the *villani* as 'lowly people lacking in substance', but it does credit them with the wergild of the *ceorl*, 200 shillings, suggestive of their basic freedom.[52] However, freedom is not the same thing as prosperity and, although the amount of land they held and the number of plough-teams assigned to them varied across the region, it is striking that the smallest average size of *villanus* holdings across England is to be found in Lincolnshire and Norfolk.[53] Manorial custom protected and defined their position and gave them a share in the arable, pasture and meadow of the village. They were all involved to a lesser or greater extent in the lord's demesne and owed heavier labour services than did the freemen and sokemen. Domesday Book does not elucidate this, but an early twelfth-century survey of Peterborough Abbey reveals that the

---

48. *DB*, fo. 283a.
49. P. Dalton, *Conquest, Anarchy and Lordship: Yorkshire 1066–1154* (1994), 33.
50. *DB*, fos. 338c–d.
51. In the same way that *tunesman* meant nothing more specific than to relate someone to the *tun* to which they pertained: Maitland, *Domesday Book and Beyond*, 86ff.; H.R. Loyn, *Anglo-Saxon England and the Norman Conquest* (2nd edn, 1991), 358.
52. S.J. Harvey, 'Domesday England' in *Ag. Hist.*, II, 45–136 at 50.
53. R.V. Lennard, *Rural England 1086–1135: a study of social and agrarian conditions* (1959), 339–92.

villani of Thurlby (Lincs) did two days' work per week and four days in August; they also had to render 33 shillings per annum and 22 hens.[54] Meanwhile the 20 *villani* of Collingham (Notts) had to perform a number of tasks:

> Each one of these works for the lord throughout the year one day in each week. And in August he performs three boon-works. And all these men bring 60 cartloads of wood to the lord's court, and they also dig and provide 20 cartloads of turves, or 20 cartloads of thatch. And they must harrow throughout the winter. And each year they pay four pounds of rent.[55]

Thus the obligations of the *villani* varied from manor to manor, and may long have done so, as the author of the *Rectitudines* implied.[56]

Cottarii/bordarii

Robert Losinga, bishop of Hereford (1079–95), described the rural population that Domesday Book intended to survey: they were to include 'those dwelling in cottages as well as those having houses and holdings in the arable fields'.[57] The latter were the *villani*, who were distinguishable from the landless and the smallholders, or *bordarii*. It is more difficult to categorize the *bordarii* (a term sometimes used interchangeably with *cottarii*, 'cottagers') of Domesday Book, but they probably had only a small amount of land; they seem not to have had a full share in the village lands, unlike the *villani*.[58] According to the surveys of the abbeys of Burton and Peterborough, the typical villein holding was two bovates (roughly 30 acres), whereas the average holding of the *bordarii* was between five and eight acres.[59] The typical holding of the *bordarii* was barely sufficient for subsistence and presumably they improved their lot by working for a lord or for other, more prosperous, peasants.[60] The term *bordarius* is unknown to pre-Domesday sources, and is but rarely used after. It is likely to have been a Latin translation of a Norman-French term. At a later date *bordiers* in northern France were smallholders who held a small amount of land and lived under very servile conditions. The close connection of their name with Old English and Old Norse *borde*, 'table', may explain

---

54. *Chronicon Petroburgense*, ed. T. Stapleton, Camden Society, 47 (1949), 160.
55. *EHD*, II, no. 177.
56. Harvey, 'Domesday England', 49–57.
57. *EHD*, II, no. 198.
58. Loyn, *Anglo-Saxon England*, 362.
59. Lennard, *Rural England*, 358, 362.
60. P.A. Stafford, *The East Midlands in the Early Middle Ages* (1985), 158–9; Harvey, 'Domesday England', 58–64.

something of their role: 'it was the seigneurial table and its needs that gave bordars and bordland their name'.[61]

Slaves

Few slaves (*servi*) are recorded in the northern Danelaw, and none in Lincolnshire and Yorkshire. However, in reality the complete absence of slaves seems unlikely. Manors with demesnes of any size would have required the labour of slaves, or of *bordarii*, to function properly, and one has to suspect omission on those manors where neither slaves nor *bordarii* are recorded.[62] The place-names Lazenby (meaning '*by*/settlement of the freedmen', found in Lincs and Yorks) and Laysingthorpe (the '*thorp*/outlying settlement of the freedmen', Lincs) indicate the freeing of slaves to becomes freedmen (*leysings*), as does the Domesday personal name Le(i)sing/Le(i)sinc.[63]

A core component of the territories controlled by lords was a relatively intensively exploited, and closely supervised, core area, sometimes known as 'inland'. The function of the people who lived on the inland was to provide the lord with supplies, and it was this that determined the lives and work of the people who lived there, including the restrictions on their freedoms, the tasks they performed and where they lived. These people were not, as we have seen, typical of the peasantry as a whole. Tracing the development of this rural group through to Domesday Book is not easy, in part because there are variations in status and obligations among this group, and in part because the terminology used in our sources is not consistent. The inhabitants of the inland, which need not have been a geographically coherent unit, include the man 'who takes a yard of land or more at a fixed money rent and cultivates it' from the laws of Ine, the *gebur* of the *Rectitudines* who was granted sown land, animals and 'tools for his work and utensils for his house' in return for certain work and payments, slaves and freed people (*coliberti*). These people are described variously by Domesday Book as *cottarii*, *bordarii*, slaves and *coliberti*. It is also apparent that the term *villanus* was used to describe some of these inland workers, but the term is so broad in its range of meanings that it must also have included people who were much less burdened.[64]

61. Faith, *The English Peasantry*, 70–4; A.J.L. Winchester, 'The distribution and significance of "bordland" in medieval Britain', *AgHR*, 34 (1986), 129–39.
62. Moore, 'Domesday slavery', 198–200.
63. *Ibid.*, 198; A.H. Smith, *English Place-Name Elements*, 2 pts, JEPNS, 25–6 (1956), 24.
64. Faith, *The English Peasantry*, 56–88.

Sokemen/liberi homines

What sets the various parts of the Danelaw apart in Domesday Book is the substantial number of 'free' peasants. Although sokemen and *liberi homines* were found in small numbers in most parts of the country, according to Domesday Book, it is in the counties of the Danelaw that they are most numerous (Fig. 5). Almost half the recorded total of sokemen are found in Lincolnshire, where *c.* 11,000 (around half the recorded population of Lincolnshire) are enumerated, although no *liberi homines* are recorded. Around 96 per cent of the total number of *liberi homines* are found in the entries for Norfolk and Suffolk.[65] In a study of the northern Danelaw it is the sokemen therefore who are of most interest, since *liberi homines* are few in number. However, although it is possible to detect differences in their status, the two groups share a number of characteristics. The following discussion will sometimes draw on evidence from the neighbouring counties of East Anglia, where evidence about the sokemen and *liberi homines* is more detailed, although it should be remembered that there is likely to have been significant regional variation in status. Nonetheless, it is likely that the origins of this stratum of the peasantry are to be found in the free peasant land-holding classes found everywhere to varying degrees in early medieval society.[66] As we shall see, these peasants owed their privileged status to their relationship with the king, to their access to public courts, and to the fact that the obligations placed on them did not derive from estate or manorial custom, as was the case for the rest of the peasantry.

As well as providing a guide to the distribution of sokemen and *liberi homines*, Domesday Book makes some reference to the dues that they owed and the rights and privileges they enjoyed. For example, it is often stated whether or not they could 'go with their land where they would' or whether they were free 'to give and sell it'. These were some of the most important rights of the sokeman and *liber homo*, although the fact that Domesday Book notes which of them could do so suggests that there were many others who could not. Even where free alienation and sale was permitted, some lord might still reserve the right to soke over the land, and this obligation would have to be met by the new recipient.[67] This interest in the right of alienation was concerned with freedom from seigneurial constraint; the capacity of the family to control alienation is a separate issue. As we have already observed, tenth-century sources from East Anglia indicate that the alienation of land by fairly humble people had been a feature of the society of the region at that time, and it does not seem that at this time, or at the time of Domesday Book, families normally sought to prevent alienation.[68] Domesday Book,

---

65. Loyn, *Anglo-Saxon England*, 357–62.
66. See Chapter 2, pp. 49–60, 72–84.
67. Maitland, *Domesday Book and Beyond*, 66–79.
68. Reynolds, *Fiefs and Vassals*, 334–5.

especially in the more detailed folios for East Anglia, also records that such free peasants were often commended to lords other than the lord of the manor to which they were attached.[69] Domesday Book records, although admittedly infrequently, that sokemen and *liberi homines* owed food renders and labour services, or equivalent payments in money, performed military service, escort duty and carrying service (services which could be commuted for a money payment), and were obliged to make suit to the lord's mill and his sheep-fold.[70] The term *consuetudines* is sometimes used to describe the burdens placed on sokemen and *liberi homines*, which seems to have incorporated a range of payments and obligations.[71] They were apparently responsible for their own geld payments. This would seem to be the implication of the instructions given to the Domesday commissioners to record not only how many sokemen and *liberi homines* there were, but how much land they held. Such information is not requested for *villani*, *bordarii* and the like.[72]

In an analysis of the distribution of sokemen and *liberi homines* the omissions of the Domesday record are a problem. For example, two early twelfth-century surveys of the estates of Burton Abbey reveal a class of rent-paying tenants (*censarii*) among the population of a number of Derbyshire manors whose status is much like that of sokemen; but no such comparable tenants are recorded on those manors in Domesday Book.[73] The *censarii* owed a money rent rather than undertaking weekly labour services, and they were obliged to do other services that were quite unlike villein service: messenger duty, hunting service and attendance at hundred and shire courts. It has been suggested that Domesday Book does not always record such people, since they owed only rents rather than labour services, but that the overall manorial assessments took their presence into account by allowing for the ploughs of the *censarii* in the calculation of ploughlands.[74] Later sources indicate that the Domesday scribes may not have been consistent in recording this class of peasant throughout the region.[75] The great royal sokes of the Derbyshire Peak District, such as Bakewell, are recorded as though they were populated by only *villani* and *bordarii*, but a class of people on the manor of Bakewell in the thirteenth century, who held land for small rents and were free to dispose of it, have the characteristics of sokemen, which suggests that

69. B. Dodwell, 'East Anglian commendation', *EHR*, 63 (1948), 289–306.
70. Maitland, *Domesday Book and Beyond*, 76–7; Stenton, *Types of Manorial Structure*, 36–7; Joy, 'Sokeright', 223–55.
71. Maitland, *Domesday Book and Beyond*, 76–9; Stenton, *Types of Manorial Structure*, 35–7.
72. Maitland, *Domesday Book and Beyond*, 23–5.
73. F. Baring, 'Domesday Book and the Burton cartulary', *EHR* 11 (1896), 98–102; Bridgeman, 'Burton Abbey twelfth-century surveys'.
74. J.F.R. Walmsley, 'The *censarii* of Burton Abbey and the Domesday population', *North Staffs. Journal of Field Studies*, 8 (1968), 73–80.
75. Roffe, *The Lincolnshire Domesday*, 20.

there may have been sokemen or their equivalent on the manor in the eleventh century.[76] The disproportionately large number of sokemen in Lincolnshire in the eleventh century is not, therefore, necessarily indicative of the fact that the peasantry of this county were uniquely privileged. In general, one might question whether Domesday Book would have taken as much notice of peasants over whom lords had only jurisdiction, or who mainly contributed rents rather than regular labour services; peasants who contributed more to the income of the lord's manor would presumably have been of greater interest. The attitude of estate administrators doubtless dictated the information rendered by the Domesday survey.[77] The nature of manorial organization was probably also another important factor. In Lincolnshire land-holding was complex and characterized by interlocking interests, with the result that it was necessary to provide detailed information about resources, the peasant population and seigneurial rights in given vills. By contrast in Derbyshire and Nottinghamshire, where many vills were held by a single lord, there was much less imperative to provide such detailed information since it was unlikely that another lord would claim rights (such as the right of soke) over a particular vill. Indeed, in some instances it appears that it was felt necessary to record only the population that worked the demesne, and to include the income from the sokemen in the assessment of the manorial resources (such as the number of ploughlands, for example), since no other lord had a claim in the soke dues of the manor.[78]

In their economic standing the Domesday sokemen and *liberi homines* were much less clearly distinguished from the rest of the rural population. The size of their holdings varied enormously.[79] Some held substantial amounts of land and had *villani* and *bordarii* beneath them: at Long Eaton (Derbs), for instance, 22 sokemen had nine *bordars* under them; and at Northorpe (Lincs) four sokemen had under them two *villani* and one *bordarius*.[80] They were virtually manorial lords, albeit on a limited scale, and in the Yorkshire folios might indeed have been assigned manors. At the other extreme, however, many were apparently no more prosperous than *villani*. Domesday Book offers little information concerning the holdings of sokemen and *liberi homines*, but near-contemporary sources reveal that on the estates of

---

76. Roffe, *The Derbyshire Domesday*, 8. Similarly, the Lincolnshire wapentake of Elloe had no recorded sokemen, but again omission should be suspected since later sources reveal that there were sokemen in Elloe, and these are unlikely to have been a newly created class: H.E. Hallam, 'Some thirteenth-century censuses', *EcHR*, 2nd ser., 10 (1958), 340–61; Roffe, *The Lincolnshire Domesday*, 19, where it is suggested that the number of *censarii*, only fourteen of whom are mentioned, may be seriously under-representative.
77. Roffe, *The Lincolnshire Domesday*, 19.
78. Roffe, 'Domesday Book and northern society', 331–3.
79. R.V. Lennard, 'The economic position of the Domesday sokemen', *Economic Journal*, 57 (1947), 179–95.
80. *DB*, fos. 273b, 345d.

the abbey of Bury St Edmunds many of the *liberi homines* had a holding assessed at no more than one acre, although a few had more than twenty.[81] In Lincolnshire sokemen rarely possessed more than 40 acres. As far as it is possible to tell, sokemen and *liberi homines* normally seem to have held land in only one place, although there were exceptions.[82] The small size of the holdings of many sokemen and *liberi homines* and the low average number of plough-beasts that they possessed prompts the conclusion that part of their continuing elevated status and their income did not primarily derive from their holding. Clearly, of major significance in maintaining their social and legal status was their access to the public courts of wapentake and shire. Obviously, economic prosperity, on the one hand, and social and legal status, on the other, are not the same thing, but a deterioration in the former may lead, in some instances, to changes in the latter. Given the small average size of the holdings of sokemen and *liberi homines*, trade in agrarian products and an emphasis on sheep-rearing have been offered as possible explanations for the continuing freedoms and prosperity of this stratum of the peasantry.[83] Unfortunately, Domesday Book is of little use in determining the significance of these factors; indeed, one attempt to compare the distribution of sokemen and recorded woodland and flocks of sheep revealed no obvious positive correlation.[84] The expansion of the cultivated area during the later Anglo-Saxon period may also help to explain the distribution of sokemen and *liberi homines*. *Liberi homines*, in particular, have been shown to be especially numerous around the East Anglian marshlands; presumably the extension of the settlement area there was undertaken by this stratum of the peasantry.[85] It has been shown at a later date that dense concentrations of population which gave rise to small land-holdings could be viable because the availability of labour rendered possible intensive methods of cultivation.[86]

It is the dues and obligations of the sokemen and *liberi homines* that most clearly distinguish them from the rest of the peasantry, and for a fuller insight into these we must turn to sources later than Domesday Book. The so-called *Kalendar* of Abbot Samson, a survey of the holdings of the abbey of Bury St Edmunds in the thirteenth century, indicates that in East Anglia the dues of the sokemen were hundredal; that is to say, they were organized and owed through the hundred rather than the manor. The stock phrase used is 'nunc de carrucatis terre istius hundredi dicendum est'.[87] These were apparently regalian

---

81. Lennard, *Rural England*, 359–60.
82. Lennard, 'The economic position of the Domesday sokemen', 194.
83. Loyn, *Anglo-Saxon England*, 361–2.
84. B. Dodwell, 'The free peasantry of East Anglia in Domesday', *Norfolk Archaeology*, 27 (1947), 145–57, at 149–51.
85. T. Williamson, *The Origins of Norfolk* (1993), 119–21.
86. B.M.S. Campbell, 'Agricultural progress in medieval England: some evidence from Norfolk', *EcHR*, 2nd ser., 36 (1983), 24–46.
87. *Kalendar of Abbot Samson*, ed. Davis, xxxii.

dues which had been granted to the abbey. Certainly these dues were collected through manors belonging to the abbey, but this was a matter of administrative convenience. The dues of the sokemen included carrying-service (*averagium*), which could be commuted for a money payment (*averpeni*), guard-service (*inguard*), which could be commuted (for *wardpenny*), and the provision of *foddercorn* (oats for the king's horses). Sokemen were able to buy and sell sokeland, although they sometimes needed the permission of the abbey, and the services incumbent on the land still had to be met.[88] By the thirteenth century the sokeman's dues were said to be fixed, as opposed to those of the *villani*, which were dependent on manorial custom and seigneurial will; as a result, the sokemen 'were said to be free'.[89] Nonetheless, the very fact that twelfth- and thirteenth-century codifications of the status of the sokemen protected them from dispossession and from arbitrary increases in the demands made of them suggests that such eventualities were at least possible.[90]

Twelfth- and thirteenth-century estate surveys from the abbeys of Burton, Ely, Peterborough and Bury St Edmunds reveal that sokemen and *liberi homines* characteristically owed lighter and less onerous labour services than did other peasant classes, if indeed they owed any at all. For example, according to the *Liber Niger* of Peterborough Abbey, there were 50 sokemen at Collingham (Notts):

> who hold two and a half carucates of land. And each one of these must work by custom each year for six days at the deer hedge. And in August each shall work three days. And all these have 14 ploughs and with them they shall work for the lord four times in Lent. ... And the aforesaid sokemen pay 12 pounds each year.[91]

A comparable burden lay upon the sokemen at Winshill (Derbyshire), who were obliged to go with the hunt on three days in a year and to lend their plough and one man for two days to the abbot of Burton, and for three days in August.[92] Sokemen commonly owed rent rather than labour service: the sokemen and their equivalent the *censarii* of Burton Abbey held their land for a money rent (*ad malam*), in contrast to the *villani*, who held their land in return for labour service (*ad opus*).[93] *Villani* commonly owed week-work whereas sokemen and *liberi homines* owed boon-work (occasional services, such as the three days in August for harvest). The labour services of the *villani* were central to the efficient running of the manor, whereas those of the sokemen

88.   *Ibid.*, xxxii–xxxv.
89.   W. Stubbs, *Select Charters and Other Illustrations of English Constitutional History from the Earliest Times to the Reign of Edward the First* (1929), 415.
90.   Harvey, 'Domesday England', 75–6.
91.   *EHD*, II, no. 177; these obligations may be compared with those of the *villani* in the same place – see p. 178 above.
92.   Bridgeman, 'Burton Abbey twelfth-century surveys', 240–2.
93.   *Ibid.*, 281–99.

were additional and, to some extent, symbolic. They seem more likely to have derived from the occasional services required by the king as part of the royal farm. Stenton's emphasis is on 'jurisdiction', which is a relatively imprecise concept, as the fundamental right enjoyed by soke lords over their lands encouraged him to depict the Danelaw as being characterized by fluid associations of free peasants; however, this seems an inappropriate statement about the social structure of the northern Danelaw in the eleventh century.[94] Even if sokemen had the right to commend themselves to other lords, or were at liberty 'to go where they would' with their land, in practice, because lords relied on the labour services and dues owed by the inhabitants of their estates – and even occasional services could be extremely important to a lord's income – by the eleventh century it is most unlikely that even the freer peasants were at liberty to withdraw unilaterally from the manors to which they and their lands were attached, whatever had been the situation at an earlier date.[95]

The very word 'sokeman' derives from the Old English word *socn*, 'the act of seeking'; the sokeman was a suitor at a court, and access to the, originally, public court of the soke was perhaps the most important defining characteristic of the sokemen.[96] The *Kalendar* of the abbey of Bury St Edmunds reveals a little about the obligations of the sokemen to render suit of court. It lists the suits of court owed from the hundred and its constituent leets (groups of vills equivalent in function to the hundred of the northern Danelaw) and vills. Sokemen owed suit of court according to the lands that they held, but if the land was subdivided among heirs, then the responsibility to render suit would be divided between them. Of course, in this instance the sokemen concerned rendered suit of court to a private ecclesiastical lord, but it was presumably an obligation that had originally been owed to public courts, but which had been granted to a private lord. As local courts and the arrangements for keeping the peace were developed, they were instrumental in defining further the distinctions between the various strata of the rural population.[97] There also is some evidence to suggest that sokemen had military obligations to meet. The Peterborough Chronicle includes a *Descriptio Militum*, compiled *c.* 1100–10, which declares that the sokemen of certain vills were obliged to serve '*cum militibus*'. No further explanation of the service is given and it is unclear whether they were expected to serve in a military capacity, or whether they provided equipment or financial

94. F.M. Stenton, 'The free peasantry of the northern Danelaw', *Bulletin de la Société Royale des lettres de Lund* (1925–6), 73–185; Stenton, 'The Danes in England'.

95. Roffe, 'The "*Descriptio Terrarum*"', 11–12; C. Stephenson, 'Commendation and related problems in Domesday', *EHR*, 59 (1944), 289–310.

96. Stenton, *Social and Economic History of the Danelaw*, cix–cx; E. Miller, *The Abbey and Bishopric of Ely: the social history of an ecclesiastical estate from the tenth to the early fourteenth century* (1951), 116–19.

97. Faith, *The English Peasantry*, 255–8.

support for the knights or served as grooms or esquires.[98] There are also occasional indications in Domesday Book that military service was required from sokemen:

S. In Old Somerby Æthelgyth [had] 6 bovates of land [assessed] to the geld taxable. ...This soke[land] was such that it used to render nothing, but used to help in the king's host [*adiuabat in exercitu regis*] on land and at sea.[99]

M. In the same vill [Swaton] Alsige and Æthelstan had 1 carucate of land [assessed] to the geld .... Ælfric their brother had the soke over them in Haceby only in the king's service [*solummodo in seruitio regis*].[100]

M. In Wilsford Siward had 9 carucates of land [assessed] to the geld. ... Of this land Atsurr his brother had 6 bovates and 1 mill quit from all service except the host [*exercitum*].[101]

Admittedly none of these entries from Lincolnshire relates directly to sokemen, but they do suggest that rights of soke involved the right to exact military service, and when combined with later references to sokemen performing military service provide compulsive, if necessarily imprecise, evidence for the performance of military service by sokemen.[102] It is to be expected that the military service comprised a range of activities that varied from region to region. There is, finally, some evidence to suggest that communities of sokemen and *liberi homines* built churches.[103] The presence of churches on sokeland where only sokemen are found, such as at Springthorpe (Lincs), or on sokeland apparently without a resident lord, such as at Mareham-le-Fen (Lincs), may indicate a similar phenomenon of the foundation of churches by sokemen.[104]

Stenton suggested that within the ranks of the sokemen there was a distinction to be drawn between intra-manorial and extra-manorial sokemen; that is, between those situated within the confines of a manor and those who inhabited the dependencies of a manor.[105] However, we have already seen that Domesday Book was not always

---

98. E. King, 'The Peterborough *"descriptio militum"* ', *EHR*, 84 (1969), 84–101; Stenton, *Types of Manorial Structure*, 28–31.
99. *DB*, fo. 368a.
100. *Ibid.*, fo. 357c.
101. *Ibid.*, fo. 366b.
102. Stenton, *Types of Manorial Structure*, 28–31.
103. Stenton, *Social and Economic History of the Danelaw*, lxx–lxxi; P. Warner, 'Shared churchyards, freemen church builders and the development of parishes in eleventh-century East Anglia', *Landscape History*, 8 (1986), 39–52.
104. *DB*, fos. 338c, 339a.
105. Stenton, *Types of Manorial Structure*, 46–9.

consistent in drawing distinctions between what is, and what is not, a manor. Moreover, the fact that the sokemen of Scotter (Lincs) owed the same dues to Peterborough Abbey, according to a contemporary survey, whether they were intra- or extra-manorial suggests that there was no significant distinction to be drawn.[106] On the other hand, it is not unlikely that a major ecclesiastical lord would seek to standardize dues and services. The day-to-day experiences of the sokemen who occupied land close to the manorial centre were likely to have been rather different from the experiences of those who were situated many miles away; the latter were doubtless less vulnerable to seigneurial pressures. It is likely that within the stratum of the peasantry described as sokemen and *liberi homines* there was an enormous range in social as well as economic status. Sally Harvey has commented on the distinction between those sokemen who had small land-holdings, were largely annexed to manors by the time of the Domesday survey and were not easily economically distinguishable from the *villani*, and the thegn-like sokemen who had substantial holdings, were almost akin to manorial lords and were more likely to owe their dues directly to the king rather than through a manor.[107] It is important to remember that legal and social status were not the same thing as economic prosperity.

Many attempts to distinguish between sokemen and *liberi homines* and to define the differences have been made. In the counties of the northern Danelaw only sokemen are recorded, and most counties surveyed by Domesday Book have a preponderance of either sokemen or *liberi homines*, suggesting that the terms may be interchangeable and that Domesday scribes chose whichever they preferred.[108] This is borne out by a comparison of Domesday Book with the *Feudal Book of Abbot Baldwin of Bury St Edmunds*, which was probably compiled shortly before Domesday Book. Where Domesday Book describes *liberi homines*, the *Feudal Book* often records sokemen: for example, at Great Barton (Suff) Domesday Book records 70 *liberi homines* whereas the *Feudal Book* records 70 sokemen.[109] However, in many East Anglian entries Domesday Book does draw distinctions between sokemen and *liberi homines*. The clearest distinction in their status is that *liberi homines* are more commonly said to be able to 'go where they will' with their land than are sokemen. However, there are also examples of sokemen who could withdraw and *liberi homines* who could not, so this distinction in status is not universal. A recent comparison of the distribution of sokemen and *liberi homines* in Norfolk suggests that sokemen seem to be more closely tied to manors than were *liberi homines* and are consequently located near the heart of the major estates, whereas the *liberi homines* tend to be located at a greater

---

106. *Chronicon Petroburgense*, ed. Stapleton, 157–83; D.R. Roffe, 'The Lincolnshire hundred', *Landscape History*, 3 (1981), 27–36, at 31.
107. Harvey, 'Domesday England', 72–8.
108. R. Welldon-Finn, *Domesday Studies: the eastern counties* (1967), 123.
109. Lennard, *Rural England*, 349, n. 1.

distance, often on marginal land or newly colonized land.[110] Despite such local distinctions it is not easy to distinguish sokemen from *liberi homines*, because neither appears to have formed a homogeneous group by the eleventh century, if indeed they ever had done. It is questionable how readily contemporaries would have been able to distinguish one group from another; had the commissioners who surveyed East Anglia also surveyed Lincolnshire, perhaps they would have found *liberi homines* lurking among the sokemen. We may conclude that sokemen and *liberi homines* were heterogeneous groups distinguished from the rest of the rural population by greater legal freedoms, which were, however, increasingly being diminished. Although sokemen and *liberi homines* were being submerged within the manorial system, vestiges of their status did survive in some regions, most notably their links to the public courts of the wapentakes and their continuing performance of specialized services.

It is worth noting that although Domesday Book employs a limited range of terms to describe and distinguish the various groups within the rural population, the reality may have been more complex and fluid. Twelfth-century charters commonly fail to distinguish the various rural classes, and often employ the general word *homo* to describe people of varying social rank.[111] The extent of the fluidity between the various classes is not entirely clear, but a comparison of Domesday entries with twelfth-century charters suggests that peasants could and did move from one group to the other. Intermarriage between people who held land in different ways was also common. Moreover, later manorial surveys reveal that, for example, the same people could hold both sokeland and villein land and as a result had to meet the obligations incumbent on both types of land. It is extremely difficult to determine the status of such people. Indeed, there is a distinction to be drawn between status and tenure; some peasants whom Domesday Book would have called sokemen also held land by villein service at a later date.[112] Domesday Book simplified society, and the terms it used reflected uneasily on the complexity of rural society.

Although the sokemen and *liberi homines* of the Danelaw have long been viewed as an anomalous group, comparison with the rest of Europe suggests that they are the descendants of a much earlier stratum of free peasant landowners. Three factors have hindered us from appreciating this: the belief that early medieval society was characterized by manorial-style exploitation and a heavily burdened, and 'unfree', peasantry; the association of the free peasants of Domesday Book with the Scandinavian settlement; and the interpretation of

---

110. Williamson, *The Origins of Norfolk*, 117–22.
111. Stenton, *Social and Economic History of the Danelaw*, lxxviii.
112. W. Hudson, 'Traces of primitive agricultural organization as suggested by a survey of the manor of Martham, Norfolk, 1101–1292', *TRHS*, 4th ser., 1 (1918), 28–58; P.R. Hyams, *Kings, Lords and Peasants in Medieval England* (1980), 55, 115, 180; J.A. Raftis, 'The East Midlands', *Ag. Hist.*, II, 634–51.

Domesday Book as depicting a rigid tenurial hierarchy, in which those at the lower end of the social scale all held their land on limited terms from someone else. Now that all these ideas have been revised it is much more plausible to draw a connection between the free peasants and sokemen of the eleventh century and the free peasant landowners of a much earlier date. Of course, this is not to deny that there were changes in those freedoms throughout the Anglo-Saxon period. What an individual might have freedom to do, or freedom from, would obviously vary according to the nature of the wider society. Domesday Book identifies certain characteristics of freedom, related to possession of land, service to a lord and status in the courts, but none of these freedoms was immutable.[113] Clearly, estate policy changed and this had implications for the services demanded of the peasantry, and freedom to sell land was proscribed by the rights that greater lords had over the land and the service owed from it, as much as by familial and social expectations. The legal requirements of courts had also developed in important ways through the tenth century. To discuss further the reasons why there were so many sokemen in the northern Danelaw we need to address more closely aspects of estate policy, as this seems to have been of central importance to their survival.

The peasantry and the manorial structure of Domesday Book

Was the Danelaw really 'the home of liberty', as Maitland maintained?[114] Is peasant freedom more prevalent in the Danelaw than elsewhere in England? And if so, why? As we have already seen, Domesday Book is not always consistent in the way that it records the inhabitants of manors. The more fragmented the tenurial arrangement in a given place, the more likely it is that the survey will record its inhabitants in great detail. Yet even taking into account the foibles of Domesday Book, there are still broad differences between the social structure of many parts of the Danelaw and that elsewhere. Not only are there more sokemen and *liberi homines* in the Danelaw than elsewhere, but there are also proportionately fewer *bordarii, cottarii* and slaves in the Danelaw. Together these figures suggest that a far smaller percentage of the rural population was closely involved in providing for the seigneurial economy than in other regions of England.[115]

Ethnic explanations for the differences in early medieval society have long since been abandoned. We now no longer believe that the sokemen were the descendants of the 'rank and file' of the

---

113. P.A. Stafford, *Unification and Conquest: a political and social history of England in the tenth and eleventh centuries* (1989), 208.
114. Maitland, *Domesday Book and Beyond*, 23.
115. Faith, *The English Peasantry*, 86–8.

Scandinavian armies, or that the peculiarities of the society of the Danelaw should be ascribed solely, or even mainly, to the Scandinavian settlement. Such ethnic explanations have been replaced with interpretations that emphasize the similarity of the characteristic features of the society of the Danelaw to those found in other early medieval societies. However, explanations are still required for the distinctiveness of the society of the Danelaw in the eleventh century when compared with other parts of England. Increasingly apparent is the importance of estate management and seigneurial policy, although this is not to deny that the Scandinavian conquest, as much as the subsequent West Saxon conquest, was significant. Even with the limited documentary evidence available for the region, it is possible to trace some of the developments that created the social structure of Domesday Book.

It is entirely appropriate that remnants of peasant liberties should survive in the northern Danelaw. It was a region which was subject to two conquests, in the ninth and tenth centuries, from which followed major upheavals in patterns of land-holding and lordship. The local power bases were severely disrupted. Fragmented patterns of land-holding prevailed, and by the eleventh century some manorial lords and their halls were located at great distances from much of the land and the peasantry they sought to exploit, rendering seigneurial involvement in the lives of the inhabitants of those vills, and the imposition of labour services, far less likely. There appears to have been a vigorous land market. Here also the communal interests of the peasantry remained strong, as is reflected in the continuing importance of the vill rather than the manor as a taxation and administrative unit. Contemporary analogy leads us to expect a higher incidence of peasant freedom and land-owning in such contexts, so the northern Danelaw is not unusual. In the previous chapter it was suggested that a number of the sokes of the northern Danelaw had come into existence since the mid-tenth century, and such transformations of territorial organization also seems to have been a contributory factor to the level of peasant freedom. Large sokes and those which appear to have been constructed in the later Anglo-Saxon period are characterized by a high percentage of sokemen, according to Domesday Book. Of course, this conclusion has to be subject to the caveat that Domesday Book is clearly not a totally reliable guide to the peasant population of the northern Danelaw. However, from the evidence that it presents it is apparent that sokemen are more common on large sokes and in vills with divided lordship. The fragmentation of tenurial organization contributed to the survival of large numbers of free peasants, doubtless in part because it rendered seigneurial domination of townships by individual lords relatively uncommon.

The survival of sokemen in the northern Danelaw may also be linked to the low level of ecclesiastical land-holding. It is difficult to establish the origins of this situation, although the Scandinavian settlement was undoubtedly a factor, as was the virtual absence of re-formed and re-endowed monasteries in the northern Danelaw in the tenth and eleventh centuries. The significance of this can be demonstrated by comparison with East Anglia, where the lands of the re-founded monasteries of the tenth century are notable as 'islands of a much more "manorialized" peasantry than was typical of the region as a whole'.[116] Other factors which may have been relevant to the survival of sokemen are less straightforward to identify. Recent work on East Anglia has suggested that the nature of the landscape and the emphasis on pastoralism may account for the high incidence of sokemen and *liberi homines*.[117] Given the difficulties of the Domesday text and the suspected level of omission, it is difficult to be sure about this factor in the northern Danelaw; the relatively unmanorialized upland areas where we might expect to find less emphasis on intensive arable exploitation, and, perhaps, as a consequence, a high proportion of sokemen, are particularly poorly dealt with by the Domesday text.

The status of the peasantry had much to do with the ability of lords to bring the peasants on their estates into dependence. Some lords, especially absentee lords, were less inclined to develop and maintain a substantial demesne on their lands, and were content to receive rents and occasional services; in such circumstances sokemen were likely to fare better. Although it is rarely possible to determine seigneurial policy at an early date, it is striking that on the lands that Wulfric Spott bequeathed in his will in the early eleventh century, there was, at the time of Domesday Book, a relatively high percentage of sokemen, as well as relatively small numbers of demesne ploughs. Certainly with extensive lands spread over the north Midlands, the largely absentee Wulfric would have been precisely the type of lord to emphasize rents on his lands, and to be less concerned to engage in intensive demesne exploitation.[118]

Clearly, by the eleventh century the sokemen of the northern Danelaw, although undoubtedly a privileged class among the peasantry, were subordinated to the manorial system and to seigneurial policy. They may have enjoyed many freedoms and privileges but they were not at liberty to live beyond the grasp of some lord or other. The increasing acquisition by lords of rights over peasant landholders cannot be traced in any great detail, but general processes in Anglo-Saxon society and analogy with contemporary societies suggest the gradual but inexorable seigneurialization of the countryside. By the eleventh century not only were sokemen and their land firmly annexed to manorial structures but lords had begun to encroach on sokeland, and in a few instances seigneurial plough-teams

---

116. *Ibid.*, 82–3.
117. Williamson, *The Origins of Norfolk*, 117–22.
118. G.T. Davies, 'The origins of the parishes of south Yorkshire', *South Yorkshire Historian*, 4 (1980), 1–18, at 7–8; on seigneurial policy, see Faith, *The English Peasantry*, 85–8, 168–77.

were to be found on sokeland. We have already noted the fact that there was much fluidity in the Domesday text concerning the concept of a manor and in the classification of types of holding; the presence of demesne ploughs on sokeland contributed to the process of manorialization. Indeed, where there was a 'subtenant' such a holding might appear in Domesday Book as a manor. The absence of sokemen from sokeland entries may also suggest the encroachment of the seigneurial hand.

The removal of sokemen and *liberi homines* from one manor to another is not uncommonly mentioned, especially in the more detailed folios for East Anglia: for example, King William placed six sokemen who belonged to Repton in the manor of Winshill.[119] The sokemen and *liberi homines* were sliding into a much less privileged position, and Domesday allows us a glimpse of the processes involved. The annexation of this section of the peasantry to the manorial structure threatened to deprive them of both access to the public authority and the capacity to perform and meet the public exactions and obligations that characterized their status. When combined with rising population and the weakening of the sokeman's economic basis, it might prove difficult to resist increased seigneurial demands. At Fersfield (Norfolk), Domesday Book notes that only the soke of those who had more than 30 acres pertained to the hundred; those who had less land remained under the lord's control.[120] Changes in status are also sometimes mentioned by Domesday Book, and it is clear that between 1066 and 1086 the number of sokemen and *liberi homines* fell. For example, in the soke of Falsgrave (Yorks) there were 108 sokemen in 1066 but in 1086 there were only 7.[121] In Cambridgeshire the number of sokemen fell from over 900 to around 200.[122] Occasionally we are given glimpses of the processes involved. At Benfleet (Essex) a freeman who had half a hide in 1066 had later been 'made one of the *villani*'. Although examples are more readily drawn from the more detailed folios of East Anglia, it is not to be doubted that such developments had been, and were still, a feature of the society of the northern Danelaw. Yet in spite of these pressures on the sokemen of the region and the fact that they were so clearly an integral part of the estate structure of the northern Danelaw in the eleventh century, their status did not derive *from* those estates – although the development of those estates certainly served to submerge their privileges.

An important feature of the manorial structure of Domesday Book and its relationship with peasant organization is the quite consistent distribution of the various peasant classes within the manorial structure (even given the caveats already expressed about omissions from the text). Sokemen are consistently located within manors or on

---

119.   *DB*, fo. 273b.
120.   *Ibid.*, II, fo. 130b.
121.   *Ibid.*, fos. 299a–b.
122.   Maitland, *Domesday Book and Beyond*, 62–3.

sokeland, but are much less commonly found on berewicks/inland. The reason for this is clearly that sokemen were not generally associated with the lord's demesne; they were located on their own land. This was either a separate vill, recorded as sokeland, or a separate part within the manor; it is notable that when sokemen are recorded on manors they are generally assigned their own plough-teams, which were separate from those of the demesne. On the manor of Kirton in Lindsey (Lincs) there were no sokemen, but spread among its sokelands there were 223 sokemen; it is notable that at the only dependency (for which populations are given) where no sokemen are recorded – Hibaldstow – there is a demesne plough, and the text notes later that Hibaldstow is in fact a berewick, not sokeland.[123] Similarly, on the soke of Caistor, sokemen are outnumbered at the manorial centre by *villani*, as they are on the dependencies described as inland; but on the sokeland they are much more numerous.[124] Such a pattern is replicated in the sokes of, for example, Mansfield, Sutton-by-Retford (Notts) and Conisbrough (Yorks).[125] The encroachment of demesne ploughs on to sokeland seems to have been detrimental to the survival of sokemen; and in this we may see part of the gradual process of manorialization.

It is also notable that sokemen were more numerous on large manors than on small manors. This is undoubtedly because on small manors the lord, in order to maximize his income, developed proportionately larger demesnes than are found on large manors, and demesnes were detrimental to the survival of sokemen. A number of examples demonstrate these points. In 1066 Keelby (Lincs) was divided into seven manors, and there was also a parcel of sokeland belonging to the manor of Caistor. On the sokeland there were 13 sokemen, but on the seven small manors there were only 6 recorded sokemen in total, and four of the manors had no sokemen at all.[126] At South Muskham (Notts), in the manor held by the archbishop of York, and assessed at four carucates and five bovates, there were 20 sokemen, whereas in the smaller manor held in 1066 by Athelstan, and assessed at only six bovates, there was only 1 sokeman.[127] In Barrow upon Humber (Lincs) there were 50 sokemen on the nine carucate manor held in 1066 by Earl Morcar, but none on the smaller manors held by Earnwine and Siward.[128] Lords of small estates are likely to have exploited their lands more intensively in order to make a living for themselves, and this is consistently associated with lower numbers of sokemen.[129]

The proportion of an estate given over to the lord's demesne varied, with concomitant implications for the peasant inhabitants of those estates. This movement towards the creation of more intensively

---

123. *DB*, fos. 338b–c.
124. *Ibid.*, fos. 338c–d.
125. *Ibid.*, fos. 281b–c, 283b, 321b.
126. Stenton, *Types of Manorial Structure*, 64–6.
127. *DB*, fos. 283a, 293b.
128. *Ibid.*, fo. 360b.
129. Faith, *The English Peasantry*, 157.

exploited inlands, or a demesne-oriented economy, seems to have continued through the tenth and eleventh centuries and beyond. W.E. Kapelle has argued that the creation of new demesnes is indicated by the Domesday record of manors with more ploughlands *in dominio* than there was ploughland for them.[130] At Pontefract (Yorks) he argues for the creation of a geld-free inland after 1066, where Ilbert de Lacy built a castle on which the *villani*, *cottarii* and *bordarii* were heavily burdened with labour services imposed since the Conquest.[131] There are a number of examples that may be cited of what appears to be the creation of a small demesne by 1086 within holdings that do not seem to have had one in 1066. The soke of Bolingbroke (Lincs) provides examples of this process. On most of the sokelands the sokemen, *villani* and *bordarii* possessed between them as many ploughs as there were ploughlands. For example, at Asgarby there was land for three ploughs, and the 20 sokemen and 2 *villani* had three ploughs between them. However, on a few of the sokelands (for example, Halton Holegate and Little Steeping, Sibsey, East Keal, and East Kirkby and Revesby) the post-Conquest holder of the soke, Ivo Taillebois, had a plough which brought the actual number of ploughs to more than the number of ploughlands.[132] Changes to the organization of this estate can be charted in the twelfth century, when a Cistercian house was founded at Revesby by William de Roumare, Earl of Lincoln, in 1142. The land of the peasants was required for the monastic grange, and the earl gave the peasant inhabitants the choice of accepting new holdings on new terms or leaving. These terms distinguished between doing regular week-work or boon-works, including annual harvest work, and this may indicate a continuing distinction between villein and sokeman status, although the peasant tenants were no longer described in these terms in 1142. This foundation charter sees a new stage in the development of a demesne at Revesby. It is not made explicit, but it is probable that the charter offered those who agreed to the exchange of land better terms than they had previously enjoyed on their holdings; this was certainly true for the three knightly tenants who accepted new terms. However, the new terms were not so favourable as to prevent most of the peasants from taking the option to leave. The negotiations that the lord embarked upon seem to derive from the fact that the land in question was former sokeland and, as the charter of 1142 states, was not *in proprio dominio*.[133]

The inland, including the demesne, of large multi-vill estates was commonly spread over a relatively wide area, and it was on such land that the most dependent and heavily encumbered peasants were to be found in the eleventh century. We know that some estates were organized in this

130. W.E. Kapelle, *The Norman Conquest of the North: the region and its transformation, 1000–1135* (1979), 153–77.
131. *DB*, 316c; Kapelle, *The Norman Conquest*, 179.
132. *DB*, fos. 351b–c.
133. Stenton, *Types of Manorial Structure*, 24–6.

manner in the northern Danelaw in or before the mid-tenth century, although not all were organized this way. Some Domesday sokes had the inland located much closer to the estate centre, and the rest of the soke consisted of widely scattered sokeland. Examples of this include Newark-on-Trent (with berewicks in adjacent Balderton and Farndon) and Pocklington (with berewicks in neighbouring Hayton, Millington and Bielby) (Yorks). In the thirteenth century this arrangement was still in force at Newark, and the bishop of Lincoln's demesne of the manor was still located in the former berewicks.[134] In the case of smaller manors we find similar variety in the distribution of inland and demesne land. There is some twelfth-century evidence to suggest that demesne land was often distributed throughout the fields of the township, alongside the lands of the peasantry. Equally, however, we do also find evidence, such as at Laxton (Notts), to reveal that the part of the demesne of the manor was separate from the land of the peasants and was located adjacent to the manorial centre.[135]

It is difficult to trace in any detail the changing circumstances of the peasantry, but there is some evidence to suggest that through the later Anglo-Saxon period and on into the post-Conquest period there were important developments in estate organization, and also in peasant status and obligations. Also clear is the importance that the policy adopted by given lords had for the inhabitants of their estates. The available written sources allow us to detect, however imperfectly, the processes by which lords moved from enjoying tribute and occasional services from the peasant population to a system in which the lord became more directly involved in the exploitation of the land, and occasional renders become transformed into regular renders, and labour services.[136] It is common to describe this process as 'manorialization', although the term 'manor' does not appear prior to Domesday Book. Manorialization was a process by which lords exploited lands and people more systematically, and which developed from below as well as from above through the initiative of great lords. This would seem to be the conclusion to be drawn from the examples of sokemen who had *villani* and *bordarii* below them, according to Domesday Book. Evidence from elsewhere for the *ceorl* who might prosper to acquire the status of a thegn suggests a similar process.[137] The numerous small manors of Domesday Book need not be envisaged as having come into being only through the dismemberment of a larger 'estate' by a great lord, and may have been created through the efforts of small lords who had no need, or likelihood, of receiving either a land-book or the sanction of great lords or the king.

---

134. M.W. Barley, *Documents Relating to the Manor and Soke of Newark-on-Trent*, Thoroton Record Society Series, 16 (1956), xliv–xlv.
135. Stenton, *Social and Economic History of the Danelaw*, lvii–lix; C.S. Orwin and C.S. Orwin, *The Open Fields* (1938), 95.
136. Maitland, *Domesday Book and Beyond*, 319–20.
137. See Chapter 2, pp. 73–5.

One final point needs to be made about the sokemen of the region. At the end of his important survey of the manorial structure of the northern Danelaw Sir Frank Stenton was left with a dilemma. Having argued for the basic freedom of the peasantry of the region and the relatively 'unmanorialized' nature of many of its vills, he acknowledged that there was a body of evidence that undermined his case:

> the place-names of the Trent basin raise a silent protest which has hitherto been too little regarded. Brooksby, Thorganby, Gamston, Skegby, are names which will not permit us to deny a primitive superiority, of whatever origin or extent, to Broc, Thorgrim, Gamel, and Skegg. We may minimize the significance of the eponymous lord; we may refuse him the ownership of the village lands; we may believe that a village of free settlers coexisted from the beginning beside his dominant homestead; but we cannot explain him away ... the reconciliation of the personal element compounded in countless place-names with the general freedom which distinguished the Danelaw villages of 1066 is a task which must be undertaken in the future.[138]

In many respects modern work and the interpretation offered here have resolved Stenton's dilemma. The stages by which lords came to dominate their estates and exploit the peasantry were many and varied and there is, in fact, no necessary dichotomy between lordship and peasant freedom. The context in which personal names entered place-names seems to have been the increasingly close relationship of lords with individual townships, and this may have been a relatively late development in the Anglo-Saxon period. Moreover, the distribution of these place-names in the eleventh century suggests that not all places that were named after someone were, or remained, separate manorial-style properties; many were berewicks or sokelands. Furthermore, it suggests that over any given block of land more than one lord might have rights of various sorts: for example, the soke lord and the eponymous immediate lord of the land. This seems to be another indication that the path towards the manorial structure of the later medieval period was neither even nor predictable. As we have seen, the rights enjoyed by lords over their lands varied, and even within a relatively small land-holding there would be land and people less fully exploited by the lord. Rather than being a problem, then, the observation made by Stenton may serve more as confirmation that lordship and peasant freedom were *not* necessarily mutually exclusive.

---

138.   Stenton, *Types of Manorial Structure*, 91.

The impact of lords and peasants on the landscape

The changing exploitation of the countryside and of its inhabitants left its mark on the landscape. The settlements and field systems of the region were both a product of, and a contributory element to, these changes. It is now widely accepted that the nucleated villages of the later Middle Ages find their origins in the period *c.* 800–1200, as do the open-field systems with which they were commonly linked.[139] However, explanations for their emergence vary. Broadly speaking there are two schools of thought: one argues that lords were responsible for planning and reordering the landscape; the other looks, instead, to the influence of peasant communities. Much ink has been spilled over this thorny issue.[140] There are good reasons to maintain that no single explanation is adequate, and that the relevant social dynamics included both relationships within the peasantry and the tensions and compromises between lords and peasants.

The archaeology of Anglo-Saxon rural settlement reveals a diversity of settlement types. Isolated hamlets and farmsteads were not uncommon, but nucleated clusters of farmsteads have also been found. Excavation has shown that many late medieval villages were not on the sites of earlier settlement, and that they did not take their late medieval form until the eleventh or twelfth century. Prior to this, nucleated settlements were formed and abandoned, and, like their later medieval counterparts, might be either irregular arrangements of buildings or more regularly laid out. Some studies have argued that there was a widespread abandonment of settlement in the Middle Saxon period, at which point the sites occupied by later villages came into occupation. This has been dubbed the 'Middle Saxon shuffle'. However, more recently it has been argued that the evidence on which the argument for sudden abandonment is based may be reinterpreted as evidence for a continual shifting of settlement location throughout the Anglo-Saxon period.[141]

Village origins in the northern Danelaw

In discussing the reasons for settlement nucleation, and for the relative stability of nucleated villages (at least until the fourteenth century), we need to be clear that villages continued to change and develop in important ways throughout the later medieval period. Therefore, the plans of villages (on post-medieval maps, or revealed by

---

139. There is a vast literature on these subjects; for a recent overview, see C. Lewis, P. Mitchell-Fox and C.C. Dyer, *Village, Hamlet and Field: changing medieval settlements in central England* (1997), 1–37.
140. See Chapter 1, pp. 33–5.
141. H. Hamerow, 'Settlement mobility and the "Middle Saxon shift": rural settlements and settlement patterns in Anglo-Saxon England', *ASE*, 20 (1991), 1–17.

earthworks of deserted villages) need not reveal the layout of the village at the point of nucleation. Indeed, recent work in Lincolnshire has revealed the extent of evidence for reorganization of villages. Parts of villages can be shown to overlie ridge and furrow, as at Coates, South Carlton, West Rasen, East Torrington and Somerby, for example. The presence of two or more distinct, and differently aligned, elements to villages suggests successive phases in the laying out of the village, as at Southrey, Scotter, Stow, Faldingworth, Tealby, Nettleham and Welton (Fig. 33).[142] The fact that some parts of villages have a more regular appearance than others may also have something to reveal about the origins and development of villages. In many instances there is a correlation between the complexity of the tenurial arrangements in a given township and the form that the respective village plan took. Multiple manorial and ecclesiastical foci are commonly associated with distinct elements of the village plan.[143] Together this evidence reveals the composite nature of many village plans. It also suggests that our discussion of the reasons for nucleation should be distinguished from our analysis of the form that the village eventually took.

The initial dynamic for settlement nucleation must lie with both lords and peasant communities. Lords seem to have had little interest in the agricultural regimes of their peasants in the later Middle Ages, and it seems unlikely that they would have been significantly more interested at an earlier date. It is not, however, improbable that lords came to have an interest in the activities of the peasants whom they most intensively exploited, and this may have extended to the places where these peasants lived, as is indicated by Ine's law-code, as we have seen.[144] Rosamond Faith has suggested that the inland of estates took on distinctive forms in many places, including the lord's *curia* and a block of regularly arranged tenements, sometimes enclosed within a boundary of some sort. This may have been associated, in some instances, with an intensively cultivated discrete field system at the centre, or an 'infield'.[145] However, such arrangements are unlikely to have extended to all the peasantry, and these elements in the landscape must have been relatively limited. Nonetheless, they may have acted, in the long term, as magnets for settlement, and such seigneurial complexes do commonly form an integral part of village plans.[146]

In the northern Danelaw, where multiple lords and manors were common in individual vills, it is to be expected that there were many more estate foci in the late Anglo-Saxon period than were to become

142. P. Everson, C.C. Taylor and C.J. Dunn, *Change and Continuity: rural settlement in north-west Lincolnshire* (1991), 13–15.
143. *Ibid.*, 16–22.
144. See Chapter 2, p. 78.
145. Faith, *The English Peasantry*, 79, 163–77.
146. Everson, Taylor and Dunn, *Change and Continuity*, 32–3, 41–3.

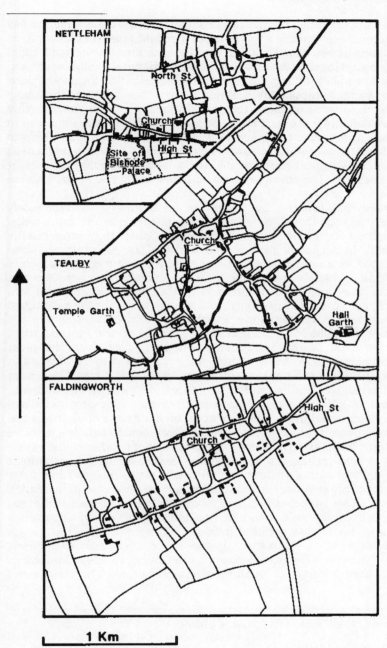

Figure 33 Polyfocal villages in Lincolnshire (after P. Everson, C.C. Taylor and C.J. Dunn, *Change and Continuity: rural settlement in north-west Lincolnshire* (1991))

features or foci of the late medieval village plan. This phenomenon has not been archaeologically explored, but a recent study in Nottingham-shire has proposed that such foci can be identified in the landscape. For example, in the three townships of Staunton, Sibthorpe and Cotham a number of foci can be identified (in the form of manor houses, moated sites, plan elements of the village) that may correspond to pre-Conquest tenurial divisions.[147] It is notable that not all of these foci are part of the village, and this raises the issue of which of the numerous seigneurial focal points in a vill are likely to have influenced village formation. The connection between seigneurial initiative and village formation may not be as straightforward, at least in the northern Danelaw, as some studies have encouraged us to believe.

The impetus for the nucleation of settlement was not solely provided by seigneurial interests. One of the reasons why lords' actions have received more attention is that they are readily identifiable in archaeological terms, whereas the peasantry tend to be regarded as a single dependent and homogeneous group which is reflected in archaeological terms by indistinguishable tenements and buildings. However, there are other ways of viewing the archaeological evidence that reveal the diversity and dynamism within the peasantry. Whatever the initial impetus to nucleation, the constant rebuilding and reorganization of buildings indicates a degree of agency on the part of those who lived in the settlement; at a later date even the most burdened members of the peasantry were charged with the upkeep of their own holdings and houses, and it is unlikely that it was different at an earlier date.[148] The shifting nature of settlement, and the abandonment of some Anglo-Saxon settlements, suggests that what-ever the seigneurial involvement in settlement organization, it was not sufficiently powerful to prevent these developments. This presents an interesting contrast with parts of the Continent, where nucleation appears in many regions to have replaced a very dispersed settlement pattern and was such a distinct transition that many villages came to be contained within defences associated with a lord's castle or defended residence. This appears to have resulted in a rather different landscape from the one found in England and may have involved a much more decisive seigneurial influence.[149]

We also need to be aware of the differences and distinctions between parts of villages: neighbours often went to great lengths to delineate their holdings through the use of banks, ditches, hedges and

---

147. Unwin, 'The Norman aggregation of estates', 61.
148. C.C. Dyer, 'English peasant buildings in the later Middle Ages', *Medieval Archaeology*, 30 (1986), 19–45, at 21.
149. J. Chapelot and R. Fossier, *The Village and House in the Middle Ages* (1985), 144; C.J. Wickham, *Early Medieval Italy: central power and local society, 400–1000* (1981), 163–7; S. Reynolds, *Kingdoms and Communities in Western Europe, 900–1300* (1984), 101–22.

fences.[150] This suggests a degree of competition and tension within the peasantry, and suggests agency on the part of peasant inhabitants in the organization of their living arrangements. Whatever the tensions between lords and peasants, they were ameliorated by the requirements of the former to make use of peasant labour and assistance in the administrative machinery of the estate, and by the desire of some of the former to perform these tasks. The pressures for members of the peasant community to distinguish themselves from their neighbours is an important dynamic, which may be identified archaeologically. It is also important to note that even in areas of settlement, nucleation-dispersed settlement is also found, and insufficient attention has been paid to this phenomenon;[151] it may have telling things to reveal about resistance, and alternatives, to nucleation, although that is not to deny that in some instances the peasantry might collude with lords in creating nucleated villages, or find such developments to their advantage.[152] This archaeological evidence contributes to the debate about the origins of settlement nucleation because it shows a more complex seigneurial contribution than has hitherto been recognized, and because it displays agency on the part of the inhabitants of the settlement. There is clearly much more archaeological and survey work that needs to be undertaken, and there is much potential in exploring the dynamics between, and within, the seigneurial and peasant classes.

Whatever the origins of village nucleation, and whatever the main impetus, it is clear that it coincided with a more intensive seigneurial exploitation of the countryside. There is also little doubt that the manorial structure had an important impact on the form that villages took. Simple, and regular, village plans are commonly associated with vills with a single manorial lord. For example, the villages in the Vale of Pickering which have regular plans commonly formed a single Domesday manor (or manorial dependency); these include Middleton, Appleton-le-Moors, Ebberston, Levisham and Ryhill (Fig. 34), whereas some of the more complex village plans are associated with a multiplicity of manors and manorial holdings: for example, Brompton, Preston, Duxford and Withernwick (Fig. 35).[153] This pattern has also been noticed in Holderness and Lincolnshire.[154] The impact of the division of a vill between two lords is pronounced at Addingham

---

150. G. Astill, 'Rural settlement: the toft and croft', in *The Countryside of Medieval England*, ed. G. Astill and A. Grant (1988), 36–61, at 51–3.

151. C.C. Taylor, 'Dispersed settlement in nucleated areas', *Landscape History*, 17 (1995), 27–34.

152. H.S.A. Fox, 'Approaches to the adoption of the Midland system', in *The Origins of Open-Field Agriculture*, ed. T. Rowley (1981), 64–111, at 77–82, 91–102; B. Yorke, *Wessex in the Early Middle Ages* (1995), 268, n. 115.

153. *DB*, fos. 299a–b, 304d, 380d; P. Allerston, 'English village development: findings from the Pickering district of north Yorkshire', *IBGT*, 51 (1970), 95–109.

154. M. Harvey, 'Irregular villages in Holderness, Yorkshire: some thoughts on their origin', *YAJ*, 54 (1982), 63–71.

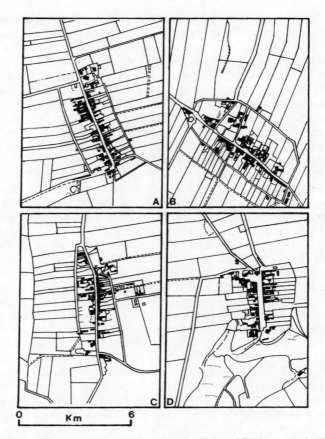

Figure 34 Regular village plans in the Vale of Pickering: A, Appleton-le-Moors; B, Middleton; C, Wombleton; D, Levisham (after P. Allerston, 'English village development: findings from the Pickering district of north Yorkshire', *IBGT*, 51 (1970), 95–109)

(Yorks), where the Marchup Beck ('boundary valley') divides the vill into two parts, each with its own field system.[155] Whatever the nature of rights that lords enjoyed over their land and its inhabitants, the creation of associations between lords and particular vills, or parts of vills, did eventually have an impact on the landscape, although this still leaves room for peasant initiative to have played a part in the form that villages eventually took.

There is also some evidence to suggest that changes to the manorial structure in the twelfth century led to changes in the layout of villages, often following the consolidation of the manorial holdings by a single

---

155. K.M. Hall, 'Pre-Conquest estates in Yorkshire', in *Yorkshire Boundaries*, ed. H.A.J. Le Patourel, M.H. Long and M.F. Pickles (1993), 25–38, at 37.

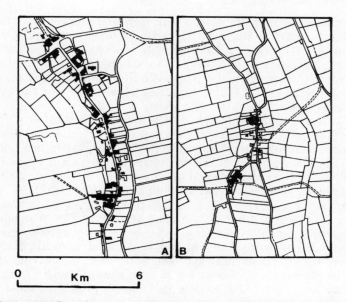

Figure 35 Complex village plans in the Vale of Pickering: A, Allerston; B, Pockley (after P. Allerston, 'English village development: findings from the Pickering district of north Yorkshire', *IBGT* 51 (1970), 95–109)

lord, or the foundations of religious houses.[156] However, as we have seen, manorial sites did not always have an impact on village plans, and many were doubtless perpetuated by isolated farmsteads or hamlets, a pattern noted in other regions also.[157] Although there may have been important advances towards nucleation by the tenth and eleventh centuries, we should not underestimate the amount of dispersed settlement that still obtained, and which often survived and may even have proliferated through the later medieval period.[158]

It has been proposed in a number of recent studies that distinctions within the peasantry may be identified in the layouts of villages. In particular, the most dependent and heavily burdened members of the peasantry may have been located in specific, regularly laid out sections of villages, associated with the manorial *curia*.[159] It has been suggested

156. Everson, Taylor and Dunn, *Change and Continuity*, 13–33.
157. J. Blair, *Anglo-Saxon Oxfordshire* (1994), 144.
158. Taylor, 'Dispersed settlement'.
159. Faith, *The English Peasantry*, 78–80, 224–34; L.H. Campey, 'Medieval village plans in County Durham: an analysis of reconstructed plans based on medieval documentary sources', *Northern History*, 25 (1989), 60–87; B.K. Roberts, 'Village plans in Co. Durham: a preliminary statement', *Medieval Archaeology*, 16 (1972), 33–56; M. Aston, 'Medieval settlement sites in Somerset', in *The Medieval Landscape of Wessex*, ed. M. Aston and C. Lewis (1994), 219–37.

that bovated holdings associated with manorial demesnes in the Vale
of York originated as planned seigneurial foundations.[160] The regular-
plan villages of Yorkshire have commonly been associated with new
seigneurial plantations after the devastation caused by William the
Conqueror's 'harrying of the North'.[161] However, doubt has recently
been cast on the extent of this supposed devastation, and the evidence
on which it was based (the Domesday entries which simply record
'waste') has been shown to relate to lack of information or vills which
did not render geld, rather than to abandoned or destroyed
settlements. In many ways the 'harrying of the North' has become a
convenient historical peg on which to hang the origins of these regular-
plan villages; 'a process in need of a cause', as David Palliser has put
it.[162] Voices of dissent have tended to offer another, equally
problematic, peg in the form of the Scandinavian settlement as a
catalyst for the laying out of the same settlements.[163] We should not
rule out *any* seigneurial planning, and it is not at all unlikely that some
parts of villages were laid out for tenants of a particular status.
However, the archaeological and fieldwork evidence reveals that we
should look not to single moments in time when all such villages plans
came into being, but rather to 'a broad range of processes and dates'.[164]

The church had an important impact on medieval settlement forms,
and churches often provided focal points for settlement. There are few
examples of isolated churches in the northern Danelaw, and at virtually
all of them there is some field evidence for the existence of former
settlement.[165] More commonly there is a close relationship between
churches and manorial centres. In some examples the church lies
within some form of manorial enclosure which includes the manorial
hall, fishponds, watermills and other features, such as at Buslingthorpe, Coates, Rand, Scampton, Toft Newton and Linwood (Lincs)
(Fig. 36).[166] Although it is often assumed that this was an original
feature of the settlement, recent work in Lincolnshire has revealed
that in a few instances there are hints that the church was founded
first, and that the manorial *curia* was a later accretion. At Rand, for
example, the manorial *curia* is clearly later than the extant village plan

160. T.A.M. Bishop, 'Assarting and the growth of the open fields', *EcHR*, 1st ser., 6
    (1935–6), 13–29 at 15.
161. J. Sheppard, 'Metrological analysis of regular village plans in Yorkshire', *AgHR*,
    22 (1974), 118–35; Allerston, 'English village development', 100, 105–6.
162. D.M. Palliser, 'Domesday Book and the "harrying of the North" ', *Northern
    History*, 29 (1993), 1–23, at 7 for the quotation.
163. M. Beresford and J.G. Hurst, *Wharram Percy Deserted Medieval Village* (1990),
    84; M. Harvey, 'Open field structure and landholding arrangements in eastern
    Yorkshire', *IBGT*, new ser., 9 (1984), 60–74.
164. D. Austin, 'Medieval settlement in the north-east of England: retrospect,
    summary and prospect', in *Medieval Rural Settlement in North-East England*, ed.
    B.E. Vyner (1990), 141–50 at 145.
165. Everson, Taylor and Dunn, *Change and Continuity*, 45.
166. *Ibid.*

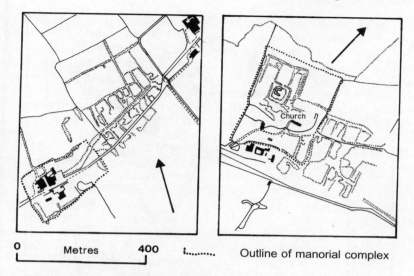

Metres 400   ⋮.......... Outline of manorial complex

Figure 36 Manorial complexes in Coates and Rand (Lincs) (after P. Everson, C.C. Taylor and C.J. Dunn, *Change and Continuity: rural settlement in north-west Lincolnshire* (1991))

as it blocks part of the village street system.[167] Such topographical relationships warrant further investigation. It is tempting to suggest that one of the ways in which manorial lords imposed their presence in settlements was by associating themselves with the village church, turning what was a community focal point into a seigneurial centre. In polyfocal villages the church is not uncommonly associated with one of the foci. It is not unusual for this part of the village to be less regularly arranged than the other part(s); this suggests that the regularly arranged parts of the village are later (planned?) additions. This may be observed at Riseholme (Lincs), for example (Fig. 37).[168] However, we ought to be aware of the phenomenon of multiple churches in settlements. Separate settlement foci might have once had their own church, and, although only future excavation is likely to be able to identify this, there are sufficient known examples of abandoned churches to make this a facet of settlement organization worth taking seriously.[169]

Another important impact of the church on local settlements concerns the impact of mother churches. These are commonly associated with large villages, and small late medieval towns. Examples

---

167. *Ibid.*
168. *Ibid.*, 46.
169. *Ibid.*, 20, 46; examples include Fillingham, Hemswell, South Kelsey, Spridlington, Waddingham and Glentworth.

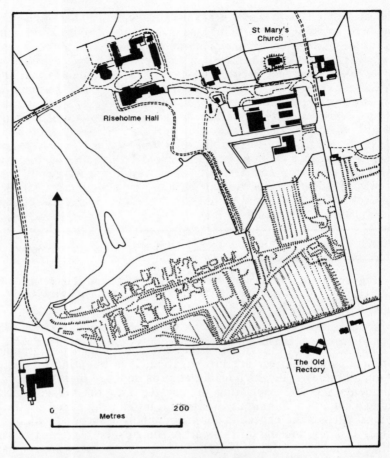

Figure 37 The village of Riseholme (after P. Everson, C.C. Taylor and C.J. Dunn, *Change and Continuity: rural settlement in north-west Lincolnshire* (1991)). Note that the southern part of the village appears to overlie ridge and furrow

include Wirksworth, Ashbourne, Bakewell, Chesterfield (Derbs), Blyth, Southwell (Notts), Barton upon Humber, Caistor, Grantham, Louth, Kirton in Lindsey (Lincs), Beverley, Howden, Pocklington, North-allerton, Pickering, Whitby, Pontefract and Ripon (Yorks).[170] That important churches became the focal point for important settlements in the pre-Conquest period is less easy to demonstrate, but recent excavation and metal-detector finds have revealed that such sites are

170.   M. Beresford and H.P.R. Finberg, *English Medieval Boroughs: a handlist* (1973), 85–6, 136–7, 185–91; *The Cartulary of Blyth Priory*, ed. Timson, c–cxiv.

often associated with concentrations of evidence for high-status settlement activity in the Middle Saxon period (including metalwork, concentrations of coinage finds, elaborate building arrangements, and so on).[171] Commonly, such places were, or became, the locations not only of early churches, but also of royal vills, major aristocratic dwellings or residences of bishops and archbishops. They were often at the centres of substantial estates, at which a range of administrative functions were exercised as a result. It is not surprising, then, that such places emerged as major settlements, sometimes of proto-urban form, in the post-Conquest period. Not all mother churches, however, became the centres of important settlements, and some of the urban centres of the later Middle Ages were not associated with such churches: for example, Castleton (Derbs), Grimsby (Lincs), Kingston upon Hull, Bootham, Drax, Harewood, Sheffield, Wakefield (Yorks), Retford, Newark and even Nottingham (Notts).[172] Nonetheless, on the whole the pattern of mother churches established in the Anglo-Saxon period did help determine the distribution of major settlements in the medieval period.

Villages and fields

The origins of the open-field system are still imperfectly understood. The debate about the relationship between field systems and village origins has tended to be circular, as they are commonly considered in isolation, and studies of either phenomenon have tended to use studies of the other to underpin their arguments, especially concerning chronology. The open-field system that characterized much of 'Midland England' comprised the organization of the agricultural land in two or more large fields, the ploughing of land in strips bundled together in furlongs, the distribution of the strips cultivated by individuals throughout the fields, arrangements for common access to pasture, which often involved the throwing open of one field to fallow, and some form of communal regulation of the system.[173] Not all these features were necessarily always in place, however, but what is common to all occurrences of this form of agricultural regime is the need for co-operation between neighbours. Many reasons have been proposed for the origins of this system; population growth, developments in technology, inheritance patterns and changes to the settlement pattern are the most commonly cited explanations. It is

---

171. See, for example, C. Loveluck, 'A high-status Anglo-Saxon settlement at Flixborough, Lincolnshire', *Antiquity*, 72 (1998), 146–61.
172. Beresford and Finberg, *English Medieval Boroughs*, 85, 137, 146–7, 186–92.
173. There is a vast literature on this subject. A useful review of the literature, that makes a case for the origins of the system in the Anglo-Saxon period, is Fox, 'The Midland system'; see also T. Williamson, 'Explaining regional landscapes: woodland and champion in southern and eastern England', *Landscape History*, 11 (1989), 5–13, where early origins for open fields, and nucleated settlement, are proposed.

clear that the system was in existence by the twelfth century and there are hints of its presence in the tenth century. This is suggested by, for example, the clause in Ine's law-code which refers to *ceorls* having 'a common meadow or other land divided in shares', some of whom had fenced this land and others of whom had not; this suggests a primitive form of open-field system, although the code also suggests that other *ceorls* dwelt in and cultivated the land in individual enclosed farmsteads.[174] Charters from Wessex suggest that land was being cultivated in an open-field system in the tenth century: three hides at Avon (Wilts) are said to consist of 'single strips (*jugera*) dispersed in a mixture here and there in common land'; five hides at Charlton (Berks) are said to lie in common land and 'are not demarcated on all sides by clear bounds because to left and right lie *jugera* in combination with one another'; and at Ardington (Berks) it is said that 'the open pasture is common and the meadow is common and the arable is common'.[175] In the northern Danelaw such a system may have been in operation, to judge from the terms of the charter granting land at Newbald (Yorks) in 963, which includes land in neighbouring Hotham, said to lie in 'every other acre', and the boundary clause of which refers to 'the headland of the fields'.[176] Recent work in the west Midlands has suggested that in the later pre-Conquest period there was a variety of agricultural systems in operation. Land organized in common fields was found alongside small enclosed fields.[177] Hence, as with villages, open-field systems may have come into existence gradually and as a result of a series of piecemeal developments. Although the wholesale reorganization of the landscape should not be ruled out in some regions, the inclusion of all, or most, of the agricultural land of a vill into a single field system may have been the final development in a gradual shift that began with piecemeal co-operation.[178]

This presents a rather different picture from previous work, which looked to a single act for the creation of open-field systems. Another reason to question the idea that there was a revolution in the organization and management of the countryside is the fact that prior to the development of open-field systems the inhabitants of the landscape were seemingly quite accustomed to co-operative under-takings, and interaction between the inhabitants of various vills appears to have been common, for purposes of sharing of resources

174. *EHD*, I, no. 32, c. 40, 42.
175. S 634 (B 925), S 691 (B 1079), S706 (B 1083); Yorke, *Wessex in the Early Middle Ages*, 269–71.
176. S 716 (B 1113); *EYC*, 1, 16–18; M.H. Long, 'Newbald', in *Yorkshire Boundaries*, ed. Le Patourel, Long and Pickles, 134–41, at 135–8.
177. D. Hooke, *Anglo-Saxon Landscapes of the West Midlands: the charter evidence* (BAR British Series, 95, 1981), 207–8; D. Hooke, 'The administrative and settlement framework of early medieval Wessex' in *The Medieval Landscape of Wessex*, ed. Aston and Lewis, 83–95, at 90.
178. Faith, *The English Peasantry*, 144.

and the provision of tribute.[179] It has been stated that the fragmentation of 'multiple estates' was a catalyst for the reorganization of the landscape, of which open fields and nucleated villages were an important element, since communities now had to rely on the resources of their own township rather than sharing with other members of the 'multiple estate'.[180] However, although that may be true of other regions, it patently is not the case in the northern Danelaw, where large sokes survived into the post-Conquest period. Moreover, many vills continued to share common resources between them right through the later Middle Ages, including land for grazing. This suggests that although the need to ensure access to grazing land may have been a reason for the organization of land in open fields in some regions, it does not everywhere explain the development. There may have been an element of necessity in some places, but of emulation in others, both by lords and communities. We have to think, perhaps, of a range of causes, which resulted in open-field agriculture being adopted at various dates and in a variety of ways, sometimes gradually, at other times more swiftly. Whatever the initial impetus to create an open-field system, the relationship between the land of the lord and that of the peasant cultivators was commonly not equal. Although they often had their land interspersed, there is some evidence to suggest that there were irregular distributions of land and that lords often had their lands scattered in whole furlongs rather than individual strips.[181]

It seems plausible that the nucleation of settlement and the laying out of open fields should have been in some way related. The fields of parts of Holderness, in which the furlongs run from the village right to the township boundary, in contrast to the patchwork of furlongs found elsewhere, must have been laid out at a single moment and at the time of, or later than, nucleation.[182] There are interesting anomalies in the field systems of the region that reveal some of the complexity of the relationship between field systems and settlement. In some instances two villages shared elements of their field system: for example, the Lincolnshire villages of Aisby and Great Corringham shared a field system, and the villages of Little Corringham and Springthorpe shared elements of the common fields. Elsewhere a single field system is shared between a number of settlements: in the township of Nettleton (Lincs), for example, a single field system was used by the inhabitants of Nettleton, Hardwick, Wykeham and Draycote.[183] In many parts of the region complex tenurial arrangements are not given expression in the agricultural organization of a township, as a single open-field

---

179.   See p. 94–101 above.
180.   Fox, 'The Midland system', 98–102.
181.   Stenton, *Social and Economic History of the Danelaw*, lii–lvii.
182.   M. Harvey, 'Planned field systems in eastern Yorkshire: some thoughts on their origin', *AgHR*, 31 (1983), 91–103; Harvey, 'Open field structure'.
183.   Everson, Taylor and Dunn, *Change and Continuity*, 9.

system may be found even where numerous manors are present. This suggests that open fields were created, and maintained, irrespective of tenurial arrangements. It can be shown that in multi-manorial villages there was still a single open-field system in which the lands of the various manorial lords, and of the peasants who pertained to each manor, were intermingled. In Staunton, Kilvington and Alverton (Notts), for example, the lands of the various manors can be traced in the thirteenth century, when they were scattered over the village fields.[184] It is also important to note that in some places there is no evidence for open fields, and, indeed, some evidence for agricultural land being organized in blocks instead.[185] Once again, we see that monocausal explanations are inadequate, and variation and diversity are prominent.

In the same way that the social structure and estate organization of Domesday Book can be shown to be less fixed than has sometimes been supposed, and the product of long-term and short-term developments, we can now see that villages and open-field systems were not immutable, nor did they all come into being through the same mechanism. There is, perhaps, less similarity in practice between superficially similar villages and field systems than has sometimes been maintained, and it is the study of the diversity, as much as the similarity, that will better enable us to understand their origins and development.

Villages in context

The daily lives of the peasantry in the northern Danelaw varied enormously from place to place. In some cases the agricultural and economic activities of the peasantry were largely limited to the vill in which they lived; that is to say, they owed their regular dues and services to a lord who had a manor-house in the vill in which they lived. The church they attended may also have been located within that vill. By way of contrast, in many other cases there were vills whose inhabitants were attached to manors located many miles away, and sometimes this involved them travelling from their village to meet the obligations they owed at the lord's manor. This was particularly common for the inhabitants of berewicks and sokeland. They were also often obliged to travel outside the village in order to attend church, as many berewicks and sokelands either had no church or had only a chapel which was not licensed to perform the major ecclesiastical functions, especially burial. We can understand something of the complex web of activities in which the inhabitants of a township were involved through the example of Waddingham (Lincs). In 1066 the tenurial structure of the township was complex: there was sokeland of

---

184. Stenton, *Types of Manorial Structure*, 66–7.
185. *Rufford Charters*, ed. C.J. Holdsworth, Thoroton Society Record Series (4 vols, 1972–81), 1, lxvi–lxix.

Type of holding	Manor to which it was attached	Wapentake of manorial centre
Sokeland (with Stainton)	Kirton in Lindsey	Corringham
Manor (with Stainton)	–	Manley
Manor (with Stainton)	–	Manley
Sokeland (with Stainton)	Snitterby	Aslacoe
Manor	–	Manley
Manor	–	Manley
Sokeland	Waddingham	Manley

Figure 38 Manorial, hundredal and wapentake organization in the vicinity of Waddingham: land-holding in 1066

Kirton in Lindsey (linked with Stainton, and held by Earl Edwin), a manor (with Stainton, held by Harthgripr), a second manor (again with Stainton, held by Steingrimr and Agmundr), sokeland of Snitterby (with Stainton, and held by Godwin), two further manors (held by Arnketill and Godric) and sokeland of Godric's manor (held by Elfin) (Fig. 38). The combined assessment of these holdings is three carucates and seven and a half bovates, which reveals that Waddingham must have belonged to a larger grouping of townships to form a twelve-carucate hundred. It is possible that this hundred included Manton, Hibaldstow and Gainsthorpe, as their combined assessment is almost twelve carucates (eleven carucates and six bovates). If this suggestion by Cyril Hart is correct – and it is persuasive, because the adjacent township to Waddingham is Redbourne, which was assessed at twelve carucates and constituted a hundred in its own right – it would result in a dispersed hundred, which is relatively uncommon.[186] Waddingham is in Manley wapentake, but the two external manors which had sokeland in Waddingham were in the wapentakes of Aslacoe (Snitterby) and Corringham (Kirton in Lindsey). Waddingham was divided in the medieval period into two parishes, one of which was apparently associated with Domesday 'Stainton'. The parish also included neighbouring Snitterby, which was, as already mentioned, in a different wapentake. The village of Waddingham comprises two distinct nuclei, one of which may represent the location of Stainton (Fig. 39). The plan of the village has two different alignments and it suggests that it came into being at different stages. Interestingly, however, the two churches were located adjacent to each other, which suggests that there was a core area at which the two communities of Waddingham and 'Stainton' came together for worship.[187] The inhabitants of Waddingham and 'Stainton' were involved in a complex

186. C.R. Hart, *The Danelaw* (1992), 354–8.
187. Everson, Taylor and Dunn, *Change and Continuity*, 13.

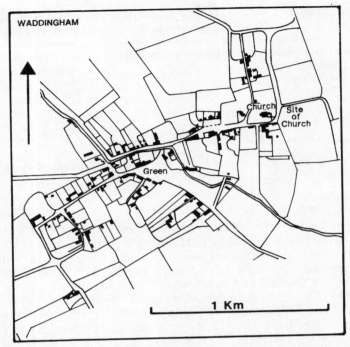

Figure 39 The village of Waddingham (after P. Everson, C.C. Taylor and C.J. Dunn, *Change and Continuity: rural settlement in north-west Lincolnshire* (1991))

web of social, manorial, ecclesiastical and administrative obligations which regularly brought them into contact with people from outside the township; moreover, the inhabitants of the township were divided between several manors and two parishes. Although there may have been much community of interest in the vill, there were also very clear distinctions. Waddingham is not unusual in the complexity of arrangements in which its inhabitants were involved. These aspects of the social organization of vills in the northern Danelaw distinguish parts of the region very clearly from elsewhere.

Although it was not unknown for all the inhabitants of a vill to owe obligations to the same lord, in many other vills groups of peasants were distinguished from each other by the fact that they and their neighbours owed obligations to a different lord. In multi-manorial vills the community of the vill may have assumed a prominent role in organizing their agricultural activities, since no one lord was dominant. Single open-field systems and nucleated villages are as common in such cases as they are in villages controlled by a single lord, although the separate manors within the township occasionally acquired their own churches: examples in Lincolnshire include Waddingham, South

Kelsey, Middle Rasen, Hemswell, Fillingham, Glentworth and Spridlington (Fig. 40).[188] Sometimes the inhabitants of vills were involved with those of neighbouring vills in agricultural activities. The twelve carucate hundreds – which are recorded more systematically in Lincolnshire but are found elsewhere – saw two or more townships combine for agricultural functions. These were almost certainly pre-manorial groupings as they commonly bear little relationship to the complex manorial structures of the region. On the fen edges the hundreds remained active for centuries, owing to their role in organizing communal resources.[189] One may add that even those communities whose manorial and agricultural obligations were limited to their own township could not have failed to have had contact with neighbouring communities. Certainly those that practised any level of agricultural specialization would by necessity have been forced to exchange goods with neighbouring communities. The importance of exchange networks and markets at an early date is unknowable, but their significance should not be underestimated. At a later date, when documentation becomes more extensive, it is apparent that rural communities were not self-sufficient, and it seems unlikely that at an earlier date they would have been.[190]

In any discussion of village origins it is important to locate the settlement in its social, ecclesiastical, estate and landscape context. Villages were not isolated, but rather part of a complex socio-economic network, and this commonly had an influence on the form that the village eventually took. Recent studies have emphasized the piecemeal nature of extant village plans. This does not mean that there were not decisive moments when village plans were reorganized, but rather that the plan as it survives represents a number of changes and developments, seemingly spread over a long period of time, from the ninth century through into the thirteenth century and beyond.

Conclusions

How unique was the social structure of the northern Danelaw? Numerous factors determined the social structure of the region in the period *c.* 800–1100. Of these, the most prominent, and easily detectable, include attitudes to land-holding, changes to the estate structure and estate management policy. What seems certain is that the peculiar social structure of the northern Danelaw is not the product of ethnic difference, neither should we underplay the importance of the evidence for free, and relatively unencumbered,

---

188. *Ibid.*, 46.
189. See Chapter 3, pp. 103–4.
190. C.C. Dyer, 'Were peasants self-sufficient? English villagers and the market, 900–1350' in *Campagnes médiévales: l'homme et son espace*, ed. E. Mornet (Paris, 1995), 653–66.

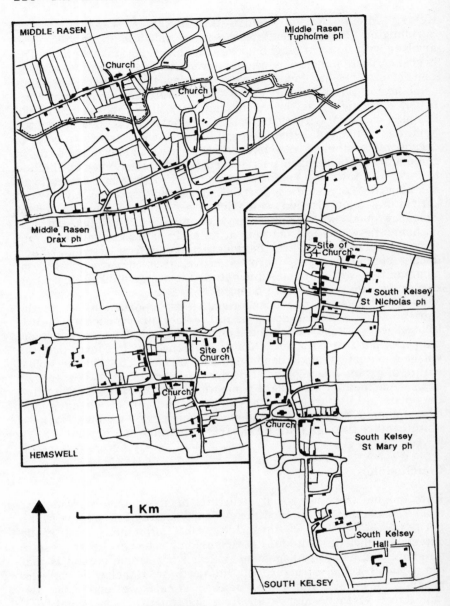

Figure 40 Villages with two churches in Lincolnshire (after
P. Everson, C.C. Taylor and C.J. Dunn, *Change and Continuity: rural
settlement in north-west Lincolnshire* (1991))

peasants, as some recent studies have attempted.[191] Such interpretations are a product of the reaction against earlier concepts of freedom which emphasized the communal nature of Anglo-Saxon society, and supposed that the basis of society was the free peasant and that lordship was only gradually imposed upon it. Anglo-Saxonists have become generally too reluctant to acknowledge the existence of a stratum of free peasant landowners, and have tended to look more to the controlling powers of lords as the force which shaped society. In Chapter 2 it was argued that free peasant landholders formed a substantial stratum of early medieval society in England, and it is not difficult to believe that the privileged sokemen and *liberi homines* of the northern Danelaw were the descendants of such peasants. The peasant freeholders identified across European society, the Anglo-Saxon *ceorl* and the sokemen and *liberi homines* of Domesday Book share a number of important basic characteristics. It ought, perhaps, to be expected that in the smaller kingdoms of Anglo-Saxon England, where there were fewer places to escape the grasp of lords, the subordination of the peasantry to estate structures was more rapidly achieved than elsewhere. Yet this was clearly not universally the case in Anglo-Saxon England, and the northern and eastern regions followed a different path.

The reasons for the discrepancies in the numbers of such free peasants across England by the eleventh century are manifold, and include royal policy, seigneurial initiative, estate organization, the amount of ecclesiastical land and, to some extent, the actions of the peasantry themselves. It is only through further localized studies that the history of social organization will be better understood. There can be little doubt that the Scandinavian settlement of parts of northern and eastern England was an important factor, but not because it introduced a stratum of free peasants, but because of the impact that it had on lordship and estate organization in the region. The response of the West Saxon kings and native lords is also important, and the rapid transfer of land and the diminution of ecclesiastical land are crucial. Also important are the policies of individual lords and the responses of the peasantry. By taking a dual approach, one wide-ranging, the other locally focused, it is clear that despite the very real similarities across much of England in the early medieval period, as indeed across Europe as a whole in this period, there were also significant regional differences.

---

191. Kristensen, 'Danelaw institutions and Danish society'; G. Platts, *Land and People in Medieval Lincolnshire* (1985), 68.

5 Ecclesiastical organization

It is not disputed that early [ecclesiastical] organization differed
from kingdom to kingdom ... a central aim of local studies must
be to map variation on a finer scale

– J. Blair[1]

This chapter traces the development of ecclesiastical provision from
the seventh to the eleventh centuries, and also considers how the
church was structured to deliver pastoral care in the northern
Danelaw. The impact of pagan Scandinavian settlement on the
ecclesiastical structure is examined in order to test by detailed local
study whether the traditional picture of the destruction of ecclesiastical structures by vikings who did not respect the sanctity of the
church has any validity. The chapter also examines the fate of the
church in the period after the Scandinavian settlement, with particular
reference to the West Saxon conquest of the region. Of course, it may
not have been simply the circumstances of successive military and
political conquests that shaped the local organization of the church;
accordingly, consideration will be given to the extent to which the
social structure and estate organization of the region determined
ecclesiastical arrangements. The chapter examines the wider role of
churches in the society of the northern Danelaw: for example, in the
relationship of churches to centres of secular authority; in the political
role of the church; in burial practices; and in the socio-economic
context of churches.

Ecclesiastical provision from the seventh to the eleventh centuries

Recent discussions of Anglo-Saxon ecclesiastical organization have
been dominated by debate about the so-called 'minster model'.[2] Yet in
many respects the 'minster model' has very few adherents in the form
in which it was first explicitly formulated in the 1980s, and much of the

---

1. J. Blair, 'Ecclesiastical organization and pastoral care in Anglo-Saxon England',
   EME, 4 (2) (1995), 193–212, at 199.
2. See Chapter 1, pp. 37–9.

recent criticism has concerned itself with a 'model' that even its former proponents have refined and moderated. Rather than follow this debate in a local context, this chapter seeks to show what the evidence from the northern Danelaw allows us to say about ecclesiastical development during this time.

Where do the origins of the late medieval parochial structure of the northern Danelaw lie? What, if anything, did the parochial system inherit from the period before the Scandinavian settlement? What developments in the ecclesiastical organization can be shown to have taken place between the seventh and the eleventh centuries? And were these developments merely evolutionary or did they involve wholesale transformations? What was the impact of successive conquests on ecclesiastical organization in the northern Danelaw? What is the relationship between parish boundaries and secular estate organization? What was the role of the aristocracy in the development of local ecclesiastical provision? In my attempt to answer these questions the minster terminology favoured by other studies has been eschewed because of its connotations. The term 'minster' may well have been the word contemporaries often used, but its use and abuse in recent scholarship renders it a loaded word, accordingly avoided here.

The analysis of the ecclesiastical organization in the northern Danelaw may best begin with a cross-section of churches in the region (Fig. 41). They may be grouped into three categories: those churches which have pre-viking origins and are mother churches in the later Middle Ages; those churches which have pre-viking origins but are not later mother churches; and mother churches without evidence for early origins. These distinctions primarily reflect the surviving evidence, but also correspond to real differences between churches. A complex pattern emerges, which serves to demonstrate both the inadequacy of previous studies of the region and the importance of examining regional diversity. John Blair did indeed once observe of the Danelaw that since studies revealed an absence of a minster network, future work would have to consider whether this reflected 'genuine regional contrasts, or merely differences in later developments, in the available evidence or in the preconceptions of local studies'.[3] This chapter serves as a response to that observation, and it reveals that all his points apply to the northern Danelaw; furthermore, it demonstrates that the preconceptions of the minster model itself have contributed to the perception that the evidence and the ecclesiastical organization of the various regions of the Danelaw are unusual.

This is not the place to list and discuss every church in the northern Danelaw, but rather this chapter discusses, in turn, a range of churches whose history may be discussed through the use of documentary, sculptural, architectural and archaeological evidence.

---

3.   J. Blair, 'Introduction: from minster to parish church', in *Minsters and Parish Churches: the local church in transition, 950–1200*, ed. J. Blair (1988), 1–19, at 2.

Figure 41 Major churches in the northern Danelaw

This is followed by a synthesis of the evidence and a discussion of what it reveals about ecclesiastical organization between *c.* 800 and 1100.

A variety of types of evidence can illuminate the ecclesiastical structure but each requires sensitive handling. First, documentary sources which describe contemporary issues can be problematic because the identification of the places to which they refer is not always secure, and they provide only partial impressions of the sorts of issues with which we are concerned. Later sources describing earlier events may sometimes appear to draw upon well-informed earlier written sources, but are sometimes largely or entirely fabricated.

Second, archaeological evidence (including both excavation and survey) has proved useful in identifying pre-Conquest churches and their layouts and resources.[4] However, many site reports are dictated by the available historical evidence: for example, doubt is often expressed about whether a site is an early church if there is no supporting documentary evidence; and viking destruction is commonly adduced as an explanation of sites abandoned, destroyed or 'in decline' at any time between the late eighth and the mid-tenth centuries. In fact, both continuity and desertion of sites are very difficult to demonstrate or to date.

Third, sculpture provides a wealth of potentially very useful evidence for the region, since hundreds of pieces of pre-Conquest sculpture survive, and it continues to accumulate. However, the dating of sculpture is necessarily subjective and depends upon inscriptions that reveal the occasion when a carving was completed, but more frequently we must rely upon similarity of design with that of illuminated manuscripts or upon the stratigraphic context in which a sculpture was discovered. The presence of Scandinavian influence on iconography or design may suggest a date after the later ninth century, although the absence of Scandinavian influence does not conversely mean that the sculpture concerned is necessarily of pre-viking date.[5] Neither the place-names of the sites where sculpture is found, nor the 'quality' of a piece of sculpture reveal anything about the sculpture's antiquity. Who is to say whether poor workmanship is 'the feeble beginnings of a style, a misunderstanding of an old style ... or just the work of a poor sculptor'?[6] The use of sculptural evidence to identify the sites of early churches requires some justification. Stone sarcophagi, shrines, panels and architectural detail are unlikely to have been positioned anywhere other than a church. Stone crosses, by contrast, might conceivably have been located in other contexts, although there is little documentary evidence to support this.[7] However, it seems reasonable to assume that they were normally found in association with churches, not least because sculpture is often found in places which other evidence reveals to have had a contemporary church. This was probably also the case even where confirmation from other sources is lacking, given that much sculpture has been discovered in, near or under churches. Moreover, if such crosses had really been erected in advance of the building of a church, we might expect to find more examples of crosses found away from churches, since the factors

---

4. J. Blair, 'Anglo-Saxon minsters: a topographical review' in *Pastoral Care before the Parish*, ed. J. Blair and R. Sharpe (1992), 226–66.
5. R.N. Bailey, *Viking Age Sculpture in Northern England* (1980), 45–75.
6. *Ibid.*, 53.
7. I.N. Wood, 'Anglo-Saxon Otley: an archiepiscopal estate and its crosses in a Northumbrian context', *Northern History*, 23 (1987), 20–38.

that determined where a church was built are unlikely to have been successfully predicted in circumstances in which a cross alone was erected.[8] The survival of Anglo-Saxon architecture is a more secure indication that a church existed, but as with sculpture, precise dates are difficult to determine.[9]

Pre-viking churches and later medieval mother churches

The first aspect of the ecclesiastical organization of the northern Danelaw to emphasize is the striking correlation, in some parts of that region, between the sites of pre-viking churches and the locations of later medieval mother churches, of the sort that served large parishes incorporating numerous chapelries. It is noticeable that many of them were royal or ecclesiastical possessions both at an early date and in the tenth and eleventh centuries. They were also often located at the centres of important Domesday estates. Did these churches survive the viking assault? There is some evidence to suggest that many of these churches were functioning in the early tenth century, often producing sculpture and continuing to attract burials. However, it is also apparent that many of these churches had experienced major transformations in their status and prosperity by the later eleventh centuries; the Scandinavian settlement undoubtedly had a fundamental impact, but the changing political circumstances of the tenth century were also important.

Repton (Derbs)

Repton was the site of a religious community ruled by an abbess, at which Guthlac, a Mercian nobleman, took the tonsure towards the end of the seventh century.[10] The community was probably founded in or before the last quarter of the seventh century, which is when Friduricus *princeps* granted land to Abbot Hædda of Breedon on the Hill (Leics) '31 *manentes* called *Hrepingas*'.[11] The close association of

---

8.   R.K. Morris, *Churches in the Landscape* (1989), 153.
9.   The standard work remains H.M. Taylor and J. Taylor, *Anglo-Saxon Architecture* (3 vols; vols 1 and 2, 1965; vol. 3, 1978); but see the discussion of ninth-century architecture in R. Gem, 'Architecture of the Anglo-Saxon church, 735 to 870: from Archbishop Ecgberht to Archbishop Ceolnoth', *JBAA*, 146 (1993), 29–66.
10.   *Life of Saint Guthlac*, c. xx and c. xxi–xxiii for his life there. The oft-used terms 'double house' or 'double monastery' are best avoided because they are not contemporary and they introduce confusion. Many communities described in this way were nunneries with associated groups of clergy: A.T. Thacker, 'Monks, preaching and pastoral care in early Anglo-Saxon England', in *Pastoral Care before the Parish*, ed. Blair and Sharpe, 137–70, at 143.
11.   The reasons why Repton is the most satisfactory identification of *Hrepingas* are discussed in A. Rumble, ' "Hrepingas" reconsidered', in *Mercian Studies*, ed. A. Dornier (1977), 169–72.

Repton with the Mercian royal house is demonstrated by the burials there of Merewalh, king of the Magonsætan and son of Penda, king of the Mercians, of King Æthelbald in 757, of King Wiglaf c. 840, and of his grandson Wystan, who was murdered in a family struggle for power in the mid-ninth century.[12] Wystan was said by Florence of Worcester to have been buried in 'the mausoleum of his grandfather Wiglaf', and this mausoleum has been identified as the crypt beneath the present parish church.[13] It has been suggested that the flow of pilgrims to the tomb of Wystan, where miracles are said to have occurred, resulted in the remodelling of the entrances to the crypt.[14]

The religious community located at Repton appears to have been a house for men and women, ruled by an abbess. When Guthlac entered the community at Repton he is recorded as having become a clerk.[15] Together the documentary evidence suggests that Repton was probably a royal nunnery which also consisted of a community entirely, or chiefly, made up of clerks.[16] It is possible that the church was the setting for a Mercian royal council at which a charter was written in the 840s (*'in venerabili monasterio ... æt Hrypadune'*).[17]

Extensive excavations at Repton have revealed that the crypt was originally free-standing and largely below ground, with ceremonial plinths built above ground. A drain leading from the east wall suggests that the crypt may have served as a baptistery. Its construction must have been later than c. 715, which is the date of a sceatta found in a layer sealed by the construction of the crypt. The crypt was preceded by a cemetery of the seventh century, and by an earlier church. A church to the west later incorporated the crypt, some time before the end of the ninth century. Further to the west a sunken two-celled building has been discovered which probably served as a mausoleum and which was dressed internally with moulded stucco, had coloured glass and a roof of lead.[18] The religious complex at Repton seems, then, to have comprised a family of ecclesiastical buildings aligned

---

12. D.W. Rollason, *The Mildrith Legend: a study in early medieval hagiography* (1982), 26, 77, 81, 93; *ASC*, C, *s.a.* 757; D.W. Rollason, 'The cults of murdered royal saints in Anglo-Saxon England', *ASE*, 11 (1983), 1–22, at 5–9.
13. D.W. Rollason, *Saints and Relics in Anglo-Saxon England* (1989), 121–9.
14. M. Biddle, 'Archaeology, architecture and the cult of saints in Anglo-Saxon England', in *The Anglo-Saxon Church*, ed. L.A.S. Butler and R.K. Morris (CBA Res. Rep., 60, 1986), 1–31, at 16–22.
15. *Life of Saint Guthlac*, c. xx.
16. C.R.E. Cubitt, 'Pastoral care and conciliar canons: the provisions of the 747 council of *Clofesho*', in *Pastoral Care before the Parish*, ed. Blair and Sharpe, 193–211, at 208.
17. S 197 (B 454); F.M. Stenton, *Anglo-Saxon England* (3rd edn, 1971), 201.
18. For this section, see H.M. Taylor, 'Repton reconsidered: a study in structural criticism', in *England before the Conquest: studies in primary sources presented to Dorothy Whitelock*, ed. P. Clemoes and K. Hughes (1971), 351–89; Biddle, 'Archaeology, architecture and the cult of saints', 16–22. One of the burials that may have belonged to the pre-crypt cemetery contained a sceatta of c. 725: H. Geake, *The Use of Grave-Goods in Conversion-Period England, c. 600–c. 850* (BAR British Series, 261, 1997), 149.

east–west on a bluff overlooking the Trent, an arrangement characteristic of major early churches.[19] In spite of the extensive excavations, however, no buildings which may have housed the monastic population have been identified at Repton. As is common at many pre-viking religious communities, Repton has produced early sculpture, including a grave slab and fragments of a cross-shaft, one of which depicts a rider on horseback and which has been assigned to an eighth-century context. It has been suggested by Martin Biddle and Birthe Kjølbye-Biddle that the rider might be King Æthelbald.[20]

Little is known from written sources of the community at Repton between the ninth and eleventh centuries, but excavation of burials around the church (some including grave goods) and the discovery of a hogback monument reveal the church to have been a focal point for burial in the ninth and tenth centuries (Fig. 42).[21] A D-shaped enclosure around the church and a mass burial containing the remains of some 249 individuals have been assigned to the late ninth century and have been linked directly with the record in the Chronicle that a viking army wintered at Repton in 873–4.[22] It is certainly possible that the church was destroyed at this time, and it is this possibility that has

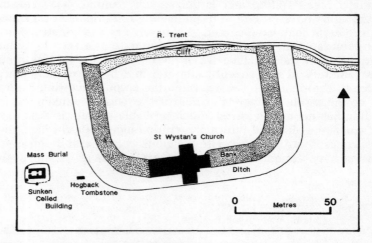

Figure 42 Excavations at Repton (after J. Graham-Campbell (ed.), *Cultural Atlas of the Viking World* (1994), 128)

19.   Biddle, 'Archaeology, architecture and the cult of saints', 22; Blair, 'Anglo-Saxon minsters: a topographical review', 227–30.
20.   M. Biddle and B. Kjølbye-Biddle, 'The Repton stone', *ASE*, 14 (1985), 233–92, at 279–90.
21.   M. Biddle and B. Kjølbye-Biddle, 'Repton and the vikings', *Antiquity*, 250 (March, 1992), 36–51; J.D. Richards, *Viking Age England* (1991), 123–6. It is not clear whether hogbacks were grave markers or commemorative memorials.
22.   *ASC*, s.a. 873.

encouraged the interpretation of the D-shaped enclosure as a viking fortress, for which the church served as a gatehouse. A handful of burials with grave goods have similarly been interpreted as a sign of the Scandinavian takeover of the site.[23] But the historical context needs to be borne in mind. The outcome of the viking foray into Mercia at that time was that Burgred lost his throne and fled to Rome, to be replaced by Ceolwulf II, 'a foolish king's thegn', as the Anglo-Saxon Chronicle puts it. The Chronicle portrays viking activity in Mercia as a series of predatory attacks upon a peaceful realm, but the events of 873–4 may have been part of a coup to remove the ruling dynasty, in which Danish support was used as a means to an end. Burgred was the last representative of a dynasty which had probably come to power in 757 with Beornred. At various times in the ninth century the authority of this dynasty had, however, been challenged by a royal line descended from Ceolwulf I (821–3), and Ceolwulf II was probably a descendant of this line. Ceolwulf II was certainly acceptable enough to the Mercian bishops and nobility to have issued charters which they witnessed.[24] That the viking army was invited into a turbulent situation and supported one side in internecine warfare is plausible, and is readily paralleled elsewhere.[25] Cast in this light, the D-shaped ditch may indeed have served a military purpose but it need not have been a symbol of the hostility between a viking army and a Mercian army, as is widely assumed.

The mass burial has consistently been interpreted in the light of the events of 873–4. Yet it is probably not a battle cemetery, given the apparent lack of visible terminal trauma (although it should be noted that not all terminal wounds need show up on skeletal remains).[26] An early eighteenth-century account of the discovery of a central burial of a 'humane body nine foot long' in a stone coffin has been pivotal to the interpretation of the site. Yet there is an absence of supporting archaeological evidence, and the notion that it was the burial of a viking leader has to be regarded with caution, as does the tenuous argument that metal artefacts found among the bones had orginally accompanied the alleged central burial.[27] The robust stature of the interred cannot be taken as an indication of the 'racial' or ethnic origin of the deceased,[28] but it may suggest that they were healthy and well fed, in

---

23. Biddle and Kjølbye-Biddle, 'Repton and the vikings', 38–40.
24. P. Wormald, 'The ninth century', in *The Anglo-Saxons*, ed. J. Campbell (1982), 132–57 at 138; D.R. Roffe, 'Nottingham 868 to 1086' (forthcoming); S 215 (B 540); S 216 (B 541).
25. See, for example, N. Lund, 'Allies of God or man? The viking expansion in a European context', *Viator*, 19 (1989), 45–59.
26. Biddle and Kjølbye-Biddle, 'Repton and the vikings', 45–8.
27. M. Biddle, B. Kjølbye-Biddle, J.P. Northover and H. Pagan, 'Coins of the Anglo-Saxon period from Repton, Derbyshire', in *Anglo-Saxon Monetary History*, ed. M.A.S. Blackburn (1986), 111–32, at 111–14.
28. *Contra* Biddle and Kjølbye-Biddle, 'Repton and the vikings', 45; see also Chapter 6, pp. 323–5.

which case it may be appropriate to assume that the deceased had belonged to a monastic or a warrior élite. That the mass burial did indeed post-date the wintering of the viking army is suggested by the discovery of a number of pennies in the mound dating to the 870s, the latest of which dates to 873–4.[29] Given the disarticulated nature of the bones, they must have been brought from elsewhere, and after a considerable length of time, whether buried or left exposed to the elements.[30] This 'burial' may be a red herring in Viking Age archaeology, despite its reputation as having 'dramatically demonstrated' the reality behind the Anglo-Saxon Chronicle entry for 873–4.[31] A less dramatic explanation may lie behind the evidence. The disarticulated remains and the fact that many bones are missing indicates that the bodies in the mass 'burial' had been moved there from earlier places of burial. Some of the bones had been stacked up against the north-east corner of the eastern compartment of the two-celled sunken building in which they were placed, and more may originally have been stacked in this way before the mound was opened in the late seventeenth century and the bones disturbed.[32] It is plausible to conclude that the mass 'burial' was, in fact, a charnel-house, and that the deposit may have been the result of steady accretion, rather than a single event (a conclusion borne out by the radio-carbon dates from the bones, which range between the eighth and tenth centuries).[33] After the mass burial was sealed, burials continued on and around it. Thus whatever the significance of the mound had once been, it was quickly incorporated into the ecclesiastical and funerary landscape of Repton.[34] In sum, the archaeology at Repton does not prove the destruction of the church in 873–4 or even the end of the religious community there. On the contrary, the archaeological evidence may be interpreted as a sign that the church retained, or regained, an important role through undoubtedly turbulent times.

That the religious community at Repton became less influential after the demise of the Mercian kingdom is suggested by the fact that in the reign of Cnut the relics of St Wystan were removed from Repton to Evesham Abbey, apparently in the belief that Wystan was descended from King Coenred of Mercia, the supposed founder of that house.[35]

---

29. Biddle *et al.*, 'Coins of the Anglo-Saxon period', 115–19.
30. I am grateful to Andrew Chamberlain for discussing this point with me.
31. P.A. Stafford, *The East Midlands in the Early Middle Ages* (1985), 110.
32. Biddle *et al.*, 'Coins of the Anglo-Saxon period', 113–14.
33. Martin Biddle allows for the possibility of a charnel-house but does not develop the argument, preferring instead to pursue a possible association with the viking army of 873–4: *ibid.* For an example of the clearance of the cemetery of a religious community, see *HE*, iv, 10, where members of the community of Barking Abbey (Essex) were exhumed and reburied in a tomb in the later seventh century.
34. Biddle and Kjølbye-Biddle, 'Repton and the vikings', 47.
35. *Chronicon Abbatiae de Evesham ad Annum 1418*, ed. W.D. Macray, Rolls Series, 29 (1863), 83, 331–2.

This event must, however, be set in its broader context; the translation of relics from northern and parts of Midland England to the south and East Anglia was relatively common in the tenth and early eleventh centuries, and was, therefore, arguably part of the politics of southern English rule.[36] Repton was, thus, not alone in suffering the loss of its relics. Indeed, it is interesting that the relics of St Wystan should have been retained for so long, given that many other relics in the immediate vicinity (such as those of St Alkmund at Derby and St Werburgh at Hanbury (Staffs)) and further afield were removed sometime in the tenth century. This may suggest that the church at Repton experienced important protection at that time.

By the time of Domesday Book the religious community at Repton had gone; although the two priests recorded may be a residual sign of its former status, a feature noted at many other early churches.[37] In the later Middle Ages Repton was a mother church with eight chapels, and the isolated position of the chapel at Measham (Leics) may reveal that the parish of Repton had once been even larger (Fig. 43).[38] In the eleventh century Repton was an important comital manor that later passed into the hands of the king; the soke attached to the manor corresponds quite closely with the parish of Repton.[39] Whatever was the fate of the religious community at Repton, it is arguable that the pastoral role of the church, and its role as a focal point for burial, remained significant through the tenth and eleventh centuries.

Derby, St Alkmund's (Derbs)

Documentary and archaeological evidence reveals the church of St Alkmund, Derby, to have origins in or before the ninth century. We know from Æthelweard's tenth-century version of the Chronicle that when Ealdorman Æthelwulf was killed while fighting the Danes at Reading in 871 his body was taken from there 'into the province of the Mercians to the place called *Northworthig*, but in the Danish tongue, Derby'.[40] This, in turn, enables us to identify the resting place of St Alkmund (Ealhmund), which is recorded in an Old English list of saints' resting-places (*Secgan be þam Godes sanctum*) as '*Northworthy*'.[41] The background to the interment of Ealhmund is provided by

---

36. D.W. Rollason, 'The shrines of saints in later Anglo-Saxon England: distribution and significance', in *The Anglo-Saxon Church*, ed. Butler and Morris, 32–43; D.W. Rollason, 'Relic-cults as an instrument of royal policy c. 900–c. 1050', *ASE*, 15 (1987), 91–103.

37. J. Blair, 'Secular minster churches in Domesday Book', in *Domesday Book: a reassessment*, ed. P.H. Sawyer (1985), 104–42, at 106.

38. Cox, III, 425–60.

39. *DB*, fo. 272d.

40. *Æthelweard*, 37.

41. D.W. Rollason, 'Lists of saints' resting-places in Anglo-Saxon England', *ASE*, 7 (1978), 61–94, at 69.

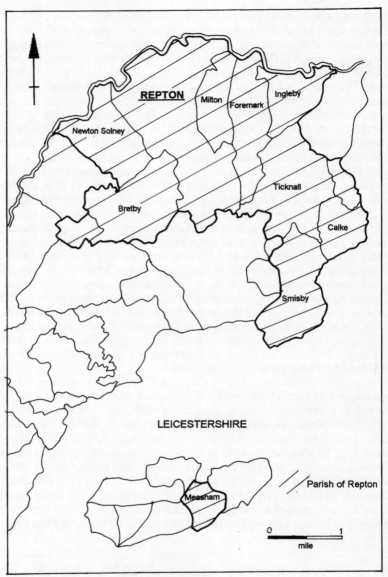

Figure 43 The parish of Repton

the twelfth-century *Historia Regum* attributed to Simeon of Durham, which seems to have drawn on a set of York annals for 732–802. It records under the year 800 that 'Alhmund, the son, as some say, of King Alhred [of Northumbria], was seized by the guards of King Eardwulf, and by his order killed along with his fellow fugitives'.[42] David Rollason has suggested that the cult of St Alkmund may have been promoted by King Coenwulf of Mercia. In the early ninth century Eardwulf was waging war on Coenwulf, having accused him of sheltering his enemies. When Eardwulf was expelled from his kingdom in 807–8, Pope Leo III blamed Coenwulf; Coenwulf's interests in Ealhmund may have been an attempt to undermine further Eardwulf's position and to marshall church support against him, because of his complicity in the murder of Ealhmund.[43] Whether or not this is the case – and it is plausible since the cults of saints were certainly subject to political manipulation – the veneration of a member of the Northumbrian royalty suggests the involvement of the Mercian royal house, and may indicate that St Alkmund's was a royal foundation.

It is not known when Ealhmund became, or how long he remained, a politically sensitive saint, or even when he was taken to Derby. A later tradition holds that he was translated there at some point from Lilleshall (Shrops).[44] Ealhmund's remains were certainly at Derby by *c.* 1031 – when the *Secgan* was compiled in its present form – and probably by the late ninth century, because that early part of the *Secgan* appears to have been based on ninth-century sources.[45] The resting-place of Ealhmund in Derby was almost certainly the church later dedicated to St Alkmund. Even if we were sceptical of the tradition recorded in the fourteenth-century *Vita Ælkmundi* that Ealhmund was buried in Derby 'in the north church built in his name' – and St Alkmund's was indeed the most northerly medieval church in Derby – excavation of this church confirms its pre-viking origins.[46] An impressive sarcophagus was discovered buried beneath the nave, and it has been dated on stylistic grounds to the ninth century. The excavator suggested that it was made for Ealhmund, but Martin Biddle has remarked that it could equally well have been a fitting resting-place for a ninth-century ealdorman, i.e. for Æthelwulf.[47] Other pieces of pre-viking sculpture and the fact that the earliest phases of the church resemble other known pre-viking churches confirm this as a pre-viking church.

---

42.   *EHD*, I, no. 3, s.a. 800; cf. M Lapidge, 'Byrhtforth of Ramsey and the early sections of the *Historia Regum* attributed to Simeon of Durham', *ASE*, 10 (1982), 97–122.
43.   Rollason, *Saints and Relics*, 122; see also A.T. Thacker, 'Kings, saints and monasteries in pre-viking Mercia', *Midland History*, 9 (1984), 1–25, at 15–16.
44.   Rollason, 'The cults of murdered royal saints', 4–5.
45.   Rollason, 'Lists of saints' resting places', 62–8.
46.   C.A.R. Radford, 'The church of St Alkmund, Derby', *DAJ*, 96 (1976), 26–61.
47.   Biddle, 'Archaeology, architecture and the cult of saints', 16 – although there may have been other churches in Derby where Æthelwulf could have been buried: see p. 273 below.

The discovery of a hogback and a fragment of a cross-shaft with Scandinavian influence on its carving suggests that the church was in use in the tenth century, possibly for burial, and certainly for some form of memorialization.[48] The loss of the relics of Ealhmund may be associated with the activities of Alfred's daughter, Æthelflaed, who is suspected of removing the relics of a number of Mercian saints in the early tenth century. Her capture of Derby in 917 may provide the context for the removal of the saints' relics, which eventually came to Shrewsbury.[49] Domesday Book records that there were two collegiate churches in Derby in the eleventh century. Although they are not named, it is evident that one of them was St Alkmund's because at a later date it was a collegiate church. It is instructive that unlike other mother churches, particularly those that retained collegiate status, St Alkmund's did not have a substantial parish. This may be linked with evidence that at least in the thirteenth century, it was in some way subordinate to another church in Derby (All Saints).[50]

Wirksworth (Derbs)

An early church at Wirksworth may be surmised from the presence there of a particularly fine piece of stone sculpture. The so-called Wirksworth slab seems originally to have been part of a shrine, although when it was discovered in 1821 it had been reused upside down over a coffin two feet beneath the floor of the church.[51] The slab has been variously dated by art historians to the seventh, eighth or ninth centuries.[52] It depicts the death of the Virgin, the descent into Hell, Ascension and the apocalyptic representation of the Lamb on the Cross; its iconography, then, represents death, judgement and resurrection.[53] Roberta Gilchrist has recently commented that the iconography of the slab may suggest that Wirksworth had once been a 'double house' for men and women. The panel is divided into parallel upper and lower registers – dominated by images of Christ and the Virgin respectively – which she interprets as having male and female associations: 'an appropriate opposition for a double house'.[54] In 835 an Abbess Cynewaru granted land at Wirksworth to Humbert, *dux*, on condition that he make an annual rent payment of 300 *solidi* of lead

---

48. Bailey, *Viking Age Sculpture*, 91; E. Roesdahl (ed.), *The Vikings in England and Their Danish Homeland* (1982), 103.
49. ASC, B, *s.a.* 917; Thacker, 'Kings, saints and monasteries', 15–16.
50. *The Cartulary of Darley Abbey*, ed. R.R. Darlington (1945), D2.
51. T.E. Routh, 'A corpus of pre-Conquest carved stones of Derbyshire', *DAJ*, 71 (1937), 1–46, at 44–6; R.W.P. Cockerton, 'The Wirksworth slab', *DAJ*, 82 (1962), 1–20.
52. Cockerton, 'The Wirksworth slab', 17–18; Rollason, *Saints and Relics*, 44.
53. Stafford, *The East Midlands*, 176.
54. R. Gilchrist, *Gender and Material Culture: the archaeology of religious women* (1994), 31–2. On the term 'double house', see n. 10 above.

from Wirksworth to Christ Church, Canterbury.[55] This association of an abbess with Wirksworth, when placed alongside the evidence of the sculpture, might suggest that it was the site of another royal nunnery, with an associated community of clerks.[56]

Little is known about any other aspects of the history of Wirksworth in the Anglo-Saxon period. Cynewaru's bequest suggests that it may have already been a focal point for lead-mining in the region, as it certainly was in the later Middle Ages, when it was the site of the Barmote court. It has also been identified as the location of the Roman lead-mining centre, *Lutudaron*, recorded in the *Ravenna Cosmography* and, in abbreviated form, on a number of inscribed lead pigs found nearby.[57] The single reference from the early ninth century to the annual supply of lead from Wirksworth to Canterbury hints that lead-mining may have provided a continuing foundation for Wirksworth's importance through the earlier Middle Ages.

There was nothing remarkable about the church at Wirksworth, according to Domesday Book. In the absence of earlier documentary evidence concerning this church it is impossible to surmise what might have happened to the church or community at Wirksworth during the pre-Conquest period. In the later Middle Ages, however, it was a wealthy church with a substantial parish, and, like a number of the superior churches of the region, it had been granted to the dean of Lincoln Cathedral in *c*. 1093.[58] The parish of Wirksworth corresponds quite closely to the Domesday soke; that is to say, most of the dependencies of the manor were located within the parish (Fig. 22).[59] The main exception to the pattern concerns Ible and Bonsall, as both were members of the manor of Matlock. However, it is notable that the church of Matlock was a possession of the dean of Lincoln from the twelfth century, even though there is no surviving record of the church being granted to him, and this may indicate that it came to the dean as one of the chapelries of Wirksworth.[60] It is tempting to surmise that the parish and the Domesday manor of Matlock had been carved out of that of Wirksworth. However, one needs to be careful when applying this logic because we would also have to conclude that the same was true of the parish of Darley, which included two of the berewicks of the manor of Matlock. It is not implausible that this whole area might once have formed a single territory and parish focused on Wirksworth, and

---

55. S 1624 (B 414).
56. It has been suggested that another abbess of Repton sent a coffin of lead for St Guthlac in the early eighth century which may plausibly have come from the lead supplies in the Wirksworth area; however, the evidence is late and unreliable (see p. 231 below).
57. I.A. Richmond and O.G.S. Crawford, 'The British section of the Ravenna Cosmography', *Archaeologia*, 93 (1949), 1–50, at 38; Cockerton, 'The Wirksworth slab', 1–2.
58. *RA*, III, no. 765; *Tithe Files*, 219; Cox, II, 417, 457; *RA*, I, no. 38.
59. *DB*, fos. 272c, 274a.
60. Cox, II, 517–18.

this might account for the overlap in the manorial and parochial geography, but we can say nothing more certain than that.

Bakewell (Derbs)

Architectural evidence suggests that there was an early church at Bakewell. Fragments of a number of pre-viking cross-shafts and sarcophagi have been found there.[61] It has been suggested that Bakewell may have been a centre of sculptural production; pieces with designs and iconography similar to the pieces found at Bakewell have been discovered elsewhere in Derbyshire at Eyam, Bradbourne and Wirksworth, and at Sheffield (Yorks).[62] The fabric of the church contains some Anglo-Saxon work, and its layout has been identified as being a typical Anglo-Saxon aisleless form, although the date of the structure is unclear.[63] There was a church at Bakewell in 949, according to a charter by which King Eadred granted land there to Uhtred for the endowment of a *coenubium*.[64] It is not stated how much land was involved, but the size of other contemporary grants to the church (particularly to the archbishop of York) in the northern Danelaw indicates that it might have been a substantial amount. By the eleventh century the church at Bakewell possessed only three carucates of land, although the two priests had two *villani* and five *bordarii* with eleven ploughs under them.[65] Although by comparison with other parts of the country this is not a very impressive mark of status, the Domesday evidence does mark Bakewell out as a church of some note in this region.

In the later medieval period the church of Bakewell served an enormous parish, with many chapelries (Fig. 20).[66] The payment of pensions from the churches at Edensor and Youlgreave to Bakewell in the thirteenth century may be an indication that they too had formerly been chapels of Bakewell.[67] The parish incorporated the Domesday manors of Bakewell and Ashford and their respective dependencies.[68]

The early relationship between Ashford and Bakewell remains unclear. In the first decade of the tenth century Uhtred had purchased land in the area which was appurtenant to Ashford, suggesting that at

61.   Routh, 'Pre-Conquest carved stones of Derbyshire', 6–19; R. Cramp, 'Schools of Mercian sculpture', in *Mercian Studies*, ed. Dornier, 191–233, at 218–25.
62.   Cramp, 'Schools of Mercian sculpture', 218.
63.   Taylor and Taylor, *Anglo-Saxon Architecture*, I, 36.
64.   S 548; *Burton Abbey Charters*, 20–1; P.H. Sawyer, 'The charters of Burton Abbey and the unification of England', *Northern History*, 10 (1975), 28–39.
65.   *DB*, fo. 272d.
66.   *Tithe Maps*, 68; Cox, II, 7, 72, 112–13.
67.   Cox, II, 178.
68.   *DB*, fo. 272d.

this date Ashford was an important territorial centre.[69] Edward the Elder built a *burh* at Bakewell in 920, although it has yet to be located, which suggests that it too was an important territorial centre at that date.[70] It is possible that there was formerly one estate which had by the early tenth century been divided in two, but which continued to form a single parish, although it is possible that the church at Bakewell had always served two separate estates. Perhaps Bakewell had always been the ecclesiastical centre and Ashford the associated secular estate centre. Whatever the case, it seems certain that by 920, when the *burh* was built, both Ashford and Bakewell were the focal points of substantial territories, and the church of Bakewell had a parish which continued to serve two distinct tenth- and eleventh-century estates.[71]

The fate of the church at Bakewell in the tenth century remains obscure. The grant to Uhtred in 949 may have extended his possessions in the Peak District, but it is equally possible that the grant was obtained to allow him to endow a religious community, perhaps newly founded or refounded, with part of his estate. The presence of tenth-century sculpture offers additional proof that Bakewell remained an important church and centre of sculpture production.[72]

Southwell (Notts)

The only evidence concerning Southwell in the pre-viking period comes from the *Secgan*. In that portion which derives from a ninth-century list it is recorded that the body of Eadburh rested at Southwell. Eadburh was possibly an early eighth-century abbess of Repton: Felix's *Life of St Guthlac* records that Abbess Eadburh sent a coffin of lead for Guthlac *c.* 715, and a later gloss identifies her as an abbess of Repton.[73] Assuming that the identification of this Eadburh with the person interred at Southwell is correct (and the name is common), we might

---

69. S 397 (B 658); F.M. Stenton, *Types of Manorial Structure in the Northern Danelaw*, Oxford Studies in Social and Legal History, ed. P. Vinogradoff, 2 (1910), 3–96, at 74.
70. *ASC, s.a.* 924; C.R. Hart, *The North Derbyshire Archaeological Survey to AD 1500* (1981), 118–21; J. Stetka, *King Edward the Elder's* Burh: the lost village of Burton by Bakewell (1997).
71. For discussion of which lands were included in the grant to Uhtred, see Sawyer, 'The charters of Burton Abbey', 31–3; D.R. Roffe, 'The origins of Derbyshire', *DAJ*, 106 (1986), 102–22 at 120–1. The association of secular and ecclesiastical sites is discussed in J. Blair, 'Minster churches in the landscape', in *Anglo-Saxon Settlements*, ed. D. Hooke (1988), 35–58, at 40–8.
72. Sawyer, 'The charters of Burton Abbey', 32; Routh, 'Pre-Conquest carved stones of Derbyshire', 8–19.
73. *Life of Saint Guthlac*, 146–7, 191; *Liber Eliensis*, ed. E.O. Blake, Camden 3rd ser., 92 (1962), xxiii–xxiv, 19. The identification of Abbess Ecgburg (Eadburh) as an abbess of Repton was an interlineation in the early thirteenth-century F manuscript of the *Liber Eliensis* 'probably inserted in response to a marginal note *cuius loci?*' in the late twelfth-century E manuscript.

suggest that Southwell was the location of another nunnery, in some way associated with Repton. Although there is little enough early evidence, this is not implausible, and groups of nunneries with close ties are known in other regions.[74] Domesday Book does not record a church at Southwell, but the presence of three clerics on the manor is indicative of one. The presence of a church is known in 1051 when the archbishop of York, Ælfric, died there, after which his successor, Archbishop Cynesige, made a gift of bells to the church. Shortly afterwards a refectory was built for the canons.[75] A tympanum there decorated with the Urnes style is possibly of pre-Conquest date.[76]

In the later Middle Ages Southwell Minster served a large parish (Fig. 21). The dependencies of Southwell named in a charter of 956 are all, except one, within the parish.[77] The church was a college of secular canons, and a prebendal system was instituted at some point in the mid-eleventh century. Each canon acted as parish priest to the church which gave its name to his prebend; the canons combined service to the collegiate community with duty as a vicar.[78]

Flawford (Notts)

Although there is no documentary evidence concerning the church of Flawford until *c.* 1150, there is some archaeological evidence to suggest that it had early origins. Excavation has revealed an Anglo-Saxon church which stood within the remains of a Roman villa. The church was on the same alignment as the villa, and the nave seems to have made use of the tessellated floor of the villa.[79] Of course, this does not prove continuity of use of the site, nor does it reveal when the church was built, but the discovery of a coin of Burgred of Mercia (852–74) at the level of the tessellated floor suggests that the church existed in the ninth century.[80]

No church is mentioned in Domesday Book, and indeed Flawford did not constitute a separate manor, probably being included under the

---

74.   Thacker, 'Monks, preaching and pastoral care', 144–5.
75.   F.M. Stenton, 'The founding of Southwell Minster', in *Preparatory to Anglo-Saxon England: being the collected papers of Frank Merry Stenton*, ed. D.M. Stenton (1970), 364–70.
76.   Although a twelfth-century date is possible: Olwyn Owen (pers. comm.). There is no other reliable evidence of pre-Conquest fabric, but see a reference in 1853 to the reuse of some late Saxon carved stones in rebuilding the central piers: N. Pevsner, *The Buildings of England, Nottinghamshire* (2nd edn, 1979), 319.
77.   S 659 (B 1029); *Tithe Maps*, 83; Stenton, 'Southwell Minster'; J. C. Cox, 'Southwell', *VCH Notts*, 152–61, at 155; P. Lyth, 'The Southwell charter of 956 AD: an exploration of its boundaries', *TTS*, 86 (1982), 49–61.
78.   Cox, 'Southwell', 152–7; *Valor*, V, 277.
79.   L.E. Webster and J. Cherry, 'Britain in 1976', *Medieval Archaeology*, 21 (1977), 211–12; W. Rodwell, *Church Archaeology* (1984), 154.
80.   Webster and Cherry, 'Britain in 1976', 212.

entry for Ruddington.[81] Yet the church of Flawford was certainly more important than many of the churches in the vicinity. It had a chapelry at Edwalton, and there is circumstantial evidence to suggest that the area served by the church may have been rather larger.[82] In order to pay the dues owed from Flawford to the Hospital of St John of Jerusalem, Durham, in the thirteenth century, payments were drawn from the parishes of Bradmore, Keyworth and Bunny.[83] Bradmore was a chapel of Bunny, and the parishioners of Keyworth are known to have paid tithe to the church of Bunny in the seventeenth century.[84] This network of dues and tithe payments does not prove what was the earlier organization, but it may suggest a complicated process of fragmentation of a once larger parish into a series of smaller parishes, the churches of which enjoyed competing and conflicting rights. Given the peculiar location of the church of Flawford on its parish boundary, it is possible that the church once included neighbouring Plumtree in its parish (with its constituent townships of Normanton and Clipston).[85]

If these disparate pieces of evidence may be relied upon, then the church of Flawford may once have served a relatively substantial parish. It is impossible to say any more than this, particularly since the parish of Flawford did not correspond to the manorial structure, but rather incorporated a number of separate manors. In comparison with mother churches elsewhere in the region, Flawford has few signs of superior status. However, in the context of southern Nottinghamshire it does emerge as one of the very few churches that has any signs of superior status at all. It was seemingly more than an ordinary village or manorial church. It seems significant that a church with some evidence for early origins should display signs at a later date of a status superior to that of a number of neighbouring churches; as such, Flawford fits into a familiar pattern, even if the nature of the available evidence is different from that for other churches.

Ripon (Yorks)

Ripon has a wealth of documentary evidence for its status and history before the ninth century, and recent re-examination of the archaeological evidence has added substantially to our understanding of the religious community based there. The *Life of St Wilfrid* written by Stephanus the priest reports that Wilfrid was given 'the monastery

81. *DB*, fos. 282c, 286a, 290d, 291d. No church is recorded under the Ruddington entries.
82. 'The register, or rolls, of Walter Gray, Lord Archbishop of York', ed. J. Raine, *Surtees Society*, 56 (1872), 18.
83. *Thoroton*, I, 128.
84. J.T. Godfrey, *Notes on the Churches of Nottinghamshire: Bingham Hundred* (1907), 25, 43, 120; *Valor*, V, 168.
85. *Tithe Maps*, 83.

(*coenobium*) at Ripon together with 30 hides of land' in the late seventh century.[86] Bede in his *Ecclesiastical History* and his *Vita Sancti Cuthberti* adds that Ripon had previously been granted by King Alhfrith of Deira to Abbot Eata of Melrose (probably sometime before 660), but this community had abandoned the site rather than give up their religious customs, which were of Irish origin.[87] It was here that Wilfrid later constructed 'a church built of dressed stones, supported with columns and complete with side aisles' some time later.[88] Archaeological and architectural analysis of the church has attempted to identify elements of the fabric which might be associated with Wilfrid's construction; most attention has been focused on the stone crypt, which is now accepted as a survival of Wilfrid's church.[89] Wilfrid was buried in his church at Ripon, although not in the crypt, as Bede records that he was buried close to the altar on the south side. Also buried at Ripon according to the earliest part of the *Secgan* were St Egbert and St Wihtberht.[90]

There are a number of sites at Ripon that have produced evidence for cemeteries or churches of the Anglo-Saxon period, and in this respect the religious community at Ripon was like many other early ecclesiastical communities in comprising several foci (Fig. 44).[91] These foci include, first, St Peter's itself with its seventh-century crypt. Second, there is a sixth/seventh- to tenth-century cemetery at Ailcy Hill, in which there was a transition from the burial of adult males and females and infants to the burial exclusively of adult males. This has been explained as the adoption of the site for monastic burial (the presence of chest-burials is significant, as they have been associated elsewhere with monastic or episcopal contexts);[92] since more than 50 per cent of the hill on which the cemetery is located had been quarried away prior to investigation it is not clear whether there was an associated chapel or other structure. Third, there is a two-celled church (known as the Ladykirk) which contained burials accompanied by combs (dated on stylistic grounds to the later Anglo-Saxon period)

---

86. *VSW*, c. 8; on the authorship of the text, see D.P. Kirby, 'Bede, Eddius Stephanus and the "Life of Wilfrid"', *EHR*, 98 (1983), 101–14, at 102–4.
87. *The Life of St Cuthbert*, ed. B. Colgrave (1940), c. 8; *HE*, iii, 25.
88. *VSW*, c. 22. R.A. Hall and M. Whyman, 'Settlement and monasticism at Ripon, North Yorkshire, from the 7th to 11th centuries AD', *Medieval Archaeology*, 40 (1996), 62–150 at 65.
89. Taylor and Taylor, *Anglo-Saxon Architecture*, 1, 302; 2, 517; R.A. Hall, 'Rescue excavation in the crypt of Ripon cathedral', *YAJ*, 49 (1977), 59–63; R.A. Hall, 'Observations in Ripon cathedral crypt, 1989', *YAJ*, 65 (1993), 39–53; Hall and Whyman, 'Settlement and monasticism at Ripon', 63–5.
90. *HE*, v, 19; Rollason, 'Lists of saints' resting places', 62–3, 89.
91. Hall and Whyman, 'Settlement and monasticism at Ripon', 136–44; on comparable examples see Blair, 'Anglo-Saxon minsters', 246; E. Cambridge and A. Williams, 'Hexham Abbey: a review of recent work and its implications', *Archaeologia Aeliana*, 5th ser., 23 (1995), 51–138, at 74–6; D. Stocker, 'The early church in Lincolnshire: a study of the sites and their significance', in *Pre-Viking Lindsey*, ed. A. Vince (1993), 101–22.
92. Hall and Whyman, 'Settlement and monasticism at Ripon', 112–13, 122.

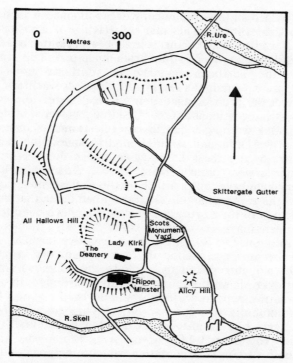

Figure 44 Excavations at Ripon (after R.A. Hall and M. Whyman, 'Settlement and monasticism at Ripon, North Yorkshire, from the 7th to 11th centuries AD', *Medieval Archaeology*, 40 (1996), 62–150)

and which cuts through earlier burials, and is associated with sculpture of probable eighth- or ninth-century date. Fourth is a burial-ground at All Hallows Hill (from which no secure dating evidence has, however, been recovered). Finally, the site known as Scott's Monument Yard certainly had a church, although of uncertain origin, which was located within the truncated remnant of an enclosure.

The fate of Ripon following the Scandinavian settlement is not well documented, but there is sufficient evidence to suggest that ecclesiastical life of some sort continued here. The presence of sculpture bearing Scandinavian-style motifs is significant, as it suggests that the church continued to play some role in local society.[93] More striking, however, is the reference in the Anglo-Saxon Chronicle for 948 to King Eadred's campaign northwards, which resulted in the burning of the monastery at Ripon. It is likely that this was the occasion when the

---

93. W.G. Collingwood, 'Anglian and Anglo-Danish sculpture in the West Riding of Yorkshire', *YAJ*, 23 (1915), 129–299, at 233–5; Bailey, *Viking Age Sculpture*, 120–1.

relics of St Wilfrid and the Ripon copy of Stephanus's *Vita Wilfridi* were removed to Canterbury.[94] This may, as David Rollason has observed, have been a raid to acquire the relics of 'a particularly self-assertive and independent-minded Northumbrian bishop'.[95] The translation of relics from the northern Danelaw to southern monasteries and cathedrals was a prominent feature of the tenth century, and must, in part, reflect the growing assertion of West Saxon domination of the North. This striking demonstration of Eadred's power was also, perhaps, meant both as a warning to northern ecclesiastics against siding with Scandinavian overlords, and as an attempt to undermine local identities and patriotism by removing the relics central to the cults around which local allegiances were often created.[96] It is remarkable that the only clear evidence we have for an attack on the ecclesiastical community at Ripon concerns a West Saxon raid. It is a reminder that whatever the fate of churches in the northern Danelaw may have been following the period of Scandinavian conquest, their fate also depended on the actions of the house of Wessex and other native lords.

After he became archbishop of York, one of the great reforming bishops, Oswald, introduced monks into the religious community at Ripon. However, it was an experiment that ended in failure. The initiative was not repeated elsewhere, and by the time of Domesday Book the community at Ripon had no surviving trace of monastic life, and it was served by an unrecorded number of canons.[97] In the later Middle Ages the church of St Peter's at Ripon was an important mother church serving a large parish, which incorporated the majority of the many berewicks and sokelands that were attached to the estate of Ripon according to documents of the later tenth and eleventh centuries (Fig. 19). However, we cannot tell how far these endowments had been held continuously since the time of St Wilfrid, and the record of losses from the estate of Ripon in a memorandum of *c.* 975 cautions against assuming continuity.[98]

Otley (Yorks)

There is sculptural evidence to suggest that Otley was an important pre-viking church, possibly belonging to the archbishops of York from an early date. The documentary evidence sometimes adduced to suggest that Otley had long been a possession of the archbishops is, however, fragmentary and hardly conclusive. The fact that Simeon of

94. N.P. Brooks, *The Early History of the Church of Canterbury: Christ Church from 597 to 1066* (1984), 227–8, 230.
95. Rollason, 'Relic-cults', 95–6.
96. Brooks, *The Early History of the Church of Canterbury*, 228.
97. 'Vita Oswaldi', *Historians of the Church of York and Its Archbishops*, ed. J. Raine (3 vols, 1879–94), I, 462; *DB*, fo. 303d.
98. *EHD*, I, no. 114; *EYC*, I, 21–3; *DB*, fo. 303d. The parish and soke of Ripon are mapped out above: Figure 19, p. 129.

Durham records that Archbishop Wulfhere fled *c.* 867 to Addingham, known to have been part of the Otley estate in the later tenth century, certainly raises the possibility that Addingham, and by extension Otley, were already episcopal possessions in the late ninth century.[99] The church of Addingham possesses a pre-viking stone panel which Ian Wood has claimed may have been an archiepiscopal commission.[100] Even if this is true, given the clear evidence from the tenth century that estates of the archbishop were regularly reconstituted, possession of Addingham *c.* 867 cannot be taken as proof of possession of Otley at that time.[101] However, that there is other early sculpture on outlying parts of the Otley estate (at Ilkley and Weston) supports the argument that this church and estate were the possession of a major lord, plausibly the archbishop of York.[102]

The best evidence for the status of the church at Otley in the pre-viking period is provided by the two stone crosses in the church, which have been dated to the eighth and ninth centuries.[103] Ian Wood has suggested that the iconography of the so-called Angel Cross is suggestive of a pastoral and evangelical context: it includes what have been interpreted as a mass-priest, angels, Evangelists and the Tree of Life.[104] The other cross at Otley may similarly depict the Evangelists, and also an olive branch, which in scriptural exegesis comes to stand for 'those who are to be brought into the church', owing to its association with the sprig brought back to the ark by the dove.[105] On this basis Wood has suggested that the community at Otley was more likely to have been of priests than of monks.[106] An archiepiscopal context for iconography relating to pastoral or evangelical work is certainly suggested in a number of sources: in Bede's letter to Archbishop Ecgbert, emphasizing the importance of preaching; in the reiteration of the need for preaching in the Legatine Council of 786; and in Alcuin's recommendation to Archbishop Eanbald II that he

---

99. *Sym. Op.*, I, 225.
100. Wood, 'Anglo-Saxon Otley', 23.
101. Other evidence from the *Life* of Wilfrid concerning the estate at *Ingaedyne* – which is commonly identified as Yeadon in the parish of Guiseley, itself a member of the Otley estate – adds nothing to the argument about the possible archiepiscopal possession of Otley, not least because the identification of *Ingaedyne* with Yeadon is open to question, but also because the context in which it is named may indicate that it was a possession of Ripon rather than York: M.L. Faull and S.A. Moorhouse, *West Yorkshire: an archaeological survey to AD 1500* (4 vols, 1981), II, 183; Wood, 'Anglo-Saxon Otley', 21-4. On the archbishop's tenth-century estate, see Chapter 3, pp. 120, 126.
102. Bailey, *Viking Age Sculpture*, 170, 189; W.G. Collingwood, *Northumbrian Crosses of the Pre-Norman Age* (1927), 50; Roesdahl (ed.), *The Vikings in England*, 92; Wood, 'Anglo-Saxon Otley', 36-7.
103. R. Cramp, 'The position of the Otley crosses in English sculpture of the eighth to ninth centuries', *Kolloquium über spätantike und frühmittelalterliche Skulptur*, 2 (Mainz, 1970), 55-63.
104. Wood, 'Anglo-Saxon Otley', 30-2.
105. *Ibid.*, 32-4.
106. *Ibid.*, 36.

make use of Gregory the Great's *Cura Pastoralis*.[107] However, it should be noted that more recent work has suggested that the preoccupations of most pre-viking sculpture are non-monastic and more concerned with the role of the church as Christ's representative on earth; therefore the Otley sculpture may not be as abnormal as Ian Wood suggested.[108] Moreover, the distinction he draws between communities involved in pastoral care and monastic communities has been shown to be somewhat anachronistic.[109]

It is not clear what happened to the church at Otley during the later Anglo-Saxon period. A religious presence at Otley in the tenth century is indicated by the survival of stone sculpture influenced by Scandinavian iconography; such a deduction may also be made about Ilkley, Weston and Addingham, where sculpture bearing Scandinavian-style iconography has also been found.[110] Whether Otley remained an episcopal possession is, however, unclear. It was certainly held by Archbishop Oswald in the later tenth century, but its fate before this is unknown. Comparison with Sherburn in Elmet, which had been granted to one Æslac in 963 before coming into the hands of the archbishop, reveals that it is not wise to assume uninterrupted archiepiscopal possession. The iconography of the tenth-century sculpture at Otley and Weston includes warrior-figures, and this might be an indication that these places were in secular hands in the earlier tenth century, although it should be noted that a comparable depiction of a horseman with shield is found on sculpture at Chester-le-Street (Co. Durham), where the community of St Cuthbert is known to have resided from *c.* 883 to *c.* 995.[111]

In the later Middle Ages the parish of Otley was substantial, and included many of the places which are listed in accounts of the lands of the archbishops of York from the late tenth and early eleventh centuries, and in Domesday Book (Fig. 18). Those places which were not in Otley parish were mainly in the immediately adjacent parishes.[112] This is significant, because some of these parishes are known from sculptural evidence to have had pre-viking churches. If there had ever been an ecclesiastical connection between these places – which Ian Wood has suggested on the fragile basis of the sculpture at each of these places – then it was one which was lost, perhaps as a result of the early foundation of the churches. Indeed, Ilkley may itself have been a particularly important early church. In addition to its pre-viking sculpture, it is striking that the church was built within the walls

---

107. *Ibid.*, 35; *EHD*, I, no. 170; A.W. Haddan and W. Stubbs (eds), *Councils and Ecclesiastical Documents Relating to Great Britain and Ireland* (3 vols, 1869–79), 3, 449–50, 505.
108. John Blair, pers. comm.
109. Blair, 'Introduction', 1.
110. Bailey, *Viking Age Sculpture*, 162, 170, 189–90, 195; Roesdahl (ed.), *The Vikings*, 92.
111. Wood, 'Anglo-Saxon Otley', 23; Roesdahl (ed.), *The Vikings*, 93.
112. *PN WRY*, 195–210; *EHD*, I, no. 114; *EYC*, I, 21–3; *DB*, fo. 303c. The parish and soke of Otley is mapped above: Figure 18, p. 128.

of a Roman fort, and has two Anglo-Saxon window-heads cut from a Roman altar.[113] Given this evidence, and the fact that we know that territorial organization in this region was relatively fluid, at least in the tenth and eleventh centuries, we should not assume that Ilkley, or Weston and Addingham for that matter, had necessarily always been associated with either the parish or the estate of Otley.

Beverley (Yorks)

Bede records that Bishop John of York retired *c.* 714 to the monastery of *inderawuda* ('in the wood of the Deirans'), where he died and was buried in 721; this has traditionally been identified as Beverley.[114] Support for this identification is provided by the *Secgan*, which records that John's burial place was *Beferlic*; it appears in that portion of the *Secgan* which David Rollason has demonstrated to be based on pre-viking sources.[115] A so-called frithstool, which was probably originally an abbot's or bishop's throne, survives at Beverley and has been attributed to the seventh century.[116]

The fate of this church after the eighth century is unclear, but there are a number of later medieval traditions concerning the events of the late ninth and early tenth centuries. Twelfth-century writers alleged that the monastery was destroyed by the vikings and that it was refounded as a secular college by King Athelstan in the 930s. However, doubt has been cast on this account, largely because it emerged late.[117] In grants and confirmations issued by Edward the Confessor, William the Conqueror and Henry I there is no mention of this tradition, and Richard Morris and Eric Cambridge interpret this as a sign that this was a settled community in the eleventh century, not one relatively newly formed, nor one which felt the need to conjure up a foundation myth. They suggest that an uninterrupted history stretching back to the eighth century would account for this lack of interest in the eleventh century in supposed recent foundations.[118]

There has also been debate about the findings of excavations to the

---

113. P. Ryder, *Medieval Churches of West Yorkshire*, South Yorkshire County Archaeology Monograph, 2 (1993), 7–9; Blair, 'Anglo-Saxon minsters', 236–9.

114. *HE*, v, 7.

115. Rollason, 'Lists of saints' resting-places', 68, 87; for a recent discussion of the evidence for the pre-Conquest history of Beverley, see D.M. Palliser, 'The "minster hypothesis": a case study', *EME*, 5 (2) (1996), 207–14.

116. R. Cramp, 'The furnishing and sculptural decoration of Anglo-Saxon churches' in *The Anglo-Saxon Church*, ed. Butler and Morris, 101–4 at 102, 104; J.T. Lang, *Corpus of Anglo-Saxon Stone Sculpture, III: York and Eastern Yorkshire* (1991), 224.

117. R.K. Morris and E. Cambridge, 'Beverley minster before the early thirteenth century', in *Medieval Art and Architecture in the East Riding of Yorkshire*, ed. C. Wilson, British Archaeological Association Conference Transactions, 9 (1989), 9–32, at 9–10.

118. *Ibid.*, 11–12.

south of the present minster, and their possible significance for understanding the Scandinavian impact. The excavators argued that there was a break in occupation from *c.* 851 to 930 as a result of viking activity. However, this assessment has been undermined by Richard Hall, who has observed that too much has been made of the supposed ninth-century date of some of the artefacts found (such as a Scandinavian-style comb and a bone pin), not least because stratigraphically these finds do not belong to the ninth century, and it is hard to see what these particular artefacts might have to do with military activity. Hall rightly concludes that 'the evidence for the viking raids is nil'.[119] Even if there was a break in occupation on a particular site, that is not evidence that the monastery as a whole was abandoned or destroyed. At best, the archaeological evidence perhaps corresponds with that at other ecclesiastical sites which have evidence for the reduction of the intensity and extent of occupation in the ninth or tenth century, but not its total abandonment.[120]

The story of Athelstan's involvement in the fortunes of Beverley is difficult to substantiate. It has been argued that the rights of the minster were probably acquired gradually but were retrospectively credited to a single royal benefactor for the sake of security and prestige.[121] In the twelfth century it was alleged that Athelstan had granted to the canons of Beverley the right to four thraves (96 sheaves) of corn from every working plough in the East Riding, and that this had previously been a royal levy for the upkeep of the king's horses and messengers. Whatever the real involvement of Athelstan in the history of Beverley Minster, there is a story that there was a functioning church there in the early tenth century. If it was indeed patronized by Athelstan, a likely context is provided by his contemporary patronage of York and the community of St Cuthbert (at Chester-le-Street).[122] Alternatively, memories of such benefactions could have been the foundation of a Beverley myth.

Bede describes the dedication by John of Beverley of two churches on the estates of *comites*, one of which adjoined its owner's house some two miles from Beverley. We are told nothing of the provision for these, and it is possible that they were served by priests from Beverley.[123] Yet a more straightforward and equally plausible reading of the evidence suggests that these churches were proprietary aristocratic churches, and it does not appear necessary to turn them into dependencies of Beverley. There is admittedly little evidence for independently functioning small churches in the seventh and eighth

---

119. P. Armstrong, D. Tomlinson and D.H. Evans, *Excavations at Lurk Lane, Beverley, 1979–82* (1991), 14, 243; the review of this excavation report by Hall is in *YAJ*, 65 (1993), 182–3.
120. Palliser, 'The "minster hypothesis" ', 209.
121. R.E. Horrox, 'Medieval Beverley', *VCH E. Riding*, VI, 2–62 at 3.
122. *HSC*, c. 26; S 407 (B 703); T.M. Fallow, 'The hospital of St Leonard, York', *VCH Yorks*, 336–45 at 336.
123. *HE*, v, 4–5; Blair, 'Ecclesiastical organization', 196, n. 15.

centuries, which creates an impression that all priests lived in communities of some sort, but it is unreasonable to assume that were no such churches.[124]

By the eleventh century Beverley was a collegiate church with a large estate and numerous privileges, and the centre of the cult of Bishop John.[125] According to twelfth-century sources, the church also had a sanctuary zone, the 'peace of St John', which extended one mile around the church and was 'free and quit of all royal custom, all payment of money and all the geld which is paid to the king'.[126] There is little to support the case that has been made for this privilege being of much earlier origin.[127]

The parish of Beverley included a number of chapels, although the minster retained rights of burial and baptism. The various chapels were served by one or other of the prebendaries of the minster.[128] The parish, although relatively sizeable, is not as large as those of other mother churches in the region. It is much smaller than the Domesday estate of Beverley, which was divided between the archbishop and the minster, and which extended far into Holderness.[129]

York

York was, of course, the location of an archbishopric about which much has been written. It is therefore necessary here only to outline the main evidence for ecclesiastical provision in York from the seventh to the eleventh centuries. There is written evidence for the presence of a church in York in the early seventh century, built in wood for the baptism of King Edwin in 627, which was incorporated in the stone church built soon afterwards under the instructions of Bishop Paulinus. After Edwin's death in 633/4 the episcopal see for Northumbria was established at Lindisfarne, but was transferred to York probably after the Synod of Whitby (664).[130] The patronage of the episcopal church of St Peter's, and its use as a place of burial are referred to in numerous sources, particularly the writings of Bede, Alcuin and those attributed to Simeon of Durham. Excavations around the minster have failed to identify traces of the pre-Conquest church,

---

124. Thacker, 'Monks, preaching and pastoral care', 142, n. 28.
125. Palliser, 'The "minster hypothesis"', 210–11; *The Historians of the Church of York and Its Archbishops*, ed. J. Raine, Rolls Series, 71 (3 vols, 1879–94), II, 343–4, 353–4.
126. *EYC*, I, 108; *English Lawsuits from William I to Richard I*, ed. R.C. van Caenegem, Selden Society, 106 (1990), 141–2.
127. But see Blair, 'Anglo-Saxon minsters', 257; Palliser, 'The "minster hypothesis"', 210–11.
128. K.J. Allison, 'Outlying townships', *VCH E. Riding*, VI, 271–313.
129. *DB*, fos. 304a–b.
130. The sequence of bishops of York can be recovered from Bede's *Ecclesiastical History* and Stephanus's *Life of Bishop Wilfrid*.

but grave-markers and crosses of the seventh to ninth century have been excavated there.[131] There were other early churches in York. At St Mary, Bishophill Junior, an inscription has been found which reads 'Hail, holy priest, on behalf of your merits' and which has been variously dated to the eighth or early ninth century, and a series of early carved stones have also been discovered there.[132] In his poem about the bishops, kings and saints of the church of York, Alcuin refers to the foundation of a church dedicated to the Alma Sophia by Archbishop Æthelbert 779/80, which was a 'lofty building, supported by strong columns/themselves bolstering curving arches ... with its many galleries ... and thirty altars'.[133]

There is no doubt of the continuity of ecclesiastical life in York during the tenth century. The preparedness of successive archbishops of York to collaborate with whoever was in control of York and its hinterland doubtless helped.[134] The minting of coins in the early tenth century bearing the legend 'St Peter' and the production of sculpture in the tenth century provide support for the documentary evidence, and reveal the forms that continuity of ecclesiastical life might take. Excavations at York have been particularly important for students of stone sculpture, as they have produced a rare example of sculpture in a stratified context that reveals that it was certainly produced before the mid-tenth century.[135]

West Gilling (Yorks)

Bede reports that a monastery was built at West Gilling as atonement for the death of King Oswin by the order of King Oswy in 651. Queen Eanfled petitioned Oswy to grant land at Gilling to Trumhere (later bishop of the Mercians) on which to build a monastery in order that prayer might be offered for the kings, both the slayer and the slain.[136] Pre-viking sculpture at West Gilling includes fragments of a cross-head and a cross-arm.[137] Fragments of two Anglo-Scandinavian crosses also survive there, suggesting that the church was functioning in the tenth century, although there is no other evidence for its fate.[138]

---

131.   *HE*, ii, 14; *VSW*, 50–1; *ASC, s.a.* 738; P. Godman, *Alcuin, the Bishops, Kings and Saints of York* (1982); *Sym. Op.*, I, 58; *ii*, 62; Lang, *York and Eastern Yorkshire*, 53–68.

132.   Lang, *York and Eastern Yorkshire*, 83–7.

133.   Godman, *Alcuin*, 118–21; for suggestions about the location of the Alma Sophia, see R.K. Morris, 'Alcuin, York and the *alma sophia*', in *The Anglo-Saxon Church*, ed. Butler and Morris, 80–9; Lang, *York and Eastern Yorkshire*, 8, 17.

134.   See pp. 312–13 below.

135.   M. Dolley, 'The Anglo-Danish and Anglo-Norse coinages of York', in *Viking Age York and the North*, ed. R.A. Hall (CBA Research Report, 27, 1978), 26–31, at 26–7; Bailey, *Viking Age Sculpture*, 50.

136.   *HE*, iii, 14 and 24.

137.   W.G. Collingwood, 'Anglian and Anglo-Danish sculpture in the North Riding of Yorkshire, *YAJ*, 19 (1907), 267–413, at 322.

138.   Collingwood, *Northumbrian Crosses*, 97–8.

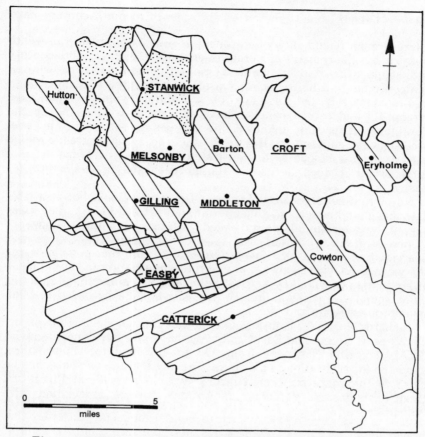

Figure 45 The parishes of Easby, West Gilling, Stanwick and Catterick

In the later Middle Ages the church of St Agatha at Gilling served a large and scattered parish.[139] It is tempting to suggest that the parish might also once have included those places interspersed between Gilling and its dependencies, not least because one of them, located in the centre, is called Middleton. However, the case ought not to be pushed, because among other reasons it begs questions about the relationship of Gilling to Stanwick St John, Melsonby and Croft, which themselves have pre-viking sculpture.[140] The Domesday estate of Gilling included those places which are in its parish, but also many others (Fig. 45).[141]

---

139. A. Russell, 'Gilling West', *VCH N. Riding*, II, 71–84.
140. See p. 270 below.
141. *DB*, fo. 309a.

Easby (Yorks)

There are no documentary references to Easby before the eleventh century, but the remains of a cross of probable eighth- or ninth-century date suggest that this late medieval mother church may have had pre-viking origins.[142] Admittedly, the existence of a church is demonstrated less conclusively by this sort of sculptural evidence than, say, sarcophagi and carved panels, since, at least in Ireland and on the Continent, it is not unknown for crosses to be found in non-ecclesiastical contexts.[143] However, since so many churches which have early crosses can be demonstrated from other evidence to be of early origin it does not seem too unreasonable a conjecture for Easby.[144]

No church is recorded at Easby in Domesday Book, but at a later date this church was clearly of superior status. Until 1152–3 Easby was served by a group of clergy called *fratres*, and when a house of Premonstratensian canons was founded at Easby the church was described as a monastery (*monasterium*).[145] From that point onwards the vicar of Easby was always one of the canons, and the care of souls at Easby was provided by a priest belonging to a community of clerks living round the parish church.[146] The parish of Easby included Aske, Brompton-on-Swale and Skeeby.[147]

Richard Morris has observed that the unusual dedication of the churches at Gilling and Easby to St Agatha is possibly connected with St Agatho, who was pope from 678 to 682, and to whom Wilfrid appealed for arbitration in a dispute. The fact that the two churches lie close to the route between Wilfrid's two monasteries at Ripon and Hexham might be a further indication of their association with Wilfrid.[148]

Northallerton (Yorks)

The church of Northallerton has yielded pre-viking stone sculpture and sculpture which displays Scandinavian-style iconography, although nothing else is known of its early history. Nonetheless, Eric Cambridge has proposed a connection with the community of St Cuthbert that warrants consideration. He has suggested that the journey from

---

142. Collingwood, 'Sculpture in the North Riding of Yorkshire', 315; Morris, *Churches in the Landscape*, 138.
143. Wood, 'Anglo-Saxon Otley', 26–30.
144. As argued in E. Cambridge, 'The early church in County Durham: a reassessment', *JBAA*, 137 (1984), 65–85.
145. *EYC*, 5, 169, 231–2.
146. G.W.O. Addleshaw, *Rectors, Vicars and Patrons in Twelfth- and Early Thirteenth-Century Canon Law* (1987), 16–17.
147. A. Russell, 'Easby', *VCH N. Riding*, II, 51–64.
148. Morris, *Churches in the Landscape*, 145, fig. 33.

Lindisfarne to York would have required more staging-posts at which the community could reside than the sole recorded one at Crayke. Pre-viking sculpture is found at a number of churches along the main route between York and Lindisfarne in a region otherwise without much sculpture of this period, and this may indicate that these churches, including Northallerton, served as staging-posts, at which religious communities were presumably also founded, as was the case at Crayke.[149]

The church had a large late medieval parish (including chapels at Brompton, Deighton, Romanby and Worsall), although it was not as substantial as the Domesday soke of Northallerton. As is a common fate for many important churches in the region, the church became a major possession of Durham Cathedral.[150]

Whitby (Yorks)

It is widely accepted that the monastery at *Streanœshalh* described in some detail by Bede was located at Whitby, an association first made in the twelfth century.[151] The house was probably founded in the 650s and arguably became the *Eigenkloster* of the Deiran royal line, where a number of the Deiran royal family were buried.[152] They include the first three abbesses – Hild, Eanfled and Ælflaed – and also Ælflaed's mother and father, Eanfled and Oswy, and her grandfather, Edwin.[153] The community at Whitby included both male and female religious under the authority of an abbess. Hild attracted ordinary people, kings and princes who sought her advice, and ruled over a religious community that trained numerous people in the religious lifestyle, including five bishops (Bosa, Ætla, Oftfor, John and Wilfrid).[154] A great synod was held at Whitby in 664 to determine the date for the observance of Easter, suggesting that the community was extremely influential in the diocese of York.[155] The involvement of the abbess in Northumbrian ecclesiastical politics outside the monastery is

---

149. E. Cambridge, 'Why did the community of St Cuthbert settle at Chester-le-Street?', in *St Cuthbert, His Cult and Community to AD 1200*, ed. G. Bonner, C. Stancliffe and D. Rollason (1989), 367–86, at 380–5; the other proposed staging-posts are Sedgefield, Chester-le-Street, Bedlington, Warkworth and Bamburgh. On Crayke, see pp. 258–61 below.
150. M. Weston, 'Northallerton', *VCH N. Riding*, II, 418–34; *DB*, fo. 299a.
151. *Sym. Op.* II, 201–2. This association is widely preferred despite the presence of the place-name Strensall near York, which has the same origin as *Streanœshalh*: Morris, 'Alcuin, York and the *alma sophia*', 87, n. 6.
152. Thacker, 'Monks, preaching and pastoral care', 143. For the foundation of the monastery, see *HE*, iii, 24.
153. *Ibid.*
154. *Ibid.*, iv, 23.
155. Thacker, 'Monks, preaching and pastoral care', 149–51.

obvious, and reveals the extent to which early religious foundations might be closely involved in affairs beyond their own precincts.[156]

The influence of the community of Whitby was extended through at least two dependent communities, one at Hackness, the other at the unidentified *Osingadun*. Both of these foundations appear to have been organized communities. Bede records that a messenger was sent from *Osingadun* 'to the greater *monasterium*' at Whitby, implying that the term '*monasterium*' was equally applicable to *Osingadun*; moreover, the description of the community as '*famuli Christi*' employs a phrase with strong monastic overtones.[157] More is known about the community at Hackness, where there was a group of nuns who had a church and a dormitory.[158]

The evidence provided by Bede and by excavation can reveal something of the layout of the community at Whitby. Bede reports that the news of the death of Hild did not reach some of the nuns of the community until the next morning, and these nuns are said to have lived '*in extremis monasterii locis*'.[159] This may suggest that the precinct of the monastery was sizeable.[160] In the eleventh century there were said to be some 40 ruined structures which were at that time interpreted as oratories; it is perhaps significant that the site was then known as *Prestebi*, 'priests' farm'.[161] In the eleventh century there were two churches at Whitby, dedicated to St Peter and St Mary respectively. St Peter's was believed to be associated with the former monastery, but it is possible that the church dedicated to St Mary also had pre-viking origins; certainly the evidence of Bede could be taken to indicate that the site of St Mary's could have been included in the precinct. Moreover, it would not be unusual for an early religious community to have had more than one church, and the existence of churches dedicated to St Peter and St Mary at an early date is documented elsewhere.[162] The excavations at Whitby were not well recorded, although there have been recent attempts to make sense of the excavation reports. The multiplicity of small rectangular structures is a feature noted at the sites of other seventh- and eighth-century religious communities. The excavations also uncovered a range of high-status personal artefacts including pins and writing styli. The range of finds is similar to those made at Monkwearmouth, Jarrow, Whithorn

156. E. Cambridge and D.W. Rollason, 'The pastoral organization of the Anglo-Saxon church: a review of the "minster hypothesis"', *EME*, 4 (1) (1995), 87–104, at 93.
157. Cambridge, 'The early church in County Durham', 74, 84; Thacker, 'Monks, preaching and pastoral care', 144, for the quotation.
158. *HE*, iv, 23; see p. 247 below.
159. *HE*, iv, 23.
160. Thacker, 'Monks, preaching and pastoral care', 144, n. 40.
161. *Chartulary of Whitby Abbey*, ed. J.C. Atkinson, Surtees Society, 69 (1878), 2.
162. For example, at Wearmouth, Lichfield and Canterbury: Blair, 'Anglo-Saxon minsters', 246–58.

and Hartlepool.[163] Pre-viking sculpture survives at Whitby, as does a stone plaque inscribed with an epitaph to Abbess Ælflæd.[164]

In the later Middle Ages Whitby had an extensive parish, and St Mary's had seven chapelries. The Domesday soke of Whitby was confined to the parish.[165]

Hackness (Yorks)

Bede informs us that there was a community of nuns at Hackness, who had a church and a dormitory, as we have seen. Two fragments from an eighth-century cross-shaft survive, and they carry Latin inscriptions and inscriptions in a form of Old Irish Ogham and in Old English runes. The Latin and Runic inscriptions all refer to Abbess Oedilburga, who is almost certainly the Abbess Æthelburh referred to in the *Life of St Wilfrid* as a witness to the death of King Aldfrith in 705.[166] Part of an early grave-cover survives, and the church of St Peter also contains some eighth-century fabric, in the form of the north impost of the chancel arch, decorated with a pair of interlaced beasts.[167]

In the later eleventh century there were three churches at Hackness, two of which are known at that time to have been dedicated to St Peter and St Mary. It is possible that this arrangement was of much earlier origin, and it echoes the arrangement at Whitby.[168] The parish of Hackness included Suffield and Everley, which were Domesday berewicks of the manor of Hackness.[169] It is notable that the parishes of Whitby and its daughter cell at Hackness are contiguous, and it is open to question whether the other known daughter cell of Whitby, at *Osingadun*, was also located adjacent to, if not within, the later medieval parish of Whitby. There are certainly a number of churches of pre-viking origin in the general vicinity, and the mother church of Pickering is also nearby, which although it lacks

---

163. *Ibid.*, 261–2; R. Cramp, 'Monastic sites', in *The Archaeology of Anglo-Saxon England*, ed. D.M. Wilson (1976), 223–41; P. Rahtz, 'Anglo-Saxon and later Whitby', in *Yorkshire Monasticism: archaeology, art and architecture from the 7th to 16th centuries AD*, ed. L.R. Hoey, British Archaeological Association Conference Transactions, 15 (1995), 1–11; R. Cramp, 'A reconsideration of the monastic site of Whitby', in *The Age of Migrating Ideas*, ed. R.M. Spearman and J. Higgitt (1993), 64–73; R. Daniels, 'The Anglo-Saxon monastery at Church Close, Hartlepool, Cleveland', *Arch. J.*, 145 (1988), 158–210.
164. Rahtz, 'Whitby', 2, 7–8.
165. A. Russell, 'Whitby', *VCH N. Riding*, II, 506–28; *DB*, fo. 305a.
166. R. Sermon, 'The Hackness cross cryptic inscriptions', *YAJ*, 68 (1996), 101–11, at 101; *VSW, c.* 60.
167. Lang, *York and Eastern Yorkshire*, 135–42; Taylor and Taylor, *Anglo-Saxon Architecture*, 1, 268–70; Cambridge, 'The early church in County Durham', 74–5.
168. *Chartulary of Whitby Abbey*, ed. Atkinson, 2–3, 31–3, 155–7, 163, 223–4; F. Rimmington, 'The three churches of Hackness', *Transactions of the Scarborough Archaeological and Historical Society*, 26 (1988), 3–4.
169. A. Russell, 'Hackness', *VCH N. Riding*, II, 528–32; *DB*, fo. 323a.

clear evidence of pre-viking origins may have been of such a date. It is clear that the area of jurisdiction of Whitby once extended beyond the limits of its own later medieval parish to include the parishes of at least two other communities in the vicinity.

Dewsbury (Yorks)

The presence of an early church at Dewsbury is suggested by the survival of fragments of crosses which are stylistically of ninth-century date. A cross-shaft displays scenes of the miracle of the loaves and the fishes, the miracle of Cana, and the Madonna and child. A cross-head depicts an angel with a cleric kneeling before it, and it carries an inscription that indicates that the cross was erected in memory of an individual whose name is now lost.[170] In the loaves and fishes panel there is a crowd of people, and this may be an indication of the evangelical context of this sculpture, alongside the angel.[171] Another piece of sculpture is a fragment of further cross-shaft, which Collingwood suggested contains part of a crucifixion scene.[172] Sections of Anglo-Saxon fabric survive above the arcading in the nave.[173] There is also sculpture, possibly of the tenth century, at Dewsbury.[174]

The late medieval church of All Saints, Dewsbury, appears to have once had an extremely large parish. A number of parishes and their constituent townships are recorded as paying annual pensions to the church in the medieval period, and the chapelry of Mirfield was also part of Dewsbury parish (Fig. 46).[175] The parish of Dewsbury corresponds more or less exactly to the Domesday and medieval manor of Wakefield.[176] Yet although the estate centre and its associated church were located in separate places, the correlation between the estate and the parish was close; how ancient this arrangement was is, however, unknown.

Lincoln

It is well known that there was early ecclesiastical provision in Lincoln, that there were a number of tenth-century churches and that in 1072 a

---

170. '... *rhtae becun aefter beornae. gibiddadd der saule*', '[Someone set this in memory of] –berht, a monument to his lord. Pray for his soul': Collingwood, *Northumbrian Crosses*, 6–7, 59, 72–3.
171. There are parallels at Collingham, Halton and Leeds: Wood, 'Anglo-Saxon Otley', 35.
172. Collingwood, *Northumbrian Crosses*, 99–101.
173. Ryder, *Medieval Churches of West Yorkshire*, 18–19.
174. Collingwood, 'Sculpture in the West Riding of Yorkshire', 169–71.
175. Faull and Moorhouse, *West Yorkshire: an archaeological survey*, 217–18; see also S.J. Chadwick, 'Notes on Dewsbury church and some of its rectors and vicars', *YAJ*, 20 (1909), 369–446.
176. Faull and Moorhouse, *West Yorkshire: an archaeological survey*, 218; *DB*, fo. 299d. The soke of Wakefield is mapped above: Figure 12, p. 110.

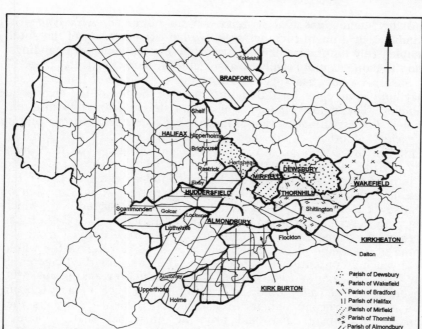

Figure 46 The parish of Dewsbury. The places named in this illustration all either possessed chapels of All Saints, Dewsbury, or paid tithe or pensions to All Saints

see was established by Bishop Remigius. However, the pre-viking ecclesiastical provision in Lincoln is difficult to unravel. In particular, there has been much debate whether the bishops of Lindsey, of whom the first was consecrated in 678, had their see and episcopal church in Lincoln.[177] Usually the bishops are referred to as bishops of the people of Lindsey, but Bishop Eadwulf (796–836 × 9) is referred to in a Canterbury document of 803 as *syddensis ciuitatis episcopus*.[178] This has excited much interest, and *syddensis ciuitas* has been interpreted as a latinized version of a lost Old English name, *Sidnace[a]ster*. A number of places in Lincolnshire have been proposed, with varying degrees of plausibility, as the site of *syddensis ciuitas/Sidnace[a]ster*, including Caistor, Horncastle, Stow in Lindsey, Louth and Lincoln. However, the etymology of the word *syddensis* is difficult to determine,

---

177. *HE*, iv, 12; for discussion of the fate of the bishopric, which was transferred to Dorchester for a time in the tenth century, and again from *c.* 1011: D.P. Kirby, 'The Saxon bishops of Leicester, Lindsey (*Syddensis*), and Dorchester', *Leicestershire Archaeological and History Society Transactions*, 41 (1965–6), 1–8.
178. B 312.

and the suggestions that it derived from either *lindensis/lyndensis*, 'Lindsey', or a name such as **sýðnaceaster*, 'Roman town of the south people', rely too implausibly on scribal errors and misunderstandings, and the name cannot readily be associated with any particular place.[179]

Steven Bassett has suggested that the etymology of Lindsey itself may hold some clues for the identification of the see of the bishops of Lindsey. The name Lindsey appears to derive from two different names: *Lindissi/Lindesse* (found in Bede's *Ecclesiastical History* and in a variety of other eighth- and ninth-century sources) and *Lindesig* (found in the D version of the Anglo-Saxon Chronicle and in Asser's *Life of King Alfred*). The latter name means 'island of the **Lindes*', and it is from this that the eventual form of Lindsey came.[180] It is often assumed that the name Lindsey referred to the whole kingdom of Lindsey, but if so, this would be unusual for a place-name in *eg*, which normally describes an island of some sort. Alternatively, as Bassett has argued, the name Lindsey might conceivably have derived from the name of a specific place, which was later used to refer to the whole area. Such a contention is supported by the entry for the kingdom in the Tribal Hidage as *Lindesfarona* (*landes*) which means 'people who resort to a place called *Lindesse/Lindesig*'.[181] For such a place, Lincoln has much to recommend it. Archaeological evidence suggests that Lincoln, a Roman town and probable episcopal seat, remained important in the post-Roman period. The church of St Paul-in-the-Bail contained a prominent burial of the pre-viking period, and its cemetery may be of fifth-century origin. It is also notable that the first convert of Paulinus in Lindsey was Blæcca, *praefectum ... Lindocolinae ciuitatis*. This suggests that success in Lincoln was regarded by Bede as being important in the history of the mission and the subsequent conversion of the whole of Lindsey, which serves to emphasize the regional importance of Lincoln.[182]

Bede tells us that Paulinus built a stone church 'of remarkable workmanship' in Lincoln in the early seventh century, and that it was ruinous by 731. It is not known where this church was located or when it fell into disrepair, nor is it known whether it was used by the bishops of Lindsey.[183] An inscription of early eighth-century date reveals that a church was dedicated to one of the apostles by the bishop as the mother seat (*almam ... sedem*) for himself and his successor bishops in an unnamed city (*urbs*). It is not, however, clear that this was

---

179. For discussion and references, see S.R. Bassett, 'Lincoln and the Anglo-Saxon see of Lindsey', *ASE*, 18 (1990), 1–32 at 4–5.
180. *Ibid.*, 6, and the note by Margaret Gelling at 31–2.
181. *Ibid.*, 8, 32. The debate over whether Lindsey was a kingdom is reviewed in S. Foot, 'The kingdom of Lindsey', in *Pre-Viking Lindsey*, ed. A. Vince (1993) 128–40.
182. *HE*, ii, 16; Bassett, 'Lincoln', 11.
183. *HE*, ii, 16; R. Gem, 'The episcopal churches of Lindsey in the early ninth century', in *Pre-Viking Lindsey*, ed. Vince, 123–7, at 125.

Lincoln.[184] The profession of canonical obedience made by Bishop Beorhtred to Archbishop Ceolnoth at the time of his consecration (836 × 9) indicates that the bishops of Lindsey then had two churches, but again it is not certain that they were in Lincoln, or indeed that they were in the same place.[185] None of the churches in Lincoln has produced archaeological evidence for pre-viking origins, and Bassett's suggestion that an episcopal church was in the southern promontory known as Wigford, an admittedly suitable location for the '*eg* of the people of **Lindes*', is not borne out by the extensive excavations in Wigford.[186] Domesday Book reveals that there was a church of St Mary in Lincoln in 1066, which may have housed the bishop's see while the new cathedral was being built, but it is not known when this church was founded or which, if any, surviving church it may have been.[187] The so-called St Martin pennies, minted in Lincoln in the early tenth century, suggest that the principal church in Lincoln was then dedicated to St Martin, in the same way that contemporary coins minted in York bear a dedication to St Peter, the dedication of the episcopal church.[188]

Although the ecclesiastical history of Lincoln is complex between the early seventh century and the later eleventh century, it is clear that there was continuing ecclesiastical activity in Lincoln through the tenth century. This is further supported by the examples of tenth-century sculpture that have been found in churches in Lincoln, most notably the collection found at St Mark's.[189] By *c.* 1100, and possibly at the time of Domesday Book, there were 35 parish churches in Lincoln, many of which seem to have had graveyards, and hence burial rites, from their inception. This is a striking testimony to the great differences in ecclesiastical organization in towns of the Danelaw when compared with other parts of England, where the dominance of mother churches over lesser foundations was much greater, often including a monopoly over burial.[190]

---

184. L. Wallach, 'The Urbana Anglo-Saxon Sylloge of Latin inscriptions' in *Poetry and Poetics from Ancient Greece to the Renaissance*, ed. G.M. Kirkwood (Ithaca, N.Y., 1975), 134–51, at 144; Stocker, 'The early church in Lincolnshire', 118–19; Gem, 'The episcopal churches of Lindsey', 125.

185. M. Richter, 'Canterbury professions', *Canterbury and York Society*, 67 (1973), 17; Gem, 'The episcopal churches of Lindsey', 123.

186. Bassett, 'Lincoln', 19.

187. *Ibid.*, 20–9.

188. I. Stewart, 'The St Martin coins of Lincoln', *British Numismatic Journal*, 36 (1967), 46–54; Bassett, 'Lincoln', 24–5.

189. B.J.J. Gilmour and D. Stocker, *St Mark's Church and Cemetery*, The Archaeology of Lincoln, 13 (1) (1986), 44–57.

190. Stafford, *The East Midlands*, 186; J. Barrow, 'Urban cemetery location in the high Middle Ages', in *Death in Towns*, ed. S.R. Bassett (1992), 78–100.

Crowland (Lincs)

Much is known about the early history of Crowland, owing to the survival of the near-contemporary *Life of St Guthlac* written by the monk Felix. Guthlac (*c.* 674–715) was a nobleman of Mercian royal stock who abandoned the aristocratic lifestyle in 698 to enter the religious life. After his period at Repton he set off to live as a hermit, and at the fen edge was taken by a local man, called Tatwine, to the island of Crowland. Here he built a hermitage, and when he died in 715 was buried there. His hermitage had attracted other hermits before his death, and the site of his relics became a focus for pilgrimage. In 716 a monastery was established by King Æthelbald of Mercia, the forged 'foundation charter' of which was probably written in the eleventh or twelfth century. The *Life* of Guthlac records that Æthelbald enriched Guthlac's shrine with 'wonderful structures and ornamentations'.[191]

Recent work by David Stocker has sought to trace the development of the site from the hermitage of St Guthlac to the monastery of Æthelbald. As he observes, Felix's account indicates that the monastery was considered to be coextensive with the whole island; Bishop Hedda consecrates the whole island, not just the church.[192] The later forged foundation charter also states that the whole island was to be set apart for the abbey, which suggests that in the eleventh or twelfth century the monastery still constituted the whole island.[193] Guthlac's cell was one of at least five cells in the early religious community, and some of them may have become foci within the eighth-century monastery. Stocker has suggested that the later medieval abbey at Crowland and its outlying chapels might resemble some of the early medieval cells of the monastery.[194] Whether this is the case or not, the early medieval island at Crowland incorporated a number of scattered religious foci, a feature of other early medieval religious communities.[195]

Unlike in the cases of other fenland monasteries such as Ely, Peterborough, Ramsey and Thorney, few reliable sources survive for the monastic revival at Crowland in the third quarter of the tenth century. A number of eleventh-century charters survive which record additional grants to Crowland, but according to Domesday Book it possessed a modest estate of five manors and their dependencies.[196]

---

191. *Life of St Guthlac*, c. li; S 82 (B 135). A number of forged charters of the twelfth century purport to be eighth- and ninth-century grants to Crowland: S 135 (B 268); S 162 (B 325); S 189 (B 409); S 200 (B 461); S 213 (B 521); S 1189 (B 331); S 1190 (B 365); S 1191 (B 383); S 1192 (not printed).
192. *Life of St Guthlac*, c. xlvii; Stocker, 'The early church in Lincolnshire', 104.
193. A.S. Canham, 'Notes on the history of Crowland: its charters and ancient crosses', *JBAA*, 46 (1890), 116–29.
194. Stocker, 'The early church in Lincolnshire', 104–5.
195. Blair, 'Anglo-Saxon minsters', 246–64.
196. R. Graham, 'The Abbey of Crowland', *VCH Lincs*, 105–18, at 105; S 1049 (K 794); S 1230 (K 795); S 538 (B 872); S 741 (B 1178); S 1294 (B 1179); *DB*, fo. 346d.

The history of the abbey is much more fully recorded from the mid-eleventh century, when it seems to have been subject to Peterborough Abbey.[197] The later medieval parish of Crowland was not extensive, but the church has been included in the category of major later medieval churches because there is just sufficient evidence to indicate that the later medieval abbey grew up out of the earlier community; there was certainly no tradition that it had been destroyed when Orderic Vitalis wrote his history of the abbey in the early twelfth century.[198] Other pre-viking churches in Lincolnshire are perpetuated by later medieval monastic houses, but they were all post-Conquest foundations, whose relationship to an earlier community is not at all clear. At Crowland the parish church was subsumed within the abbey, which is a further indication that it was the direct successor to the earlier community.

Caistor (Lincs)

In 1770 a fragment from a stone panel was found at Caistor which bore an inscription recording the dedication of an altar. This panel is now lost, but on the basis of the record made in the eighteenth century it has been suggested that it may date from the eighth century.[199] The fabric of the church indicates that this was a major late Anglo-Saxon church. It appears to preserve the remains of a large building with lateral porticus, of a type identified as typical of churches of senior status in the later pre-Conquest period. The west tower also contains considerable amounts of Anglo-Saxon fabric.[200] Although the manor of Caistor was held by the king in 1086, it was noted that the church had been granted by King William to the bishop of Lincoln, a fate shared by many of the major churches of the northern Danelaw. An additional sign of its superior status is the record that the church of Caistor possessed half a carucate of land in Grasby, two bovates in Caistor and soke of one carucate in Hundon.[201] In the later Middle Ages Caistor had a relatively large parish with chapels at Clixby and Holton le Moor, although the parish was much smaller than the soke of the manor of Caistor.[202] The church stands within a Roman walled town, a location which is characteristic of many major early churches.[203]

---

197. The sources for the later history of the abbey are discussed in Graham, 'The Abbey of Crowland', 105–18.
198. *The Ecclesiastical History of Orderic Vitalis*, ed. M. Chibnall (6 vols, 1968–80), I, 46; II, xxvi–xxvii, 338–50.
199. C.A.R. Radford, 'A lost inscription of pre-Danish age from Caistor', *Arch. J.*, 103 (1946), 95–9; Stocker, 'The early church in Lincolnshire', 117.
200. Blair, 'Secular minster churches', 121; Taylor and Taylor, *Anglo-Saxon Architecture*, I, 127–8.
201. *DB*, fos. 338c–d, 375d.
202. D.M. Owen, 'Medieval chapels in Lincolnshire', *LHA*, 10 (1975), 15–22, at 17; *DB*, fos. 338c–d.
203. B. Whitwell, *Roman Lincolnshire* (1970; revised edn, 1992), 69–72; Blair, 'Anglo-Saxon minsters', 235–46.

Other mother churches with pre-Viking origins

We have now exhausted the most substantive evidence concerning the pre-viking origins of late medieval mother churches in the northern Danelaw. However, many more have surviving pre-viking sculpture or later written traditions of varying reliability which suggest pre-viking origins. These may be described briefly.

Bede implies that Catterick (Yorks) was a place of some importance when he states that *c.* 627 Paulinus baptized many in the river Swale, which flows near to Catterick, and when he later indicates that a village was 'near to Catterick'; it is unlikely that he would have identified the river and the village in relation to anywhere other than a major and well-known place.[204] This implication is confirmed by the *Historia Regum* attributed to Simeon of Durham, which records that King Æthelwold and Queen Æthelthryth were married at Catterick in 762, and that King Æthelred and Queen Ælflaed, daughter of Offa, were married there in 792.[205] This suggests that Catterick was a royal vill. The presence of a contemporary church is suggested by the presence there of possible pre-viking sculpture.[206] The later medieval parish of Catterick was substantial and it was significantly larger than the Domesday estate of Catterick (Fig. 45).[207]

The fabric of the church of St Peter's, Conisbrough (Yorks), is certainly of Anglo-Saxon date, and it has been suggested that it may have pre-viking origins, on account of the similarity of its plan to those of Northumbrian churches of eighth-century date.[208] A fragment of a tenth-century cross-shaft has been found at Conisbrough, but nothing more is known of the church before the eleventh century, when, according to Domesday Book, it was served by a single priest.[209] In the later Middle Ages the church of Conisbrough served a large and scattered parish and drew tithe from numerous other parishes in the vicinity (Fig. 47). The large parish corresponds closely with the soke of Conisbrough, but it is difficult to say whether the soke or the parish had ever included the places in between Conisbrough and their more far-flung members.[210] These include Laughton-en-le-Morthen, itself the centre of a big parish and the location of pre-Conquest sculpture, and Doncaster, which was sufficiently important to be listed in the *Historia Regum* as a place devastated by fire in 764 alongside *Hamwic* (Southampton), London and York. Given the status of the other places listed there, it has been surmised that Doncaster might have been a similarly proto-urban

---

204. *HE*, ii, 15; ii, 20.
205. *EHD*, I, no. 3.
206. Collingwood, 'Sculpture in the North Riding of Yorkshire', 305.
207. M. Curtis, 'Catterick', *VCH N. Riding*, II, 301–13; *DB*, fo. 310c.
208. P. Ryder, *Saxon Churches in South Yorkshire*, South Yorkshire County Archaeology Monograph, 2 (1981), 45–56, 123.
209. *Ibid.*, 109; *DB*, fo. 321b.
210. G.T. Davies, 'The origins of the parishes of south Yorkshire', *South Yorkshire Historian*, 4 (1980), 1–18 at 6-8; see Chapter 3, p. 140.

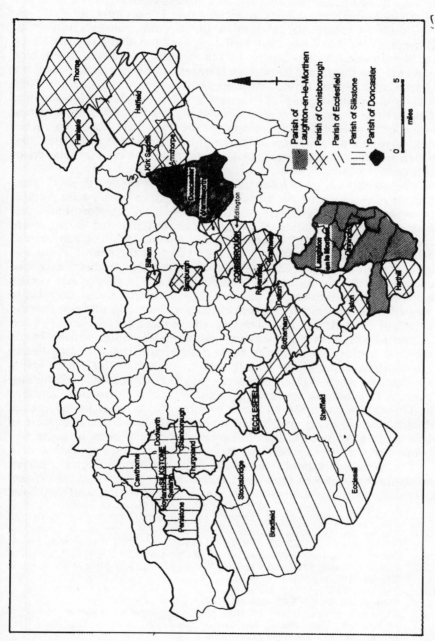

Figure 47 Parishes in south-western Yorkshire

Parish of Laughton-en-le-Morthen
Parish of Conisborough
Parish of Ecclesfield
Parish of Silkstone
Parish of Doncaster

0   5
miles

Thorpe
Hatfield
Fishlake
Kirk Sandall
Armthorpe
Edlington
Conisborough Cast.
Loversall-en-le-Morthen
Braithwell
Rossington
Doncaster
Dinnington
Barnburgh
Bilham
Rotherham Conisborough
Dalton
Rotherham
Aston
Harthill
ECCLESFIELD
Sheffield
Bradfield
Stockbridge
Penistone
Cawthorne
SILKSTONE
Dodworth
Silkstone
Royston
Swaith
Hoyland
Stainborough
Thurgoland
Ecclesall

place, and the possibility that it was a *burh* is raised by the excavation of a double ditch resembling those of other known *burhs*.[211]

Giraldus Cambrensis, writing in the twelfth century, states that Howden (Yorks) had been the burial place of the sister of King Osred of Northumbria in the early eighth century.[212] In the tenth and eleventh centuries the estate at Howden, and presumably also the church, was held by various royal and ecclesiastical lords, and in 1086 was held by the bishop of Durham.[213] The parish of Howden was relatively sizeable and included many of the dependencies of the estate recorded in the mid-tenth century and in Domesday Book. The other dependencies were mostly in the neighbouring parish of Eastrington, which as the 'eastern *tun*' clearly acquired its name in relation to Howden.[214]

The twelfth-century *Liber Eliensis* records the journey through Lincolnshire taken by St Ætheldreda, a member of the East Anglian royal family who was married to King Ecgfrith of the Northumbrians. She crossed the Humber at Wintringham and founded a monastery somewhere in the vicinity, *c.* 670. This has been located by a number of scholars at West Halton on the fragile basis that the church there was dedicated to St Etheldreda.[215] There were two late medieval manorial chapels in the parish of West Halton, and while this is not secure evidence for mother-church status it is striking that these chapels are located some distance from West Halton, which might indicate that the parish of West Halton had once once been more extensive.[216]

The *Life* of the seventh-century abbess St Werburg, written in the eleventh century by Gocelin of Canterbury, states that the saint died in a religious community at Threekingham (Lincs), *c.* 700. There was a substantial Anglo-Saxon cemetery at Threekingham, which may suggest a significant ecclesiastical site.[217] There were two churches at Threekingham in the eleventh century, the present parish church dedicated to St Peter, and St Mary, which possessed half a carucate of land. It is possible that these churches may have been in some way connected with the earlier foundation.[218]

The name Ecclesfield ('open country of the British church, *ecles') suggests that this was the site of a British church. Ecclesfield (Yorks) served a substantial parish in the later medieval period, and may be of

211. Collingwood, 'Sculpture in the West Riding of Yorkshire', 209; Morris, *Churches in the Landscape*, 137, 258–9; *Sym. Op.*, II, 42 (trans. *EHD* I, no. 3); M.S. Parker, 'Some notes on the pre-Norman history of Doncaster', *YAJ*, 59 (1987), 29–43.
212. *Gerald of Wales, The Journey through Wales and The Description of Wales*, ed. L. Thorpe (1978), 84–5.
213. See Chapter 3, pp. 119, 152–3.
214. *Tithe Maps*, 83; *PN ERY*, 245–56.
215. *Liber Eliensis*, ed. Blake, 30; D.R. Roffe, 'The seventh-century monastery of Stow Green, Lincolnshire', *LHA*, 21 (1986), 31–3.
216. Owen, 'Medieval chapels in Lincolnshire', 18.
217. Roffe, 'Stow Green', 32.
218. Rollason, *The Mildrith Legend*, 26; Roffe, 'Stow Green', 31; *DB*, fos. 341d, 357b, 356a, 370b.

early origin, although the earliest indication of a church there comes from sculpture of the tenth or eleventh century.[219]

A number of the mother churches of the later Middle Ages in Yorkshire have pre-viking sculpture suggesting early origins. Aldborough possesses four fragments of an eighth- or ninth-century cross-shaft, and like a number of other important early churches was built within a Roman town, seemingly directly upon the remains of a Roman building.[220] In the eleventh century the church was located on a major royal manor and it had an extensive late medieval parish.[221] Leeds was clearly an important place in the seventh century, and Bede refers to events taking place in the *regio* of 'Loidis', including the building of a church by the successors of the murdered King Edwin.[222] It is not clear whether this was actually at Leeds, but pre-viking sculpture survives there. Another cross-shaft, which depicts the legend of Weland the Smith and Sigurd, carries Scandinavian-style braiding, and indicates that sculpture was also produced for this site in the tenth century (Fig. 48).[223] In the later Middle Ages Leeds served a substantial parish.[224] The remains of a cross suggest that there was a pre-viking church at Masham, which, like Leeds, served a substantial parish in the later Middle Ages.[225] Hunmanby has pre-viking sculpture and it was a later medieval mother church with five chapels.[226] Excavation at Wharram Percy has produced sculpture of the eighth century and also moulds for casting decorated metalwork which might conceivably have had an ecclesiastical context. In the later Middle Ages the church at Wharram served a substantial parish.[227]

Other pre-viking churches

In addition to those churches with pre-viking origins that were mother churches at a much later date, there are many other churches with

---

219. M. Gelling, *Signposts to the Past* (1978), 96–7; Davies, 'The origins of the parishes of south Yorkshire', 9–10; Ryder, *Saxon Churches in South Yorkshire*, 110–11; P. Sidebottom, 'The Ecclesfield cross and "Celtic" survival', *Transactions of the Hunter Archaeological Society*, 19 (1997), 43–55.
220. Collingwood, 'Sculpture in the West Riding of Yorkshire', 133–5; Rodwell, *Church Archaeology*, 122. A sundial suggests rebuilding in the eleventh century, when 'Ulf ordered the church to be put up for himself and for Gunwaru's soul',
221. *DB*, fos. 299d–300a, 301c, 326d, 328c, 329c, 330b; *PN NRY*, 296–7.
222. *HE*, ii, 14; iii, 24.
223. Collingwood, 'Sculpture in the West Riding of Yorkshire', 209–19; A. McGuire and A. Clark, *The Leeds Crosses* (1987); J.T. Lang, 'Sigurd and Welland in pre-Conquest carving from northern England', *YAJ*, 48 (1976), 83–94; the legend could have been depicted prior to the tenth century but here it is argued that the surviving examples from Yorkshire were carved in the tenth century.
224. *The Registers of the Parish of Leeds*, ed. W. Brigg, YPRS, 33 (1908), vi.
225. Collingwood, *Northumbrian Crosses*, 6–7, 43, 72; Bailey, *Viking Age Sculpture*, 265; *PN NRY*, 230–5.
226. Lang, *York and Eastern Yorkshire*, 148–9; *EYC*, 2, 266, 428.
227. M. Beresford and J.G. Hurst, *Wharram Percy Deserted Medieval Village* (1990), 26, 82–4.

Figure 48 Sculpture at Leeds (shown at a scale of 1:20) (after P. Ryder, *Medieval Churches of West Yorkshire* (1993), based on a reconstruction by Peter Brears of the Leeds cross-shaft held at Leeds City Museum)

evidence for early origins which at a later date are little more than ordinary parish churches. As was the case with the churches already discussed, many of the following churches have tenth-century sculpture, which indicates that they were in use during the early to mid-tenth century. Unless otherwise stated, these churches have little evidence for superior status in Domesday Book or later.

Crayke (Yorks)

The *Historia de Sancto Cuthberto* alleges that in the late seventh century Crayke was granted to Cuthbert in the presence of King Ecgfrith and Archbishop Theodore, who gave to him the vill [*mansio*] which was called Crayke, and three miles around that vill, so that he might have a dwelling-place, however many times he might go to York, or return from there. And there the Holy Cuthbert established a community of monks and ordained an abbot.[228]

There has been some speculation that Crayke was the site of the religious community described in the early ninth-century poem *De Abbatibus*, which describes a community founded in the reign of Osred (704/5–16) and which was a cell of the community of St Cuthbert.[229] However, it is probably better not to replace the reasonably reliable evidence of the *Historia de Sancto Cuthberto* with such speculation;[230] and although the topographical description of *De Abbatibus* fits Crayke, in reality the site might be any place near a small hill in the north of England.[231]

Excavations at Crayke have added to our understanding of the site in the pre-viking period (Fig. 49). Two fragments of a stone cross of the ninth century have been discovered.[232] The possibility that there was once a church on a different site from the parish church has been raised following the excavation of a number of Anglo-Saxon male and female burials at Castle Garth. The burials are in alignment not with the parish church but with the south-east slope of the hill in the vicinity of Crayke Hall, and it has been suggested that they may be following the alignment of a focal point in that area, some 66 yards away, which may have included a church.[233]

The *Historia Regum* attributed to Simeon of Durham states that in 767 Etha the Anchorite died at Crayke.[234] The *Historia de Sancto Cuthberto* claims that King Ælle seized Crayke in 867 because of his hatred of the community of St Cuthbert, and proceeded to live there.[235] However, the community of St Cuthbert soon regained the church, as can be seen from the fact that they visited Crayke in 882 or 883, during their seven years of wandering with the body of their patron. They were looked after by Abbot Geve, and since Geve is a female name this

---

228. *HSC*, 199; the translation is provided in K.A. Adams, 'Monastery and village at Crayke, North Yorkshire', *YAJ*, 62 (1990), 29–50, at 32. A charter which purports to record this grant is 'an obvious forgery' probably produced in the late eleventh century: S 66 (B 66); *EYC*, 2, 256. For discussion of the reliability of the *Historia*, see E. Craster, 'The patrimony of St Cuthbert', *EHR*, 69 (1954), 177–99; A.T. Thacker, 'Lindisfarne and the origins of the cult of St Cuthbert', in *St Cuthbert* ed. Bonner, Stancliffe and Rollason, 103–22, at 115–16.
229. The debate is described in Adams, 'Monastery and village at Crayke', 32–3; for the text, see *Æthelwulf de Abbatibus*, ed. and trans. A. Campbell (1967).
230. Adams, 'Monastery and village at Crayke', 32–3.
231. *Æthelwulf de Abbatibus*, ed. Campbell, xvi.
232. T. Sheppard, 'Viking and other relics at Crayke, Yorkshire', *YAJ*, 34 (1939), 273–81 at 278–9.
233. Adams, 'Monastery and village at Crayke', 39–44.
234. *Sym. Op.*, II, 43.
235. *HSC*, 202.

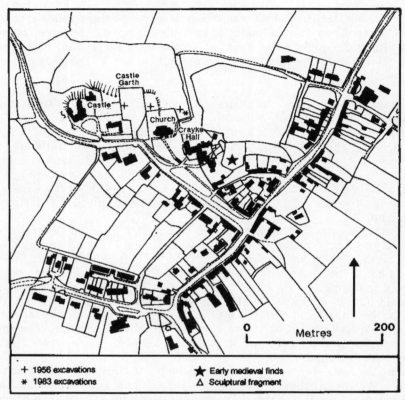

Figure 49 Excavations at Crayke (after K.A. Adams, 'Monastery and village at Crayke, North Yorkshire', *YAJ*, 62 (1990), 29–50)

has prompted speculation that Crayke housed a community of male and female religious at that date.[236] The final pre-Conquest reference to Crayke concerns a grant made by Earl Thured of two hides of land at Crayke to the community of St Cuthbert in the late tenth century.[237] It has been suggested that this grant might have been an addition to the earlier grant of three hides, given that the Domesday assessment for Crayke is six hides, and the boundary of Crayke parish includes an anomalous piece of land on the opposite bank of the river Foss.[238]

Nothing more is known of the fate of the religious community at Crayke. Given the reasons for the foundation of the community at Crayke, according to the *Historia de Sancto Cuthberto*, it is not implausible that it was never intended to do anything more than

---

236.   *Ibid.*; *EHD*, I, no. 6.
237.   S 1660 (B 1255); A.J. Robertson, *Anglo-Saxon Charters* (2nd edn, 1956), 124–5.
238.   J. Kaner, 'Crayke and its boundaries' in *Yorkshire Boundaries*, ed. H.E.J. Le Patourel, M.H. Long and M.F. Pickles (1993), 103–11.

provide Cuthbert with somewhere to stay on his way to and from York, and pastoral care for the wider district was never its concern.

Stonegrave, Coxwold and Donaemuthe (Yorks)

In a letter written by Pope Paul I in 757 or 758 to Eadberht, king of Northumbria, it is stated that an abbot called Forthred had complained to the pope that three monasteries which had been granted to him by an abbess had been taken away from him by the king. These monasteries, which may have included female religious given the association with an abbess, are named as Stonegrave, Coxwold and *Donaemuthe*.[239] The last has not been securely located. *Donaemuthe* cannot be the place at 'Donmouth' which Simeon of Durham suggests is Jarrow, because, as Dorothy Whitelock has observed, Jarrow was neither under secular control in the eighth century nor did it have an abbess.[240] *Donaemuthe* has consequently been sought in the vicinity of the Yorkshire river Don, and Adlingfleet, which sits at the mouth of that river, has recently been identified as a possible location.[241]

Stonegrave has surviving pre-viking sculpture and also tenth-century sculpture which reveals continuity of style with the earlier sculpture, in sharp contrast to the sculpture produced elsewhere in the vicinity, which may reflect some level of ecclesiastical continuity.[242]

Ledsham (Yorks)

Elements of the fabric of the church at Ledsham have been dated to the seventh and eighth centuries. The nave walls, west porch and south *porticus* of a building of that date survive in the present fabric of the church, although in the late Anglo-Saxon or early Norman period the west porch was converted into a tower, and in the later Middle Ages the south *porticus* was reduced in height and converted into a south porch.[243] Architectural detail on the imposts of the chancel arch reveals an influence that may be dated to the seventh or early eighth century.[244] Its plan, with an unaisled nave and flanking porticus, is of a type regarded as having been of eighth- or ninth-century date.[245]

---

239. *EHD*, I, no. 184.
240. *Ibid.*, no. 3.
241. W. Richardson, 'The Venerable Bede and a lost Saxon monastery in Yorkshire', *YAJ*, 57 (1985), 15-22.
242. M. Firby and J.T. Lang, 'The pre-Conquest sculpture at Stonegrave', *YAJ*, 53 (1981), 17-29; Lang, *York and Eastern Yorkshire*, 215-20.
243. R.N. Bailey, 'Ledsham', *Bulletin of the CBA Churches Committee*, 18 (1983), 6-8; M.L. Faull, 'The decoration of the south doorway of Ledsham church tower', *JBAA*, 139 (1986), 143-7; L.A.S. Butler, 'Ledsham church: the south doorway of the tower', *JBAA*, 140 (1987), 199-203; Ryder, *Medieval Churches of West Yorkshire*, 15-16.
244. Gem, 'Architecture of the Anglo-Saxon church, 735 to 870', 48-9.
245. *Ibid.*, 46, 49.

Lastingham (Yorks)

According to Bede, a religious community was founded at Lastingham by Cedd, who became bishop of the East Saxons, at the request of King Æthelwald, who wanted to have a monastery at which he could go to pray and at which he might be buried.[246] Cedd died in 664 and was buried at first outside, but was later reburied inside a stone church dedicated to Mary, to the right of the altar. It is not clear whether the stone church itself was built after 664, as opposed to Cedd's reburial taking place after this date.[247] Bede cites the monks of Lastingham as his major source of information about Cedd and his brother Chad.[248] The corpus of stone sculpture at Lastingham dates from the eighth, ninth and tenth centuries, and some of the earlier fragments include part of what may be a liturgical chair and sections of two door jambs.[249] At a later date Lastingham served as an ordinary parish church; the large size of its parish is accounted for by the fact that it stretched up on to the North York Moors (Fig. 9).

Thornhill (Yorks)

Fragments of a grave slab have been found at Thornhill, on which an inscription including the name 'Osberht' is to be found.[250] The remnants of a cross-shaft bear a runic inscription which Collingwood interpreted as revealing that it was a grave monument put up to one Berhtsuith, although runic inscriptions are notoriously problematic. This sculptural evidence indicates the presence not only of a church in the pre-viking period, but of one at which burials took place. At a later date the parish church of Thornhill paid annual pensions to the church at Dewsbury, which suggests that it was in some way subordinate to it.[251]

Kirkdale (Yorks)

Two grave slabs from Kirkdale reveal the probable existence of an early church at which burial took place (Fig. 50). Recent excavations at Kirkdale have uncovered a series of graves in the field to the north of the churchyard, an area that was cultivated subsequently, and which has produced *c.* 500 sherds of eleventh- and twelfth-century pottery.

---

246. *HE*, iii, 23.
247. *Ibid.*; R. Gem and M. Thurlby, 'The early monastic church of Lastingham' in *Yorkshire Monasticism*, ed. Hoey, 31–9, at 31.
248. *HE*, preface.
249. Lang, *York and Eastern Yorkshire*, 167–74.
250. Attempts to associate this common name with King Osberht, killed at the hands of a viking army in 867, carry little conviction; Collingwood, *Northumbrian Crosses*, 17, 61.
251. See p. 248 above.

Figure 50 Kirkdale grave slab (shown at a scale of 1:12) (after J.T. Lang, *Corpus of Anglo-Saxon Stone Sculpture*, Volume III: *York and Eastern Yorkshire* (1991))

Also discovered was a fragment of a lead sheet with an inscription of eighth- or ninth-century date, and a tiny glass rod believed to have been made to decorate elaborate glass vessels or jewellery, and of a type found before in England only at Barking Abbey (Essex). A boundary identified by geophysical surveying in this field has been interpreted as a possible *vallum monasterii*. More certain is the fact that the present

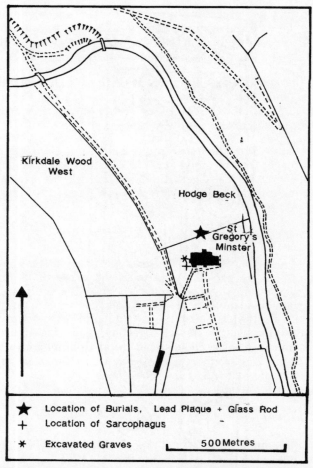

Kirkdale Wood
West

Hodge Beck

St
Gregory's
Minster

★ Location of Burials, Lead Plaque + Glass Rod
+ Location of Sarcophagus
✳ Excavated Graves   500 Metres

Figure 51 Excavations at Kirkdale (after P. Rahtz and L. Watts, 'Kirkdale Anglo-Saxon minster', *Current Archaeology*, 155 (1998), 419–22)

churchyard at Kirkdale is the remnant of a larger religious complex. Further burials were excavated on either side of the tower of St Gregory's; they were on a different orientation from that of the church, and were on a similar alignment to those in the north field, suggesting that there may have been a major reorganization at some point in the pre-Conquest period. A stone sarcophagus was also excavated on the south side of the tower, although its date is uncertain (Fig. 51).[252]

252.   P. Rahtz and L. Watts, 'Kirkdale Anglo-Saxon minster', *Current Archaeology*, 155 (1998), 419–22.

Tenth-century sculpture survives at Kirkdale, and elements of late Anglo-Saxon fabric survive in the church, which we know to have been rebuilt in the decade before the Norman conquest. An inscription on a sundial (which may be a reused section of a sarcophagus) reveals that

> Orm, the son of Gamel, bought St Gregory's church when it was broken and fallen, and had it made anew from the ground in honour of Christ and St Gregory, in the days of Edward the king and Tosti the earl.[253]

This serves as a reminder that the period of the viking raids and settlement was not the only point at which churches might fall into ruin or decay. In the later Middle Ages Kirkdale served as an ordinary parish church, although it was habitually known as St Gregory's Minster.

Collingham (Yorks)

Fragments of at least two cross-shafts suggest that there was a church at Collingham in the pre-viking period. One cross-shaft depicts the Apostles, and this might be an indication that this sculpture belongs within an evangelical milieu, as Ian Wood has argued for the Otley sculpture of a similar period.[254] A second cross-shaft reveals Scandinavian influence in its iconography, and this indicates that there was some level of ecclesiastical life at Collingham in the tenth century.[255] Some Anglo-Saxon fabric remains in the nave and in the western part of the chancel.[256]

Bardney (Lincs)

Bede provides much information about Bardney, which had been founded by the late seventh century, possibly by King Æthelred and Queen Osthryth of Mercia, who were certainly patrons of the house. Æthelred retired to Bardney in about 704, following the murder of his wife.[257] Æthelred and Osthryth were buried at Bardney; and their relics were obviously important, as they are listed in the *Secgan*.[258] Bardney is particularly well known for its possession of the relics of

---

253. Lang, *York and Eastern Yorkshire*, 158–66; L. Watts *et al.*, 'Kirkdale – the inscriptions', *Medieval Archaeology*, 41 (1997), 51–99, at 89.
254. See p. 237 above.
255. T.J. Pettigrew, 'The monumental crosses at Ilkley and Collingham', *JBAA*, 20 (1864), 308–14; Collingwood, *Northumbrian Crosses*, 6, 25, 50; Collingwood, 'Sculpture in the West Riding of Yorkshire', 155–61.
256. Taylor and Taylor, *Anglo-Saxon Architecture*, I, 166–7; Ryder, *Medieval Churches of West Yorkshire*, 16–17.
257. *HE*, iii, 11; *ASC*, s.a. 704.
258. Rollason, 'Lists of saints' resting-places', 89.

King Oswald of Northumbria, who was the uncle of Osthryth.[259] The
political significance of relics is again demonstrated by the response of
the monks at Bardney to the arrival of Oswald's relics. They initially
refused to receive them because Oswald had conquered the province of
Lindsey; however, during the night a heavenly sign indicated to the
monks that they should accept the relics, and they did so the next
morning.[260] The cult was also influential at another, unnamed,
monastery nearby, where an Abbess Æthelhild used dust from the
pavement on which Oswald's bones had been washed to treat a man
possessed by evil spirits.[261]

The description of Bardney by Bede and the topography of the area
suggest that, as in the case of Crowland, Bardney consisted of a series of
religious foci located on an island. David Stocker has suggested that some
or all of the late medieval churches of Bardney – including the abbey of
Bardney, the parish church of SS Peter and Paul, the chapels of St
Andrew and St Leonard and a further, unnamed, chapel – might reveal the
locations of early medieval religious foci. This likelihood is strengthened
by the close relationship between the abbey and the parish church, and
the resultant confusion of rights in SS Peter and Paul.[262]

Although there is a late medieval local tradition that the monastery
at Bardney was destroyed by the Danes, it seemingly survived until at
least 909, at which point the relics of St Oswald were removed by West
Saxon agency to Gloucester.[263] This, as we have seen, is but one of a
number of examples of the house of Wessex removing the relics of
saints from churches in the Danelaw to churches in Wessex or Mercia.
Peter Sawyer has suggested that the unusually low number of
Scandinavian place-names in the vicinity of Bardney is a further
indication of the survival of the abbey and of the fact that it may have
retained some of its lands; which contrasts with, for example, Whitby,
which has a number of Scandinavian place-names nearby.[264] However,
another interpretation of this evidence is possible. It is likely that if an
estate were broken up in the tenth century its individual members
might come to acquire new place-names, and that these might include a
high proportion of Scandinavian place-names given that these were in
common currency at this time. If the various manors in the vicinity of
Bardney had once belonged to the religious community there, they are

---

259.   *HE*, iii, 11–13.
260.   *HE*, iii, 11; the cult is discussed in Thacker, 'Kings, saints and monasteries', 2–
       4.
261.   *HE*, iii, 13.
262.   Stocker, 'The early church in Lincolnshire', 108–9. The site of the later abbey
       was excavated in the twentieth century, but no evidence for earlier occupation
       was discovered; this may be because of the techniques of excavation employed,
       or because the early monastery was spread out around the island; on the
       excavation, see C.E. Laing, 'Excavations on the site of Bardney Abbey', *AASRP*,
       32 (1914), 20–34; S.A.J. Brakspear, 'Bardney Abbey', *Arch. J.*, 79 (1922), 1–92.
263.   *ASC*, Mercian Register, *s.a.* 909.
264.   P.H. Sawyer, *Kings and Vikings: Scandinavia and Europe, AD 700–1100* (1982),
       104.

more likely to have been lost to it *before* the Scandinavian settlement, which would explain why they have Old English names rather than Scandinavian place-names.

Nothing more is known of the fate of Bardney until 1087, when Gilbert de Ghent founded a Benedictine priory there, which later became an abbey.[265]

Partney and 'Near Partney/Bardney' (Lincs)

Bede reveals that there was an early monastery at Partney, and at least one of its seventh-century abbots was known to him.[266] Deda and Aldwine were abbots at the time when Bede was writing, and the latter was the brother of Æthelhild, who was abbess of an unnamed house near to Partney and Bardney.[267] David Stocker has suggested that the monastic complex at Partney was similar to that at Crowland and Bardney, in that it was located on an island in the fen and incorporated a number of religious foci, possibly perpetuated by the later medieval monastery. He has also argued that this link between the heads of the neighbouring houses of Partney and that ruled by Abbess Æthelhild, and the fact that Æthelhild came to visit when Queen Osthryth was at Bardney, might indicate that there was a network of monasteries centred on Bardney ruled by a group of aristocratic clerics.[268] This does not stretch the evidence, but his additional suggestion that these monasteries were daughter foundations of Bardney is more speculative, although such a relationship finds parallels elsewhere, as we have seen in the case of Whitby. Abbess Æthelhild's community drew on the cult of St Oswald in its work, and took dust to use for healing purposes from the pavement at Bardney on which Oswald's bones had been washed. The story Bede tells of that incident reveals that the community consisted of nuns and priests, housed separately.[269]

Barrow upon Humber (Lincs)

Barrow upon Humber has long been identified as the location of the monastery built by St Chad on the 50 hides of land given to him by King Wulfhere in the late 660s *æt Bearuwe* in the province of Lindsey.[270] Bishop Wynfrid of the Mercians retired to the monastery there and remained until his death in the 670s.[271] The precise location of the monastery is unknown, although David Stocker has argued that

---

265. S. Elspeth, 'The abbey of Bardney', *VCH Lincs*, 97–103, at 97–8.
266. *HE*, ii, 16.
267. *Ibid.*, iii, 11.
268. Stocker, 'The early church in Lincolnshire', 111.
269. *HE*, iii, 11.
270. *Ibid.*, iv, 3.
271. *Ibid.*, iv, 6.

in common with other religious communities founded at that time, an island site might be expected, for which there is a possible candidate east of the castle.[272]

Excavation has revealed a number of middle to late Saxon burials in both Barrow and neighbouring Barton upon Humber, although the earliest excavated churches at both places do not pre-date the tenth century. It is conceivable that these burial sites were in some way connected to the pre-viking religious community, and there is circumstantial evidence that there may have been an early connection between Barton and Barrow. In a charter of 971 King Edgar granted to Bishop Æthelwold an estate *æt Bearuwe* which 'St Chad had formerly possessed', which was possibly intended to endow Æthelwold's foundation at Peterborough. The boundary clause reveals that the estate included both Barrow and Barton, and it is not at all unlikely that this was a relationship of some antiquity.[273] The place-name Barton ('barley-farm') is indicative of a subsidiary settlement. Rosamond Faith has also suggested that the name may have been applied to the home-farm of a major estate, especially monastic estates, and 'Bartons' have indeed been found in the vicinity of a number of early religious foundations.[274]

In the later medieval period neither Barrow nor Barton displays any evidence for superior status. A three-celled church of late Saxon date has been excavated at Barrow, which comprised a nave, chancel and apse; a series of unaccompanied inhumation burials preceded the building of the church.[275] The tenth-century church at Barton was also a three-celled structure, with a central nave over which a two-storey tower was constructed, plus a chancel and a baptistery. Immediately adjacent to the church was a manorial complex, and this has encouraged speculation that the church was a proprietary foundation. According to Domesday Book, Barton was a substantial place with a market and a valuable ferry, and a population much greater than the manors in the immediate vicinity; it seems unlikely that St Peter's was its only ecclesiastical provision, although the chapel of All Saints (later known as St Mary's) does not appear to be any earlier in date than *c.* 1100.[276]

Hibaldstow (Lincs)

Bede refers to an abbot of a monastery in the province of Lindsey, called Hygbald, who is almost certainly the same person as the Hygbald

272. Stocker, 'The early church in Lincolnshire', 114.
273. S 782 (B 1270); P. Everson, 'The pre-Conquest estate at *æt Bearuwe*', in *Studies in Late Anglo-Saxon Settlement*, ed. M. Faull (1984), 123–7.
274. R. Faith, *The English Peasantry and the Growth of Lordship* (1997), 36–7.
275. J.M. Boden and J.B. Whitwell, 'Barrow-upon-Humber', *LHA*, 14 (1979), 66–7.
276. W. Rodwell and K. Rodwell, 'St Peter's church, Barton-upon-Humber: excavation and structural study, 1978-81', *Antiq. J.*, 62 (1982), 283–315; G. Bryant, *The Early History of Barton-upon-Humber* (1994), 31–53; *DB*, fo. 354c.

who is said by the *Secgan* to rest at *Cecesege* on the river *Oncel* in Lindsey.[277] The resting-place of St Hygbald has been identified as Hibaldstow; in part because of the place-name ('Hygbald's holy place'), in part because Hibaldstow is near to the river Ancholme, with which *Oncel* has been identified, and in part because three of the four church dedications to St Hygbald are at Hibaldstow and neighbouring Manton and Scawby.[278] It is not, of course, certain that he was buried in the monastery of which he had been abbot, but he was almost certainly interred at a religious community. There is no other evidence for the existence of a pre-Conquest church at Hibaldstow, and by comparison with the sites of other known early religious communities in Lindsey, David Stocker has argued that the location of the early church may have been not where the present parish church is located, but on an island between it and the river Ancholme.[279]

Flixborough (Lincs)

Recent excavations at Flixborough have revealed a so-called 'high-status' site, interpreted variously as a monastic site, a secular site, or an aristocratic site that included a church at least during part of its existence. The excavation has revealed a series of some 38 buildings which were rebuilt on different alignments, over ten different phases of the site's occupation, and that the site appears to have been occupied from the seventh century into the post-Conquest period. The large number of metal finds, especially the dress-pins, of which there are over 300, together with pottery, coins and vessel-glass, indicate wide-ranging national and international contacts. An inhumation cemetery containing eleven graves has been excavated close to the settlement, and it has been dated, as a result of this juxtaposition and the presence of the iron fittings of a coffin, to the seventh to ninth centuries. One building, intepreted as a church, contained four burials and had a fifth immediately outside, and has produced a lead plaque containing seven or eight personal names. The presence of a church is also suggested by some of the artefacts discovered at the site, which may all have belonged to an ecclesiastical context. These include items suggestive of literacy, such as styli; a lead plaque inscribed with personal names, which may have been a book-mount or attached to a reliquary; two other book-mounts and an alphabet ring; and evidence for glazed windows, including pieces of window came and window glass. The finds from Flixborough are similar to those found at other

---

277. *HE*, iv, 3; Rollason, 'Lists of saints' resting-places', 89.
278. Seemingly the association with Hygbald resulted in the earlier place-name being superseded: M. Gelling, 'Some meanings of Stow', in *The Early Church in Western Britain and Ireland*, ed. S.M. Pearce (BAR British Series, 102, 1982), 187–96 at 189; E. Venables, 'The dedications of the churches of Lincolnshire', *Arch. J.*, 38 (1881), 365–90, at 369–70.
279. Stocker, 'The early church in Lincolnshire', 113–14.

excavated religious complexes, but thus far there is no evidence of a stone church or of stone sculpture, and burial appears to have been limited. Given the location of the site part-way down a slope and the limited nature of the excavated area, it is not implausible, however, that we have only a partial impression of the Middle Saxon site.[280]

If the building with the burials was indeed a church, it may have undergone a change of function at some point when a hearth was inserted into the eastern end of the building, sometime before the mid-ninth century, when the building was demolished.[281] It should also be noted that the artefacts associated with an ecclesiastical foundation are found at Flixborough only from the mid-eighth century, which may reflect another change in the nature of the site.[282] It is not clear why the church at Flixborough went out of use, although the fact that the later medieval church is close to the site may indicate that it was relocated.

Churches with pre-viking sculpture

Sculptural evidence permits us to identify the locations of many other pre-viking churches, many of which display few signs at a later date of being of superior status. In Yorkshire these include the churches at Wycliffe, Croft, Melsonby, Stanwick St John, West Tanfield, Middleton, Kirkby Moorside, Hovingham, Kirkby Misperton, Darfield, Sheffield, High Hoyland, Cundall and Kirkby Hill, and in Derbyshire at Eyam.[283] Of these, Hovingham is especially notable for its sculpture, a frieze which may have been the side of a shrine. It has been suggested that the iconography of the frieze, which includes the Annunciation, the dialogue between Elizabeth and Mary, and the three Marys at the Holy Sepulchre, is appropriate for the shrine of a female saint.[284] Tenth-century sculpture has also been found at Hovingham, as, indeed, at many of the other churches in this group.[285] The distribution of these churches is noteworthy. Many are located close to other major pre-viking churches and late medieval mother churches. It is unclear whether any of these churches had once been in any way connected, as

---

280. B. Whitwell, 'Flixborough', *Current Archaeology*, 126 (1991), 244–7; C. Loveluck, 'A high-status Anglo-Saxon settlement at Flixborough, Lincolnshire', *Antiquity*, 72 (1998), 146–61. The claim that the lead plaque carried the word 'nunna' has now been discounted.
281. Loveluck, 'Anglo-Saxon settlement at Flixborough', 159.
282. *Ibid.*
283. Collingwood, *Northumbrian Crosses*, 8, 17, 37, 42–3, 46–8, 72, 82, 92; Collingwood, 'Sculpture in the West Riding of Yorkshire', 172, 239; Lang, *York and Eastern Yorkshire*, *passim*; Ryder, *Saxon Churches in South Yorkshire*, 109–11, 118–19; Routh, 'Pre-Conquest carved stones of Derbyshire', 29–31; Cramp, 'Schools of Mercian sculpture', 193, 218–19, 224.
284. Gilchrist, *Gender and Material Culture*, 31; J. Hawkes, 'Mary and the cycle of Resurrection: the iconography of the Hovingham panel', in *The Age of Migrating Ideas*, ed. Spearman and Higgitt, 254–60.
285. Lang, *York and Eastern Yorkshire*, 144–8.

mother and daughter foundations for example. But it is striking that Sheffield was in the parish of Ecclesfield in the later Middle Ages, and Eyam appears to have been subordinate to Hope.[286]

In Lincolnshire the churches of South Kyme, Edenham and Redbourne all possess stone sculpture which has been assigned to the eighth century. The six sculptural fragments found at South Kyme appear to have once been part a shrine, which might indicate that it was the site of some now lost cult. The location of South Kyme on an island is common to other known early foundations.[287] At Edenham, in addition to two pre-viking carved roundels built into the south wall of the nave, there survives a section of a pre-viking cross-shaft. The latter depicts a standing male figure on the front and a female on the reverse, but whether this is an indication of the presence of male and female religious is complicated by the likelihood that the female figure was a later addition.[288] There is little to suggest that any of these churches were superior churches in the later Middle Ages. Domesday Book records two churches at South Kyme, but the prospect that this was a sign of superior status is lessened by the possibility that one of the churches was at North Kyme.[289] The late medieval parish of Edenham included four chapels in the later Middle Ages (at Grimsthorpe, Scottlethorpe, Elsthorpe and Southorpe), but they were all initially twelfth-century manorial chapels of local landowners, of which only Scottlethorpe became a parochial chapel.[290]

Written sources for pre-viking churches

Adlingfleet (Yorks) has been identified as 'Aelfet.ee', where the Anglo-Saxon Chronicle records that Pehtwin was consecrated bishop of Withorn in 763. It has also been identified as the site of a monastery in the Humber area called *Cornu Vallis* by the early eighth-century *Vita Ceolfridi. Cornu* refers to the branches of a river and the angle between them, a description that would fit the Humber–Trent–Don area. It has also been identified as the site of a monastery at *Donaemuthe* in the late eighth century, on the grounds that it is located at the mouth of the Yorkshire river Don. If Adlingfleet was indeed an early church, then although this was an exceptionally wealthy church in the later Middle Ages, it was not otherwise a remarkable one.[291]

286. Davies, 'The origins of the parishes of south Yorkshire', 9; Cox, II, 187.
287. A.H. Clapham, 'Six early carved stones from South Kyme, Lincolnshire', *Antiq. J.*, 3 (1923), 118–21; Stocker, 'The early church in Lincolnshire', 112–13.
288. J. Taylor and H.M. Taylor, 'The Anglo-Saxon church at Edenham, Lincolnshire', *JBAA*, 26 (1963), 6–10.
289. *DB*, fos. 337c, 353c, 357c; Stocker, 'The early medieval church in Lincolnshire', 112–13.
290. Owen, 'Medieval chapels in Lincolnshire', 17; D.M. Owen, *Church and Society in Medieval Lincolnshire* (1971), 8.
291. *ASC, s.a.* 763; *EHD*, I, no. 157; Richardson, 'A lost Saxon monastery in Yorkshire'.

There are late medieval written traditions concerning the existence of early religious foundations in Lincolnshire at Stow-by-Threekingham and Louth, neither of which displays obvious mother-church characteristics. The twelfth-century *Liber Eliensis* records that St Ætheldreda, having founded a monastery in northern Lindsey, *c.* 670, set off for Ely, but had to rest because of the heat, and there her staff took root and sprouted. Afterwards the place was known as Ætheldreda's Stow, and a church was built there in honour of the saint. It has been suggested that this church was founded at Stow Green, where there is a church dedicated, at least from the twelfth century, to St Ætheldreda and where a medieval market was held on the feast day of St Ætheldreda.[292] Stow Green is located near to Threekingham, where St Werburgh, the great-niece of St Ætheldreda, is alleged to have died.[293]

The late eleventh- or early twelfth-century F manuscript of the Anglo-Saxon Chronicle written at Canterbury refers to the archbishop elected in 792, Æthelheard, as an abbot of Louth (Lincs) (*Hludensis monasterii*).[294] A late eleventh-century text, 'Concerning the Translation of the Saints who rest in the Monastery of Thorney', states that 'the blessed Herefrith bishop of Lincoln resting in Louth chief town of the same church' was removed from Louth to Thorney in the 970s following the refoundation of Thorney by Æthelwold.[295] Herefrith clearly cannot have been a bishop of Lincoln (as the bishopric was not founded until 1072), but it has been suggested by A.E.B. Owen that he might have been a bishop of Lindsey, perhaps in the later ninth century.[296] Louth was clearly an important place: it was a Domesday market and had burgesses, and the place-names Ludford (*Ludeforde/Ludesforde*, 'ford on the way to Louth') and Ludborough (*Ludeburg*, '*burh* belonging to Louth'), which are eight miles and six miles respectively from Louth, indicate its regional importance.[297]

292. *Liber Eliensis*, 30; Roffe, 'Stow Green', 31–3.
293. See p. 256 above; Roffe, 'Stow Green', suggests that St Werburg may have died at Stow, and that Gocelin used the estate name rather than the name of the precise location of the monastery.
294. *ASC*, F, *s.a.* 792.
295. *Liber Vitae: register and martyrology of New Minster and Hyde Abbey, Winchester*, ed. W. de Gray Birch (1892), Appendix F, 286–90. The evidence is discussed at length in A.E.B. Owen, 'Herefrith of Louth, saint and bishop: a problem of identities', *LHA*, 15 (1980), 15–19.
296. Owen, 'Herefrith of Louth', 16. His tentative suggestion that Louth (*Hludensis*) might be the site of the elusive *Syddensis*, the seat of the bishops of Lindsey, has not been considered by other authors, who have assembled more evidence for Lincoln being the primary site of the bishops of Lindsey (see p. 249–50 above).
297. *DB*, fo. 345b; Owen, 'Herefrith of Louth', 17.

Later medieval mother churches without evidence for early origins

There are a number of important churches in the northern Danelaw in the later medieval period for which we do not have any evidence of origins before the tenth or eleventh centuries. This may simply be due to loss of earlier evidence. However, it may stem from the later foundation of some of these important churches. We know that such foundations occurred in other, better-documented regions in the tenth century and they may also have been a feature of the northern Danelaw.[298] It is difficult to speculate which of the churches described below might have had pre-viking origins; some surely did, but not necessarily all.

Derby, All Saints

The mother church of late medieval Derby was All Saints. It was a late medieval Royal Free Chapel, and these have consistently been shown to have been important churches of early origins.[299] It had a largely coherent parish, including most of the town and the Roman site at Little Chester. The urban parts of the parishes of several churches in Derby appear to have been carved out of that of All Saints, and three (St Mary's, St Michael's and St Peter's) had large rural parishes, which might once have been part of the parish of the mother church of Derby (Fig. 24). All Saints was also the heir to the lands recorded in Domesday Book as the possessions of the two collegiate churches of Derby, the other being St Alkmund's.[300] The canons of All Saints appear to have served St Alkmund's in the later medieval period, and in a dispute of 1253 the canons of All Saints spoke on behalf of 'their churches of All Saints and St Alkmund', suggesting that All Saints had control over the other church.[301] The early relationship between the two churches is unknown, but it may be that All Saints was the original church at *Northworthy* and St Alkmund's an additional construction of the ninth century to accommodate the cult of Ealhmund.

Chesterfield (Derbs)

Chesterfield was the site of another important late medieval mother church. No church is recorded in Domesday Book, and our earliest evidence comes from a writ of *c.* 1093 when the church – along with other major churches in Derbyshire – was granted to the Dean of

---

298. Blair, 'Secular minster churches', 118–19; Blair, 'Introduction', 3.
299. J.C. Cox, 'The collegiate church of All Saints, Derby', *VCH Derbs*, 88–9; J.H. Denton, *English Royal Free Chapels 1100–1300* (1970), 110–12.
300. Cox, 'The collegiate church of All Saints', 88.
301. *The Cartulary of Darley Abbey*, ed. Darlington, no. D2.

Lincoln.[302] We know that in the late twelfth century the church was served by two portionary vicars, and that in 1546, and perhaps earlier, the gild-priests of the town helped to serve the large parish. In 1546 the gild-priests were said to exist partly

> for the help and ministration of all manner of sacraments and sacramentals within the said parish, and other charitable deeds, forasmuch as the said parish is very large ... and is divided into many hamlets and villages, being distant some two miles, some three miles or more from the said parish church, so that the vicar and his parish priest in the time of Lent and Easter and some other times cannot suffice to the ministration of behoveful matters.[303]

John Blair has noted that the religious life of towns often shows continuing links with service of the old *parochiae*, and has suggested that gilds may have coexisted with multi-priest minsters.[304] The parish of Chesterfield was extensive and included most of the Domesday soke of Newbold (Fig. 30).[305] We know that Chesterfield was an estate centre in 955 when land there was granted to Uhtred *cild*.[306] The origins of the important church at Chesterfield are obscure, although the church occupies a location, within a Roman fort, commonly favoured for the foundation of early churches.[307]

Ashbourne (Derbyshire)

The earliest evidence for a church at Ashbourne is provided by the survival of a fragment of a cross-shaft of the tenth century.[308] The late medieval mother church at Ashbourne had numerous chapelries, and its parish incorporated the Domesday soke of Ashbourne and many other separate manors (Fig. 22).[309] It may also once have included the parishes of Parwich and Bradbourne and their respective chapelries.[310] Its rights as a mother church are especially well documented: it

---

302.   *RA*, I, no. 14.
303.   *The Records of the Borough of Chesterfield*, ed. P. Riden and J. Blair (1980), 105; *RA*, III, nos. 691, 703–5. The three gilds are known to have been in existence in the thirteenth century.
304.   Blair, 'Secular minster churches', 141.
305.   *DB*, fos. 272b, 276c, 277d, 278c; there was also sokeland in a number of now unidentifiable places.
306.   S 569 (B 911); *RA*, I, no. 14.
307.   P. Riden, 'Roman Chesterfield', *DAJ*, 109 (1987), 51–130; Blair, 'Anglo-Saxon minsters', 230.
308.   Routh, 'Pre-Conquest carved stones of Derbyshire', 5, where it is noted that there was once another stone, now lost.
309.   *DB*, fos. 272c, 273c, 274d, 275b, 276d, 277c; *RA*, III, nos. 677, 683, 685, 688; *Tithe Maps*, vol. 68.
310.   See Chapter 3, p. 133.

received annual pensions from the chapels; it reserved the right of presentment to them on the occurrence of a vacancy; it received the oblations and obventions due to the chapels; and it retained control over the pastoral activities of the chapels, including burial.[311]

Mansfield (Notts)

Mansfield had a wealthy late medieval church, which along with other important churches in the region was granted to the Dean of Lincoln *c.* 1093.[312] It served a large late medieval parish, and had chapels at Sutton in Ashfield and Skegby (which itself had a chapel at Hucknall).[313] It is also likely that there was another chapel at Edwinstowe; this church seems to have come into the possession of the dean of Lincoln following the grant of the church of Mansfield and 'all the chapels in the berewicks of the manor'.[314] Edwinstowe itself had a relatively large parish.[315] Although there is some correspondence between the parish of Mansfield and the dependencies of the manor, there are also many of its dependencies that do not lie within the parish.

Blyth (Notts)

The church of Blyth was a Royal Free Chapel in the later Middle Ages, a status commonly associated with important early churches.[316] There is, however, no pre-Conquest evidence concerning a church at Blyth, and even Domesday Book fails to record a church there.[317] Indeed, Blyth was merely a sokeland of the manor of Hodsock, and displays very little similarity with the sites of other major churches which were commonly at the centre of large Domesday estates. Nonetheless, when Roger de Buisli founded an alien priory there in 1088 he granted to the priory the church and the vill of Blyth, which indicates that there was a church there in the eleventh century.[318] The parishioners of Blyth used the nave of the priory church for their worship and the priory provided the clerks to meet the needs of the parishioners.[319] The late medieval

311. Cox, II, 363–416, 463–72, 489–94, 505–16, 531–8.
312. *RA*, I, no. 14.
313. *Lists of the Clergy of Central Nottinghamshire*, ed. K.S.S. Train, Thoroton Record Society, 15, 3 pts (1953), pt 1, 70.
314. *RA*, I, no. 14; Edwinstowe was a Domesday berewick of Mansfield, as were Sutton and Skegby: *DB*, fo. 281b.
315. *RA*, III, nos. 972–3; *Tithe Maps*, 83.
316. Denton, *English Royal Free Chapels*, 75–6.
317. *DB*, fo. 285b.
318. *The Cartulary of Blyth Priory*, ed. R.T. Timson, Thoroton Record Society, 27 (2 vols, 1968), I, xxix.
319. *Ibid.*, lii–liii, lvii; for comparable examples of this phenomenon, see M.J. Franklin, 'St Augustine's, Daventry', in *Minsters and Parish Churches*, ed. Blair, 97–104, at 99 for comparison with Blyth.

parish of Blyth was substantial and included chapels at Austerfield and Bawtry in Yorkshire, and may possibly have once included Sutton-by-Retford.[320]

Orston (Notts)

Orston was a major royal manor in Domesday Book, and the church at Orston displays some superior characteristics, according to the survey, which records that there were two priests with their own lands in the manor.[321] This church was another of that group of important churches granted to the dean of Lincoln, *c.* 1093, together with all of its possessions 'in the time of King Edward'.[322] Orston had four chapels at Scarrington, Thoroton, Screveton and Staunton (the parish of which included the township of Flawborough).[323] This scattered group of chapels possibly indicates that the medieval parish of Orston was the remnant of a once larger parish, perhaps including Whatton and its chapel at Aslockton, and the parishes of Elton, Alvington, Kilvington and Hawksworth.

Sherburn in Elmet (Yorks)

The church at Sherburn in Elmet had a substantial late medieval parish (Fig. 17).[324] The church was a possession of the archbishops of York, and the estate of Sherburn had been held by the archbishop since the tenth century, although in 963 it had been held by one Æslac.[325] It has been suggested that Sherburn was a royal centre in the ninth century following the discovery there of a ring of Queen Æthelswith (probably the sister of Alfred and the wife of Burgred of Mercia). This is not strong evidence, but it is not too fanciful to believe that Sherburn might have been a sufficiently important vill in the ninth century to have enjoyed a royal visit, or, perhaps, a royal gift in the form of the ring of a queen.[326]

Grantham (Lincs)

The church at Grantham was clearly very important in the eleventh century. It had eight plots of land, of which the priest held seven, and it

---

320. *Tithe Maps*, 83; *Tithe Files*, 225; *The Cartulary of Blyth Priory*, ed. Timson, I, xxix.
321. *DB*, fo. 281d.
322. *RA*, I, n. 14.
323. *Ibid.*, III, no. 975.
324. *PN WRY*, pt 4, 53–63.
325. *EYC*, 1, 18–21.
326. R.A. Smith, 'Anglo-Saxon remains', *VCH N. Riding*, I, 98–9; Wormald, 'The ninth century', 139.

had all the tithes and customary church dues (*ecclesiasticas consuetu-dines*) from all the berewicks and sokelands held by the king in the wapentakes of Winnibriggs and Threo.[327] It had a substantial parish which included the chapels of Braceby, Gonerby, Londonthorpe, Sapperton, Spittlegate and Towthorpe.[328] A Latin list of saints' resting-places contained in the *Chronicle of Hugh Candidus*, which was completed around 1155, states that Wulfrannus, Symphorianus and Etritha lay at Grantham.[329] Hugh Candidus may have based his list on other lists of saints' resting-places, perhaps including a northern list, as he includes many more saints than are listed in the early eleventh-century *Secgan*, including many northern saints, and, as David Rollason has observed, he is unlikely to have added them all himself.[330] However, it is impossible to know when these saints were translated to Grantham, and their presence there in the mid-twelfth century does not prove the existence of an early church at Grantham.

Castle Bytham (Lincs)

Castle Bytham was at the centre of a large parish, and until 1284 the church had three canonries, or portions in the churches of Castle Bytham, Little Bytham and Holywell. It also had chapels at Counthorpe and Aunby, and a number in the village of Bytham itself (dedicated to St Mary, St Thomas, St Mary Magdalen and St John the Baptist).[331] The church is not recorded in Domesday Book, although surviving fragments of a tenth-century cross-shaft indicate that there was a church there at that date.[332]

Other mother churches

There are many other mother churches in the northern Danelaw. These include Silkstone, Snaith, Old Malton, Kilham, Pocklington, Pickering, Topcliffe and Driffield (Yorks), Horncastle, Stow St Mary, Witham on the Hill, Wragby (Lincs), Hope (Derbs), Dunham and West Markham (Notts).[333] All served large parishes, and a few have other signs of superior status. For example, Topcliffe had two priests,

---

327. *DB*, fos. 337d, 377a.
328. Owen, 'Medieval chapels in Lincolnshire', 18.
329. *Chronicle of Hugh Candidus*, ed. W.T. Mellows (1949), 59–64. Symphorianus was an early Christian martyr at Autun (Cornwall): G.H. Doble, *St Symphorian*, Cornish Saints, 27 (1931).
330. Rollason, 'Lists of saints' resting-places', 71.
331. Owen, *Church and Society*, 8; Owen, 'Medieval chapels in Lincolnshire', 17.
332. D.S. Davies, 'Pre-Conquest carved stones of Lincolnshire', *Arch. J.*, 83 (1926), 1–20, at 9.
333. Morris, *Churches in the Landscape*, 134–5; Owen, 'Medieval chapels in Lincolnshire', *passim*; Cox, II, 187–98, 227–58; *The Cartulary of Blyth Priory*, ed. Timson, I, xxxv.

according to Domesday Book.[334] As was a common fate for mother
churches, several were granted to ecclesiastical lords in the post-
Conquest period: Pocklington and Pickering were granted to the
deanery of York, Horncastle was granted to the bishop of Carlisle, and
Dunham was granted to the archbishop of York by Henry I in order to
make it a prebend of Southwell Minster.[335] Churches with known early
origins are commonly located on royal vills or within former Roman
towns, and it may be significant that Driffield was a royal vill where
King Aldfrith died in 705, and Horncastle was located within a Roman
walled town.[336] It is possible that the community of secular clerks
founded in the early eleventh century at Stow St Mary perpetuated an
earlier community, but such a suggestion is supported only by the
circumstantial evidence that Leofric and Godiva elsewhere patronized
existing churches, and that the place-name 'Stow' is sometimes
associated with early churches.[337]

There are other churches in the northern Danelaw which exhibit
signs of superior status, and which were certainly more than
'ordinary' parish churches, but which do not have the full range of
attributes to warrant describing them as mother churches. Many have
a small number of chapels, or some other mark of superior status. In a
few instances some of these churches seem likely to have been in
some way subordinate to another church, either through the payment
of pensions or tithes to other churches or because their parish
appears to have been carved out of that of another church. These
churches include Bradbourne (possibly carved out of Ashbourne
parish); Dronfield; Longford; Duffield; Sawley; Stapenhill; St Peter's,
Derby (possibly carved out of the parish of All Saints, Derby); Edensor
and Youlgreave (subordinate to Bakewell) (Derbyshire); East Drayton;
Kneesall; Stoke; Newark (possibly carved out of Stoke); Lenton
(which was possibly the mother church of at least two churches in
Nottingham) (Notts); Winghale; Withcall; Boothby Graffoe; Well-
ingore; Brant Broughton; Cadney; Ingham; and Scott Willoughby
(Lincs).[338]

---

334. *DB*, fo. 323b; M. Weston, 'Topcliffe', *VCH N. Riding*, II, 70–80, at 70.
335. *EYC*, 1, no. 427; 'The register, or rolls, of Walter Gray', ed. Raine, 211–13;
     Owen, *Church and Society*, 2; *Thoroton*, III, 235.
336. *ASC*, D, *s.a.* 705; Whitwell, *Roman Lincolnshire*, 72–5.
337. Leofric and Godiva also patronized Leominster, Wenlock, and St John's and St
     Werburh's, Chester: Blair, 'Secular minster churches', 121; D. Whitelock, M.
     Brett and C.N.L. Brooke (eds), *Councils and Synods with Other Documents
     Relating to the English Church, I: AD 871–1204*, 2 vols (1981), II, 538–43. On
     the name, see Gelling, 'Some meanings of Stow'.
338. The churches in Derbyshire and Nottinghamshire are discussed, with
     references, in D.M. Hadley, 'Danelaw society and institutions: east midlands'
     phenomena?' (Ph.D. thesis, University of Birmingham, 1992), ch. 5, *passim*; the
     Lincolnshire churches and their chapels, along with other examples, are listed
     in Owen, 'Medieval chapels in Lincolnshire'.

Synthesis

The pattern of ecclesiastical organization detectable in the later medieval period in some areas of the northern Danelaw had its origins in the pre-viking period. There is a group of churches in the region which exhibit a series of variables, including pre-viking documentary references and sculpture, distinctive topography and complex planning at an early date, royal and episcopal patronage, saints' cults, superior status in Domesday Book, royal or episcopal ownership in the eleventh century, residual staffs of clergy, and mother-church rights over large parishes, which suggest the relative antiquity and stability of those churches as a broad but distinct class.[339] These churches are distributed at regular intervals across the region, and whatever else the Scandinavian settlement may have done, it did not apparently result in the eventual disruption or destruction of this layer of ecclesiastical organization. This is not to deny that there may have been great changes, but much of the basic organizational framework clearly survived the Scandinavian settlement. Those mother churches with no evidence for early origins may well have been pre-viking foundations, and it is notable that many display characteristics in Domesday Book and later that are similar to those of churches of known pre-viking origin.

Another significant feature of these mother churches is that most are located at the centre of large Domesday estates, of the type with a central manor and numerous dependent berewicks and sokelands. There is commonly a close correspondence between the dependent properties and the parishes of the respective churches. This pattern adds substantial support to recent studies which have argued that the parishes of major early churches were framed around secular territorial units.[340] Nonetheless, it is important to note that the coincidence between parishes and Domesday estates is not always exact, and this suggests that estates went on being adapted after parish boundaries had been fixed. Accordingly, we should be wary of aggregating the evidence of Domesday estates and parish boundaries as we seek to identify earlier patterns of estate structure and ecclesiastical organization.

Not all churches of pre-viking origins were mother churches in the later Middle Ages. There are two possible reasons for this. They either lost their mother-church characteristics – perhaps as a result of Scandinavian or other disruption – or they had never had them. We know that some of these churches had communities of clergy at an early

---

339. Blair, 'Ecclesiastical organization', 199.
340. S.R. Bassett, 'In search of the origins of Anglo-Saxon kingdoms', in *The Origins of Anglo-Saxon Kingdoms*, ed. S.R. Bassett (1989), 3–27, at 18, discusses the grant of 20 hides to a church at Wootton Wawen (Warwickshire) in the early eighth century by Æthelbald of Mercia, which gives no indication where those 20 hides lay, but which the author proposes may be identified since the church can be reasonably assumed to have taken it as its parish.

date, and the loss of these communities must have had much to do with the nature of the protection received by these churches. Surviving communities of clergy are found most commonly at churches held by successive archbishops of York through the tenth and eleventh centuries. It has been traditional to ascribe the absence of important mother churches in some regions to the Scandinavian settlement. This is not necessarily a suggestion that ought to be completely dismissed, but it is only one of the factors that emerge about this group of churches that are worthy of further consideration. Others are the close proximity in which some of them are found; their fate in the ninth century before the Scandinavian settlement; the actions of the West Saxon kings and their followers in the tenth century; and the proliferation of seigneurial church-building in the tenth and eleventh centuries.

The distribution of pre-viking churches

A number of the churches of early origin which have no obvious signs of superior status at a later date are located very close together. Richard Morris has drawn attention to this phenomenon in north Yorkshire: Stonegrave and Hovingham are just two miles apart, Gilling East is located about three miles from Stonegrave, and Coxwold is about nine miles from Stonegrave.[341] Furthermore, within ten miles to the north-east of Stonegrave are the churches of Kirkdale, Kirkby Moorside and Lastingham, and also in the vicinity are the pre-viking churches of Middleton and Kirkby Misperton, and the major late medieval church of Pickering, which possibly had earlier origins. This is a significant clustering of churches of pre-viking date, made all the more remarkable by the fact that our evidence for their existence – which is largely sculptural, and, in the documented case of Stonegrave and Coxwold, incidental – suggests, as Morris observes, that many more such unrecorded early foundations might have existed. Clusters of early churches, some of which are mother churches in the later Middle Ages, others of which are not, are found elsewhere: West Gilling, Catterick, Easby, Stanwick St John, Wycliffe, Melsonby and Croft (Yorks); Ripon, Aldborough, Cundall and Kirby Hill (Yorks); Redbourne and Hibaldstow (Lincs); and Stow-by-Threekingham and Threekingham (Lincs).

This clustering of early churches raises questions about their roles, and the influences on their foundation. It is, of course, possible that some of the closely sited churches were daughter foundations of some other community, of the type that we know that Whitby had.[342] Indeed, the parishes of some of these churches appear to have been carved out of the parishes of neighbouring churches. There are also a few

---

341. Morris, *Churches in the Landscape*, 121–2, fig. 26.
342. This is the explanation favoured in Cambridge, 'The early church in County Durham', 73–6.

examples of pre-viking sculpture at churches known to be dependent churches of another church (Hackness, Thornhill, Sheffield and Eyam, for example). However, we should not assume that all churches located in close proximity were necessarily related to other churches in the area, as mother and daughter foundations.[343]

Although the distribution of churches is not the soundest of starting-points for a discussion of the motives and backgrounds of the patrons of pre-viking churches, it becomes more significant when one realizes that there are other differences between the churches concerned. Some do not appear to have the same range of attributes as the great royal and episcopal foundations of the region, such as Repton, Ripon, Whitby or Otley, which were founded on large estates that spawned large parishes that were maintained into the later Middle Ages. It is, then, worth considering whether the clustering of early churches provides, in some instances, a material manifestation of the impact of a variety of influences on foundation, including that of the aristocracy. It is in Yorkshire that we are, as yet, most clearly able to uncover this pattern because of the trend for the provision of stone sculpture; in time, excavation such as that undertaken at Flixborough might lead to the discovery of yet more such early foundations. Other foundations might have been like those at Crayke and Addingham, which originated as temporary residences for bishops or archbishops.

The religious communities about which we are most fully informed at an early date tend to be royal or episcopal foundations; accordingly, the aristocratic involvement in church foundation has tended to be overlooked. This does not stem solely from the nature of the evidence, but is, in part, the result of the prevailing debates, which have tended to focus on the deliberate and organized manner in which the seventh- and eighth-century network of 'minsters' was established, a process which has been typically attributed to royal and episcopal intervention. Recent discussion of the early medieval church and its organization has tended to focus on the actions of kings and bishops, and such evidence as King Oswy's vow in 655 to give twelve ten-hide estates *ad construenda monasteria*, six of which were to be in Deira and six in Bernicia, has been understood to imply royal planning.[344] Yet we need to take account of individual initiatives by local lords with smaller-scale, regional authority.[345] It is widely recognized that the proliferation of churches from the tenth century had much to do with aristocratic initiative, but the importance of aristocratic initiative at an earlier date has not been explored in depth. Yet Bede's letter to

---

343. As is often assumed – a point discussed in Cambridge and Rollason, 'The pastoral organization of the Anglo-Saxon church', 97.
344. Blair, 'Ecclesiastical organization', 207; *HE*, iii, 24.
345. A point made by C.R.E. Cubitt, *Anglo-Saxon Church Councils, c. 650–c. 850* (1995), 117; see also J. Campbell, 'Bede's *reges* and *principes*' in his *Essays in Anglo-Saxon History* (1986), 85–98.

Bishop Ecgbert indicates that this was rife, although he did not approve of these aristocratic foundations:

> those who are totally ignorant of the monastic life have received under their control ... many places in the name of monasteries ... having usurped for themselves estates and villages ... they gratify their own desires alone, laymen in charge of monks; nay, rather, it is not monks that they collect there, but whomsoever they may perchance find wandering anywhere, expelled from true monasteries for the fault of disobedience, or whom they can allure out of the monasteries, or, indeed, those of their own followers whom they can persuade to promise to them the obedience of a monk and receive the tonsure.[346]

Despite his disapproval, Bede's comments suggest not only that such foundations were common but that they met their patron's standards. Before we are tempted to suggest that these standards were not very high we might do well to recall Patrick Wormald's comments on the 'serious and sober community' described by the early ninth-century poem *De Abbatibus*, probably the type of foundation of which Bede did not approve, yet meeting high standards in Latin literacy and manuscript production.[347]

It is not unlikely that it was through this type of community, heavily involved with the lay aristocracy, that Christianity was brought to the Anglo-Saxon countryside. The Anglo-Saxon church was successful precisely because it did embrace the secular world. Wormald has pointedly observed that *Beowulf* (with its mixture of pagan mythology, warrior and aristocratic culture, worldly concerns and Christian ideology) may be seen as being as representative of the early medieval church as is the writing of Bede, because it represents the 'aristocratic environment of early English Christianity'.[348] The aristocracy seem to have been avid founders of churches, although they are unlikely to have been involved in some great plan to provide churches and pastoral care across the kingdoms. Their dynastic ambitions were probably one important factor (as they sought to preserve family lands through the privileges of ecclesiastical tenure), and their foundations both provided a hereditary abbacy and offered the spiritual support of a saint's cult.[349]

Whether we may identify aristocratic foundations on any other grounds is debatable. It is noteworthy, for example, that churches of

---

346. *EHD*, I, no. 170.
347. P. Wormald, 'Bede, "Beowulf" and the conversion of the Anglo-Saxon aristocracy' in *Bede and Anglo-Saxon England*, ed. R.T. Farrell (BAR British Series, 46, 1978), 32–95, at 54.
348. *Ibid.*, 57.
349. Blair, 'Introduction', 2–3; P. Sims-Williams, *Religion and Literature in Western Britain, 600–800* (1990), 144–76; Brooks, *The Early History of the Church of Canterbury*, 175–206.

pre-viking origin that are not mother churches at a later date include a large number at places which have names incorporating the element 'kirk' (ON *kirkja*), such as Kirkby or Kirby. It may be that such names came to be coined for the sites of aristocratic churches, rather than for the more prominent royal and episcopal foundations.[350] It has also been suggested that aristocratic churches might have a different layout and range of attributes as compared with a major royal or episcopal foundation. Sites such as Flixborough and the comparable site at Brandon (Suffolk) have been variously interpreted as aristocratic or monastic sites, but in fact they may be aristocratic sites, of which a church was an integral part.[351] Perhaps such sites are the early medieval forerunners of the later manorial centre–church complexes.

However, although there are likely to have been differences in the origins, patronage and fate of churches, we have to be cautious in describing particular pre-viking churches as royal, episcopal or aristocratic. Only in a handful of cases is it possible to say anything certain about the foundation and patronage of a church. Moreover, although a few churches apparently remained in archiepiscopal or royal hands, we cannot be sure that this was a common pattern. A royal, archiepiscopal or aristocratic foundation need not have continued to be supported or endowed by the successors of its founder: the evidence concerning Stonegrave, Coxwold and *Donaemuthe* demonstrates that churches could pass from an abbess to an abbot, to the king and to his brother. Nonetheless, when we combine the available evidence, from the very general to the very specific evidence revealed by local studies, we may conclude that there were many influences on the development of ecclesiastical provision between the seventh and ninth centuries, which gave rise to uneven distributions of churches in the northern Danelaw. Furthermore, the absence in some regions of mother churches located at the centre of major Domesday manors and serving large parishes may as often have derived from early foundations of limited scope as from destruction or impoverishment in the ninth and tenth centuries.

The ninth century

The evidence for the fate of early foundations in the ninth century is sparse, but there are signs that the church experienced significant transformations in its fortunes at this time. There is, for example, little evidence for the building of churches during the ninth century, which may suggest that investment in churches diminished. However, Richard Gem has recently observed that one reason why we tend to think of the ninth century as a period of stagnation is that we simply do

---

350. Morris, *Churches in the Landscape*, 159–61.
351. Loveluck, 'Anglo-Saxon settlement at Flixborough', 159–60; R.D. Carr, A. Tester and P. Murphy, 'The middle Saxon settlement at Staunch Meadow, Brandon', *Antiquity*, 62 (1988), 371–7; Blair, 'Anglo-Saxon minsters', 262.

not know how to identify ninth-century architecture, yet he has identified a number of major church-building projects which suggest that there was both continuity and innovation in architectural development at that time. Architectural details from ninth-century buildings have been identified in the northern Danelaw at Ledsham and Lastingham, and the church at Conisbrough may, to judge from its form (an unaisled church with porticus), be of such a date.[352] Nonetheless, there is documentary evidence to suggest that the ninth century witnessed struggles between kings and bishops for control over churches and their lands, and that the church often lost land as a result.[353] This is easier to document in Kent and western Mercia, but there are hints that it was also a feature of the northern Danelaw. The *Historia de Sancto Cuthberto* alleges that the Northumbrian kings Osbert and Ælle were robbing the community of St Cuthbert of land (including Crayke) in the period immediately preceding the Scandinavian settlement of Northumbria. Patrick Wormald has interpreted this, and the contemporary monetary collapse, as a possible indication that the wealth of Northumbrian kings had been undermined by civil war and that they sought to make good their losses at the expense of the church.[354]

A number of late eighth- and ninth-century commentators indicate that there had been a decline in Christian standards and practices. Alcuin clearly believed that the sins of the people had caused the viking assault on Lindisfarne in 793:

> Consider carefully, brothers, and examine diligently, lest perchance this unaccustomed and unheard-of evil was merited by some unheard-of evil practice ... from the days of King Ælfwold fornications, adulteries and incest have poured over the land, so that these sins have been committed without any shame and even against the handmaids dedicated to God. What may I say about avarice, robbery, violent judgments? – when it is clearer than day how much these crimes have increased everywhere, and a despoiled people testifies to it.[355]

---

352. Gem, 'Architecture of the Anglo-Saxon church', at 48–9 for comments on the Northumbrian evidence.
353. Brooks, *The Early History of the Church of Canterbury*, 184–6, 201–6, discusses the policies of the Mercian king Coenwulf towards Kentish churches and the interference of Archbishop Wulfred, the stuggle between Abbess Selethryth and the archbishop over the lands of Minster-in-Thanet, and the transfer of wealth from ecclesiastical to lay hands in the later ninth century. King Berhtwulf of Mercia restored land to the bishop of Worcester in 840 which he had earlier given to his own men: S 192 (B 430) (trans. *EHD*, I, no. 86), and discussed in Wormald, 'The ninth century', 139.
354. *EHD*, I, no. 6; Wormald, 'The ninth century', 135.
355. *EHD*, I, nos. 193–4.

Asser comments on the apathy of potential recruits and the disrespect into which the monastic life came as a result of the abundance of riches which people had, and offers them as explanations for the condition of the Anglo-Saxon church.[356]

Archaeological evidence reveals changes to ecclesiastical sites in the ninth and tenth centuries, including abandonment and the contraction of the area in use (as we have seen at Beverley, Repton and Flixborough).[357] It has recently been proposed that there was often a secular transformation of ecclesiastical sites in the ninth and tenth centuries, reflecting the fact that churches were coming under pressure from the secular authorities who came to control them.[358] The events of the ninth and tenth centuries may have made this secular usurpation of ecclesiastical sites all the more likely in the northern Danelaw, although it is found everywhere.

In interpreting this evidence, however, we have to be careful not to confuse change and development with decline. Increasing secular involvement in ecclesiastical organization need not be an indication of decline; indeed, the early medieval church was firmly wedded to secular society in its organization, patronage and values. In relation to the documentary evidence of the seventh and eighth centuries Patrick Wormald has commented that evidence for secular involvement has commonly been taken as evidence for the 'decline' of the Anglo-Saxon church during and after the age of Bede, but that this is to misunderstand the nature of the church and its relationship to aristocratic customs and values.[359]

Tenth-century politics

The tenth century witnessed important developments in ecclesiastical fortunes in the northern Danelaw. It is clear that monastic revival was unsuccessful in this area, in contrast with other parts of the country. It may be that there was very little effort to re-establish the regular life in the northern Danelaw. One reason for this might have been a lack of royal land with which churches could be endowed. The impact of the West Saxon conquest on patterns of land-holding seems to have resulted in the acquisition of large tracts of land either by kings or by their leading followers. In the areas where the latter acquired land, the momentum for

---

356. Asser, c. 93.
357. See, for example, Carr, Tester and Murphy, 'Staunch Meadow, Brandon', 371–7; V. Fenwick, 'Insula de Burgh: excavations at Burrow Hill, Butley, Suffolk, 1978–81', in *ASSAH*, 3, ed. D. Brown (1984), 35–54; Cramp, 'Monastic sites', 223–41.
358. J. Blair, 'Palaces or minsters? Northampton and Cheddar reconsidered', *ASE* 25 (1996), 97–121; Loveluck, 'Anglo-Saxon settlement at Flixborough', 159–60.
359. Wormald, 'Bede, "*Beowulf*" and the conversion of the Anglo-Saxon aristocracy', 50–8.

re-endowment of communities or the establishment, or re-establishment, of the regular life at those places may have been inhibited.[360]

Direct assaults on the church are also recorded, most famously Eadred's attack on Ripon in 948, which ironically almost certainly was the result of the success of northern ecclesiastics in coming to terms with Scandinavian settlers, as it seems to have been a punitive measure following Archbishop Wulfstan's change of allegiance to Eric Bloodaxe. The acquisition of relics from churches may also be interpreted as an attack on their prosperity. The relics of St Oswald were taken from Bardney into Mercia in 909, and Alfred's daughter Æthelflæd may have been behind the transfer of the relics of St Ealhmund from Derby to Shrewsbury, and those of St Werburgh to Chester.[361] Although the pious motives of the house of Wessex should not be overlooked, there was clearly also political capital to be gained through the acquisition of relics. The movement of some relics was almost certainly related to the establishment of West Saxon *burhs* in western Mercia. This transfer of cults may have served the dual role of satisfying Mercian pride and of establishing more firmly West Saxon control in Mercia, perhaps by reminding the Mercians of the fact that some of their major saints' cults had long involved them in looking up to foreign royalty, since Oswald and Ealhmund were from Northumbrian royal families and Werburgh had been associated with that of Kent.[362] According to William of Malmesbury, Glastonbury acquired the relics of many northern saints, including those of Hild of Whitby, Ceolfrith of Monkwearmouth–Jarrow and Aidan of Lindisfarne.[363] This transfer of relics was possibly associated with the military campaigns of Edmund, and served to benefit a monastery long associated with the West Saxon kings.[364] The importance of saints' relics should not be underestimated. Cults and religious communities were intimately linked. Cults provided a focal point for pilgrimage and patronage, they conferred prestige, they were central to local pastoral work and they were important to regional traditions and identities.[365] In addition to the recorded removal of relics, one wonders what happened to the relics undoubtedly associated with the remains of shrines discovered at, for example, Wirksworth, South Kyme and Hovingham.

---

360. D. Dumville, 'Between Alfred the Great and Edgar the Peaceable: Athelstan, first king of England', in his *Wessex and England from Alfred to Edgar* (1992), 141–72, at 161.
361. *ASC*, Mercian Register, *s.a.* 909; Rollason, *The Mildrith Legend*, 26–7; A.T. Thacker, 'Chester and Gloucester: early ecclesiastical organization in two Mercian *burhs*', *Northern History*, 18 (1982), 199–211, at 203–4 and 209–11; Thacker, 'Kings, saints and monasteries', 18.
362. Rollason, 'Relic-cults', 95.
363. *Willelmi Malmesbiriensis Monachi, De Gestis Pontificum Anglorum, Libri Quinque*, ed. N.E.S.A. Hamilton, Rolls Series, 52 (1870), 198.
364. Rollason, 'Relic-cults', 95.
365. Thacker, 'Monks, preaching and pastoral care', 166–9; Rollason, 'Relic-cults', 91–5.

The proliferation of churches in the tenth century

The proliferation of churches in the tenth century also appears to have been instrumental in determining the fate of some of the pre-existing churches in parts of the northern Danelaw. The point can be explored by looking at the evidence from two regions: north Lincolnshire and Ryedale (Yorks). North Lincolnshire is striking in having so few mother churches of note in the later Middle Ages, and the small size of parishes in this region has already been noted.[366] The evidence for the existence of tenth-century churches is, admittedly, patchy, but there are hints of a clustering of such foundations. Tenth-century sculpture has been found in all four of the adjacent churches of Aisthorpe, Brattleby, Cammeringham and Hackthorn, and there are four churches of known tenth-century date in the adjacent parishes of Barton upon Humber, Barrow upon Humber, Thornton Curtis and Burnham. The extant evidence may indicate that there were many more churches of that date, evidence for which has failed to survive. The sculpture of tenth-century date found north of Lincoln and the regular arrangement of parishes in that area have given rise to the suggestion that the pattern may have been established by the mid-tenth century.[367] Obviously, the presence of tenth-century sculpture does not prove that churches were founded at that time, as opposed to being earlier foundations for which no evidence survives. Nonetheless, it remains the case that areas with few surviving mother churches are sometimes characterized by significant numbers of 'ordinary' churches in the tenth century. Yet in other areas mother churches retained control over the various churches that came to be founded in the vicinity. Examples of Yorkshire churches with tenth-century sculpture that are within the parish of some other church include Forcett (in Gilling parish), Brompton (Northallerton), Ellerburn and Levisham (Pickering), Middlesmoor (Kirkby Malzeard), Pateley Bridge (Ripon), Harrogate (Knaresborough) and Hawkser (Whitby).[368] The absence of mother churches with large parishes across most of north Lincolnshire must be, in part, due to the inability of major churches to retain control over these newer foundations. The demands for ecclesiastical provision made as a result of the fragmented tenurial geography of the region (many vills were divided among two or more lords and even the large sokes sometimes included only parts of vills) arguably gave rise to the proliferation of churches, and may have marked the point at which any preceding pattern of major churches serving large areas ceased to be socially relevant.[369] This is a process that was inhibited

---

366. Sawyer, *Kings and Vikings*, 107.
367. D. Stocker, 'Five Towns funerals: decoding diversity in Danelaw stone sculpture', in *Proceedings of the Thirteenth Viking Congress*, ed. J. Graham-Campbell, R. Hall, J. Jesch and D. Parsons (forthcoming).
368. Lang, *York and Eastern Yorkshire*, 126–30, 175–8.
369. A process described as 'competitive church-building' in T. Williamson, *The Origins of Norfolk* (1993), 184–7.

elsewhere by the survival of large sokes in which the church at the manorial centre remained responsible for ecclesiastical provision for the members of the soke.

The impact of the Scandinavian settlement on ecclesiastical provision in the northern Danelaw was arguably not simply restricted to attacks on churches and their resources, but may also have given rise to changes in estate organization that, in turn, had implications for ecclesiastical organization. Furthermore, the resultant political circumstances of the tenth century may also have had an impact on the church in Lincolnshire. Tenth-century stone monuments are now known at over 100 locations in Lincolnshire, and since the majority of them are not found at churches which display any obvious superior characteristics, David Stocker has argued that they are found at the sites of 'newly created parochial churches'. Irrespective of whether this claim is correct, it is clear that there was a transformation in the form and ornamentation of the monuments of northern Lincolnshire in the tenth century away from styles typical of the North towards styles of ornamentation much more reminiscent of southern styles. Stocker has linked this with both the capture of Lincolnshire by King Edmund and attempts to reunite the province of Lindsey with southern England and the diocese of Canterbury (the most significant development of which was the re-establishment of a bishop of Lindsey); he describes the later tenth-century monuments of northern Lincolnshire as 'the colonial monuments of the southern church'. The élite of northern Lincolnshire appear to have been memorializing themselves in distinctive regional fashions through which they reflected their cultural and political allegiances.[370] As they sought to consolidate their authority they may have used the church, and their patronage seemingly extended beyond the major churches of the region to a new group of local or manorial churches. We might justifiably conclude that, rather than reflecting a church in crisis, this evidence is commensurate with a thriving church or with a church being reasserted after a pagan interlude, which was significantly patronized, and which was regarded as an integral part of lordship in northern Lincolnshire, as lords used their churches to convey messages to far-flung audiences of peers.

The distribution of sculpture in the Ryedale area reveals that the full complement of later medieval parish churches had been reached by the tenth century. This suggests that a combination of a dense distribution of pre-viking churches followed by the foundation of new churches in the tenth century contributed to an absence of large parishes. This, combined with the slight information provided by Domesday Book about churches in the region, has given rise to the conclusion that the church had suffered greatly at the hands of the Scandinavians. Of course, it may have done, but it is apparent that in Ryedale, and other

---

370.   Stocker, 'Five Towns funerals'.

areas in Yorkshire (around Gilling and in south Yorkshire, for example), continuous coverage of ecclesiastical provision existed in the tenth century, although it was different from that characteristic of other regions of England.

The Scandinavian impact

The implication of much of the discussion in this chapter has been that the period of Scandinavian conquest and settlement was not as disruptive to the organization of the church as has been traditionally believed. Some aspects of the late medieval parochial structure have been shown to have their origins in the pre-viking period, but this is not to deny that there were important developments and innovations throughout the period c. 800–1100. Regional diversity has also been highlighted. However, although the Scandinavian impact can now be seen as but one factor which shaped ecclesiastical organization in the northern Danelaw, we do need to address more carefully how and why ecclesiastical organization survived the period of settlement of a group of incomers who were not initially Christian, and how individual churches may have continued to have a role during this settlement.

The evidence for the survival of ecclesiastical life from the mid-ninth to the mid-tenth centuries is disparate. The careers of successive archbishops of York demonstrate that collaboration with Scandinavian leaders could be both possible and desirable. Archbishop Wulfstan I (931–56) accompanied Olaf Guthfrithson as he headed into the north Midlands in 940, and both were besieged by King Edmund at Leicester; later, although he had previously pledged himself to King Eadred in 947, he quickly changed his allegiance to Eric Bloodaxe.[371] These actions probably had much to do with attempts to maintain independence for the kingdom of York and the ecclesiastical province of York in the face of West Saxon expansionism. Moreover, the minting of coins at York and Lincoln in the late ninth or early tenth century was clearly under ecclesiastical influence, as the coinage bearing the names of St Peter and St Martin reveals. This is further evidence for the importance of ecclesiastical lordship in northern England, and is also an indication of the capacity of the church to be effective under viking overlordship.[372]

The large corpus of Anglo-Scandinavian stone sculpture indicates that many churches were in use for burial and commemoration in the earlier part of the tenth century, and it also suggests that the church was central to lordship in the northern Danelaw at this time. The corpus of Anglo-Scandinavian sculpture has recently been assigned to a much smaller period of production than was once the case, and to a

---

371. *ASC, s.a.* 943, 947–8; D.W. Whitelock, 'The dealings of the kings of England with Northumbria in the tenth and eleventh centuries', in *The Anglo-Saxons: studies presented to Bruce Dickins*, ed. P. Clemoes (1959), 70–88, at 71–3; see also Chapter 1, pp. 14–15 on the problem of dating events in the late 940s and early 950s.
372. See Chapter 1, pp. 9, 12 and 29 above.

much earlier date.[373] The production of stone sculpture and its display, which were intimately associated with the church, indicates a thriving church. This is not to deny that there may have been a period of disruption, and the sculpture may attest to the subsequent reassertion of the church in some areas. It is indeed difficult to use the sculpture to demonstrate continuity in ecclesiastical organization, although the fact that so many churches with earlier sculpture also have tenth-century sculpture suggests that, whatever the levels of disruption following Scandinavian settlement, the basic framework of ecclesiastical provision survived. Yet there were certainly changes. New styles of sculpture surely reflect new influences in local society: in Ryedale, for example, tenth-century sculpture is very different from earlier sculpture, and animal ornamentation and figure carving (including warriors and huntsmen) are prominent. Yet in the middle of this region of distinctive Scandinavian cultural influence the sculpture produced at Stonegrave maintains much of the earlier styles, and makes few concessions to Scandinavian style. Jim Lang has suggested that there may be a distinction to be drawn between the new 'secular' influence on sculptural iconography in Ryedale and the more overtly ecclesiastical patronage of sculpture at Stonegrave.[374] Clearly, we have to be careful about drawing distinctions between secular and ecclesiastical patronage; but the iconography may be interpreted as an indication of continuity of patronage, and perhaps also of continuity of ecclesiastical organization at this site.

It would be rash to deny that the church in the northern Danelaw suffered during the Scandinavian settlement. We cannot ignore the disruption to the dioceses of the region, or the loss of most of the early books and charters of the Danelaw.[375] Although land may have been taken from the church prior to the Scandinavian settlement, and later in the tenth and eleventh centuries, it is implausible to suppose that the church in the northern Danelaw did not also lose land as a result of the Scandinavian settlement.[376] This need not invariably mean that land was taken directly from the church: further north, the community of St Cuthbert lost land when the viking Ragnald seized the lands of its tenants, Alfred and Eadred, in the second decade of the tenth century. It should be noted, however, that all this land eventually came back to

---

373. J.T. Lang, 'Recent studies in the pre-Conquest sculpture of Northumbria', in *Studies in Medieval Sculpture*, ed. F.H. Thompson (1983), 177–89, at 185–6.
374. M. Firby and J.T. Lang, 'The pre-Conquest sculpture at Stonegrave', *YAJ*, 53 (1981), 17–29.
375. P. Wormald, 'Viking studies: whence and whither?', in *The Vikings*, ed. R.T. Farrell (1982), 128–53, at 137–41.
376. On the ninth century, see nn. 235 and 254 above. On the tenth and eleventh centuries, see Blair, 'Secular minster churches', 118–19; Blair, 'Introduction', 3–5; R. Fleming, 'Monastic lands and England's defence in the viking age', *EHR*, 100 (1985), 247–65; D. Dumville, 'Ecclesiastical lands and the defence of Wessex in the first Viking-Age', in his *Wessex and England*, 29–54.

the community, and this is possibly only the best-documented example of a wider phenomenon.[377]

Although many churches doubtless suffered, others may have survived, albeit in an altered state. Repton clearly retained a role for burial and commemoration in the tenth century, whatever may have been the implications of a viking army over-wintering in 873–4; the distribution of tenth-century sculpture suggests that this was the case at many churches, although this does not preclude an earlier period of disruption. The fate of religious communities is less clear. A community survived at Crayke for some time, as it was there that the community of St Cuthbert resided in 882 or 883. Indeed, it has been suggested by Gerald Bonner that the community may have resided subsequently at Chester-le-Street rather than trying to return to Lindisfarne, where they could have enjoyed the patronage and protection of the native rulers at Bamburgh, precisely because they wanted to benefit from Danish patronage.[378] Political factors may have been important in determining the fates of churches. The churches of the archbishops of York seem likely to have survived largely because of the archiepiscopal support given to successive viking rulers. The archbishops may have retained many of their estates, as would seem to be suggested by the relative absence of Scandinavian place-names on those estates they held in the tenth and eleventh centuries, and this may in turn provide the context for the survival of their churches, which continued to provide pastoral care for the surrounding area.[379] The fact that many churches retained the relics of saints, at least until they were removed by the West Saxon kings, may also indicate an element of institutional continuity.

There is evidence from other areas of the Danelaw for the survival of churches in areas of Scandinavian settlement, which also offers some insights into the contexts in which churches survived. A passage in the *Libellus Æthelwoldi* states that at the time of the Scandinavian conquest there was a monastery at Horningsea (Cambs) under a priest called Coenwald and 'later the people of the place who gathered together from paganism in the grace of baptism gave this minster five hides at Horningsea and two in Eye'. Coenwald's successor was said to have been a follower of Athelstan, suggesting that he remained in post for many years. This evidence indicates, as Dorothy Whitelock put it, that there was thought to have been little, if any, breach of continuity

---

377. C.D. Morris, 'Viking and native in northern England: a case-study', in *Proceedings of the Eighth Viking Congress*, ed. H. Bekker-Nielsen (Odense, 1981), 223–44.

378. G. Bonner, 'St Cuthbert at Chester-le-Street', in *St Cuthbert*, ed. Bonner, Stancliffe and Rollason, 387–95, at 388–9; the *Historia de Sancto Cuthberto* alleges that the viking king Guthfrith bestowed on the community land between the Tyne and the Wear, and it may have been this patronage that was a significant factor in the decision to remain at Chester-le-Street.

379. See Chapter 3, p. 139.

at this church.[380] The existence of numerous small religious foundations by the middle of the tenth century in East Anglia may also suggest that Christianity was thriving in the eastern Danelaw.[381] The East Anglian king Edmund, who had been martyred at the hands of the great viking army of 870, was already venerated as a saint, as is shown by the production of East Anglian coinage bearing the name of the saint. This indicates a tolerance for, if not an actual promotion of, Christianity, and it doubtless also reflects the importance of the church in the legitimation of secular authority in the areas of England which experienced Scandinavian settlement.[382]

A tentative case can be made, then, from a variety of types of evidence for elements of continuity in ecclesiastical organization through the period of Scandinavian settlement. Why was this the case? It has been normal to point to the readiness of the pagan belief-system to admit the Christian God into its pantheon; but although this might begin to explain *how* integration was facilitated, it does not explain *why* it happened. This aspect of Scandinavian activity will be addressed in the next chapter on the wider issues concerning Scandinavian settlement. However, it would not be controversial to state that the Anglo-Saxon church and the Scandinavian settlers eventually adapted themselves to each other; in some instances they did so relatively rapidly, but our evidence also suggests ongoing processes of adaptation and a gradual transition by the settlers from one belief system to another. Paganism is not an easily definable belief-system, and there is much to debate over the matter of what it was to be a Christian in the ninth century; as a result, we may have been too hasty to draw a clear distinction between paganism and Christianity. We also should not assume that Christians and pagans could not interact with each other, trade, marry and live together; there may in any case have been a wide range of religious beliefs held by the various inhabitants of the Danelaw during the late ninth and tenth centuries.[383] Whatever the difficulties faced by the church in the wake of the Scandinavian settlement, in the long run Christianity may have been less a factor which distinguished the indigenous population from the Scandinavian settlers than a force for their integration.

Conclusions

It is apparent that in the seventh, eighth and ninth centuries there was great variety in the size and composition of ecclesiastical communities

---

380. D.W. Whitelock, 'The conversion of the eastern Danelaw', *Saga-Book of the Viking Society for Northern Research*, 12 (1937–45), 159–76, at 169.
381. *Ibid.*, 169–75.
382. *Ibid.*, 164–8; P. Grierson and M.A.S. Blackburn (eds) *Medieval European Coinage, I: The early Middle Ages (5th–10th centuries)* (1986), 319–23.
383. I.N. Wood, 'The conversion of the barbarian peoples', in *The Christian World*, ed. G. Barraclough (1981), 85–98.

of the northern Danelaw, as elsewhere. The functions they performed may also have varied, although it is difficult to be precise in anything more than a handful of cases. It is now thought that most communities were involved in providing some form of pastoral care, and that it is implausible that they should have been entirely inward-looking.[384] It is clear from Bede's letter to Ecgbert, for example, that religious communities and bishops were both greatly involved in secular affairs.[385] Admittedly, little is said in early written sources about the pastoral role of communities, but that has much to do with the fact that these sources are more concerned with the activities of monks and nuns than with the ordained priests who were responsible for pastoral care.[386] Nonetheless, these sources suggest that pastoral care included the following functions: preaching and teaching; baptism; visiting the sick; receiving the faithful into the church on Sundays and major feast days; the prohibition of clearly pagan activities (such as sacrifice to pagan gods, incantation, divination and the taking of auguries); penance and confession; seeking out those who had not recently received clerical ministrations; and an obligation to leave behind a priest 'for the offices of the church' if a minster was moved.[387] It is in the later Anglo-Saxon period that we first hear of control over burial, as the foundation of local churches with graveyards threatened to usurp the parochial rights of the older foundations and reduced their revenues, including tithe and soul-scot. However, excavation of churchyards suggests that centralized burial, and presumably therefore control over burial, was exercised by the major early foundations from the eighth century.[388] The effectiveness and the appeal of these various aspects of pastoral care must have varied, as Bede's complaints reveal.[389] However, it is clear that the church councils of the eighth and early ninth centuries went to great lengths to reinforce the pastoral role of churches, and to 'incorporate the independent proprietary *monasteria* into a coherent pastoral framework'.[390] The written sources give the impression that the ecclesiastical network and the roles of churches were developed and reinforced through the Anglo-Saxon period, rather than being established firmly at a single moment at an early date.[391]

---

384. Thacker, 'Monks, preaching and pastoral care', 142–3.
385. *EHD*, I, no. 170.
386. Blair, 'Ecclesiastical organization', 207–8; Thacker, 'Monks, preaching and pastoral care', 139–60.
387. Thacker, 'Monks, preaching and pastoral care', 138–64.
388. Blair, 'Introduction', 8–9; J. Blair, *Anglo-Saxon Oxfordshire* (1994), 72–3; Biddle, 'Archaeology, architecture and the cult of saints', 16–22.
389. Thacker, 'Monks, preaching and pastoral care', 152–66; Cambridge and Rollason, 'The pastoral organization of the Anglo-Saxon church', 93–4; Blair, 'Ecclesiastical organization', 208–9.
390. Thacker, 'Monks, preaching and pastoral care', 165.
391. For discussion of the ways in which the systematic provision of mother churches emerged gradually, see Sims-Williams, *Religion and Literature*, 168–72; J. Haslam, 'Parishes, churches, wards and gates in eastern London', in *Minsters and Parish Churches*, ed. Blair, 35–43.

Did early communities minister first to a recognized *parochia* or first to those who lived in the immediate vicinity? The late seventh-century charters relating to Breedon on the Hill (Leics) reveal that the priest was indeed responsible for the local *populus*, whereas the Council of *Clofesho* (747) refers rather to districts (*loca et regiones*), but it is unclear whether these two sources of information should be interpreted as relating to different responsibilities.[392] Moreover, it is not certain whether early communities served only their own estates, or larger territories, or what the implications might be of their acquisition of additional lands at subsequent dates. Estates and administrative units were liable to change, and this may have had implications for any early 'parishes' that were based upon them. It is clear, however, that by the tenth century churches did habitually have a defined territory attached to them, and that the area to which they ministered often extended beyond that of their own property, and might include two or more separate estates. Provisions in tenth-century law-codes protect the vested interests of 'old minsters' against newer foundations in the territories they served, and there is little reason to believe that these provisions were recent innovations.[393] The frequent correlation of parish boundaries (recorded in post-medieval sources) with the boundary clauses recorded in Anglo-Saxon charters also suggests that ecclesiastical parishes may be expected, in general, to correspond to some extent with secular territorial units which existed at some point in the Anglo-Saxon period.[394] Although estates continued to be adapted, parishes proved more conservative, and they were seemingly more likely to fragment into smaller parishes than to expand (parishes were not finally crystallized until the twelfth century).

The imprecise usage of terminology by contemporary commentators has encouraged the conclusion that the term 'minster' is 'the most appropriate word for describing pre-[Benedictine] reform religious houses in England'.[395] This has elicited the not unreasonable response that it is a 'lowest common denominator approach',[396] although attempts to distinguish churches on the basis of the words employed by contemporaries is an exercise doomed to failure.[397] The use of the all-encompassing term 'minster' is also a potential route to circularity

---

392. Thacker, 'Monks, preaching and pastoral care', 146–7.
393. *EHD*, I, nos. 40, 44.
394. There have been many studies of this phenomenon; see, for example, *PN Berks*, 617–22; C.C. Taylor, *Dorset* (1970), 49–72; D. Hooke, *Anglo-Saxon Landscapes of the West Midlands: the charter evidence* (BAR British Series, 95, 1981), 34–8; D. Hooke, *The Landscape of Anglo-Saxon Staffordshire: the charter evidence* (1983), 32–7, 63–109; J. Blair, *Early Medieval Surrey: landholding, church and settlement before 1300* (1991), 31–4.
395. S. Foot, 'Anglo-Saxon minsters: a review of terminology', in *Pastoral Care before the Parish*, ed. Blair and Sharpe, 212–25, at 225.
396. Cambridge and Rollason, 'The pastoral organization of the Anglo-Saxon church', 91.
397. *Ibid.*, 88–91; on the futility of the semantic debate, see Blair, 'Ecclesiastical organization', 195–6.

of argument: even if in contemporary usage the term was used of a variety of establishments, it has taken on a specific set of connotations in recent studies, of which the provision of pastoral care at an early date in a defined territory is paramount. It would be a mistake to lump together all pre-viking establishments under the term 'minster', as it implies that we expect all to have shared a similar range of functions. The very fact that a minster could include 'anything from Monkwearmouth or Barking to a head-priest with two or three clerics' should give cause for concern about our use of the term.[398] There is also a tendency to use the term to refer both to churches for which there is some evidence of pre-viking origins and to churches which display 'mother-church' characteristics in the later medieval period. Certainly, some churches have evidence for both pre-viking origins and mother-church status, but others do not, and we would be advised to keep sight of the distinctions; the conflation of distinguishing characteristics may lead us to obscure important differences between churches, and undermine our efforts to trace the emergence of the parochial system.

There are likely to have been many more Anglo-Saxon churches than we are currently able to identify. Some certainly survived to become the parish churches of a later date, but excavation has revealed a number of churches that were abandoned during the Anglo-Saxon period, and also later, in the northern Danelaw, about which we otherwise know little or nothing. The development of ecclesiastical organization was more complex than was once believed, and there was no simple and orderly growth from a network of major pre-viking religious communities to a pattern of local parish churches. Many churches were lost along the way. In the northern Danelaw excavation has revealed that this was the case at Flixborough in the pre-Conquest period and at Barrow upon Humber in the thirteenth century, for example. The inscription at Kirkdale records that the church had fallen into ruin, but in this case it was rebuilt, although on a different scale and alignment, as recent excavation has revealed. Other churches may not have been rehabilitated, but have fallen down and passed out of memory.[399] It is also clear that burial grounds also often went out of use. Many of these, although not all, were adjacent to churches.

The processes by which churchyard burial became the norm varied, both socially and geographically. Whatever the control exercised by mother churches over burial, this did not invariably result in burial at the mother church from the seventh or eighth century. The inhabitants of religious communities, bishops and kings were certainly sometimes buried in churchyards, or within churches, from an early date: King Oswy was buried at Whitby in 670, and the bodies of Kings Edwin (d.

---

398. Blair, 'Ecclesiastical organization', 196, where this fact is used to support the use of the term.
399. The ephemeral nature of pre-Conquest churches is discussed in R.K. Morris, 'The church in the countryside: two lines of enquiry', in *Medieval Villages: a review of current work*, ed. D. Hooke (1985), 47–60, at 55.

633/4) and Oswald (d. 642/3) were removed from the battlefields where they fell to Whitby and Bardney, respectively, in the 680s or 690s.[400] It also seems likely that the aristocracy sought to provide burial for their kindred in and around churches; we might note here the *praefectus* in the *Vita Sancti Cuthberti* who sought to ensure burial in 'holy ground', not implausibly near to a church, and certainly a consecrated cemetery.[401] The excavation of seventh- and eighth-century burials in churchyards and the survival of pre-viking grave slabs and funerary monuments indicate that many churches were focal points for burial and commemoration by the eighth or ninth century for some members of society. However, it is striking that written sources demonstrate a marked lack of interest in provision for, or restrictions on, burial in the Anglo-Saxon centuries, and burial in a cemetery belonging to the mother church may not have been either expected or demanded.[402] Indeed, some of the elaborate barrow burials in the Peak District and elsewhere (such as at Caenby, Lincs) clearly belong within a Christian milieu, and John Blair has seen in such burials a direct parallel with the aristocratic fashion for churchyard burial; those who chose elaborate burial, often in barrows, did so because they did not have strong family ties to any particular 'minster', which would have obliged their kin to take them there and the religious communities to accept them.[403]

Until recently archaeologists had failed to identify graveyards of the eighth to eleventh centuries that were not within churchyards. Small, short-lived eighth- to eleventh-century Anglo-Saxon cemeteries have been found in parts of the northern Danelaw located in the general vicinity of churches but not in surviving churchyards. These include cemeteries at Addingham, Whitby (Abbey Lands Farm), Crayke (north of the churchyard), Pontefract (The Booths), Kirkdale, Ripon and Flixborough.[404] Any or all of these burials may once have been in a churchyard, and the fact that they were later not included in a churchyard may have been because either the church went out of use, or the churchyard contracted in size, perhaps as a result of the various daughter churches of the mother church acquiring their own burial grounds.[405] Elsewhere there are a number of small ninth- or tenth-century burial grounds which preceded the building of a church, as at

---

400.   *HE*, ii, 20; iii, 11–12; iii, 24.
401.   Bede, *Vita S. Cuthberti*, ch. 16; discussed in Thacker, 'Monks, preaching and pastoral care', 148.
402.   *Ibid.*
403.   J. Blair, *The Church in Anglo-Saxon Society, 600–1100* (forthcoming).
404.   M. Adams, 'Excavation of a pre-Conquest cemetery at Addingham, West Yorkshire', *Medieval Archaeology*, 40 (1996), 151–91; Adams, 'Monastery and village at Crayke', 36–40; Loveluck, 'Anglo-Saxon settlement at Flixborough', 148; Rahtz and Watts, 'Kirkdale Anglo-Saxon minster'; Hall and Whyman, 'Settlement and monasticism at Ripon', 63.
405.   For comparable examples, see J. Blair, *Anglo-Saxon Oxfordshire* (1994), 72–3.

Barton upon Humber and Holton-le-Clay (Lincs).[406] The Sites and Monuments Records of the region contain numerous reports of small groups of unaccompanied inhumation burials, aligned west–east, often near to the sites of medieval settlements, any or all of which could belong to the later Anglo-Saxon centuries. Future attention to this group of burials may have important things to reveal about the processes by which the transition to churchyard burial occurred. In sum, the evidence demonstrates that the role of the church in meeting the need for, and influencing the form and location of, burial varied and continued to develop through the later Anglo-Saxon period.

Recent discussions of early medieval ecclesiastical organization have not sufficiently accounted for diversity, preferring, instead, to project single explanatory models. We must allow for the probability that the network of ecclesiastical provision based on a series of mother churches which may be uncovered in later medieval sources owes its form to organic development over a considerable period of time. The best we can hope to achieve, therefore, is an understanding of some of the stages by which the ecclesiastical network was created, an undertaking best achieved on a local scale. The evidence from the northern Danelaw is consistent with that from other regions, which reveals a group of churches founded by the ninth century, serving areas based on the estates on which they sat, that survived to form the mother churches of the later Middle Ages. The nature and efficacy of the pastoral care they provided at an early date are open to debate, but it is evident that the parish structure of the later medieval period finds its origins in the seventh, eighth and ninth centuries, even in the northern Danelaw, where Scandinavian settlement certainly had a disruptive effect. It also seems clear that there was much diversity in early medieval ecclesiastical organization, both in terms of the roles of the churches founded in the seventh, eighth and ninth centuries, and in terms of their subsequent fate. There has been a tendency to highlight royal and episcopal foundations, but it seems clear that aristocratic initiative must also be taken into account. Finally, attention to local detail may help us to move out of the impasse which the debate between the adherents and the critics of the 'minster model' has led us towards. It is certain that ecclesiastical organization was not uniform throughout Anglo-Saxon England, and any attempt to construct a universal model is doomed to failure. This is not to deny that there were broadly similar trends in ecclesiastical development throughout England, but the pace at which ecclesiastical provision proceeded varied. An appropriate model for the development of the Anglo-Saxon church must take account of regional diversity and acknowledge that such diversity may not be simply the product of differences in evidence but may also have much to reveal about real regional variation.

---

406. Rodwell and Rodwell, 'St Peter's church, Barton-upon-Humber', 290–4; J. Sills, 'St Peter's church, Holton-le-Clay, Lincolnshire', *LHA*, 17 (1982), 29–42, at 30–1.

6   The Scandinavian impact

And that year Halfdan shared out the land of the Northumbrians,
and they proceeded to plough and to support themselves
– *The Anglo-Saxon Chronicle*, s.a. 876[1]

This chapter examines the Scandinavian impact on the society of the
northern Danelaw in the ninth and tenth centuries. The previous
chapters have demonstrated that much that was once directly ascribed
to the Scandinavian settlement can now be seen either to have had
earlier origins or to have been the result of later developments.
However, the recent tendency to play down the Scandinavian influence
on the region fails to do justice to the Scandinavian impact. It is clear
that a number of issues have become confused in the study of the
Scandinavian conquest and settlement, and that debate has for too long
revolved around the same set of issues, including the scale of the
Scandinavian settlement, the attempt to identify the precise locations
where Scandinavians settled, the 'Danishness' of the Danelaw, the
paganism of the settlers and the general question of continuity.
Although these issues are related, the nature of the relationship is far
from clear-cut, and too often inadequately supported hypotheses about
one of these aspects of the settlement are used to draw conclusions
about the others.[2] This chapter reconsiders some of the fundamental
principles on which the study of the Scandinavian settlement has been
based, clarifies our preconceptions and brings a new approach to the
evidence.

Ethnic identity

Many interpretations of the Scandinavian impact on Anglo-Saxon
society have been informed by a fairly simplistic understanding of
ethnic identity. The debate about the scale of the Scandinavian
settlement has, whatever the divergent views of the contributors,
generally hinged on a basic understanding that being Danish was a

---

1.   *EHD*, I, no. 1.
2.   D.M. Hadley, ' "And they proceeded to plough and to support themselves": the
     Scandinavian settlement of England', *ANS*, 19 (1997), 69–96.

distinctive identity, and that we can therefore readily 'find the Danes' and their settlements through the use of distribution maps of artefacts bearing Scandinavian motifs, of apparently 'pagan' – and therefore Scandinavian – burials and of Scandinavian place-names, for example. However, the purpose, or the potential for success, of such an undertaking is dubious. There have been numerous recent challenges to the notion that 'national' and 'ethnic' groups were internally homogeneous, historically continuous entities that can be objectively defined by their cultural, linguistic and racial distinctiveness. The manifestation of such groups in the archaeological record in the form of sharply delineated distributions of artefacts has also been open to much critical reappraisal.[3] It is apparent that 'ethnic identity' is not innate and unvarying, and it is now defined less as a concrete or objective fact than as a subjective process by which individuals and groups identified themselves and others within specific contexts.[4] Such contexts might include contact with external forces, a developing awareness of common interests, the maintenance of group cultural conformity, competition for access to resources, and so on. An ethnic group is now understood, then, as a community bound together primarily by a shared and subjective sense of common interests, often, although not invariably, *vis-à-vis* others. Ethnic groups may be characterized by a distinct language, culture, territory or religion, but these characteristics are not necessary or predictable.[5] It is also sometimes the case that there are differences between the self-identification of peoples and their behaviour, on the one hand, and the labels imposed by external commentators, on the other.[6] These ideas have been applied to many regions of early medieval Europe, but have not been discussed explicitly in the context of the Scandinavian settlement of Anglo-Saxon England. Such discussion proves instructive, not least because we are forced to reconsider the appropriateness

---

3. S. Shennan, 'Introduction: archaeological approaches to cultural identity', in *Archaeological Approaches to Cultural Identity*, ed. S. Shennan (1989), 1–32; S. Jones and P. Graves-Brown, 'Introduction: archaeology and cultural identity in Europe', in *Cultural Identity and Archaeology*, ed. P. Graves-Brown, S. Jones and S. Gamble (1996), 1–24; S. Jones, 'Discourses of identity in the interpretation of the past', *ibid.*, 62–80.
4. Recent British and American scholarship has followed in the wake of German scholarship, notably R. Wenskus, *Stammesbildung und Verfassung: das Werden des frühmittelalterlichen Gentes* (Cologne, 1961); H. Wolfram, *History of the Goths* (Berkeley, trans. 1988); H. Wolfram and W. Pohl (eds) *Typen der Ethnogenese unter besondere Berücksichtigung der Bayern* (Vienna, 1990); P. Geary, 'Ethnic identity as a situational construct in the early Middle Ages', *Mitteilungen der Anthropologischen Gesellschaft in Wien*, 113 (1983), 15–26; S. Reynolds, 'What do we mean by "Anglo-Saxon" and "Anglo-Saxons"?', *Journal of British Studies*, 24 (1985), 395–414; P. Amory, 'The meaning and purpose of ethnic terminology in the Burgundian Laws', *EME*, 2 (1) (1993), 1–28; P. Amory, 'Names, ethnic identity and community in fifth- and sixth-century Burgundy', *Viator*, 25 (1994), 1–30; P. Heather, *The Goths* (1996).
5. Jones, 'Discourses', *passim*.
6. Amory, 'Ethnic terminology'.

of the questions we have hitherto asked of our evidence: can we continue to ask whether this or that site is 'Scandinavian' or 'English'? or to use place-name evidence to plot the locations and movements of peoples? or to argue over whether this or that feature of the society and culture of the Danelaw is Danish? We need to address the issue of how language, names and material culture were manipulated by groups and individuals in the ninth and tenth centuries, and the extent to which they both reflected and were used to construct ethnic identities.

'Danes' and the 'Danelaw'

References to 'Danes' in the Anglo-Saxon Chronicle and other written sources, and the existence of the term 'Danelaw' to describe the regions of Scandinavian settlement, have formed the basis for many deductions about the nature of Scandinavian settlement and the 'ethnic' identity of the inhabitants of those regions. However, there are good reasons why this evidence is not a very sound starting-point for such discussions. References to the Danes and the Danelaw appear infrequently and in specific contexts, particularly during times of military or political conflict, or when aspects of the law are being discussed. When we examine these contexts it becomes apparent that they have little to reveal about the majority of the inhabitants of the region, in terms either of how they were perceived or of how they identified themselves.

Although it is common to call the main areas of Scandinavian settlement the 'Danelaw', the term is not recorded earlier than a law-code compiled in 1008, and is most common in legal codes of the eleventh and twelfth centuries, where it is used to distinguish a region in which Danish as opposed to Mercian or West Saxon law was thought to prevail.[7] These uses of the term seem to stem from a recognition that certain regional differences in law coincided with an area known to have once been under some form of Danish control.[8] There is, in fact, little in the law of the region that can be claimed as a Scandinavian creation, and the Scandinavian influence seems to have been largely terminological.[9] Nonetheless, the legal personality of the region was thought to have been Danish: as far back as the mid-tenth century Edgar had legislated in his fourth law-code that 'there should be in force among the Danes such good laws as they best decide on'.[10] Why

---

7.   *EHD*, I, no. 44; J.M. Kaye, 'The Sacrabar', *EHR*, 83 (1968), 744–58; O. Fenger, 'The Danelaw and the Danish law', *Scandinavian Studies in Law*, 16 (1972), 85–96.

8.   P.A. Stafford, 'The Danes and the Danelaw', *History Today* (October, 1986), 17–23, at 19.

9.   Fenger, 'The Danelaw and the Danish law', 94; Kaye, 'The Sacrabar'; F.M. Stenton, *Anglo-Saxon England* (3rd edn, 1971), 506–7; P.H. Sawyer, *The Age of the Vikings* (2nd edn, 1971), 153–4; Stafford, 'The Danes', 19.

10. *EHD*, I, no. 41.

did Edgar legislate separately for 'the Danes', and what does this reveal about ethnic identities in tenth-century England?

The background to Edgar's law-code of 962 × 3 arguably lies in the circumstances of his accession. Although it might appear to imply that society was divided into distinctive 'ethnic' groups which could be identified in objective, legal terms, Edgar's interest in 'the Danes' can be shown to have had a political currency. Edgar succeeded to the former kingdoms of Mercia, Northumbria and East Anglia two years before he succeeded to southern England, on the death of his brother, Eadwig.[11] Between 957 and 959 Edgar's support was located north of the Thames, as the charters he issued confirm, whereas Eadwig's support came from the bishops and ealdormen from south of the Thames. Edgar's accession to the north occurred when he was only 14, and just three years after the expulsion of Eric Bloodaxe from York, and it has been argued that Edgar was set up by the northern magnates to protect their privileges against royal usurpation. Therefore, Edgar's fourth law-code was arguably a measure designed to help a southern king handle the regionalism of the northern part of his kingdom, maintaining a semblance of political unity by recognizing the regional legal traditions of his kingdom.[12] It was also arguably a recognition of the support he had received from the magnates of those regions between 957 and 959; the law-code could be seen as a confirmation of his intention to honour their privileges.[13] The circumstances of his accession, and political reality, provide the context for Edgar's separate legal provision for northern England. Therefore, we have to be wary of using this as evidence for ethnic relations and identities in northern England. Nonetheless, it is reasonable enough to enquire why such 'ethnic' terminology was employed in this and other law-codes.

Patrick Amory has recently discussed the application of ethnic labels in legal contexts in the early medieval period. He has shown that they were often used to identify territories, and that, increasingly, ethnicity was defined by territorial origin and adherence to a particular law-code rather than by blood or descent alone. He has commented that 'law was not so much a result as a major determining factor' of the new ethnic identities forged in the Carolingian period.[14] That is to say, the use of an ethnic label may reveal something of the previous history of the region, the way in which it was perceived from an external perspective, and something of the common legal experience of the inhabitants of that region, but it may reveal little about the biological descent of the inhabitants of the region. It may also have little to reveal

---

11. Stenton, *Anglo-Saxon England*, 364–72; N. Lund, 'King Edgar and the Danelaw', *Mediaeval Scandinavia*, 9 (1976), 181–95.
12. S. Keynes, 'The vikings in England, *c.* 790–1016', in *The Oxford Illustrated History of the Vikings*, ed. P.H. Sawyer (1997), 48–82, at 72.
13. Lund, 'King Edgar', 182.
14. Amory, 'Ethnic terminology', 23.

about the ways in which the inhabitants of a region saw themselves. This argument has resonance for the Danelaw. Following unification of England under a single king and the codification of the various laws of the country, aspects of the history of the three legal regions of England were called upon in labelling these laws: they became known as the areas of West Saxon, Mercian and Danish law. In northern and eastern England pre-existing regionalism had been reinforced by successive political conquests, the arrival of settlers from Scandinavia, and, arguably, the circumstances of Edgar's accession in the mid-tenth century, which further emphasized the autonomy of the northern regions. Edgar's separate legislation for the region was a recognition of political reality, and the employment of ethnic terminology derives from a recognition of the regionalism within England as a whole, and is not primarily a reflection of a perceived binary division – between 'Danes' and 'English' – north of the Thames. The reason for the use of an ethnonym must derive in part from the recognition that there had recently been a conquest from Scandinavia, partly from the fact that some of the leading magnates in the region were recognizably of Scandinavian origin, and partly from the adoption of Old Norse in legal and administrative contexts.[15] The ruling élite of northern England in the tenth century were assuredly not all of Scandinavian extraction, but the conquests of successive armies from Scandinavia, when combined with pre-existing separate regional identities and a determination from the leading magnates (of whatever origin) to maintain regional autonomy, gave vent to expression of a regional political and legal identity which borrowed much from the newcomers. In sum, historical process in the tenth century saw new 'ethnic' identities formed, and these were both informed by and derived from the language of law and of territorial identification.[16] This is not to say, however, that the inhabitants of the Danelaw were, or were considered to be, largely of Danish origin.

It is important to note that the region is not always identified as the Danelaw. It is often referred to as Northumbria, East Anglia or *Norðleoda*. Clearly the 'Danishness' of the region was called into play only at certain times: in some legal contexts and often during times of political or military conflict.[17] Moreover, kings did not always note that their subjects included 'Danes'.[18] Nonetheless, the ongoing legally recognized 'Danishness' of northern England was clearly fostered by

---

15. J. Geipel, *The Viking Legacy: the Scandinavian influence on the English and Gaelic languages* (1971), 70; B.H. Hansen, 'The historical implications of the Scandinavian element in English: a theoretical valuation', *Nowele*, 4 (1984), 53–95; D. Kastovsky, 'Semantics and vocabulary', in *The Cambridge History of the English Language*, ed. R.M. Hogg (1992), I, 290–408, at 320, 332–5.
16. Amory, 'Ethnic terminology', 23; I.N. Wood, 'Ethnicity and ethnogenesis of the Burgundians', in *Typen der Ethnogenese*, ed. Wolfram and Pohl, 53–69, at 53–5, 63–4.
17. Reynolds, ' "Anglo-Saxon" and "Anglo-Saxons" ', 408.
18. Keynes, 'The vikings in England', 70–3.

successive kings: by Æthelred II, who legislated directly for the region in his overtly Danish Wantage code; by Cnut, who confirmed the laws of Edgar; and by Edward the Confessor, who confirmed the laws of Cnut. The recognition of a 'Danish' political constituency in northern England was a useful means for dealing with the élite of that region, and it was also a means by which the latter could foster a sense of regional identity within the English kingdom and in their dealings with the king.[19]

'Danishness' is noticeably often commented upon in England in the context of the new threat from Scandinavia in the later tenth and early eleventh centuries. However, it is not the descendants of Danish immigrants of the late ninth century who are referred to as Danes in sources of this period but, rather, recent arrivals: the Danish raiders, merchants and nobles who arrived from the mid-tenth century, for example. It is revealing that when Æthelred II ordered the massacre of Danes in 1002 the only place in which it can be shown to have taken effect was Oxford, a town far from the regions in which earlier Danish settlement had taken place. For this reason, it has been suggested that the most readily identifiable Danes in England in the early eleventh century were recently arrived urban merchants.[20] As far as the chroniclers were normally concerned, the subjects of the kings of England were English; Danes were invaders and enemies – 'recent Danes', as Susan Reynolds has put it – people who had come recently from Denmark and who might be going back there.[21] The situation after the Norman Conquest provides a point of comparison: in the later eleventh century it can be seen that it was those great lords who maintained strong links with Normandy who, according to the chroniclers, retained their Norman identity longest: lesser men with little or no property in Normandy quickly became known as 'English', although they may have considered themselves to be Norman.[22] Patrick Geary has recently remarked that in the early Middle Ages ethnicity tended to be invoked when an individual seemed 'out of place' in terms of geography or religion, and this observation may be of relevance to understanding some of the references to Danes in England in the tenth and eleventh centuries.[23] To set this in context, it is notable that in the early eleventh century Archbishop Wulfstan added to a panegyric on Edgar in the northern recension of the Anglo-Saxon Chronicle that 'he did one ill-deed too greatly. He loved evil foreign customs and brought too firmly heathen manners within the land, and attracted hither foreigners and enticed harmful people to this

---

19. For a discussion, see M. Innes, 'Danelaw identities: ethnicity, regionalism and political allegiance', in *Cultures in Contact: Scandinavian settlement in England*, ed. D.M. Hadley and J.D. Richards (forthcoming).
20. P.A. Stafford, *Unification and Conquest: a political and social history of England in the tenth and eleventh centuries* (1989), 66.
21. Reynolds, ' "Anglo-Saxon" and "Anglo-Saxons" ', 409.
22. A. Williams, *The English and the Norman Conquest* (1995), 1–6, 187–219.
23. Geary, 'Ethnic identity as a situational construct', 23.

country'.[24] There was clearly a perception, then, in the early eleventh century that foreigners – almost certainly including 'Danes' – had made their presence felt in English society and that some were not well received. Yet although there were complaints about the disruptive effect of recent Danish arrivals 'who had sprung up in this island, sprouting like cockle amongst the wheat' (as is lamented in a charter of Æthelred II), there is little evidence to suggest that there was normally thought to have been anything markedly Scandinavian about eleventh-century society; intermarriage was common and the descendants of these Danish immigrants quickly came to be identified as English.[25]

Nonetheless, the political events of the tenth and early eleventh centuries have frequently been cited as evidence for the reality of ethnic difference in the Danelaw. In the early tenth century successive viking rulers captured York, and in 940 Olaf Guthfrithson used this as a basis to expand control south of the Humber.[26] Certainly, previous Scandinavian settlement may have aroused the ambitions of such rulers, but in practice they relied upon indigenous support, such as that provided by Archbishop Wulfstan, and there is little evidence that Olafwas attempting to unite 'Danish' England. If Olaf was capitalizing on any pre-existing sense of identity it was as likely to have been the claims of earlier Deiran kings of York, who had sometimes ruled south of the Humber.[27] 'Ethnic' differences have also been seen behind the later activities of Swegn, who in 1013 acquired the submission of England north of Watling Street before ravaging southwards.[28] However, there are good reasons to question this assessment. Perhaps the area of earlier Scandinavian settlement did shape the aspirations of Swegn, but there is no evidence that his support was anything other than regional. In fact, unlike Olaf, Swegn did not launch his assault from York, the focal point of earlier Scandinavian rule, but from Gainsborough (Lincs) on the river Trent; this decision may have been encouraged by knowledge of the disaffection of leading noble families in the north Midlands and by the presence of recently arrived Danish merchants in the urban centres of the region.[29] If Swegn harboured any notions of mobilizing Danish support in the region (and there is little evidence that he did), then we should not suppose that he simply called on the descendants of the earlier settlers. After a century and a half of intermarriage and social mixing, it is difficult to see how

24. *ASC*, D, *s.a.* 959; Stenton, *Anglo-Saxon England*, 371, n. 2.
25. A. Williams, ' "Cockles amongst the wheat": Danes and English in the western Midlands in the first half of the eleventh century', *Midland History*, 11 (1986), 1–22.
26. Stenton, *Anglo-Saxon England*, 323–43, 356–8.
27. Stafford, *Unification and Conquest*, 65.
28. W.E. Kapelle, *The Norman Conquest of the North: a region and its transformation 1000–1135* (1979), 14–15; Stenton, *Anglo-Saxon England*, 384–5; Reynolds, ' "Anglo-Saxon" and "Anglo-Saxons" ', 406–7, 410–1.
29. Stafford, *Unification and Conquest*, 65–6.

he could have done so. However many settlers there were, they surely could not have maintained a completely separate existence and identity which could be readily mobilized by Swegn. It is improbable that it would have been possible at that date to distinguish people of exclusively English or Danish descent: to reduce the issue to the terms in which it has commonly been discussed, were the 'Danes' those with Danish personal names, or those who wore Danish-style jewellery, or those who lived in places with Danish names? Certainly there may have been some who considered themselves to be Danish, or of Danish descent, but if Swegn wanted to draw on 'Danish' support, it would have to be from people who had become firmly wedded to indigenous society.[30] Swegn's activities were, in any case, part of an attempt to capture the English kingdom from the north; there is no evidence that it was a movement to unite the 'Danish' parts of England. The areas that submitted to him did not do so in terms of 'ethnic' affiliation but as administrative units: the ealdormanries of Lindsey and Northumbria, and the Five Boroughs. Moreover, the inhabitants of places outside the Danelaw, such as Oxford, Winchester and Bath, also readily surrendered to him. Pauline Stafford has observed the absence of what she calls an 'ethnic voice' in the various recorded disputes of the late tenth and early eleventh centuries; regional grievances are more prominent.[31] Recent studies of the construction of ethnic identity have rejected the notion that ethnicity was an objective phenomenon which invariably created antagonism, and instead have explored the extent to which ethnicity might be mobilized in the context of political conflict; as a means of moulding an identity and a sense of community in opposition to one's enemies.[32] Such reasoning may be applicable to the northern Danelaw. Regional disputes and political manoeuvring do not provide evidence for innate ethnic difference; the documentary evidence suggests that the former processes may have revived memories of the diverse ancestry of inhabitants of parts of England in the tenth and eleventh centuries, not that existing 'ethnic' differences were the cause of such antagonisms.

References to Danes and the 'Danishness' of eastern and northern England in the tenth and eleventh centuries have more than one context: the political disunity of the English kingdom; and the continuing arrival of merchants and political opportunists from Denmark. The meaning and purpose of ethnic terminology are often related to specific situations of conflict in England, used as 'the instrument of political agendas'.[33] It also arguably became simply a useful label for the region and its inhabitants. The mere existence of

---

30.   Reynolds, ' "Anglo-Saxon" and "Anglo-Saxons" ', 407.
31.   P.A. Stafford, 'The reign of Æthelred II: a study in the limitations on royal policy', in *Ethelred the Unready*, ed. D. Hill (BAR British Series, 59, 1978), 17–21.
32.   Wolfram, *History of the Goths*; Geary, 'Ethnic identity as a situational construct', 25.
33.   Amory, 'Ethnic terminology', 28.

the 'Danelaw' and references to 'Danes' in England do not, it may be suggested, provide a very sound basis for any argument concerning the ethnic affiliations of the inhabitants of northern and eastern England. There is, indeed, little in the documentary evidence to suggest that the descendants of the Danish settlers of the late ninth century continued to be regarded as such through the tenth and eleventh centuries. That is not to say, however, as Susan Reynolds has observed, that no one in the Danelaw ever felt themselves to be 'Danish', or 'English', but rather that the documentary evidence we have for such feelings is less substantive than is sometimes supposed.[34]

Who were the Scandinavian settlers and did they have a common identity?

Many interpretations of the Scandinavian settlement have been predicated on the notion that the Scandinavian settlers had some sort of common identity and purpose. Yet it is unlikely that even the smaller war-bands were composed exclusively of people who thought of themselves as Danes, or of people from the same region. We ought not to be misled by the chroniclers who lumped together the raiders under the title 'Danes' or 'Northmen', not least because it can often be seen that there were divergent interests within those groups.[35] Viking armies operated all over the place and their war-bands are likely to have been ethnically mixed, not least because of their ability to attract allies and followers from the regions they raided. The lack of consistency in viking activity is another indication that interests could and did change, and armies were not averse to changing sides in a dispute: as Niels Lund has put it, 'the vikings were not united against anything or anybody, and were as pleased to fight other vikings as they were to fight Christians or Muslims if the prospects of booty were good'.[36] This is not to say that viking armies did not have common interests, only that it seems inappropriate to describe them as 'Danish' or 'Scandinavian' when their interests sometimes clearly coincided with those of the people they had formerly been raiding. The fact that the Danish territories did not yet constitute a consolidated kingdom does not in itself preclude the possibility that those who came to England developed some sense of group solidarity in the face of other peoples, but the political circumstances of their activities were sufficiently complex for us to hesitate to describe them using ethnic labels. It is arguable that the ultimate origin of viking leaders and their followers became irrelevant after settlement began, and any feelings of common ethnic identity and military solidarity were overlain by those

---

34. Reynolds, ' "Anglo-Saxon" and "Anglo-Saxons" ', 411.
35. J.L. Nelson, 'The Frankish Empire', in *The Vikings*, ed. Sawyer, 19–47, at 35.
36. N. Lund, 'Allies of God or man? The viking expansion in a European context', *Viator*, 19 (1989), 45–59, at 47 for the quotation.

of political and social reality, which often involved accommodation with indigenous leaders and their followers.

The division between conquerors and conquered in the Danelaw would have been difficult to maintain once settlement began. The notionally divergent interests of the indigenous population and the Scandinavian settlers must have been thrown into confusion by subsequent conquest of the region by the kings of Wessex and of Dublin. Given the political context, it is difficult to envisage a separate 'Scandinavian' identity being long sustained, by either the leaders of the Scandinavian settlement or their followers. Indeed, we ought to remember that the Scandinavian settlement was a protracted affair, led by a diversity of individuals who often came via other parts of Britain and Ireland. In the face of continuing conquest and rapidly changing political circumstances a commonality of interest might be forged between peoples who initially had divergent interests, and following the incorporation of Mercia, Northumbria and East Anglia into the English kingdom the sense of difference from other parts of the kingdom can only have served to further the creation of a society, and a set of interests and concerns, that are best, if awkwardly, summed up as Anglo-Scandinavian.[37] Under this label we might include a whole range of regional interests relating both to the former history of the regions, and to the circumstances of conquest and settlement by Scandinavian peoples. The political situation of northern England was sufficiently complex between the 870s and the mid-tenth century for it to have been difficult to maintain clear divisions between 'Danish' and 'English' interests; moreover, one of the interested parties in northern England, the house of Wessex, had hijacked Englishness for its own purposes. It is perhaps not, then, so surprising that aspects of Scandinavian culture were so readily adopted in northern England, as part, among other things, of a process of marking out the political and cultural distinctiveness of the region. If a distinctive Scandinavian culture was maintained in the Danelaw, it was one that was promoted and utilized by individuals of diverse backgrounds, not simply those whose ancestors were from Scandinavia.

Of course, some of the Scandinavian settlers may have wished to maintain some form of 'Scandinavian' identity, but in doing so they did not simply draw on the culture from which they had come, and they borrowed much from the indigenous cultures of England and Britain. There was also much that was new, and although we often label it Danish or Scandinavian we have to remember that there are often no direct antecedents in Scandinavia. None of these observations about ethnic identity and the common interests of the settlers depends on decisions about the numbers of Scandinavian settlers, and it does not help to confuse the two issues.

The emphasis on what Stenton called the 'particularism of the Danes' does not take account of the divergent interests among the

---

37. For comparison with the situation after the Norman Conquest, see Williams, *The English and the Norman Conquest*, 1–6, 187–219.

Scandinavian settlers, determined by such factors as social status, age, gender, family connections, profession, and so on.[38] It is unlikely that the leaders of viking armies should have had exactly the same interests as the peasant hordes who supposedly followed in their wake; and we know that viking armies were adept at picking up a wide variety of followers who had divergent interests. Moreover, the leaders of the Scandinavian settlers quickly adapted themselves to indigenous modes of authority and formed allegiances with indigenous rulers; that is where their interests more surely lay, rather than with peasant immigrants. Whatever communal interests the Scandinavian settlers may have had, through their shared language, place of origin, common purpose, and so on, those interests must have been thrown into confusion by the circumstances of conquest and settlement, and in the face of continuing conquests and settlements of the region from Scandinavia, Dublin and Wessex. We should not expect the Scandinavian settlers to have responded in a uniform manner to the circumstances of conquest and settlement, any more than we should expect a uniform indigenous response.[39] Neither should we assume that the settlers and their descendants remained a self-consciously different ethnic group within the society of the Danelaw; this is a matter to be demonstrated, and not assumed.

Ethnic identity, language and material culture

The documentary evidence does not, then, provide very much evidence about the ethnic identities of the majority of the inhabitants of the Danelaw, and it also gives reasons to doubt the notion that the Scandinavian settlers shared or maintained a long-standing common identity. Linguistic evidence and the material culture from the northern Danelaw have commonly been cited as proof that the Scandinavian settlers were a recognizable element within society and that they retained a separate identity through the tenth century and beyond. This evidence is considered below in detail. Here it is necessary only to make two preliminary points. First, it is now widely recognized that language was an important element in the construction and negotiation of ethnic identities, but that there is no necessary or predictable correlation between language and ethnic identity. Recent research in socio-linguistics has highlighted the ways in which language might be manipulated in given cultural contexts, as an act of identity, and the ways in which it was culturally variable.[40] Second,

---

38.   F.M. Stenton, 'The Danes in England', *Proceedings of the British Academy*, 13 (1927), 1–46, at 46.
39.   Hadley, 'Scandinavian settlement of England', 87–8, 95.
40.   See, for example, J. Hines, 'Focus and boundary in linguistic varieties in the North-West Germanic continuum', in *Friesische Studien II*, ed. V.F. Faltings, A.G.H. Walker and A. Wilts (Odense, 1995), 35–62.

although individuals and groups actively used material culture in the processes of group identification, it is now widely recognized that the distribution of given artefact-types is not necessarily consistent with the location of self-conscious ethnic groupings.[41]

Two issues have emerged from the previous discussion. First, there is reason to doubt that the Scandinavian settlers retained a separate and self-consciously Scandinavian or Danish identity through the tenth and into the eleventh century, as was once thought. Moreover, 'Danishness' was not a term restricted in its contemporary use to the descendants of the settlers, becoming, rather, a label for the whole region and all its inhabitants at various times. Chroniclers were sometimes able to identify groups of Danes, but they did not do so consistently, and generally did so when describing conflict or political issues. Second, a case has been made in other branches of linguistics and archaeology for doubting whether ethnic groups may be identified straightforwardly through linguistic traits or the distribution of artefacts. In order to discuss further the Scandinavian settlement we need to address the following questions: how was the settlement achieved? how did the Scandinavian rulers establish control? how did indigenous lords respond? what was the impact of the settlement on language and material culture? and how far does this evidence reflect the nature of the Scandinavian settlement?

The role of the church in the northern Danelaw

The previous chapter argued that the ecclesiastical organization of the region suffered less long-term disruption at the hands of the Scandinavians than has often been supposed, although that is not to deny the damage suffered by many individual churches and ecclesiastics.[42] How did the Scandinavians respond to the church, and how did ecclesiastics respond to the Scandinavians? Clearly there were differences between the religious beliefs and practices of the indigenous populations and the newcomers, and there was undoubtedly disruption to the Anglo-Saxon church and an apparent crisis of confidence among some ecclesiastics. Nonetheless, the church, its role in society and the material culture with which it was associated were ultimately of great importance for the integration of the settlers into indigenous society.

Although much damage may have been done to the interests of the church – for which there is, however, in consequence little enough specific evidence – ultimately the church did accommodate the

---

41. A useful recent review of archaeological approaches to ethnicity is S. Jones, *The Archaeology of Ethnicity: constructing identities in the past and present* (1997).
42. For a recent critical response of the tendency to downplay viking destruction of churches, see D. Dumville, *The Churches of North Britain in the First Viking-Age*, Fifth Whithorn Lecture (1997), 8–10.

Scandinavian settlers. It is, then, essential first to discuss the ways in which the church responded to the challenges posed by the arrival of a group of non-Christians in society. A few documented incidents provide some possible insights: the baptism of 'pagans' in the vicinity of Horningsea (Cambs) by the priest Coenwald: the baptism of Guthrum following his defeat by Alfred at Edington in 878; the baptism of the wife and sons of the viking lord Hæsten sometime before 893; the election of Guthfrith as king by the community of St Cuthbert; the acceptance of Christianity by Sihtric, king of York, following his marriage to King Athelstan's sister; and the baptism of Olaf Guthfrithson and the confirmation of King Ragnald, at which King Edmund stood sponsor.[43] These incidents suggest that the role of kings and individual ecclesiastics was central to the conversion of the Scandinavian leaders, and to the integration of them into Christian forms of lordship and kingship. It is noteworthy that there is no tradition of missionary activity from Wessex to the Danelaw. This absence may be significant, especially when we remember that there *is* a written tradition about West Saxon missionary activity in Scandinavia.[44] The fact that most of the bishoprics of northern and eastern England were left vacant between the later ninth and mid-tenth centuries and the accompanying apparent disappearance of many religious communities make it difficult to envisage how the church managed to deal with the Scandinavian settlers and their paganism, since the bishops and religious communities between them had been responsible for both providing pastoral care and training new recruits to the religious life. Nonetheless, it seems plausible to assume that the conversion of the Scandinavian settlers was achieved within the Danelaw itself, and through the efforts of the ecclesiastics of that region.[45]

However, we need to consider what we think the process from 'paganism' to 'Christianity' actually involved. We know very little about pagan beliefs in the ninth and tenth centuries, and our earliest recorded evidence is undoubtedly heavily influenced by contact with Christianity. Equally, it is not entirely clear what being a good Christian would have entailed, although baptism, attendance at church, adherence to the ecclesiastical hierarchy and restraint from certain prohibited practices might be expected. Furthermore, there are distinctions to be drawn between baptism, which might be an immediate event, and an individual's and a group's daily practices thereafter. Conversion to Christianity might be achievable in some sense through baptism, but the broader Christianization of a person's

---

43. See pp. 291–2 above; *ASC*, D, *s.a.* 893, 925, 943.
44. L. Abrams, 'The Anglo-Saxons and the Christianization of Scandinavia', *ASE*, 24 (1995), 213–49.
45. For discussion, see L. Abrams, 'Conversion and assimilation', in *Cultures in Contact*, ed. Hadley and Richards; J. Barrow, 'Survival and mutation: ecclesiastical institutions in the Danelaw in the ninth and tenth centuries', *ibid.*

behaviour and of wider society might be a more protracted process. The success of the church in combating what Richard Morris has called the 'cobweb of superstitions, tendencies, customs and relatively simple propitiatory rituals' of paganism is unknown, but comparison with other parts of Europe in the early Middle Ages, where condemnations of 'superstitious' practice were common, suggests that it may have been extremely difficult to prohibit practices that probably had more to do with social relations than with any structured religion.[46] Indeed, it may be that other factors, such as the growth of urbanism in the northern Danelaw, played a more important role in dissolving pagan practices, as they gave rise to new economic, social and institutional relationships which were expressed through new forms of popular culture and practice.[47] Acceptance of some aspects of Christianity (such as models of kingship, art styles, material culture, iconography) need not signify total abandonment of other practices and beliefs. The receptiveness of individuals to Christianity doubtless varied according to social status, and what leaders might do need not necessarily determine what their followers and the rest of society did.[48] Although in some circumstances groups may have been regarded as, and perhaps even to some extent thought of themselves as, Christian if their leaders converted and accepted the trappings of Christianity, this may have had little impact on the ways in which most people conducted themselves on a daily basis, or on their burial practices.[49]

The paganism of the Scandinavian settlers must have initially distinguished them from the indigenous population. Yet it is well known that viking armies commonly found allies among the peoples they were raiding, and their paganism did not always prevent alliance with lay lords or even ecclesiastics.[50] The latter may have preferred to deal with Christians – and alliance between pagan vikings and Christians often led to baptism into the Christian faith – but ultimately the importance of the alliance lay in the advantages that viking leaders and their followers could offer, which was commonly to add their weight to one side in some power struggle. Paganism was hence not an insurmountable obstacle to interaction with Christians.

We have seen that a number of studies have argued that there was some continuity in ecclesiastical life: attention has focused upon the alliances forged between Scandinavian lords and ecclesiastics, the known survival of a handful of communities alongside the overwhelming

---

46. R.K. Morris, *Churches in the Landscape* (1989), 61–2.
47. *Ibid.*, 62; on urbanism, see p. 327 below.
48. E.A. Thompson, 'The Visigoths from Fritigern to Euric', *Historia*, 12 (1963), 105–26; I.N. Wood, 'Christians and pagans in ninth-century Scandinavia', in *The Christianization of Scandinavia*, ed. B. Sawyer, P.H. Sawyer and I.N. Wood (Alingsas, 1987), 36–67, at 59.
49. A series of models are explored in R.A. Fletcher, *The Conversion of Europe: from paganism to Christianity, 371–1386* (1997).
50. Lund, 'Viking expansion', 50–1.

evidence for the coincidence between the locations of pre-viking religious communities and later mother churches, the issuing of coinage in the Danelaw bearing the names of Christian saints, the proliferation of stone sculpture in the tenth century, which is generally found in ecclesiastical contexts, and upon the general lack of evidence for 'pagan' practices.[51] However, any argument for continuity in ecclesiastical organization needs to do more than to cite a handful of miscellaneous examples. Continuity may not, in any case, be the most pertinent term to employ to describe a situation which may have involved, rather, restoration after a period of disruption. How did the church, or individual churches and ecclesiastics, to be more accurate, manage to remain relevant and to find a role in the changing socio-political circumstances of the later ninth and the tenth centuries?

The emergence of 'royal' dynasties in parts of Scandinavia during the Viking Age caused a great deal of competition for power and commonly led to the exile or departure of disaffected followers or offshoots of the various dynasties, who went off in search of somewhere to rule. Once removed from their background, as Patrick Wormald has observed, it is not perhaps surprising that they should have readily accepted aspects of Christianity, as they sought to establish themselves in an unstable environment – in which other Scandinavian leaders and indigenous lords were vying for power – since the church could offer models for kingship and the exercise of power.[52] In short, the church offered a means for the Scandinavian rulers, as much as indigenous lords, to legitimate their rule.

It was also in the interests of the church for such a situation to obtain: by promoting the interests of a handful of Scandinavian rulers it echoed a well-worn policy for instilling order into a turbulent situation. The expansionist policies of the house of Wessex may have focused the minds of individual ecclesiastics in the northern Danelaw, because it seems evident that an independent kingdom of Northumbria was not part of the West Saxon agenda. So, the documentary sources indicate that on a broad level there were pressures from both sides for some sort of accommodation to be made between the church and the new arrivals from Scandinavia. There had been a long tradition of the church waiting to see which way political upheaval would go before taking sides, as can be seen in the behaviour of Archbishop Wulfhere, who is said to have waited at Addingham (Yorks) while the struggle between Osberht and Ælla and a viking army was taking place in 867 and who then managed to make accommodation with the viking appointment as king, Egbert, with his successor Ricsige (who were probably both local men) and with the viking promoted by the community of St Cuthbert, Guthfrith, to whom he permitted burial in

---

51. See Chapter 5, pp. 289–92.
52. P. Wormald, 'Viking studies: whence and whither?', in *The Vikings*, ed. R.T. Farrell (1982), 128–51, at 144–7.

the Minster at York.[53] This policy towards the raiders and settlers was continued by his successor, Archbishop Wulfstan.[54]

There is little more documentary evidence for the relationship between the church and the Scandinavian settlers, and the role of the church in the political struggles of the ninth and tenth centuries, but these issues may be explored further through an examination of the sculptural and burial evidence from the northern Danelaw.

Stone sculpture in the northern Danelaw

Although the body of stone sculpture from the northern Danelaw is widely regarded as belonging to a Christian milieu because of its association with churches, there has been much debate about whether aspects of the sculpture should be described as 'pagan' or 'secular' (Fig. 52). This debate has focused on those panels which display scenes apparently derived from Norse mythology, or depict figures involved in what may be regarded as non-ecclesiastical activities such as hunting or wearing armour. Richard Bailey has recently argued, however, that many of the scenes commonly described as 'pagan' could be interpreted as Christian teaching and art 'being presented in Scandinavian terms', in which parallels were drawn between Christian themes and Scandinavian mythology and pagan beliefs. There are, for example, possible parallels between depictions of the Sigurd legend and eucharistic images, as both involve enlightenment through consumption, of the dragon's blood and the host respectively. Other images, such as those involving snakes, may have had resonance for both Christian and pagan viewers, and may have been deliberately multivocal images.[55] Bailey has also urged us to think in terms of a 'fusion' of styles rather than the 'overwhelming of one by the other', and to think of the motifs as 'secular' rather than 'pagan'.[56] This is a useful way of thinking about the sculpture as it begins to break down some of the rather blunt categories traditionally used. In general, however, it may be that discussions of the significance of this type of sculpture have been, and are still, based on a fundamental misunderstanding of the nature of early medieval élite behaviour and the role of Christianity in society, and have set up a false dichotomy between 'secular' and 'Christian' values and images. The debate about stone sculpture in the northern Danelaw is reminiscent of the debate

---

53. *Æthelweard*, 35; A.P. Smyth, *Scandinavian York and Dublin: the history and archaeology of two related kingdoms* (2 vols, 1975), I, 44–6.
54. D.W. Whitelock, 'The dealings of the kings of England with Northumbria in the tenth and eleventh centuries', in *The Anglo-Saxons: studies presented to Bruce Dickins*, ed. P. Clemoes (1959), 70–88.
55. R.N. Bailey, *England's Earliest Sculptors* (1997), 77–94; see also J.T. Lang, 'Sigurd and Welland in pre-Conquest carving from northern England', *YAJ*, 48 (1976), 83–94.
56. R.N. Bailey, *Viking Age Sculpture in Northern England* (1980), 83–4.

Figure 52 Examples of Anglo-Scandinavian sculpture from Kirklevington, Levisham and Brompton (Yorks) (shown at a scale of 1:20)

over the poem *Beowulf*. Its mixture of pagan rites, secular subject matter and biblical citations makes it hard to classify from a modern Christian standpoint. Patrick Wormald resolved these debates to a large extent by emphasizing the extent to which the Anglo-Saxon church had absorbed the values of the nobility and their heroic ethos. The 'aristocratic environment of early English Christianity' makes the creation and the enjoyment of the poem understandable, even within a monastic environment. A further point to note is the fact that this is, of course, only one perspective on the poem, and that there was clearly a strain of ecclesiastical thought that did not find such poems acceptable.[57] In many ways the stone sculpture of the Danelaw reflects values similar to those of *Beowulf*, and both our and contemporary responses to it will depend on what perspective we take on what constituted appropriate Christian behaviour. The church in the northern Danelaw was doing what it was well equipped to do, and adapting itself to new circumstances, even if some of its members might have disproved of its methods. It is arguable that there is little, if anything, about the sculpture that can be regarded as un-Christian, assuming that we take a sufficiently, and appropriately, broad view of what was acceptable Christian behaviour.

The sculpture is a material manifestation of a period of contact and acculturation. It is, of course, rarely possible to say who the patron of the sculpture was, but its symbolism reflects a number of possible contexts for production. It may have been the product of indigenous patronage by a lord, perhaps even an ecclesiastic, trying to understand the culture of the newcomers and expressing newly formed allegiances. Or it was the product of the patronage of a Scandinavian lord trying to record his presence and to legitimate his authority by establishing links with the past and with indigenous traditions. Or perhaps it was produced for someone who was of mixed Scandinavian and indigenous origins. Crucially, patrons of whatever origins recognized that if you were anybody in the society of the northern Danelaw, you patronized stone sculpture and utilized a well-known repertoire of symbols, and in this way the stone sculpture did not simply passively reflect social relations and cultural interaction, but played an active role in creating them. The fusion of motifs and ideas from different traditions was undoubtedly part of the processes by which cultural assimilation was achieved. This is not to say, however, that sculpture was invariably commissioned and displayed for self-consciously political or cultural reasons; the role of emulation needs to be considered, and many may have commissioned particular sculptural forms simply because they were what was available, or it was what everyone else in their social world did.

It is not easy to determine the self-conscious choices made by those

---

57. P. Wormald, 'Bede, "Beowulf" and the conversion of the Anglo-Saxon aristocracy' in *Bede and Anglo-Saxon England*, ed. R.T. Farrell (BAR British Series, 46, 1978), 32–95, at 57 for the quotation.

who commissioned and produced sculpture, but in context it is possible to suggest a range of possibilities. Recent attempts to establish a chronology for the sculpture of the region have tended to suggest that it can be assigned to a much shorter period of production than was allowed for by older chronologies which attempted to identify steadily evolving processes of production spread over a wide time-span. The art-historical approach has been subject to critical re-evaluation by studies that have attempted to place monuments more securely in their historical and cultural context. The general absence of later tenth-century Scandinavian styles (Mammen and Ringerike) and the recognition that the same workshop could produce radically different designs prompted James Lang to ascribe most of the Anglo-Scandinavian sculpture to the late ninth or early tenth century.[58] Recent detailed work on cutting techniques, the methods of laying out the decorative scheme and the dimensions of particular motifs has provided new insights into sculpture production. These elements of sculptural production are precise and idiosyncratic, and their study has permitted the recognition that the same workshop could produce monuments with radical differences in ornament and form: for example, it has been shown that the round cross-shaft at Masham was produced by the same hand as the squared cross-shaft from Cundall (Yorks), whereas previously these monuments had been ascribed very different chronologies because of the differences in design.[59] The implications of this redefinition of typologies have a wider currency. The establishment of typologies of many types of artefact has, in fact, been dependent on the perceived truism that people who live close together in time and space are more likely to do things in a similar manner than those who are more distant from one another. Many of our typologies may require reconsideration, because it is becoming apparent that people in one region at any one time may actually do things very differently. Those who created artefacts were able and inclined to produce them in a range of styles, and those who commissioned, bought and used material objects were offered a choice.

We should not expect the response to the Scandinavian settlement to have everywhere been the same, nor for it to have been everywhere articulated in similar ways through sculpture production. It should be noted, for example, that not all sculpture produced in the later ninth and tenth centuries adopted Scandinavian motifs, and it has recently been suggested by Phil Sidebottom that a reason for this in the Peak District may be the survival of regional polities which expressed shared cultural identity through the display of similar iconographic schemes on stone sculpture. The advance of West Saxon rule may have rendered inappropriate the adoption of the Scandinavian-influenced

58.   J.T. Lang, 'Recent studies in the pre-Conquest sculpture of Northumbria', in *Studies in Medieval Sculpture*, ed. F.H. Thompson (1983), 177–89.
59.   *Ibid.*, 185.

iconography currently fashionable further north.[60] Furthermore, David Stocker has argued, as we have seen, that the stone sculpture produced in northern Lincolnshire in the earlier part of the tenth century had very close affiliations with that produced in York, but that later, after incorporation into the English kingdom, a more southern influence may be observed.[61] These transitions in sculptural motifs arguably reflect the changing political map of the region, and emphasize the ways in which sculpture both was central to lordship and was used to convey messages over wide areas.

The use of a variety of iconographic systems found in the northern Danelaw may have been deliberate, and perhaps deliberately ambiguous, allowing those who saw it to derive varied impressions from it. The context was a period of rapidly changing political allegiances, successive conquests, and settlement by people from different cultural backgrounds, so the diversity of motifs employed is not surprising. In time, perhaps, some motifs and styles may have become simply the 'fashion' for sculptural design in parts of northern England. It is notable that differences in sculptural style between northern and southern England continued well into the eleventh century (even following the second Scandinavian conquest and the reign of Cnut), and perhaps formed part of the way in which northern lords, whatever their origins, continued to display their sense of separateness from southern rule. This is a reason for maintaining that whatever regional identities were expressed through the sculpture of the northern Danelaw, they were not primarily reflecting a self-consciously Scandinavian identity. If that were the case we might expect to find a more receptive home for eleventh- and twelfth-century Danish, Swedish and Norwegian styles in northern England, but we do not, and they are found mostly in southern and eastern England: for example, the sarcophagus at St Paul's, and another from All Hallows (London) decorated with the Ringerike style; the architectural fragment decorated with the Urnes style from St Andrew's, Jevington (Sussex); the capital from Norwich Cathedral decorated in the Urnes style; and the apparent Scandinavian influence on the decorated stone, possibly from a shrine, at Winchester (Hants). Indeed, the infiltration of later Scandinavian styles (Ringerike and Urnes, in particular) can be found in a number of media in southern England, on items of jewellery and in manuscript illuminations produced at Winchcombe Abbey (Glos). Such styles are rarely found in the northern Danelaw: exceptions include the grave slab from Otley (Yorks) and the possible book

---

60. This interpretation depends on revision of the dates traditionally assigned to this sculpture: P. Sidebottom, 'Schools of Anglo-Saxon stone sculpture in the north Midlands' (Ph.D. thesis, University of Sheffield, 1994); P. Sidebottom, 'Monuments that mark out viking land', *British Archaeology*, 23 (April 1997), 7; P. Sidebottom, 'The Ecclesfield cross and "Celtic" survival', *Transactions of the Hunter Archaeological Society*, 19 (1997), 43–55.
61. See Chapter 5, p. 288.

mounts found at Lincoln.[62] Although sculptural production in the northern Danelaw may have adopted Scandinavian styles and iconography initially in response to the conquest of the region by groups from Scandinavia, many of these motifs were retained despite the growing pressure of West Saxon domination. 'Scandinavian' cultural motifs may, then, have become in parts of northern society either a mark of the difference of the region – rather than serving to denote or create 'Scandinavian' identity – or simply fashion.

There are distinct regional patternings in the distribution of particular forms of sculpture and iconography.[63] One influence on these distributions must have been the desire on the part of some lords to memorialize themselves through the use of region-wide symbols and motifs. This may have much to do with regional political groups and influence. But other determinants include the location of schools of sculpture, and possibly also the nature of the churches at which this sculpture was displayed. We have noted that the sculpture at Stonegrave (Yorks) is markedly different from that at other churches in the vicinity, where there is a much wider range of new designs in the tenth century.[64] One interpretation would be that the sculpture displayed at newly founded 'manorial' churches was more receptive to new social and cultural trends than were some of the older-established churches, which also had a concern to maintain past traditions, as well as to respond to new developments. In other words, we should not focus solely on the 'ethnicity' paradigm or even on the religious history of the region when interpreting the sculpture from the region; political and seigneurial issues were as, if not more, important.

In sum, the sculpture is a testament to regional lordship and its displays of authority, patronage and allegiance. It appears to be an art form which both Scandinavian and indigenous lords commissioned and displayed. It also serves as an important reminder of the role that the church occupied during the ninth and tenth centuries. We should not, however, assume that it necessarily represents rapid conversion and Christianization, not least because the sculpture cannot be closely dated; nonetheless, it does provide an insight into some of the mechanisms by which the settlers were converted, and adopted and adapted aspects of indigenous culture.

---

62. Bailey, *England's Earliest Sculptors*, 95–104; E. Roesdahl (ed.), *The Vikings in England and Their Danish Homeland* (1982), 84, 180, 182–4; J. Graham-Campbell (ed.) *Cultural Atlas of the Viking World* (1994), 139.
63. Sidebottom, 'Schools of Anglo-Saxon stone sculpture'; D. Stocker, 'Five Towns funerals: decoding diversity in Danelaw stone sculpture', in *Proceedings of the Thirteenth Viking Congress*, ed. J. Graham-Campbell, R. Hall, J. Jesch and D. Parsons (forthcoming).
64. See Chapter 5, p. 290.

Burial

The interpretation of the evidence for Viking Age burials in the northern Danelaw has long been a controversial issue, associated with different interpretations of the fate of the church and of the form of ecclesiastical organization following the period of Scandinavian settlement. There are a small number of ninth- and tenth-century burials from the Danelaw (and a few others from other parts of England) which are accompanied by grave goods and a few cremation burials which have been interpreted as 'pagan', and therefore Scandinavian (Fig. 6). The problem has always been that there are very few, and that the furnished inhumations have a habit of turning up in churchyards. Various rival explanations have been offered: loss of evidence due to the churchyard context; the observation that 'pagan practice remains pagan practice' wherever it occurs; the rapid conversion of the Scandinavians; a small-scale settlement of Scandinavians.[65] There may, however, be more to be said in the light of the wider social context, and through an examination of the various forms of burial practice in the northern Danelaw in the ninth and tenth centuries.

In order to identify Scandinavian settlement on the basis of burial evidence it would be necessary to establish that the settlers and the indigenous populations had differing burial rites. It is often supposed that by the later ninth century in England burials were normally located in churchyards and were unaccompanied by grave goods, and that this contrasts with Scandinavian burials, which included inhumations accompanied by grave goods, cremations and burial in barrows.[66] However, burial in churchyards was not universal in the ninth century in the northern Danelaw, and may have been restricted to the élite in many instances.[67] Moreover, artefacts – whether the product of clothed burial or deliberate deposition – are sometimes found in burials of the ninth century in the Danelaw.[68] Burial in or near to prehistoric barrows is also occasionally found in the Danelaw.[69] The ritual deposition of artefacts may provide one plausible explanation for the hoards found in the region, which have commonly been attributed

---

65. J. Graham-Campbell, 'Pagans and Christians', *History Today*, 36 (October, 1986), 24–8.
66. D.M. Hadley, 'Burial practice in the northern Danelaw, *c.* 600–1100' (forthcoming).
67. See Chapter 5, pp. 295–7.
68. H. Geake, *The Use of Grave-Goods in Conversion-Period England,* c. *600–c. 850* (BAR British Series, 261, 1997), 125, 139; R. A. Hall and M. Whyman, 'Settlement and monasticism at Ripon, North Yorkshire, from the 7th to 11th centuries AD', *Medieval Archaeology*, 40 (1996), 62–150, at 124–30; J.D. Richards, *Viking Age England* (1991), 115–16; R.K. Morris, *The Church in British Archaeology* (CBA Res. Rep., 47, 1983), 60–1.
69. P. Phillips, *Archaeology and Landscape Studies in North Lincolnshire* (2 vols, BAR British Series, 208, 1989), I, 169–70; C. Loveluck, 'A high-status Anglo-Saxon settlement at Flixborough, Lincolnshire', *Antiquity*, 72 (1998), 146–61, at 148.

to the failure of the owner to return to collect them.[70] Hence, the burial practices of the northern Danelaw were not entirely uniform prior to the Scandinavian settlement. This complicates our ability to identify Scandinavian burials, a situation made even more difficult by the diversity of burial practices that the Scandinavians employed in their homelands, including inhumation with and without grave goods, cremation, ship-burials and barrow-burials.[71] By concentrating discussion of Scandinavian burials in the northern Danelaw on evidence retrieved from churchyards, on burials with grave goods and on cremations, we may be dealing with an unrepresentative sample and we may be encouraging a rather circular argument which ignores the great wealth of burial evidence from the region. Furthermore, it is not true that 'pagan practice is pagan practice wherever it is found', when the practice in question is furnished burial – a form of burial that is certainly found among pagan peoples, but is also consonant with Christianized communities.[72] We must also remember that burials were not the only means by which individuals and communities expressed their religious affiliations: others include the funeral ritual itself, which is normally archaeologically invisible (except on rare occasions where evidence for feasting, for example, is found); the use of funerary monuments and grave markers; and an individual's daily practices. Thus, we should not over-emphasize the burial evidence that does survive in discussions of religious beliefs in the northern Danelaw. Finally, burial rite is not solely concerned with religious belief, even within a churchyard setting; it is also central to expressions of social status and identity.[73]

In the northern Danelaw in the period following the Scandinavian settlements, a variety of burial strategies were employed. These included inhumation with or without grave goods, and with or without stone or wooden coffins, both in churchyards and elsewhere; cremation; burial within new or existing barrows; and perhaps also ritual hoards and votive offerings in rivers, if this is how we may interpret the number of weapons and other artefacts found in rivers, and such finds as the skeletons of

---

70. G. Halsall, 'The viking presence in England? The burial evidence reconsidered', in *Cultures in Contact*, ed. Hadley and Richards.
71. E. Roesdahl, 'The archaeological evidence for conversion', in *The Christianization of Scandinavia*, ed. Sawyer *et al.*, 2–3; Graham-Campbell (ed.), *Cultural Atlas of the Viking World*, 68–73; L. Ersgard, 'The change of religion and its artefacts: an example from Upper Dalarna', *Papers of the Archaeological Institute*, new ser., 10 (Lund, 1993–4), 79–94.
72. B. K. Young, 'Paganisme, christianisme et rites funéraires mérovingiens', *Archéologie Médiévale* 7 (1977), 5–81; G. Halsall, *Settlement and Social Organization: the Merovingian region of Metz* (1995), 246–7; J. Blair, *The Church in Anglo-Saxon Society, 600–1100* (forthcoming).
73. G. Halsall, 'Female status and power in Merovingian central Austrasia: the burial evidence', *EME*, 5 (1) (1996), 1–24, at 13; for a fuller discussion, although relating to a different period, see I. Morris, *Death-Ritual and Social Structure in Classical Antiquity* (1992), 1, which describes burial as 'part of a funeral, and a funeral [as] part of a set of rituals by which the living deal with the dead'.

animals, Scandinavian metalwork and weapons excavated at Skerne (Lincs).[74] The corpus of stone sculpture may also indicate that whatever form of burial was adopted, commemoration with sculpture in a churchyard often accompanied it. It seems plausible to suggest that the indigenous populations continued to employ a variety of burial rites following the Scandinavian settlements, and that the settlers both continued to use traditional burial practices and adopted new ones, doubtless influenced by their new social milieu and contact with differing religious and cultural beliefs.

Nonetheless, in spite of these remarks it may well be that some of those ninth- and tenth-century burials with grave goods in the northern Danelaw are indeed those of Scandinavian settlers. The reasons why churchyard burial might have been chosen by the Scandinavian élite doubtless had much to do with the burial practices of the indigenous élite. The Scandinavians consistently adopted and manipulated aspects of indigenous behaviour, and it is plausible that this extended to burial practice. It was a means of exerting control over the indigenous population by associating themselves with pre-existing forms and loci of authority, and may also have been a means to emphasize claims to newly won land. On the other hand, we ought not to rule out completely the possibility that Scandinavian influence temporarily encouraged the revival of burial with grave goods among the indigenous population. For it is intriguing that of those known furnished burials, some do have distinctly 'native' items among their grave goods: for example, Anglo-Saxon coins and weapons are found in some of the burials at Repton; an 'Anglo-Saxon' sword was interred with a body in the churchyard at Wensley (Yorks); and 'straightforward Anglo-Saxon products', including a pendant and a strap-end, were found in a grave at Saffron Walden (Essex).[75] The local élite signified their status in the northern Danelaw in the later ninth and earlier tenth centuries by reference to a variety of forms of burial rite, and through the use of a number of symbols of authority, including weapons, riding equipment, weighing-scales, agricultural implements, stone sculpture, barrows and churches.[76] Whatever the views of a community about the after-life, burial rite is arguably primarily concerned with the living community. It is a time when social standing is reinforced and the fractures in society caused by a death begin to be healed. During times of great social stress, burials are prone to be marked with elaborate displays of grave goods. The use of grave goods need not be an expression of 'pagan' beliefs so much as a means by which the position of a person in local society was signalled at the moment of burial.

---

74. J.D. Richards, M. Jecock, L. Richmond and C. Tuck, 'The viking barrow cemetery at Heath Wood, Ingleby, Derbyshire', *Medieval Archaeology*, 39 (1995), 51–70.; Phillips, *Archaeology and Landscape*, 169–70; Richards, *Viking Age England*, 116–17.
75. M. Biddle and B. Kjølbye-Biddle, 'Repton and the vikings', *Antiquity*, 66 (1992), 36–51, at 40–3; Roesdahl *et al.* (eds) *The Vikings in England*, 77.
76. Halsall, 'The viking presence in England?'.

These displays, however, are, by their very nature, temporary and aimed at a local audience.[77] Messages for a wider audience are unlikely to be conveyed through this medium. Individuals and groups may have marked their allegiances over greater distances through, for example, the use of particular iconographic systems on stone sculpture. Indeed, it is possible that one reason why there is so little evidence for furnished burial, even after the settlement of people who were used to this tradition, is that stone sculpture was utilized to mark the burials of the élite, and to commemorate and convey messages about the dead.

Cremation, by contrast, is unlikely to have been a choice exercised by individuals and groups who had converted to Christianity.[78] Therefore, the cremation cemetery at Heath Wood, Ingleby (Derbs) seems likely to be the burial ground of a group of pagan Scandinavians. The cemetery comprised 59 barrows, of which around a third have been excavated. Some of the barrows covered the site of a funeral pyre upon which calcinated human bones remained. A number of metal items, some of Scandinavian type, and cremated animals have been found inside the barrows. The barrows are mostly clustered into four distinct groups, which recent earthwork survey suggests is a real phenomenon rather than the product of differential survival.[79] These may have been for distinct family or kinship groups. Not all of the barrows contain human remains, and it has been suggested that these were 'cenotaph mounds' put up to commemorate individuals buried elsewhere. The cenotaph mounds appear to have had more effort invested in them, as they are enclosed by ditches, while those with human remains are not.[80] Recent work at Ingleby has shown that the two types of mound were contemporary with each other, rather than belonging to separate phases of the cemetery's existence, indicating that two distinct burial practices were employed at the same time.[81]

The visibility of the mounds, which showed up black against the surrounding red-coloured soils, and the investment in the cremation cemetery at Ingleby, which included the possible use of ship strakes as funerary biers in addition to the raising of mounds and the creation of ditches, may be indicative of 'instability and insecurity of some sort ... a statement of religious, political and military affiliation in unfamiliar and inhospitable surroundings'.[82] This combination of ship symbolism,

---

77. Halsall, 'Female status and power', 12–13.
78. B. Effros, '*De Partibus Saxoniae* and the regulation of mortuary custom: a Carolingian campaign of Christianization or the suppression of Saxon identity?', *Revue Belge de Philologie et d'Histoire* 75, fasc. 2 (1995), 267–86, where it is pointed out, however, that the condemnation of cremation by the church was not as common as is often supposed.
79. Richards *et al.*, 'Ingleby', 58.
80. M. Posnansky, 'Heath Wood, Ingleby: a preliminary excavation report', *DAJ*, 75 (1955), 140–4, at 143; M. Posnansky, 'The pagan-Danish barrow cemetery at Heath Wood, Ingleby: 1955 excavations', *DAJ*, 76 (1956), 40–51, at 50–1.
81. Richards *et al.*, 'Ingleby', 59.
82. *Ibid.*, 66.

cremation, mound burial and sacrifice is perhaps the most overt statement of 'Scandinavianness', of 'otherness', found in the northern Danelaw. Here, for once, we probably can see the Scandinavian settlers behaving in a self-consciously 'Scandinavian' manner. Yet this is not the whole story. Those for whom cenotaphs were raised must have been buried somewhere, and it has recently been suggested that the cenotaphs commemorated individuals buried at Repton, visible some two and a half miles away. If so, the cemetery at Ingleby is also an important testimony to the acculturation process.[83] Moreover, this was not a linear process, and cremation and inhumation with associated cenotaph occurred simultaneously. It is also notable that the place-name 'Ingleby' is a Scandinavian name that means 'farmstead/village of the English'. This cannot easily be related to the archaeological evidence, and highlights the danger of trying to use place-name or archaeological evidence alone to discuss the Scandinavian settlement. The combined evidence from Ingleby may indicate that it was a place that was recognized locally for attributes that changed over time.

For evidence of Scandinavian burial we have been encouraged to look for burials accompanied by grave goods, but given the circumstances of settlement, the apparent use of the church to legitimate power, the undoubted conflict of belief systems, and the ultimate transition from one form of religious expression to another, it would not be surprising to find that Scandinavian newcomers to England concerned themselves with a variety of burial practices. Our evidence suggests that the Scandinavian settlements were followed by ongoing processes of adaptation, by both the settlers and the indigenous populations to each other – processes which are mirrored to some extent in the varied and changing burial practices and forms of commemoration used by both groups. The elaborate burials in the northern Danelaw that appear to date to a generation either side of 900 doubtless reflect a society undergoing major transition in political authority and in religious organization: studies of other regions and periods of early medieval society have suggested that social crisis and competition for power were often manifest in elaborate burial displays.[84] If this is so, the tensions of the period around 900 in the northern Danelaw may not have been cataclysmic, and our evidence suggests that the élite had recourse to means other than burial display for establishing their authority.

Scandinavian bones

Recently, hopes have been raised that 'scientific' analysis of skeletal material will enable us to answer questions about the location of Scandinavian settlement, and maybe even its density, as it may allow

83.   *Ibid.*, 68.
84.   G. Halsall, *Settlement and Social Organization* (1995), 262–82.

us to identify the biological origins of the deceased.[85] However, if not a false hope, it is definitely a premature one. It is certainly the case that aspects of skeletal morphology, such as height, body proportions and genetic traits, may be useful to a discussion of, for example, diet and health in early medieval populations, and we may then be able to say something about the social and cultural context of the skeletal evidence. However, it is virtually impossible to use skeletal morphology to discuss the racial affinities of the deceased: it is certainly possible to distinguish between people at a very broad level, and Caucasians, sub-Saharan Africans and Mongoloids do have distinctive skeletal morphologies, but within those categories it is not possible to make any further distinctions.[86] There is, sadly, no such thing as an identifiable 'Scandinavian' skeleton. It might be possible to analyse skeletons found in Scandinavia from the Viking Age and to compare their characteristics with those found in England and to develop an argument that similarities might be an indication of Scandinavian settlement. But that is not primarily because there is anything diagnostically Scandinavian about those bones, but because it means that the people we have identified shared some basic similarities as a result of, say, diet and health. Moreover, to adduce it as evidence for Scandinavian settlement depends on the settlers having been typical of the population who remained in Scandinavia, and also on people in England enjoying markedly different standards of living. In any case, we know that skeletal morphology might change rapidly in a very short time in response to changed conditions.

The other type of skeletal evidence which has excited interest is that of genetic characteristics, of which blood-group types and DNA are the most publicized examples. Recent work in northern England has demonstrated that there are similarities in gene frequencies between some modern inhabitants of the region and patterns found in parts of Scandinavia.[87] However, it is nigh on impossible to determine when the contact between the two groups occurred, and it certainly cannot be isolated to the ninth or tenth centuries. The extraction of ancient DNA from skeletons excavated in Viking Age cemeteries both in England and in

---

85. See, for example, Biddle and Kjølbye-Biddle, 'Repton and the vikings', 45; R.A. Hall, 'Vikings gone west? A summary review', in *Developments around the Baltic and the North Sea in the Viking Age*, ed. B. Ambrosiani and H. Clarke (Stockholm 1994), 32–49, at 32; A. Rogerson, 'Vikings and the new East Anglian towns', *British Archaeology*, 35 (June 1998), 8–9, at 8.
86. See, for example, the statement issued by the American Association of Physical Anthropologists, 'AAPA statement on biological aspects of race', *American Journal of Physical Anthropology*, 101 (1996), 569–70; H. Nelson and R. Jurmain, *Introduction to Physical Anthropology* (5th edn, New York 1991), 161–3; W.M. Krogman and M.Y. Iscan, *The Human Skeleton in Forensic Medicine* (Springfield, Ill., 1988), 268–301.
87. D.F. Roberts, R.J. Mitchell, C.K. Green and L.B. Jorde, 'Genetic variation in Cumbrians', *Annals of Human Biology*, 8 (2) (March–April 1981), 135–44; M. Evison, 'All in the genes? Evaluating the biological evidence of contact and migration' in *Cultures in Contact*, ed. Hadley and Richards.

Scandinavia has yet to provide statistically valid results, and the significance of any parallels between gene frequencies is as yet unproven. No matter what happens over the next few years we have to remember that the aims of physical anthropologists are very different from those of historians: they are not fundamentally setting out to answer the questions historians have formulated, and we should be wary of the newspaper headlines that claim the contrary. In any case, it should hardly need to be stated that 'biology is not culture', and the biological affinities of a person cannot predict what socio-cultural attributes and affinities they may have displayed.[88]

Material culture

How may we use the evidence of metalwork, coinage, pottery and settlement from the region to discuss the location, density and nature of the Scandinavian settlement? Moreover, what does it reveal about indigenous responses? In discussions of the locations of Scandinavian settlement it is common to produce distribution maps of finds bearing Scandinavian-style ornamentation. However, such an approach is problematic, and we cannot realistically make such simplistic connections between material culture and the origins of the people who created, commissioned and used it. The fact that the distributions of sculpture, metalwork and other artefacts displaying Scandinavian-style motifs, of Scandinavian place-names, and of Scandinavian terms for social institutions are inconsistent is prima-facie evidence that the Scandinavian impact on material culture and language was not consistent. The indigenous response to this influence must also therefore have varied.

Was material culture invariably used self-consciously to signify social status and identity? This has been argued for some of the corpus of stone sculpture, and it may be a plausible interpretation of the evidence given the cost of the sculpture, its élite status and the fact that it was to intended be put on display in a relatively visible context. However, other types of material culture are likely to have been readily diffused, and may not have been intended to make any overt statements about the status or identity of those who made or used them. This has recently been argued for the corpus of jewellery and strap-ends that has been discovered in the Danelaw, because not only was this body of metalwork ubiquitous, but many of the jewellery forms and strap-ends were familiar to both the Scandinavian settlers and the indigenous populations. Recent discoveries of metalwork reveal complex combinations of style and ornamentation, with, for example, indigenous forms of jewellery acquiring Scandinavian or even

---

88. I am grateful to Andrew Chamberlain, Martin Evison, Pia Nystrom and Andy Tyrrell for their help with this section.

Carolingian styles of ornamentation. For example, the strap-ends discovered at Coppergate and St Mary Bishophill Senior (York) are typical in form of Anglo-Saxon strap-ends, but are decorated with Borre-style ornamentation. The larger finds of strap-ends also indicate that traditional styles remained in use alongside strap-ends which display new Scandinavian and Carolingian influences.[89] Individual sites have produced mixtures of types of metalwork, suggesting that different styles and designs were in use at the same time. In addition, styles common in Wessex, especially in the vicinity of Winchester, have been found in the Danelaw, and a mould for making this sort of jewellery has been found at York.[90] These finds urge caution in using the metalwork as an index of the location or density of Scandinavian settlement: it is simply too common, easily made and easily transported for us to interpret it in this manner, and it is clear that there was much diversity in the styles of metalwork being made and used in the region. This evidence is a useful reminder that although the presence of distinct ethnic and social groups is sometimes marked by distinctive distributions of artefacts, the distribution of other forms of material culture does not necessarily respect any such boundaries between groups.

We cannot, then, simply plot distributions of artefacts bearing Scandinavian motifs in order to identify the locations of Scandinavian settlement. Furthermore, distribution maps of finds mean little unless we consider the context in which they were found: material objects were used and understood differently according to whether used in a domestic setting, in a communal location, in an ecclesiastical context, or as part of a burial. A number of the rural settlement sites excavated in northern England are in what Richard Hall has described as 'isolated places', rather than in locations where wealth was concentrated or displayed through a rich variety of types of material culture (such as at estate centres or near churches).[91] Perhaps it is not surprising that we cannot 'find the Scandinavians' in such isolated locations. If it was not the type of site at which identities were expressed through lavish displays – such as the production of stone sculpture or a distinctive burial rite – and if any newcomers replicated this mode of behaviour, then their arrival will probably have remained archaeologically undetectable. In both rural and urban contexts it is striking that finds and buildings displaying Scandinavian influence are found in combination with

89.   Roesdahl (ed.), *The Vikings in England*, 105–8, 121, 126–7; D. Haldenby, 'An Anglian site on the Yorkshire Wolds', *YAJ*, 62 (1990), 51–62; D. Haldenby, 'An Anglian site on the Yorkshire Wolds', *YAJ*, 64 (1992), 25–40; R.N. Bailey, 'An Anglo-Saxon strap-end from Wooperton', *Archaeologia Aeliana*, 5th ser., 21 (1993), 87–91.
90.   R.A. Hall, *Viking Age York* (1994), 110. I am grateful to Gabor Thomas for his help with this section: further discussion of the finds is in G. Thomas, 'A new survey of late Saxon and viking age strap-ends' (Ph.D. thesis, University of London, forthcoming).
91.   Hall, 'Vikings gone west?', 33.

distinctly indigenous-looking artefacts and buildings. This suggests either that the settlers adopted the material culture of the indigenous population, or that the indigenous population adopted the material culture of the settlers. Either way, the evidence has much to reveal about the ways in which the culture of the settlers and the local populations became intermingled, and suggests the emergence of a common 'Anglo-Scandinavian' culture.[92] This is not necessarily to say that individuals and communities ceased to think of themselves as Danish, English, Northumbrian, Mercian, and so on, but rather that such distinctions are not easily identifiable and distinguishable, and may not necessarily have been signified, in the material evidence from the region.

There is clear evidence for urban expansion in the northern Danelaw during the late ninth and the tenth centuries, and for the growth of trading contacts.[93] However, archaeologists have found the Scandinavians to be somewhat elusive, because they have sought artefacts from Scandinavia. Many of the urban sites of the northern Danelaw reveal the importance of local, national and international trade, suggesting that the Scandinavian influence on urban life in England was not simply restricted to developing contacts with Scandinavia.[94] This evidence also has much to reveal about the adaptation of Scandinavian settlers to local ways of life, rather than the long-term maintenance of links with Scandinavia. Moreover, it shows that if the Scandinavian influence is archaeologically detectable, it is through items from far-flung regions of Europe which it may be presumed that they were responsible for introducing into the Danelaw: for example, the steatite bowls and vessels from the Shetland Islands, jewellery and dress accessories from Scotland and Ireland, lava quern stones from the Mayen region (Germany), pottery vessels from the Rhineland, twilled and dyed cloths of a type commonly found in Frisia, and Byzantine silk found at York.[95] The growth of towns and trading networks may also have served in the long run to create new social groupings which served to blur the distinctions between the local populations and the settlers.

It is ironic, but telling, that some of the evidence commonly adduced as indicative of Scandinavian influence comprises artefacts which are, in origin or style, indigenous or from elsewhere in Europe. For example, coinage and pottery influenced by Carolingian motifs and methods of production have been highlighted by Richard Hodges as indicative of the 'Scandinavian' impact, and the corpus of metalwork which has come to light recently displays, as we have seen, some Scandinavian influence but also Carolingian influences.[96] Some of the

---

92. For similar views on a different region of Scandinavian settlement, see J. Bradley, 'The interpretation of Scandinavian settlement in Ireland', in *Settlement and Society in Medieval Ireland*, ed. J. Bradley (1988), 49–78.
93. See Chapter 1, p. 31.
94. R.A. Hall, 'The Five Boroughs of the Danelaw: a review of present knowledge', *ASE*, 18 (1989), 149–206, at 185, 200; Hall, *Viking Age York*, p. 31, 83–7.
95. Hall, *Viking Age York*, 84–6.
96. R. Hodges, *The Anglo-Saxon Achievement* (1989), 160–2.

accompanied burials interpreted as 'Scandinavian' contain Anglo-Saxon coins, weapons and accessories, and some of the coinage minted in the Danelaw bears the names of Christian saints, while the coinage of Guthrum bears his baptismal name, Athelstan; there was even an issue of coinage in East Anglia that copied coins of Alfred, including that king's name.[97] Scandinavian iconography on sculpture also has some indigenous features, and buildings said to be possibly of Scandinavian type are typically found in association with indigenous forms of material culture. For example, at Ribbleshead, Simy Folds, Bryant's Gill (Yorks) and Lindisfarne long-houses 'similar to those found in Norway' have been excavated, yet the range of finds includes artefacts 'of everyday types common throughout early medieval Europe'.[98] In other words, even when it is argued that we may be able to see the Scandinavians archaeologically, it is not uncommonly through artefacts that bear few or no Scandinavian-style motifs, or are from regions other than Scandinavia.

In interpreting the material culture from the region there is a tendency to concentrate upon its antecedents in pre-viking England or Scandinavia. Yet there is much that cannot be directly paralleled, and it seems apparent that much was entirely new in the tenth century, including both the form and the ornamentation and iconography of artefacts. If those who created sculpture or jewellery, for example, were looking back to past traditions, they were at the same time also adapting their creations for a new context and audience, and developing or leading taste or fashion. If the form and ornamentation of artefacts was meant to make reference to the past traditions of England and Scandinavia, then it was a reference to a past that never quite existed. In the case of stone sculpture, although it certainly existed in pre-viking England, new forms emerged following the Scandinavian settlement (such as hogbacks, and certain types of wheel-heads), and although many of the traditions of ornamentation found on the sculpture are known in Scandinavia, they were not, on the whole, found on stone. A comparable example of the manipulation of pre-existing cultural and artistic traditions following political conquest has been discussed recently in the light of the Norman Conquest. Lisa Reilly has suggested that the architectural forms of Durham Cathedral

---

97.   D.M. Metcalf, 'The monetary history of England in the tenth century viewed in the perspective of the eleventh century', in *Anglo-Saxon Monetary History: essays in memory of Michael Dolley*, ed. M.A.S. Blackburn (1986), 133–58, at 140.

98.   A. King, 'Gauber High Pasture, Ribblehead: an interim report', in *Viking Age York and the North*, ed. R.A. Hall (CBA Res. Rep., 27, 1978), 31–6; D. Coggins, K.J. Fairless and C.E. Batey, 'Simy Folds: an early medieval settlement in Upper Teesdale', *Medieval Archaeology*, 27 (1982), 1–26; S. Dickinson, 'Bryant's Gill, Kentmere: another "viking period" Ribblehead?', in *The Scandinavians in Cumbria*, ed. J.R. Baldwin and I.D. White (1985), 83–8; Graham-Campbell (ed.) *Cultural Atlas of the Viking World*, 135 for the quotations.

drew on 'Saxon artistic tradition in a very general way, which may be why specific precedents have not been found', and others have observed that 'Norman architecture in England was always Norman architecture with a difference', being greatly influenced by traditions from elsewhere in Europe.[99] This argument may be extended to other aspects of late eleventh- and early twelfth-century society – history-writing and legal codification in particular – as it can be seen that the concern to record and define the past saw the past manipulated and transformed to fit the needs of the new political and cultural regime.[100] The demands of living in the present often encourage a very selective, and sometimes greatly invented, remembrance of the past.

Recent research in prehistoric archaeology has questioned the extent to which ethnic identity may ever be identified archaeologically, but this has yet to have a significant impact on Viking Age archaeology. The material culture of the northern Danelaw has much to reveal about the processes by which the Scandinavian culture was disseminated through the region, but it is hazardous to use it to speculate on the extent to which the settlers retained any separate sense of ethnic identity, or conversely were integrated into indigenous society. If anything, the artefactual evidence from the northern Danelaw reminds us of the continuing importance of regional identities and cultures, and signifies the emergence of new local identities, all of which may have been as important to the settlers as to the indigenous populations.

The cultural interaction between the settlers and the local populations was undoubtedly great, but this does not preclude the possibility that the settlers retained a separate sense of community and group, or 'ethnic', identity for a considerable time. Linguistic and onomastic evidence offers us some insights into this.

Language change and cultural change

Place-names

When Snorri Sturluson observed in the thirteenth century that some of the places in eastern England have Scandinavian names he could scarcely have known how the debate over this subject would develop![101] The distribution of Scandinavian place-names has been central to two main debates: the scale of the Scandinavian settlement and the locations of that settlement. These debates are tired and in need of new approaches, since it is now apparent that the distribution

---

99. L. Reilly, 'The emergence of Anglo-Norman architecture: Durham Cathedral', *ANS*, 19 (1997), 335–51, at 345.
100. Williams, *The English and the Norman Conquest*, 155–86.
101. Keynes, 'The vikings in England', 64.

of Scandinavian place-names cannot tell us much about either issue.[102]

Place-names have much to reveal about naming practice and about the language and vocabulary in which that process was conducted; but they do not necessarily tell us anything about settlement. Neither the age of a settlement nor the processes or density of Scandinavian settlement can be recovered from place-name distribution maps. It may be true on a very broad level that the large numbers of Scandinavian place-names and of Scandinavian words for landscape features are the result of a significant influx of Scandinavians; that is, they reflect heavily scandinavianized vocabulary or speech. However, when we attempt to move from such generalizations to specific examples of the nature of the Scandinavian settlement the situation proves to be more problematic. The context in which Scandinavian place-names were coined is obscure, and it is difficult to offer more than a handful of unequivocal examples of the processes involved.[103] The intensification of settlement in previously underexploited regions may provide one context for the coining of new place-names. A number of recent studies have argued that new place-names were coined between the tenth and twelfth centuries for settlements in upland and woodland regions which had become separated from their parent settlements in the more fertile river valleys and lowlands; in regions where Scandinavian elements were in current use in place-name formation, such a process might well have been the catalyst for the proliferation of Scandinavian place-names.[104] This is not to say, however, that such areas were necessarily settled only by Scandinavians or that Scandinavians were responsible for coining those names. It may be true that an influx of new settlers was broadly responsible for increasing pressure on available land and resources, although it should be noted that similar transformations in land use have been noted in regions for which there is no suggestion of Scandinavian settlement.[105]

Another context for the coining of Scandinavian place-names may be that of changes to estate organization. The Scandinavian place-name

---

102.   For recent reviews, see C.D. Morris, 'Aspects of Scandinavian settlement in northern England: a review', *Northern History*, 20 (1984), 1–22, at 8–9, 12–16; G. Fellows Jensen, 'Scandinavian settlement in Yorkshire: through the rearview mirror', in *Scandinavian Settlement in Northern Britain*, ed. B. Crawford (1995), 170–86; Hadley, 'The Scandinavian settlement of England', 71–5.

103.   An oft-cited example of a place renamed with a Scandinavian place-name is Derby (formerly *Norðworðig*). For this and other examples of the complete or partial replacement of Old English place-names with Scandinavian names, see G. Fellows Jensen, *Scandinavian Settlement Names in the East Midlands* (Copenhagen, 1978), 12, 37, 43, 60, 67, 292–4.

104.   A. Everitt, 'River and wold: reflections on the historical origins of regions and pays', *JHG*, 3 (1977), 1–19; A. Everitt, 'The wolds once more', *JHG*, 5 (1979), 67–78 ; H.S.A. Fox, 'The people of the wolds in English settlement history', in *The Rural Settlements of Medieval England*, ed. M. Aston, D. Austin and C.C. Dyer (1989), 77–101; Fellows Jensen, 'Scandinavian settlement in Yorkshire', 181–3.

105.   Fox, 'The people of the wolds', 85–96.

element *thorp* is widely agreed to carry the meaning of a 'secondary settlement, an outlying farmstead or a small hamlet dependent on a larger place'.[106] It is not difficult to see why this should have become a widely used generic term for settlements in the context of estate division; such an interpretation carries much more conviction than the uncorroborated, and sometimes refutable, claim that they represent Scandinavian 'colonization in the strict sense'.[107] If places acquired names appropriate to their status within some larger estate or territorial grouping, then this suggests that their names may have been given by the lord of the area. Furthermore, changes to the composition of estates, or the status or function of parts of those estates, doubtless provided an important catalyst to place-name transformation, although it is difficult to provide any unequivocal examples of this process.[108] The most readily detectable transformation in place-name forms is the proliferation of personal names as the first element, or specific, of names. In regions for which more numerous documentary sources survive it can be seen that the closer association of a lord with a particular estate was commonly accompanied by the transfer of the lord's name into the place-name.[109] Another indication of the relationship between changes in territorial organization and changes in placenames derives from the distribution of particular types of place-names within the sokes recorded by Domesday Book. There are patterns in the distribution of Scandinavian place-names that coincide with aspects of the Domesday estate structure.[110] These include the following: soke centres rarely have Scandinavian place-names; many of the large sokes, which may be of some antiquity, have comparatively few Scandinavian place-names; Scandinavian place-names are most common as the names of separate manors or of townships with divided lordship; and Scandinavian place-names are also common among the members of sokes that appear to have been acquired since the mid-tenth century, or at least are first separately recorded after that date. It seems clear that estate structure and patterns of land-holding and lordship were dominant contexts for the formation of place-names, although this is not to deny that differences in the density of Scandinavian settlement or the vagaries of record-keeping also determined the eventual

---

106. K. Cameron, 'Scandinavian settlement in the territory of the Five Boroughs: the place-name evidence, part II: Place-names in thorp', *Mediaeval Scandinavia*, 3 (1970), 35–49' at 35; cf. A.H. Smith, *English Place-Name Elements*, 2 pts, EPNS, 25–6 (1956), I, 214–16. Some examples of Thorpe may derive from Old English *throp*: N. Lund, '*Thorp*-names', in *Medieval Settlement: Continuity and Change*, ed. P.H. Sawyer (1976), 223–5.
107. Cameron, 'Place-names in thorp', 43.
108. Fox, 'The people of the wolds', 92.
109. P.H. Sawyer, 'Medieval English settlement: new interpretations', in *English Medieval Settlement*, ed. P.H. Sawyer (1978), 1–8; M. Gelling, *Signposts to the Past* (1978), 123–4, 180–3. O. Von Feilitzen, *The Pre-Conquest Personal Names of Domesday Book* (Uppsala, 1937), 32–3, comments on the occurrence of the name of manorial lords in Domesday place-names.
110. See Chapter 3, p. 139.

distribution of Scandinavian place-names. Place-names cannot be used as straightforward guides to either the density or the precise locations of Scandinavian settlement, and since place-names arose and were recorded in multifarious contexts, to concentrate on only one context for place-name formation is inappropriate.

There are other reasons why it is inappropriate to expect a direct correlation between the distribution of Scandinavian place-names and the areas of Scandinavian settlement. We cannot, of course, assume that any settlement with a Scandinavian name ever contained only people of Scandinavian descent, as this would demand all sorts of assumptions about 'ethnic' separateness that do not stand up to scrutiny. The Scandinavian place-name Ingleby ('farmstead/village of the English') is, moreover, a stark reminder of the fallaciousness of such assumptions. Indeed, the implications of the name 'Ingleby' are made more complex by the fact that Ingleby (Derbs) is, as we have seen, the site of a cremation cemetery at which Scandinavian-style artefacts have been found.[111] By contrast, we know that Scandinavian lords took over estates without causing the name of the estate centre to change: for example, Uhtred purchased a substantial estate in the Peak District at Hope and Ashford 'from the heathen', yet none of the major estate centres in that region has a Scandinavian place-name, and Scandinavian place-names are generally rare in that area.[112] Regions with few or no Scandinavian place-names may nevertheless have experienced some Scandinavian settlement or influence, to judge from the occurrence in these same areas of large numbers of Scandinavian names for landscape features.[113] Furthermore, the fact that stone sculpture displaying Scandinavian motifs is commonly located at sites with Old English place-names similarly highlights problems in associating Scandinavian settlement with Scandinavian settlement names; not all the patrons of such sculpture were necessarily of Scandinavian origin, but some surely were.[114] At the very least, the sculpture betokens some contact with Scandinavian settlers in the vicinity. These examples establish that it is not appropriate to make a simple connection between Scandinavian place-

---

111. *PN Derbs*, Pt 3, 639; Richards *et al.*, 'Ingleby'.

112. F.M. Stenton, *Types of Manorial Structure in the Northern Danelaw*, Oxford Studies in Social and Legal History, ed. P. Vinogradoff, 2 (1910), 3–96, at 74–5.

113. G. Fellows Jensen, *Scandinavian Settlement Names in Yorkshire* (Copenhagen, 1972), 118; K. Cameron, 'Early field-names in an English-named Lincolnshire village', in *Otium et Negotium*, ed. F. Sandgren (Stockholm, 1973), 38–43, at 41; N. Lund, 'The settlers: where do we get them from – and do we need them?', in *The Eighth Viking Congress*, ed. H. Bekker-Nielsen (Odense, 1981), 147–71, at 156–67.

114. G. Fellows Jensen, 'Place-names and the Scandinavian settlement in the North Riding of Yorkshire', *Northern History*, 14 (1978), 19–46, at 38; Morris, 'Scandinavian settlement', 10–11.

names and places of Scandinavian settlement.[115] Used in isolation, place-name distribution maps are too blunt an instrument with which to identify the location or movements of peoples.

The question of who coined place-names is difficult to answer but is crucial to an understanding of their historical significance. Presumably it was not the inhabitants of the actual settlement but those of the district who gave it its name; this, however, opens up the possibility that any given settlement may have been known by more than one name, and the names given by neighbouring communities and local lords were not necessarily identical. It is the latter that are more likely to have entered the written record, which blurs still further the long-held connection between place-names and the scale of the Scandinavian settlement. The replacement of Old English place-name elements with cognate Scandinavian words also clouds the issue: a scandinavianization of the existing place-name corpus presents a rather different proposition from the wholesale replacement of place-names, or from the coining of place-names for new settlements.[116]

It is important to consider the ways in which place-names were coined. Place-names are a means by which an individual and a community address and refer to the places around them, and the means by which they establish their social and geographical orientation. The transfer of topographical terms from Scandinavia to England must, in origin, have been the result of Scandinavian settlement, and it is a common trait of colonists who when 'making a living in a new environment ... discern new landscapes in terms of the homeland and create a familiar habitat within the framework of these perceptions'.[117] However, the replication of those names need not be ascribed solely to Scandinavian activity. It is, for example, possible to cite examples from elsewhere of speakers of one language taking with them names from another language when they move on: for example, the place-name *Dímun* (signifying a mountain with two peaks), which is found in several areas of the North Atlantic region, derives from a Celtic name, but was transferred to other regions along with Scandinavian names by Scandinavian- rather than Celtic-speaking people.[118] In other words, it is perfectly possible for speakers of one language to adopt and use place-names in another language, and if they

---

115.   G.R.J. Jones, 'Early territorial organization in northern England and its bearing on the Scandinavian settlement', in *The Fourth Viking Congress*, ed. A. Small (1965), 67–84, at 77, 83; P.H. Sawyer, *Kings and Vikings: Scandinavia and Europe, AD 700–1100* (1982), 106. Old English place-names often became 'scandinavianized' in pronunciation and spelling: Morris, 'Scandinavian settlement', 7–8.

116.   This problem has been extensively considered in respect of field-names: Lund, 'The settlers', 162–5.

117.   W.F.H. Nicolaisen, 'Imitation and innovation in the Scandinavian place-names of the northern isles of Scotland', *Nomina*, 11 (1987), 75–85, at 84.

118.   S. Brink, 'The onomasticon and the role of analogy in name formation', in *Namn och Bygd: Tidskrift för Nordisk Ortnamnsforskning*, ed. T. Andersson (Uppsala, 1996), 61–84, at 67–8.

can do that when they move, then presumably they can do so in the original context in which they encounter such names. The role of analogy in place-name formation has not been seriously considered in the northern Danelaw, yet it has been shown elsewhere that it played an important role in naming-strategies, and that the person or people who coined a name did not necessarily have to speak the language from which the name was drawn or to fully understand its etymology to be able to use it. They need only recognize that it was an appropriate name for such a place: such naming processes might occur in a situation in which the etymological meaning of a name is no longer of any interest to the namer, but, rather, it is the connotations that go with the name that count, even if that name is in a foreign language.[119] The desire to follow, even unconsciously, fashion cannot be discounted from our range of interpretations of Scandinavian place-names in the northern Danelaw. Rather than viewing the place-name distribution map as an index of Scandinavian settlement, then, we can see it as a palimpsest of changes to the place-name corpus and as the product of the conscious and unconscious decisions made by the inhabitants of the northern Danelaw.[120] The distribution of types of place-names in the northern Danelaw, as elsewhere, reflects something of the changing cultural landscape.

It is notable that place-names formed with -by in Scandinavia have a much lower incidence of personal names as their first element than is the case in England: around 10 per cent in Denmark, in contrast to 68 per cent in the territory of the Five Boroughs.[121] This suggests that in England there was a more developed tendency to associate individuals with land, and that the place-names formed with a personal name and -by in the Danelaw were coined either by the indigenous population or by settlers who had come into contact with indigenous attitudes to land and naming practices. Together with the fact that a person bearing a Scandinavian name was not necessarily of Scandinavian origin, this dictates that this group of place-names cannot be taken in isolation as an index of exclusively Scandinavian activity. The personal names contained in place-names in the Danelaw include both names that had long since dropped out of use and names currently fashionable at the time of Domesday Book, reinforcing the notion that the Scandinavian influence on naming patterns (which was sometimes effected by people of indigenous or mixed descent who had acquired Old Norse personal names) extended over a long period, and again we can see that the place-name distribution map provides a palimpsest of change rather than access to clearly definable or datable events.[122]

---

119. Brink, 'The onomasticon', 68; T. Ainiala, 'On change in place-names', in *Namn och Bygd: Tidskrift för Nordisk Ortnamnsforskning*, ed. T. Andersson (Uppsala, 1997), 75–92, at 86.
120. Brink, 'The onomasticon', 81.
121. K. Hald, *Vore Stednavne* (Copenhagen, 1965), 109–13; Fellows Jensen, *East Midlands*, 15–17, 27–8.
122. Fellows Jensen, 'Scandinavian settlement in Yorkshire', 178–9.

In short, the place-name evidence is inconclusive as an indicator of the scale of the Scandinavian settlement and as a guide to the nature of that settlement. Moreover, the occurrence of Scandinavian place-names clearly has many explanations, and we should also remember that there is a distinction to be drawn between the *coining* of place-names and the *recording* of place-names. The institutional context, especially that of estate structures, offers a useful perspective on place-name formation. Meanwhile, questions about the interaction of groups of peoples and about the construction of ethnic and cultural identities must also be considered. The indigenous population eventually adopted and continued to use Scandinavian place-names (and, indeed, lexical terms and personal names, as we shall see), and the proliferation of Scandinavian place-names reveals a certain amount about the interaction between people of Scandinavian and indigenous origin. It should be noted that it is the place-name evidence above all else that continues to be interpreted along 'ethnic' lines. Many of the points made here are not easily transformed from generalizations in order to explain individual place-names, but what they do allow us to do is to consider the place-name evidence in the same light as we are able to examine the documentary and archaeological evidence for settlement, social interaction and cultural diffusion. It remains for those whose specialism is the study of place-names to take up this challenge.

Language change

The linguistic impact of the Scandinavians who settled in England was undoubtedly great, and this may well be indicative of numbers of people who spoke Scandinavian languages. The fact that people spoke different languages would initially have made them distinctive from one another. Indeed, both the chronicler Æthelweard and the homilist Ælfric observed that Danes spoke Danish and had different names from English speakers for places and gods, which suggests that language was one factor that made Danes distinctive.[123] However, both were writing long after the initial settlement began and may have been referring to more recent arrivals from Denmark. Moreover, a simple correlation between language, on the one hand, and ethnic or cultural identity, on the other, does not pay sufficient regard to the logistics of conquest and settlement, and to the needs of the newcomers to form a *modus vivendi* with the indigenous population. No matter how many Scandinavians migrated to England, they were still in the minority, and in such circumstances it is difficult to imagine, and is indeed unlikely, that

---

123. *Æthelweard*, 37; J.C. Pope, *Homilies of Ælfric: a supplementary collection*, Early English Text Society (2 vols, 1967–8), II, 683–4, 686. For discussion of this evidence, see M. Townend, 'Viking Age England as a bilingual society', in Hadley and Richards, *Cultures in Contact*.

they maintained a separate existence which was not in any way reliant on interaction with the indigenous population. As Scandinavian leaders took over estates and had them cultivated, they must have relied on indigenous labour, and perhaps also on indigenous estate administrators. The Scandinavian leaders were generally politically in the ascendancy until the mid-tenth century, but this was coupled with a reliance on indigenous support and a need to mix with the indigenous populations from the very start, a need which was increased as the tenth century progressed and the settlers were drawn more firmly into the realm of English politics.[124] This level of social mixing appears to have operated at every level of society, and provides the backdrop for linguistic change.

The intensity of the Scandinavian influence on Old English is not in doubt, but its temporal deployment and the relationship between linguistic influence and the scale of the Scandinavian settlement is open to debate. Part of the problem concerns the date of the sources in which the Scandinavian influence is apparent. Old English sources contain *c.* 150 loans from Scandinavian languages, but in Middle English sources there are many thousands.[125] It is the late appearance of the vast majority of the linguistic borrowings that hampers analysis of the type of language contact likely to have brought about this influence. In Old English sources most of the Scandinavian loans are found in the technical vocabulary: legal, seafaring and military terms, and words for ranks, measures and coinage.[126] It is not until the twelfth or thirteenth century that the full impact of the Scandinavian influence can be monitored, although we can be sure that the period of greatest linguistic borrowing lay much earlier than this. The technical nature of the borrowings into Old English marks them out as 'cultural loans', which are 'compatible with a socially superior, more prestigious status of Scandinavian in the Danelaw'.[127] By contrast, the Middle English borrowings can be accounted for only by 'assuming the existence of a mixed speech community operating on the basis of social and cultural equality'; in other words, they assume the settlement of more than a few hundred aristocrats, and suggest more than one context for language contact and change.[128]

The Scandinavian influence on Old English is not, of course, limited to loan words, and extends to matters of grammar. Concentration on loan words is, in many ways, as unsatisfactory as an attempt by an archaeologist to make sense of a box of unprovenanced and undated artefacts. Moreover, an understanding of the significance of linguistic change involves consideration of the cultural function of language: as

---

124. Keynes, 'The vikings in England', 68–70.
125. Geipel, *The Viking Legacy*, 70; Hansen, 'The Scandinavian element in English'; Kastovsky, 'Semantics and vocabulary', 320, 332–6.
126. Kastovsky, 'Semantics and vocabulary', 332–6.
127. L. Bloomfield, *Language* (1935), 461; Kastovsky, 'Semantics and vocabulary', 324.
128. Kastovsky, 'Semantics and vocabulary'; see also Hansen, 'The Scandinavian element in English', 79.

Angus McIntosh has commented, 'fundamentally what we mean by "languages in contact" is "users of language in contact"'.[129] John Hines has drawn on linguistic and extralinguistic data and on analogy with what is known of comparable situations of language contact, in order to suggest how and why language developed in the way that it did in the Danelaw. In the earliest years of settlement the Scandinavians were in the political ascendancy and it is plausible that this placed pressures on the indigenous populations to learn and adopt aspects of Scandinavian speech to facilitate communication, but that once the political tide turned, so too did the linguistic tide.[130] Much space has been devoted to debating the extent to which Old Norse and Old English were mutually intelligible, but this debate has largely missed the point: where there is social pressure for individuals and communities to communicate with each other, then any two individuals who are able to interact with each other using, among other means, speech become mutually intelligible even if they do not fully understand or speak each other's language.[131] The acculturation process, which is more readily detectable in the archaeological record, as we have seen, appears to have extended to language. As Hines has observed, Anglo-Scandinavian acculturation was not simply the product of 'the thoughtless confusion of cultures in contact' but was consciously articulated through the creation of distinctive forms of material culture and the elaborate range of Scandinavian English. Socio-linguists now discuss language change as a product of, and a contributory factor to, cultural change, and Hines has observed of language change in the Danelaw that the distinctive language forms found there may have been used as '"acts of identity" for individuals and groups, embodying an identity of speakers as members of a particular group'.[132] If it is true that Scandinavian settlement continued over many years or decades, it may not be appropriate to think in terms of two speech communities in the Danelaw, but rather to imagine that there may have been a series of speech communities, speaking varying forms of English, Old Norse or 'Anglo-Scandinavian'. Thus, although language certainly may be an important element in the construction of ethnic or social identities, it may not be appropriate to think in terms of a dichotomy between the indigenous populations and the settlers. Furthermore, the infiltration of Old Norse into Old

---

129. A. McIntosh, 'Codes and cultures', in *Speaking in our Tongues*, ed. M. Laing and K. Williamson (1994), 135–7, at 137.
130. J. Hines, 'Scandinavian English: a creole in context', in *Language Contact in the British Isles*, ed. P.S. Ureland and G. Broderick (Tübingen, 1991), 403–27 at 415–17.
131. On the debate about mutual intelligibility, see Kastovsky, 'Semantics and vocabulary', 328–9; Geipel, *The Viking Legacy*, 57; A.C. Baugh and T. Cable, *A History of the English Language* (3rd edn, 1978), 95; P. Poussa, 'The evolution of early Standard English: the creolization hypothesis', *Studia Anglica Posnaniensia*, 14 (1982), 69–85, at 72.
132. Hines, 'Scandinavian English', 417–18.

English must have both reflected, and contributed to, a sense of the regional distinctiveness of the Danelaw within England.

We may also consider the deployment of Scandinavian personal names in this light. Personal names in the Danelaw are not a reliable guide to descent; the very fact that the same family might have some members who bore Old English names and others with Scandinavian names urges caution.[133] It is nonetheless instructive that indigenous families began to employ the personal names of the newcomers. The same thing also happened after the Norman Conquest and one can but conclude that, as well as simply starting a new fashion in nomenclature, these conquests encouraged people to align themselves – or, strictly, their children – self-consciously with their new overlords.[134] It is, however, important to note that many of the 'Scandinavian' personal names found in the Danelaw are rather different from personal names recorded in Scandinavia, and it seems that in the Danelaw new names were created out of the individual elements of compound names. There is, for example, a much greater variety of compound names formed with *-brandr, -grímr, -hildr, -steinn* and *-ulfr* in the Danelaw than is found in Scandinavia.[135] If the individuals who bore these names considered them to be Scandinavian names, then they were Scandinavian names with a difference. The form of the Scandinavian names found in the Danelaw suggests that once the settlers had left their home environment and been freed from the restrictions imposed by inherited naming-principles they became more adventurous in their choices of names.[136]

It is also notable that names of Scandinavian origin were often written – in texts, on coins and on sculpture – to conform with either Old English or Latin spelling.[137] This tranformation in presentation of names may have more to reveal about scribal conformity than social practice, but it may reveal something about both pronunciation and perception of names of Scandinavian origin. Examples drawn from Domesday Book reveal differences in the ways in which essentially the

---

133. F.M. Stenton, *Documents Illustrative of the Social and Economic History of the Danelaw* (1920), cxiv–xv; Von Feilitzen, *The Pre-Conquest Personal Names of Domesday Book*, 18–26; E. Ekwall, 'The proportion of Scandinavian settlers in the Danelaw', *Saga-Book of the Viking Society*, 12 (1937–45), 19–34; R.H.C. Davis, 'East Anglia and the Danelaw', *TRHS*, 5th ser., 5 (1955), 23–39, at 29; D.W. Whitelock, 'Scandinavian personal names in the *Liber Vitae* of Thorney Abbey', *Saga-Book of the Viking Society*, 12 (1937–45), 127–53; G. Fellows Jensen, *Scandinavian Personal Names in Lincolnshire and Yorkshire* (Copenhagen 1968).

134. C. Clark, 'Clark's first three laws of applied anthroponymics', *Nomina*, 3 (1979), 13–19; Williams, *The English and the Norman Conquest*, 206–7.

135. G. Fellows Jensen, 'From Scandinavia to the British Isles and back again: linguistic give-and-take in the viking period', in *Developments around the Baltic and North Sea*, ed. Ambrosiani and Clarke, 253–68, at 259.

136. *Ibid.*, 262.

137. G. Fellows Jensen, 'Of Danes – and thanes – and Domesday Book' in *People and Places in Northern Europe, 500–1600*, ed. I.N. Wood and N. Lund (1991), 107–21, at 114.

same or similar names are presented: for example, the tenant of Flixton (Suffolk) was called *Osketellus*, an anglicized and latinized version of the Scandinavian name *Asketil*. The uncontracted form of names ending in *-ketil* has been shown by John Insley to have been virtually confined to East Anglia, whereas further north the contracted forms *-kel* or *-kil* are common, which betokens adaptation to more modern forms of names which developed in Scandinavia, and may suggest either ongoing contact with Scandinavia or that individuals who bore such names were relatively recent immigrants. An anglicized version of *-ketil* is *-cytel*, and some individuals in the Danelaw who bore such names seem likely to have regarded themselves as English, or at least were acculturated to English society: they include Oscytel, bishop of Dorchester and archbishop of York (d. 971), and Ulfcytel, who died fighting the Danes in 1016. In such contexts the anglicized presentation of names and the roles fulfilled by those who bore them may have undermined the impression of the name and its bearer as Scandinavian or of Scandinavian origin. The contemporary perception of personal names cannot be regarded simply as a matter of etymology: pronunciation, spelling and the associations which a name carried from having been borne by someone else previously encountered or known of, associations which might be genealogical, historical, legendary, familiar or non-familiar, must have served to determine the way in which individuals and their names were perceived.[138] Some of the Scandinavian names which were brought into England in the eleventh century were associated almost exclusively with the rural land-holding classes, and as such may have been regarded as élite names as much as Danish names.[139] Social factors and 'class' difference need to be considered alongside ethnic factors when examining personal names.[140]

It is also striking that many of the moneyers attested on coins produced across England in the tenth century had Frankish personal names. It may be that a group of Carolingian moneyers came to England following the Scandinavian conquest, but the continuing use of such names might be because such names came to be regarded as appropriate to someone of this profession, rather than indicating an ongoing influx of Carolingian moneyers. This argument may be supported by the fact that some of the coins from East Anglia present Old Norse or Old English names in a Continental guise.[141]

---

138. C. Clark, 'Personal-name studies: bringing them to a wider audience', *Nomina*, 15 (1991), 21–34, at 26.
139. J. Insley, 'Regional variation in Scandinavian personal nomenclature in England', *Nomina*, 3 (1979), 52–60, at 54; V. Smart, 'Scandinavians, Celts and Germans in Anglo-Saxon England: the evidence of moneyers' names', in *Anglo-Saxon Monetary History*, ed. Blackburn, 171–84, at 179–80.
140. Amory, 'Names', 3.
141. O. Von Feilitzen and C.E. Blunt, 'Personal names on the coinage of Edgar', in *England before the Conquest: studies in primary sources presented to Dorothy Whitelock*, ed. P. Clemoes (1971), 183–214; V. Smart, 'The moneyers of St

In conclusion, language forms and language change indirectly reflect social change and the migrations of peoples, but are mediated by many political and social factors. The linguistic evidence suggests that the use of language, place-names and personal names was central to the emergence of an Anglo-Danish society and culture in the northern Danelaw.

Conclusions

The traditional notion that society in the northern Danelaw was divided in the long term into 'Scandinavian' and 'English' cannot be sustained, although that is not to deny that some individuals and families long retained memories of their Scandinavian ancestry and culture. It is not easy to identify very much about the society of the region that can be said to have been especially Scandinavian, although this is not to deny that the Scandinavians had an important impact on society in the regions where they settled. Moreover, the fact that we are able to identify elements of continuity in the ecclesiastical, administrative and agrarian institutions of the northern Danelaw does not mean that there were not at the same time important transformations in social organization and in social and cultural identities. The ethnicity paradigm has for too long been used in an outdated manner; moreover, it has tended to divert our attentions from what the indigenous populations and the newcomers had in common, and how they proceeded to forge a *modus vivendi*. Furthermore, many studies of the impact of the Scandinavian settlement have regarded the numerical question, the distinctiveness of the region and the level of continuity as being directly related to each other. Yet as has been demonstrated in the present volume, neither the distinctiveness of the society and institutions of the region nor the degree of continuity can be used as an index of the numbers of Scandinavians who came to England. As Niels Lund aptly put it, 'it is misleading to arrange "numbers", "influence" and "permanent effects" co-ordinately: the latter two are the premises, the first is the conclusion drawn from these'.[142]

It has often been overlooked that estate structures, the ecclesiastical network, trading networks, the legal and administrative structure and most of the documentary evidence from the northern Danelaw are largely indicative of the activities and the practices of the élites of the region. For the activities of the masses the linguistic evidence, and perhaps in time the archaeological record, have more to offer. It seems clear that the Scandinavian conquest was more than a simple political

---

contd.

Edmund', *Hikuin*, 11 (1985), 83–90; Smart, 'Scandinavians, Celts and Germans', 174–7.
142.   Lund, 'The settlers', 167.

conquest, and involved a relatively substantial settlement in many areas. Yet in many ways it was the political conquests of the Scandinavians that determined the Scandinavian impact, as much as, if not more so than, the scale of the settlement. The needs of Scandinavian lords as they sought to establish control determined much of the perceivable political and cultural impact of the Scandinavian settlement. In many ways, then, the old debates about the scale of the settlement are redundant, and much of the evidence that has been central to these debates has in fact little to tell us about this issue.

One of the distinctive features of the northern Danelaw following the Scandinavian conquests and settlement is the emergence of a society that, although it owed much to antecedents in the region and in Scandinavia, radically transformed the society and culture both of the inhabitants of the region and of the newcomers. The circumstances of successive conquests gave rise to new challenges. Reference to the past was clearly important in securing control in the region, yet the realities of living in the present witnessed substantial transformations in the way in which the past was remembered and maintained.

By rethinking the premises on which our investigations of the Scandinavian settlement are based, the subject is thrown wide open to new interpretations. A debate that had become stale, faction-ridden and restrictive is now ripe for revival. Mad, bad or dangerous to know the Scandinavians may have been, but they were also destined to stay, and it is the mechanisms by which their settlement and accommodation were achieved that, in particular, necessitate a truly interdisciplinary approach.

Epilogue

There is every reason why the explorers of ancient English
history should be hopeful. We are beginning to learn that there
are intricate problems to be solved and yet they are not insoluble
— F.W. Maitland [1]

This study has revealed and discussed a number of historiographical
and methodological problems related to the study of the northern
Danelaw in particular, and early medieval society more generally. It
has highlighted new approaches that may be taken to a cross-section of
types of evidence, and the value of studying the period and aspects of
social organization from a variety of perspectives, and on a variety of
scales, has been revealed. The Scandinavian settlement of the
northern Danelaw was clearly important in shaping the society of
the region, but our understanding of the impact of this settlement has
changed immeasurably in recent years, and it can now be placed in
context and seen as but one event that shaped the social structure and
institutions of the region. By reformulating our questions and adopting
new approaches to evidence that has been discussed and debated many
times, in addition to drawing on newly available bodies of evidence, we
can continue to make important advances in our understanding of early
medieval societies. There is little doubt that the scholar of the early
medieval period is required to adopt an interdisciplinary approach, but
in doing so to ensure that we do not gloss over the very clear
inconsistencies that emerge from divergent evidence. The early
medieval period was not a simple and ordered world, in which everyone
normally followed the same rules; rather than trying to reconstruct such
a world — which has been a feature of research in recent decades — we
must strive to identify the locally divergent, inconsistent and changing
features of given societies. The value of local studies has been
emphasized throughout this study, as has the importance of placing
them firmly in a wider context. There are numerous 'interpretative
inconveniences' that must be addressed in attempting to write such
localized studies, especially in Anglo-Saxon England. Yet the potential
remains to overcome them, and to contribute to a richer, more nuanced
understanding of early medieval societies.

---

1. F.W. Maitland, *Domesday Book and Beyond* (1897), 2–3.

Bibliography

Primary sources

Æthelwulf de Abbatibus, ed. and trans. A. Campbell (1967).
Anglo-Saxon Charters, II: charters of Burton Abbey, ed. P.H. Sawyer (1979).
The Annals of Ulster (to AD 1131), ed. S. MacAirt and G. MacNiocaill (1983).
Asser's Life of Alfred the Great and Other Contemporary Sources, trans. S. Keynes and M. Lapidge (1983).
Barley, M.W., *Documents Relating to the Manor and Soke of Newark-on-Trent*, Thoroton Record Society Series, 16 (1956).
Bede's Ecclesiastical History of the English People, ed. B. Colgrave and R.A.B. Mynors (1969).
Birch, W. de G., *Cartularium Saxonicum* (3 vols, 1885–93).
Bridgeman, C.G.O., 'Burton Abbey twelfth-century surveys', *Collections for a History of Staffordshire*, new ser., 23 (1918 for 1916), 209–300.
Caenegem, R.C. van (ed.) *English Lawsuits from William I to Richard I*, Selden Society, 106 (1990).
The Cartulary of Blyth Priory, ed. R.T. Timson (2 vols, 1968).
The Cartulary of Darley Abbey, ed. R.R. Darlington (2 vols, 1945).
The Cartulary of Tutbury Priory, Collections for a History of Staffordshire, 4th ser., 4, ed. A. Saltman (1962).
Chartulary of Whitby Abbey, ed. J.C. Atkinson, Surtees Society, 69 (1878).
The Chronicle of Æthelweard, ed. A. Campbell (1962).
The Chronicle of Hugh Candidus, ed. W.T. Mellows (1949).
The Chronicle of John of Worcester, II: The Annals from 450 to 1066, ed. R.R. Darlington, P. McGurk and J. Bray (1995).
Chronicon Abbatiae de Evesham ad Annum 1418, ed. W.D. Macray, Rolls Series, 29 (1863).
Chronicon Abbatiae Ramesiensis, ed. W.D. Macray, Rolls Series, 83 (1886).
Chronicon Petroburgense, ed. T. Stapleton, Camden Society, 47 (1949).
Cubbin, G.P. (ed.), *The Anglo-Saxon Chronicle: a collaborative edition, Volume 6.* MS D (1996).
Domesday Book: 27 Derbyshire, ed. P. Morgan (1978).
Domesday Book: 28 Nottinghamshire, ed. C. Parker and S. Wood (1977).
Domesday Book: 30 Yorkshire, ed. M. Faull and M. Stinson (2 vols, 1986).
Domesday Book: 31 Lincolnshire, ed. P. Morgan and C. Thorn (2 vols, 1986).
Douglas, D.C. and Greenaway, G.W. (eds) *English Historical Documents II, 1042–1189*, (1953; 2nd edn 1981).
The Ecclesiastical History of Orderic Vitalis, ed. M. Chibnall (6 vols, 1968–80).
Felix's Life of Saint Guthlac, ed. B. Colgrave (1956).
Flores Historiarum: Rogeri de Wendover, Chronica sive flores historiarum, ed. H. Coxe, Rolls Series, 84 (4 vols, 1841–2).
Foster, C.W., *The Registrum Antiquissimum of the Cathedral Church of Lincoln*, 3 parts, Lincoln Record Society, vols 27–9 (1931–5).
Gerald of Wales, The Journey through Wales and The Description of Wales, ed. L. Thorpe (1978).
Haddan, A.W. and Stubbs, W. (eds) *Councils and Ecclesiastical Documents Relating to Great Britain and Ireland* (3 vols, 1869–79).

Harmer, F.E. (ed.) *Anglo-Saxon Writs* (1952).
The Kalendar of Abbot Samson of Bury St. Edmunds, ed. R.H.C. Davis, Camden 3rd ser., 84 (1954).
Liber Eliensis, ed. E.O. Blake, Camden 3rd ser., 92 (1962).
Liber Vitae: register and martyrology of New Minster and Hyde Abbey, Winchester, ed. W. de Gray Birch (1892).
The Life of Bishop Wilfrid by Eddius Stephanus, ed. B. Colgrave (1927).
The Life of St Cuthbert, ed. B. Colgrave (1940).
The Old English Orosius, ed. J. Bately, Early English Text Society, Suppl. ser., 6 (1980).
Pope, J.C., *Homilies of Ælfric: a supplementary collection*, Early English Text Society (2 vols, 1967–8).
Raine, J., *The Historians of the Church of York and Its Archbishops*, Rolls Ser., 71 (3 vols, 1879–94).
J. Raine, 'The register, or rolls, of Walter Gray, Lord Archbishop of York', *Surtees Society*, 56 (1872).
Riden, P. and Blair, J., *The Records of the Borough of Chesterfield* (1980).
Robertson, A.J., *Anglo-Saxon Charters* (2nd edn, 1956).
Rufford Charters, ed. C.J. Holdsworth, Thoroton Society Record Ser. (4 vols, 1972–81).
Stubbs, W., *Select Charters and Other Illustrations of English Constitutional History from the Earliest Times to the Reign of Edward the First* (1929).
Symeonis monachis Opera omnia, ed. T. Arnold, Rolls Series (2 vols, 1882–5).
A Terrier of Fleet, Lincolnshire, ed. N. Neilson (1920).
Valor Ecclesiasticus temp. Henr. VIII (5 vols, 1817).
Venerabilis Baedae Opera Historica, ed. C. Plummer, (2 vols 1896).
'*Vita Oswaldi*', *Historians of the Church of York and Its Archbishops*, ed. J. Raine (3 vols, 1879–94).
Whitelock, D.W., *Anglo-Saxon Wills* (1930).
Whitelock, D.W. (ed.) *English Historical Documents I, c. 500–1042* (1955; 2nd edn 1979).
Whitelock, D.W., Brett, M. and Broke, C.N.L. (eds) *Councils and Synods with Other Documents Relating to the English Church, I: AD 871–1204*, 2 vols (1981).
Willelmi Malmesbiriensis Monachi. De Gestis Pontificum Anglorum, Libri Quinque, ed. N.E.S.A. Hamilton, Rolls Series, 52 (1870).
Willelmi Malmesbiriensis Monachi. De Gestis Rerum Anglorum, ed. W. Stubbs, Rolls Series, 90 (2 vols, 1887–9).

References

Brigg, W. (ed.) *The Registers of the Parish of Leeds*, YPRS, 33 (1908).
Cameron, K., *The Place-Names of Derbyshire*, 3 pts, EPNS, 27–9 (1959).
Fasti Parochiales, ed. A.H. Thompson and C.T. Clay, YAS Record Society (1933).
Gelling, M., *The Place-Names of Berkshire*, 3 pts, EPNS, 50–2 (1974–6).
Glover, J.E.B., Mawer, A. and Stenton, F.M., *The Place-Names of Nottinghamshire*, EPNS, 17 (1940).
Hart, C., *The Early Charters of Eastern England* (1966).
——*The Early Charters of Northern England and the North Midlands* (1975).
Sawyer, P.H., *Anglo-Saxon Charters: an annotated list and bibliography*, Royal Historical Society Guides and Handbooks 8 (1968).
Smith, A.H., *The Place-Names of the North Riding of Yorkshire*, EPNS, 5 (1928).
——*The Place-Names of the East Riding of Yorkshire*, EPNS, 14 (1937).
——*English Place-Name Elements*, 2 pts, EPNS, 25–6 (1956).
——*The Place-Names of the West Riding of Yorkshire*, 8 pts, EPNS, 33 (1961–3).
Tithe Files, 1836–c. 1870. Bedfords. to Leics., List and Index Society, 219 (1986).
Tithe Files, 1836–c. 1870. Lincs. to Southampton, List and Index Society, 225 (1987).
Tithe Maps and Apportionments. Part I, Bedfords. to Lincolns., List and Index Society, 68 (1971).
Tithe Maps and Apportionments. Part II, Notts. to Yorks., List and Index Society, 83 (1972).

Train, K.S.S. (ed.) *Lists of the Clergy of Central Nottinghamshire*, Thoroton Record Society, 15 (3 pts, 1953).

Secondary sources

Abels, R., *Lordship and Military Obligation in Anglo-Saxon England* (1988).

Abrams, L., 'The Anglo-Saxons and the Christianization of Scandinavia', *ASE*, 24 (1995), 213–49.

——'Conversion and assimilation' in *Cultures in Contact: Scandinavian settlement in England*, ed. D.M. Hadley and J.D. Richards (forthcoming).

Adams, K.A., 'Monastery and village at Crayke, North Yorkshire', *YAJ*, 62 (1990), 29–50.

Adams, M., 'Excavation of a pre-Conquest cemetery at Addingham, West Yorkshire', *Medieval Archaeology*, 40 (1996), 151–91.

Addleshaw, G.W.O., *Rectors, Vicars and Patrons in Twelfth- and Early Thirteenth-Century Canon Law* (1987).

Ainiala, T., 'On change in place-names' in *Namn och Bygd: Tidskrift för Nordisk Ortnamnsforskning*, ed. T. Andersson (Uppsala, 1997), 75–92.

Allerston, P., 'English village development: findings from the Pickering district of north Yorkshire', *IBGT*, 51 (1970), 95–109.

Allison, K.J., 'Outlying townships', *VCH E. Riding*, VI, 271–313.

American Association of Physical Anthropologists, 'AAPA statement on biological aspects of race', *American Journal of Physical Anthropology* 101 (1996), 569–70.

Amory, P., 'The meaning and purpose of ethnic terminology in the Burgundian Laws', *EME*, 2 (1) (1993), 1–28.

——'Names, ethnic identity and community in fifth- and sixth-century Burgundy', *Viator* 25 (1994), 1–30.

Aris, R., *History of Political Thought in Germany from 1789 to 1815* (1936).

Armstrong, P., Tomlinson, D. and Evans, D.H., *Excavations at Lurk Lane, Beverley, 1979–82* (1991).

Arnold, C.J., *An Archaeology of the Early Anglo-Saxon Kingdoms* (1988).

——'Territories and leadership: frameworks for the study of emergent polities in early Anglo-Saxon southern England', in *Power and Politics in Early Medieval Britain and Ireland*, ed. S.T. Driscoll and M.R. Nieke (1988), 111–27.

Arnold, C. and Wardle, P., 'Early medieval settlement patterns in England', *Medieval Archaeology*, 4 (1981), 145–9.

Astill, G., 'Rural settlement: the toft and the croft' in *The Countryside of Medieval England*, ed. G. Astill and A. Grant (1988), 36–61.

Aston, M., 'Medieval settlement sites in Somerset' in *The Medieval Landscape of Wessex*, ed. M. Aston and C. Lewis (1994), 219–37.

Aston, T.H., 'The origins of the manor in England', *TRHS*, 5th ser., 8 (1958), 59–83.

——'The origins of the manor in England' (reprinted with a postscript), in *Social Ideas and Relations: essays in honour of R.H. Hilton*, ed. T.H. Aston, P.R. Coss, C.C. Dyer and J. Thirsk (1983), 1–43.

Atkin, M., Ayers, B. and Jennings, S., 'Thetford-type ware production in Norwich' in *Norfolk: waterfront excavations and Thetford ware production*, ed. P. Wade-Martins (East Anglian Archaeology Report, 17, 1983), 61–104.

Austin, D., 'Medieval settlement in the north-east of England: retrospect, summary and prospect', in *Medieval Rural Settlement in North-East England*, ed. B.E. Vyner (1990), 141–50.

Bailey, R.N., *Viking Age Sculpture in Northern England* (1980).

——'Ledsham', *Bulletin of the CBA Churches Committee*, 18 (1983), 6–8.

——'An Anglo-Saxon strap-end from Wooperton', *Archaeologia Aeliana*, 5th ser., 21 (1993), 87–91.

——*England's Earliest Sculptors* (1997).

Baring, F., 'Domesday Book and the Burton cartulary', *EHR*, 11 (1896), 98–102.

Barley, M.W., 'Excavations on the medieval defences of Newark, 1972', *TTS*, 78 (1974), 68–72.

Barley, M.W. and Train, K.S.S. (eds) *The Antiquities of Nottinghamshire. Robert Thoroton. Edited and enlarged by John Throsby* (first published 1790–6; this edn, 3 vols, 1972).

Barlow, F., *Edward the Confessor* (1970).

Barrow, G.W.S., *The Kingdom of the Scots: government, church and society from the eleventh to the thirteenth century* (1973).

——*The Anglo-Norman Era in Scottish History* (1980).

Barrow, J., 'Urban cemetery location in the high Middle Ages', in *Death in Towns*, ed. S.R. Bassett (1992), 78–100.

——'Oscytel', in *The New Dictionary of National Biography* (forthcoming).

——'Survival and mutation: ecclesiastical institutions in the Danelaw in the ninth and tenth centuries', in *Cultures in Contact: Scandinavian Settlement in England*, ed. D.M. Hadley and J.D. Richards (forthcoming).

Barth, F., *Ethnic Groups and Boundaries: the social organization of cultural difference* (Oslo, 1969).

Bassett, S.R., *Saffron Walden: excavations and research, 1972–80* (CBA Research Report, 45, 1982).

——'In search of the origins of Anglo-Saxon kingdoms', in *The Origins of Anglo-Saxon Kingdoms*, ed. S.R. Bassett (1989), 3–27.

——'Lincoln and the Anglo-Saxon see of Lindsey', *ASE*, 18 (1990), 1–32.

——'Church and diocese in the West Midlands: the transition from British to Anglo-Saxon control', in *Pastoral Care before the Parish*, ed. J. Blair and R. Sharpe (1992), 13–40.

——'The administrative landscape of the diocese of Worcester in the tenth century', in *St Oswald of Worcester: life and influence*, ed. N.P. Brooks and C.R.E. Cubitt (1996), 147–73.

Bately, J., 'The compilation of the Anglo-Saxon Chronicle 60 BC to AD 890: vocabulary as evidence', *Proceedings of the British Academy*, 64 (1980 for 1978), 93–129.

Baugh, A.C. and Cable, T., *A History of the English Language* (3rd edn, 1978).

Beresford, G., *The Medieval Clay-Land Village: excavations at Goltho and Barton Blount*, Society for Medieval Archaeology Monograph Series, 6 (1975).

——*Goltho: the development of an early medieval manor, c. 850–1150* (1987).

Beresford, M. and Finberg, H.P.R. (eds), *English Medieval Boroughs: a handlist* (1973).

Beresford, M. and Hurst, J.G., *Wharram Percy Deserted Medieval Village* (1990).

Biddle, M., 'Archaeology, architecture and the cult of saints', in *The Anglo-Saxon Church*, ed. L.A.S. Butler and R.K. Morris (CBA Research Report, 60, 1986), 1–31.

——'A parcel of pennies from a mass-burial associated with the Viking wintering at Repton in 873–4', *British Numismatic Journal*, 56 (1986), 25–30.

Biddle, M. and Kjølbye-Biddle, B., 'The Repton stone', *ASE*, 14 (1985), 233–92.

——'Repton and the vikings', *Antiquity*, 250 (March, 1992), 36–51.

Biddle, M., Kjølbye-Biddle, B., Northover, J.P. and Pagan, H., 'Coins of the Anglo-Saxon period from Repton, Derbyshire', in *Anglo-Saxon Monetary History*, ed. M.A.S. Blackburn (1986), 111–32.

Binns, A.L., 'The navigation of Viking ships around the British Isles in Old English and Old Norse sources', in *The Fifth Viking Congress*, ed. W.F.H. Nicolaisen (1968), 107–8.

Bishop, M.W., 'Multiple estates in late Anglo-Saxon Nottinghamshire', *TTS*, 85 (1981), 37–47.

Bishop, T.A.M., 'Assarting and the growth of the open fields', *EcHR*, 1st ser., 6 (1935–6), 13–29.

Blair, J., 'Secular minster churches in Domesday Book', in *Domesday Book: a reassessment*, ed. P.H. Sawyer (1985), 104–42.

——'Local churches in Domesday Book and before', in *Domesday Studies*, ed. J.C. Holt (1987), 265–78.

——'Introduction: from minster to parish church', in *Minsters and Parish Churches: the local church in transition, 950–1200*, ed. J. Blair (1988), 1–19.

——'Minster churches in the landscape', in *Anglo-Saxon Settlements*, ed. D. Hooke (1988), 35–58.

——*Early Medieval Surrey: landholding, church and settlement before 1300* (1991).

——'Anglo-Saxon minsters: a topographical review', in *Pastoral Care before the Parish*, ed. J. Blair and R. Sharpe (1992), 226–66.

——*Anglo-Saxon Oxfordshire* (1994).

——'Ecclesiastical organization and pastoral care in Anglo-Saxon England', *EME*, 4 (2) (1995), 193–212.
——'Palaces or minsters? Northampton and Cheddar reconsidered', *ASE*, 25 (1996), 97–121.
——*The Church in Anglo-Saxon Society, 600–1100* (forthcoming).
Blair, J. and Sharpe, R. (eds) *Pastoral Care before the Parish* (1992).
——'Introduction', in *Pastoral Care before the Parish* (1992), 1–10.
Bloch, M., *Feudal Society* (2 vols, trans., 1961).
Bloomfield, L., *Language* (1935).
Böckenförde, E.W., *Die deutsche verfassungsgeschichtliche Forschung im 19. Jahrhundert: Zeitgebundene Fragestellungen un Leitbilder*, Schriften zur Verfassungsgeschichte 1 (Berlin, 1961).
Boddington, A., 'Modes of burial, settlement and worship: the final phase reviewed', in *Anglo-Saxon Cemeteries: a reappraisal*, ed. E. Southworth (1990), 177–99.
Boden, J.M. and Whitwell, J.B., 'Barrow-upon-Humber', *LHA*, 14 (1979), 66–7.
Bois, G., *The Transformation of the Year One Thousand* (trans. 1992).
Bonnassie, P., *La Catalogne du milieu du Xe siècle à la fin du XIe siècle: croissance et mutations d'une société* (Toulouse, 1975).
——'La croissance agricole du haut moyen âge dans la Gaule du Midi et le nord-est de la péninsule ibérique', in *Croissance agricole du haut moyen âge: chronologie, modalités, géographie, Flaran*, 10 (Auch, 1990), 13–35.
——*From Slavery to Feudalism in South-Western Europe* (1991).
Bonner, G., 'St Cuthbert at Chester-le-Street', in *St Cuthbert, His Cult and Community to A.D. 1200*, ed. G. Bonner, C. Stancliffe and D. Rollason (1989), 387–95.
Bonney, D., 'Pagan Saxon burials and boundaries in Wiltshire', *Wiltshire Archaeological and Natural History Magazine*, 61 (1966), 25–30.
——'Early boundaries and estates in southern England', in *English Medieval Settlement*, ed. P.H. Sawyer (1979), 41–51.
Bradley, J., 'The interpretation of Scandinavian settlement in Ireland', in *Settlement and Society in Medieval Ireland*, ed. J. Bradley (1988), 49–78.
Bradley, R., 'Time regained: the creation of continuity', *JBAA*, 140 (1987), 1–17.
Brakspear, S.A.J., 'Bardney Abbey', *Arch. J.*, 79 (1922), 1–92.
Brink, S., 'The onomasticon and the role of analogy in name formation', in *Namn och Bygd: Tidskrift för Nordisk Ortnamnsforskning*, ed. T. Andersson (Uppsala, 1996), 61–84.
Brooke, C.N.L., 'Rural ecclesiastical institutions in England: the search for their origins', *Settimane*, 28 (2) (1982), 685–711.
Brooks, N.P., 'The development of military obligations in eighth- and ninth-century England', in *England before the Conquest*, ed. P. Clemoes and K. Hughes (1971), 69–84.
——'England in the ninth century: the crucible of defeat', *TRHS*, 5th ser., 29 (1979), 1–20.
——*The Early History of the Church of Canterbury* (1984).
——'Rochester Bridge, AD 43–1381', in *Traffic and Politics*, ed. N. Yates and J.M. Gibson (1994), 1–40.
Brooks, N.P. and Graham-Campbell, J., 'Reflections on the Viking-Age silver hoard from Croydon, Surrey', in *Anglo-Saxon Monetary History*, ed. M.A.S. Blackburn (1986), 91–110.
Brooks, N., Gelling, M. and Johnson, D., 'A new charter of King Edgar', *ASE*, 13 (1984), 137–55.
Brown, R.A., 'The Norman Conquest', *TRHS*, 5th ser., 17 (1967), 109–20.
Brunner, O., *Land und Herrschaft: Grundfragen der territorialen Verfassungsgeschichte Österreichs im Mittelalter* (Vienna, 1939).
Bryant, G., *The Early History of Barton-upon-Humber* (1994).
Bullough, D., 'Burial, community and belief in the early medieval West', in *Ideal and Reality in Anglo-Saxon and Frankish Society*, ed. P. Wormald, D. Bullough and R. Collins (1983), 177–201.
Butler, L.A.S., 'Ledsham church: the south doorway of the tower', *JBAA*, 140 (1987), 199–203.
Cadman, G. and Foard, G., 'Raunds: manorial and village origins', in *Studies in Anglo-Saxon Settlement*, ed. M.L. Faull (1984), 81–100.

Cam, H.M., '*Manerium cum hundredo*: the hundred and the hundredal manor', *EHR*, 57 (1932), 353–76.
——*Liberties and Communities in Medieval England: collected studies in local administration and topography* (1944; reprinted 1963).
——'The community of the vill', in *Medieval Studies presented to Rose Graham*, ed. V. Ruffer and A.J. Taylor (1950), 1–14.
Cambridge, E., 'The early church in County Durham: a reassessment', *JBAA*, 137 (1984), 65–85.
——'Why did the community of St Cuthbert settle at Chester-le-Street?', in *St Cuthbert: His Cult and Community to AD 1200*, ed. G. Bonner, C. Stancliffe and D.W. Rollason (1989), 367–86.
Cambridge, E. and Rollason, D.W., 'The pastoral organization of the Anglo-Saxon church: review of the "minster hypothesis"', *EME*, 4 (1) (1995), 87–104.
Cambridge, E. and Williams, A., 'Hexham Abbey: a review of recent work and its implications', *Archaeologia Aeliana*, 5th ser., 23 (1995), 51–138.
Cameron, K., *Scandinavian Settlement in the Territory of the Five Boroughs: the place-name evidence* (1965).
——'Linguistic and place-name evidence', *Mediaeval Scandinavia*, 2 (1969), 176–7.
——'Scandinavian settlement in the territory of the Five Boroughs: the place-name evidence, part II: Place-names in thorp', *Mediaeval Scandinavia*, 3 (1970), 35–49.
——'Scandinavian settlement in the territory of the Five Boroughs: the place-name evidence, part III: The Grimston-hybrids', in *England before the Conquest*, ed. P. Clemoes and K. Hughes (1971), 147–63.
——'Early field-names in an English-named Lincolnshire village', in *Otium et Negotium*, ed. F. Sandgren (Stockholm, 1973), 38–43.
——'The minor names and field names of the Holland division of Lincolnshire', in *The Vikings*, ed. T. Andersson and K.I. Sandred (Uppsala, 1978), 81–8.
Campbell, B.M.S., 'Agricultural progress in medieval England: some evidence from Norfolk', *EcHR*, 2nd ser., 36 (1983), 24–46.
Campbell, J., 'Bede's words and places' in *Names, Words and Graves: early medieval settlement*, ed. P.H. Sawyer (1979), 34–53.
——'Epilogue', in *The Anglo-Saxons*, ed. J. Campbell (1982), 240–6.
——'The first Christian kings', in *The Anglo-Saxons*, ed. J. Campbell (1982), 45–69.
——*Essays in Anglo-Saxon History* (1986).
Campey, L.H., 'Medieval village plans in County Durham: an analysis of reconstructed plans based on medieval documentary sources', *Northern History*, 25 (1989), 60–87.
Canham, A.S., 'Notes on the history of Crowland: its charters and ancient crosses', *JBAA*, 46 (1890), 116–29.
Carle, M. del C., *Del concejo medieval castellano-leonés* (Buenos Aires, 1968).
Carr, R.D., Tester, A. and Murphy, P., 'The middle Saxon settlement at Staunch Meadow, Brandon', *Antiquity*, 62 (1988), 371–7.
Chadwick, H.M., *Anglo-Saxon Institutions* (1905).
Chadwick, S.J., 'Notes on Dewsbury church and some of its rectors and vicars', *YAJ*, 20 (1909), 369–446.
Chapelot, J. and Fossier, R., *The Village and House in the Middle Ages* (1985).
Charles-Edwards, T.M., 'Kinship, status and origins of the hide', *Past and Present*, 56 (1972), 3–33.
——'The distinction between land and moveable wealth in Anglo-Saxon England', in *English Medieval Settlement*, ed. P.H. Sawyer (1979), 97–104.
——'Early medieval kingships in the British Isles', in *The Origins of Anglo-Saxon Kingdoms*, ed. S.R. Bassett (1989), 28–37.
Clanchy, M., *From Memory to Written Record: England 1066–1307* (2nd edn, 1993).
Clapham, A.H., 'Six early carved stones from South Kyme, Lincolnshire', *Antiq. J.*, 3 (1923), 118–21.
Clark, C., *The Peterborough Chronicle 1070–1154* (2nd edn, 1970).
——'Clark's first three laws of applied anthroponymics', *Nomina*, 3 (1979), 13–19.
——'Personal-name studies: bringing them to a wider audience', *Nomina*, 15 (1991), 21–34.
Cockerton, R.W.P., 'The Wirksworth slab', *DAJ*, 82 (1962), 1–20.

Coggins, D., Fairless, K.J. and Batey, C.E., 'Simy Folds: an early medieval settlement in Upper Teesdale', *Medieval Archaeology* 27 (1982), 1–26.
Collingwood, W.G., 'Anglian and Anglo-Danish sculpture in the North Riding of Yorkshire, *YAJ*, 19 (1907), 267–413.
——'Anglian and Anglo-Danish sculpture in the West Riding of Yorkshire', *YAJ*, 23 (1915), 129–299.
——*Northumbrian Crosses of the Pre-Norman Age* (1927).
Coppack, G., 'St Lawrence church, Burnham, South Humberside: the excavation of a parochial chapel', *LHA*, 21 (1986), 39–60.
Costen, M., 'Huish and worth: Old English survivals in a later landscape' in *ASSAH*, 5, ed. W. Filmer-Sankey (1992), 65–83.
Cox, B., 'The significance of the distribution of the English place-names in *ham* in the Midlands and East Anglia', *JEPNS* 5 (1973), 15–73.
Cox, J.C., *Notes on the Churches of Derbyshire* (4 vols, 1875).
——'On an early Christian tomb at Wirksworth', in *Bygone Derbs*, ed. W. Andrews (1892), 19–32.
——'The collegiate church of All Saints, Derby', *VCH Derbyshire* 88–9.
——'Southwell', *VCH Notts*, 152–61.
Cramp, R., 'The position of the Otley crosses in English sculpture of the eighth to ninth centuries', *Kolloquium über spätantike und frühmittelalterliche Skulptur*, 2 (Mainz 1970), 55–63.
——'Monastic sites', in *The Archaeology of Anglo-Saxon England*, ed. D.M. Wilson (1976), 223–41.
——'Schools of Mercian sculpture' in *Mercian Studies*, ed. A. Dornier (1977), 191–233.
——'The furnishing and sculptural decoration of Anglo-Saxon churches' in *The Anglo-Saxon Church*, ed. L.A.S. Butler and R.K. Morris (CBA Res. Rep., 60, 1986), 000–000.
——'A reconsideration of the monastic site of Whitby', in *The Age of Migrating Ideas*, ed. R.M. Spearman and J. Higgitt (1993), 64–73.
Craster, E., 'The patrimony of St Cuthbert', *EHR*, 69 (1954), 177–99.
Crawford, S., 'The Anglo-Saxon cemetery at Chimney, Oxfords.', *Oxoniensia*, 54 (1989), 45–56.
Croom, J.N., 'The minster *parochiae* of south-east Shropshire', in *Minsters and Parish Churches: the local church in transition, 900–1250*, ed. J. Blair (1988), 67–82.
Cubitt, C.R.E., 'Pastoral care and conciliar canons: the provisions of the 747 council of *Clofesho*', in *Pastoral Care before the Parish*, ed. J. Blair and R. Sharpe (1992), 193–211.
——*Anglo-Saxon Church Councils c. 650–c. 850* (1995).
Curtis, M., 'Catterick', *VCH N. Riding*, II, 301–13.
Dalton, P., *Conquest, Anarchy and Lordship: Yorkshire 1066–1154* (1994).
Daniels, R., 'The Anglo-Saxon monastery at Church Close, Hartlepool, Cleveland', *Arch. J.*, 145 (1988), 158–210.
Dannenbauer, H., *Grundlagen der mittelalterlichen Welt* (Stuttgart, 1958).
Darby, H.C. and Maxwell, I.S., *The Domesday Geography of Northern England* (1962).
Davies, D.S., 'Pre-Conquest carved stones in Lincolnshire', *Arch. J.* 83 (1926), 1–20.
Davies, G.T., 'The origins of the parishes of south Yorkshire', *South Yorkshire Historian*, 4 (1980), 1–18.
——'The Anglo-Saxon boundaries of Sutton and Scrooby, Nottinghamshire', *TTS*, 87 (1983), 13–22.
Davies, W., *Wales in the Early Middle Ages* (1982).
——*Small Worlds* (1988).
Davies, W. and Vierck, H., 'The contexts of Tribal Hidage: social aggregates and settlement patterns', *Frühmittelalterliche Studien*, 8 (1974), 223–93.
Davis, R.H.C., 'East Anglia and the Danelaw', *TRHS*, 5th ser., 5 (1955), 23–39.
——'Alfred and Guthrum's frontier', *EHR*, 97 (1982), 803–10.
Delort, R. (ed.) *La France de l'an mil* (Paris 1990).
Denton, J.H., *English Royal Free Chapels 1100–1300* (1970).
Devroey, J.P., 'Les premiers polyptyques remois, viie–viiie siècles', *Études sur le grand domaine carolingien*, ed. J.P. Devroey (1993), 78–97.

Dickinson, S., 'Bryant's Gill, Kentmere: another "viking period" Ribblehead?', in *The Scandinavians in Cumbria*, ed. J.R. Baldwin and I.D. White (1985), 83–8.
Ditchum, B.G.H., 'The feudal millennium? Social change in rural France *circa* 1000 in recent French historiography', *Medieval History* 3 (1993), 86–99.
Doble, G.H., *St Symphorian*, Cornish Saints, 27 (1931).
Dockès, P., *Medieval Slavery and Liberation* (trans. Chicago, 1982).
Dodgshon, R., *The European Past: social evolution and spatial order* (1987).
Dodgson, J.McN., 'The significance of the distribution of English place-names in *-ingas* and *-inga-* in south-east England', *Medieval Archaeology* 10, (1966), 27–54.
Dodwell, B., 'The free peasantry of East Anglia in Domesday', *Norfolk Archaeology* 27 (1947), 145–57.
——'East Anglian commendation', *EHR*, 63 (1948), 289–306.
Dolley, M., *Viking Coins of the Danelaw and of Dublin* (1965).
——'The Anglo-Danish and Anglo-Norse coinages of York', in *Viking Age York and the North*, ed. R.A. Hall (CBA Research Report, 27, 1978), 26–31.
Dopsch, A., *Die Wirtschaftsentwicklung der Karolingerzeit vornehmlich in Deutschland* (Darmstadt, 1912–13).
——*Wirtschaftliche und soziale Grundlagen der europäischen Kulturentwicklung aus der Zeit von Cäsar bis auf Karl den Grossen* (Aalen, 1918–20).
Douglas, D.C., *The Social Structure of Medieval East Anglia*, Oxford Studies in Social and Legal History, ed. P. Vinogradoff, 9 (1927).
Drew, C.D., 'The manors of the Iwerne Valley, Dorset: a study of early country planning', *Proceedings of the Dorset Natural History and Archaeological Society*, 69 (1948), 45–50.
Duby, D., *Rural Economy and Country Life in the Medieval West* (trans. 1968).
——*The Early Growth of the European Economy: warriors and peasants from the seventh to the twelfth century* (trans. 1974).
Dumville, D., *Wessex and England from Alfred to Edgar* (1992).
——*The Churches of North Britain in the First Viking-Age*, Fifth Whithorn Lecture (1997).
Dyer, C.C., *Lords and Peasants in a Changing Society* (1980), 25.
——'Power and conflict in the medieval English village', in *Medieval Villages: a review of current work*, ed. D. Hooke (1985), 27–32.
——'English peasant buildings in the later Middle Ages', *Medieval Archaeology*, 30 (1986), 19–45.
——'Were peasants self-sufficient? English villagers and the market, 900–1350' in *Campagnes médiévales: l'homme et son espace*, ed. E. Mornet (Paris 1995), 653–66.
——'St Oswald and 10,000 west Midland peasants', in *St Oswald of Worcester: life and influence*, ed. N.P. Brooks and C.R.E. Cubitt (1996), 174–93.
Eagles, N. and Evison, V., 'Excavations at Harrold, Bedfordshire', *Bedfordshire Archaeological Journal*, 5 (1970), 17–55.
Ecclestone, M., 'Townships with detached parts', in *Yorkshire Boundaries*, ed. H.E.J. Le Patourel, M.H. Long and M.F. Pickles (1993), 75–84.
Effros, B., '*De Partibus Saxoniae* and the regulation of mortuary custom: a Carolingian campaign of Christianization or the suppression of Saxon identity?', *Revue Belge de Philologie et d'Histoire*, 75, fasc. 2 (1995), 267–86.
Ekwall, E., 'The proportion of Scandinavian settlers in the Danelaw', *Saga-Book of the Viking Society*, 12 (1937–45), 19–34.
Ellis, P., 'Roman Chesterfield', *DAJ*, 109 (1987), 51–130.
Elspeth, S., 'The abbey of Bardney', *VCH Lincs*, 97–103.
——'The abbey of Stow', *VCH Lincs*, 118.
English, B., *The Lords of Holderness, 1086–1260: a study in feudal society* (1979).
Ersgard, L., 'The change of religion and its artefacts: an example from Upper Dalarna', *Papers of the Archaeological Institute*, new ser., 10 (Lund, 1993–4), 79–94.
Everitt, A., 'River and wold: reflections on the historical origins of regions and pays', *JHG*, 3 (1977), 1–19.
——'The wolds once more', *JHG*, 5 (1979), 67–78.
——*Continuity and Colonization: the evolution of Kentish settlement* (1986).
Everson, P., 'The pre-Conquest estate at *æt Bearuwe*', in *Studies in Late Anglo-Saxon Settlement*, ed. M. Faull (1984), 123–7.

——'What's in a name? "Goltho", Goltho and Bullington', *LHA*, 23 (1988), 93–9.
——'Pre-Viking settlement in Lindsey', in *Pre-Viking Lindsey*, ed. A. Vince (1993), 91–100.
Everson, P., Taylor, C.C. and Dunn, C.J., *Change and Continuity: rural settlement in north-west Lincolnshire* (1991).
Evison, M., 'Lo, the conquering hero comes (or not)', *British Archaeology*, 23 (April 1997), 8–9.
Faith, R., 'Estates, demesnes and the village', in *The Origins of the Midland Village*, Papers prepared for a discussion at the Economic History Society's annual conference, Leicester (1992), 11–35.
——*The English Peasantry and the Growth of Lordship* (1997).
Fallow, T.M., 'The hospital of St Leonard, York', *VCH Yorks*, 336–45.
Farrer, W., 'Introduction to the Yorkshire Domesday', in *The Victoria History of the County of York*, vol. II, ed. W.M. Page (1912), 210.
Faull, M.L., 'The decoration of the south doorway of Ledsham church tower', *JBAA*, 139 (1986), 143–7.
Faull, M.L. and Moorhouse, S.A., *West Yorkshire: an archaeological survey to AD 1500* (4 vols, 1981).
Fellows Jensen, G., *Scandinavian Personal Names in Lincolnshire and Yorkshire* (Copenhagen, 1968).
——*Scandinavian Settlement Names in Yorkshire* (Copenhagen, 1972).
——'The vikings in England: a review', *ASE* 4 (1975), 181–206.
——'Place-names and the Scandinavian settlement in the North Riding of Yorkshire', *Northern History*, 14 (1978), 19–46.
——*Scandinavian Settlement Names in the East Midlands* (Copenhagen, 1978).
——'Lancashire and Yorkshire names', *Northern History*, 19 (1983), 231–7.
——'Of Danes – and thanes – and Domesday Book', in *People and Places in Northern Europe, 500–1600*, ed. I.N. Wood and N. Lund (1991), 107–21.
——'Place-names in -þorp. In retrospect and in turmoil', *Nomina*, 15 (1991–2), 35–52.
——'From Scandinavia to the British Isles and back again: linguistic give-and-take in the viking period', in *Developments around the Baltic and North Sea in the Viking Age*, ed. B. Ambrosiani and H. Clarke (Stockholm, 1994), 253–68.
——'Scandinavian settlement in Yorkshire – through the rear-view mirror', in *Scandinavian Settlement in Northern Britain*, ed. B.E. Crawford (1995), 170–86.
Fenger, O., 'The Danelaw and the Danish law', *Scandinavian Studies in Law*, 16 (1972), 85–96.
Fenwick, V., 'Insula de Burgh: excavations at Burrow Hill, Butley, Suffolk, 1978–81', in *ASSAH*, 3, ed. D. Brown (1984), 35–54.
Finberg, H.P.R., *Lucerna: studies of some problems in the early history of England* (1964).
——'Anglo-Saxon England to 1042' in *Ag. Hist.*, I.II, 385–525.
Firby, M. and Lang, J.T., 'The pre-Conquest sculpture at Stonegrave', *YAJ*, 53 (1981), 17–29.
Fleming, R., 'Monastic lands and England's defence in the viking age', *EHR*, 100 (1985), 247–65.
——'Domesday Book and the tenurial revolution', *ANS*, 9 (1987), 86–102.
——*Kings and Lords in Conquest England* (1991).
Fletcher, R.A., *The Conversion of Europe: from paganism to Christianity, 371–1386* (1997).
Foot, S., 'Parochial ministry in early Anglo-Saxon England: the role of monastic communities', in *The Ministry*, Studies in Church History, 26, ed. W. Sheils and D. Wood (1989), 43–54.
——'Anglo-Saxon minsters: a review of terminology', in *Pastoral Care before the Parish*, ed. J. Blair and R. Sharpe (1992), 212–25.
——'The kingdom of Lindsey', in *Pre-Viking Lindsey*, ed. A. Vince (1993), 128–140.
Fossier, R., *La Terre et les hommes en Picardie jusqu'à la fin du XIIe siècle* (Paris, 1968).
Fox, H.S.A., 'Approaches to the adoption of the Midland system', in *The Origins of Open-Field Agriculture*, ed. T. Rowley (1981), 64–111.
——'The people of the wolds in English settlement history', in *The Rural Settlements of Medieval England*, ed. M. Aston, D. Austin and C.C. Dyer (1989).

——'The agrarian context', in *The Origins of the Midland Village*, Papers prepared for a discussion at the Economic History Society's annual conference, Leicester (1992), 36–72.

Franklin, M.J., 'The identification of minsters in the Midlands', *ANS*, 7 (1985), 69–88.

——'St Augustine's, Daventry', in *Minsters and Parish Churches: the local church in transition, 950–1200*, ed. J. Blair (1988), 97–104.

Friedman, P., *The Origins of Peasant Servitude in Medieval Catalonia* (1991).

Geake, H., *The Use of Grave-Goods in Conversion-Period England*, c. *600*–c. *850* (BAR British Series, 261, 1997).

Geary, P., 'Ethnic identity as a situational construct in the early Middle Ages', *Mitteilungen der Anthropologischen Gesellschaft in Wien*, 113 (1983), 15–26.

Geipel, J., *The Viking Legacy: the Scandinavian influence on the English and Gaelic languages* (1971).

Gelling, M., *The Names of Towns and Cities in Britain* (1971).

——*Signposts to the Past* (1978).

——'Some meanings of Stow', in *The Early Church in Western Britain and Ireland*, ed. S.M. Pearce (BAR British Series, 102, 1982), 187–96.

Gem, R., 'Architecture of the Anglo-Saxon church, 735 to 870: from Archbishop Ecgberht to Archbishop Ceolnoth', *JBAA*, 146 (1993), 29–66.

——'The episcopal churches of Lindsey in the early ninth century', in *Pre-Viking Lindsey*, ed. A. Vince (1993), 123–7.

Gem, R. and Thurlby, M., 'The early monastic church of Lastingham' in *Yorkshire Monasticism: archaeology, art and architecture from the 7th to 16th centuries AD*, ed. L.R. Hoey, British Archaeological Association Conference Transactions, 15 (1995), 31–9.

Genicot, L., 'Sur le domaine de Saint-Bertin à l'époque carolingienne', *Revue d'Histoire Ecclésiastique*, 71 (1976), 69–78.

Gilchrist, R., *Gender and Material Culture: the archaeology of religious women* (1994).

——'Ambivalent bodies: gender and medieval archaeology', in *Invisible People and Processes: writing gender and childhood into European archaeology*, ed. J.M. Moore and E. Scott (1997), 42–58.

Gilmour, B.J.J. and Stocker, D., *St Mark's Church and Cemetery*, The Archaeology of Lincoln, 13 (1) (1986).

Gneuss, H., 'The origin of Standard Old English and Æthelwold's school at Winchester', *ASE*, 1 (1972), 63–83.

Godfrey, J.T., *The History of the Parish and Priory of Lenton* (1884).

——*Notes on the Churches of Nottinghamshire: Bingham Hundred* (1907).

Godman, P., *Alcuin, the Bishops, Kings and Saints of York* (1982).

Goodier, A., 'The formation of boundaries in Anglo-Saxon England: a statistical study', *Medieval Archaeology*, 28 (1984), 1–21.

Graham, R., 'The Abbey of Crowland', *VCH Lincs*, 105–18.

Graham-Campbell, J., 'The Scandinavian Viking-Age burials of England: some problems of interpretation', in *Anglo-Saxon Cemeteries*, ed. P. Rahtz, T. Dickinson and L. Watts (BAR British Series, 82 (1980)), 379–82.

——'Pagans and Christians', *History Today*, 36 (October 1986), 24–8.

——(ed.) *Cultural Atlas of the Viking World* (1994).

Gregson, N., 'The multiple estate model: some critical questions', *JHG*, 11 (1985), 339–51.

Grierson, P. and Blackburn, M.A.S. (eds) *Medieval European Coinage, I: the early Middle Ages (5th–10th centuries)* (1986).

Hadley, D.M., 'Danelaw society and institutions: east midlands' phenomena?' (Ph.D. thesis, University of Birmingham, 2 vols, 1992).

——'The historical context of the inhumation cemetery at Bromfield, Shropshire', *Transactions of the Shropshire Archaeological and Historical Society* 70 (1995), 145–55.

——'Multiple estates and the origins of the manorial structure of the northern Danelaw', *JHG*, 22 (1) (1996), 3–15.

——' "And they proceeded to plough and to support themselves": the Scandinavian settlement of England', *ANS*, 19 (1997), 69–96.

——'In search of the vikings: the problems and the possibilities of interdisciplinary approaches', in *The Vikings and the Danelaw*, ed. J. Graham-Campbell, R. Hall, J. Jesch and D. Parsons (forthcoming).

——'Burial practices in the northern Danelaw, *c.* 600–1100' (forthcoming).

Hadley, D.M. and Richards, J.D. (eds) *Cultures in Contact: Scandinavian settlement in England* (forthcoming).

Hald, K., *Vore Stednavne* (Copenhagen, 1965).

Haldenby, D., 'An Anglian site on the Yorkshire Wolds', *YAJ*, 62 (1990), 51–62.

——'An Anglian site on the Yorkshire Wolds', *YAJ*, 64 (1992), 25–40.

Hall, K.M., 'Pre-Conquest estates in Yorkshire' in *Yorkshire Boundaries*, ed. H.E.J. Le Patourel, M.H. Long and M.F. Pickles (1993), 25–38.

Hall, R.A., 'Rescue excavation in the crypt of Ripon cathedral', *YAJ*, 49 (1977), 59–63.

——'The Five Boroughs of the Danelaw: a review of present knowledge', *ASE*, 18 (1989), 149–206.

——'Observations in Ripon cathedral crypt, 1989', *YAJ*, 65 (1993), 39–53.

——*Viking Age York* (1994).

——'Vikings gone west? A summary review', in *Developments around the Baltic and North Sea in the Viking Age*, ed. B. Ambrosiani and H. Clarke (Stockholm, 1994), 32–49.

——'Antiquaries and archaeology in and around Ripon minster', in *Yorkshire Monasticism: archaeology, art and architecture from the 7th to 16th centuries AD*, ed. L.R. Hoey, British Archaeological Association Conference Transactions, 15 (1995), 12–30.

Hall, R.A. (ed.) *Viking Age York and the North* (CBA Research Report, 27, 1978).

Hall, R.A. and Whyman, M., 'Settlement and monasticism at Ripon, North Yorkshire, from the 7th to 11th centuries AD', *Medieval Archaeology* 40, (1996), 62–150.

Hallam, H.E., 'Some thirteenth-century censuses', *EcHR*, 2nd ser., 10 (1958), 340–61.

——*Settlement and Society: a study of the early agrarian history of south Lincolnshire* (1965).

Halsall, G., *Settlement and Social Organization: the Merovingian region of Metz* (1995).

——'The Merovingian period in north-east Gaul: transition or change?', in *Europe between Late Antiquity and the Middle Ages*, ed. J. Bintliff and H. Hamerow (BAR International Series, 617, 1995), 38–57.

——'Female status and power in Merovingian central Austrasia: the burial evidence', *EME* 5 (1) (1996), 1–24.

——'The origins of Anglo-Saxon kingdoms: a Merovingianist speaks out' (forthcoming).

——'The viking presence in England? The burial evidence reconsidered', in *Cultures in Contact: Scandinavian Settlement in England*, ed. D.M. Hadley and J.D. Richards (forthcoming).

Hamerow, H., 'Settlement mobility and the "Middle Saxon shift": rural settlements and settlement patterns in Anglo-Saxon England', *ASE*, 20 (1991), 1–17.

Hamshere, J.D., 'Domesday Book: estate structures in the west Midlands', in *Domesday Studies*, ed. J.C. Holt (1987), 155–182.

Hansen, B.H., 'The historical implications of the Scandinavian element in English: a theoretical valuation', *Nowele*, 4 (1984), 53–95.

Harley, J.B., *The Historian's Guide to Ordnance Survey Maps* (1964).

——*Maps and the Local Historian* (1972).

Hart, C.R., *The North Derbyshire Archaeological Survey to AD 1500* (1981).

——*The Danelaw* (1992).

Harvey, M., 'Irregular villages in Holderness, Yorkshire: some thoughts on their origin', *YAJ*, 54 (1982), 63–71.

——'Planned field systems in east Yorkshire: some thoughts on their origins', *AgHR*, 31 (1983), 91–103.

——'Open field structure and landholding arrangements in eastern Yorkshire', *IBGT*, new ser., 9 (1984), 60–74.

Harvey, P.D.A., 'Initiative and authority in settlement change', in *The Rural Settlements of Medieval England*, ed. M. Aston, D. Austin and C.C. Dyer (1989), 31–43.

——'Rectitudines Singularum Personarum and Gerefa', *EHR*, 108 (1993), 1–22.
Harvey, S.J., 'Royal revenue and Domesday terminology', *EcHR*, 2nd ser., 20 (1967), 221–8.
——'Domesday Book and its predecessors', *EHR*, 86 (1971), 753–73.
——'The extent and profitability of demesne agriculture in England in the late eleventh century', in *Social Relations and Ideas*, ed. T.H. Aston, P. Coss, C.C. Dyer and J. Thirsk (1983), 45–72.
——'Domesday England', *Ag. Hist*, II, 45–136.
Hase, P.H., 'The development of the parish in Hampshire' (Ph.D. thesis, University of Cambridge 1975).
——'The mother churches of Hampshire' in *Minsters and Parish Churches: the local church in transition, 950–1200*, ed. J. Blair (1988), 45–66.
——'The church in the Wessex heartlands', in *The Medieval Landscape of Wessex*, ed. M. Aston and C. Lewis (1994), 47–81.
Haslam, J., 'Parishes, churches, wards and gates in eastern London', in *Minsters and Parish Churches: the local church in transition, 950–1200*, ed. J. Blair (1988), 35–43.
Hawkes, J., 'Mary and the cycle of Resurrection: the iconography of the Hovingham panel', in *The Age of Migrating Ideas*, ed. R.M. Spearman and J. Higgitt (1993), 254–60.
Heather, P., *The Goths* (1996).
Higham, N., *The Origins of Cheshire* (1993).
Hill, D., *An Atlas of Anglo-Saxon England* (1981).
Hines, J., 'Scandinavian English: a creole in context', in *Language Contact in the British Isles*, ed. P.S. Ureland and G. Broderick (Tübingen 1991), 403–27.
——'Focus and boundary in linguistic varieties in the North-West Germanic continuum', in *Friesische Studien II*, ed. V.F. Faltings, A.G.H. Walker and A. Wilts (Odense, 1995), 35–62.
Hinton, D., *Archaeology, Economy and Society: England from the fifth to the fifteenth century* (1990).
Hodges, R., *The Anglo-Saxon Achievement* (1989).
Hooke, D., *Anglo-Saxon Landscapes of the West Midlands: the charter evidence* (BAR British Series, 95, 1981).
——*The Landscape of Anglo-Saxon Staffordshire: the charter evidence* (1983).
Horrox, R.E., 'Medieval Beverley', *VCH E. Riding*, VI, 2–62.
Hoskins, W.G., *The Making of the English Landscape* (1955; 3rd edn, 1988, with a commentary by C.C. Taylor).
Hudson, W., 'Traces of primitive agricultural organization as suggested by a survey of the manor of Martham, Norfolk, 1101–1292', *TRHS*, 4th ser., 1 (1918), 28–58.
Huggins, R., 'The significance of the place-name *wealdham*', *Medieval Archaeology*, 19 (1975), 198–201.
Hunke, H., *Germanische Freiheit im Verstandnis der deutschen Rechts- und Verfassungsgeschichtsschreibung* (Göttingen 1972).
Hyams, P.R., *Kings, Lords and Peasants in Medieval England* (1980).
Innes, M., 'Danelaw identities: ethnicity, regionalism and political allegiance', in *Cultures in Contact: Scandinavian settlement in England*, ed. D.M. Hadley and J.D. Richards (forthcoming).
Insley, J., 'Regional variation in Scandinavian personal nomenclature in England', *Nomina*, 3 (1979), 52–60.
——'Toponymy and settlement in the North-West', *Nomina*, 10 (1986), 69–76.
James, E., *The Origins of France* (1982).
John, E., *Land Tenure in Early England*, Studies in Early English History, 1, ed. H.P.R. Finberg (1960).
——*Orbis Britanniae and Other Studies*, Studies in Early English History, 4, ed. H.P.R. Finberg (1966).
——'The age of Edgar', in *The Anglo-Saxons*, ed. J. Campbell (1982), 160–91.
Jolliffe, J.E.A., *Pre-Feudal England: the Jutes* (1933).
Jones, G., *A History of the Vikings* (2nd edn, 1984).
Jones, G.R.J., 'Early territorial organization in northern England and its bearing on the Scandinavian settlement', in *The Fourth Viking Congress*, ed. A. Small (1965), 67–84.

——'The multiple estate as a model framework for tracing early stages in the evolution of rural settlement', in *L'Habitat et les paysages ruraux d'Europe*, ed. F. Bussat (Liège, 1971), 251–67.

——'Early territorial organization in Gwynedd and Elmet', *Northern History*, 10 (1975), 3–25.

——'Multiple estates and early settlement', in *English Medieval Settlement*, ed. P.H. Sawyer (1979).

——'Some donations to Bishop Wilfrid in northern England', *Northern History*, 31 (1995), 22–38.

Jones, S., 'Discourses of identity in the interpretation of the past' in *Cultural Identity and Archaeology*, ed. P. Graves-Brown, S. Jones and S. Gamble (1995), 62–80.

——*The Archaeology of Ethnicity: constructing identities in the past and present* (1997).

Jones, S. and Graves-Brown, P., 'Introduction: archaeology and cultural identity in Europe', in *Cultural Identity and Archaeology*, ed. P. Graves-Brown, S. Jones and S. Gamble (1995), 1–24.

Joy, C.A., 'Sokeright' (Ph.D. thesis, University of Leeds 1972).

Kaner, J., 'Crayke and its boundaries', in *Yorkshire Boundaries*, ed. H.E.J. Le Patourel, M.H. Long and M.F. Pickles (1993), 103–11.

Kapelle, W.E., *The Norman Conquest of the North: the region and its transformation, 1000–1135* (1979).

Karras, R., *Slavery and Society in Medieval Scandinavia* (New Haven, Connecticut 1988).

Kastovsky, D., 'Semantics and vocabulary' in *The Cambridge History of the English Language*, ed. R.M. Hogg (1992), vol. 1, 290–408.

Kaye, J.M., 'The Sacrabar', *EHR*, 83 (1968), 744–58.

Kemble, J.M., *The Saxons in England* (2 vols, 1849).

Kemp, B.R., 'The mother church of Thatcham', *Berkshire Archaeological Journal*, 63 (1967–8), 15–22.

——'The churches of Berkeley Hernesse', *Transactions of the Bristol and Gloucester Archaeological Society*, 87 (1968), 96–110.

Keynes, S., 'The Fonthill letter', in *Words, Texts and Manuscripts: studies in Anglo-Saxon culture presented to Helmut Gneuss*, ed. M. Korhammer (1992), 53–97.

——'The vikings in England, *c.* 790–1016', in *The Oxford Illustrated History of the Vikings*, ed. P.H. Sawyer (1997), 48–82.

King, A., 'Gauber High Pasture, Ribblehead: an interim report', in *Viking Age York and the North*, ed. R.A. Hall (CBA Research Report, 27, 1978), 31–6.

King, E., 'The Peterborough "*descriptio militum*"', *EHR*, 84 (1969), 84–101.

Kirby, D.P., 'The Saxon bishops of Leicester, Lindsey (*Syddensis*), and Dorchester', *Leicestershire Archaeological and History Society Transactions* 41 (1965–6), 1–8.

——'Bede, Eddius Stephanus and the "Life of Wilfrid"', *EHR*, 98 (1983), 101–14.

Krieger, L., *The German Idea of Freedom: history of a political tradition* (1957).

Kristensen, A.K.G., 'Danelaw institutions and Danish society in the viking age: *sochemanni, liberi homines* and *königsfreie*', *Mediaeval Scandinavia*, 8 (1975), 27–85.

——'Free peasants in the early Middle Ages: freeholders, freedmen or what?', *Mediaeval Scandinavia*, 12 (1988), 76–106.

Krogman, W.M. and Iscan, M.Y., *The Human Skeleton in Forensic Medicine* (Springfield, Ill., 1988).

Laing, C.E., 'Excavations on the site of Bardney Abbey', *AASRP*, 32 (1914), 20–34.

Lancaster, L., 'Kinship in Anglo-Saxon society, I', *British Journal of Sociology*, 9 (1958), 230–50.

——'Kinship in Anglo-Saxon society, II', *British Journal of Sociology*, 9 (1958), 359–77.

Lang, J.T., 'Sigurd and Welland in pre-Conquest carving from northern England', *YAJ*, 48 (1976), 83–94.

——'Anglo-Scandinavian sculpture in Yorkshire', in *Viking Age York and the North*, ed. R.A. Hall (CBA Research Report, 27, 1978), 11–20.

——'Recent studies in the pre-Conquest sculpture of Northumbria', in *Studies in Medieval Sculpture*, ed. F.H. Thompson (1983), 177–89.

——*Corpus of Anglo-Saxon Stone Sculpture, III: York and Eastern Yorkshire* (1991).

——(ed.) *Anglo-Saxon and Viking Age Sculpture and Its Context* (BAR British Series, 49, 1978).

Lapidge, M., 'Byrhtforth of Ramsey and the early sections of the *Historia Regum* attributed to Simeon of Durham', *ASE*, 10 (1982), 97–122.

Latouche, R., *The Birth of Western Economy: economic aspects of the Dark Ages* (trans. 1961).

Lauranson-Rosaz, C., *L'Auvergne et ses marges du VIIIe au XIe siècle: la fin du monde antique?* (Le-Puy-en-Velay, 1987), 397–9.

Lennard, R.V., 'The economic position of the Domesday sokemen', *Economic Journal* 57, (1947), 179–95.

——*Rural England 1086–1135: a study of social and agrarian conditions* (1959).

Lewis, C., Mitchell-Fox, P. and Dyer, C.C., *Village, Hamlet and Field: changing medieval settlements in central England* (1997).

Long, M.H., 'Howden and Old Drax', in *Yorkshire Boundaries*, ed. H.E.J. Le Patourel, M.H. Long and M.F. Pickles (1993).

——'Newbald' in *Yorkshire Boundaries*, ed. H.E.J. Le Patourel, M.H. Long and M.F. Pickles (1993), 134–41.

Long, M.H. and Pickles, M.F., 'Patrington', in *Yorkshire Boundaries*, ed. H.E.J. Le Patourel, M.H. Long and M.F. Pickles (1993), 143–50.

Loveluck, C., 'A high-status Anglo-Saxon settlement at Flixborough, Lincolnshire', *Antiquity*, 72 (1998), 146–61.

Loyn, H.R., *Anglo-Saxon England and the Norman Conquest* (2nd edn, 1991).

Lund, N., 'The secondary migration', *Mediaeval Scandinavia* 1 (1969), 196–201.

——'King Edgar and the Danelaw', *Mediaeval Scandinavia*, 9 (1976), 181–95.

——'Personal-names and place-names: the persons and the places', *Onoma*, 19 (1976), 468–86.

——'*Thorp*-names', in *Medieval Settlement: continuity and change*, ed. P.H. Sawyer (1976), 223–5.

——'The settlers: where do we get them from – and do we need them?', in *Proceedings of the Eighth Viking Congress*, ed. H. Bekker-Nielsen *et al.* (Odense, 1981), 147–71.

——'Allies of God or Man? The viking expansion in a European context', *Viator*, 19 (1989), 45–59.

——'Scandinavia, *c.* 700–1066', in *The Cambridge New Medieval History, II*, c. 700–c. 900, ed. R. McKitterick (1995), 202–27.

Lyth, P., 'The Southwell charter of 956 AD: an exploration of its boundaries', *TTS*, 86 (1982), 49–61.

McGovern, J.F., 'The meaning of "gesette land", in Anglo-Saxon land tenure', *Speculum* 45 (1971), 589–96.

McGuire, A. and Clark, A., *The Leeds Crosses* (1987).

McIntosh, A., 'Codes and cultures', in *Speaking in Our Tongues*, ed. M. Laing and K. Williamson (1994), 135–7.

Magnou-Nortier, E., *La Société laïque et l'Église dans la province ecclésiastique de Narbonne de la fin du VIIIe siècle à la fin du XIIe siècle* (Toulouse, 1974).

Mainman, A.J., *Anglo-Scandinavian Pottery from Coppergate* (CBA Archaeology of York, 16/5, 1990).

Maitland, F.W., *Domesday Book and Beyond* (1897).

Mayer, T., *Mittelalterliche Studien: gesammelte Aufsätze* (Lindau 1959).

Metcalf, D.M., 'The monetary history of England in the tenth century viewed in the perspective of the eleventh century' in *Anglo-Saxon Monetary History: essays in memory of Michael Dolley*, ed. M.A.S. Blackburn (1986), 133–58.

Metz, W., *Das karolingische Reichsgut: eine verfassungsgeschichtliche Untersuchung* (Berlin, 1960).

Miller, E., *The Abbey and Bishopric of Ely: the social history of an ecclesiastical estate from the tenth to the early fourteenth Century* (1951).

——'La Société rurale en Angleterre (Xe–XIIIe siècles)', *Settimane*, 13 (1966), 111–34.

Moore, J., 'Domesday slavery', *ANS*, 11 (1988), 191–220.

Moore, R.I., 'The first European peace movement, or virtue rewarded', *Medieval History*, 2 (1) (1992), 16–25.

Morris, C.D., 'Northumbria and the viking settlement: the evidence for land-holding', *Archaeologia Aeliana*, 5th ser., 4 (1977), 81–103.

——'Viking and native in northern England: a case study', in *Proceedings of the Eighth Viking Congress*, ed. H. Bekker-Nielsen *et al.* (Odense, 1981), 223–44.

——'Aspects of Scandinavian settlement in northern England: a review', *Northern History* 20 (1984), 1–22.

Morris, I., *Death-Ritual and Social Structure in Classical Antiquity* (1992).

Morris, R.K., *The Church in British Archaeology* (CBA Res. Rep., 47, 1983).

——'The church in the countryside: two lines of enquiry', in *Medieval Villages: a review of current work*, ed. D. Hooke (1985), 47–60.

——'Alcuin, York and the *alma sophia*', in *The Anglo-Saxon Church*, ed. L.A.S. Butler and R.K. Morris (CBA Res. Rep., 60, 1986), 80–9.

——'Churches in York and its hinterland: building patterns and stone sources in the 11th and 12th centuries', in *Minsters and Parish Churches: the local church in transition, 950–1200*, ed. J. Blair (1988), 191–200.

——*Churches in the Landscape* (1989).

Morris, R.K. and Cambridge, E., 'Beverley Minster before the early thirteenth century', in *Medieval Art and Architecture in the East Riding of Yorkshire*, ed. C. Wilson, British Archaeological Association Conference Transactions, 9 (1989), 9–32.

Morton, A., 'Burial in middle Saxon Southampton', in *Death in Towns*, ed. S.R. Bassett (1992), 68–77.

Moulden, J. and Tweddle, D., *Anglo-Scandinavian Settlement South-West of the Ouse* (CBA Archaeology of York, 8/1, 1986).

Müller-Mertens, E., *Karl der Grosse, Ludwig der Fromme und die Freien: wer waren die 'Liberi Homines' der karolingischen Kapitularien 742/743–832? Ein Beitrag zur Sozialgeschichte und Sozialpolitik des Frankenreiches*, Forschungen zur mittelalterlichen Geschichte, 10 (Berlin, 1963).

Murray, A.C., *Germanic Kinship Structure* (1983).

Nelson, H. and Jurmain, R., *Introduction to Physical Anthropology* (5th edn, New York 1991).

Nelson, J.L., 'The Frankish Empire', in *The Oxford Illustrated History of the Vikings*, ed. P.H. Sawyer (1997), 19–47.

Nicolaisen, W.F.H., 'Imitation and innovation in the Scandinavian place-names of the northern isles of Scotland', *Nomina*, 11 (1987), 75–85.

North, J.J., *English Hammered Coinage, I: early Anglo-Saxon to Henry III, c. 650–1272* (1994).

O'Hare, P., 'Yorkshire boundaries and their development', in *Yorkshire Boundaries*, ed. H.E.J. Le Patourel, M.H. Long and M.F. Pickles (1993), 9–23.

Orwin, C.S. and Orwin, C.S., *The Open Fields* (1938).

Owen, A.E.B., 'Herefrith of Louth, saint and bishop: a problem of identities', *LHA*, 15 (1980), 15–19.

Owen, D.M., *Church and Society in Medieval Lincolnshire* (1971).

——'Medieval chapels in Lincolnshire', *LHA*, 10 (1975), 15–22.

——'Chapelries and rural settlement: an examination of some of the Kesteven evidence' in *English Medieval Settlement*, ed. P.H. Sawyer (1979), 35–40.

Page, R.I., 'How long did the Scandinavian language survive in England? The epigraphical evidence', in *England Before the Conquest: studies in primary sources presented to Dorothy Whitelock*, ed. P. Clemoes and K. Hughes (1971), 165–180.

——*A Most Vile People: early English historians on the vikings* (1987).

Page, W., Some remarks on the churches of the Domesday Survey', *Archaeologia*, 2nd ser., 16 (1915), 61–102.

Palliser, D.M., 'Domesday Book and the "harrying of the north"', *Northern History*, 29 (1993), 1–23.

——'The "minster hypothesis": a case study', *EME*, 5 (2) (1996), 207–14.

Parker, M.S., 'Morthern reconsidered', *YAJ* 58 (1986), 23–9.

——'Some notes on the pre-Norman history of Doncaster', *YAJ*, 59 (1987), 29–43.

Pelteret, D., *Slavery in Medieval England: from the reign of Alfred to the twelfth century* (1995).

Perrin, C., 'Observations sur le manse dans la région parisienne au début du ixe siècle', *Annales d'histoire économique et sociale* 2 (1945), 39–52.

Perring, D., *Early Medieval Occupation at Flaxengate, Lincoln* (CBA, Archaeology of Lincoln, 9, 1981).

Pettigrew, T.J., 'The monumental crosses at Ilkley and Collingham', *JBAA* 20 (1864), 308–14.

Pevsner, N., *The Buildings of England: Nottinghamshire* (2nd edn, 1979).

Phillips, P., *Archaeoogy and Landscape Studies in North Lincolnshire* (2 vols, BAR British Series, 208, 1989), I, 169–70.

Phythian-Adams, C., *Continuity, Fields and Fission: the making of a Midland parish*, Department of English Local History, no. 8 (1975).

Platts, G., *Land and People in Medieval Lincolnshire* (1985).

Poly, J.P., *La Provence et le société féodale, 879–1166* (Paris, 1976).

Poly, J.P. and Bournazel, E., *The Feudal Transformation 900–1200* (1991).

Posnansky, M., 'Heath Wood, Ingleby: a preliminary excavation report', *DAJ*, 75 (1955), 140–4.

——'The pagan-Danish barrow cemetery at Heath Wood, Ingleby: 1955 excavations', *DAJ*, 76 (1956), 40–51.

Poussa, P., 'The evolution of early Standard English: the creolization hypothesis', *Studia Anglica Posnaniensia*, 14 (1982), 69–85.

Radford, C.A.R., 'A lost inscription of pre-Danish age from Caistor', *Arch. J.*, 103 (1946), 95–9.

——'The church of St Alkmund, Derby', *DAJ*, 96 (1976), 26–61.

Raftis, J.A., 'The East Midlands', *Ag. Hist.*, II, 634–51.

Rahtz, P., 'Anglo-Saxon and later Whitby', in *Yorkshire Monasticism: archaeology, art and architecture from the 7th to 16th centuries AD*, ed. L. R. Hoey, British Archaeological Association Conference Transactions, 15 (1995), 1–11.

Rahtz, P. and Watts, L., 'Kirkdale Anglo-Saxon minster', *Current Archaeology* 155 (1998), 419–22.

Reed, M., 'Buckinghamshire Anglo-Saxon charter boundaries', in *The Early Charters of the Thames Valley*, ed. M. Gelling (1979), 168–87.

Reilly, L., 'The emergence of Anglo-Norman architecture: Durham Cathedral', *ANS*, 19 (1997), 335–51.

Reuter, T., *Germany in the Early Middle Ages, 800–1056* (1991).

Reynolds, S., *Kingdoms and Communities in Western Europe, 900–1300* (1984).

——'What do we mean by "Anglo-Saxon" and "Anglo-Saxons"?', *Journal of British Studies* 24 (1985), 395–414.

——'Bookland, folkland and fiefs', *ANS*, 14 (1992), 211–27.

——*Fiefs and Vassals: the medieval evidence reinterpreted* (1994).

Richards, J.D., *Viking Age England* (1991).

Richards, J.D., Jecock, M., Richmond, L. and Tuck, C., 'The viking barrow cemetery at Heath Wood, Ingleby, Derbyshire', *Medieval Archaeology*, 39 (1995), 51–70.

Richardson, W., 'The Venerable Bede and a lost Saxon monastery in Yorkshire', *YAJ* 57 (1985), 15–22.

Richmond, I.A. and Crawford, O.G.S., 'The British section of the Ravenna Cosmography', *Archaeologia*, 93 (1949), 1–50.

Richter, M., 'Canterbury professions', *Canterbury and York Society*, 67 (1973), 17.

Riden, P., *History of Chesterfield* (1984).

——'Roman Chesterfield', *DAJ*, 109 (1987) 51–130.

Riley, D.N., *Early Landscapes from the Air: studies of crop marks in south Yorkshire and north Nottinghamshire* (1980).

Rimmington, F., 'The three churches of Hackness', *Transactions of the Scarborough Archaeological and Historical Society*, 26 (1988), 3–4.

Roberts, B.K., 'Village plans in Co. Durham: a preliminary statement', *Medieval Archaeology*, 16 (1972), 33–56.

——*The Making of the English Village* (1987).

——'Late -by names in the Eden Valley, Cumberland', *Nomina*, 13 (1989–90), 25–40.

Roberts, D.F., Mitchell, R.J., Green, C.K. and Jorde, L.B., 'Genetic variation in Cumbrians', *Annals of Human Biology*, 8 (2) (March–April, 1981), 135–44.

Rodwell, W., *Church Archaeology* (1984).

Rodwell, W. and Rodwell, K., 'St Peter's church, Barton-upon-Humber: excavation and structural study, 1978–81', *Antiq. J.*, 62 (1982), 283–315.

Roesdahl, E., 'The archaeological evidence for conversion', in *The Christianization of Scandinavia*, ed. P.H. Sawyer, B. Sawyer and I.N. Wood (Alingsas, 1987), 2–3.

Roesdahl, E. *et al.* (eds) *The Vikings in England and Their Danish Homeland* (1982).

Roffe, D.R., 'The Lincolnshire hundred', *Landscape History*, 3 (1981), 27–36.
——*Domesday Derbyshire* (1986).
——'The origins of Derbyshire', *DAJ*, 106 (1986), 102–22.
——'The seventh-century monastery of Stow Green, Lincolnshire', *LHA*, 21 (1986), 31–3.
——*The Derbyshire Domesday*, Alecto Historical Editions (1990).
——'Domesday Book and northern society: a reassessment', *EHR*, 105 (April 1990), 310–36.
——'From thegnage to barony: sake and soke, title and tenants-in-chief', *ANS*, 12 (1990), 157–76.
——'Place-naming in Domesday Book: settlements, estates and communities', *Nomina*, 14 (1990–1), 47–60.
——'The *Descriptio Terrarum* of Peterborough Abbey', *Historical Research*, 65 (1992), 1–16.
——*The Lincolnshire Domesday*, Alecto Historical Editions (1992).
——*The Nottinghamshire Domesday*, Alecto Historical Editions (1995), 30–2.
——'Great Bowden and its soke', in *Anglo-Saxon Landscapes in the East Midlands*, ed. J. Bourne (1996), 107–20.
——'The early history of Wharram Percy' (forthcoming).
——'Lissingleys and the meeting-place of Lindsey' (forthcoming).
——'Nottingham 868 to 1086' (forthcoming).
Rogers, A., 'The origins of Newark: the evidence of local boundaries', *TTS*, 77 (1974), 13–26.
Rogerson, A., 'Vikings and the new East Anglian towns', *British Archaeology*, 35 (June 1998), 8–9.
Rollason, D.W., 'Lists of saints' resting-places in Anglo-Saxon England', *ASE*, 7 (1978), 61–94.
——*The Mildrith Legend: a study in early medieval hagiography* (1982).
——'The cults of murdered royal saints in Anglo-Saxon England', *ASE*, 11 (1983), 1–22.
——'The shrines of saints in later Anglo-Saxon England: distribution and significance', in *The Anglo-Saxon Church*, ed. L.A.S. Butler and R.K. Morris (CBA Res. Rep., 60, 1986), 32–43.
——'Relic-cults as an instrument of royal policy c. 900–c. 1050', *ASE*, 15 (1987), 91–103.
——'S. Cuthbert and Wessex: the evidence of Cambridge, Corpus Christi MS 183', in *St Cuthbert, His Cult and Community to AD 1200*, ed. G. Bonner, C. Stancliffe and D.W. Rollason (1989), 413–424.
——*Saints and Relics in Anglo-Saxon England* (1989).
Routh, T.E., 'A corpus of pre-Conquest carved stones of Derbyshire', *DAJ*, 71 (1937), 1–46.
Rumble, A., '*Hrepingas* reconsidered', in *Mercian Studies*, ed. A. Dornier (1977).
Runciman, W.G., 'Accelerating social mobility: the case of Anglo-Saxon England', *Past and Present*, 104 (1984), 3–30.
Russell, A., 'Gilling West', *VCH N. Riding*, II, 71–84.
——'Hackness', *VCH N. Riding*, II, 528–32.
——'Pickering', *VCH N. Riding*, II, 461–76.
——'Whitby', *VCH N. Riding*, II, 506–28.
Russell, A. *et al.*, 'Easby', *VCH N. Riding*, II, 51–64.
Ryder, P., *Saxon Churches in South Yorkshire*, South Yorkshire County Archaeology Monograph, 2 (1981).
——*Medieval Churches of West Yorkshire*, South Yorkshire County Archaeology Monograph (1993).
Saunders, T., 'The feudal construction of space: power and domination in the nucleated village', in *The Social Archaeology of Houses*, ed. R. Samson (1990), 181–96.
Sawyer, B. and Sawyer, P., *Medieval Scandinavia: from conversion to Reformation, c. 800–1500* (Minneapolis 1993).
Sawyer, P.H., 'The density of the Danish settlement in England', *University of Birmingham Journal*, 6 (1) (1957), 1–17.
——'The two viking ages: a discussion', *Mediaeval Scandinavia*, 2 (1969), 163–207.
——*The Age of the Vikings* (2nd edn, 1971).
——'The charters of Burton Abbey and the unification of England', *Northern History*, 10 (1975), 28–39.

——*From Roman Britain to Norman England* (1978).
——'Some sources for the history of Viking Northumbria', in *Viking Age York and the North*, ed. R.A. Hall (CBA Research Report, 27, 1978), 3–7.
——'English medieval settlement: new interpretations' in *English Medieval Settlement*, ed. P.H. Sawyer (1979), 1–8.
——'Conquest and colonization: Scandinavians in the Danelaw and in Normandy', in *Proceedings of the Eighth Viking Congress*, ed. H. Bekker-Nielsen *et al*. (Odense 1981), 123–31.
——*Kings and Vikings: Scandinavia and Europe, AD 700–1100* (1982).
——'The royal *tun* in pre-Conquest England', in *Ideal and Reality in Frankish and Anglo-Saxon Society*, ed. P. Wormald, D. Bullough and R. Collins (1983), 273–99.
——'1066–1086: a tenurial revolution?', in *Domesday Book: a reassessment*, ed. P.H. Sawyer (1985), 71–85.
——'The last Scandinavian kings of York', *Northern History*, 31 (1995), 39–44.
Schlesinger, W., *Die Entstehung der Landesherrschaft: Untersuchungen vorwiegend nach mitteldeutschen Quellen* (Darmstadt 1941).
——'Herrschaft und Gefolgschaft in der germanisch–deutschen Verfassungs-geschichte', *Historische Zeitschrift*, 176 (1953), 225–75.
Schmitt, J., *Untersuchungen zu den Liberi Homines der Karolingerzeit*, Europäische Hochschulschriften, Reihe III, Geschichte und ihre Hilfswissenschaften, Band 83 (Frankfurt, 1977).
Schulze, H.K., *Die Graftschaftverfassung der Karolingerzeit in den Gebieten östlich des Rheins*, Schriften zur Verfassungsgeschichte 19 (Berlin, 1973).
——'Rodungsfreiheit und Königsfreiheit: zur Genesis und Kritik neuerer verfassungs-geschichtlicher Theorien', *Historische Zeitschrift*, 219 (1974), 529–50.
Seebohm, F., *The English Village Community* (1883).
Sermon, R., 'The Hackness cross cryptic inscriptions', *YAJ* 68 (1996), 101–11.
Shanin, T., 'Introduction: peasantry as a concept' in *Peasant and Peasant Societies*, ed. T. Shanin (2nd edn, 1988), 1–14.
Shennan, S., 'Introduction: archaeological approaches to cultural identity', in *Archaeological Approaches to Cultural Identity*, ed. S. Shennan (1989), 1–32.
Sheppard, J., 'Metrological analysis of regular village plans in Yorkshire', *AgHR*, 22 (1974), 118–35.
——'Medieval village planning in northern England: some evidence from Yorkshire', *JHG*, 2 (1) (1976), 3–20.
Sheppard, T., 'Viking and other relics at Crayke, Yorkshire', *YAJ*, 34 (1939), 273–81.
Sidebottom, P., 'Schools of Anglo-Saxon stone sculpture in the north Midlands' (Ph.D. thesis, University of Sheffield, 1994).
——'The Ecclesfield cross and "Celtic" survival', *Transactions of the Hunter Archaeological Society*, 19 (1997), 43–55.
——'Monuments that mark out viking land', *British Archaeology*, 23 (April 1997), 7.
Sills, J., 'St Peter's church, Holton-le-Clay, Lincolnshire', *LHA*, 17 (1982), 29–42.
Simpson, L., 'The King Alfred/St Cuthbert episode in the *Historia de Sancto Cuthberto*: its significance for mid-tenth-century English history', in *St Cuthbert, His Cult and Community to AD 1200*, ed. G. Bonner, C. Stancliffe and D.W. Rollason (1989), 397–411.
Sims-Williams, P., *Religion and Literature in Western Britain, 600–800* (1990).
Smart, V., 'The moneyers of St Edmund', *Hikuin* 11 (1985), 83–90.
——'Scandinavians, Celts and Germans in Anglo-Saxon England: the evidence of the moneyers' names', in *Anglo-Saxon Monetary History*, ed. M.A.S. Blackburn (1986), 171–84.
Smith, R.A., 'Anglo-Saxon remains', *VCH N. Riding*, I, 98–9.
Smyth, A.P., *Scandinavian York and Dublin: the history and archaeology of two related kingdoms* (2 vols, 1975–9).
Spratt, D.A., 'Prehistoric boundaries on the North York Moors', in *Prehistoric Communities in Northern England*, ed. G. Barker (1981), 87–103.
——'Prehistoric and medieval boundaries on the North York Moors', in *Yorkshire Boundaries*, ed. H.E.J. Le Patourel, M.H. Long and M.F. Pickles (1993), 85–94.
Staab, F., 'A reconsideration of the ancestry of modern political liberty: the problem

of the so-called "king's freemen" (königsfreie)', *Viator*, 11 (1980), 51–69.

Stafford, P.A., 'The reign of Æthelred II: a study in the limitations on royal policy', in *Ethelred the Unready*, ed. D. Hill (BAR British Series, 59, 1978), 17–21.

——'The "farm of one night" and the organization of King Edward's estates in Domesday', *EcHR*, 2nd ser., 33 (1980), 491–502.

——*The East Midlands in the Early Middle Ages* (1985).

——'The Danes and the Danelaw', *History Today* (October 1986), 17–23.

——*Unification and Conquest: a political and social history of England in the tenth and eleventh centuries* (1989).

Steane, K. and Vince, A., 'Post-Roman Lincoln: archaeological evidence for activity in Lincoln from the fifth to the ninth centuries', in *Pre-Viking Lindsey*, ed. A. Vince (1993), 71–9.

Stenton, F.M., *Types of Manorial Structure in the Northern Danelaw*, Oxford Studies in Social and Legal History, ed. P. Vinogradoff, 2 (1910), 3–96.

——*Documents Illustrative of the Social and Economic History of the Danelaw from Various Collections* (1920).

——'The free peasantry of the northern Danelaw', *Bulletin de la Société Royale des lettres de Lund* (1925–6), 73–185.

——'The Danes in England', *Proceedings of the British Academy*, 13 (1927), 1–46.

——*Latin Charters of the Anglo-Saxon Period* (1955).

——'The founding of Southwell Minster', in *Preparatory to Anglo-Saxon England: being the collected papers of Frank Merry Stenton*, ed. D.M. Stenton (1970), 364–70.

——*Anglo-Saxon England* (3rd edn, 1971).

Stephenson, C., 'Commendation and related problems in Domesday', *EHR*, 59 (1944), 289–310.

——*Medieval Institutions* (1954).

Stetka, J., *King Edward the Elder's Burh: the lost village of Burton by Bakewell* (1997).

Stewart, I., 'The St Martin coins of Lincoln', *British Numismatic Journal* 36 (1967), 46–54.

——'CVENNETTI reconsidered', in *Coinage in Ninth-Century Northumbria*, ed. D. Metcalf (1987), 345–59.

Stocker, D., 'The early church in Lincolnshire: a study of the sites and their significance', in *Pre-Viking Lindsey*, ed. A. Vince (1993), 101–22.

——'Five Towns funerals: decoding diversity in Danelaw stone sculpture', in *Proceedings of the Thirteenth Viking Congress*, ed. J. Graham-Campbell, R.A. Hall, J. Jesch and D. Parsons (forthcoming).

Stubbs, W., *The Constitutional History of England in Its Origin and Development* (3 vols, 1880).

Taylor, C.C., *Dorset* (1970).

——'Polyfocal settlement and the English village', *Medieval Archaeology* 21 (1977), 189–93.

——'Aspects of village mobility in medieval and later times', in *The Effect of Man on the Landscape: the lowland zone*, ed. S. Limbrey and J.G. Evans (CBA Res. Rep., 21, 1979), 126–34.

——*Village and Farmstead* (1984).

——'Dispersed settlement in nucleated areas', *Landscape History*, 17 (1995), 27–34.

Taylor, H.M., 'Repton reconsidered: a study in structural criticism', in *England before the Conquest: studies in primary sources presented to Dorothy Whitelock*, ed. P. Clemoes and K. Hughes (1971), 351–89.

Taylor, H.M. and Taylor, J., *Anglo-Saxon Architecture* (3 vols; vols 1–2, 1965; vol. 3, 1978).

Taylor, J. and Taylor, H.M., 'The Anglo-Saxon church at Edenham, Lincolnshire', *JBAA* 26 (1963), 6–10.

Thacker, A.T., 'Some terms for noblemen in Anglo-Saxon England, *c.* 650–900', in *ASSAH*, II, ed. D. Brown (BAR British Series, 92, 1981), 201–36.

——'Chester and Gloucester: early ecclesiastical organization in two Mercian *burhs*', *Northern History*, 18 (1982), 199–211.

——'Kings, saints and monasteries in pre-viking Mercia', *Midland History*, 9 (1984), 1–25.

——'Lindisfarne and the origins of the cult of St Cuthbert', in *St Cuthbert, His Cult and*

Community to AD 1200, ed. G. Bonner, C. Stancliffe and D.W. Rollason (1989), 103–22.

——'Monks, preaching and pastoral care in early Anglo-Saxon England' in *Pastoral Care before the Parish*, ed. J. Blair and R. Sharpe (1992), 137–70.

Thomas, G., 'A new survey of late Saxon and Viking Age strap-ends' (Ph.D. thesis, University of London, forthcoming).

Thompson, E.A., 'The Visigoths from Fritigern to Euric', *Historia*, 12 (1963), 105–26.

Toubert, P., 'L'Italie rurale aux viie-ixe siècles: essai de typologie domaniale', *Settimane*, 20 (1973), 95–132.

——*Les Structures du Latium médiéval: le Latium méridional et la Sabine du IXe à la fin du XIIe siècle* (Paris 1973).

——'La Part du grand domaine dans le décollage économique de l'Occident (viiie–ixe siècles)', in *Croissance agricole du haut moyen âge: chronologie, modalités, géographie, Flaran*, 10 (Auch 1990), 53–86.

Townend, M., 'Viking Age England as a bilingual society', in *Cultures in Contact: Scandinavian settlement in England*, ed. D.M. Hadley and J.D. Richard (forthcoming).

Tyler, A., *Survey of Roman Sites in North Yorkshire* (1980), 28–9.

Unwin, T.H., 'Townships and early fields in north Nottinghamshire', *JHG*, 9 (4) (1983), 341–6.

——'The Norman aggregation of estates and settlement in eleventh-century Nottinghamshire', *Landscape History*, 9 (1987), 53–64.

——'Towards a model of Anglo-Scandinavian rural settlement in England' in *Anglo-Saxon Settlements*, ed. D. Hooke (1988), 77–98.

Venables, E., 'The dedications of the churches of Lincolnshire', *Arch. J.*, 38 (1881), 365–90.

——'Traces of early Christianity in north Lincolnshire', *AASRP*, 17 (1883–4), 318–25.

Verhulst, A., 'La Genèse du régime domanial classique en France au haut moyen âge', *Settimane*, 13 (1965), 135–60.

——'Die Grundherrschaftsentwicklung im ost-frankischen Raum vom 8. bis 10. Jahrhundert', in *Strukturen der Grundherrschaft im frühen Mittelalter*, ed. W. Rösener (1989), 29–46.

——Étude comparative du régime domanial classique', in *Croissance agricole du haut moyen âge: chronologie, modalités, géographie, Flaran*, 10 (Auch, 1990), 87–101.

——(ed.) *Le Grand Domaine aux époques mérovingienne et carolingienne* (Ghent, 1985).

Vinogradoff, P., *Villeinage in England* (1892).

Von Feilitzen, O., *The Pre-Conquest Personal Names of Domesday Book* (Uppsala, 1937).

Von Feilitzen, O. and Blunt, C.E., 'Personal names on the coinage of Edgar', in *England before the Conquest: studies in primary sources presented to Dorothy Whitelock*, ed. P. Clemoes (1971), 183–214.

Waas, A., *Herrschaft und Staat im deutschen Frühmittelalter*, Historische Studien, 335 (Munich, 1938).

Wallach, L., 'The Urbana Anglo-Saxon Sylloge of Latin inscriptions', in *Poetry and Poetics from Ancient Greece to the Renaissance*, ed. G.M. Kirkwood (Ithaca, N.Y. 1975), 134–51.

Walmsley, J.F.R., 'The *censarii* of Burton abbey and the Domesday population', *North Staffs. Journal of Field Studies*, 8 (1968), 73–80.

Warner, P., 'Shared churchyards, freemen church builders and the development of parishes in eleventh-century East Anglia', *Landscape History*, 8 (1986), 39–52.

Watts, L., Rahtz, P. Okasha, S., Bradley, S. and Higgitt, J. 'Kirkdale: the inscriptions', *Medieval Archaeology*, 41 (1997), 51–99.

Watts, V.E., 'Place-names of the Darlington area', in *Darlington: a topographical review*, ed. P.A.G. Clark and N.F. Pearson (1978), 40–3.

Webster, L.E. and Cherry, J. 'Britain in 1976', *Medieval Archaeology*, 21 (1977), 211–12.

Weinrich, U., *Languages in Contact: findings and problems* (1953).

Welldon-Finn, R., *Domesday Studies: the eastern counties* (1967).

Wenskus, R., *Stammesbildung und Verfassung: das Werden des frühmittelalterlichen Gentes* (Cologne 1961).

Weston, M., 'Northallerton', *VCH N. Riding*, II, 418–34.

——'Topcliffe', *VCH N. Riding*, II, 70–80.

Wheeler, H. (ed.) 'Roman Derby', *DAJ*, 105 (1986), *passim*.

Whitelock, D.W., 'The conversion of the eastern Danelaw', *Saga-Book of the Viking Society for Northern Research*, 12 (1937–45), 159–76.
——'Scandinavian personal names in the *Liber Vitae* of Thorney Abbey', *Saga-Book of the Viking Society for Northern Research*, 12 (1937–45), 127–53.
——'The dealings of the kings of England with Northumbria in the tenth and eleventh centuries', in *The Anglo-Saxons: studies presented to Bruce Dickins*, ed. P. Clemoes (1959), 70–88.
Whitwell, B., 'Flixborough', *Current Archaeology*, 126 (1991), 244–7.
——*Roman Lincolnshire* (1970; revised edn 1992).
Wickham, C.J., *Early Medieval Italy: central power and local society, 400–1000* (1981).
——'Land disputes and their social framework in Lombard-Carolingian Italy', in *The Settlement of Disputes in Early Medieval Europe*, ed. W. Davies and P. Fouracre (1986), 105–24.
——'European forests in the early Middle Ages: landscape and land clearance', *Settimane*, 37 (1990), 479–45.
——'Problems of comparing rural societies in early medieval western Europe', *TRHS*, 6th ser., 2 (1992), 221–46.
——'Rural society in Carolingian Europe', in *The New Cambridge Medieval History, II, c. 700–c. 900*, ed. R. McKitterick (1995), 510–37.
Williams, A., ' "Cockles amongst the wheat": Danes and English in the western Midlands in the first half of the eleventh century', *Midland History*, 11 (1986), 1–22.
——*The English and the Norman Conquest* (1995).
Williamson, T., 'Explaining regional landscapes: woodland and champion in southern and eastern England', *Landscape History*, 11 (1989), 5–13.
——*The Origins of Norfolk* (1993).
Wilson, D.M., 'Scandinavian settlement in the north and west of the British Isles: an archaeological point-of-view', *TRHS*, 5th ser., 26 (1976), 95–113.
——'The Scandinavians in England', in *The Archaeology of Anglo-Saxon England*, ed. D.M. Wilson (1976), 393–403.
Winchester, A., 'The medieval vill in the western Lake District: some problems of definition', *Transactions of the Cumberland and Westmorland Archaeological and Antiquarian Society*, 78 (1978), 55–69.
——'The distribution and significance of "bordland" in medieval Britain', *AgHR*, 34 (1986), 129–39.
Wolfram, H., *History of the Goths* (Berkeley, Calif., trans. 1988).
Wolfram, H. and Pohl, W. (eds) *Typen der Ethnogenese unter besonderer Berücksichtigung der Bayern* (Vienna 1990).
Wood, I.N., 'The conversion of the barbarian peoples', in *The Christian World*, ed. G. Barraclough (1981), 85–98.
——'Anglo-Saxon Otley: an archiepiscopal estate and its crosses in a Northumbrian context', *Northern History*, 23 (1987), 20–38.
——'Christians and pagans in ninth-century Scandinavia', in *The Christianization of Scandinavia*, ed. B. Sawyer, P.H. Sawyer and I.N. Wood (Alingsas 1987), 36–67.
——'Ethnicity and ethnogenesis of the Burgundians', in *Typen der Ethnogenese unter besondere Berucksichtigung der Bayern* 1, ed. H. Wolfram and W. Pohl (Vienna, 1990), 53–69.
Wormald, P., 'Bede, "Beowulf" and the conversion of the Anglo-Saxon aristocracy', in *Bede and Anglo-Saxon England*, ed. R.T. Farrell (BAR British Series, 46, 1978), 32–95.
——'The age of Bede and Æthelbald' in *The Anglo-Saxons*, ed. J. Campbell (1982), 70–100.
——'The ninth century', in *The Anglo-Saxons*, ed. J. Campbell (1982).
——'Viking studies: whence and whither?', in *The Vikings*, ed. R.T. Farrell (1982), 128–53.
——*Bede and the Conversion of England* (1984).
——'A handlist of Anglo-Saxon law-suits', *ASE*, 17 (1988), 247–81.
——'Lordship and justice in the early English kingdom', in *Property and Power in the Early Middle Ages*, ed. W. Davies and P. Fouracre (1995), 114–36.
Yorke, B., *Wessex in the Early Middle Ages* (1995).
Young, B.K., 'Paganisme, christianisme et rites funéraires mérovingiens', *Archéologie Médiévale*, 7 (1977), 5–81.

Index